*Francine Williamon 3/3/90 (Personal)*

# COMMANDS AND FUNCTIONS—LISTED ALPHABETICALLY

W9-BNW-212

| COMMAND | KEY SEQUENCE | PAGE | COMMAND | KEY SEQUENCE | PAGE |
|---|---|---|---|---|---|
| Move, copy, delete, append rectangle | Alt-F4 Ctrl-F4 3 | 420 | Set line spacing | | 102 |
| Move, copy, delete, append sentence, paragraph, or page | Ctrl-F4 1 (or 2 or 3) | 131 | Set margins | | 87 |
| Move key | Ctrl-F4 | 130 | Set tabs | Shift-F8 1 8 | 103 |
| Name search (file name) | F5 ←N | 481 | Setup key | Shift-F1 | 661 |
| Odd/even page numbers | Shift-F8 2 7 | 162 | Sheet feeder bin number | Shift-F7 S 3 3 | 170 |
| Outline mode (on/off) | Shift-F5 4 | 342 | Shell key | Ctrl-F1 | 508 |
| Overstrike | Shift-F8 4 5 | 239 | Short form, Table of Authorities | Alt-F5 4 | 337 |
| Page break | Ctrl-← | 15 | Soft hyphen | Ctrl-(hyphen) | 214 |
| Page format | Shift-F8 2 | 159 | Sort (select) | Ctrl-F9 2 | 567 |
| Page number (new) | Shift-F8 2 6 | 162 | Sorting sequence (select) | Ctrl-F9 3 | 569 |
| Page number position | Shift-F8 2 7 | 159 | Space (hard space) | Home-Space bar | 226 |
| Page size | Shift-F8 2 8 | 166 | Speller key | Ctrl-F2 | 97 |
| Paragraph numbering | Shift-F5 5 | 351 | Split screen into windows | Ctrl-F3 1 | 510 |
| Password protection | Ctrl-F5 2 | 502 | Start a macro | Alt-F10 | 599 |
| Pitch | Ctrl-F8 4 | 302 | Stop printing | Shift-F7 4 5 | 274 |
| Print a page | Shift-F7 2 | 268 | Strikeout | Ctrl-F8 2 9 | 242 |
| Print color | Ctrl-F8 5 | 307 | Style key | Alt-F8 | 250 |
| Print defined block | Alt-F4 Shift-F7 Y | 138 | Subdocument (create) | Alt-F5 2 | 357 |
| Print from disk | Shift-F7 3 (or F5 ← 4) | 268 | Subscript | Ctrl-F8 1 2 | 232 |
| Print full text | Shift-F7 1 | 51 | Superscript | Ctrl-F8 1 1 | 232 |
| Print key | Shift-F7 | 51 | Suppress formatting for current page | Shift-F8 2 9 | 180 |
| Print multiple copies for current session | Shift-F7 N | 299 | Switch key (switch between documents) | Shift-F3 | 81 |
| Print quality (text or graphics) | Shift-F7 (T or G) | 299 | Tab Align key | Ctrl-F6 | 220 |
| Print selected pages | Shift-F7 3 <page numbers> | 270 | Tab ruler | Ctrl-F3 1 23 ← | 114 |
| Printer control | Shift-F7 4 | 273 | Table of authorities (define) | Alt-F5 5 4 | 340 |
| Printer selection | Shift-F7 S | 288 | Table of authorities (edit full form) | Alt-F5 5 5 | 337 |
| Proportional spacing | Ctrl-F8 4 | 302 | Table of authorities (mark text for) | Alt-F4 Alt-F5 4 | 335 |
| Protect a document | Ctrl-F5 2 | 502 | Table of contents (mark text for) | Alt-F4 Alt-F5 1 | 323 |
| Redline | Ctrl-F8 2 8 | 242 | Tabs (set) | Shift-F8 1 8 | 103 |
| Release left margin | Shift-Tab | 231 | Text box | Alt-F9 3 | 459 |
| Remove redline and strikeout text | Alt-F5 6 1 | 244 | Text column definition (newspaper, parallel) | Alt-F7 4 | 386 |
| Rename file | F5 ← 3 | 485 | Text column on/off toggle | Alt-F7 3 | 391 |
| Repeat a command n number of times | Esc <n> <command> | 76 | Text In/Out key | Ctrl-F5 | 498 |
| Replace key (search and replace) | Alt-F2 | 198 | Thesaurus key | Alt-F1 | 646 |
| Retrieve copied or cut text | Ctrl-F4 4 | 130 | Time/Date format | Shift-F5 3 | 228 |
| Retrieve DOS text file | Ctrl-F5 1 2 | 501 | Top margin setting | Shift-F8 2 5 | 174 |
| Retrieve file from disk | Shift-F10 (or F5 ← 1) | 108 | Typeover mode (toggle) | Ins | 57 |
| Retrieve locked document | Shift-F10 (or F5 ← 1) | 503 | Type-through | Shift-F7 5 | 282 |
| Retrieve Text key | Shift-F10 | 108 | Undelete key | F1 | 67 |
| Rewrite screen | Ctrl-F3 0 | 44 | Underline (double) | Ctrl-F8 2 3 | 307 |
| Reveal Codes key (on/off) | Alt-F3 | 112 | Underline key | F8 | 94 |
| Reverse Search key | Shift-F2 | 195 | Units of measure | Shift-F1 8 | 298 |
| Rush print job | Shift-F7 4 2 | 275 | Uppercase conversion | Alt-F4 Shift-F5 1 | 143 |
| Save DOS text file | Ctrl-F5 1 1 | 498 | View document | Shift-F7 6 | 277 |
| Save file in WordPerfect 4.2 format | Ctrl-F5 4 | 507 | Widow/orphan protection | Shift-F8 1 9 | 184 |
| Save key | F10 | 47 | Windows | Ctrl-F3 1 | 510 |
| Screen attributes | Shift-F1 3 2 1 | 662 | Word count | Ctrl-F2 6 | 640 |
| Screen key | Ctrl-F3 | 510 | Word search | F5 ← 9 | 491 |
| Search and Replace key | Alt-F2 | 198 | | | |
| Search (extended) | Home F2 | 206 | | | |
| Search for text in files | F5 ← 9 | 491 | | | |
| Search key (forward search) | F2 | 192 | | | |
| Select print options | Shift-F7 | 290 | | | |
| Select printer | Shift-F7 S | 288 | | | |

# Mastering WordPerfect 5

*Francine William* 3/3/90

Go to PFS first on main menu to "Format Disks"

# Mastering WordPerfect® 5

*Susan Baake Kelly*

San Francisco • Paris • Düsseldorf • London

Cover design by Thomas Ingalls + Associates
Cover photography by Michael Lamott
Series design by Julie Bilski
Chapter art and layout by Eleanor Ramos
Screen reproductions produced by XenoCopy

3Com Etherseries and 3Comm 3+ are trademarks of 3Com.
Accord is a trademark of Honda Corp.
Alps ALQ is a trademark of Alps Electric, Inc.
Apricot is a trademark of Apricot, Inc.
AST-PCnet and TurboLaser are trademarks of AST Research, Inc.
AutoCAD is a trademark of Autodesk, Inc.
Blaser is a trademark of Blaser Industries, Inc.
Bronco is a trademark of Ford Motor Co.
Brother HR1 is a trademark of Brother International.
Canon is a trademark of Canon, U.S.A.
Centronics is a trademark of Genicom.
Chevy Blazer and Chevy Citation are trademarks of General Motors Corp.
Citizen MSP and 120D are trademarks of Citizen America Corp.
Data General is a trademark of Data General Corp.
dBASE is a trademark of Ashton-Tate.
DEC Rainbow is a trademark of Digital Equipment Corp.
Dr. Halo II is a trademark of IMSI.
Epson LQ-1500, Epson RX-80, and Epson FX-85 are trademarks of Epson America, Inc.
Etch-a-Sketch is a trademark of The Ohio Art Co.
GEM Paint is a trademark of Digital Research, Inc.
HP LaserJet is a trademark of Hewlett-Packard Co.
Hyperion is a trademark of Bytec-Comterm, Inc.
IBM PC, IBM PC/XT, IBM PC/AT, IBM 3270-PC, PC-DOS, TopView, IBM Monochrome Monitor, PS/2, DisplayWrite and PC Network are trademarks of
  International Business Machines Corp.
Imagewriter, Macintosh Paint, and Laserwriter Plus are trademarks of Apple Computer Co.
Jeep Cherokee is a trademark of American Motors Corp.
Lotus 1-2-3, Symphony, and Freelance Plus are trademarks of Lotus Development Corp.
MPI Printmate is a trademark of Micro Peripherals, Inc.
MS-DOS, Word, Microsoft Windows are trademarks of Microsoft Corp.
MultiMate is a trademark of Multimate International Corp.
Novell NetWare is a trademark of Novell, Inc.
OfficeWriter is a trademark of Office Solutions, Inc.
Okidata 84 and Okidata ML 192 + are trademarks of Okidata.
PageMaker is a trademark of Aldus Corp.
PC Paint Plus is a trademark of Mouse Systems Corp.
PFS:Professional is a trademark of Software Publishing Corp.
PicturePak is a trademark of Marketing Graphics.
ProWriter and ProWriter Jr. Plus are trademarks of C. Itoh Digital Products, Inc.
Publisher's Paintbrush and PC Paintbrush are trademarks of Z-Soft Corp.
SammaWord is a trademark of Samma Corp.
Silver Reed is a trademark of Silver Reed Corp. of America.
STARLAN is a trademark of AT&T Information Systems.
Tandy 1000 and 2000 are trademarks of Tandy Corp.
Tapestry is a trademark of Torus System, Inc.
Texas Instruments PC and TI 855 are trademarks of Texas Instruments, Inc.
UPS is a trademark of United Parcel Service.
Ventura Publisher is a trademark of Xerox Corp.
Victor 9000 is a trademark of Victor Technologies.
Volkswriter is a trademark of Lifetree Software.
Volvo GL is a trademark of Volvo Corp.
Wang PC is a trademark of Wang Laboratories.
WordPerfect, WordPerfect Library, Personal WordPerfect, WordPerfect Jr., PlanPerfect, WordePerfect Executive, WordPerfect Office, and
  Repeat Performance are trademarks of WordPerfect Corp.
Wang PC is a trademark of Wang Laboratories
WordStar and MailMerge are trademarks of MicroPro International.
XenoCopy is a trademark of XenoSoft.
SYBEX is a registered trademark of SYBEX, Inc.

SYBEX is not affiliated with any manufacturer.

Every effort has been made to supply complete and accurate information. However, SYBEX assumes no responsibility for its use, nor for any infringements of patents or other rights of third parties which would result.

Copyright©1988 SYBEX Inc., 2021 Challenger Drive #100, Alameda, CA 94501. World rights reserved. No part of this publication may be stored in a retrieval system, transmitted, or reproduced in any way, including but not limited to photocopy, photograph, magnetic or other record, without the prior agreement and written permission of the publisher.

Library of Congress Card Number: 88-60606
ISBN 0-89588-500-X
Manufactured in the United States of America
10 9

*To my wonderful husband Jim, with love*

*Personally I'm always ready to learn, although I do not always like being taught.*

*Winston Churchill*

# ACKNOWLEDGMENTS

Special thanks to Mom, for everything.

Thanks also to Greg Harvey, for getting me started, for being there when I needed to talk, and for all his assistance and advice throughout the project.

I also wish to thank developmental editor Cheryl Holzaepfel; copy editor Eric Stone; technical reviewer Brian Atwood; word processors Scott Campbell, Bob Myren, and Jocelyn Reynolds; layout artist Eleanor Ramos; typesetter Olivia Shinomoto; proofreader Lynne Bourgault; screen illustration producer Sonja Schenk; and indexer Debbie Burnham-Kidwell. Also, thanks to Dianne King and Dr. Rudolph Langer for their support.

Many thanks to Jeff Acerson, Rebecca Mortensen, and Dan Lunt of WordPerfect Corporation, and all the folks on WordPerfect Corporation's technical support line who have been so helpful, including Sherry, Lynn, Robin, Debbie, Stuart, Kelly, Becky, Lisa, and Kevin. Also, thanks to Karen Acerson for her enthusiasm and support.

I wish to thank the following companies for providing copies of their products: Mouse Systems Corporation, PowerMax Company, Yolles Development, Hercules Computer Technology, American Training International, Inc., SoftCraft, Inc., Technical Support Software Inc., M/H Group, Systems Compatibility Corporation, and ZyLAB.

Finally, thanks and much appreciation to Kathy and Manny Sotomayor; Pam Warriner and Elizabeth Chatham of Bay Area Business Services for their wonderful advice about word processing and legal terms; Suzanne Statler, who helped me understand and incorporate the learning process of a computer novice into Chapter 1; Sharon and Ron Bealle; the law firm of Varni, Fraser, Hartwell, and Rodgers for help with line numbering and tables of authorities and for being such enthusiastic students; Patrick Corrigan of the Corrigan Group for his help with DOS and networking applications; Harvey W. Jorgenson, Jr. P. E. for help with one of the macros in Chapter 19; Valerie Franke of Diablo Valley College for her pertinent observations and suggestions about the book and her strong enthusiasm; and to the many outstanding professors at San Francisco State University's School of Business for giving me a great education.

# CONTENTS AT A GLANCE

# TABLE OF CONTENTS

*C H A P T E R*   *3:*    ***MORE EDITING TIPS AND TECHNIQUES***    **54**

# P A R T  2  *ADVANCED WORD PROCESSING FEATURES*

# *INTRODUCTION*

WordPerfect is one of the most powerful and comprehensive word processing programs available for the IBM PC and compatibles. The manufacturer, WordPerfect Corporation, has constantly been making improvements in the program since it was first released in 1982, demonstrating their willingness to satisfy user requests and to incorporate suggestions from reviewers. Over the years, the program has earned lavish and well-deserved praise from the critics, and is now widely acclaimed as one of the best word processors on the market. Whether you are a new user, or are already familiar with WordPerfect, you will find this book an invaluable tool to help you take advantage of its many features.

## *WHY A BOOK ABOUT WORDPERFECT?*

The manual that comes with WordPerfect is clear and well written, but it often assumes that you are already familiar with the word processing concepts being demonstrated, and it sometimes lacks explanations that are detailed enough to help you master the many exceptional features. This is especially noticeable in the explanations of the more complex and unfamiliar operations. Rather than focusing on the necessary background so that you will understand what you are doing and why, the manual concentrates on giving you the precise keystrokes necessary to use each feature in one or more specific examples.

The manual may also be incomplete as a learning tool for those of you who have never used a word processor. Although the introductory lessons are easy to follow as they lead you through the proper sequence of keystrokes, the individual steps do not define the basic concepts being illustrated. For example, the manual tells you precisely how to flush a header at the right margin, but it doesn't explain what a header is or what flush means.

*Mastering WordPerfect 5* is designed to fill this need, and is valuable as both a tutorial and as a reference guide. Although it is not intended to replace your manual, you'll find this book more comprehensive. The book's goal is to help you understand the concepts behind each function: that is, not just how they work, but when, where, and why they are used, so that you are better equipped to explore WordPerfect and expand your understanding of its powerful features on your own.

*Mastering WordPerfect 5* is designed to be an aid to users from a broad range of experience. It is excellent for the beginner because it assumes no prior knowledge of word processing; it explains the purpose and significance of WordPerfect's basic operations as they are introduced, in a logical step-by-step approach. For users who have had some experience with the program, this book fills in the gaps and makes it easier to explore and use some of the more sophisticated features you may have not been taking advantage of. For the skilled user, the book explains the advanced features in depth and provides many examples and ideas to incorporate into your work.

## *HOW TO USE THIS BOOK*

Users of all levels of experience can benefit from this book, but not all readers will want to use it the same way. The Fast track section at the beginning of each chapter summarizes the chapter's contents, lists the steps or keystrokes needed to complete specific tasks, and points you to the page where you can find a tutorial presentation or more detailed explanation. In some cases, the Fast Track entry will be all you need to get going. In other cases, you can use the Fast Track to pick out the points you are interested in and then go directly to the information you need. Also note that the Fast Tracks cover the chapters' primary topics; they do not cover every option, exception, or caveat discussed in the text.

Part One helps new WordPerfect users to get acquainted with the basics of the program before being introduced to more complex topics. It will teach you how to create, edit, format, print, and save commonly used documents such as letters and memos. Then you'll examine some of the fancier offerings such as the spell checker, block operations, and automatic hyphenation. If you follow the lessons in sequence, by the end of the fifth chapter you should be comfortable with all of WordPerfect's basic word processing operations, and you will be equipped to skip to any other chapter that interests you.

Part Two teaches advanced word processing operations, providing extensive examples and detailed explanations. It covers formatting features such as justification and proportional spacing, fonts, styles, and headers and footers, as well as search and replace, printer control, and much more. It also explores some of the more unusual features that distinguish WordPerfect from most other word processors on the market, including footnotes and endnotes, line and box drawing, indexing, newspaper and parallel columns, outlining and paragraph numbering, and the new desktop publishing features.

Part Three covers WordPerfect's supplemental features such as math, macros, sort and select, merges, the spelling checker and thesaurus, document locking, and the many file management functions.

Three appendices complete the book. They describe installation and system requirements, cursor movement and ASCII charts, and companion programs for WordPerfect.

### *A WORD ABOUT KEY NAMES*

If you are familiar with the WordPerfect manual, you know that it assigns names to commonly used keystrokes. (For example, the keystroke combination that is used to center text on a line is called the Center key.) These names will be used throughout this book and will always be capitalized. The manual frequently directs you to use these named keys, but doesn't tell you the corresponding keys to press, such as Shift-F6 for the Center key. However, in this book, whenever you are instructed to use such a key, both the key name and the exact keystroke combination required to execute it will always be listed. Even though this approach may seem redundant, it will help you learn the combinations and save you a lot of time flipping back through pages. Also, in case you don't read the chapters in the order they appear (and thereby learn each combination as it is introduced), this may save you some frustration.

### *ASSUMPTIONS ABOUT YOUR HARDWARE AND SOFTWARE*

This book was written for IBM and highly compatible computers that use MS-DOS or PC-DOS, including the PC, XT, AT, and PS/2 models. Although there have been several versions of WordPerfect, this book assumes you are using version 5. Earlier versions used different keystroke combinations for certain functions, so if you are not using version 5, you may need to check your manual or keyboard template for the correct keystrokes. In addition, many important features were introduced in version 5, so many of the features discussed in this book will be unavailable to users of earlier versions. I strongly recommend that you upgrade to version 5 because it contains significant improvements and additions. WordPerfect Corporation charges a very reasonable fee for the upgrade, which includes the new manual and diskettes.

## *WORDPERFECT FEATURES*

WordPerfect is an amazing package. It is fast, efficient, and a genuine pleasure to use. However, the program is best known for an abundance of useful features and the fact that WordPerfect Corporation keeps adding more to each version. All of the fundamental word processing functions are available, such as automatic word wrap, which creates a new line when the cursor reaches the right margin and moves both the cursor and any words that would have exceeded the right margin to the new line; search and replace, which can locate and change a word or phrase; block commands to copy, move, and delete sections of text; and automatic rewrite, which reformats your paragraphs after any editing changes such as additions or deletions.

WordPerfect's abilities extend beyond the basics, though, to include such special features as macros, which can automate your most commonly used keystrokes and commands; the ability to index a document and create a table of contents for it; outlining and paragraph numbering; basic mathematical functions; protection of confidential files; document switching, which enables you to shift back and forth and even exchange data between two documents that are in the computer's memory simultaneously; and a built-in spelling checker.

Version 4.1 added more features to this collection, including windows, to split the screen horizontally so that two documents can be viewed simultaneously; newspaper columns, in which text flows from one column to the next; the ability to create parallel columns of text that appear side by side on screen and can be edited independently of one another; a thesaurus; the ability to sort text or numbers in ascending or descending order; the ability to select specified kinds of items from a list; the Line Draw feature that enables you to draw lines, boxes, and graphs; a word search feature that can check all documents on the data disk for a word or phrase; and an improved Undelete command that can remember and restore the last three deletions.

WordPerfect 4.2 added the Line Numbering and Table of Authorities features, which are especially helpful to users in law offices; nonprinting Document Comments; a Document Summary that can include the file name, date, author, typist, and comments; left, right, center, and decimal tabs; document preview so you can view margins, page numbers, headers, footers, footnotes, and endnotes on screen; and the concordance feature to simplify indexing.

WordPerfect 5 is the most significant upgrade of all, and it elevates WordPerfect to a new standard of excellence that others will have to work hard to achieve. A summary of the differences and new features appears in the next section.

## *WHAT'S NEW IN WORDPERFECT 5*

The most publicized additions to WordPerfect 5 are the desktop publishing features. The program now includes many of the important functions that you need to create sophisticated looking documents. These new features can give your newsletters, brochures, flyers, manuals, and other documents that polished appearance that used to be possible only with professional typesetting and printing. With WordPerfect 5, you can easily incorporate drawings and illustrations from other programs or from scanners, change the position and size of a graphic image in your document, rotate and invert it, and add a text caption. You can create four different types of boxes: figure boxes for graphics images, diagrams, and charts; table boxes for numeric tables, maps, and statistical data; text boxes for quotations, sidebars, and other text that you want to set off from the rest of the document; and user-defined boxes for anything else. You can create horizontal and vertical rules of varying widths, including vertical rules that separate columns of text.

You won't be able to see the graphics on your editing screen, but you will see an outline of the box and the figure number, and the rest of the text on the page will wrap around it. If your monitor is capable of producing graphics, you can use View Document to see the entire page of text and graphics on screen as it will appear when printed, and preview features such as type size, subscript, superscript, small caps, and italics. You can also enlarge a page and view it at close range, or look at two facing pages of text simultaneously. If your printer does not have enough memory to print graphics and text simultaneously, you can print the text first, then reinsert the paper and print just the graphics.

Important desktop publishing features such as kerning, line height, and word and letter spacing are now available. You can mix a large variety of fonts, and are no longer limited to eight. When you change fonts, WordPerfect automatically adjusts margins and tabs, line height, the number of characters in a line, and the number of lines on a page. You also can download soft fonts from within WordPerfect before printing, or designate them as fonts that Word-Perfect will download while the document is being printed.

WordPerfect 5 also has a number of formatting changes. Formatting features that used to be on three keys have been combined into a single Format key with four submenus. The new features on these submenus enable you to create variable spacing between lines; to force a page to be numbered odd or even; to tell WordPerfect which form you are using in your printer; to enlarge or reduce the size of individual characters on the screen (useful when you are working with multiple columns); to change the default formatting for a document and save the codes with the file; to change the way redline markings are printed; to change the language files used with the spell checker, thesaurus, and hyphenation (you can obtain these files in other languages from WordPerfect Corporation, but they aren't included); to reduce space between specific letter pairs; to adjust the printed space of each character and/or word; and to adjust the amount of space between words.

WordPerfect 5 also has added more formatting features with the Font and Styles keys. The Font key has submenus that enable you to change the size of your text; add enhancements such as bold, italic, redline, strikeout, and small capitals; select a font for your base, or regular, text; and select the color you want to use for printing (if your printer can print in color). The Styles key helps standardize your formatting, enabling you to easily change formatting characteristics throughout the document with just a few keystrokes. This gives you the ability to quickly see how a document will look if you change fonts or other formatting.

WordPerfect is easier to use now because it gives you the choice of using letters or numbers to choose menu options. Selecting options by letters is more natural for many users, and if you are a user of earlier WordPerfect versions, you may find it hard to go back to the number selection method.

Options on the Setup key have also improved WordPerfect's ease-of-use. The unit of measurement now is inches, so when you make formatting changes such as margins, tabs, and paper size, the settings are displayed and changed in inches. If you prefer another unit of measurement, you can change it from inches to centimeters, points, or back to the line and pitch measurements used in the earlier versions of WordPerfect. The Setup key can also be used to vary the cursor speed; to change the default formatting; to change the key assignments for your function keys (or other keys); to save your documents without formatting using Fast Save so that saving won't take as long; and to change various display options.

New reference tools are also included in WordPerfect 5. You can insert a reference to another page number, footnote number, endnote number, or graphics box caption anywhere in your document and easily update the reference numbers if their position changes. Document Compare enables you to compare a disk file with the edited screen version of a document. Master Document lets you link several files together and generate a table of contents, index, list, and so forth that will include marked items from each file as though they were all contained in one file. Other features give you the ability to convert a Document Comment into text, and to convert text in your document into a Document Comment.

Other new features enable you to use extended parallel columns to span a page break, and to create special characters and symbols such as accent marks over letters. The Macro Editor lets you alter a macro that has been defined and the Macro Commands key lets you insert programming commands into your macros. WordPerfect's unique Reveal Codes screen is different in this version because you can actually type and edit in it. The List Files menu now includes an option to move a document from one directory or disk to another, and the Word Search option has been improved to let you search files by file date, and to search by the document summary, the first page, or the entire document.

As you can see, WordPerfect 5 offers an impressive array of features. With *Mastering WordPerfect 5* as your guide, you can use the program to its fullest advantage to meet all your word processing needs, from basic letters to complex desktop-published documents.

*I.*

# PART I

## ALL THE FUNDAMENTALS

# 1.

# *INTRODUCTION TO WORDPERFECT*

# FAST TRACK

BEFORE YOU START USING WORDPERFECT YOU NEED to learn a few fundamentals, such as how to start the program on your computer system, what you see on your screen when WordPerfect is running, where to locate important keys on your keyboard, and how to use these keys to perform certain essential tasks. If you aren't already familiar with these basic procedures, you'll be glad you invested the effort to master them because it will undoubtedly save you precious time and energy in the future. I realize that most users don't have much time to spend learning the fine points of WordPerfect and really needed to know how to use it yesterday, but if you really want to learn the program and use it efficiently, everything in this chapter is indispensable.

Learning the WordPerfect keyboard is especially important. This chapter introduces you to the keys that you will use most often in WordPerfect and therefore will see frequently throughout this book. Those of you who have never used a computer will find that you'll have to discard many of the habits you acquired using a typewriter and learn new ones. To minimize confusion, read this chapter carefully and work through the exercises, then refer back to it as often as necessary. Those of you who have worked with other popular software programs such as Lotus 1-2-3 or dBASE III will find that many keys have different and unfamiliar applications in WordPerfect. Although you will recognize their names and locations on your keyboard, you should still skim this chapter to be sure you understand how these keys work in WordPerfect.

If you have already worked with WordPerfect and feel comfortable with the keyboard and basic startup procedures, you may wish to skip this chapter for now. Please be aware, though, that you may find some useful advice in this chapter, so I advise you to skim through it when you have the time.

# STARTING WORDPERFECT

When it comes to learning a word processing program, there is no substitute for experience. Actual hands-on practice is worth a million words, so you'll have plenty of exercises to work through in this book. However, before proceeding to the lessons that teach you about the WordPerfect keyboard, you must learn how to start the program. Those of you who already know how to do this on your computer system can skip ahead to the section entitled ''The WordPerfect Editing Screen.''

## STEP ONE: UNDERSTANDING DOS AND RAM

The first step is to turn on your computer and load the disk operating system, either PC-DOS or MS-DOS, into the computer's on-line memory. This memory is called *random access memory,* or RAM, and the process of starting the computer and loading the necessary DOS instructions into the computer's RAM is often called ''booting the system.'' Loading DOS is easy.

DOS is the master software that is used to start your IBM or compatible computer. It also works in the background to manage operations like loading and running applications software (such as WordPerfect or Lotus 1-2-3), coordinating the flow of data to and from the keyboard, screen, and printer, and saving and retrieving files to and from the disk drives. Although DOS is an independent program that must be purchased separately from your WordPerfect program, it is required in order to run WordPerfect.

When you hear people say ''you need at least 256K to run this program'' or ''my computer has a megabyte'' they are referring to the amount of RAM in their computers. The ones with a megabyte are bragging, since they have 1000K! You can think of RAM as the computer's on-line or working area, the place where characters are *temporarily* stored as you are typing and editing. Don't confuse it with the disk memory, either floppy or hard, which is where you *permanently* store your files. RAM is located on chips that you can see if you open up the computer, and it is only activated when the computer is turned on. All data contained in RAM is obliterated when the computer is turned off, whether intentionally or by a mishap such as a power failure, so it's essential that you save and retrieve files to and from the disk drive (which you'll learn to do in the next chapter).

If you have a hard disk (a C drive) in your computer system, it probably has been set up so that you can load DOS just by turning on the computer. If your system contains only floppy drives (A and B), you will have to turn on the computer and load DOS using a different procedure. The two approaches are summarized in the next two sections.

## STARTING WORDPERFECT ON A TWO FLOPPY DISK SYSTEM

If your computer system has two floppy disk drives (but no hard disk), you need to follow a few simple steps to start your computer and load DOS. Note that if you have just opened your WordPerfect package and have not yet made a copy of the WordPerfect System diskette with the necessary DOS files on it, you should turn to Appendix A and follow the instructions in the section called ''Installing WordPerfect on a Floppy Drive System'' before continuing.

Are you ready? Here are the three steps in detail:

1. Place your copy of the DOS diskette into the A drive and close the door or latch. If your disk drives are side-by-side, the A drive is usually the one on the left; if one is on top of the other, the A drive is usually on top.

2. Turn on the computer's power switch and, if necessary, the monitor switch. Some monitors plug directly into the computer and use it as their source of power, so they do not have a separate on/off switch. If yours has a power cord that plugs into an electrical outlet, look for the switch somewhere on the monitor (usually in the lower front panel) and turn it on now.

3. If a message appears asking for the date and time, be sure to type them correctly so that you'll know exactly when your files were created and saved. Enter the date by typing one- or two-digit numbers for the month, day, and year, separated by hyphens or slashes, as in 11/20/88 or 11-20-88 for November 20, 1988. Type the time using the 24-hour format, separating the hour from the minutes with a colon. For instance, if it is 3:45 in the afternoon, you must type *15:45;* if you type *3:45,* DOS will interpret it to mean 3:45 a.m. You could just press the ⏎ key twice to accept the defaults for the

date and time (usually January 1, 1980 at 0:00), but you'll need to enter the correct date in order to use WordPerfect's built-in Date function, which is explained in the following chapter. Some computers have battery-operated clocks that maintain the correct time and date even when the computer is turned off. If you are fortunate enough to have one, you can just ignore this step.

After DOS has been loaded, the disk drives will be silent and their red lights will be off. You should then see the following symbol, called the *A prompt,* on your screen:

   **A>**

This is your signal that DOS is loaded and ready to work for you, so you can now start your applications software, WordPerfect.

To start WordPerfect, all you need to do now is remove the DOS disk, insert the WordPerfect 1 disk and type *WP*, then insert the WordPerfect 2 disk when prompted and press any key. However, if you learn to start the program from drive B it will greatly simplify the tasks of saving and retrieving your files, so bear with me as I explain how and why.

***CHANGING THE DEFAULT DRIVE***   Since your WordPerfect diskettes have very little (if any) free space left to store your new documents, you must get into the habit of storing them on a diskette in drive B. This section will teach you how to make WordPerfect do this automatically. When you start WordPerfect from the B drive it becomes the *default drive,* meaning that the program will automatically store all your documents there (on B) and will always go there to save and retrieve them unless you indicate otherwise. By starting WordPerfect from the B drive instead of the A drive, you can save yourself a few keystrokes each time you save or retrieve a file because you won't have to type the name of the drive before typing the file name. Furthermore, you won't ever have to figure out how to correct the mistake of unintentionally saving a document on A or, even worse, what to do if you get an error message indicating that the disk in drive A is full and cannot store the document that you just spent hours creating!

Now follow these steps to switch to the B drive (this is often called "logging onto the B drive") and start WordPerfect:

1.  To switch to the B drive, type

    **B:**

    then press the Return/Enter key (◄━━┛). You should see this prompt on the screen:

    **B>**

    Remove the DOS disk

2.  Place the disk labelled *WordPerfect 1* into drive A.

3.  Now start WordPerfect by typing

    **A:WP**

    then press the ◄━━┛ key.

4.  You'll see this message prompting you to place the other WordPerfect disk in the drive:

    Insert diskette labeled "WordPerfect 2" and press any key

    so remove the WordPerfect 1 disk and replace it with Word-Perfect 2, then press any key.

If your screen resembles the one shown in Figure 1.1, you have succeeded in starting WordPerfect. Congratulations!

You're ready to skip to the section called "The WordPerfect Editing Screen" and learn about the screen you now see. It doesn't look like much, though, does it?

## STARTING WORDPERFECT ON A HARD DISK

If your system has a hard disk, starting your computer and loading DOS will be easy. Note that if you have just opened your WordPerfect package and have not yet copied WordPerfect onto your hard disk, you should turn to Appendix A and follow the instructions in the section entitled "Installing WordPerfect on a Hard Disk System" before proceeding.

Follow these steps:

1.  Turn on the computer's power switch and, if necessary, the monitor switch. Some monitors plug directly into the com-

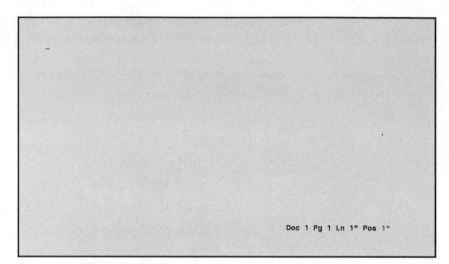

Doc 1 Pg 1 Ln 1" Pos 1"

*Figure 1.1:* The WordPerfect editing screen

puter and use it as their source of power, so they do not have a separate on/off switch. If yours has a power cord that plugs into an electrical outlet, look for the switch somewhere on the monitor (usually in the lower front panel) and turn it on now.

2. If a message appears asking for the date and time, be sure to enter them correctly so that you will know exactly when your files were created and saved. Enter the date by typing one- or two-digit numbers for the month, day, and year, separated by hyphens or slashes, as in 11/20/88 or 11-20-88 for November 20, 1988. Type the time using the 24-hour format, separating the hour from the minutes with a colon. For instance, if it is 3:45 in the afternoon you must type *15:45;* if you type 3:45, DOS will interpret it to mean 3:45 a.m. You could just press the ← key twice to accept the defaults for the date and time (usually January 1, 1980 at 0:00), but you'll need to enter the correct date in order to use WordPerfect's built-in Date function, which is explained in the following chapter. Some computers have battery-operated clocks that maintain the correct time and date even when the computer is turned off. If you are fortunate enough to have one, you can just ignore this step.

Hard disks have so much storage capacity that they are usually divided into smaller areas called *subdirectories.* DOS creates the main directory, called the *root directory,* when the hard disk is formatted. You create the subdirectories either by using a DOS command or by using one of the options in the WordPerfect List Files menu.

A *batch file* is a short file containing a sequence of DOS commands. You can easily recognize batch files because their names always end with *.bat.* When you type the first part of the file name, the DOS commands are performed automatically, saving you the trouble of typing several lines of instructions each time you want to execute a routine task.

What happens next depends on how your computer system has been set up. If you see a menu on your screen, you will have to follow its instructions to start WordPerfect. If you do not see a menu, the C prompt should appear on your screen:

    C>

This is your signal that DOS is loaded and ready to work for you, so you can now load your applications software, WordPerfect. To start it, you have to move to the subdirectory that contains the WordPerfect system files (unless a special type of file called a *batch file* has been created for you that can automatically start WordPerfect from your root directory). If you followed the directions in Appendix A and in the WordPerfect Appendix when setting up the program, the name of this subdirectory on your hard disk will be WP50. To move to the WP50 subdirectory, type

    **CD WP50**

and press Return.  The screen should now look like this:

    C> CD WP50
    C>

You can then start the WordPerfect program by typing

    **WP**

and pressing the ◀── key. If you see a message like this after you've typed *WP:*

    **Invalid directory**

or one like this:

    **Bad command or file name**

it probably means that your WordPerfect program is located in a subdirectory with a different name (instead of WP) or that the program is not yet on your hard disk.

If you see the screen shown in Figure 1.1, you have succeeded in starting WordPerfect. Congratulations!

## THE WORDPERFECT EDITING SCREEN

While WordPerfect is being loaded into your computer's RAM, you will see a startup screen with the program name and version, the name of the subdirectory it is using, and some copyright information, but this screen disappears automatically after a moment. In fact, on speedy computers like the PC/AT, it happens so quickly that you have to watch the monitor carefully or you'll never see it. After the program has been loaded and the startup screen has vanished, you'll see nothing but the line shown in the lower right corner of the editing screen in Figure 1.1.

### THE STATUS LINE

Your screen should now be blank except for a line of information in the lower right corner and a cursor in the upper left corner. The *cursor* is a small blinking underline character that marks the position where the next character you type will appear. The line of information in the lower right is called the *status line*. Its primary purpose is to provide information about the cursor's current location, but it sometimes provides messages, warnings, and other prompts.

***THE DOCUMENT INDICATOR*** The notation *Doc* tells you which document you are currently working on. WordPerfect can retain two files in the computer's memory simultaneously, an unusual and convenient feature that allows you to do things like copy paragraphs from a letter in the Doc 1 workspace into another letter in the Doc 2 area, refer to an outline in Doc 2 as you are typing an important document in Doc 1, and much more. Although you can only work on one document at a time, you can easily switch back and forth between documents and even exchange blocks of text between them. If you often make notes to yourself while writing, you'll like this feature since it lets you keep notes in one document while editing the other.

If you're typing a document and you press a few keys, then notice that your document has disappeared, don't panic! Simply check the status line to see if the document number has changed and looks like this:

**Doc 2 Pg 1 Ln 1 "Pos 1"**

If this happens to you, just press the Shift key and hold it down while pressing F3 once; this combination is called the Switch key. This will place you back in Doc 1, and whatever you were typing at the time will reappear. You'll learn more about this feature and try it out in Chapter 3.

The document indicator on the status line will always show either Doc 1 or Doc 2, with a few exceptions that you'll study in later chapters.

***THE PAGE INDICATOR*** As you would expect, the *Pg* notation represents the number of the physical page where the cursor is located. In other words, the page number shown on screen corresponds to the actual page where that text will appear when it is printed. In WordPerfect, a page is 11 inches long, but not all is for text, since WordPerfect leaves 1 inch of blank space for both the top and bottom margins. The page indicator will change to *Pg 2* after you do one of the following:

1. Type a full page of text.

2. Press the ⏎ key enough times to move the cursor to page 2.

3. Press Ctrl-⏎ to start a new page at the position where the cursor is located.

Try pressing the ⏎ key until you reach page 2, where you will see a line of dashes representing the page break. The page indicator will confirm that the cursor has reached *Pg 2,* as shown in Figure 1.2.

The type of page break that you just created is called a *soft page break.* On screen, it is represented by a single line of dashes. If you were to type a full page of text, you would see another single line of dashes, since WordPerfect would automatically create a soft page break at that point.

There is another type of page break called a *hard page break.* You use it whenever you want to force a page to end before the cursor reaches the natural end of the page, such as on a title page or a very short letter; for this reason, it's sometimes called a *forced page break.* As you'll see, it's much easier to create a hard page break than to press ⏎ over and over until you reach the natural end of the page (and create a soft page break). To make one, you press the Ctrl-⏎ combination, which produces a double line of dashes across the screen.

Try it now: press the Ctrl key and hold it down while pressing ⬅⅃. Do you see a double line of dashes, as shown in Figure 1.3?

To delete this extra page break, leave the cursor where it is (under the dashes) and press the Backspace key (the gray key with a bold left arrow symbol, usually on the top row of the keyboard above the Return key). The double dashes should be gone and the page indicator should have changed back to *Pg 2*. As you've just seen, when you

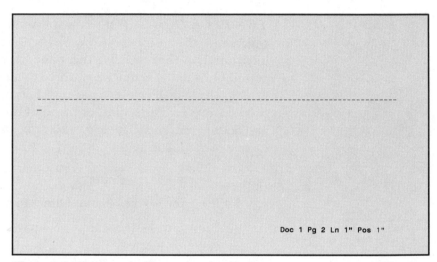

*Figure 1.2:* The page indicator showing Pg 2

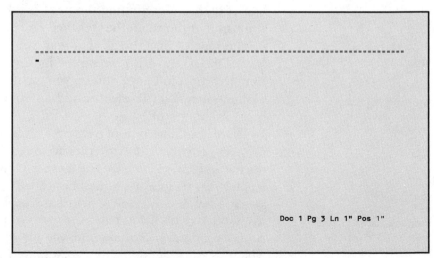

*Figure 1.3:* A hard page break, represented by a double line of dashes

want to delete a page break (either hard or soft), you just move the cursor to the left edge of the line that's just underneath the double line of dashes, then press Backspace.

***THE LINE INDICATOR*** The notation *Ln* tells you the position in inches of the line where the cursor is currently located. The line indicator changes when you do one of the following:

1. Type until the line is filled with text and the cursor automatically moves to the next line.

2. Press ←—.

3. Use the up arrow or down arrow (↑ or ↓) keys to move the cursor up or down line-by-line through existing text.

Try pressing the ↓ key. If you haven't moved the cursor since performing the exercise in the previous section (''The Page Indicator''), it will be at the bottom of the document and you'll discover that nothing happens. This occurs because there is no place left for the cursor to go, and it's one of the idiosyncrasies that many users may find perplexing. Here's why it happens: Since the cursor is located on the last blank line that you created (when you pressed ←— repeatedly to get to page 2) and you haven't typed any text below that point, the cursor has reached the end of the document and can't move down any further. As you've just seen, the ↓ key does *not* work like the carriage return key on a typewriter, and you can't move the cursor down any farther unless you press ←—.

Now press the ↑ key until the cursor moves back up to line 1. Notice the status line telling you that the cursor is now at the 1-inch position on page 1. (It starts at 1 inch because of the blank space left for the top margin.)

***THE POSITION INDICATOR*** The *Pos* notation shows the current position of the cursor. You start typing at the 1-inch position because this leaves 1 inch for the left margin on the printed page. WordPerfect also maintains 1 inch of blank space at the right side of the printed page.

Each time you type a character or press the Space bar, the number shown by the position indicator changes. It also changes if you use

WordPerfect's margins are normally 1 inch each on the left and the right. These are known as the *default margins* because they are in effect unless you use a menu option to change them. Many of WordPerfect's defaults, such as margins and tab settings, can be changed to suit your needs. If you find that your margins vary from this standard, it is possible that someone changed the *defaults* on your system.

one of the arrow keys to move the cursor over existing text. Try this exercise:

1. Type your first and last name.
2. Observe the number on the position indicator.
3. Press the Space bar twice and watch the number increase.
4. Press ← several times, watching the number on the position indicator decrease each time you press a letter.

There are times when you cannot move the cursor by pressing the → key. Remember when the cursor was at the bottom of the document and you pressed the ↓ key, only to find that it did not move the cursor? The same thing happens when you're on a blank line and there's no text or blank spaces (i.e. blank spaces created by pressing the Space bar) for the cursor to move onto. You can verify this if you wish by moving the cursor to the bottom of the document and pressing → until it won't move any further.

# THE WORDPERFECT KEYBOARD

To use WordPerfect to the fullest advantage, take a few minutes now to become familiar with the keyboard. WordPerfect is designed so that each key can be used to make word processing quick and convenient. Let's take a closer look at the keyboard.

## THE ARROW KEYS, BACKSPACE KEY, AND DELETE KEY

In the last section you discovered how to use the left and right arrow keys to move the cursor one position at a time to the left or right, and the up and down arrow keys to move up or down a line. On PC/XT-style keyboards, the arrow keys are found on the numeric keypad. Some keyboards include an extra set of arrow keys (in the middle section of keys, between the numeric keypad and the letter keys) that you can also use. Experiment with these keys until you feel comfortable with them.

Make sure you try the ← key because it's important that you understand the difference between it and the Backspace key (the one above the ◄┘ key). While both keys move the cursor to the left, the Backspace key also erases whatever it's backspacing over! Let's try it. Is your cursor still at the end of your name? If not, move it there.

1. Press the Backspace key three times. This should have deleted the three characters to the left of the cursor.

2. Press the ← key three times. As you can see, it moves the cursor to the left without deleting.

Remember this important rule: Use the ← key to move the cursor to the left, but use the Backspace key to move the cursor while erasing the text or blank spaces to the left of the cursor.

Now let's try something different.

3. Press the Delete key three times. Do you see that each time you press it, Delete erases the character that your cursor is on and pushes the text following the deleted character leftward to fill in the empty space?

The Delete key works like the Backspace key, erasing one character (or space) each time you press it. The difference is that Backspace erases the character (or space) to the left of the cursor, while Delete erases the character (or space) the cursor is positioned on.

## THE SHIFT KEY

There are two Shift keys on the keyboard, but they function identically. They are usually gray and feature an outlined arrow pointing upward. On most keyboards the right Shift key is located close to the Return/Enter (◄┘) key and the left one is near the Alt and Ctrl keys, as shown in Figure 1.4. You can distinguish them from the other keys that have arrows because their arrows are open, not solid black.

The Shift keys are used like they are on a typewriter, to type individual letters in uppercase and to type symbols such as the question mark, colon, exclamation point, and parentheses. Many new users think they can type these symbols by pressing the Caps Lock key.

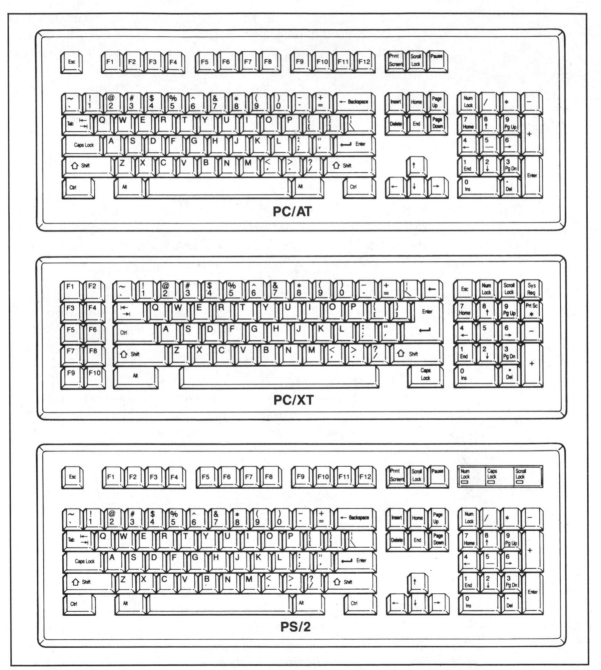

*Figure 1.4:* The PC/AT, PC/XT, and PS/2 keyboards

However, they learn quickly that Caps Lock doesn't do the job, for its only purpose is to convert the letters A to Z into uppercase. Even with Caps Lock activated, Shift must be used to type symbols such as the dollar sign or percent sign found on the numeric keys above the letter keys, as well as to type symbols such as the question mark and colon that are found next to the letter keys.

To see how it works:

1. Press Caps Lock once and type a question mark without pressing Shift. As you can see, you've typed a slash instead.

2. Now press Shift and hold it down while typing the question mark; it works!

Another purpose of the Shift key is to convert the keys on the numeric keypad so that instead of using them for cursor movement, you can use them to type numbers. Note that the procedure described below does not work on all keyboards. It should work on ones like the IBM PC and XT keyboards shown in Figure 1.4; on these keyboards all of the cursor movement keys are on the numeric keypad. Computers such as the PC/AT and PS/2 family feature a set of cursor movement keys that are separate from the ones on the numeric keypad, so this feature is not needed and may not work. On some keyboards, Shift reverses the keypad only if the Num Lock key is on, in which case pressing a key like 4 moves the cursor instead of entering the number 4.

To try it:

1. Move the cursor to the right side of the line your name is on. Make sure the Num Lock key is turned off before continuing. To do this, look at the Pos indicator on the status line; if it's blinking on and off, press Num Lock.

2. Press the ← key on the numeric keypad (number 4). This moves the cursor left one space.

3. Now press the Shift key and hold it down while pressing the ← key again. You should have typed a 4! (If not, your keyboard is the type that doesn't need this feature because it has separate cursor movement keys.)

The Shift keys have many other applications when pressed in combination with the function keys; you'll learn about these shortly.

## ALT AND CTRL

The Alt and Ctrl keys are easy to identify since they are actually labelled Alt and Ctrl on most keyboards. Generally, these keys are gray and are located at the left side of the keyboard, as shown in Figure 1.4. (Some keyboards, such as the IBM PS/2, feature an extra set on the right side.) Although Alt stands for *alternate* and Ctrl stands for *control,* these full names are virtually never used and the keys are always written as Alt and Ctrl.

Like the Shift keys, the Alt and Ctrl keys don't do anything when pressed by themselves. They are always used in combination with another key, giving that key a meaning it would not have by itself. In WordPerfect, the most important keys used in conjunction with Alt, Ctrl, and Shift are the *function keys.* You'll study them next.

## THE FUNCTION KEYS

The function keys are the ten keys labelled F1 through F10, as illustrated in Figure 1.4. On the IBM PC and XT keyboards, they are located in two vertical rows at the left side. On the PC/AT and PS/2 keyboards, they are on the top row.

Each function key has four distinct applications in WordPerfect, depending on whether it is used by itself or in combination with Shift, Alt, or Ctrl. To use one of the combinations, you press the Shift, Alt, or Ctrl key first and continue holding it down while pressing the appropriate function key once. We indicate such key combinations in the book with a hyphen, as in *Shift-F8* and *Ctrl-F2.* A proper name has been assigned to each of the four applications, such as *Format* for the combination of Shift-F8 and *Spell* for the combination of Ctrl-F2.

Try this exercise:

1. Press the Shift-F8 combination (hold Shift down while pressing and releasing F8 once).

As you can see on your screen and in Figure 1.5, a full-screen menu appears that offers several numbered choices including Line, Page,

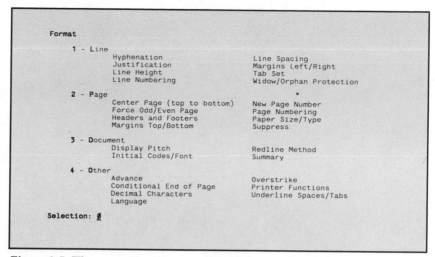

```
Format

    1 - Line
                Hyphenation                    Line Spacing
                Justification                  Margins Left/Right
                Line Height                    Tab Set
                Line Numbering                 Widow/Orphan Protection

    2 - Page                             •
                Center Page (top to bottom)    New Page Number
                Force Odd/Even Page            Page Numbering
                Headers and Footers            Paper Size/Type
                Margins Top/Bottom             Suppress

    3 - Document
                Display Pitch                  Redline Method
                Initial Codes/Font             Summary

    4 - Other
                Advance                        Overstrike
                Conditional End of Page        Printer Functions
                Decimal Characters             Underline Spaces/Tabs
                Language

    Selection: 0
```

*Figure 1.5:* The menu that appears after you press Shift-F8

Document, and Other. Notice that the cursor has moved and is at the lower left, next to the word *Selection:* and it is on the option 0. If you were to press the Space bar or ◄━ key once, you would be selecting option 0, the *default,* which causes the menu to disappear and the cursor to move back to the character it was on before you pressed Shift-F8. Nearly all prompts and menus offer a default, and the cursor waits underneath this number until you press another key. The default choice is almost always 0, which means exit; this removes the prompt or menu so you can continue typing or editing. You can usually invoke the default by simply pressing a key like the Space bar or ◄━, or by typing the number 0 (unless you type another number first).

2. Since you will not be studying any of these options until the next chapter, press either the Space bar, the ◄━ key, or **0** to eliminate the menu.

While many function key combinations replace the entire screen with menus like this, there are others that invoke prompts at the bottom of the screen, and a few that execute a command immediately with no display of choices. To see an example of each one, try the following exercises:

1. Press the Ctrl-F8 combination. This brings up the Font prompt shown in Figure 1.6.

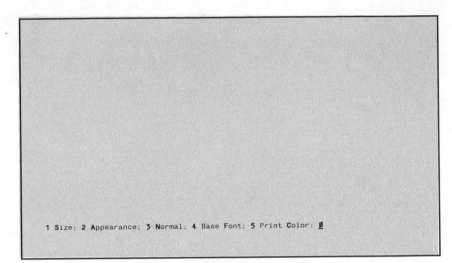

1 Size; 2 Appearance; 3 Normal; 4 Base Font; 5 Print Color: 0

*Figure 1.6:* The Font prompt

Notice the cursor at the bottom of the screen, under the *0*. As you may have guessed, if you press the Space bar or ← key the menu will disappear and the cursor will be back where it was before you pressed Ctrl-F8.

2. Press the Space bar to get back to the editing screen.

Shift-F6 is an example of a combination that executes a command as soon as you press it, automatically centering a line of text between the left and right margins. To try it:

1. Move the cursor to a blank line (press ← if necessary to get to one).

2. Press Shift-F6, then type your name.

3. Press ← again.

Notice that your name is centered. You can also center text after it has been typed, but I'll explain that in detail later.

You'll learn the proper names and the applications that have been assigned to the function keys and their combinations with Shift, Alt, and Ctrl in the chapters that pertain to each specific application. Don't worry about memorizing all these key combinations. You'll find that it won't take long to remember the ones you use most often, such as those that are used to save, retrieve, and print. Furthermore, you don't have to memorize the ones you use less frequently since you can look them up anytime using WordPerfect's on-line Help feature or glance at your function key template to find them. You'll study the WordPerfect Help key (F3) and take a look at several of the Help menus in Chapter 3.

*THE TEMPLATE COLOR SCHEME* The WordPerfect function key template, supplied with the program, fits around the function keys and helps remind you of what each one does. The template uses a color scheme to identify the forty key names for F1 through F10 and their combinations with Shift, Ctrl, and Alt. It works like this:

**RED**  When a name is listed in red on the template, the function key is used with the Ctrl key. For example, to use WordPerfect's spelling checker you press Ctrl-F2. Notice the word *Spell* shown in red on the template, by the F2 key.

**GREEN**  When a name is listed in green, the function key is used with the Shift key. For instance, to retrieve a document from disk you press Shift-F10. Notice the word *Retrieve* in green on the template, by the F10 key.

**BLUE**  When a name is listed in blue, the function key is used with Alt. To use WordPerfect's Thesaurus, for example, you press Alt-F1. Observe the word *Thesaurus* in blue on the template, next to F1.

**BLACK**  When a name is listed in black, the function key is used alone. To exit WordPerfect, for instance, you press F7, so the word *Exit* is shown in black on the template.

On the template, the words *Ctrl, Shift,* and *Alt* are written in their corresponding colors of red, green, and blue. If your function keys are on the left side of the keyboard, you'll see this color scheme in the upper left corner of the template. If your function keys are on top of the keyboard, it's between F4 and F5 and F8 and F9. In case you lose your keyboard template, you can display it on screen by pressing F3 (the Help key) twice. Go ahead and try it:

1.  Press F3 twice.

2.  As you now know, pressing the Space bar or ◄— brings the cursor back to Edit mode. Press ◄— when you finish looking at the template.

An alphabetical list of all WordPerfect commands and functions appears in the inside front cover of this book.

For many function keys and combinations, the proper names really tell you what will happen if you press them, so the template is quite helpful. Some examples are the Spell key (Ctrl-F2), the Date/Outline key (Shift-F5), and the Print key (Shift-F7). However, there are a few keys whose names are not very descriptive. Generally, these keys bring up menus or prompts that allow you to use a variety of features, so there isn't enough room to list them all on the template. One example is the Text In/Out key (Ctrl-F5), which you can use to convert files to and from other programs or to WordPerfect 4.2, place password protection on a document, create a document comment, and more. If you use them enough, you'll gradually learn these proper key names and the features they provide. Even though you may never memorize the actual keystrokes, once you know what the names stand for, you can easily find them by glancing at the template.

## THE RETURN KEY AND WORD WRAP

The Return key is the large gray key labelled ◄— and located just below the Backspace key on most keyboards, as shown in Figure 1.4. On some keyboards it is labelled *Enter,* since it's also known as the Enter key. Throughout this book it will appear as ◄—. In WordPerfect, the Return key does *not* work like the carriage return key on a typewriter, so those of you who are new to word processing should pay close attention to this section in order to unlearn an old habit.

Let's digress for a minute. Like most word processing programs, WordPerfect has an automatic carriage return feature known as *word wrap* that operates in place of ◄— when a line has been filled with text. Whenever you are typing a new line and the cursor reaches the right margin, word wrap automatically creates a new line and moves both the cursor and any words that would have exceeded the right margin position down to the new line. This feature also helps ensure that paragraphs will be realigned correctly to fit within the right and left margins after you add or delete text in the middle of a line. To use WordPerfect's word wrap feature, you must follow this important rule: *Never press* ⏎ *to end a line that appears in the middle of a paragraph, but always press it to end a paragraph.* In case you accidentally press ⏎ before the end, you can just press the Backspace key to cancel it and move the cursor back to the previous line.

To see word wrap in action, type the following sentences without pressing ⏎. But first, a word of caution. WordPerfect normally operates in *Insert* mode, pushing existing text to the right to make room for new words as you type them or if you press the Space bar to insert a blank space. However, it won't work this way if the default was changed to Typeover mode on your system. You'll learn more about Typeover in Chapter 3, but for now if you see the word *Typeover* in the lower left corner of your screen, press the key labelled *Ins* or *Insert* so that the Typeover message disappears.

Notice as you're typing that when your cursor reaches the right margin, it will automatically move down to the next line and the word you were typing may also move down with it (if that word would have extended past the right margin). Don't worry if the lines end in different places on your screen—just keep typing!

1. Type

   > WordPerfect's abilities extend way beyond basic word processing features to include such special features as a spelling checker, thesaurus, automatic footnotes, newspaper columns, and mathematical functions such as addition, subtraction, multiplication, division, and averaging.

2. When you get to the last word, press ⏎ to end the paragraph.

3. Use the ↑ key to move the cursor back to the word thesaurus. Place it on the t at the beginning of *thesaurus* and type the following phrase:

   > alphabetical and numeric sorting,

   After typing the comma, be sure to press the Space bar once. This will insert a space separating *sorting* from the next word (*thesaurus*).

As you saw, *thesaurus* was pushed to the right to make room for the new words you were typing, and it or the words that came after it may have been pushed beyond the right margin. In many cases, they will automatically move to the line below. However, sometimes you have to assist WordPerfect in this task by pressing the ↓ key.

4.  Press the ↓ key if some of your text has disappeared or is sticking out beyond the right margin. Did you see it move down to the next line?

The ←┘ key has a few other important functions that have no equivalent on a typewriter, so pay close attention! As you'll see from the brief exercise below, it's also serves to insert blank lines into your document, above the cursor. To insert a blank line above an existing paragraph, for example, you simply move the cursor to the first character on the paragraph's first line, then press ←┘. To test this feature:

1.  Move the cursor to the *W* in the word *WordPerfect's* and press ←┘ three times. Watch the cursor and your paragraph move down. Did you also notice the line indicator on the status line increase?

2.  Now move the paragraph back up and delete the blank lines. To do this, leave the cursor on the *W* in *WordPerfect's* and press the Backspace key once for each time you pressed ←┘.

Pressing ←┘ inserts a special, invisible character into your text, so each time you pressed Backspace you were simply deleting that character and the blank line that it represented. You'll learn much more about invisible characters, including how you can view them when necessary, in Chapter 4.

Another way you can use ←┘ is to divide a single paragraph in two. Test this now:

1.  Move the cursor to the beginning of the word *newspaper* in your paragraph and press ←┘.

2.  Press it once more to insert a blank line separating the two paragraphs.

3. Can you guess how to join the two paragraphs back together? If you guessed pressing the Backspace key, you're doing well! Go ahead and press Backspace twice now.

Last but not least, ← often works as an Enter key that must be pressed after certain commands are issued through a menu or prompt. In these cases, it serves as a confirmation to WordPerfect that you want it to begin executing the command. For instance, you can view a list of all the files stored on your default data disk or subdirectory by pressing F5, which is called the List Files key. To see how:

1. Press F5. You should see a message in the lower left corner of the screen that resembles the DOS command DIR. If you are using drive B to store files, it will appear as follows:

   Dir B:\*.*

   If you are using drive C, it will be similar to this:

   Dir C:\WP\*.*

   After you see this message you must press ←, now functioning as an Enter key. If you do not press ←, nothing will happen and you'll be looking at the DIR message indefinitely.

2. Press ←. A directory listing will then appear on your screen.

3. Press the Space bar or 0 to exit from this screen. Notice that pressing ← will not work since the default option on this menu is 6, Look. If the cursor is highlighting one of the directory names such as <CURRENT> <DIR>, you'll get stuck in an endless loop if you press ← repeatedly.

When using WordPerfect you are frequently asked to type something such as a file name and then press ←. I will often refer to these two steps (typing the name and pressing ←) as a unit by saying *"Enter the file name"* without explicitly reminding you to press ←. Below are the four distinct functions of the Return key.

1. Press ← to end a paragraph, but never to end a line that appears in the middle of a paragraph.

2. Press ← to insert a blank line above the cursor position.

3. Press ⏎ to divide a paragraph in two at the cursor position.

4. Press ⏎ to confirm to WordPerfect that you want it to begin executing a command you have selected from a menu or prompt.

## *THE NUM LOCK AND CAPS LOCK KEYS*

The Num Lock (numeric lock) and Caps Lock (capital lock) keys are important because of the effects they have on other keys. The Caps Lock key is labelled *CapsLock* and on most PC/XTs and PC/ATs it is usually a gray key to the immediate right of the Space bar, as shown in Figure 1.4. (On some keyboards, such as the PS/2, it is on the left side, above the Shift key.) When Caps Lock is turned on, all alphabetical keys that you type will be entered in uppercase. As explained earlier in the section about the Shift keys, Caps Lock only affects the A to Z keys and cannot completely substitute for the Shift key, which is still required for entering such symbols as the percent sign and dollar sign.

Both the Num Lock and Caps Lock keys are what we call *toggle* keys, meaning that you press them once to turn them on and press them again to turn them off.

The Num Lock key, also shown in Figure 1.4, is located on the top row of the numeric keypad. This key serves to activate the numeric keypad so that when you press one of its keys, the corresponding number will be entered. When Num Lock is off, many of these keys are used for cursor movement, as you will see in the next section.

On many keyboards, the Shift keys reverse the action of the Caps Lock and Num Lock keys. In other words, if the Caps Lock key is turned on and you hold down one of the Shift keys, any alphabetical character you type will appear in lowercase. Likewise, if the Num Lock key is on and you hold down Shift while pressing a key on the numeric keypad, you will not see a number on your screen. Instead, you may find yourself in some other section of the document, such as the next page, because this action converts the number keys into their corresponding cursor movement functions such as Page Up and Page Down (with the exception of the 5 key, which has no cursor movement function).

***THE CAPS LOCK AND NUM LOCK INDICATORS*** The position indicator on the status line corrects a significant deficiency in some PC keyboards (i.e., those that don't have lights or other indicators to tell you whether Caps Lock and Num Lock are on or off) because its appearance tells you the current status of the Caps Lock and Num Lock keys. When Caps Lock is on, the word *Pos* in the lower right corner of the screen appears in uppercase, like this:

POS 1"

When you turn Caps Lock off again (by pressing Caps Lock) the position indicator switches to lowercase, and looks like this:

Pos 1"

A blinking *Pos* message shows that the Num Lock key is on and the numeric keypad is activated. To turn it off, just press Num Lock once.

## EXITING FROM WORDPERFECT

Since you have just covered so much material, you're probably ready to turn off the computer and take a well-deserved break. Though exiting from WordPerfect isn't hard, it does involve more than just turning off the power switch and walking away. In fact, there is only one correct method of exiting from the WordPerfect program and that is to use the Exit key, F7. If you try to turn off the program using any other method, you'll create unnecessary problems. To understand why, you'll need to learn a little about how WordPerfect manages files.

### FILE MANAGEMENT AND OVERFLOW FILES

As you're typing and editing, WordPerfect is constantly moving data back and forth between the disk drives and your computer's on-line memory, RAM. RAM can be thought of as the computer's workspace. If your computer is equipped with a large amount of memory (640K or more) and you're working on a short document, you won't notice this movement because the system probably has enough RAM for both the WordPerfect instructions and the text you're editing. However, if you're working on a long document and/ or your computer has a more limited amount of memory, it can slow you down. As you move the cursor to different sections of the file, for example, WordPerfect moves the parts of the document that you aren't presently working on from the memory (RAM) to the disk, and this process takes a few seconds.

The movement of data to and from RAM creates temporary disk files called *overflow* files. Here's how they work: Text that appears on screen above the cursor position is stored in an overflow file called WP{WP}.TV1, while text that appears below the cursor is stored in a file called WP{WP}.BV1. (If you're using the document 2 area, you'll also have a WP{WP}.TV2 file and WP{WP}.BV2 file.) If you look at a directory listing of your files while using WordPerfect (which you'll learn how to do in Chapter 15) you actually see these file names.

To close the overflow files when you finish using WordPerfect, you must use the Exit key (F7). If you don't, the next time you start WordPerfect you will see an error message like this:

**Are other copies of WordPerfect currently running? (Y/N)**

and you'll have to press N to start WordPerfect. Pressing N also erases the overflow files. If you press Y, though, you go back to the DOS prompt, such as *A>* or *C>*, or to your menu if that's how your system starts, and you can rename those overflow files and retrieve them the next time you start WordPerfect.

You will explore this issue further in the chapter that covers file management, and you'll also learn how to set up WordPerfect to create backup files as you are working, in case the computer is unexpectedly turned off due to a power failure or some other unpredictable cause.

Now that you understand why, use the Exit key (F7) to turn the program off.

1. Press F7. You should see the following prompt in the lower left corner of the screen:

**Save document? (Y/N) Yes**

Notice that the message ends in *Yes*. WordPerfect inserts the Yes because it assumes your answer will be yes, and if you were to press any key other than N (or n) it would try to save the file. (Don't press anything yet, though.) For your benefit, the program is being cautious and making sure you don't lose your work by accidentally exiting without saving. Isn't that considerate?

2. Since you don't need to save the work you did in this chapter, press **N.**

3. Next, you will be asked if you wish to exit from WordPerfect, and this prompt will appear:

**Exit WP? (Y/N) No**

Once again, WordPerfect is double-checking to make sure you really want to leave the program, so the prompt ends in *No.* You'll find that if you press any key other than Y or y you'll remain in WordPerfect, ready to work on a new document, and the screen will be clear.

4. Press **Y** or **y.**

You should find yourself back in the operating system (or your computer's startup menu) with a DOS prompt such as B> or C> on the screen. Now it is safe to turn off the computer and relax!

## CONVENTIONS USED IN THIS BOOK

The WordPerfect manual frequently directs you to use named keys and combinations without telling you the corresponding physical keys to press, such as the Center key for Shift-F6 and the Date/Outline key for Shift-F5. In this book, both the key name and the exact keystroke combination required to execute it will always be listed. Although it may sometimes be redundant, this will help you memorize the combinations faster and save you a lot of time flipping back through the pages. This will also be useful in case you don't read the chapters in the order they appear and therefore don't learn each combination as it's introduced.

## *SUMMARY*

In this chapter you've seen how to start WordPerfect on your computer and how to exit from the program when you're finished using it. You've also learned about the editing screen, which shows the status line indicators, and about the many keys you'll use when working with WordPerfect. You've even learned a few basics about file management. Armed with all this knowledge, you're all set to go! In the next chapter you'll learn much more about WordPerfect by creating and revising a short letter, then saving and printing it.

**2.**

*CREATING, EDITING, AND
PRINTING YOUR FIRST
DOCUMENT*

# FAST TRACK

**To insert the date automatically**,         **40**

> press the Date/Outline key (Shift-F5), then press *1*. WordPerfect will insert the current system date at the cursor location (if you entered it correctly when you turned on the computer).

**Word wrap**         **42**

> is WordPerfect's automatic carriage return feature. When the cursor reaches the right margin as you're typing, word wrap automatically moves it down to the next line, along with any text that would have exceeded the right margin. Word wrap also helps realign paragraphs after additions, deletions, or alterations to the text. To use it properly, you press the ⏎ key only to end a paragraph or to insert a blank line, never to end a line in the middle of a paragraph.

**To insert text**,         **43**

> move the cursor to the place you want the new text to appear and type it in. Word wrap will automatically realign the paragraph when text is inserted.

**To delete text**,         **45**

> you can use the Del key or the Ctrl-Backspace key combination. To delete a character, place the cursor on the character and press Del. To delete a word, place the cursor on the word and press Ctrl-Backspace.

**To save a document**,         **46**

> press the Save key (F10) and enter a new file name. After the document is saved, it will remain on the screen so you can continue to work on it.

**To print a document,**

press the Print key (Shift-F7). You will then have the option of printing the entire file (press *1* or *F*), or printing only the page where the cursor is currently located (press *2* or *P*).

**To exit WordPerfect or clear the screen,**

use the Exit key (F7). At the prompt, type *Y* to save the document if it hasn't been saved yet. At the *Document to be saved:* prompt, press ⏎ to accept the name, or type a new file name. At the next prompt, type *Y* to exit WordPerfect or *N* to clear the screen and work on another document.

WORDPERFECT IS POWERFUL AND SOPHISTICATED, but that does not mean it has to be difficult. You already know that it's loaded with helpful features, which is probably the reason you purchased it in the first place, but it isn't necessary to learn every one of them in order to get some work done. In fact, you'll be amazed at how little you really have to know in order to produce documents such as letters, memos, and even lengthy reports.

The next four chapters are designed to teach you WordPerfect's essential word processing operations, and if you follow them carefully you'll be producing meaningful documents in no time. In fact, in less than one hour you will have succeeded in creating, saving, and printing your very first letter. Let's get started!

## A WORD ABOUT INTIMIDATION

I have a few words of advice to those of you who are beginners: Please don't make it hard on yourself. After all, Rome wasn't built in a day, and you shouldn't expect to learn and remember everything there is to know about WordPerfect in a day. As you know from reading the first chapter, there are over 40 different keystroke combinations that you can use to make formatting changes such as line spacing, margins, tabs, page numbering, and underlining; to perform important operations such as saving and retrieving files; and to move the cursor. Trying to memorize the keystrokes for every command and function the first time you use them would be a formidable task. I think it's infinitely more valuable that you use these exercises to learn about WordPerfect's many features and what they can do for you. Later, when you find yourself needing a particular one, you can easily go back and look up the exact keystrokes required.

There are many ways to look up the keystrokes. For example, WordPerfect's Help key (which you'll learn about in the next chapter) can provide you with on-screen, alphabetized lists of all WordPerfect features and operations, and the keys that you press to execute them. Therefore, as long as you know the name of the feature (Indent, Underline, Save, Retrieve, etc.), you can always find out how to use it by pressing F3 followed by the first letter of the feature. You can also locate features alphabetically and learn their corresponding keystrokes in the reference section of the WordPerfect manual, the reference card that comes with the manual, the inside cover of this book, or even the index of this book.

My goal is to help you understand what features are available in WordPerfect, how they work, and where to look them up when you need them. So relax, work through the exercises at your own pace, and have fun!

## CREATING A SAMPLE LETTER

Now that you've read Chapter 1 and studied all the preliminaries such as starting WordPerfect, using the keyboard, moving the cursor with the arrow keys, and using Backspace and Delete to erase unwanted characters, you're ready to create your first document. Figure 2.1 illustrates the letter you'll be typing.

Some computers have battery operated clocks that keep the current date in your computer's memory at all times. If your computer does not have such a clock, you were probably asked to enter the date and time when you turned it on. If you did not enter today's date correctly, WordPerfect's Date key will probably enter an incorrect date.

### ENTERING THE DATE WITH THE DATE KEY

As you see, the date will appear on the first printed line of the letter, so check the status line in the lower right corner of the screen to see if the cursor is on line 1, at the left margin (the 1-inch position). If not, move the cursor there using the arrow keys.

Instead of the date you see in Figure 2.1, let's place today's date in your letter. To do this, you can use a special WordPerfect key, named the Date/Outline key. This keystroke combination automatically enters the current date (as it exists in your computer), saving

```
April 15, 1988

Mr. Raymond Vaughn
Western District Sales Manager
2134 Main Street
San Ramon, California 90122

Dear Ray:

We sure are proud of you!  Once again you've outdone everyone in
the district with phenomenal sales figures.  Keep up the good
work and you'll soon be drinking Mai Tais on a beach in Maui: the
contest ends next month!

Best regards,

Janet Jones
National Sales Manager
```

*Figure 2.1:* Sample letter 1

you several keystrokes. Try it now:

1. Press the Date/Outline key, Shift-F5. (Remember to hold down the Shift key while pressing F5 once.) You should see this prompt in the lower left corner of your screen:

   **1 Date Text; 2 Date Code; 3 Date Format; 4 Outline; 5 Para Num; 6 Define: 0**

2. Press **1** or **T** to select the first option: Date Text.

The current date will appear at the cursor position and the Date/Outline prompt at the bottom of the screen will disappear. If you accidentally pressed any key other than 1, 2, 3, 4, 5, or 6 (or T, C, F, O, P, or D), you actually selected option 0. As a result, you exited from the prompt without using it and will have to repeat the two steps above. You'll learn about the other Date/Outline key options in other chapters.

## TYPING THE INSIDE ADDRESS AND SALUTATION

The next step is to move the cursor down a few lines and type the inside address.

1. Press ⟵ twice to move the cursor down two lines, then type this address:

   Mr. Raymond Vaughn
   Western District Sales Manager
   2134 Main Street
   San Ramon, California 90122

   Be sure to press ⟵ after typing each line.

2. Skip another line by pressing ⟵, then type this salutation:

   Dear Ray:

   Press ⟵ twice.

## USING WORD WRAP

Before you type the body of the letter, I want to remind you about a feature introduced in the last chapter: word wrap, WordPerfect's automatic carriage return feature. Whenever you're typing and the cursor reaches the right margin position, word wrap automatically creates a new line and moves both the cursor and any words that would have exceeded the right margin down to the new line. To take advantage of word wrap, you must not press ⟵ until you've finished typing the last word in the paragraph. If you accidentally press ⟵

before that, simply press the Backspace key. This will cancel the Return, and the cursor (and the word you were typing) will move back to the preceding line. As you'll see later in this exercise, word wrap also helps ensure that paragraphs will be realigned correctly to fit within the right and left margins after you add or delete text in the middle of a line.

3. Now type the body of the letter. Don't worry if the line breaks on your screen differ from those shown below, just keep typing.

> **We sure are proud of you! Once again you've outdone everyone in the district with phenomenal sales figures. Keep up the good work and you'll soon be drinking Mai Tais on a beach in Maui: the contest ends next month!**

## INSERTING A NEW SENTENCE INTO YOUR PARAGRAPH

Now let's see how easy it is to insert text and realign the margins.

1. Move the cursor to the *K* in *Keep*.

2. Type the following sentence and watch the screen carefully as you're typing. Stop as soon as you've reached the end of the last word.

> **In fact, if you close the deal with Johnson next week, you'll probably set a new national sales record, unprecedented for the month of January.**

As you typed, you probably saw some of the text disappear off the right side of the screen, but the lost words eventually reappeared on the line below, pushing the rest of the paragraph to the right and/or down to the next line to make room. After you finished typing the sentence, though, your screen may have looked something like Figure 2.2. Notice that several words are extended beyond the right margin and that a few seem to be missing. In fact, the last sentence now seems nonsensical:

> **Keep up the good work an beach in Maui: the contest ends next month!**

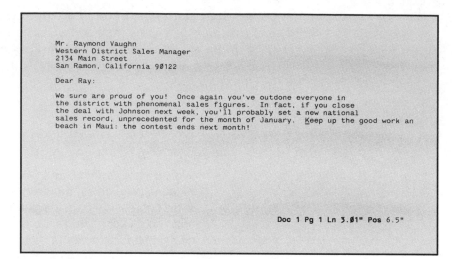

```
Mr. Raymond Vaughn
Western District Sales Manager
2134 Main Street
San Ramon, California 90122

Dear Ray:

We sure are proud of you!  Once again you've outdone everyone in
the district with phenomenal sales figures.  In fact, if you close
the deal with Johnson next week, you'll probably set a new national
sales record, unprecedented for the month of January.  Keep up the good work an
beach in Maui: the contest ends next month!
```

                                                    **Doc 1 Pg 1 Ln 3.01" Pos** 6.5"

*Figure 2.2:* Before rewriting the screen

Don't worry. Whenever you insert text and some words appear to be missing, just press the ↓ key. This action will move the cursor down one line and automatically realign the paragraph. WordPerfect calls this *rewriting the screen.*

3. Press the ↓ key to realign your paragraph correctly.

Now you're beginning to understand the power of word wrap. If you had pressed ⬐ after typing each line instead of letting word wrap move the cursor for you, you would not have been able to perform this feat. Instead, your paragraph would have ended up resembling the one below:

We sure are proud of you! Once again you've outdone
everyone in the district with phenomenal sales figures. In fact,
if you close the deal with Johnson next week, you'll probably
set a new national sales record, unprecedented for the month
of January! Keep up the good
work and you'll soon be drinking Mai Tais on a beach in Maui:
the contest ends next month!

To fix it, you would have had to find and delete the unwanted Returns, such as the ones after the words *probably* and *good*. This is because pressing ←⏎ actually inserts into your text an invisible character represented by the code [HRt]. It can only be seen in the Reveal Codes screen, which you'll study in Chapter 4. When you place the cursor on a blank line and press Delete, you erase the [HRt] code and delete the blank line. In our example, if you were to place the cursor right after the word *good* and press Delete, it would delete the Return character that marks the end of the line and bring up the remaining words from the line below to fill in the empty space.

## DELETING WORD BY WORD

Now let's see how word wrap works when we delete the same sentence. As you recall, you can delete text character-by-character. Try it now.

1. Move the cursor to the first character of the sentence (to the *I* in *In*) then press Delete. Keep pressing it until the first two words and the comma that follow them have disappeared.

See Chapter 3 for a complete discussion of how to delete text.

As you can see, this method erases one character at a time, so it would be quite tedious for deleting the whole sentence. In fact, you'd have to press it over 100 times! Fortunately, there are more efficient ways to erase text, including the Ctrl-Backspace combination that deletes a whole word at once. Let's use that to erase the rest of the sentence.

2. Press Ctrl-Backspace five times until you've erased the following words:

   **if you close the deal**

As you see, the rest of the sentence has moved up to fill in the empty space created by the deletion. Word wrap is again helping you realign your paragraph.

3. Continue pressing Ctrl-Backspace until you've erased the entire sentence. Press the ↓ key when you're done, in case any misalignment remains.

### *TYPING THE COMPLIMENTARY CLOSE*

Let's finish your letter by typing the complimentary close and author's name.

1.  Move the cursor down a few lines (using ◄┘), then type

    **Best regards,**

2.  Press ◄┘ a few more times to insert some blank lines, then type the name and title:

    **Janet Jones**
    **National Sales Manager**

See how easy that was! Now that you have perfected your sample letter, it's time to save it.

## *SAVING THE LETTER TO DISK*

Although you can see your letter on screen, it actually exists only in your computer's on-line memory (RAM) and is not permanent until you save it to disk. Since this type of memory disappears as soon as the computer is turned off (whether you do it intentionally or through a power failure), it is imperative that you save your letter to a disk file if you ever want to use it again. Likewise, if you later retrieve the file from the disk and make some changes to it, those changes will not be stored on the disk unless you save it once more.

Before I explain how to save files, let me offer a warning based on years of experience with microcomputers: Save your documents frequently while you're typing, especially if you live in an area where the power supply is unstable or if you're working during a storm. Losing five minutes worth of work is much less traumatic than losing a few hours worth. It's happened to me more than once, so now I'm in the habit of pressing F10 and saving my work every few minutes. I also use WordPerfect's automatic backup feature every five minutes; you'll learn how to use it in the chapter that covers file management.

There are two different keys you can use to save your letter, the Save Text key (F10) and the Exit key (F7). Both are easy to use.

## *THE SAVE TEXT KEY*

Use the Save Text key whenever you want to save the document on your screen in its current form and then continue working on it. After you use this method to save, your file will remain on the screen and in the computer's RAM (memory).

1.  Press the Save Text key (F10) once. You should see this prompt in the lower left corner of your screen:

**Document to be saved:**

The List Files key (F5) enables you to see all the file names that have a particular extension, such as *ltr* or *mem* or all files that begin with a specific character or characters. You can then ask WordPerfect to copy, delete, print, retrieve, or rename one or more of the files.

This message means WordPerfect is waiting for you to enter a name for your new file. You can type as many as eleven characters for your file name, divided into two parts. The first part can have from one to eight characters, either letters or numbers. The second part, which is optional, can consist of one to three characters. The last three characters are called the *file extension,* and they are often used as a means of identification. For example, I often add extensions such as *ltr* to identify letters or *mem* to identify memos. To type a file name with an extension, you enter the first one to eight characters then press the period key and enter one to three more characters. For example, if you were to name your letter VAUGHN.LTR, you'd type VAUGHN then press the period key and type LTR. You'll find it helpful to use meaningful names and extensions for your files, especially if you use a hard disk. This practice will help you enormously in the future when you have to keep track of hundreds of different file names on your disk(s).

Let's name the letter VAUGHN1.LTR in case you type any more letters to Mr. Vaughn in the future.

2.  Type

**VAUGHN1.LTR**

then press ⬅.

It doesn't matter whether you use uppercase or lowercase when entering your file name. Any lowercase letters will be converted into uppercase automatically.

While the file is being saved, watch the lower left corner of your screen carefully and you'll see a message on the prompt line (although on some computers it happens so fast you may miss it). If you're using a system with floppy disk drives only (assuming you followed the instructions in Chapter 1 to start WordPerfect), the message will appear as follows:

**Saving B:\VAUGHN1.LTR**

Note that *B* is the name of the drive where the file is being stored on disk and *VAUGHN1.LTR* is the name of the file.

If you're using a hard disk, the message will look like this:

**Saving C:\WP50\VAUGHN1.LTR**

*WP50* is the name of the subdirectory where your WordPerfect files are located. Your documents will automatically be stored in the same subdirectory, assuming you followed the instructions in your Word-Perfect manual and in Appendix A of this book, otherwise, your sub-directory may have a different name.

After the file has been saved, a new message will appear in the lower left corner of the screen, telling you the name of the file and the name of the drive and subdirectory where it has been saved.

When you save your document to a disk file, WordPerfect saves the formatting and information about the printer you are using along with the document.

## THE EXIT KEY

The second method of saving to disk is with the Exit key (F7). You may recall that you used this method in Chapter 1. This key has two functions when you use it to save:

- To save your work, then clear the screen so that you can either start typing a new document or retrieve an old one to edit

- To save your work, then exit from WordPerfect so that you can either turn off your computer or use a different program

To review how it works, follow these steps:

1. Press the Exit key (F7) once. You should see this message in the lower left corner of the screen:

**Save document? (Y/N) Yes**

Notice that the prompt ends in *Yes*. This is called the *default choice*. WordPerfect assumes that you really do want to save, so if you were to press any key other than N (either uppercase or lowercase) you would be answering *yes*.

If you have not made any changes since saving the document in the previous section, you'll also see this prompt in the lower right corner of the screen:

**(Text was not modified)**

This message means that no revisions have been made since you last saved the file, so the file on disk is identical to the copy on your screen. If you see it, you'll know that you do not need to save your letter before exiting. However if you've made any changes at all since you last saved it, even something as minor as pressing the Space bar or Delete key one time, you won't see the message because the version on screen differs from the one on disk.

Regardless of whether you see the *Text was not modified* prompt, let's see what happens the second time you save a file.

2. Press **Y** to indicate that you want the letter saved. Since you saved this letter previously (in the last section) under the name VAUGHN1.LTR, that name should now appear on your prompt line.

   If your system has only floppy disks, it will look like this:

   **Document to be saved: B:\VAUGHN1.LTR**

   If you have a hard disk, the message will be:

   **Document to be saved: C:\WP50\VAUGHN1.LTR**

3. Press ⏎ to indicate that you want to use the same file name. You should now see another prompt asking if you want to replace the VAUGHN1.LTR. The message for floppy disk users is

   **Replace B:\VAUGHN1.LTR? (Y/N) No**

   On a hard disk, the message will be

   **Replace C:\WP50\VAUGHN1.LTR? (Y/N) No**

This prompt is a warning and it's very important that you understand what it means so you'll know what to do the next time you encounter it. WordPerfect is alerting you to the fact that there is already a file on your disk named VAUGHN1.LTR (which may or may not be the same as the one on your screen) and asking if you wish to erase that disk file and replace it with the screen version. Be aware that the disk file could be something completely different, such as a letter someone else in your office wrote to Mr. Vaughn, so erasing it may be inappropriate.

If you ever see this Replace message text the first time you try to save a file (whether you were using the Save Text key, F10, or the Exit key, F7) and you know (or even just suspect) that you've never saved the document on screen, always play it safe and type N at this point. WordPerfect will then allow you to type a different name for your new file.

Since we know the letter on screen matches the one on disk, it's all right for you to replace it now.

4. Type **Y** (either uppercase or lowercase) and WordPerfect will then save the file, erasing the previous disk version.

As the file is being saved, the message in the lower left corner will change. Floppy disk users will see

    Saving B:\VAUGHN1.LTR

and hard disk users will see

    Saving C:\WP50\VAUGHN1.LTR

This happens so fast on some computers that you have to look closely or you'll miss it!

Next you'll be asked if you wish to exit from WordPerfect or if you'd rather cancel and return to your letter. You'll see this prompt:

    Exit WP? (Y/N) No          (Cancel to return to document)

At this point, you have three options: no, yes, or cancel. Don't press anything for now so that I can explain them all.

- If you were to press N or any other key except Y or the Cancel key (which you'll learn about in a minute), your letter would disappear from the screen. You'd remain in WordPerfect, but the screen would be cleared so that you could type a new document or retrieve an existing one from disk. This is like removing a finished letter from a typewriter and inserting a blank sheet of paper to begin a new one.

- If you were to press Y you'd find yourself out of WordPerfect and back in the operating system, with a DOS prompt (B> or C>) on the screen. As you learned in the last chapter, this is the only correct way to turn off WordPerfect when you have finished using it.

- If you were to press the Cancel key (F1) you'd cancel the Exit command and your letter would remain on the screen.

Since you are going to continue working with the letter in the next section, choose the last option.

5. Press the Cancel key, F1.

## PRINTING

Now you can print your letter and see the results of all your hard work! Make sure your printer is on and contains at least one sheet of paper. If you haven't installed your printer yet, please turn to Chapter 9 and complete the installation process before continuing.

### THE PRINT KEY

As you'll see in a minute, the Print key (Shift-F7) provides you with many options, all of which will be examined in detail in an upcoming chapter. For now, let's just learn how to print the letter that's on your screen. It's very easy.

1. Press Shift-F7. You should see the menu shown in Figure 2.3.

2. Select option 1, Full Document, by pressing **1** (not F1) or **F**.

Your printer should start operating. If not, check to make sure it's

Although the text on screen has a ragged right margin, it will have an even, or justified, margin on your printed copy. Right justification is WordPerfect's default setting; you can turn it off using the Format key (Shift-F8 1 3 N).

```
Print

      1 - Full Document
      2 - Page
      3 - Document on Disk
      4 - Control Printer
      5 - Type Through
      6 - View Document
      7 - Initialize Printer

Options

      S - Select Printer             HP LaserJet Series II
      B - Binding                    Ø"
      N - Number of Copies           1
      G - Graphics Quality           Medium
      T - Text Quality               High




   Selection: Ø
```

*Figure 2.3:* The Print key menu

turned on and ready to go. (Some printers have a button on the front or top with a light on it, labeled something like *on-line* or *ready,* and you may have to press it.) If your printer isn't working yet, don't repeat steps 1 and 2 again because it won't work. Instead, turn to Appendix A and make sure your printer has been set up properly.

## EXITING FROM WORDPERFECT

Now that you have created, saved, and printed your first letter, you may want to turn off the computer and take a well deserved break. To do this you'll use the Exit key (F7) again, not to clear the screen (as before) but to exit from WordPerfect.

1. Press F7. You'll see this prompt:

   Save document? (Y/N) Yes        (Text was not modified)

2. Since you haven't altered your letter since you last saved it, press **N.**

3. The next prompt asks if you wish to exit from WordPerfect.

   Exit WP? (Y/N) No        (Cancel to return to document)

   If you want to quit WordPerfect, go ahead and type **Y** for *yes.*

## *SUMMARY*

You should feel proud of yourself! You just succeeded in creating, editing, saving, and printing a document, and you explored some of WordPerfect's most important features, including word wrap and automatic paragraph reforming. Armed with all this knowledge, you can really get some useful work done.

At this point you may wish to practice creating, saving, and printing a few letters of your own. If not, go right ahead to Chapter 3, where you'll learn about some editing and cursor movement tricks as well as how to use WordPerfect's on-line Help feature.

3.

# MORE EDITING TIPS AND TECHNIQUES

# FAST TRACK

NOW THAT YOU'RE GETTING FAMILIAR WITH WORD-Perfect, I'd like to teach you some new tricks that will help you use it more efficiently. For instance, you'll learn several cursor movement methods so that you can quickly move word-by-word, to the beginning or end of a line, to the top or bottom of the screen, to the next or previous page, to the beginning or end of the document, and more. You'll also learn how to delete large sections of text, including whole words, lines, and pages, and you'll discover an exciting feature that you can use to bring back any of the last three deletions. Let's get started!

## INSERTING TEXT

As you've seen, WordPerfect is usually in *Insert* mode. This means that when you type new text or press the Space bar in the middle of a line of existing text, the new text or blank space will be inserted at that point, pushing any existing text and/or blank spaces to the right (and, if necessary, down to the next line) to make room. To turn this feature off, you use the Insert key (Ins).

On most keyboards the Insert key is located on the numeric keypad, on the same key as the *0*. Keyboards such as the PS/2 and compatibles have a second Insert key located in a small row of keys between the numeric keypad and letter keys. Insert is a *toggle* key, which means you press it once to turn the feature on and once more to turn it off. It's a bit confusing because when you press Insert, the feature you are turning on is actually Typeover, not Insert!

## USING THE TYPEOVER MODE

When Typeover is on, this prompt appears in the lower left corner of your screen:

Typeover

and new characters that you enter actually type over and replace existing text while you type. If there is nothing but blank space you won't notice it, but if there are existing characters they will disappear. To see how it works, try this exercise:

1. Move the cursor to a blank line and type this sentence:

   **WordPerfect is now in insert mode.**

2. Press ← to move the cursor back to the beginning of the word *insert.*

3. Press the Insert key once, watching for the Typeover message in the lower left corner of the screen. Now type

   **typeover**

As you can see in Figure 3.1, the word *typeover* erased the word *insert* as well as the blank space and the *m* in the word *mode.* If you pressed the Space bar after typing it, it also erased the second letter *(o).*

Some keys, including Tab and Backspace, work differently when you're in Typeover mode. The Tab key moves the cursor over existing text, without inserting tabs, and Backspace deletes characters but does not delete the spaces they were occupying. You'll see how the Backspace key works in the next section. For now, let's see how the Tab key works.

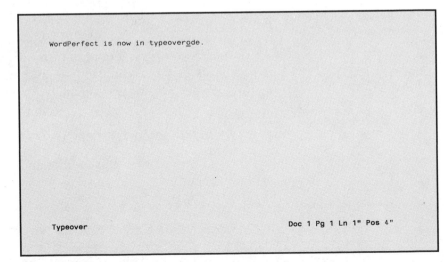

*Figure 3.1:* Using Typeover

The Tab key is usually found on the left side of the keyboard, next to the letter Q. Sometimes it is labelled *Tab,* but on certain keyboards it can only be identified by a set of two arrows, one pointing left and one pointing right. Unless you are in Typeover mode, the Tab key works just like the one on a typewriter, indenting the line five spaces.

1. Move the cursor to the left side of the sentence you typed in step 1 of the previous exercise.

2. If you don't see the Typeover message in the lower left corner of the screen, press Insert.

3. Press Tab. The cursor moves to the next tab stop, 1/2 inch. Press it again and it moves another 1/2 inch.

Now let's see what happens when we switch back into Insert mode and repeat the steps.

4. Move the cursor back to the left side of the sentence.

5. Press the Insert key so that the Typeover message disappears.

6. Press Tab.

Did you see that pressing the Tab key moved the text to the right? That's the way Tab usually works, inserting a tab stop and indenting the text, except when you're in Typeover mode.

The Insert key is often puzzling to beginners because pressing it takes you out of Insert mode, just the opposite of what you'd expect. However, it you remember to keep an eye on the lower left corner of the screen and watch for the Typeover prompt, you'll do just fine. If you see it (Typeover), you'll know that you're in Typeover mode and that typing will erase existing text. If this is not what you want, just press Insert once so that the Typeover prompt disappears, and new text you type will then be inserted into your document without erasing anything.

## DELETING TEXT

WordPerfect has several methods for deleting text that can save you considerable time and effort. These fast and easy techniques enable you to delete entire words, lines, pages—even special formatting codes.

## THE DELETE, BACKSPACE, AND ARROW KEYS

As you learned in Chapter 1, WordPerfect has two keys that you can use to delete a single character or blank space: the Delete key to erase the character or blank space the cursor is positioned on, and the Backspace key to erase the character or blank space to the left of the cursor. You may also remember that the ← key is the one to use when you want to move the cursor to the left one character at a time without erasing text.

When you use Typeover, the Backspace key works differently. While it still deletes the character or blank space to the left of the cursor, it does not move the cursor leftward to fill in the empty space. Let's try it.

1. Press ← to start on a blank line.

2. Type

   **The Backspace key works differently in Typeover mode**

3. Press ←.

4. Press Insert so that the Typeover message appears.

5. Move the cursor onto the *T* in *Typeover*.

6. Press Backspace three times. Notice that *in* is erased, but the blank space remains, as shown in Figure 3.2.

7. Type **in** again.

8. Press Insert to get rid of the Typeover prompt.

9. Press Backspace three times, watching the screen carefully. Notice that this erases the word *in* and closes up the blank space by moving the remaining words to the left.

## DELETING HIDDEN CODES

When using the Backspace and Delete keys, you may find that they sometimes bump into the hidden codes that control formatting

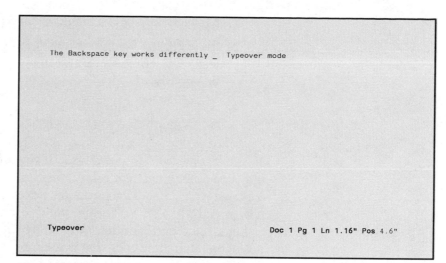

The Backspace key works differently _  Typeover mode

Typeover                                    Doc 1 Pg 1 Ln 1.16" Pos 4.6"

*Figure 3.2:* Using Backspace in Typeover mode

features such as boldface and underline, and a peculiar message will appear on your screen. Although you'll learn all about these codes in Chapter 4, I want to provide a brief explanation here so you'll understand the message if it happens to you earlier.

When you make formatting changes such as underlining, setting new tab stops, or centering a line, you are actually inserting special codes into your document that direct WordPerfect to make these modifications. These codes are not visible on the Editing screen because they would clutter it up and make it difficult to read (nor are they visible in the printed version). It's easy to insert a formatting code accidentally, unless you are extremely agile and never make typing mistakes. Since you cannot see these codes, it's easy to bump into them by mistake when using the Backspace or Delete key.

When you see a prompt such as this in the lower left corner of your screen:

Delete [BOLD]? (Y/N) No

it means that the cursor has moved onto a hidden code, in this case the code that controls WordPerfect's Bold feature. As you can see, WordPerfect assumes you don't want to delete the code and is asking whether you really want to.  Let's try it.

1.  Move the cursor to a blank line and press the Space bar once.

2.  Press F8, the Underline key. This action turns on WordPer-fect's Underline feature so that whatever you type next will be underlined.

3.  Type

    **hello**

Notice that the word is underlined. (If you are using a color monitor, it may appear in a different color instead of underlined.) If you were to continue typing and did not want the next word underlined, you would now press F8 to turn it off again (but don't do it for this exercise).

Let's remove the underlining from *hello*. To do this, you must delete the Underline code that caused it.

4.  Press the ← key five times to move the cursor back to the *h* in *hello*.

5.  Watch the screen closely and press the ← key one more time.

Did it look like the cursor stayed in the same place? In reality, it moved from the *h* onto the invisible Underline code. Look at the position indicator in the lower right corner of your screen, and remember the number.

6.  Press the → key once.

It also appears to remain stationary, doesn't it? Now look at the position indicator, where you'll see that the number has not changed. By pressing the → key, you just moved the cursor over a hidden code, but codes don't use up positions so it appears that the cursor is not moving. Notice that the number in the position indicator is under-lined (or in a different color).

7.  Press the ← key again.

It looks as though the cursor has not moved, but you can tell that it has because the number in the position indicator is no longer under-lined (or in a different color). Pressing ← caused the cursor to move to the left over the hidden underline code.

8. Now press the Delete key once.

You should see the following prompt in the lower left corner of the screen asking if you wish to delete the code:

**Delete [UND]? (Y/N) No**

As you can see, the name of the code, UND, appears in brackets and the message is followed with a (Y/N) prompt. Notice that it assumes *No*, so you must press *Y* or *y* if you want to delete it.

9. Press **Y** or **y** to delete the code.

The underlining should disappear immediately from the word *hello* (or the color should change if you have a color monitor).

Here's another exercise you can try. This one uses WordPerfect's Bold feature and deletes the Bold code with the Backspace key.

1. Move the cursor to a blank line and press the Space bar once.

2. Press F6, the Bold key. Type your first name. If you have a monochrome monitor, your name should appear in bold. (If not, try adjusting the contrast knob.) If you have a color monitor, your name should be in a different color.

3. Press F6 again, then press the Space bar. Now type your last name. Notice that your last name does not appear in bold; pressing F6 the second time turned the Bold function off again.

4. Use the ← key to move the cursor onto the space separating your first and last name.

5. Press the Backspace key. You should now see this prompt:

**Delete [bold]? (Y/N) No**

6. Press **Y** to delete the bold and notice that your first name is no longer in bold.

WordPerfect's hidden codes are summarized in a chart in the inside cover of this book.

Whenever you make formatting changes such as bold, underline, or double spacing, hidden codes are automatically inserted into your document. If you bump into them when using Backspace or Delete, you'll see a prompt asking if you wish to delete that code. If you don't want to delete it, press *N* or any other key except *Y*. However, if you placed it there accidentally and don't really want it, press *Y* (either uppercase or lowercase) and it will be erased. In Chapter 4 you'll learn much more about these codes, including how to view them and change them if they are disrupting your document's appearance.

## DELETING WORDS, LINES, AND PAGES

You already know how to delete characters using the Backspace and Delete keys, but WordPerfect has many other useful methods, most of which are quicker. In this section, you'll learn how to delete whole words, lines, and pages.

***DELETING A WORD***    To delete a word, you place the cursor on any character in the word or on the first space following it, then press Ctrl and hold it down while pressing and releasing Backspace once. To try it:

1. Type your first and last name on a blank line.

2. Position the cursor on any character in your first name.

3. Press Ctrl and hold it down while you press the Backspace key once. Is it erased?

4. Press Ctrl-Backspace once again. Now your last name should be deleted as well.

To delete several consecutive words, you would just hold Ctrl down and press Backspace repeatedly until the last word is deleted. To delete a word to the left of the cursor, place the cursor at the beginning of a word and press Home, then Backspace. Pressing Home and then Del deletes from the cursor position to the right until it reaches the end of a word.

***DELETING FROM CURSOR TO THE END OF LINE***    To delete from the cursor to the end of a line, you press Ctrl and hold it down while pressing the End key once. The End key is found on the numeric keypad, on the same key as the number 1 (and on AT and PS/2 style keyboards, in the small middle section of keys as well). To see how it works:

1. Type this phrase:

   **I have just learned how to delete word by word and
   to the end of a line!**

2. Move the cursor onto the *d* in *delete*. Press Ctrl and hold it down while pressing End once.

The rest of the line should be erased, as shown in Figure 3.3. Notice that this action also moved the word(s) that were on the second line up to the first line.

To delete an entire line, be sure to place the cursor at the extreme left side before pressing Ctrl-End.

***DELETING FROM CURSOR TO THE END OF PAGE***  To delete from the cursor to the end of the page, press Ctrl and hold it down while pressing the key labelled PgDn (or Page Down) once. The Page Down key is on the numeric keypad (and on the small middle section of keys for AT and PS/2 keyboards). The Ctrl-PgDn combination is called the *Delete To End Of Page key.* Since it has the potential to delete so

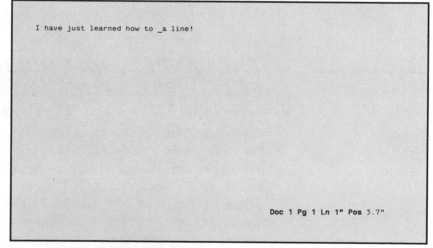

*Figure 3.3:* Using Ctrl-End to delete

much text, when you press Ctrl-PgDn, WordPerfect always double-checks to make sure you really want to do it. You'll see this prompt in the lower left corner of the screen:

**Delete Remainder of page? (Y/N) No**

If you press any key other than *Y* (either uppercase or lowercase), the action will be cancelled and the page will not be erased.

To try it:

1. Move the cursor to the left edge of the line you typed earlier.

2. Press Ctrl and hold it down while you press Page Down once.

You should see the *Delete Remainder of page* prompt in the lower left corner. Since the cursor is on the word *No,* if you press any key other than the uppercase or lowercase *Y,* WordPerfect will assume you do *not* want to delete the rest of the page.

3. Press **Y** to delete it.

Be careful with these keys, since they erase larger sections of text than Backspace and Delete. In the next section you'll learn how to *undelete* text (bring it back into your document) if you change your mind after using any of the deletion methods you've studied.

## THE CANCEL AND UNDELETE FEATURES OF THE F1 KEY

The Cancel key (F1) is the one of the function keys you should learn immediately because it can be a lifesaver. If you press F1 after having pressed one of the function keys (or combinations) that summons a menu or prompt, that menu or prompt will be cancelled and you can return to your work. This is especially helpful if you accidentally press the wrong key—which is easy to do—and see something unexpected at the bottom of the screen, or if your work disappears entirely and an unfamiliar screen appears in its place. F1 has another function that you'll love. When you press it alone (with no WordPerfect menu or prompt on the screen) it can undelete text and/or hidden codes that you erased recently. When used this way, it's called the *Undelete key*.

## THE CANCEL FEATURE

First let's see how Cancel works.

1. Press F10, the Save Text key. You should see this prompt:

   **Document to be saved:**

2. Press F1. As you see, the prompt disappears and you are returned to the editing screen.

If you had pressed the Space bar or ⏎, you would have gotten an error message (assuming the document on screen had never been saved) telling you this was an invalid file name. If you had pressed a letter or number key, WordPerfect would have used that as the file name. Pressing F1 is the best way to back out of a prompt like the *Document to be saved* message.

## THE UNDELETE FEATURE

The Cancel key's Undelete function is useful both to restore erased text and to move words, sentences, and even whole paragraphs or pages. When the cursor is in Edit mode and you press F1 (that is, with no other prompt or menu on the screen) you see the most recently deleted text (or blank spaces if you deleted those) in a highlighted block. You can then choose to restore it or to view text from any of the last two delete actions and restore that instead. Undelete only applies to deletions of text, blank spaces, or codes that you've made since you last turned on WordPerfect. As you'll see, text is always restored at the position where the cursor was located when you pressed F1, which is not necessarily the same place you deleted it from!

So far you have learned several ways to delete text, including the Backspace and Delete keys, and the Ctrl-Backspace, Ctrl-End, and Ctrl-Page Down combinations, and you'll learn others. As you learn them, keep in mind that the Undelete command works with all of them except for those methods that use the Cut options on the

Move key, Ctrl-F4 (which you'll study in Chapter 5).
Let's learn how Undelete works.

1. Type the following sentence:

   **I can't wait to learn how to use the Undelete key!**

2. Press ← once, then press Backspace four times to erase the word *key* and the blank space that came before it.

3. Press ← until the cursor is on the first character of the word *Undelete.*

4. Press Backspace four times until the word *the* has been erased.

5. Press F1. You should now see the characters you just erased (*the*) reappear in a highlighted block. You'll also see a prompt line like the one shown in Figure 3.4 at the bottom of the screen.

6. Press **R** or **1** to restore the word *the*.

7. Press F1 again and select option 2, *Previous Deletion*, by pressing either **P** or **2**. Notice that the word *key* is highlighted.

8. Since this is not where the word *key* belongs, move the cursor to the end of the sentence and position it on the exclamation point. (As soon as you press →, the Undelete prompt disappears.)

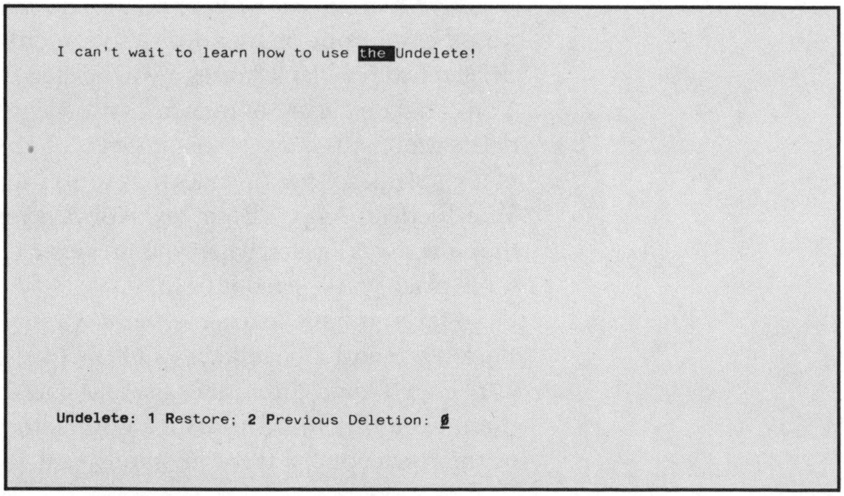

*Figure 3.4:* The Undelete prompt

9. Press F1 again and select option 2, Previous Deletion, by pressing either **P** or **2**. You should see the word *key* again. Since this is where it belongs, press **R** or **1** to restore it.

Up to three levels of deleted text can be restored using the Undelete key. In our example, level 1 was the word *the,* since it was the most recently deleted text. The word you deleted before that, *key,* was level 2. If you had deleted something before *key,* it would have been level 3, and to restore it you could have pressed F1 2 2 1. (You may find that you can use F1 2 2 1 to restore the text you deleted in the last section, when you pressed Ctrl-PgDn.)

## ADVANCED CURSOR MOVEMENT

The many cursor movement methods available in WordPerfect are listed in Appendix B.

As you type and edit your documents, you'll find yourself constantly moving the cursor to add, change, and delete text, or just to review your work. So far you've only learned how to use the arrow keys to move the cursor character-by-character and line-by-line; imagine how slow these methods would be if you needed to move the cursor to the end of a line, paragraph, or page, or to the bottom of a twenty-page report! Fortunately, WordPerfect has a large variety of keys that you can use for cursor movement, and you'll be amazed at how much faster you can move the cursor around once you know them. With only a few keystrokes, you can move word-by-word, to the beginning or end of a line, to the top or bottom of the screen or the page, to the beginning of the next or previous page, all the way to the beginning or end of the document, to a specific character or word, to a specific page, and much more. If it sounds like a lot, don't worry because you won't learn them all at once. Instead, we'll concentrate on learning the most helpful and frequently used methods now, and I'll introduce others in later chapters.

In Chapter 1 you learned how to use the ← and → keys to move the cursor one position at a time to the left or right, and the ↑ and ↓ keys to move up or down one line. On PC/XT style keyboards, you must use these keys for cursor movement; some keyboards include an extra set of arrow keys in the middle section of keys (between the numeric keypad and letter keys) that you can also use. If you aren't comfortable with these keys yet, experiment with them for a while, because they're definitely the most fundamental cursor movement keys.

## *AUTO REPEAT*

Like most keys on the IBM PC keyboard, the arrow keys are affected by a feature known as *auto repeat*. When you press an arrow key and continue holding it down after the cursor has moved one position, the cursor will continue moving until you let go of the key. Auto repeat also works when you press a character key such as a letter or number. Let's see how auto repeat works:

1. Move the cursor to a blank line.

2. Press **T** and hold it down until the cursor reaches the right margin, filling the line with T's. Use Backspace to get back to the right edge of the line if you went too far.

3. Press ⏎.

4. Press ↑ to move the cursor back up to the beginning of the line of T's.

5. Press →. Continue holding it down until the cursor has reached the right edge of the line.

6. Press → once more. Notice that the cursor moves to the beginning of the line below.

7. Press ← once and notice that the cursor "wraps" back up to the right side of the previous line.

## *MOVING WORD-BY-WORD*

As you've probably noticed, moving the cursor character-by-character can be tedious, so WordPerfect has two key combinations that are invaluable. We call them *Word Left* and *Word Right*. By pressing the Ctrl key and holding it down while pressing the ← or → key, you can move the cursor a whole word to the left or right. Let's try it.

1. Type this sentence:

   **I can move the cursor word-by-word to the left by pressing Ctrl and Left Arrow.**

2. Press Ctrl and hold it down while pressing ← once. The cursor should move to the beginning of the word *arrow*.

3. Keep holding Ctrl and pressing ← until you reach the beginning of the sentence. Isn't that easy?

4. Press Ctrl-→ until you reach the end of the sentence.

I consider the Word Left and Word Right combinations to be essential time savers, and I urge you to memorize them. Once you start using them frequently, you'll understand why I think it's so laborious and (often) unnecessary to move character-by-character!

## *MOVING TO THE BEGINNING OR END OF A LINE*

Now that you know how to move the cursor word-by-word, moving to the beginning or end of a line will be easy. Instead of pressing Ctrl first, you press and release Home and then press the ← or → key. Try it on the sentence you typed in the last section.

1. Move the cursor to the beginning of the sentence.

2. Press Home and release it, then press → once. The cursor should jump to the last position on the line (usually a blank space).

3. Press Home and release it, then press ← once. The cursor should jump back to the first position on the line.

You may wish to know that the End key does the same thing as Home →, moving the cursor to the last position on the line. However, since it's easier to memorize Home → and Home ←, I suggest you stick with Home → until you have memorized these two combinations.

## *MOVING BY PAGES AND SCREENS*

If your documents are lengthy and you want to move the cursor quickly from page to page or screen to screen, WordPerfect has four important keys to serve you: Page Up, Page Down, Screen Up, and Screen Down.

***PAGE UP AND PAGE DOWN***    The Page Up and Page Down keys are clearly marked *PgUp* and *PgDn* on the numeric keyboard and (only if you have an AT or PS/2 style keyboard) *Page Up* and *Page Down* on the keys in the middle row. As you would expect, Page Up and Page Down are used to move the cursor page-by-page, automatically bringing the first line of the next or previous page to the top of the screen.

We'll try Page Up and Page Down, but since you haven't filled a whole page with text and/or blank lines, Page Down will only move the cursor to the last line in the document. To overcome this, you will insert enough blank lines to fill a page by pressing ←⏎ until the line indicator shows that the cursor is on line 1 (the 1-inch position) of page 2. Let's see how these keys work.

1. Press Page Up until the status line tells you that the cursor has reached line 1 (the 1-inch position) of page 1.

2. Press Page Down.

If the cursor does not move to page 2, as shown on the status line, your document is less than one page in length. If so, you should now be on the last line of the document. (You can verify this by pressing ↓, which will not be able to move the cursor down any further.)

Refer to the section in Chapter 1 called *The Page Indicator* for more information about page breaks.

3. If you do not have a second page, press ←⏎ and hold it down until you see the line of dashes that represents the page break. The status line should now tell you that the cursor is on page 2.

4. Press Page Up. This should move the cursor to the first line of page 1 (at the 1-inch position).

5. Press Page Down. The cursor should now be on line 1 of page 2 (at the 1-inch position).

Fairly straightforward, wasn't it?

***SCREEN UP AND SCREEN DOWN*** What do you think would have happened if you had been trying to find a certain paragraph in your document using the Page Up and Page Down keys? Since the visible screen consists of only 24 lines (about 4.83″), you may have never seen it! In fact, if the paragraph had been located between the 5-inch line position and the last line on page 1, you definitely would have missed it.

Here's why: When the cursor was on the first line of the first page, you were looking at lines 1 through 24 (lines at the 1″ through 4.83″ positions on the status line), which is one screenful. When you pressed the Page Down key, the cursor moved to the first line of the second page, completely skipping the line at the 5-inch position through the last line on the page. Therefore, if the paragraph you were trying to find had started at the 5-inch position and ended at the 7-inch position, you wouldn't have seen it at all!

Fortunately, WordPerfect has *Screen Up* and *Screen Down* keys to help you solve this problem. There are two sets of them. The first is found on the numeric keypad, where Screen Up is the gray key marked only with a minus sign ( – ), and Screen Down is the key below it, marked only with a plus sign ( + ). The other Screen Up key is Home ↑, and the Screen Down key is Home ↓. Pressing Screen Up moves the cursor to the first line currently visible on your screen. If you press it again right after that, it moves the cursor up one more screenful (24 lines), bringing the new screen into view with the cursor at the top. Note that the last screenful will have disappeared altogether. Screen Down works exactly the same way, except in the opposite direction. Be aware that when Num Lock is on, these keys are converted into minus and plus keys and numeric keys, and don't work for cursor movement.

Let's try them.

1. Start by pressing F7 N N to clear the screen.
2. Press ⏎ until you reach page 3, as shown on the status line.
3. Use Page Up to move the cursor to the first line of page 1.
4. Type your first name.
5. Press the Screen Down key ( + or Home ↓). The status line should now indicate that the cursor is at the 4.83-inch position.

Note that this is the last line of the screen you were viewing when you began this exercise (although it may be hard to tell if the screen has little or no text on it).

6. Type the following:

Line 4.83

7. Press Screen Down ( + or Home ↓) once more. The cursor should have moved down to the 8.83-inch position (equal to one screenful). The words you typed in step 6 will no longer be visible.

8. Type your last name.

9. Press Screen Down ( + or Home ↓) a third time. Is the cursor on page 2 and has your last name disappeared?

10. Type **hello**.

11. Press Screen Up ( – or Home ↑). You just moved the cursor up one screen, to the first line of the screen that had *hello* on it. You should still see *hello* at the bottom.

12. Press Screen Up again ( – or Home ↑). Now the cursor will be on the next screen up and you should see your last name at the bottom.

13. Press Screen Up ( – or Home ↑) one last time.

The cursor should have returned to the first line of the first screen and the status line will say *Pg 1 Ln 1''*. Do you remember the words you typed in step 6 (*Line 4.83*)? They should be visible at the bottom of this screen, and your first name should be at the top.

I really depend on Screen Up and Screen Down, and I think you will too if your documents are lengthy and if you edit your work as much as I do. (Being a writer is tough!) If you're still unclear about how to use these important keys, try the exercise again later when you have typed a document that is a page or more in length—having several screens full of text makes it much easier to understand.

## MOVING TO THE TOP OR BOTTOM OF THE DOCUMENT

WordPerfect has two key combinations that you can use to move to the top or bottom of the document: Home Home ↑ to take you to page 1, line 1 (the 1-inch position), and Home Home ↓ to take you to the end of the document, wherever that may be. These methods should be easy for you to remember, because they use a familiar combination of Home and arrow keys.

To try them:

1.  Move the cursor to the end of the document by pressing

    **Home Home ↓**

    Try pressing the ↓ key—it won't move now because the cursor is at the bottom.

2.  Move the cursor to the top of the document by pressing

    **Home Home ↑**

    Notice that the status line says *Pg 1, Ln 1''*.

The Home Home ↓ combination can only move the cursor to the last place that you typed text (or pressed ↵ or the Space bar to insert blank spaces). For instance, if you stopped typing on line 4'' of page 1, that's where the cursor will be after you press Home Home ↓.

## *MOVING THE CURSOR WITH THE GO TO KEY*

The Go To key is the combination of Ctrl-Home, and it's always followed by another key or keys. It has several important functions, but only a few are relevant now.

1.  Go To followed by the number of a page in your document moves the cursor to the top of that page. This is useful when your document is very long.

2.  Go To followed by ↑ moves the cursor to the first line of the page the cursor is on. (Don't confuse it with Page Up, which moves to the first line of the *previous* page.)

3.  Go To followed by ↓ moves the cursor to the last line of the page the cursor is on (whereas Page Down moves the cursor to the top of the following page).

4.  Go To followed by a letter places the cursor right after the next occurrence of that letter.

To move to a specific page with the Go To key, you press Ctrl-Home and watch for this prompt in the lower left corner of the screen:

Go to

Next, you type the number of the page you want to move to and press ←.

To use the Go To key to move to the top or bottom of the page your cursor is on, you press Ctrl-Home then ↑ or ↓ (you do not press ← after the arrow key).

To use the Go To key to move to the next occurrence of a letter, press Ctrl-Home then type the letter (don't press ←). The cursor moves to the position following the next incidence of that letter (which must be to the right of or below the cursor, since Go To can't move up or to the left). Also, Go To is case-sensitive, so if you type an uppercase *R*, the cursor will move to the position after the next uppercase *R*. Although this can be helpful, once you learn about the Search keys (F2 and Shift-F2) in Chapter 6, you probably won't use it because Go To can only find a single character and move forward, while the Search keys can move the cursor to an entire word or phrase and move either forward or backward.

## THE ESCAPE KEY

The Escape key is found on the upper left side of most keyboards, and is usually labelled *Esc*. It serves as a repeat key, and when used with one of the arrow keys it moves the cursor multiple times in that direction. When you press Esc, you see this message:

Repeat Value = 8

and the next arrow key you press will move the cursor eight times instead of one. For example, if you press Esc then ↑, the cursor moves up eight lines. Try it:

1. Press Page Down.

2. Press Esc.

3. Press ↑.

You can use the Setup key to change the default for the numeric value that appears when you press the Esc key (it's currently set to 8). Press the Setup key (Shift-F1), select Initial Settings (*5* or *I*), select Repeat Value (*5* or *R*), type the number that you want to use, then press ← and Exit (F7). This change will be permanent unless you use the Setup key to change it again.

The cursor should have moved up eight lines (if there were eight lines above the cursor).

If you press Esc ←, the cursor moves to the left eight positions. You should try this one as well.

1. Move to the right edge of the line you typed earlier.

2. Press Esc.

3. Press ←.

The cursor should have moved left eight positions on the line. Incidentally, if you try this with the cursor at the left margin, it wraps up to the right edge of the previous line.

To move more than eight times, press Esc, type the number, then press the arrow key. Let's see how.

1. Press Esc.

2. Type **15** (don't press ←⏎).

3. Press ↓.

That should have moved the cursor down 15 lines (1½inches) (if there were 15 lines to move through). If you had pressed ←⏎ in step 2, this would have changed the number to 15 and made the prompt disappear. The next time you pressed Esc, the prompt would have been

Repeat Value = 15

Lastly, if you press Esc followed by a character, it types that character eight times (or whatever number you've entered). Let's try an example.

1. Press Esc.

2. Press **a**.

This types the letter *a* eight times (or the equivalent of your repeat value if you changed it).

I know we've just covered a lot of cursor movement methods, but so many involve the arrow keys that they shouldn't be too hard to remember. Here's a rule that may help: Pressing an arrow key alone moves once to the left, right, up, or down, whereas pressing Home followed by an arrow key takes you to the edge of the visible screen in that direction. For example, ↑ takes you up one line, but Home ↑ takes you to the top of the screen. Table 3.1 summarizes the most important arrow key methods, and these are the ones I suggest you memorize. You already know the first two pairs, so that leaves only four more!

*Table 3.1:* Cursor Movement with the Arrow Keys

| | |
|---|---|
| ← | Left 1 character or space |
| → | Right 1 character or space |
| ↑ | Up 1 line |
| ↓ | Down 1 line |
| | |
| Home ← | Left edge of screen |
| Home → | Right edge of screen |
| | |
| Home ↑ | Top of screen |
| Home ↓ | Bottom of screen |
| | |
| Home Home ↑ | Top of document |
| Home Home ↓ | End of document |
| | |
| Ctrl ← | Word left |
| Ctrl → | Word right |

## GETTING HELP

The Help key (F3) provides a fast and easy way to get information about any of WordPerfect's features. For example, if you forget which keys to press to make a formatting change such as double spacing, you just press a few keys and presto, there's your answer! Let's see how it works.

## *STARTING HELP ON A FLOPPY DRIVE SYSTEM*

If you have floppy disk drives but no hard disk, remove your data disk from drive B and replace it with the WordPerfect disk labelled *WordPerfect 1*. Press the Help key (F3). You should see a prompt at the bottom of the screen asking for the letter of the drive that the Learning diskette is in. Type (without a colon, in either uppercase or lowercase):

**B**

## *STARTING HELP ON A HARD DISK SYSTEM*

If your system has a hard disk, just press the Help key (F3) once.

## *USING HELP*

As you just saw, pressing Help (F3) temporarily replaces whatever is on your Edit screen with the initial Help screen. Notice the message *Press Enter or Space bar to exit Help*. This is how you will exit from the Help menus when you finish. Now follow these steps to view specific Help screens:

1. Type **S**. This brings up a screen of information about all the WordPerfect features that begin with the letter *S*, as shown in Figure 3.5.

Notice that the screen is organized alphabetically by the name of the feature shown in the middle column, such as *Save Text* (notice the column title, *Feature*). The keys you press in order to implement the feature are listed in the first column, so its heading is *Key*. The third column, *Key Name*, refers to the proper name which the authors of WordPerfect have assigned to that keystroke combination.

Do you see how useful this screen would be if you knew a certain feature was available but didn't know how to implement it (or just forgot)? For example, if you forget how to run WordPerfect's Search and Replace feature, look for *Search and Replace* in the middle column, then look to the first column to find out which function keys to press (Alt-F2). Let's find out how to change margins. Can you guess what to do?

```
Key              Feature                           Key Name

F1Ø              Save Text                         Save
Ctrl-F3          Screen                            Screen
+(Num Pad)       Screen Down                       Screen Down
-(Num Pad)       Screen Up                         Screen Up
Shft-F1          Screen Setup                      Setup,3
Alt-F2           Search and Replace                Replace
F5               Search for Text in File(s)        List Files,9
Ctrl-F9          Secondary File, Merge             Merge/Sort
Alt-F3           See Codes                         Reveal Codes
Shft-F7          Select Printer(s)                 Print
Shft-F8          Set Pitch (Letter/Word Spacing)   Format,4,6,3
Ctrl-F8          Shadow Print                      Font,2
Shft-F7          Send Printer a "GO"               Print,4
Shft-F7          Sheet Feeder                      Print,S,3
Alt-F5           Short Form, Table of Auth.        Mark Text,4
Shft-F1          Side-by-side Columns Display       Setup,3
Ctrl-F8          Size of Print                     Font
Ctrl-F8          Small Capitalized Print           Font,2
Ctrl-F8          Small Print                       Font,1
Ctrl "-"         Soft Hyphen                       Soft Hyphen

              Type 1 for more help: Ø
```

*Figure 3.5:* Help screen for the letter S

2. Type **M** (uppercase or lowercase). Note that if you exited from the Help menu back to the Edit screen, you have to press F3 first. This brings up a new screen similar to the last one but listing features that begin with *M*.

3. Look for *Margins Left and Right* in the center column, then look in the first column for the key combination you must press to change them—it's Shift-F8.

4. Type **E**. (If you exited from the Help menu back to the Edit screen, you'll have to press F3 first.) Can you figure out which key to use to exit from WordPerfect? It's F7.

Now let's try something different. As you saw in step 4 above, the Help screen can tell you that the Exit key is F7. However, that doesn't really tell you how to use it because pressing Exit gives you four options (as you'll see in a minute). To find out more about them while still in Help mode, you can press the function key itself.

5. Press F7, the Exit key. (If you exited from the Help menu back to the Edit screen, you'll have to press F3 first.) As you can see, the various uses of the Exit key are explained.

Many function key combinations bring up menus or prompts, which in turn offer several choices. When you call up their Help screens you see a list of these choices and (sometimes) brief explanations of what they mean. To get more information about one of the specific options, you can then press the number that appears next to it on the Help screen. That action will bring up another Help screen devoted to that feature. To try it:

6. Press the Format key, Shift-F8, then select one of the options shown.

The last way you can use the Help key is to view a copy of the keyboard template. To do this, you just press F3 twice. If you're already in one of the Help menus, you only need to press F3 once.

7. Press F3 (or press F3 twice if you exited from the Help menu back to the Edit screen).

When you're finished looking at the Help menus, remember that you have to press either the Space bar or ⏎ to get back to Edit mode.

8. Press the Space bar or ⏎ to exit from the Help screen.

You can print a copy of the function key template shown in the Help menu by pressing the Print Screen key (usually with Shift, depending on your keyboard configuration).

## *SWITCHING TO THE DOC 2 AREA*

As you may remember from Chapter 1, the Doc message tells you which document you are currently working on. WordPerfect can retain two files in the computer's memory simultaneously, so that you can use the Switch key (Shift-F3) to move back and forth between them and exchange blocks of text, refer to notes, and more. You'll find that it's easy to accidentally press this key (Shift-F3) because you must use the other F3 combinations such as Help and Reveal Codes so frequently. When you do press Switch, the screen changes and anything you were typing disappears. Since this will undoubtedly happen to you sooner or later, let's be sure you understand how it works so you know exactly what to do when it happens.

1. Press F7 N N to clear the screen.

2. Type your first and last name wherever the cursor is located.

3. Press the Shift key and hold it down while pressing F3.

Notice that your name is gone. Look for the message *Doc 2* on the status line, which tells you that you've switched into the second area of the computer's memory. You can now type a second distinct document or retrieve another one from the disk to edit. To prove it:

4. Type

   **I just used the Switch key!**

You got to the Doc 2 area by pressing Shift-F3 and can return to the first document (the one with your name in it) by pressing the same two keys.

5. Press Shift-F3. You should see your name again.

Notice that the status line now says *Doc 1*. Did the sentence you typed in step 4 vanish? Actually it's still in the Doc 2 area, and you can use the Switch key to see it again.

6. Press the Switch key, Shift-F3. You should see the sentence again.

## COPYING TEXT FROM DOC 2 TO DOC 1

Let's copy your sentence from Doc 2 into Doc 1.

1. Place the cursor on the left edge of the line and press

   **Ctrl-End**

2. Use the Cancel key, F1, to restore it here in Doc 2. Press

   **F1 1**

3. Press the Switch key, Shift-F3, to get back to Doc 1.

4. Use Cancel (F1) again to make a copy in the Doc 1 area. Press

   **F1 1**

## CLOSING DOC 2

Let's close the Doc 2 area before continuing. To do this, you'll switch back there and use the Exit key, F7.

1. Press the Switch key, Shift-F3. You should be in Doc 2.

2. Press F7 now and you'll see this message:

   **Save document? (Y/N) Yes**

   Notice that the cursor is under the *Yes.* WordPerfect always assumes you want to save your documents.

3. Since you really don't need to save this phrase, type **N**. Now you'll see this message:

   **Exit doc 2? (Y/N) No**

4. Type **Y** for yes.

You should now be back in Doc 1 where you typed your name and copied the sentence. Do you see them?

The document indicator on the status line always shows either Doc 1 or Doc 2, with a few exceptions that you'll study in later chapters. If you accidentally switch to Doc 2 and your work disappears, you now know exactly what to do: press Switch again, Shift-F3.

## *SUMMARY*

We've covered much material in this chapter, and I don't expect you to memorize it all at once. You can use this as a reference chapter and come back to it whenever you need a refresher on one of the many techniques you just learned.

The next chapter will be fun, because you'll be typing another letter and learning many new formatting techniques such as how to double-space, change margins and tabs, and use WordPerfect's automatic hyphenation feature to smooth out the right margins. Also, you'll study WordPerfect's spelling checker, a wonderful tool that can improve your productivity and accuracy enormously.

**4.**

# TEXT FORMATTING TO ADD EMPHASIS AND VARIETY

# FAST TRACK

**To change the left and right margins,**     87

press the Format key (Shift-F8). The Format menu lists four options; choose Line, which brings up the Format: Line menu, then choose Margins. Type the left and right margins, then press *0* or ⬅ twice to return to the editing screen.

**Center a line of text before you type it**     92

by moving the cursor to the left margin, then pressing the Center key (Shift-F6). Simply type your text then press ⬅. WordPerfect centers it as you type.

**To boldface text,**     93

press the Bold key (F6) once, type your text, then press F6 again to turn off Bold.

**To underline text,**     94

press the Underline key (F8) once, type your text, then press F8 again to turn off Underline.

**To indent the first line of a paragraph,**     95

press the Tab key, then type your text. The first line of the paragraph will be indented $1/2$ inch, but the rest of the paragraph will align with the left margin.

**To indent an entire paragraph,**     95

press the Indent key (F4), then type your text; the entire paragraph will be indented $1/2$ inch from the left margin. Press ⬅ when you've completed the paragraph to end indenting.

**To change tab settings,**     101

press the Format key (Shift-F8), select the Line option, then select the Tab Set option. You'll see a menu that marks each tab stop setting with a bright *L*. You may add or delete individual tab settings, or clear the old settings and replace them with new Tabs.

**To set line spacing,**  102

press the Format key (Shift-F8), select Line, then select Line Spacing and enter the number you want.

**To check for spelling and typing errors,**  97

use WordPerfect's spelling checker. If you have a floppy disk system, insert the Speller disk into drive B, then press the Spell key (Ctrl-F2), then *1*, then type *B:* at the prompt. If you have a hard disk, just press the Spell key. A menu will appear offering six choices: choose *3* to check the entire document, *2* for the current page, or *1* for the word the cursor is on. If WordPerfect stops on a misspelled word, press the letter next to the correct choice on the list, or press *4* to enter another spelling.

**Retrieve a saved file from the disk**  108

by pressing the Retrieve Text key (Shift-F10). WordPerfect prompts you to enter the name of the file. Type it in, then press ←┘. The file will appear on your screen.

**To automatically hyphenate text,**  109

press the Format key (Shift-F8), then select the Line option. From this menu, choose Hyphenation then select one of the two types of hyphenation assistance, manual or automatic.

**The Reveal Codes key (Alt-F3)**  112

enables you to locate and delete or change the formatting codes in your text. These codes are not shown on the editing screen. When you press Reveal Codes, you see a split screen that shows both the text and the codes, as well as the Tab Ruler. Press Alt-F3 to return to normal editing.

NOW THAT YOU'VE GOTTEN A TASTE OF THE WORD-Perfect program and are beginning to get comfortable with the basic editing techniques, it's time to introduce some new tools that can improve the appearance of your documents. If you're an experienced typist you're already familiar with concepts such as underlining, double spacing, and setting margins and tabs, but you'll soon see how much more powerful these features are on a computer. You'll also learn some tricks that you can't do with ordinary typewriters, including automatic hyphenation, automatic centering, flush right alignment, and spell checking.

Start your computer and load WordPerfect, referring to Chapter 1 if you need a refresher. You'll be typing the letter shown in Figure 4.1.

## FORMATTING YOUR TEXT

WordPerfect's powerful formatting functions enable you to easily produce polished, attractive documents. For example, you can bold-face a line of text, indent an entire paragraph, underline a heading—and much more. In the following exercises you'll discover one of the advantages of computerized word processing—text formatting.

### CHANGING LEFT AND RIGHT MARGINS

Business correspondence often requires wider left and right margins than the 1 inch (each) that WordPerfect provides by default, so let's change yours before typing. Although you can change margins anytime and as often as you want in a document, it's usually easier to do it before you type. The new margins you create will stay in effect the whole time you're typing that document (unless you change them again later), but they will not alter any other documents. It's important that you understand why.

Like all formatting changes, each time you change margins Word-Perfect places a special hidden code into your document. The code is saved with the file, so it cannot affect other documents. As soon as you clear the screen, the margins revert to the default settings, 1 inch on both sides. In the next chapter, you'll learn more about these invisible codes, including how to find and delete them if necessary.

```
                                        1001 First Street
                                 San Mateo, California 91123
                                        November 16, 1989


Mr. William B. Taylor
Service Manager
ABC Parts, Inc.
423 Main Street
Santa Ana, California 90124


                            URGENT NOTICE

Dear Mr. Taylor:

     As I told you on the phone this morning, there was
an apparent misunderstanding in the order we placed on
Thursday, November 7, and we recieved the wrong parts.

     As you will see on the enclosed copy of our purchase
order, we requested a replacement interface and cable for
a PC 110 and were instead sent parts for a PC 110B. We
were fairly certain that they would not work, but just
to be sure we went ahead and tested them anyway. As we
suspected, they do not work at all in the 110.

     Our customer is furious and in dire need of her
computer. If you wish to continue to do business with us,

            PLEASE RUSH THE FOLLOWING PARTS:

     A PC 110 interface, part# 66A and a PC 110
     cable, part# 76A, as listed in your catalog of
     November 1, 1988.

As soon as we receive them, I'll return the others.



                    Sincerely,


                    Sam Jones
```

*Figure 4.1:* Sample letter 2

You change the width of the margins by using the Format key (Shift-F8). Let's see how.

1. Press Shift-F8. The Format menu shown in Figure 4.2 should appear.

As you see, it offers four options: Line, Page, Document, and Other. Underneath each option is a list of formatting features. For instance, the Line option includes margins, tab set, and hyphenation. You select one of the four options by typing either the number next to it or the letter that is highlighted, such as *L* for Line. When you press *1* or *L*, you see a submenu containing the formatting features shown: hyphenation, justification, line numbering, line spacing, left and right margins, tab set, line height, and widow/orphan protection.

2. Press either **1** or **L** to select Line. You should see the Format: Line menu shown in Figure 4.3.

You'll learn about some of the other options later in this chapter, and by the time you finish this book I promise you'll know them all! For now, let's just change the margins. Notice that choice 7 is Margins, and that the margins are currently set to 1 inch on both the left and right sides. These settings are called the defaults. WordPerfect always uses these settings unless you change them, so you are using them by default

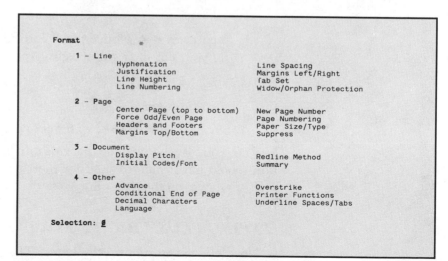

*Figure 4.2:* The Format menu

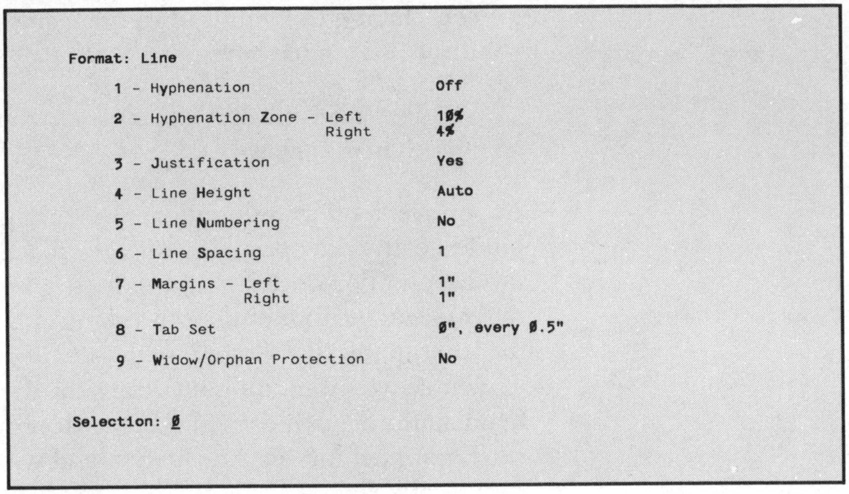

```
Format: Line

    1 - Hyphenation                        Off

    2 - Hyphenation Zone - Left            10%
                           Right           4%

    3 - Justification                      Yes

    4 - Line Height                        Auto

    5 - Line Numbering                     No

    6 - Line Spacing                       1

    7 - Margins - Left                     1"
                  Right                    1"

    8 - Tab Set                            0", every 0.5"

    9 - Widow/Orphan Protection            No


Selection: 0
```

*Figure 4.3:* The Format: Line menu

(although someone may have changed the defaults in your version of WordPerfect, through a menu you'll learn about later).

Let's change the margin settings so that you'll have 1.5-inch margins on both sides. To do this,

3. Press either **7** or **M** for margins. The cursor jumps to the current left margin setting.

4. For the left margin, type

    **1.5**

    then press ◄┘. Notice that WordPerfect enters the ″ mark for you. For the right margin, type

    **1.5**

    then press ◄┘.

5. Press either **0** or ◄┘ two times to get back to Edit mode.

Since you just changed the margins to 1.5 inches, the cursor position should have changed, and for most users it will be at position 1.5″, as shown on the status line.

## TYPING FLUSH RIGHT TEXT

Now let's get started on the letter. The first step is to type the return address and date in the upper right corner of the page. Do you see how the three lines are aligned against the right margin in Figure 4.1? WordPerfect has a Flush Right key (Alt-F6) that will do this automatically for you. When you press it, the cursor moves one position beyond the right margin, and whatever you type after that will be pushed to the left until you press the ◄━┘ key. The last letter on the line (or blank space inserted with the Space bar) will end up at the right margin.

Go ahead and try it.

1. Press the Flush Right key (Alt-F6). You should see the cursor jump to the position just beyond the right margin.

2. As you type the first line, watch the characters move leftward from the right side. Type

    **1001 First Street**

    then press ◄━┘. Since the ◄━┘ key signals the end of the flush right action, the cursor moves back to the left margin.

3. Since the Flush Right feature operates on only one line at a time, you'll have to press the Flush Right key again before typing the next line. Press Alt F6 and type

    **San Mateo, California 91123**

    then press ◄━┘.

Do you remember the Date/Outline key from the last chapter? Let's use it again to "type" today's date into this letter.

4. Since the date will be aligned against the right margin, press Alt-F6.

5. Press the Date/Outline key (Shift-F5). To select option 1—Date Text—type either **T** or **1** (remember to press the number *1*, not F1).

Did you see how the date was inserted and pushed to the left?

The Flush Right key is a useful feature, but you have to be careful with it. It was designed for short lines of text, such as the ones you just typed, in which all the words are right aligned. Although you can type a few words before pressing Flush Right, if you type too many you could get strange results. Some of your text could disappear altogether! This happens only if the total number of characters exceeds

Remember that this date matches the date in your computer's memory. If you did not type the correct date (if asked) when you first turned on the computer, the date you'll see when you use WordPerfect's Date key probably will be January 1, 1980.

You can also use WordPerfect's Flush Right feature on text that has already been typed, if the line ends in a hard return (i.e., you pressed ← after typing it). To do this, move the cursor to the first character on the line, press Alt-F6, then press the ↓ key.

the total number of positions available for text on a line. Here's why: You type several words, then press the Flush Right key and continue typing. The new words are pushed to the left and, as you keep typing, they finally bump into the ones which had been typed before you pressed Flush Right. Since there is no room left on the line, they vanish from the Edit screen (but can still be seen in Reveal Codes).

You'll be learning more about the hidden codes later in this chapter, including how to use the Reveal Codes screen to get you out of such dilemmas, so don't worry about it now. Just be careful not to type more than a few words on a line before pressing the Flush Right key and you'll stay out of trouble.

6. Move the cursor down by pressing ← three times, and type this inside address:

> Mr. William B. Taylor
> Service Manager
> ABC Parts, Inc.
> 423 Main Street
> Santa Ana, California 90124

7. Press ← several times to skip three lines.

Since the next phrase, *URGENT NOTICE,* must grab the reader's attention, it will be centered, capitalized, and printed in boldface. That sounds like a lot to learn, but it's actually just a matter of pressing a few keys.

## CENTERING TEXT

To center an existing line of text, you move the cursor to the first character, press the Center Key (Shift-F6), then press the ↓ key to realign it. The line you wish to center must end in a hard return (i.e., you must have pressed the ← key after typing it).

You can center a line of text either before or after typing it, but it's easier to do it before. Be sure that the cursor is at the left margin before you begin.

1. Press the Center key, Shift-F6. You'll see the cursor move to the middle of the page, to position 4.2″. Don't start typing yet.

## TYPING UPPERCASE CHARACTERS

The easiest way to type the phrase in capital letters is to press the Caps Lock key before you begin. Be sure to turn it off (by pressing it once more) when you want to start typing in lowercase again.

2. Press Caps Lock once. Do you see that the position indicator (Pos) on the status line changed to uppercase (POS)? It will stay this way until you press Caps Lock once again (don't do it yet though) to turn off the feature.

## *BOLDFACING TEXT*

Boldfacing is easy, and it works just like Caps Lock: you press the Bold key (F6) once to switch it on before you start typing, then press it once again to turn it off after you finish typing the word or words you want in bold. When it's on, the number next to the position indicator will appear bolder on your screen, or in color if you have a color monitor. Although you can boldface text after it has been typed, it's much easier to do it before you begin typing it.

You can boldface text that has already been typed, as well as convert it from lowercase to uppercase, using WordPerfect's Block key. You'll learn how to do this in Chapter 6.

3. Press the Bold key (F6) once. The position indicator number should appear brighter or in another color, like the rest of the text on the status line.

4. Type the following *without pressing* ⬅:

   **URGENT NOTICE**

The phrase should be centered, capitalized, and brighter than the rest of the text (or in a different color if you have a color monitor); if you have a monochrome screen and it's not bolder, try adjusting the contrast button on your monitor.

The Caps Lock and Bold keys are toggle commands, so they stay in effect until you press them again to turn them off. Since you are finished using them, let's deactivate them.

5. Press the Caps Lock key once, then press the Bold key (F6) once. Check the position indicator and the number following it to confirm that they are turned off.

6. Press ⬅ twice to skip a line then type this salutation:

   **Dear Mr. Taylor:**

followed by ⬅ twice.

## *USING TABS*

As you see, the first line in each paragraph of the letter is indented five spaces. You should use the Tab key to do this, just like you would on a

It's particularly important to use the Tab key, not the Space bar, to indent your text if you use proportional spacing. In such a case, using the Space bar instead of Tab results in spaces that look much different in the printed document than they do on screen. You'll learn more about proportional spacing and other special printer effects in Chapter 9.

typewriter. Since tab stops are initially set for every ½ inch, each time you press the Tab key the cursor will jump to the right ½ inch.

The Tab key is usually found on the left side of the keyboard, next to the letter Q. Sometimes it is labelled *Tab,* but on certain keyboards it can only be identified by a set of two arrows, one pointing left and one pointing right.

Type the next three paragraphs of the letter, using the Tab key before you start typing the first line in each paragraph. By the way, you may have noticed that the word *received* is spelled incorrectly as *recieved.* I did this deliberately so that you can correct it later with the spelling checker, so be sure you misspell it!

1.  Press Tab once, then type

    As I told you on the phone this morning, there was an apparent misunderstanding in the order we placed on Thursday, November 7, and we recieved the wrong parts.

2.  Press ← to end the paragraph. Press it again to leave a blank line separating this from the next paragraph.

3.  Press Tab once and type

    As you will see on the enclosed copy of our purchase order, we requested a replacement interface and cable for a PC 110 and were instead sent parts for a PC 110B. We were fairly certain that they would not work, but just to be sure we went ahead and tested them anyway. As we suspected, they do not work at all in the 110.

4.  Press ← twice, to end the paragraph and leave a blank line.

5.  Press Tab once and type

    Our customer is furious and in dire need of her computer. If you wish to continue to do business with us,

## *UNDERLINING TEXT*

The phrase after ''If you wish to continue to do business with us,'' will be capitalized, underlined, and centered. The Underline key works exactly like the Bold key; you press it once to turn it on, type the text, then press it again to turn it off and continue typing.

When you press F8 to begin underlining, the number that follows the position indicator (*Pos*) will appear underlined (or in a different color on some color monitors). This signal will always appear when you turn on underlining, or if your cursor is positioned on a character that has been underlined.

1. Press ← twice to skip a line, then press Caps Lock, Underline (F8), and Center (Shift-F6). You should see *POS* on the status line in uppercase, the number next to it should be underlined or in a different color, and the cursor should have jumped to the middle of the line. Type

**PLEASE** <u>RUSH</u> **THE** <u>FOLLOWING</u> **PARTS:**

2. Now turn off Underline and Caps Lock before typing the rest of the letter. Press the Underline key (F8) once, then press Caps Lock once. The underline should have disappeared from the number next to the position indicator, and the *Pos* message should be in lowercase.

## *THE TAB AND INDENT KEYS*

Look at the next three lines; do you see that the entire paragraph is indented 1 inch from the left margin? WordPerfect does this automatically for you when you use the Indent key (F4). It's important that you understand the difference between WordPerfect's Tab and Indent keys. To indent only the first line in a paragraph, you press the Tab key, as you did at the beginning of the first three paragraphs. However, if you want every line in the paragraph to automatically begin at an indented position, you use the Indent key. Let's see how it works.

1. Press ← three times to skip two lines.

2. Press the Indent key (F4) two times (to indent the paragraph two tab stops instead of just one), then type the following sentence. Do not press ← until you have typed the very last word, *1988*.

> A PC 110 interface, part# 66A and a PC 110 cable, part# 76A, as listed in your catalog of November 1, 1988.

Wasn't that easy? Did you see how the cursor automatically wrapped to the indented position after it reached the right margin? The real advantage of using the Indent key is that it makes the process of realigning your margins completely automatic if you add or delete text in the middle of the paragraph. Let's try it by splitting the sentence in two and changing the second sentence to read as follows:

> **These parts are listed on page 20 in your catalog of**
> **November 1, 1988.**

3. Type a period after *76A,* then press the Space bar twice to insert two blank spaces. Press Delete to erase the comma.

4. Type

> **These parts are**

5. Use the Delete key to erase the word *as.*

6. Move the cursor to the *i* in the word *in,* press the Space bar once, then type

> **on page 20**

7. Press the ↓ key when you are finished in case the text needs to be realigned.

If you had used the Tab key at the beginning of each line in the indented paragraph, the new text would not have been aligned correctly to fit into the indented margins.

8. Press ⏎ twice. Press Tab once then type

> **As soon as we receive them, I'll return the others.**

Since the paragraph you just typed consisted of only one line, you used Tab instead of Indent to insert the five blank spaces. If you were to insert several more words or another sentence into this paragraph and it spilled over to a second line, you *would* want the second line to start at the regular left margin (15) instead of the indented position (20). This only happens if you use the Tab key instead of Indent.

9. Now press ⏎ four times, then press Tab seven times and type

> **Sincerely,**

10. Press ⏎ several times.

11. Press Tab seven times and type

    Sam Jones

## USING THE SPELLER

Now that the letter is finished, it would be a good idea to check it for typing and spelling errors. WordPerfect has a built-in spelling checker that can do the job very easily and quickly.

If you're using a floppy disk system, you'll have to insert your Speller disk into drive B before continuing. (If you have a hard disk, the Speller should already be copied onto it.) Follow these steps:

1. If you're using a floppy disk system, place the Speller disk into drive B.

2. Press the Spell key, Ctrl-F2, then (if you have a floppy system) press **1** to select Enter Path. Type **B:** in response to the prompt asking for the temporary dictionary path.

You now should see a menu on the status line that resembles the one below:

**Check: 1 Word; 2 Page; 3 Document;**
**4 New Sup. Dictionary; 5 Look up; 6 Count: 0**

The first three options pertain to spell checking; you can check either the word the cursor is positioned on, the page the cursor is on, or the entire document.

3. Since you want to check the entire document, press either *3* or **D**.

As WordPerfect begins to check your letter, you may see a *Please Wait* message on the status line (but on some computers it happens so fast you'll miss it if you don't watch carefully). Soon you will see the word *Mateo* highlighted, as shown in Figure 4.4.

If you see an error message after you press the Spell key, refer to the Setup menu (Shift-F1).

```
                                           1001 First Street
                           San Mateo, California 91123
                                           November 16, 1989

         Mr. William B. Taylor
         Service Manager
         ABC Parts, Inc.
         423 Main Street
         Santa Ana, California 90124


         ==================================================================

            A. mate            B. mated           C. mater
            D. mates           E. matzo           F. mad
            G. made            H. maid            I. mat
            J. math            K. matt            L. matte
            M. mayday          N. mead            O. meadow
            P. meadowy         Q. meat            R. meaty
            S. med             T. media           U. mediae
            V. medii           W. meed            X. meet
         Press Enter for more words

         Not Found: 1 Skip Once; 2 Skip; 3 Add Word; 4 Edit; 5 Look Up: 0
```

*Figure 4.4:* The Speller in action

The Speller contains over 100,000 words, including many common names such as Smith and Jones, but it does not include all proper names (such as city names) so it assumes that *Mateo* is misspelled. Notice the *Not Found* message on the status line—it does not necessarily mean that the word is misspelled, just that it was not found in the dictionary. Above the prompt you see a section that lists several possible replacements such as *mate, mates, made, math,* and *mayday.* As you may have guessed, none of these choices is correct, for the word is properly spelled. Therefore, you should ask the Speller to skip it and move to the next misspelled word.

Notice the two Skip options, Skip Once and Skip. If you select option 2, Skip, the Speller will skip the word *Mateo* anywhere else it appears (assuming it's spelled exactly the same). If you select option 1, Skip Once, the Speller will stop the next time it encounters *Mateo* and give you the *Not Found* message. However, the next time you run the Speller it will stop on that word regardless of whether you used Skip or Skip Once, so if you were planning to use this word frequently in other documents, the best option would be to add it to your dictionary. To do this, you'd select option 3, Add Word. This would add the word to a supplemental dictionary so that the Speller would never again stop on that word.

4. Since the word is correct and you don't need to replace it, press **2** to choose the Skip option. The next highlighted word will be *Taylor,* another proper name.

5. Press **2** again to skip the word *Taylor.*

The cursor will then stop at the word *recieved,* and your screen will resemble Figure 4.5. This time the word is definitely misspelled: remember the rule "i before e except after c"? Notice that *A* is the correct choice.

6. Press **A** to choose the correct spelling, *received.*

The misspelled word will be corrected in your document and the Speller will continue. The "word" to be highlighted will be *110B,* as shown in Figure 4.6. The WordPerfect Speller does not recognize words containing numbers (the presence of a letter makes *110B* a word) so you must choose 1 or 2 to skip this word. Press *2,* and repeat for the next two *NOT FOUND* prompts.

When the Speller is finished you'll see a count of the total number of words that were checked, along with this message:

Word Count: 191      Press any key to continue

7. Press any key to get back to Edit mode.

Wasn't that fun? Now you know enough to use the Speller effectively, and since it's so easy I'm sure you'll want to use it each time you finish typing a document. In Chapter 20 you'll learn more about

```
Dear Mr. Taylor:

        As I told you on the phone this morning, there was
an apparent misunderstanding in the order we placed on
Thursday, November 7, and we recieved the wrong parts.

        As you will see on the enclosed copy of our
purchase order, we requested a replacement interface
and cable for a PC 110 and were instead sent parts for
a PC 110B.  We were fairly certain that they would not

================================================================

    A. received            B. relieved




Not Found: 1 Skip Once; 2 Skip; 3 Add Word; 4 Edit; 5 Look Up: 0
```

*Figure 4.5:* A misspelled word

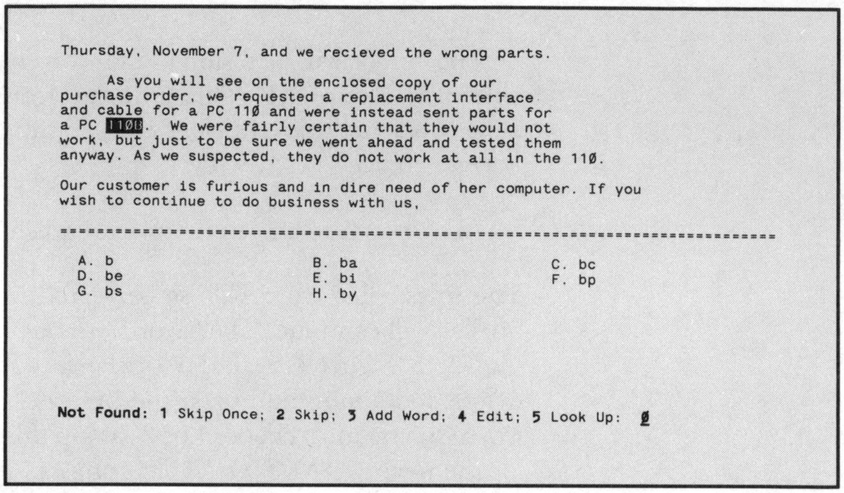

```
Thursday, November 7, and we recieved the wrong parts.

     As you will see on the enclosed copy of our
purchase order, we requested a replacement interface
and cable for a PC 110 and were instead sent parts for
a PC [110]. We were fairly certain that they would not
work, but just to be sure we went ahead and tested them
anyway. As we suspected, they do not work at all in the 110.

Our customer is furious and in dire need of her computer. If you
wish to continue to do business with us,
=============================================================================

    A. b                        B. ba                    C. bc
    D. be                       E. bi                    F. bp
    G. bs                       H. by




Not Found: 1 Skip Once; 2 Skip; 3 Add Word; 4 Edit; 5 Look Up: 0
```

*Figure 4.6:* Words containing numbers

the Speller, including how to check just a portion of your document, look up words before typing them, and add or delete words from the dictionary.

8. If you're using a floppy disk system, be sure to remove the Speller disk from drive B and replace it with your data disk before continuing.

## SAVING AND PRINTING THE LETTER

You learned how to save and print your work in Chapter 2, but you may need a refresher. To save the letter, you press the Save Text key (F10), type a name for the file, then press ◄┘. Let's call this letter *Taylor.ltr.*

1. Press the Save Text key, F10, and type the file name

   TAYLOR.LTR

then press ←⎯. You should see the *Saving* message as Word-Perfect saves the document on your disk drive. When the status line clears, you can print the letter using the Print key, Shift-F7. Be sure that your printer is on before proceeding.

2. Press Shift-F7.

3. Select option 1, Full Document, by typing either **1** or **F**.

Incidentally, you can print before saving, and the order in which you do these two operations is not important.

## CHANGING MARGINS, LINE SPACING, AND TAB SETTINGS

Now that your letter is safely stored on disk, let's experiment with it and learn how to make some more formatting changes.

### SETTING MARGINS

You've already changed the margins once, so let's begin by converting them back to the original ones, 1 inch each. To do this, you'll need to move the cursor up.

1. Move the cursor to the 1-inch line position. Press ← once to be sure that the cursor is to the left of the code for flush-right alignment (it should be on position 1.5″ or this procedure will not work).

2. Press the Format key (Shift-F8) and select option 1, Line, by pressing either **1** or **L**.

3. Select option 7, Margins, from the Format: Line menu by pressing either **7** or **M**.

4. For the new left margin, type **1** then press ←⎯. For the right margin, type **1** then press ←⎯.

5. Press ←⎯ or **0** twice to get back to the Edit screen.

The prompt disappears; press ↓ until you reach the last line in the letter and you should see the effects of this change, as the entire letter is adjusted to fit the new margins. Remember, WordPerfect allows you to change margins anytime and as often as you want throughout your document. Let's prove it by changing them again, this time to 1/2 inch each.

6. Move the cursor to the beginning of the first paragraph in the body of the letter, placing it in the blank space at the left margin. Be sure the cursor is at the 1-inch position. (Do not place it on the word *As.*)

7. Press the Format key (Shift-F8) and select option 1, Line, by pressing either **1** or **L**.

8. Press **7** or **M** to change the margins.

9. Enter **.5** for the left margin and **.5** for the right margin.

10. Press ⏎ or **0** twice, then press ↓.

The text should expand to fit into these new margins. However, the lines above the first paragraph have not changed. In case you can't tell by looking at them, move the cursor up to the salutation, *Dear Mr. Taylor.* Place the cursor on the *D* at the beginning of the line and notice that the position indicator on the status line shows position 1″.

What you've just demonstrated is a very important fact about margin changes: they do not affect that part of the document that is above or to the left of the position where the cursor was located when you initiated the change. Like other formatting changes, when you change margins, a hidden code is inserted into your document at the cursor position, directing WordPerfect to change the margins from that point forward. If you had wanted to change the margins for the entire document, you would have had to place the cursor at the top of the document before changing them, like you did the first time. This rule is also true for the other formatting changes (line spacing and tab settings) that you'll make in this section.

We'll return to this subject later, so let's leave the margin settings as they are for now.

## *CHANGING LINE SPACING*

Line spacing is another variable formatting feature that can improve the appearance of your letter. Let's change the body of the letter to double spacing and see how it looks. WordPerfect's default is single spacing, but you can change it for individual documents using the Format key (Shift-F8).

Move the cursor to the beginning of the first paragraph, which starts with *As I told you.* To change spacing, you use the same key that you used to change margins, the Format key (Shift-F8).

1. Press the Format key (Shift-F8).

2. Press either **1** or **L** to select option 1 for the Line menu.

3. Press either **6** or **S** to select option 6 for Line Spacing.

4. Change to double spacing by typing **2**, then press ◄─┘ or **0** three times.

The rest of the letter will be double spaced and it may spill over to a second page. Isn't it easier to read? Remember, formatting changes such as line spacing only affect the document from the cursor position forward, so the salutation and all other text above the cursor is still single spaced.

As you know, you can use different spacing for different parts of your document, so let's change the paragraph that describes the missing items back to single spaced. To do this, move the cursor to the beginning of the paragraph (to the *A* in *A PC 110 interface*).

5. Press the Format key (Shift-F8) and select **L** or **1** for the Format: Line menu.

6. Press **6** or **S** for Line Spacing.

7. Type **1** for single spacing, then press ◄─┘ three times.

Now the rest of the letter is single spaced, as shown in Figure 4.7. (Note that I deleted the extra blank lines under *PLEASE RUSH THE FOLLOWING PARTS:* to make it fit on one page.)

## CHANGING TAB SETTINGS

As you may recall, earlier in this chapter you indented the first line of each paragraph in the body of the letter by using the Tab key, except you used the Indent key (F4) to indent all the lines in the paragraph

You can also set line spacing in increments of half spaces, but you'll have to test your printer to see if it's capable of printing this way. Thus, you could change to 1.5, 2.5, or even .5 spacing. When you do, what you see on screen may not resemble the printed version, so you have to keep an eye on the status line. For instance, if you change to 1.5 spacing, your text will appear double spaced on the screen. However, if you place the cursor at the 1-inch position and press ↓ or ◄─┘ once, the line indicator on the status line will say that the cursor is on line 1.25″.

about the missing items. Each time you pressed Tab or Indent, the cursor jumped ½ inch. Remember, tabs are set for every ½ inch, starting at position 0. Let's try changing them.

1.  Move the cursor to the blank line above the first paragraph.

```
                                              1001 First Street
                                       San Mateo, California 91123
                                             November 16, 1989


         Mr. William B. Taylor
         Service Manager
         ABC Parts, Inc.
         423 Main Street
         Santa Ana, California 90124


                            URGENT NOTICE

         Dear Mr. Taylor:

             As  I told  you  on  the  phone  this morning,  there  was an  apparent
         misunderstanding in the  order we placed  on Thursday, November  7, and  we
         received the wrong parts.


             As  you  will see  on  the enclosed  copy  of our  purchase  order, we
         requested a  replacement interface and cable for a  PC 110 and were instead
         sent parts for a PC 110B.  We were fairly certain that they would not work,
         but just to be sure we went ahead and tested them anyway.  As we suspected,
         they do not work at all in the 110.


             Our customer is furious and in dire need of her computer.  If you wish
         to continue to do business with us,


                        PLEASE RUSH THE FOLLOWING PARTS:

             A PC  110 interface,  part# 66A and  a PC 110 cable,  part# 76A.
             These parts are  listed on page 20  in your catalog of November 1,
             1988.

         As soon as we receive them, I'll return the others.


                            Sincerely,

                            Sam Jones
```

*Figure 4.7:* The letter with mixed spacing

2. Press the Format key (Shift-F8) and select option 1, Line, by pressing either **1** or **L**.

3. Select option 8, Tab Set, by pressing either **8** or **T**.

By default, Word-Perfect sets a left tab stop every ½ inch, beginning at position 0″ and extending to position 8.5″. You'll learn more about tab settings in Chapter 8, including how to make right aligned, centered, and decimal tabs, and how to set up dot leaders between tabs.

The lower part of your screen will then be filled with the Tab menu, illustrated in Figure 4.8, which marks each tab stop setting by placing a bright *L* above it. The *L* means left tab, which is the standard type of tab used for text. This is how a left tab works: when you press the Tab key and type a word, the first letter of the word ends up in the same position as the tab stop (so that it's left justified against the tab stop). Notice the inch marks at 1, 2, 3, 4, 5, 6, 7, and 8 and the caret signs ( ^ ) at ½-inch intervals.

Let's delete all the tab stops and replace them with different ones. Notice the message on the tab screen that tells you to press *Delete EOL* to clear tabs. The combination of Ctrl and End is called the Delete EOL key in WordPerfect, and it means delete from the cursor to the *End Of* the *Line*. Before we use it, though, we need to move the cursor to position 0″, which is where the first tab setting is located.

4. Type **0** then press ⬅.

5. Now delete all the tab stops using the Delete EOL key. Press the Ctrl key and hold it down while pressing the End key once.

```
ABC Parts, Inc.
423 Main Street
Santa Ana, California 90124


                        URGENT NOTICE

Dear Mr. Taylor:

As I told you on the phone this morning, there was an apparent

misunderstanding in the order we placed on Thursday, November 7,

and we received the wrong parts.

As you will see on the enclosed copy of our purchase order, we

requested a replacement interface and cable for a PC 110 and were

instead sent parts for a PC 110B.  We were fairly certain that they
L....L....L....L....L....L....L....L....L....L....L....L....L....L....L...
    !    ^    !    !    ^    !    !    ^    !    !    ^    !    !    ^    !
    1"        2"        3"        4"        5"        6"        7"        8"
Delete EOL (clear tabs); Enter Number (set tab); Del (clear tab);
Left; Center; Right; Decimal; .= Dot Leader
```

*Figure 4.8:* The Tab menu

Now you have no tab stops at all, and all the L's have disappeared. To reset them at even intervals such as every 2 inches beginning at position 0″, you type the beginning position number, 0, followed by a comma and the interval number, 2. This means that the first setting would be at position 0″. Placing tab stops to the left of the margin position like this will let you use WordPerfect's Margin Release key, Shift-Tab, to move the cursor and text to the left of the regular margin.

6. Reset the tabs for every 2 inches starting at position 0″ by typing **0,2** then press ⏎.

As you see, the *0* places the first tab stop at position 0″, and the 2 inserts another every 2 inches. You should see an *L* at positions 0″, 2″, 4″, and 6″.

To exit from this screen, you must press the Exit key (F7). If you press another key to get out of this menu (such as Esc or Cancel, F1), the changes will be ignored.

7. Press the Exit key twice.

Your paragraphs should be indented 2 inches, and the word *As* begins at position 2″. However, above the cursor position the old tabs remain in effect. You can verify this by moving the cursor to the blank line above *Dear Mr. Taylor,* starting at position 1″, and pressing the Tab key. This will move the cursor to position 1.5″, and the next time you press it, the cursor will move to 2″.

It's not necessary to delete all settings to make changes such as adding or deleting one tab setting. Let's try adding a tab stop at the 1-inch position and erasing one from the 2-inch position. Move the cursor to the end of the first paragraph for this exercise.

8. Press Shift-F8 and select 1, Line, by pressing either **1** or **L**.

9. Select option 8, Tab Set, by pressing either **8** or **T**.

10. Add a tab stop at 1 inch by typing **1** and pressing ⏎.

The cursor in the Tab menu should have moved to 1 inch and you should see an *L* there. Now delete the tab at 2 inches. You can get there either by using the → key or by entering the number 2.

11. Press the → key to move to the 2.

12. Press the Delete key. The *L* should have disappeared.

13. Press Exit (F7) twice.

When you inserted an *L* at 1 inch, the paragraphs below the cursor were correctly indented again, ½ inch from the left margin.

## *SAVING THE LETTER AND CLEARING THE SCREEN*

Now that we've finished experimenting, let's save the letter again. As you know, the changes you have made on screen have not yet been saved to disk (you saved it before changing the margins, tabs, and spacing) so if the power were to fail right now, you'd lose the changed version. Instead of replacing the disk version with this screen version, you'll save this one under a different name so that you'll have two separate files. Later in this chapter you'll be using this version again to learn about the Reveal Codes screen.

To save the letter:

1. Press F10, the Save Text key.

You should see the *Document to be Saved* prompt and the file name under which you saved it earlier, *Taylor.ltr,* next to the prompt. The new file name will be *Taylor2.ltr.* Be careful not to press the Space bar when you type the name, because file names cannot have spaces. Don't worry about erasing the old name; as soon as you type the first letter, *T,* it will disappear from your screen.

2. Type

   Taylor2.ltr

   then press ◄┘.

Now clear the screen so that you can retrieve the original letter. To do this:

3. Press the Exit key, F7. WordPerfect asks if you want to save the document on your screen.

Notice the prompt *(Text was not modified)* in the lower right corner of your screen. Since you just saved it and have made no further changes, this message tells you that you don't have to save it again.

4. Type **N** to indicate that you don't want to save the letter again.

Now you should see a prompt asking if you wish to exit from Word-Perfect: *Exit WP (Y/N)? No.*

5. Type **N** to indicate that you do not want to exit from Word-Perfect.

The screen should now be cleared. Try pressing the ↓ key; since there is no place to go, the cursor does not move at all.

## RETRIEVING A SAVED FILE FROM THE DISK

Since you will be using the original version of the letter (Taylor.ltr) to study WordPerfect's hyphenation feature, you need to retrieve it from the disk. One way is to use WordPerfect's Retrieve Text key, Shift-F10.

1. Press the Retrieve Text key, Shift-F10. You should see this prompt in the lower left corner:

   **Document to be retrieved:**

   WordPerfect is asking for the name of the file, all you have to do is type it in and press ←⎯.

2. Type

   **Taylor.ltr**

   and press ←⎯.

The original letter should now be on your screen.

## *HYPHENATING TEXT*

WordPerfect has a built-in hyphenation system that you can use to improve your document's appearance. When right justification is on, hyphenation helps reduce the extra blank spaces that the program inserts between words to create even right margins. Hyphenation is also useful if you use a ragged right margin because it eliminates the most noticeable blank gaps at the right side and makes the right margin look less ragged. When you turn it on, this feature helps you decide where to hyphenate words and inserts a special type of hyphen, called a *soft hyphen,* that disappears if the word moves away from the right margin as you add or delete text.

You may have noticed the Hyphenation Zone option on the Format: Line menu. The *hyphenation zone* refers to the area between two positions that serve as flags to activate hyphenation assistance. The left boundary, called the left hyphenation zone, is set to 10% from the right margin. The right boundary, called the right hyphenation zone, is set at 4% from the right margin. This means that on a standard line of 6½ inches (the default), the left hyphenation zone will be .65 inches and the right hyphenation zone will be .26 inches. Whenever a word begins *before* or *at* the left hyphenation zone and extends past the right hyphenation zone, you will be asked to hyphenate it (if hyphenation is turned on). By contrast, if the word begins *after* the left hyphenation zone and extends past the right margin, word wrap will move it to the next line as you type. In Chapter 8 you will learn how and why to alter these positions; for now it is only necessary to understand how they work.

If you were to print the letter you just retrieved, you'd find that it has several large blank spaces between words; you may be able to reduce them by using hyphenation help. Let's turn on hyphenation and see what happens. To ensure that you will be asked to hyphenate a few words, we'll first change the left and right margins to .5 inches each, and change the hyphenation zone.

1. Move the cursor to the left margin, and be sure it is on position 1.5".

2. Press the Format key (Shift-F8).

3. Select Line by pressing either **1** or **L**.

The left and right margins you see in this menu should be 1.5; if they are not, press ◄┘ twice to get back to your document, press → once, then repeat steps 2 and 3 again.

4. Select Margins by pressing either **7** or **M** and change them both to .5.

5. Select option 2, Hyphenation Zone, by pressing either **2** or **Z**.

6. Change the left zone to 9% by typing **9**, then press ◄┘ twice.

7. Select option 1, Hyphenation, by pressing either **1** or **Y**.

You should see this prompt on the status line:

**1** Off; **2** Manual; **3** Auto: **0**

WordPerfect has two types of hyphenation help, automatic and manual. The automatic method hyphenates words, without asking for your permission, using a set of rules incorporated into the program (except in certain cases where the rules don't apply and you are asked to decide where the hyphen belongs). By contrast, the manual method stops at each word that could be hyphenated and suggests a location for the hyphen, but lets you change it or eliminate the hyphen altogether from that word.

8. Press **2** or **M** to turn manual hyphenation on, then press ◄┘ twice.

9. Press the ↓ key until you reach the end or are asked to hyphenate a word. (You may not get a chance to press ↓ at all.)

WordPerfect checks your letter and may ask you to hyphenate a word. In my case, it stopped to hyphenate *misunderstanding,* as illustrated in Figure 4.9.

If WordPerfect tries to hyphenate one of your words, you have three choices:

- If you don't want the word hyphenated, you can press the Cancel key (F1) to prevent hyphenation of this word.

- If the suggested position is acceptable, you just press the Esc key to hyphenate it there.

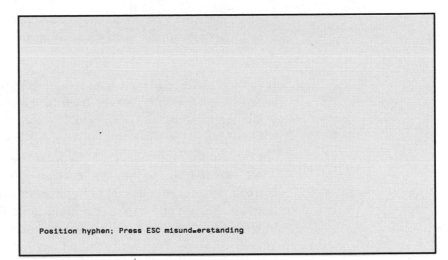

Position hyphen; Press ESC misund≡erstanding

*Figure 4.9:* Hyphenation in action

- If you don't like the suggested position, you can use the ← and → keys to move the cursor to the position where you want the hyphen inserted, then press Esc. However, sometimes you can't move the cursor to the right as far as you'd like because if the word were hyphenated at that point, it would exceed the right margin.

10. In my case, I wanted to hyphenate *misunderstanding* between *misunder* and *standing,* but WordPerfect wouldn't let me move the cursor that far to the right. Instead, I moved the cursor between the *s* and the *u* and pressed Esc, so that the word was split between *mis* and *understanding.*

11. WordPerfect then asked me to split *requested,* and I hyphenated it between *re* and *quested* by pressing Esc.

If you add or delete text in the sentence with the hyphenated word and that word moves away from the right margin, the soft hyphen will no longer be visible. However, it will remain there as an invisible code and reappear if the word ever moves back to the right margin. Let's try it.

12. Delete *apparent* and change *an* to *a.*

13. Press the ↓ key. This causes the paragraph to realign, and the hyphen in the word *misunderstanding* disappears since it's no longer at the right margin.

If you were to change the sentence back to the original version and *misunderstanding* were to be moved back to the right margin, the hyphen would reappear and the word would be split between the two lines.

If you're in the habit of using hyphens as you type, you should always use this special type of hyphen (the soft hyphen), but you don't have to resort to the Hyphenation option on the menu to do it. Instead, whenever you want to hyphenate a word, press the Ctrl key first, then press the hyphen (minus) key. This inserts the type of hyphen that disappears if the word moves away from the right margin. You'll study this feature more thoroughly and learn about other types of hyphens in Chapter 8.

## THE REVEAL CODES SCREEN

Earlier in this chapter, you learned that WordPerfect places special codes into your text when you make formatting changes such as double spacing, and I promised to teach you more about them. Nearly all of WordPerfect's formatting features insert codes, including several of the ones you have just studied such as underline, center, boldface, line spacing, margins, and tabs. These codes are not shown on the regular Edit screen; that way the document on your screen resembles the printed version as closely as possible. However, it's often necessary to see where the codes are located in case you want to remove an unwanted one that's disrupting your document's appearance.

Let's consider the Underline key (F8) as an example. As you know, you have to press this key once to begin underlining as you type, then press it again when you're ready to turn it off and stop underlining. When you do this, you're actually inserting a pair of codes that turn underlining on and off. Let's see how they work.

1. Clear the screen using the Exit key: press F7 N N.

2. Press ← once.

3. Press the Underline key (F8) once.

4.  Type the following phrase:

    <u>THE</u> <u>WORDPERFECT</u> <u>REVEAL</u> <u>CODES</u> <u>SCREEN</u>

5.  Press ◄─┘ and type

    <u>testing</u>

As you can see, the word *testing* is underlined. In fact, until you press F8 again WordPerfect will continue to underline anything you type. What if you want to remove underlining from the word *testing*? The easiest way is to locate and delete the Underline code from the Reveal Codes screen, so let's look at it now.

6.  Press the Reveal Codes key (Alt-F3) and don't panic!

Although it looks confusing the first time, this screen is actually quite logical. It is shown in Figure 4.10.

The screen is divided into two parts, separated by a thick band with triangles and other symbols on it. The section above the band displays several lines of text around and including the one on which the cursor is located. The same text appears in the lower part, along with several formatting codes that are surrounded by brackets. The cursor is located in the same position in both sections. The one in the lower section is a box, and it should be highlighting the bracketed Underline code.

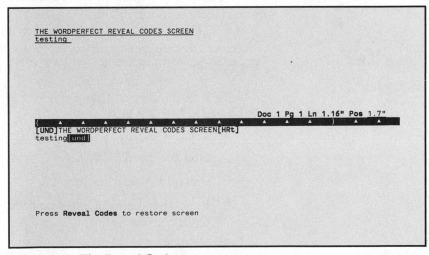

*Figure 4.10:* The Reveal Codes screen

The band is called the *Tab Ruler,* and it shows you where each tab stop and margin setting is located. The triangles represent tab stops, and a brace or bracket represents the margins. If a margin coincides with a tab stop it appears as a brace (as do both margins in our example); otherwise it appears as a bracket.

The first bracketed code on the screen is [HRt], symbolizing a hard return. This means that you pressed the ⏎ key at that position, to create a blank line. Next you see the first underline symbol, [UND]. A capitalized Underline code is the signal to begin underlining.

The [UND] is followed by the text *THE WORDPERFECT REVEAL CODES SCREEN,* which appears underlined (or in a different color) above the Tab Ruler but not below it. The text is followed by another [HRt] code, since you pressed ⏎ at that point. The word *testing* appears on the next line, followed by a lowercase Underline code in brackets [und]. This code ends the underlining. Underlined text is always surrounded by a pair of bracketed Underline codes, the first in uppercase and the second in lowercase.

This is what happened when you typed the phrase: When you pressed F8 to begin underlining, the uppercase and lowercase underline codes were created simultaneously and the cursor was positioned between them. As you typed the phrase, all your text was underlined because the cursor remained between the pair of codes. If you had pressed F8 a second time before typing the word *testing,* the cursor would have jumped past the ending Underline code, and underlining would have been turned off.

As you've probably figured out by now, if you don't want the word testing underlined, the lowercase code should be at the end of the first line, after the word *SCREEN.* To fix it:

7. Exit the Reveal Codes screen by pressing the Reveal Codes key (Alt-F3) again.

8. Move the cursor to the end of the first line and position it just after the word *SCREEN.*

9. Press the Underline key, F8.

10. Press the Reveal Codes key (Alt-F3) to check the Reveal Codes screen again.

Because you pressed the Underline key (F8) in the midst of text that was already underlined, you created a second pair of bracketed underline codes, with the cursor between the two pairs.

To remove underlining from the word *testing,* you can now delete the extra pair, which begins with the second uppercase Underline code. Since the cursor is right next to it, all you have to do is press the Delete key. You can do this from within the Reveal Codes screen.

11.  Press the Delete key once.

As soon as you erased the uppercase [UND] code, the lowercase one was erased as well, and the underlining disappeared from the word *testing* above the Tab Ruler. Now you can return to the Edit screen by pressing the Reveal Codes key, Alt-F3.

12.  Press Alt-F3 to exit from the Reveal Codes screen.

The Reveal Codes screen is extremely helpful and it's important to become comfortable with it, so you will be directed to use it frequently throughout the rest of this book. Many of the codes are in plain English with very obvious meanings, such as [Tab], which signifies the Tab key was pressed, [Hyph On], which means that WordPerfect's hyphen help is on, and [L/R Mar:1.5",1.5"] which shows that you changed the margin settings. To help you decipher the more unfamiliar ones, they are summarized inside the cover of this book.

## USING REVEAL CODES

Now let's look at more situations where the Reveal Codes screen can help you. To do this, we'll retrieve the Taylor2.ltr and fix it so that it's all single spaced, the margins are set to 1.5 inch throughout the letter, and the tab settings are appropriate for those margins.

Before retrieving the letter, clear the screen using the Exit key (F7).

1.  Press Exit (F7).

2.  Press **N** since you don't need to save this work.

3.  Press **N** so that you do not exit from WordPerfect.

Now retrieve the letter.

4. Press the Retrieve Text key (Shift-F10).

5. Type the file name

    **Taylor2.ltr**

    then press ◄─┘.

Before typing the letter, you set the margins to 1.5 inches each and you later changed them to 1 inch each. What if you moved the cursor to line 1 (1″)and used the Format key (Shift-F8) to set .75-inch margins throughout the document, but nothing happened? (If you want to try it, move to line 1, then press Home Home Home ← to move the cursor to the extreme left edge of the line before any hidden codes, then change the margins.) You would have to consult the Reveal Codes screen to see what went wrong, and what you'd find is three sets of Margin codes in a row, like this:

[L/R Mar:0.75″,0.75″][L/R Mar:1.5″,1.5″][L/R Mar:1″,1″]

The code for the margin setting you just selected would be to the left of the original one (1.5″), and the code that set 1-inch margins would follow. In such a case, WordPerfect would use the 1-inch setting because it reads them in order and follows the last one. If you wanted to use the .75-inch setting, you'd have to delete the other two.

Let's look in the Reveal Codes screen to see the codes that are affecting the letter now, and change to 1.5-inch margins. To do this:

1. Press the Reveal Codes key (Alt-F3). Your screen should resemble Figure 4.11.

Notice that the first two codes are margin setting codes, one for 1.5-inch margins and the next one for 1-inch margins. Let's move the cursor so that it is on the 1-inch code.

2. Press ← (not Backspace, which as you know, deletes text and codes) until the cursor is on the 1-inch Margin code. It looks like this:

    [L/R Mar:1″,1″]

3. Press Delete once to erase the code.

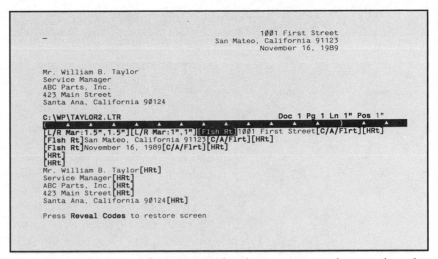

```
                                            1001 First Street
                                 San Mateo, California 91123
                                       November 16, 1989

Mr. William B. Taylor
Service Manager
ABC Parts, Inc.
423 Main Street
Santa Ana, California 90124

C:\WP\TAYLOR2.LTR                              Doc 1 Pg 1 Ln 1" Pos 1"
[        ^       ^    ^      ^      ^     ^         ^        ^       ^
[L/R Mar:1.5",1.5"][L/R Mar:1",1"][Flsh Rt]1001 First Street[C/A/Flrt][HRt]
[Flsh Rt]San Mateo, California 91123[C/A/Flrt][HRt]
[Flsh Rt]November 16, 1989[C/A/Flrt][HRt]
[HRt]
[HRt]
Mr. William B. Taylor[HRt]
Service Manager[HRt]
ABC Parts, Inc.[HRt]
423 Main Street[HRt]
Santa Ana, California 90124[HRt]

Press Reveal Codes to restore screen
```

*Figure 4.11:* The Reveal Codes screen showing two consecutive margin codes

4.  Press the Reveal Codes key (Alt-F3) to exit the Reveal Codes screen.

Now check your letter to see what has happened to the margins. If you move the cursor to the second line in the first paragraph, you'll notice that the margins are not at 1.5 inches; instead they begin at .5 inches. Do you remember that you changed the margins to ½ inch each before that paragraph? Let's delete the code that WordPerfect inserted when you made that change.

5.  Press the Reveal Codes key (Alt-F3).

6.  Move the cursor to the beginning of the paragraph. You should see the margin setting code for .5″ margins to the left of the word *As.* Move the cursor until it is on top of the code.

7.  Press the Delete key to erase it.

8.  Press the Reveal Codes key (Alt-F3) to exit the Reveal Codes screen.

Now the margins for the entire letter are 1.5 inches, but press ↓ repeatedly to see what's happened to your other paragraphs! Since you changed the tab settings at the end of the first paragraph, the first line in the remaining paragraphs begins at position 4″, except for the indented paragraph *(A PC 110 interface...)* which is at position 6″! To fix it, let's find the Tab Set code and erase it.

9. Move the cursor to the end of the first paragraph, then press the Reveal Codes key (Alt-F3).

10. Position the cursor on the Tab Set code. It looks like this:

    **[Tab Set:0″,1″,4″,6″]**

    and it tells you that the tab settings are at positions 0, 1, 4, and 6.

While experimenting with tabs, we set them for every 2 inches beginning at 0, then deleted the one at the 2-inch position and inserted one at 1 inch. The code you're looking at represents the second change.

11. Press Delete to erase the code.

12. Press Alt-F3 to exit Reveal Codes, then press ↓ repeatedly to view the rest of the letter.

Oops! The indented paragraph is now at position 4″, so there must be another Tab Set code affecting it. In fact, a Tab code was inserted in the blank line under *Dear Mr. Taylor,* where you changed the tab settings to every 2 inches starting at position 0.

13. Press ↑ to move the cursor to the blank line above the salutation, then press the Reveal Codes key (Alt-F3).

14. Position the cursor on the code, then press Delete to erase it. It looks like this:

    **[Tab Set:0″, every 2″]**

15. Press the Reveal Codes key (Alt-F3) to exit the Reveal Codes screen.

Now the indented paragraph looks like it did originally, and it starts at position 2.5″.

The last change you'll make is to convert the entire letter back to single spacing. What happens if you move the cursor to the top of the letter and change to single spacing there? Let's find out.

16. Move the cursor to line 1″ and press the Format key (Shift-F8).

17. Press **1**, Line, then **6**, Line Spacing. It already says *1!*

18. Press ◄─┘ three times to get back to the letter.

Nothing happens! As you may remember, you changed the line spacing twice in the document, once in front of the first paragraph and once before the indented paragraph. Changing the spacing at the top only affects text up to the position where you switched to double spacing. In situations like this, you really have to use the Reveal Codes screen to find and erase the code, so let's do that now.

19. Move the cursor to the beginning of the first paragraph and press the Reveal Codes key (Alt-F3).

20. Place the cursor on the Line Spacing code, which looks like this:

    **[Ln Spacing:2]**

21. Press Delete.

22. Press the Reveal Codes key (Alt-F3) to exit the Reveal Codes screen.

Now the entire document should be single spaced, and it looks like it did originally.

As you've seen, the Reveal Codes screen is very helpful when you're having trouble making formatting changes because it allows you to look behind the scenes at the otherwise hidden codes and find out which ones are affecting your document. That way, you can easily delete the ones that are no longer needed and/or enter new ones in the correct position.

## SUMMARY

You've covered a great deal of material and should feel very accomplished. By now you're getting comfortable with commonly used formatting techniques such as margins, tabs, indentation, hyphenation, and line spacing. Furthermore, you won't have to use a dictionary to check your spelling; as you've seen, WordPerfect can do it much faster!

You've also been introduced to the Reveal Codes screen, which I'll be discussing frequently in the remaining chapters. It's crucial that you understand Reveal Codes, for it's almost impossible to use

WordPerfect efficiently unless you do. In Chapter 7 I'll teach you how to use another method, Search and Replace, to find and delete unwanted codes, and you may find that method easier.

The next chapter will introduce block operations, which allow you to mark a section of text and perform many different operations on it such as cutting and pasting sentences, making copies of paragraphs, converting a section of text to uppercase or lowercase, saving and printing a block of text, and underlining and boldfacing text that has already been typed. You'll learn how to use the Block key with features you've already studied such as underline, delete, and print, as well as with new ones such as move and copy.

5.

# EXPANDING YOUR EDITING
# POWER WITH THE BLOCK
# FEATURE

**To delete a text block,**    126

move the cursor to the beginning of the text you want to delete, then press the Block key (Alt-F4). Highlight the text block with the cursor movement keys, then press the Delete key. At the *Delete block* prompt, type *Y*. The block will be deleted.

**To cut and paste with the Block and Move keys,**    130

move the cursor to the beginning of the text you want to cut, press Block (Alt-F4), then move the cursor to the end of the block. Press the Move key (Ctrl-F4) and select Block from the menu, then select Move from the next menu. Move the cursor to the place you want the cut text to appear and press ←┘. The cut text appears at the cursor location.

**Move a sentence, paragraph, or page with the Move key (Ctrl-F4).**    131

First, place the cursor in the sentence, paragraph, or page you want to move. Press the Move key and select the Sentence, Paragraph, or Page option. You then are prompted to move, copy, delete, or append the text. Select Move and move the cursor to the place you want the text to appear. Press ←┘. The text appears at the cursor location.

**To copy a block of text,**    135

place the cursor at the beginning of the text to be copied, then press the Block key (Alt-F4). Highlight the text block, press the Move key (Ctrl-F4), then select the Block option and select Copy. Move the cursor to the place you want the text to appear, then press ←┘.

**To copy a sentence, paragraph, or page,**                                      136

place the cursor in the sentence, paragraph, or page you want
to copy. Press the Move key (Ctrl-F4) and select the Sentence,
Paragraph, or Page option. At the next prompt, select Copy.
Move the cursor to the place you want the text copied and press
←┘. The text appears at the cursor position.

**To print a text block,**                                                        138

place the cursor at the beginning of the block, then press the
Block key (Alt-F4). Highlight the block, then press the Print
key (Shift-F7) and select *Y*; the block will then be printed.

**To boldface or underline a text block,**                                        145

place the cursor at the beginning of the text and press the Block
key (Alt-F4). Highlight the block and press the Underline (F8)
or Bold (F6) key.

**To keep a text block together on the same page,**                               147

use the Block Protection feature. Place the cursor at the beginning of the block you want kept together and press the Block
key (Alt-F4). Highlight the text, then press the Format key
(Shift-F8). At the *Protect Block? (Y/N) No* prompt, type *Y*.

THE BLOCK KEY IS ONE OF WORDPERFECT'S MOST useful features and you'll undoubtedly be using it often. Simply stated, it allows you to mark off a block of text, ranging in length from one character to the entire document, in order to perform operations that affect only that section of text. For instance, you can mark a block to be saved to disk, sent to the printer, copied, deleted, moved to another location, or converted from lowercase to uppercase.

Block mode is more than an amenity, though; in many cases it's a necessity. In the last chapter you learned how to use the Underline and Boldface keys when entering text and I mentioned that neither of these features can be used by itself to underline or boldface text once it has been entered. Instead, such text must first be defined as a block.

Alt-F4 is the Block key. It's worth memorizing because you will use it often.

## USING THE BLOCK KEY

Despite its power, the Block key is not hard to use. After you type the following paragraph, you'll use Block mode to delete a phrase and find out just how easy it can be. Make sure that your screen is clear before you begin; press F7 N N if you need to clear it.

Type

> WordPerfect fully utilizes the PC keyboard and cursor control is outstanding. The arrow keys are used the most frequently in WordPerfect, to move one space to the left or right and one line up or down. You can get to the beginning of a document by pressing the Home key twice followed by the Up Arrow key and to the end of the document by pressing the Home key twice followed by the Down Arrow key. The Ctrl-Home combination allows you to select a page number and the cursor will quickly jump to the top of that page.

Be sure to press ◄─┘ when you finish.

## *BLOCKING AND DELETING TEXT*

Now we'll learn an easy block operation—how to block and delete text. You'll be erasing this phrase, which is in the second sentence:

the most frequently in WordPerfect,

1.  Move the cursor to the *t* in *the* (before *most*).

2.  Press the Block key, Alt-F4. Notice the message that appears in the lower left corner of the screen:

    Block on

3.  Press the → key and keep pressing it until the cursor and highlighting reach the comma after *WordPerfect*. Watch the screen carefully to see the text being highlighted as you move the cursor.

This highlighted area is the currently defined block. When you finish, it should look like Figure 5.1.

4.  Press the Delete key and watch for this prompt in the lower left corner of the screen:

    Delete Block? (Y/N) No

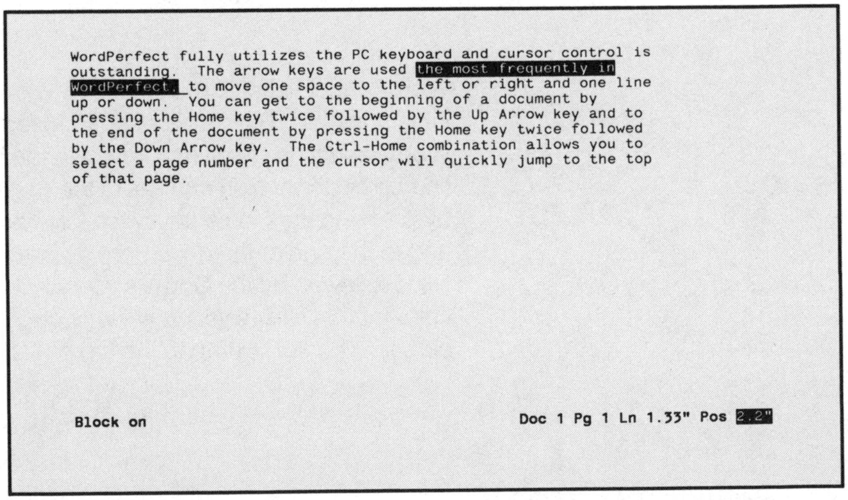

```
WordPerfect fully utilizes the PC keyboard and cursor control is
outstanding.  The arrow keys are used the most frequently in
WordPerfect, to move one space to the left or right and one line
up or down.  You can get to the beginning of a document by
pressing the Home key twice followed by the Up Arrow key and to
the end of the document by pressing the Home key twice followed
by the Down Arrow key.  The Ctrl-Home combination allows you to
select a page number and the cursor will quickly jump to the top
of that page.




Block on                                    Doc 1 Pg 1 Ln 1.33" Pos 2.2"
```

*Figure 5.1:* The blocked text

As you know, when you press the Delete key it usually erases the character that the cursor is on without asking your permission, but when the *Block on* message is flashing, you see a different prompt and Delete operates differently. There are many other keys whose meanings are altered when the Block key is on, and you'll learn more of them in this chapter.

> 5. Press **Y** to delete the block, then press ↓ if any misalignment remains.

Incidentally, you could have used the Backspace key instead of the Delete key in the exercise above, and it would have worked exactly the same way.

As you learned in Chapter 3, when you erase text with the Delete key, it can be restored using the Undelete function of the Cancel key (F1). Let's review it.

> 6. Move the cursor back to the previous position, after the word *used.*
>
> 7. Press the Cancel key, F1, and select either **1** or **R** to restore the highlighted text.

This brings back the blocked text that you deleted in step 5. Remember, this text will remain in memory and can be undeleted again using the Cancel key (F1) until you make three more deletions using either the Delete, Backspace, Ctrl-End, or Ctrl-PgDn (Page Down) keys. To prove it:

> 8. Press F1 again.

Unless you've deleted something else since step 7, the phrase *the most frequently in WordPerfect,* appears in a highlighted block, and if you were to press *1* or *R*, you would create another copy of it at the current cursor position.

> 9. Press ⟵ to remove the Undelete prompt, then press ↓ if you need to realign the text.

### *CURSOR MOVEMENT IN BLOCK MODE*

Some unique methods of cursor movement are available in Block mode. For example, once Block is on you can press ↑ or ← to move the cursor up or to the left and shrink the block, press any character to move the cursor to the first position after that character's next appearance in the text, or press the Cancel key to get out of Block mode altogether. Let's experiment with them.

1. Move the cursor to the beginning of the first word in the paragraph and press the Block key, Alt-F4.

2. Press the ↓ key twice to move the cursor down a few lines.

3. Type a comma (,) and you'll see that the cursor and highlighting move to include all the text up to the next comma (after *WordPerfect*).

4. Press the period key (.) and the cursor and highlighting will move to the end of the sentence.

5. Press the letter **k** (lowercase) and the cursor will move one position after the *k* in *key,* highlighting everything up to and including *k.*

6. Press ←┘. This moves the cursor and highlighting to the end of the paragraph (provided you pressed ←┘ when you typed it).

7. Press ↑ twice. This moves the cursor up two lines.

8. Press the Cancel key (F1). As with most other operations, this terminates the Block mode altogether and the *Block on* message disappears.

## *CUTTING AND PASTING TEXT*

There are several methods you can use in WordPerfect to cut text from one location and move it to another (called *cutting and pasting*). One method we'll study uses the Block and Delete keys, another uses the Block and Move keys, and one uses only the Move key. All accomplish the task, but some are safer than others. Let's take a closer look at each method.

## *USING BLOCK AND DELETE TO CUT AND PASTE*

This method can be dangerous because if you cut some text and then delete three more times before you try to paste it back at another location, you'll lose it. Let's try an example. Suppose we wanted to move this sentence to the end of the paragraph:

**You can get to the beginning of a document by pressing the Home key twice followed by the Up Arrow key and to the end of the document by pressing the Home key twice followed by the Down Arrow key.**

Before we do it, let's save the paragraph.

1. Press the Save Text key, F10.

2. Type

   **keys**

   for the file name, then press ◄––▐.

Now let's cut and paste it.

1. Move the cursor to the first letter in the third sentence, *Y,* and press the Block key, Alt-F4.

2. Press the period key (.) to move the highlighting to the end of the sentence.

3. Press the Delete key and press **Y** when asked if you want to delete it.

4. Press Delete one more time to delete the blank space that was left when you deleted the sentence.

5. Move the cursor up to the word *PC* in the first line and press Delete three times to delete *PC* and the blank space that follows it.

6. Move the cursor down a line and delete *the most.*

7. Place the cursor after the period at the end of the paragraph, where we want to paste the sentence back in.

8. Press the Cancel key, F1. The first block of text you see is *the most,* which you just deleted in step 6.

9. Press **2** or **P** to see the previous level of deleted text. It should be *PC*.

10. Press **2** or **P** to see the third level of deleted text. It should be the space you deleted in step 4.

Guess what: the sentence you deleted in step 3 is lost forever. Now you know why I made you save it first!

## CUTTING AND PASTING WITH THE BLOCK AND MOVE KEYS

WordPerfect has another more practical cut and paste method that uses the Block (Alt-F4) and Move (Ctrl-F4) keys. If you had used this method in the exercise above, you wouldn't have lost the sentence because the deleted block would have been placed in a separate memory location from the one used by the Cancel key (F1), and pressing keys like Delete, Backspace, and Ctrl-End has no effect on it. Let's clear the screen and retrieve the original paragraph to learn how this method works.

1. Press the Exit key, F7 N N, to clear the screen without saving.

2. Use the Retrieve Text key to bring back the entire original paragraph. Press Shift-F10 and enter the file name, **keys**, at the *Document to be retrieved* prompt.

Now block the same sentence ("You can get to the beginning of a document. . ."").

3. Move the cursor to the first letter in the third sentence, *Y,* and press the Block key, Alt-F4.

4. Press the period key (.) to move the highlighting to the end of the sentence.

5. Press the Move key, Ctrl-F4.

You should see this prompt at the bottom of the screen:

Move: 1 Block; 2 Tabular Column; 3 Rectangle: 0

6. Press either **1** or **B** for the highlighted block.

7. Next you'll see this prompt:

   **1 Move; 2 Copy; 3 Delete; 4 Append: 0**

   Select the Move option and this prompt will appear:

   **Move cursor; Press Enter to retrieve.**

8. Move the cursor to the end of the paragraph and press the ⏎ key.

The deleted sentence reappears at the cursor location. The sentence remains in memory, and you could keep making copies of it, regardless of any other deletions you make with Delete, Backspace, Ctrl-End, or Ctrl-PgDn, because it remains in this special memory location until the next time you delete or copy text with the Block and Move keys. You can retrieve it again by pressing the Move key (Ctrl-F4) and selecting the Retrieve option, then selecting the Block option from the next prompt.

## USING THE MOVE KEY ALONE TO MOVE TEXT

The Move key has two sets of functions, depending on whether it's used alone or while the Block key is in operation. As you just saw, when you use it with Block, it serves to cut or copy a user-defined section of text. However, if you want to cut and paste a sentence, paragraph, or page, you can save a few steps because you don't have to highlight them with the Block key first. When you press Move alone (without pressing the Block key first), the first three choices allow you to designate a sentence, paragraph, or page to be cut or copied. The next few sections will teach you how.

***MOVING A SENTENCE***  In the next exercise, you'll move the sentence from the end of the paragraph back to its original location. The cursor can be anywhere in the sentence when you press the Move key, since WordPerfect can figure out where it starts and ends by searching for periods, exclamation points, or question marks, which normally designate the beginning and end of a sentence. The only difficulty arises when there is an abbreviated word such as *Mrs.*

in the middle of a sentence, in which case WordPerfect will consider it the end of the sentence.

Before continuing, make sure that the last sentence is separated from the previous one by at least one blank space, because otherwise WordPerfect will consider the two sentences to be a single one. If not, move the cursor to the *Y* in *You* and press the Space bar once.

1. To prove that it doesn't matter where you begin, start by moving the cursor to the *b* in *beginning.*

2. Press the Move key, Ctrl-F4.

3. Select option 1, Sentence, by pressing either **1** or **S**.

Notice that WordPerfect highlights the entire sentence. Now you have four choices—Move, Copy, Delete, or Append—as shown in Figure 5.2. Let's be sure you understand the difference between them.

The Move and Delete options both erase the highlighted sentence from the screen. The difference between them is that when you use the Move option (1), you'll see the *Move cursor; press Enter to retrieve.* prompt and can retrieve the sentence right away by moving the cursor to the new location and pressing ←┘. You can also press F1 to cancel the prompt, then retrieve the text later using Ctrl-F4 4 (Retrieve), then 1 (Block). When you use the Delete option (3), you restore the sentence with the Undelete function on the Cancel key

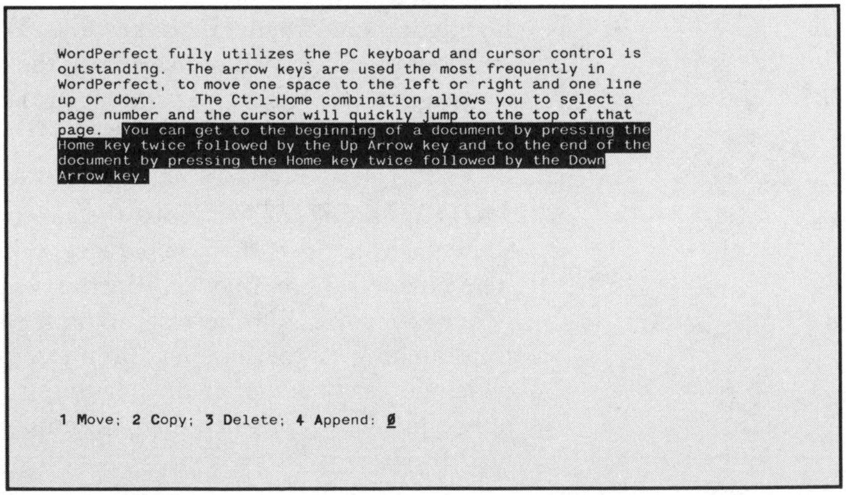

```
WordPerfect fully utilizes the PC keyboard and cursor control is
outstanding.  The arrow keys are used the most frequently in
WordPerfect, to move one space to the left or right and one line
up or down.   The Ctrl-Home combination allows you to select a
page number and the cursor will quickly jump to the top of that
page. You can get to the beginning of a document by pressing the
Home key twice followed by the Up Arrow key and to the end of the
document by pressing the Home key twice followed by the Down
Arrow key.
```

`1 Move; 2 Copy; 3 Delete; 4 Append: 0`

*Figure 5.2:* The Move, Copy, Delete, and Append options on the Move key

(F1). You can do this anytime. The Copy option (2) copies the sentence into memory and tells you to move the cursor and press ⬅, but this option leaves the original intact where it is.

4. Press either **1** or **M** to move the text. The *Move cursor* prompt appears.

5. Move the cursor back to the beginning of the last sentence ("The Ctrl-Home combination allows you. . .") and place it on the *T.*

6. Press ⬅.

The sentence reappears and the paragraph looks like it did originally. Note that you could have pressed F1 to get rid of the *Move cursor* prompt, then retrieved it later using Ctrl-F4 4 1.

I use the Move key constantly to delete sentences, even if I have no intention of pasting them back in somewhere else, because it's the easiest and fastest way to do it. If you use Block first, at least eight keystrokes are required (Alt-F4, move cursor, Ctrl-F4 1 3) and if you were to start at the beginning of the sentence and delete word by word using Ctrl-Backspace, it would probably take much more than six. However, if you use Move alone, only three keystrokes are needed (Ctrl-F4 1 3).

***MOVING A PARAGRAPH*** Let's see what happens when we use the Move key to highlight the paragraph and delete it with the Delete option. The cursor can be anywhere in the paragraph when you begin.

1. Press the Move key, Ctrl-F4.

2. Select Paragraph by pressing either **2** or **P**. The entire paragraph should be highlighted.

This time let's try the Delete option.

3. Press either **3** or **D** to delete the paragraph.

The entire paragraph is erased, and the screen is empty. Since you used the Delete option instead of the Cut option, you can only bring it back by using the Cancel key (F1). To prove it, try the Retrieve Text option on the Move key (Ctrl-F4) first.

4. Press Move (Ctrl-F4) and select **4**, Retrieve, then select **1** Block.

This only retrieves the sentence you cut earlier, in the previous exercise. Now try the Cancel key (F1).

5. Press Cancel (F1). The paragraph should reappear in a highlighted block. If it doesn't, try pressing option 2, *Previous Deletion,* once or twice until you see it.

6. Press either **1** or **R** to restore the paragraph.

*MOVING A PAGE*   Now let's try deleting and moving a page. Before we begin, let's make a hard page break so that we'll have two pages on screen.

1. Move the cursor to the end of the document (use Home Home ↓).

2. Press Ctrl-← to force a page break there.

3. Type your first and last name, then press ←.

4. Move the cursor back to the previous page using the Page Up key. The cursor can be anywhere on the page.

5. Press the Move key, Ctrl-F4.

6. Select option 3, Page, by pressing either **3** or **A**.

7. Select option 1, Move, by pressing either **1** or **M**.

This leaves only your name on the screen, and the first page has disappeared. Let's move the cursor down under your name and retrieve the page.

8. Move the cursor to the blank line under your name.

9. Press ←.

This brings back the text and the page break you had created at the bottom of the page. The screen should resemble Figure 5.3.

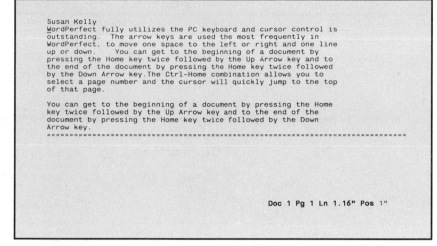

```
Susan Kelly
WordPerfect fully utilizes the PC keyboard and cursor control is
outstanding.  The arrow keys are used the most frequently in
WordPerfect, to move one space to the left or right and one line
up or down.   You can get to the beginning of a document by
pressing the Home key twice followed by the Up Arrow key and to
the end of the document by pressing the Home key twice followed
by the Down Arrow key.The Ctrl-Home combination allows you to
select a page number and the cursor will quickly jump to the top
of that page.

You can get to the beginning of a document by pressing the Home
key twice followed by the Up Arrow key and to the end of the
document by pressing the Home key twice followed by the Down
Arrow key.
=====================================================================

                                    Doc 1 Pg 1 Ln 1.16" Pos 1"
```

*Figure 5.3:* After retrieving a page

## COPYING TEXT

Now that you know how to use the Block and Move keys to move text around, copying will be easy. The steps are almost the same except that when you select Copy instead of Move or Delete, the highlighted text is copied into memory but the original is left intact where it is.

The four brief exercises that follow will teach you how to use the Block and Move keys to copy a phrase and how to use the Move key alone to copy a sentence, paragraph, and page. We'll use the original paragraph, so clear the screen and retrieve it before continuing.

> If you use the Block and Move keys or the Move key alone to move or copy text, there are two ways to retrieve it: by pressing Move (Ctrl-F4) and selecting Retrieve (*4* or *R*) then Block (*1* or *B*), or by pressing the Retrieve Text key (Shift-F10) and pressing ← (instead of typing a file name) when the *Document to be retrieved* prompt appears.

1. Press F7 N N to clear the screen.

2. Press the Retrieve Text key, Shift-F10, and enter the file name, **keys**.

### COPYING A BLOCK OF TEXT

We'll begin by copying the phrase *the PC keyboard* and placing it in the second sentence so that it reads

**The arrow keys on the PC keyboard are used the most frequently in WordPerfect, to move one space to the left or right and one line up or down.**

1. Move the cursor to the beginning of the phrase *the PC keyboard* and place it on the first letter, *t.*

2. Press the Block key, Alt-F4.

3. Press the letter **d** to extend the highlighting to the end of the word *keyboard.*

4. Press the Move key, Ctrl-F4.

5. Select Block by pressing either **1** or **B**, then select Copy (**2** or **C**). You'll see the *Move cursor* prompt. Press F1 to cancel it.

6. Move the cursor to the second sentence, after the word *keys,* and type

   **on**

7. Press the Space bar twice, then press ← to place the cursor in the blank space before *are.*

8. Make a copy of the phrase by pressing the Move key, Ctrl-F4, and selecting the Retrieve option (press either **4** or **R**), then press **B** or **1** for Block.

I told you that was going to be easy!

## COPYING A SENTENCE

Let's use the Move key to make a copy of the first sentence and place it at the end of the paragraph. Remember, when text you want to cut or copy falls into the category of sentence, paragraph, or page, you don't have to block it first with the Block key because the Move key can do the blocking for you.

1. Place the cursor anywhere on the first sentence.

2. Press the Move key, Ctrl-F4.

3. Select Sentence by pressing either **1** or **S**. The sentence should be highlighted.

4. Select Copy by pressing either **2** or **C**.

Once again, the highlighting disappears and the *Move cursor* prompt appears.

5. Move the cursor to the end of the paragraph, after the last period.

6. Press ←⏎.

Now you have a copy of the first sentence at that end of your paragraph.

## *COPYING A PARAGRAPH*

In this exercise we'll make another copy of the entire paragraph, but this time we'll do something different and retrieve the extra copy into the Doc 2 work area.

1. Press the Move key, Ctrl-F4. The cursor can be anywhere in the paragraph.

2. Select Paragraph by pressing either **2** or **P**. The paragraph should be highlighted.

3. Select Copy by pressing either **2** or **C**.

4. Switch to Doc 2 by pressing the Switch key, Shift-F3. You should see *Doc 2* on the status line and the screen should be blank except for the *Move cursor* prompt.

5. Press ←⏎ to retrieve the paragraph.

Now you've made an extra copy of the paragraph and placed it into the Doc 2 area.

## *COPYING A PAGE*

Now let's make an extra copy of the page. Before we begin, let's make a hard page break so that we'll have two pages on screen.

1. Move the cursor to the end of the document (use Home Home ↓).

2. Press Ctrl-←⏎ to force a page break there.

3. Type **Page 2**, then press ←⏎.

4. Move the cursor back to the previous page using ↑. The cursor can be anywhere on the page when you copy it.

5. Press the Move key, Ctrl-F4.

6. Select option 3, Page, by pressing either **3** or **A**. The page should be highlighted.

7. Select option 2, Copy, by pressing either **2** or **C**.

8. Move the cursor to the end of the document by pressing Home Home ↓.

9. Press ↵.

You just made an extra copy of the page and placed it on page 2. If you move the cursor to the bottom (press Home Home ↓ again), you'll see that the page break was included with the copied text, so that the document ends on page 3.

Before we continue, let's close the Doc 2 area.

1. Press the Exit key and exit without saving (F7 N). You should now see this prompt:

   Exit doc 2? (Y/N) No    (Cancel to return to document)

2. Press **Y**.

> The Block key also can be used to cut, copy, or move a rectangular block such as a line drawing (see Chapter 13).

Table 5.1 summarizes the many methods you've learned in this chapter to cut, copy, and move text using the Block and Move keys.

## PRINTING A BLOCK OF TEXT

The Print key (Shift-F7) is another example of a key whose meaning is altered when the Block key is on. Pressed alone, the Print key allows you to print an individual page or an entire document from the Edit screen, but nothing smaller than a page and nothing in between a page and a document. It's often desirable to print a section of your work that does not fit into one of these categories; the Block key makes this possible. When the *Block on* message is flashing and you press the Print key, instead of bringing up the Print menu (shown in Figure 2.3), WordPerfect asks if you want to print the block that you've highlighted.

Printing by blocks is especially useful when you're working with long documents. If you're in the habit of printing and proofreading

*Table 5.1:* Cutting, Copying, and Moving Text

| **To delete a** | **Use these keystrokes:** |
|---|---|
| Sentence | Ctrl-F4 1 3 |
| Paragraph | Ctrl-F4 2 3 |
| Page | Ctrl-F4 3 3 |
| Block of text | Alt-F4, use arrow keys to mark the block, Ctrl-F4 1 3 |
| **To copy a** | **Use these keystrokes:** |
| Sentence | Ctrl-F4 1 2, move cursor to new location, ← |
| Paragraph | Ctrl-F4 2 2, move cursor to new location, ← |
| Page | Ctrl-F4 3 2, move cursor to new location, ← |
| Block of text | Alt-F4, use arrow keys to mark the block, Ctrl-F4 1 2, move cursor to new location, ← |
| **To move a** | **Use these keystrokes:** |
| Sentence | Ctrl-F4 1 1, move cursor to new location, ← |
| Paragraph | Ctrl-F4 2 1, move cursor to new location, ← |
| Page | Ctrl-F4 3 1, move cursor to new location, ← |
| Block of text | Alt-F4, use arrow keys to mark the block, Ctrl-F4 1 1, move cursor to new location, ← |

each section after it's been typed, this will save you a lot of paper. Rather than printing the entire document after finishing each section, you can block, print, and proofread the sections individually.

Let's try printing the first two sentences of the sample paragraph. Be sure that your printer is turned on before you proceed.

1. Move the cursor to the beginning, to the *W* in *WordPerfect.*

2. Press Block (Alt-F4), then press the period key twice to move the cursor to the end of the second sentence.

3. Press the Print key, Shift-F7.

3. Press the Print key, Shift-F7.

A message will appear on the status line asking if you wish to print the block, as illustrated below:

**Print block? (Y/N) No**

4. Press **Y**.

A message will appear briefly on the status line, saying

**\* \* Please wait \* \***

and then the block will be printed.

If you had pressed *N* or any key other than *Y* or *y* in step 4, the *Block on* message would still be flashing but the *Print block?* prompt would be gone. If this happens, you can either press the Print key (Shift-F7) and try again or cancel Block mode by pressing the Cancel key, F1.

## *SAVING A TEXT BLOCK*

Saving a block of text is equally simple and can serve many purposes. You may decide to delete a section because it doesn't really fit or doesn't sound right, but still wish to retain it in a separate file just in case you change your mind. You may have a paragraph that you use frequently without any changes. Rather than retyping it each time you use it, you can save it to its own disk file and insert copies of it as often as you wish.

Let's save the two sentences you just printed.

1. Move the cursor to the beginning of the paragraph (on the *W*).

2. Press Alt-F4, then press the period key twice to highlight both sentences.

3. Press the Save Text key (F10).

Instead of asking if you want to save the document, as it does when you press the Save Text key without having pressed the Block key first, WordPerfect asks you to assign a name to the block. You should see this prompt on the status line:

**Block name:**

Once you type a name and press ←, the block will be saved in a separate file under that name. As with any file, you should try to assign a logical name that you will remember easily. Let's call it *testbloc*.

4. Type

    **testbloc**

    then press ←.

The file is now stored permanently on the default disk. Let's try retrieving it from the disk file. Move the cursor to the end of the document first.

5. Press the Retrieve Text key (Shift- F10).

6. Type the file name, testbloc, and press ←.

The block will appear at the cursor location with the cursor on the first word. Since we didn't clear the screen before retrieving it, the *testbloc* file was added to the text on screen. If you had a standard paragraph that you used frequently and had saved in a disk file, this is how you would insert it into other documents. Remember, though, that when you retrieve a file, you are only bringing up a copy of the file, and any changes you make to it will have no effect on the disk version until you save it again. Thus, if you were to clear the screen right now and retrieve the *testbloc* file again, you'd see that it contains only the two highlighted sentences that you blocked and saved rather than the entire paragraph. Let's prove it.

7. Press F7 N N to clear the screen.

8. Press the Retrieve Text key, Shift-F10, type the file name, **testbloc**, and press ←.

The two sentences you originally blocked and saved should appear by themselves on the screen.

# ADDING A TEXT BLOCK TO THE END OF A FILE

The Block and Move keys can also be used together to add a block of text to the end of an existing file on disk. Unlike the block save method you just learned, this does not create a separate file for the block of text, but just adds it to the end of an existing file. To try it, we'll type a new sentence and add it to the end of your *testbloc* file. Clear your screen (F7 N N) before continuing.

1. Type this sentence:

    **I will add this to the end of my testbloc file using the Block and Move keys.**

2. Place the cursor on the first word, *I,* and press the Block key, Alt-F4.

3. Press the period key to move the highlighting to the end of the sentence.

4. Press the Move key, Ctrl-F4.

5. Select Block by pressing **1** or **B**.

6. Select the Append option by pressing either **4** or **A**.

You should see this prompt:

**Append to:**

WordPerfect is waiting for you to type the name of the file that you want to add the highlighted text to.

7. Type the file name, **testbloc**, and press ◄┘.

Now clear the screen and we'll retrieve the *testbloc* file to see if it worked.

8. Press the Exit key to clear the screen without saving (F7 N N).

9. Press the Retrieve Text key, Shift-F10, and enter the file name, **testbloc**.

You should see the file on screen, with your sentence at the end. It should look like this:

> WordPerfect fully utilizes the PC keyboard and cursor control is outstanding. The arrow keys are used the most frequently in WordPerfect, to move one space to the left or right and one line up or down.I will add this to the end of my testbloc file using the Block and Move keys.

## CONVERTING TEXT BLOCKS BETWEEN UPPERCASE AND LOWERCASE

Have you ever been typing along with your eyes glued to the paper, when you suddenly looked up at the screen to discover that all of your characters had been entered in uppercase because the Caps Lock key was on? WordPerfect has a wonderful feature that will switch the text to lowercase, saving you the effort of deleting and retyping all your work. As you've probably guessed, it works with the Block key.

To see how it works, let's convert your sample paragraph to uppercase. Before continuing, use the Exit key to clear the screen (F7 N N) then use the Retrieve key to retrieve the file (Shift-F10 *keys* ◄┘).

1. Move the cursor to the first character and press Block (Alt-F4).

2. Press ◄┘ to highlight the whole paragraph.

3. Press the Switch key (Shift-F3).

This prompt will appear on the status line, asking if you wish to use lowercase or uppercase:

**1 Uppercase; 2 Lowercase: 0**

As you know from reading Chapters 1 and 3, the Switch key usually moves you into the Doc 2 work area. However, when you press it after turning on Block mode, it serves a different purpose: to switch text between uppercase and lowercase.

4. Select Uppercase by pressing either **1** or **U**.

The entire paragraph will now be capitalized. However, when you switch it back to lowercase, you are going to have a problem. Try it now and see if you can discover what the problem is.

5. Press Page Up to move the cursor to the beginning.

6. Press Block, Alt-F4, then press ⟵ to highlight the entire paragraph.

7. Press the Switch key, Shift-F3 and select lowercase by pressing either **2** or **L**.

The results appear in Figure 5.4.

The paragraph contains several words that were originally capitalized, such as *PC* and *Ctrl*. With the text converted back to lowercase, the only words that remain capitalized are those that follow a period, with one notable exception, the first word in the paragraph. WordPerfect recognizes that words immediately following a period, question mark, or exclamation point are supposed to remain capitalized, but it is unable to capitalize the other words correctly. In fact, the *w* in

```
     wordperfect fully utilizes the pc keyboard and cursor control is
     outstanding.  The arrow keys are used the most frequently in
     wordperfect, to move one space to the left or right and one line
     up or down.  You can get to the beginning of a document by
     pressing the home key twice followed by the up arrow key and to
     the end of the document by pressing the home key twice followed
     by the down arrow key.  The ctrl-home combination allows you to
     select a page number and the cursor will quickly jump to the top
     of that page.
     _




     C:\WP5\KEYS                              Doc 1 Pg 1 Ln 2.5" Pos 1"
```

*Figure 5.4:* The sample paragraph converted back to lowercase

the paragraph's first word, *WordPerfect,* is no longer capitalized because it does not follow a period.

As long as you recognize this limitation, the Switch feature can be very useful. In most cases, it will still be quicker than deleting and retyping the entire text.

## *BLOCK UNDERLINING AND BOLDFACING*

As mentioned earlier, the Block key must be used to underline or boldface text that has already been entered. The next exercise will teach you how. You'll type a title for the paragraph, then use Block mode to boldface and underline it. Before continuing, clear the screen (F7 N N) and retrieve the original paragraph (Shift-F10 *keys* ←⏎).

1. Move the cursor to the beginning of the paragraph (to the *W*) and press ←⏎ twice to insert two blank lines.

2. Press the Caps Lock key to turn Caps Lock on.

3. Move the cursor back to the first line and type the following title.

   **INTRODUCTION TO WORDPERFECT'S CURSOR CONTROL FEATURES**

4. Move the cursor back to the first character, the *I* in *INTRO-DUCTION.*

5. Press the Block key (Alt-F4).

6. Press Home → and watch the cursor jump to the end of the line, highlighting the whole title.

7. Press the Underline key (F8) once. The title should be underlined or in another color, and the highlighting and the *Block on* prompt should disappear.

As you saw, pressing Underline in Block mode both begins and ends the underlining, so you did *not* have to press F8 a second time to turn underlining off, as you did when you underlined text as you entered it.

Now try repeating the steps again to boldface the title.

1. Press the Block key, Alt-F4.

```
┌─────────────────────────────────────────────────────────────┐
│                                                              │
│   INTRODUCTION TO WORDPERFECT'S CURSOR CONTROL FEATURES      │
│   WordPerfect fully utilizes the PC keyboard and cursor control is │
│   outstanding.  The arrow keys are used the most frequently in │
│   WordPerfect, to move one space to the left or right and one line │
│   up or down.  You can get to the beginning of a document by  │
│   pressing the Home key twice followed by the Up Arrow key and to │
│   the end of the document by pressing the Home key twice followed │
│   by the Down Arrow key.  The Ctrl-Home combination allows you to │
│   select a page number and the cursor will quickly jump to the top │
│   of that page.                                              │
│                                                              │
│                                                              │
│                                                              │
│                                                              │
│   C:\WP5\KEYS                          Doc 1 Pg 1 Ln 1" POS 1" │
│                                                              │
└─────────────────────────────────────────────────────────────┘
```

*Figure 5.5:* The transformed title

2. Press Home ← to move the cursor back to the left edge of the line.

3. Press the Bold key (F6) once.

Your title should be both underlined and boldfaced, and it should resemble Figure 5.5.

## SPELL CHECKING A BLOCK

See Chapter 4 if you need more information on how to use Word-Perfect's speller.

Another key that works differently when you're in Block mode is the Spell key. When used in this mode, Spell immediately begins spell checking the highlighted text. Imagine if you had typed a 40-page report, spell checked it and corrected all the errors, then added a few paragraphs in the middle. Rather than having to recheck the entire document, which takes several minutes even if there are no errors, you can use Block and Spell to highlight and check just the new paragraphs. I use this feature all the time, and it's much faster. Let's learn how.

We'll begin by deliberately misspelling a few words.

1. Change *fully* in the first line to *fuley*.

2. Change *utilizes* to *utilizs*.

3. Move the cursor to the beginning of the paragraph and press the Block key, Alt-F4.

4. Press the period key so that the highlighting includes the first sentence.

5. Press the Spell key, Ctrl-F2.

WordPerfect will immediately begin checking your document and should stop on the first misspelled word, *fuley*. (Remember, if the Block key were not on, you'd see a prompt asking if you wanted to check the word, page, or document.)

6. Select the letter next to the correct spelling, *fully*. This replaces the word in your document.

7. The next misspelled word, *utilizs,* should be highlighted. Select the letter next to the correct spelling.

If there are any more misspelled words in the block, WordPerfect will try to correct them also. When the speller is finished, you'll be told the number of words in the block, and asked to press any key to continue.

8. When the prompt appears telling you the word count, press any key to exit from spell checking.

## KEEPING TEXT TOGETHER WITH THE BLOCK PROTECTION FEATURE

Block Protection is a wonderful feature that keeps a block together so that it doesn't get split into separate pages as you add and delete text. For instance, you could use it to keep headings on the same page as the text that follows them, or use it to preserve the integrity of charts, tables, and similar groupings. For example, look at Figure 5.6, which is part of a marketing survey. The entire last rating question, number 8, should have been printed on one page, which would have been the case if block protection had been used. In this format, it's difficult for respondents to grade the brands on page 2 since they have to keep turning back to the previous page to see the original question and explanation of the rating scale. (Market researchers have enough trouble just finding willing participants for these surveys, so why make their task more difficult?)

```
6. Please rate the overall quality of products that are produced
by the following corporations.  Circle the number corresponding
to your answer, 1 being the lowest quality and 10 being the
highest.

Product Quality

Company #1          1    2    3    4    5    6    7    8    9    10

Company #2          1    2    3    4    5    6    7    8    9    10

Company #3          1    2    3    4    5    6    7    8    9    10

Company #4          1    2    3    4    5    6    7    8    9    10

Company #5          1    2    3    4    5    6    7    8    9    10


7. Please rate these brands according to how good a value they are
for the money.  Again, the scale of values is from 1 to 10 with
#10 being the highest value and #1 the lowest.

Value for the Money

Brand #1            1    2    3    4    5    6    7    8    9    10

Brand #2            1    2    3    4    5    6    7    8    9    10

Brand #3            1    2    3    4    5    6    7    8    9    10

Brand #4            1    2    3    4    5    6    7    8    9    10

Brand #5            1    2    3    4    5    6    7    8    9    10


8.Please rate these brands according to whether you think they are
important items to own.  Rate them on a scale of 1 to 10, with 1
being the least important and 10 being the most important.
```

*Figure 5.6:* The marketing survey with list split over two pages

Like many other keys you've studied, the Format key (Shift-F8) operates differently when you're in Block mode, serving to protect the highlighted block. Let's see how it works by block-protecting your paragraph and the heading you created for it, then moving them to the end of the page to see what happens.

| Importance | | | | | | | | | | |
|---|---|---|---|---|---|---|---|---|---|---|
| Brand #1 | 1 | 2 | 3 | 4 | 5 | 6 | 7 | 8 | 9 | 10 |
| Brand #2 | 1 | 2 | 3 | 4 | 5 | 6 | 7 | 8 | 9 | 10 |
| Brand #3 | 1 | 2 | 3 | 4 | 5 | 6 | 7 | 8 | 9 | 10 |
| Brand #4 | 1 | 2 | 3 | 4 | 5 | 6 | 7 | 8 | 9 | 10 |
| Brand #5 | 1 | 2 | 3 | 4 | 5 | 6 | 7 | 8 | 9 | 10 |

*Figure 5.6:* The marketing survey with list split over two pages (continued)

1. Move the cursor to the first character in the heading and press ⏎ to move it down a line.

2. Press the Block key (Alt-F4).

3. Press the period key four times to move the cursor to the end of the paragraph, so that the heading and the entire paragraph are highlighted.

4. Press the Format key (Shift-F8). You should see the following message:

   Protect Block? (Y/N) No

5. Type **Y**.

The block highlighting will immediately disappear. Now let's see if the block protection works. To do this, we'll make an extra copy of the paragraph at the top of the page, then press ⏎ until the blocked section is moved as a unit to the second page.

6. Place the cursor anywhere in the paragraph and press the Move key, Ctrl-F4.

7. Select the Paragraph option by pressing either **2** or **P**.

8. Select Copy by pressing either **2** or **C**. You'll see the *Move cursor Press Enter* prompt.

9. Press Page Up to move the cursor to the beginning of the page and make sure it's on a blank line.

10. Press ⏎.

11. Use the Format key to double-space the document. Press Shift-F8 L S 2, then press ⏎ three times to exit from the Format: Line menu.

12. Move the cursor down and place it in the blank line above the heading (to guarantee that it is before the Block Protection code).

13. Press ⏎ repeatedly until the paragraph and heading have been moved to the next page.

You should see the entire blocked section moved as one unit to page 2. When I tried it, I only had to press ⏎ six times before the section moved to the next page. After that, my page 1 ended at line 6" instead of the usual position.

As you can imagine, this tool can be very valuable, particularly if your documents are quite long and contain tables, headings, and other text that must be kept together.

## *SUMMARY*

Block mode is a powerful and valuable feature for which there are innumerable applications. Instead of disfiguring your work with the physical cut and paste method, you can use this remarkable tool to copy, move, delete, and rearrange to your heart's content, and your documents will always look terrific. Before long, you'll wonder how you ever managed without it.

You have performed many operations with the Block key, and by now you should feel comfortable enough to experiment by using it with other features. For instance, you might try using it with the Flush Right key (Alt-F6) or the Center key (Shift-F6) to right-align or center a block of text. In later chapters you will learn how to use the Block key with some new features. For instance, in the next chapter you'll learn how to use it with WordPerfect's Search and Replace function to find and replace text and/or hidden codes in a highlighted block. In the chapter about line drawing you'll learn how to cut, copy, or move a rectangular block, such as a box. In the math chapter, you'll learn how to block a column of text or numbers. The Block key is also used to mark text to be included in an index, list, table of contents, or table of authorities, and you'll study these in the chapter on reference tools.

**II.**

# PART II

## ADVANCED WORD PROCESSING FEATURES

# 6.

# *CONTROLLING PAGE LAYOUT*

# FAST TRACK

**To create a ragged right margin,**                                158

turn justification off (right justification is WordPerfect's default). Press the Format key (Shift-F8), then press *1* or *L* to reach the Format: Line menu. At this menu, turn justification off by selecting Justification (*3* or *J*) and pressing *N*. Be sure that the cursor is at the top of the document if you want to turn off justification for the entire document.

**Place page numbers in your document**                             159

by pressing the Format key (Shift-F8), then pressing *2* or *P* to reach the Format: Page menu. At this menu, press *7* or *P* for Page Numbering and you'll see the Page Number Position menu, which offers eight choices for the page number position. Choose the desired option by pressing the number next to it, such as *1* for top left. When the document is printed, the page numbers will appear in that position. The cursor must be on line 1 when you choose a page number position.

**Center text between the top and bottom margins**                  164

by placing the cursor on the first line on the page, then pressing the Format key (Shift-F8) and selecting *2* or *P*. Next, press *1* or *C*, then press the Exit key (F7). The text will not appear centered on screen, but will be centered when you print your document or use View Document (Shift-F7 V) to preview it.

**Set the top and bottom margins**                                  174

by placing the cursor on line 1 of the page you are changing, pressing the Format key (Shift-F8), selecting *2* or *P*, then *5* or *M*. Enter the new measurement (in inches) for the top margin and press ←⟵, then enter the measurement for the bottom margin.

You will not see the margins change until you print the document or use View Document (Shift-F7 V).

**Create headers and footers**                                          174

by placing the cursor on line 1 of the first page you want the header or footer to appear on, pressing the Format key (Shift-F8), selecting *2* or *P*, then *3* or *H* for a header, or *4* or *F* for a footer. At the prompt, select *1* to create your first header or footer, or *2* to create a second one. At the next menu, indicate the pages on which you want the header (or footer) to appear. You can choose every page, odd pages, or even pages. Type the header or footer text and press Exit (F7) twice to return to the Edit screen. Headers and footers only appear in the printed version or in View Document (Shift-F7 V).

**To create a page break**                                              180

before the normal end of a page, press Ctrl-←.

**Keep lines of text from being divided between two pages**             183

if they appear at the end of a page by moving the cursor to the first character in the block of text you want kept together, then pressing the Block key (Alt-F4). Use cursor movement keys to highlight the text you want kept together, then press the Format key (Shift-F8) and *Y*.

**Change the default format settings for all documents**                185

by pressing the Setup key (Shift-F1), pressing *5* or *I*, then pressing *4* or *I*. You will see a screen that looks like the Reveal Codes screen. To change settings, press the appropriate format keys and select the desired menu options, then press Exit (F7) twice.

WORDPERFECT HAS FOUR FORMATTING MENUS attached to the Format key (Shift-F8): Line, Page, Document, and Other. Up to this point, you've only been introduced to one, the Format: Line menu. This chapter will acquaint you with a few new options on this menu as well as all of the options on the Format: Page menu. The Format: Page options control features that affect the number of text lines on the printed page: the top and bottom margins, paper size and type, page numbering, and headers and footers. In addition, you will learn about Widow/Orphan Protection (on the Format: Line menu) and Conditional End of Page (on the Format: Other menu), both of which can help you avoid "widows and orphans" in the paging of the document. Don't worry if some of these terms sound strange to you; you'll know them all quite well by the time you finish this chapter!

## THE FORMAT KEY

Unlike many of the other keys you've studied, the Format key completely replaces your Edit screen with a full-screen menu. The four menu options that appear on the Format screen have full-screen menus of their own, each of which presents you with various formatting options. Press Shift-F8 and you'll see the Format menu, as shown in Figure 6.1.

## FORMAT: LINE OPTIONS

The first option on the Format menu is Line. If you select Line by pressing *1* or *L,* the options shown in the two columns below it (from Hyphenation to Widow/Orphan Protection) become available. You have already used many of these options while studying basic document formatting in earlier chapters. In this chapter, which is concerned primarily with page formatting, we will explore only two

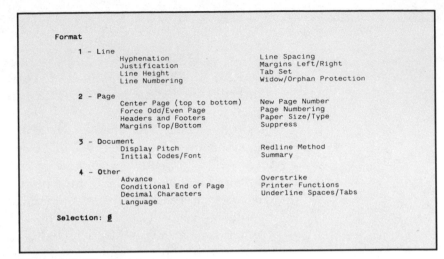

*Figure 6.1:* The Format menu

options on the Format: Line menu: Justification and Widow/
Orphan Protection. Let's begin by examining the Justification
option and its effect on the appearance of the printed page. You will
learn about Widow/Orphan Protection a little later, in the section
about controlling page breaks in a document.

## JUSTIFICATION

The Justification option on the Format: Line menu is set to Yes by
default. This means that the printed version of the document will have
an even *(justified)* right margin. Although the text on the screen appears
to be uneven, it will always be justified when printed unless you use this
option to turn Justification off. When it is off, the right margins will be
ragged, just like the margins produced by typewriters.

WordPerfect creates even right margins by expanding or com-
pressing the blank space between words. In short lines where the
blank space is expanded, this sometimes results in large gaps between
words (especially if you are not using hyphenation). If you find this
unattractive, you can turn off Justification by placing the cursor at
the top of the document, selecting the Justification option on the Format: Line menu, and typing *N* to change it to No. When you do this,
the following code will be inserted into your document (visible only in
the Reveal Codes screen):

[Just Off]

If you prefer to turn off Justification permanently, you can change the default setting in your program. We will examine how to change initial settings such as this at the end of the chapter.

## FORMAT: PAGE OPTIONS

The second option on the Format menu is Page. When you select Page, another menu appears, as shown in Figure 6.2, with options to center text vertically on a page, force odd or even page numbering, change top and bottom margins, change the paper size that you are using, add page numbers, change the page number, and add headings at the top or bottom of your pages. We will begin examining the options available on this menu by looking at the page numbering options.

### SELECTING A PAGE NUMBER POSITION

Unlike many other word processors, WordPerfect does not print page numbers on your documents unless you tell it to. You do this by using the Page Numbering option from the Format: Page menu to select a location on the page where you want the numbers printed.

```
Format: Page

     1 - Center Page (top to bottom)       No

     2 - Force Odd/Even Page

     3 - Headers

     4 - Footers

     5 - Margins - Top                     1"
                   Bottom                  1"

     6 - New Page Number                   1
         (example: 3 or iii)

     7 - Page Numbering                    No page numbering

     8 - Paper Size                        8.5" x 11"
              Type                         Standard

     9 - Suppress (this page only)

  Selection: 0
```

*Figure 6.2:* The Format: Page menu

To view the Format: Page Numbering menu, press the Format key (Shift-F8), press *2* or *P* for Page, then press *7* or *P* to select Page Numbering. As shown in Figure 6.3, this submenu offers you eight possible locations for the page number: 1—each page at the top left; 2—the top center; 3—the top right; 5—the bottom left; 6—the bottom center; 7—the bottom right; 4—the top but alternating left and right; or 8—the bottom but alternating left and right.

Most of these alternatives are self-explanatory. For instance, selection 1 inserts a code that causes page numbers to be printed at the upper left corner of each page. The number will be aligned with the left margin of your document; if your left margin setting is set to 1 inch, the number will appear exactly one inch from the left side of the paper.

Selection 2 inserts a code that causes a page number to be printed at the top center; that is, centered between the current left and right margin settings. Selection 3 inserts a code that causes a page number to be printed at the top right, aligned with the right margin of the document text. Selections 5, 6, and 7 place the numbers at the bottom of each page, in the same column positions as at the top (left margin, center, and right margin).

If you select *4* from the Format: Page Numbering menu, the first page number will be printed on the top right side of the first page (aligned with the right margin), the second page number will be printed on the top left side of the second page (aligned with the left margin), the

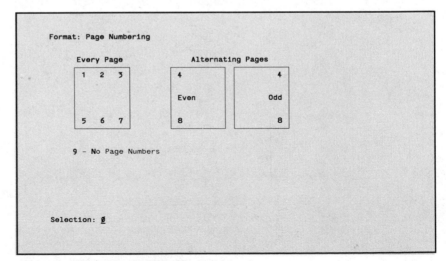

*Figure 6.3:* Possible page number positions

third page number will be printed on the top right side of the third page, and so forth, alternating like this throughout the document. Selection 8 will do the same, except that the page numbers will be placed alternatively at the *bottom* left and *bottom* right of the pages.

This alternating format is often used in books, manuals, and similar publications to allow page numbers to appear at the outer edge of the left and right facing pages. To present your document like this you must have text on both sides of the page, which you can accomplish by making two-sided copies on a copy machine.

The No Page Numbers option (9) on the Format: Page Numbering menu is the default. It is included on the menu so that you can change back to it if necessary after choosing another option. For example, if you wanted to limit page numbering to the first five pages of your document, you would insert a Page Numbering code on the first page, as usual. However, before typing the sixth page, which you do not want numbered, you would select option 9 to turn the Pagination feature off. This procedure would ensure that the sixth and subsequent pages would be printed without page numbers (unless you inserted another Page Numbering code later in the document).

For example, to add a page number, make sure that the cursor is on line 1 of the page and press option 1 on the Format: Page Numbering menu to select numbering at the top left of every page. This action will restore the Format: Page menu, where you will see Top Left listed after the Page Numbering heading on this screen. You can then press the Exit key to return directly to your document. Page numbers appear only on the printed document (or in the View Document option of the Print key), so don't be alarmed if a number does not appear at the top of your screen. To verify that the change was actually made, check the Reveal Codes screen by pressing the Reveal Codes key (Alt-F3). You should see the following code at the top left of the Reveal Codes screen, confirming that you selected Top Left for the page number position:

[Pg Numbering: Top Left]

When the document is printed, the program will place the appropriate page number in the top margin. Also, WordPerfect subtracts a small amount of space from the amount of text space on the page (equal to the line height of the font in use plus one sixth of an inch). To preview how page numbers will appear when printed, you can use WordPerfect's View Document feature (Shift-F7 6 or V).

## *SPECIFYING ODD/EVEN PAGE NUMBERING*

When you need to ensure that the page numbering begins with an odd or even number, you can use the Force Odd/Even Page option on the Format: Page menu. This is often used to make sure that the first page of a book or report begins with an odd number (because page 1 is normally a right-hand or facing page when a document is bound).

To use the Force Odd/Even Page option, move the cursor to the first line of the page you want to affect, select the Format key (Shift-F8), Page (*2* or *P*), then Force Odd/Even Page (*2* or *O*). You will see these options at the bottom of the Format: Page screen:

**1 Odd; 2 Even: 0**

Press *1* or *O* to force the current page to be odd-numbered, or press *2* or *E* to force the current page to be even-numbered. After you select one of these options, the number next to the New Page Number option may have changed to reflect the selection you made. For example, if you were on page 1 and selected Even, the number will change to 2. If you return to the Edit screen and use the Reveal Codes key, you will see either

**[Force:Odd]**

or

**[Force:Even]**

depending upon the option you selected. Also, the page number indicator on the status line may have changed to accommodate your selection. For instance, if the cursor was on the first line of page 1 and you selected Even, it will now say *Pg 2* on the status line. However, if the cursor was on page 4 and you selected Even, it will not change the page number indicator.

## *NEW PAGE NUMBER*

You can use the New Page Number option on the Format: Page menu to start the page numbering with a number other than 1. For example, if you were writing an exceptionally long document such as a book, you would probably save each chapter as a separate file so that the document wouldn't become too cumbersome. However, you would not want the first page of each chapter to be numbered as page 1 when printed. The New Page Number option allows you to place the desired page number on the first page of each chapter, so that all of the following pages in the chapter are renumbered in the correct sequence.

To try this, press the Format key (Shift-F8) and select *2* or *P* for Page. Next, press *6* or *N* (for New Page Number). Your cursor will be positioned on the current starting number, which is the number of the page the cursor is on now. Here, you enter the new starting number you want on the current page and press ←. If you want the entire document renumbered, remember to move the cursor to the first line of the document's first page before starting this procedure. Changing the number inserts a code like this into your document:

[Pg Num: 5]

where *5* is the new page number that was selected. Also, the page number indicator on the status line changes to reflect the number you've chosen, and all pages that follow are renumbered sequentially. Numbers will not appear in the printed version of your document unless you use the Page Numbering option described earlier or place them in a header or footer (which you'll learn about shortly).

## CHOOSING A NUMBERING STYLE

The New Page Number option is used not only to set a new starting page number but also to change the style of numbering, that is, to switch between Arabic and Roman numerals. *Arabic* describes the type of numerals normally used: 1, 2, 3, 4, 5, 6, 7, 8, 9, and 0; this style is WordPerfect's default. *Roman* numerals such as i, ii, iii, iv, v, vi, and vii are probably familiar to you, since they are frequently used in the prefaces, forewords, and tables of contents of books. To use the Roman style of numbering, you simply select the New Page Number option and enter the starting number in this style. For instance, if you want to switch to Roman numerals and to change the page number to 5, you enter *v* instead of *5* for the new page number. When you choose this style by entering your starting number in its appropriate Roman numeral equivalent, the letters that represent the numbers appear in lowercase (i, ii, iii, iv, etc.).

If you type *5* (instead of *v*) for the new page number, you automatically select Arabic numbering at the same time you set a new beginning page number. When you select the Roman style of page numbering, it inserts a code similar to this:

[Pg Num:v]

where *v* represents the new page number you choose (5). Remember, page numbers still won't be printed unless you use the Page Numbering option or place them in a header or footer.

## CENTERING TEXT BETWEEN TOP AND BOTTOM MARGINS

The purpose of the *Center Page (top to bottom)* option is to center the text on a page vertically between the top and bottom margins, which is useful for title pages, tables of contents, very short letters, and other such documents. It only affects the printed version of the document, so don't expect to see a centered page on your screen (however, you can preview it with the View Document option on the Print key). It is pointless to use this feature when the page is full because if it is, the text will automatically be centered between the normal top and bottom margins.

To see how page centering works, try the following exercise:

1. Type the text of the title page illustrated in Figure 6.4. A word of advice about *horizontal* centering: Instead of centering each individual line as you type, it is easier to use the Block (Alt-F4) and Center (Shift-F6) keys to center the entire text in one operation after you have typed it.

2. Move the cursor to the first line on the page. If your cursor is not on line 1, the Center Page code will have no effect.

3. Press the Format key (Shift-F8) and press **2** or **P** to select Page. Next, press **1** or **C** to select *Center Page (top to bottom)*. This changes *No* to *Yes* next to the option at the top of the screen.

4. Press the Exit key (F7) to return to the editing screen.

When you switch to the Roman numeral style of numbering, the page number displayed on the status line of the editing screen after the Pg prompt is still shown in the Arabic style, even though it reflects the number of the page set with Roman numerals in the New Page Number option. For example, if you enter *iii* for the new page number, the Pg indicator will display *Pg 3* (not *Pg iii*) on the Edit screen.

```
                    THE UNIVERSITY OF CALIFORNIA

                  WORD PROCESSING AND CORPORATE POLITICS


                       A DISSERTATION SUBMITTED TO
                    THE FACULTY OF THE BUSINESS SCHOOL
                     IN CANDIDACY FOR THE DEGREE OF
                          MASTER OF BUSINESS



                                  BY

                            JANET R. SMITH


                            SAN FRANCISCO
                            MARCH, 1989
```

*Figure 6.4:* The sample title page

5. Since page centering only appears in the printed version of your document or in the View Document option of the Print key, check the Reveal Codes screen to verify that the code for centering has been inserted into your document. Press Alt-F3 and look for the code

   [Center Pg]

and make sure that it is on line 1. To verify that the page will be centered when printed, you could also check View Document by pressing Shift-F7 V.

6. Print the title page to see how professional it looks when it's centered on the page. If you want, save the practice file at this point.

7. Clear the screen using the Exit key (F7) but don't exit from WordPerfect.

## *PAPER SIZE AND TYPE*

WordPerfect assumes that you will be printing your document on the standard 8½″ by 11″ page. When this is not the case, you can use the Paper Size/Type option on the Format: Page menu to change it to any form that your printer is capable of printing. You select this option by pressing the Format key (Shift-F8), selecting the Page option (*2* or *P*), then the Paper Size/Type option (*8* or *S*). When you do, you'll see the Format: Paper Size menu shown in Figure 6.5.

As soon as you select a paper size from this menu, you'll see another screen called the Format: Paper Type menu, and you use it to select the paper type. This screen is shown in Figure 6.6.

```
Format: Paper Size

     1 - Standard                (8.5" x 11")

     2 - Standard Landscape      (11" x 8.5")

     3 - Legal                   (8.5" x 14")

     4 - Legal Landscape         (14" x 8.5")

     5 - Envelope                (9.5" x 4")

     6 - Half Sheet              (5.5" x 8.5")

     7 - US Government           (8" x 11")

     8 - A4                      (210mm x 297mm)

     9 - A4 Landscape            (297mm x 210mm)

     0 - Other


  Selection: 1
```

*Figure 6.5:* The Format: Paper Size menu

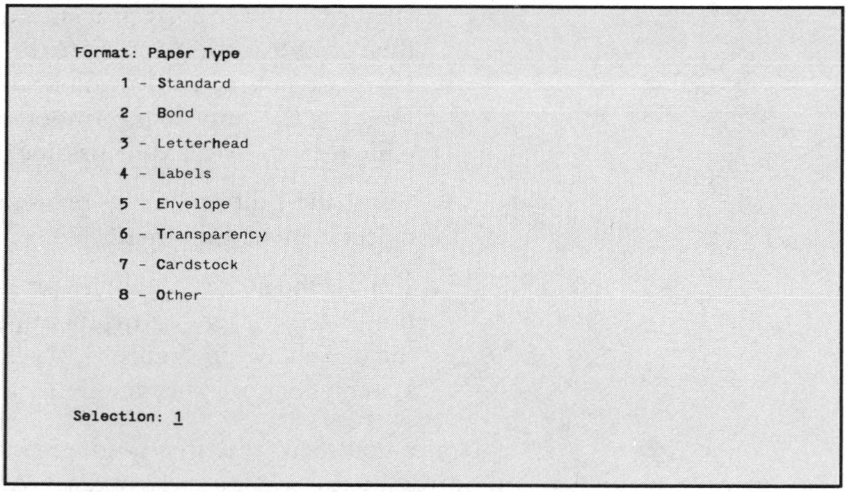

```
Format: Paper Type

     1 - Standard

     2 - Bond

     3 - Letterhead

     4 - Labels

     5 - Envelope

     6 - Transparency

     7 - Cardstock

     8 - Other




Selection: 1
```

*Figure 6.6:* The Format: Paper Type menu

When you choose a paper size and type from these two menus, WordPerfect inserts a form change code into your document at the cursor position, similar to this example:

**[Paper Sz/Typ:8.5″ x 11″,Letterhead]**

When you print this document, WordPerfect tries to match this code with a form definition in your printer definition file. If the form definition doesn't exist, the program looks for a form definition called *All Others* and uses that definition. If WordPerfect does not find *All Others,* it uses the form that is the most comparable. Forms are defined in the printer definition file because many of the settings they contain are dependent upon your printer's capabilities. This means that you define a form using the Print key, then use it in a specific document with the Format key.

To find out what forms have already been established for your printer or to define new forms, you use the Select Printer option on the Print key. Let's try it.

1. Clear the screen (using F7) and press the Print key (Shift-F7).

2. Press **S** for Select Printer.

3. The name of your printer should appear on the list at the top of the screen with an asterisk ( *) next to it. If not, move the

˙cursor bar to the correct printer name and type **S** for Select, then press **S** again to return to the Print-Select Printer menu. If you do not see your printer name on the list, and *Standard Printer* is the only name under Printer Selection, refer to Chapter 9 to install your printer before proceeding.

4. Select the Edit option by pressing **3** or **E**. You will see the Select Printer: Edit menu.

5. Choose the Forms option by pressing **4** or **F**. This brings up the Select Printer: Forms menu, which should be similar to the one shown in Figure 6.7 (which is the menu for an HP LaserJet Series II printer).

Notice that there are already some forms that have been defined for this printer: envelope and standard. Also, this printer comes with an *All Others* option that will be used if you select a Paper Size and Paper Type option (from the Format key) that doesn't fall into any of these categories.

Let's try adding a form definition for letterhead with a 2.5″ top margin. Here are the steps to define the form:

1. Select the Add option by pressing **1** or **A**. The Select Printer: Form Type menu shown in Figure 6.8 appears on your

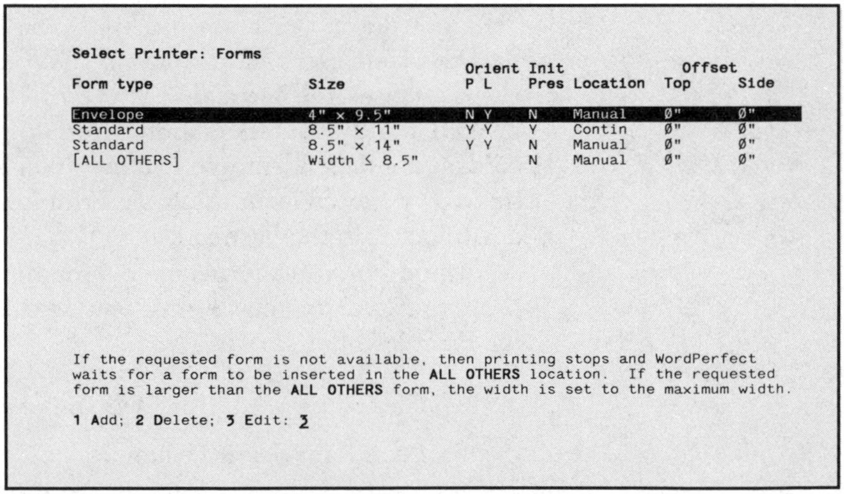

```
Select Printer: Forms
                                        Orient Init           Offset
Form type              Size             P L    Pres Location  Top    Side

Envelope               4" x 9.5"        N Y    N    Manual     Ø"     Ø"
Standard               8.5" x 11"       Y Y    Y    Contin     Ø"     Ø"
Standard               8.5" x 14"       Y Y    N    Manual     Ø"     Ø"
[ALL OTHERS]           Width ≤ 8.5"            N    Manual     Ø"     Ø"




If the requested form is not available, then printing stops and WordPerfect
waits for a form to be inserted in the ALL OTHERS location.  If the requested
form is larger than the ALL OTHERS form, the width is set to the maximum width.

1 Add; 2 Delete; 3 Edit: 3
```

*Figure 6.7:* The Select Printer: Forms menu for the HP LaserJet Series II printer

screen. If this menu looks familiar, it's because it is almost the same as the one you see when you select Paper Type using the Format: Page menu (as shown in Figure 6.6) except that it has one additional option: [ALL OTHERS].

2. To create a definition for Letterhead, press **3** or **H**. You will then see a screen that resembles Figure 6.9.

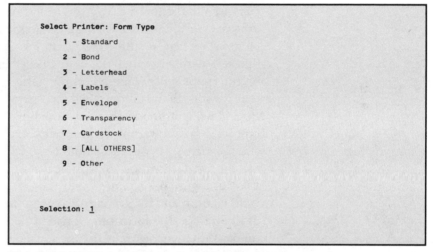

```
Select Printer: Form Type

     1 - Standard

     2 - Bond

     3 - Letterhead

     4 - Labels

     5 - Envelope

     6 - Transparency

     7 - Cardstock

     8 - [ALL OTHERS]

     9 - Other



Selection: 1
```

*Figure 6.8:* The Select Printer: Form Type menu

```
Select Printer: Forms

          Filename            HPLASEII.PRS

          Form Type           Letterhead

     1 - Form Size            8.5" x 11"

     2 - Orientation          Portrait

     3 - Initially Present    Yes

     4 - Location             Continuous

     5 - Page Offsets - Top   0"
                       Side   0"



Selection: 0
```

*Figure 6.9:* The Select Printer: Forms screen

The Form Size option on this menu allows you to change the form size if your new form is other than the standard 8½" by 11". For instance, if you were defining a form for 4" x 2" labels, you would enter the correct dimensions here.

The Orientation option allows you to switch between Portrait and Landscape, or to select Both. Portrait mode prints the regular way, so that the longest edge of the form corresponds to the vertical axis. It is called portrait because portraits of people in photos and paintings usually orient the subject's body with the long side of the paper or canvas. Landscape mode prints sideways on the page, so that the longest edge of the form corresponds to the horizontal axis. It is called landscape because landscape paintings usually place the horizon so that it is parallel to the long edge of the canvas. Landscape mode is useful for printing wide columnar tables, graphics, and other text that is wider than standard 8.5-inch paper. When you use it, Word-Perfect will automatically adjust the line length to maintain the top, bottom, left, and right margins that you are using (1 inch unless you change them). If you select Both (Landscape and Portrait), you can use the form definition to print either way (not both ways at once!). Look at Figure 6.7 again. Under the *Orient* heading, both the *P* (portrait) column and the *L* (Landscape) column are set to *Y* for the Standard form, so the form can be used in either Landscape or Portrait mode. When you actually use the form definition by selecting it from the Paper Size and Type menus on the Format key, you decide which mode to use.

The Initially Present option lets you decide if this paper form should be present in your printer when you issue the command to print it. If you change it to No, WordPerfect will pause after you issue the print command to let you manually feed or load the correct paper for this type of form.

The Location option allows you to indicate where the paper will come from when you issue a print command, and you can select continuous, sheet feeder, or manual feed. The default is continuous, which means that you are using either paper that is fed through the printer with a tractor feed, or individual sheets fed by a single tray (as on the HP LaserJet Series II printer). If your printer is equipped with multiple trays, you can select Location, then use the Bin Number option from the next menu to tell WordPerfect which tray or bin holds the paper for this form. For example, if you keep company let-terhead paper in one bin and plain bond in another, you could use this option to indicate the tray number that holds the letterhead paper. Select Location, then use the Manual option if you will insert these forms manually (one at a time) into your printer.

The Page Offsets option is used to indicate where you want the printer to begin printing when this form is used, so that if you are printing on a form that is loaded into the printer at a different hori-zontal or vertical position, WordPerfect can still print with the correct margins. For example, most printers that use tractors position the top edge of the paper right at the printhead and WordPerfect rolls it up 1 inch before printing (for the 1 inch top margin). If your printer posi-tions the printhead 1 inch under the top edge of the paper, you should use this option to tell WordPerfect that there is a 1-inch top offset, otherwise you will end up with a 2-inch top margin. This option is also useful when you are creating a definition for a form such as let-terhead, which usually requires a top margin of 2 or more inches. As you can see from Figure 6.9, there are two settings, Top and Side. Notice that both are set to 0″. If you change an offset to a negative number such as − 1, the offset ( − 1 inch) is *added* to the current mar-gin setting, and if you change it to a positive number such as 1, the offset (1 inch) is *subtracted* from the current margin setting. If you leave them at 0, the printer will begin printing at the position desig-nated by the current top and left margin settings (usually 1″ each, provided your printer initially positions the paper correctly to print a 1-inch top margin). Since you're defining a form for letterhead and you want printing to begin 2.5″ from the top edge of the paper, you'll use this option to change the top offset to 1.5″, thereby adding 1 inch to the current top margin.

3. Select Page Offsets by pressing **5** or **P**, then type − **1.5** for the top offset and press ⏎ twice.

4. Check your new definition to make sure that the settings are correct. For instance, you may wish to change Location to manual if you intend to hand feed the letterhead stationery into your printer. If you won't be changing any of the other options on this menu, press Exit (F7).

5. Now you see the Select Printer: Forms menu again (as in Fig-ure 6.7). You should see that your new Letterhead form

definition has been added. When you finish looking at it, press Exit (F7) four times to return to Edit mode.

## USING A FORM DEFINITION

Now that you have created a form definition for printing on letterhead stationery, let's apply it to a document using the Paper Size and Type option on the Format key's Format: Page menu. If you still have the document named Vaughn.ltr that you created in Chapter 2, you'll use it for the next exercise. If not, you can use any short letter you have on disk.

1. Use the List Files key (F5) or the Retrieve Text key (Shift-F10) to retrieve the file named Vaughn1.ltr (or any short letter you've created).

2. Make sure that the cursor is on the first line of the document (press Home Home ↑ if necessary to get it there) so that the settings in your Letterhead form definition apply to the entire letter.

3. Press the Format key (Shift-F8), then press **2** or **P** to select Page.

4. Select Paper Size/Type by pressing **8** or **S**.

5. On the Format: Paper Size menu, select Standard by pressing **1** or **S**.

6. On the Format: Paper Type menu, select Letterhead by pressing **3** or **H**.

You should now be back in the Format: Page menu shown in Figure 6.10. Notice that the paper type has been changed to Letterhead, and check to be sure that the top margin setting is 1″.

7. Press the Exit key (F7) to return to your document.

You may wish to check the Reveal Codes screen to verify that the Form Change code has been inserted into your document. To do this, press the Reveal Codes key (Alt-F3) and look for this code at the left side of line 1:

[Paper Sz/Typ:8.5″ x 11″,Letterhead]

```
Format: Page

       1 - Center Page (top to bottom)    No

       2 - Force Odd/Even Page

       3 - Headers

       4 - Footers

       5 - Margins - Top                  1"
                     Bottom               1"

       6 - New Page Number                1
           (example: 3 or iii)

       7 - Page Numbering                 No page numbering

       8 - Paper Size                     8.5" x 11"
              Type                        Letterhead

       9 - Suppress (this page only)

Selection: 0
```

***Figure 6.10:*** The Format: Page menu after selecting the Letterhead form type

This code instructs WordPerfect to find the Letterhead form definition that you created through the Print key and to apply its settings to the text that follows.

> 8. Complete the exercise by printing the letter. Press the Print key (Shift-F7) and select Page by pressing **2** or **P**.

The letter should have started printing 2.5″ down from the top of the paper. If not, you may need to edit the Letterhead form definition, checking all of your settings and changing any that are incorrect. To do this, press the Print key, choose Select Printer, choose Edit, choose Forms, then move the cursor bar down to the Letterhead definition and choose Edit from the Select Printer: Forms menu. After making the necessary changes, print the document again to see if it worked.

If you use the Letterhead form to print a letter that's longer than one page, be sure to change the paper size and type on the first line of the second page, or that page will also be printed with a 2.5″ top margin. To change back to standard paper with 1″ top, bottom, left, and right margins, use the Format: Page menu (Shift-F8 P), select Paper Size/Type, select Standard from the Format: Paper Size menu and Standard from the Format: Paper Type menu. This inserts another Form Change code into your document:

[Paper Sz/Typ:8.5″ x 11″,Standard]

This code cancels the letterhead settings.

This may have seemed like a lot of work just to change the top margin setting for your letterhead stationery, but for other forms such as labels there will probably be more than just a margin setting that has to be changed. Once you have defined a form, all the work is done and you can easily use it whenever you need to by selecting the paper size and type from the Format key.

## SETTING TOP AND BOTTOM MARGINS

The default for the top and bottom margins in a document is 1 inch. The top margin is measured down from the top edge of the paper, and the bottom margin is measured up from the bottom edge of the paper. You can change these settings for any page in a document or for the entire document (by moving the cursor to the top of the document before changing the margin settings).

To change the top or bottom margin, place the cursor on line 1 of the page you are changing, press the Format key (Shift-F8), select Page (*2* or *P*), then select Margins (*5* or *M*). Next, enter the new measurement (in inches) for the top margin, press ◄┘, and enter the new measurement for the bottom margin.

When you use this option to change top or bottom margins in a document, WordPerfect inserts a code at the cursor position. For example, if you were to change the Top margin to 2″ and leave the Bottom margin at 1″, you would see the code

[T/B Mar:2″,1″]

in the Reveal Codes screen. You will not see the actual margin change until you print the document or use View Document on the Print key (Shift-F7 V).

If your printer must be hand-fed, the top and bottom margin changes work a little differently. WordPerfect assumes that you will advance the paper manually so that the printhead is positioned 1 inch below the top edge of the paper before you start printing. If your top margin setting is less than 1 inch, the printer will begin printing at the printhead. If your top margin setting is more than 1 inch, the printer will advance 1 inch less than the top margin measurement, so if your top margin is 2″, the printer will advance only 1″.

## HEADERS AND FOOTERS

A header is one or more lines of standard text that appears at the top of each page, and a footer is one or more lines that appear at the bottom. They are often used in books, reports, and reference works to insert titles, labels, and page numbers. The titles at the tops of the pages of this book are an example of a header. WordPerfect has the ability to place headers and footers at the top or bottom of every page, every odd-numbered page, or every even-numbered page.

There is no practical limit to the number of lines that headers and footers can contain except common sense. A header of 25 lines is possible but certainly not practical, since it would leave very few text lines on each page for the rest of the text. You can create two different headers and two footers per page, or you can create a header and footer for the even-numbered pages and different headers and footers for the odd-numbered pages. If they are short enough, and you're sure they won't run into each other, you can enter two headers or footers on the same line, but you should use the Flush Right key (Alt-F6) before entering the second one, so that the first aligns against the left margin and the second aligns against the right margin.

Each header or footer uses a minimum of two lines, at least one for the text itself and another one to separate it from the main text on the page. WordPerfect subtracts these lines from the text lines on the page, not from the top and bottom margins.

## CREATING HEADERS AND FOOTERS

Creating headers and footers is quite easy. To enter a header, start on line 1 of the page, press the Format key (Shift-F8), select Page (*2* or *P*), then select Headers (*3* or *H*) from the Format: Page menu. The following prompt appears at the bottom of the screen:

**1** Header **A**; **2** Header **B**: **0**

To create or edit your first header, you select *1* or *A*. To create or edit your second header, you select *2* or *B*. If there are no other headers in your document, press *1* to select Header A. Selecting either header brings up these options:

**1** Discontinue; **2** Every **P**age; **3** **O**dd Pages; **4** **E**ven Pages;
**5** Edit: **0**

You use these options to choose a location for the header (or footer) you just specified. Option 2 causes the header or footer to be printed on every page in the document; with option 3, they will be printed only on odd-numbered pages; with option 4, they will be printed only on even-numbered pages. You use option 1 when you want to permanently discontinue a header or footer which you had previously entered. It will be discontinued on all remaining pages (starting from the page on which the cursor is located). You use option 5 when you want to edit a header or footer after it has been entered. Note that creating a footer for the document involves the same procedure; the only difference is that you select the Footers option (*4* or *F*) on the Format: Page menu.

To experiment with these features, try the following exercise.

1. Type the following paragraph:

    **The word ambition has an interesting history. The Latin noun ambitio was used by the Romans to describe a political candidate; it meant the act of going around or going about to get votes. It came from the verb ambire, which literally means "to go about." Like their modern counterparts, Roman politicians were probably as interested in the power and wealth that came with the office as they were with the honors, but the word ambition came to describe their craving for fame and honors.**

2. Move the cursor back to the top of the page (Home Home ↑).

3. Press the Format key (Shift-F8), select Page (**2** or **P**), and then select Headers (**3** or **H**) from the Format: Page menu.

4. Select Header A by pressing **1** or **A**.

5. Select Every Page by pressing **2** or **P**. You will then see a blank screen with the following message on the status line:

    **Press EXIT when done**               **Ln 1″ Pos 1″**

6. For your header, type

    **CHAPTER FIVE
    THE HISTORY AND MEANING OF WORDS**

7. When you're done, press Exit (F7) and you will return to the Format: Page menu. Notice that after the Headers option on the screen you now see this message: *HA Every Page.* It tells you that you have a Header A, which is going to be printed on every page of the document. Press the Exit key (F7) to return to the document on your Edit screen.

## *VIEWING HEADERS*
## *IN THE REVEAL CODES SCREEN*

Like page numbers, headers and footers are invisible on the editing screen. They only appear when printed or when viewed with the View Document feature of the Print key (discussed in Chapter 9), but you can use the Reveal Codes key to verify that they have been correctly added to your document. Let's try it.

1.  Press Alt-F3 now and your screen will resemble Figure 6.11.

The code *Header A:2;* inside the brackets confirms the choices you just made: *A* for Header A and *2* for Every Page. You will also see the text of your header, and the two lines will be separated by the Hard Return code, [HRt], signifying that you pressed ⟵ after the first line.

2.  Since you can only see how your header actually looks in the printed version of your document (or in View Document), go ahead and print the page now or press Shift-F7 V to view it. It should resemble Figure 6.12. However, if the cursor was not on line 1 when you selected the Header option, it will not be seen. (The header would be visible on subsequent pages, if there were any.) Save this paragraph for a later exercise.

Note that you could have used boldface, underline, centering, or a different font when creating the header to distinguish it further from the text that follows it on the page. If you wish, you can still add any of them using the Edit option (5) on the Header menu.

To do this, press the Format key (Shift-F8), select Page (*2* or *P*), select Headers (*3* or *H*), then select 1 or A for Header A and 5 or E for Edit. You will be back in the header screen and you'll see the text of your header. Make the formatting changes you want, then press Exit (F7) when you are finished. The Reveal Codes screen will show the formatting codes for these changes.

A problem may arise when you change the margins in a document. Existing headers and/or footers will not be updated unless the code that changes margins is inserted before the header or footer code in the document. Therefore, when you want to change the margin settings for a document in which you have already created headers and/or footers, use the Reveal Codes screen to position the cursor on

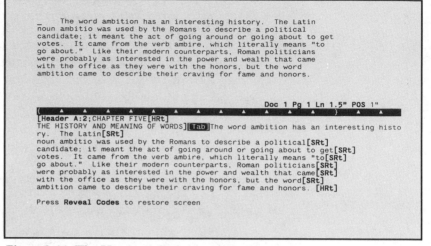

*Figure 6.11:* The Header A Definition code

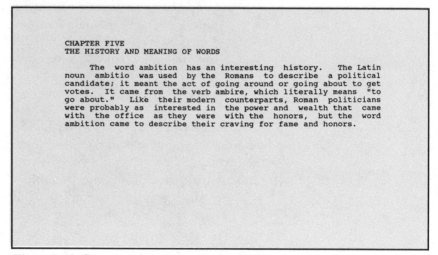

*Figure 6.12:* Sample printed paragraph with Header A

or before the first Header or Footer code before changing your margins. Remember that you can always use the View Document feature (Shift-F7 V) to make sure that the headers and/or footers are properly aligned with the body of the text, and it's a good idea to do so before printing.

## *PLACING A PAGE NUMBER IN A HEADER OR FOOTER*

If you are using headers or footers in your document and are also including page numbers, you can avoid using two lines specifically for the page numbers by placing the number within the header or footer itself. (Remember that page numbers require two lines, one for the page number and one that separates it from the rest of the text.)

To do this, use the method already described to create a standard header or footer and insert a special code for the page number:

^B

or

^N

(both work the same). This is done by pressing the Ctrl key with the *B* or *N* key, and it can be placed anywhere you choose in the header or footer. For example, to create a footer that will print the correct page number on each page of your document, you would follow these steps:

1.  Place the cursor on page 1, line 1, and press the Format key (Shift-F8), then select Page (**2** or **P**).

2.  Select Footers (**4** or **F**).

3.  Select Footer A (**1** or **A**).

4.  Select Every Page (**2** or **P**).

5.  Press the Ctrl key and type **B**, skip a few spaces, then type the text of your footer. You may wish to surround the code with hyphens, as in -^B-, so that the printed number for page 1 will look like this:

    -1-

    Note that you do *not* have to type text—the page number code can be the sole contents of the footer.

6.  Press Exit (F7) twice to return to the editing screen.

Incidentally, you can add the page number code (^B or ^N) any-where in your document; its use is not limited to footers and headers. It is no substitute, though, for standard page numbering (Shift-F8 P P) or page numbering in a header or footer, because as you add or delete text, the page number code will move with the text instead of retaining its position at the page break. You may end up with printed pages that have page numbers everywhere except where they're supposed to be!

## USING THE SUPPRESS (THIS PAGE ONLY) FEATURE

You may want headers, footers, and/or page numbers to be omitted from a specific page in your document, such as one that contains a chart or illustration. Option 9, *Suppress (this page only)* on the Format: Page menu prevents any or all of these from appearing on an individual page, but it does not omit the page from the page count, so subsequent pages will still be numbered correctly.

Press the Format key (Shift-F8), select Page (*2* or *P*), then select *Suppress (this page only)* (*9* or *U*). You will see the screen illustrated in Figure 6.13, with eight options. Most of these are self-explanatory except for option 3, which is used to print the page number at the bottom center of the current page and which overrides any other page number position code in the document. The cursor must be on line 1 of the page when you use one of these options to insert a Suppress code.

If you wish to prevent headers, footers, and/or page numbers from appearing on any of the remaining pages in your document, do not use this option. Instead, to discontinue headers or footers, select the header or footer from the Format: Page menu, then select option 1 (Discontinue). To discontinue page numbers, select the Page Number Position option (*7* or *P*) on the Format: Page menu and select No Page Numbers (*9* or *N*) from that screen.

## CONTROLLING PAGE BREAKS

As you may have noticed, you never need to specify page breaks when using WordPerfect. Like most word processors, the program has a feature known as *Soft Page,* which works at the end of each page as word wrap does at the end of each line. When you have typed enough lines to fill a page, a Soft Page code is inserted and the program automatically creates a new page while you are typing. You will see a dashed line appear across the entire screen, and your cursor will then move down to the new page as you continue typing. You can easily recognize the Soft Page code on the Reveal Codes screen:

[SPg]

This feature is not always desirable, though, because after editing changes it can break up lines and paragraphs you want kept together on the same page. For instance, the very last line of a paragraph may start a new page, or numeric expressions such as formulas may be split between two pages.

To force a page break at a particular line, you can always resort to entering a hard page break. To do this, you press Ctrl-⏎ and WordPerfect inserts the code

[HPg]

in the Reveal Codes screen and a line of equal signs on the Edit screen. However, sometimes using the hard page break can cause

```
Format: Suppress (this page only)

     1 - Suppress All Page Numbering, Headers and Footers

     2 - Suppress Headers and Footers

     3 - Print Page Number at Bottom Center    No

     4 - Suppress Page Numbering               No

     5 - Suppress Header A                      No

     6 - Suppress Header B                      No

     7 - Suppress Footer A                      No

     8 - Suppress Footer B                      No




Selection: 0
```

**Figure 6.13:** The *Format: Suppress (this page only)* screen

problems as you edit your document. For instance, say the cursor is on page 1, line 5″, and you press Ctrl-⏎ to create a hard page break there. Later, you move the cursor to line 4″ of page 1 and type another paragraph of 10 lines. You move the cursor to page 2 and discover that it ends on line 3″! Here's why: As you type the new paragraph on line 4″, it is inserted at the cursor position and pushes all other text down to make room. Eventually the page becomes full, and WordPerfect creates a soft page break. Meanwhile, the hard page break remains where you originally inserted it, on what used to be line 5″, but that line has now been moved down to line 3″ of page 2, so that's where the second page ends.

Fortunately, WordPerfect provides three superior methods for keeping text together so that it is not split by page breaks: Conditional End of Page, Block Protection, and Widow/Orphan Protection.

## CONDITIONAL END OF PAGE

The Conditional End of Page option, located on the Format: Other menu on the Format key (Shift-F8), does just what its name implies: it forces a page break when a certain condition is met. You define the condition as a certain number of lines you want kept together on the same page. If these lines are moved near the end of a page as you edit, rather than divide the protected group of lines between two pages, WordPerfect will push the entire block down to the next page.

To use this feature, move the cursor to the line before the first line of the block you wish to keep together. Press the Format key (Shift-F8), select Other (*4* or *O*), then select Conditional End of Page (*2* or *C*). In response to this prompt:

**Number of Lines to Keep Together:**

type the total number of lines in the block you want to keep together. Blank lines (that is, those in multiple spacing) are considered to be the same as text lines and must be counted in your calculation of the number of lines that are to be kept together. Thus, if you are using double spacing and want to keep four lines of text together, press *8* in response to the prompt.

## *USING BLOCK PROTECTION TO KEEP TEXT TOGETHER*

Fortunately, there is an easier way to protect a group of lines from being separated other than struggling to calculate the exact number of lines you want to keep together: block protection. To do this, you use the Block and Format keys. You've studied this feature in Chapter 5, so this will be a brief review.

Like many other keys you've studied, the Format key (Shift-F8) operates differently when you're in Block mode, serving to protect the highlighted block from being split between two pages. Here are the steps you take to protect a block.

1. Move the cursor to the first character in the block of text you want to protect.

2. Press the Block key (Alt-F4).

3. Use the cursor movement keys to highlight all the text you want kept together on a page. Do *not* include a hard return code at the end of a paragraph. If you are protecting a paragraph, be sure to start with the first word and end with the last word.

4. Press the Format key (Shift-F8). You should see the following message:

   **Protect block? (Y/N) No**

5. Type **Y**.

The block highlighting will immediately disappear. If you look in the Reveal Codes screen, you'll see a pair of Block Protection codes, [Block Pro:On] at the beginning of the section you protected and [Block Pro:Off] at the end. If this block is moved near the bottom of the page as you insert text above it, the entire blocked section will move as one unit to the next page.

As you can imagine, this tool can be very valuable, particularly if your documents are quite long and contain charts, tables, headings, and similar groupings that must be kept together on the same page.

## *PREVENTING WIDOWS AND ORPHANS IN TEXT*

*Widows* and *orphans* are the most demonstrative terms used in word processing, so their meanings are not as cryptic as you might think. A widow is the first line of a paragraph that is left alone (widowed) at the bottom of a page when the Soft Page feature pushes the rest of the paragraph to the next page. Orphans are also created by the Soft Page feature. When the last line of a paragraph is pushed to a new page, that line becomes an orphan, stranded alone at the top of the page without the rest of its paragraph. (I am following WordPerfect's terminology here, though it departs somewhat from the standard definitions.)

The Widow/Orphan feature is a toggle key, meaning it is either on or off. To use it, you select Widow/Orphan Protection (*9* or *W*) from the Format: Line menu (Shift-F8 1 or L) and change the *No* to *Yes* by typing *Y*.

The default setting is off (that is, no widow/orphan protection) so you'll always see the *No* unless it has been changed earlier in the document. If you enter a *Y*, WordPerfect will protect widows and orphans from that point forward in your document, so you should start at the top of the document if you want to protect all of it. If you use the Reveal Codes key (Alt-F3) after changing it to Yes, you will see that WordPerfect has inserted the code

[W/O On]

to indicate where widow/orphan protection begins.

Protection means that widow lines will always be moved to the next page, and orphan lines will never appear alone at the top of a page because the line that comes before them in the paragraph will also be moved to the new page. You can turn this feature on and off whenever you wish, but if you want widow/orphan protection for the entire document, you should move the cursor to the beginning before turning it on.

Using widow/orphan protection will decrease the number of lines on any page that is affected by the feature, so don't worry if you have several pages with fewer than the normal number of text lines. These pages will be reformatted if you add or delete text, and the protected lines will readjust in the normal manner.

# CHANGING
# INITIAL FORMAT SETTINGS

In this chapter we have examined many of WordPerfect's formatting settings that affect the layout of the printed page, and as you saw, all of them have defaults that will be in effect unless you change them. If any of the defaults are unsuitable for the kind of work you do most often and you want to change them permanently, you can do so using the Setup key (Shift-F1).

To change the defaults, press Shift-F1 and select Initial Settings (*5* or *I*). You then see the menu shown in Figure 6.14. You can use this menu to change many default settings, such as the Date Format, which controls the way the date appears when you insert it with the Date/Outline key (Shift-F5); *Repeat Value*, which you see when you press the Escape key; several Beep options, which you can use to turn off the beep you hear when you make a mistake, when WordPerfect is trying to hyphenate a word, or when a search fails; and the initial codes.

When you want to permanently change format settings such as initial margins, you select Initial Codes (*4* or *I*) from this menu. When you do, you see a blank screen that is automatically split in half by the Tab Ruler, with the Edit screen on top and the Reveal Codes screen below it (incidentally, you can't make the Reveal Codes screen disappear with Alt-F3 when setting new initial settings). Once you are in this screen, you can make changes to the default format settings by pressing the appropriate keys and selecting the menu options as you would in a document. As you make changes, WordPerfect inserts codes just as it does when you make changes in the document, only you see them here.

To see how this procedure works, look at Figure 6.15, which shows three changes to WordPerfect's default format settings. You can see the format codes WordPerfect inserted when the changes were made.

The first code, [Just Off], turns off Justification so that all printed documents will have a ragged right margin by default. This code was entered by pressing the Format key (Shift-F8), selecting the Line option, then selecting the Justification option and typing *N* for No. The second code, [LnSpacing: 2], changes the line spacing, making double spacing the default. This was accomplished by pressing the Format key (Shift-F8), selecting the Line option, then selecting the Line Spacing option and typing *2* to set double spacing. The third code, [Pg Numbering: Bottom Center], turns on page numbering,

You cannot use the Initial Codes option on the Setup key to change the default font. Instead, you have to use either the Initial Font option on the Print key's *Select Printer: Edit* menu (Shift-F7 S E I), or the Initial Font option on the Format: Document menu of the Format key (Shift-F8 D F). The Print key method affects all *new* documents that you create, but the Format key method affects only the document you are working on when you use it.

```
Setup: Initial Settings

    1 - Beep Options

    2 - Date Format                    3 1, 4

    3 - Document Summary

    4 - Initial Codes

    5 - Repeat Value                   8

    6 - Table of Authorities




Selection: 0
```

***Figure 6.14:*** The Setup: Initial Settings menu

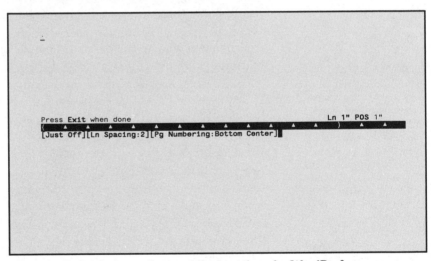

***Figure 6.15:*** Setting new format default settings for WordPerfect

so that page numbers that are centered at the bottom of each page will always appear in your printed documents by default. It was entered by pressing the Format key (Shift-F8), selecting the Page option, then selecting Page Numbering and typing *6* (to create page numbers that are centered at the bottom of each page).

If you make a mistake during this process, you can move the cursor onto the incorrect code in the Reveal Codes screen and delete it by pressing Delete (as you do in any document). When you are finished making all of your changes, press the Exit key (F7) twice to return to the Edit screen (you can't press the Cancel key to leave this screen—only the Exit key will work). There will be a slight delay as the program writes these new default settings to the disk. Thereafter, whenever you create a new document, the initial settings you selected will be in effect (although, like other defaults, you do not see them in the Reveal Codes screen).

The fact that you have set new default format settings doesn't mean that you can't override them ( just as you do currently when you use the various format commands). For example, even if you make double spacing the default, you still can use single spacing (or triple, or any other) by selecting the Line Spacing option on the Format: Line menu and typing *1* (or any other desired line spacing value).

WordPerfect also allows you to change the default format settings just for the document you are currently working on. The procedure is similar to the one described above to make changes using the Initial Codes option, except that you use the Initial Codes option on the Format: Document menu instead of the Initial Codes option on the Setup: Initial Settings menu. To do this, press the Format key (Shift-F8), select Document (*3* or *D*), then select Initial Codes (*2* or *C*) and use the appropriate keys to enter the codes you want to use. These settings override initial settings you may have entered using the Setup key, but they do not place a code in the Reveal Codes screen.

## *SUMMARY*

Congratulations again! You just experienced a thorough study of many of WordPerfect's page formatting features, and have  progressed beyond the rank of novice. In fact, some of these features are quite complex and tricky to use, so unless you have unusual needs, you may never have to alter the settings established by the program. The standard form and top and bottom margins, for instance, were designed to conform to standard business usage, so they are acceptable for many applications.

Other settings, such as page numbering, are used frequently but not in one standard manner, so WordPerfect assumes nothing and provides several different methods for you to choose from.

All of the features covered in this chapter share a common characteristic: they affect the layout of the printed page. Consequently, it is important that you understand them and learn how to use them properly so that your work appears as attractive and cohesive as possible.

7.

# SEARCH AND REPLACE: AN INDISPENSABLE TOOL

**To search for characters or hidden function codes,**     192
use the Forward Search (F2) or Reverse Search (Shift-F2) key.
To search forward through the document, press the Forward
Search key (F2). To search backward, press the Reverse Search
key (Shift-F2), or press the Forward Search key (F2) followed
by ↑ to reverse the direction of the arrow in the *Srch:* prompt.
Whichever direction you choose, the next step is to type the text
you're trying to find, which is called the *search string*. If you want
WordPerfect to ignore case when searching, type the search
string in lowercase letters. When you finish typing it, press
either F2 or Esc to begin the search. If WordPerfect finds the
search string in your document, it will stop on the first character or space that follows it. To search forward for another occurrence, press F2 F2; press Shift-F2 F2 or F2 ↑ F2 to search
backward. To search for text which you're unsure of the wording, use the wild-card character (Ctrl-X), which can substitute
for any single character except the first one in the search string.
Enter it as part of your search string by pressing Ctrl-V then
Ctrl-X.

**To locate a search string and either replace it or erase it,**     198
use the Replace key (Alt-F2). At the *w/Confirm? (Y/N) No* prompt,
type *N* to have WordPerfect make all the replacements automatically, or type *Y* if you want the program to stop at each occurrence
and wait for your permission to change it. Whichever method you
choose, the *Srch:* prompt will appear, and in response you type the
text you are searching for (the search string) then press F2 or Esc.
In response to the *Replace with:* prompt, type the text you want to
change it to, or, if you want to erase the search string, leave it

blank. Press F2 or Esc to begin the procedure. If you selected *N* in response to the *w/Confirm* prompt, all the changes will be made automatically and the cursor will stop after the last one. If you selected *Y*, the cursor will stop at the first occurrence of the search string, and you'll see the *Confirm? (Y/N) No* prompt. Choose *N* or *Y*, and WordPerfect will continue searching and asking for your confirmation until it has found all occurrences, stopping after the last one.

**To find and delete codes,**                                                          202

use the Replace key (Alt-F2). Select *Y* or *N* for Confirm. In response to the Search prompt, press the function key or combination that is normally used to enter the code into your text, such as Shift-F8 L M for a Margin Setting code or F6 for a Bold code. The bracketed code will appear next to the Search prompt. Press F2 or Esc. In response to the *Replace with:* prompt, press F2 or Esc to leave it blank and begin the procedure.

**To search and replace within a limited section of your document,**     207

place the cusor at the beginning of it and turn on Block mode by pressing Alt-F4. Use the cursor movement keys to highlight all the text you want to include. Press the Replace key (Alt-F2), then proceed, as usual, to choose *Y* or *N* for Confirm, type the search string, press F2, type the replacement string, and press F2.

THIS CHAPTER WILL INTRODUCE WORDPERFECT'S Search feature as well as Search and Replace, two closely related operations that are among WordPerfect's most useful features. Search enables you to locate any word, any combination of words up to 59 characters, or any hidden function code(s) wherever they appear in your document. Search and Replace can find the text or code and either erase it or replace it with something else. Since the Search feature automatically moves the cursor to the located text, it is often the fastest method for cursor movement, particularly in larger documents. WordPerfect can search through your document either forward or backward, ignore uppercase and lowercase when performing the operation (if the search is conducted using lowercase), and use a wild-card character to substitute for any other character, so that you can search for similar but not identical text (for example, when you're unsure of the exact spelling that was used).

Type in the following paragraphs so you can experiment with these commands:

Unlike other word processors, with WordPerfect it is difficult, if not impossible, to lose files when you run out of disk space. If you try to save a file and receive a message indicating there is not enough room on the default disk, don't worry. By pressing the List Files key (F6), you can search the directory for files you don't need anymore and delete them to make more space available. However, it is usually easier and always safer to insert another formatted disk that has some room left on it into the drive and then save the file.

The List Files key (F6) has many other functions. It can be used to retrieve, delete, rename, print, or copy a file, or perform operations like print and delete on any number of files that you have marked. If you forget the name of a file you wish to retrieve, you can use the List Files key (F6) to perform a word search, and the program will then find and list all files containing a certain word or combination of words. You can also use the List Files key (F6) to import a DOS text file into WordPerfect, to change the default directory, or to look at a file without retrieving it for editing.

# SEARCHING FOR TEXT

These paragraphs contain a significant error: the List Files key is incorrectly identified as F6, whereas it is actually F5. Let's locate and fix the problem with WordPerfect's Search feature.

Make sure that the cursor is located before the first word of the first paragraph before you begin.

1. Press F2, the Forward Search key. You should see the following prompt:

→ Srch:

The cursor will appear to the right of this prompt, indicating that you can now type the word or words that you want to find. The word or combination that you enter is called the *search string;* in this case it will be *F6.* Note that you do not have to capitalize the F, because whenever you enter lowercase letters, the program searches for both lowercase and uppercase matches. However, the reverse is not true; uppercase letters in a search string will only locate uppercase letters. If you're searching for a word that is not capitalized, you must type only lowercase characters in the search string.

2. Now type

F6

Note that you can type it in either uppercase or lowercase. (Incidentally, you should type **F6**, not press the F6 key!)

At this point, do not press ←. If you do, you'll actually enter the code for a hard return, [HRt], which will appear next to the *F6* on your prompt line and become part of what WordPerfect searches for (the search string). In case you did this by mistake, press the Backspace key to erase the code.

The next step is to press either F2 or Esc to signal WordPerfect that you want it to begin searching.

3. Press F2. The cursor should now be in the position just after the first *F6* in your text, which is a close parenthesis character. Let's change the *6* to a *5*.

4. Press Backspace once to erase the *6*.

5. Type *5* to replace it.

## REPEATING THE SEARCH

As you can see, *F6* appears three more times in the second paragraph. Let's find the other occurrences.

1. To repeat the search action, press the Forward Search key (F2).

You should see that the last search string you entered, *F6*, will already be in place next to the prompt. The program always remembers the last string you searched for and assumes you want to continue using it unless you type something else. If you type any other character at this point, the old string will be replaced immediately by the new character(s). However, since you want to continue searching for *F6,* you can accept it by pressing either F2 or Esc. Note that you could use the regular cursor movement and editing keys if you wanted to change the search string. For example, you could use → and ← to move the cursor, and Delete or Backspace to erase.

2. Press either Esc or F2 to proceed with the search. The cursor will move to the next appearance of F6. This time, you won't delete it. Instead, you'll keep pressing Forward Search (F2) until you reach the last F6.

3. Press F2 F2. The cursor should be on the next *F6,* before the words *to perform.*

4. Press F2 F2 again. Now the cursor should be on the last *F6,* before the words *to import.*

5. Press Forward Search (F2) twice and the following message should appear briefly:

**\* Not found \***

and the cursor will reappear at the last occurrence of the string.

The **\*** *Not found* **\*** prompt indicates that there are no more occurrences of the search string in the document; you can confirm this by looking at the paragraph.

Whenever you see the Search prompt, you can change the direction of your search by pressing the ↑ or ↓ key. Let's try it.

1. Press the Forward Search key, F2. Since the cursor is near the bottom, WordPerfect won't find any more occurrences of your search string.

2. Press ↑. You should see the direction of the arrow change.

3. Press ↓ then ↑ again to switch back to a forward search.

4. Press Cancel (F1) to cancel the search operation.

You can use the arrow keys to change the direction of the search regardless of whether you're using Forward Search or Reverse Search.

Search is particularly helpful for cursor movement in longer documents. Although you may move the cursor page-by-page and screen-by-screen with the Page Up, Page Down, Screen Up, and Screen Down keys, these are relatively slow methods. You can also move the cursor to a specified page using the Go To key (Ctrl-Home), but this method is only useful if you know which page contains the text you wish to move to. On the other hand, with the Search key you can almost immediately find a section that has a particular subheading or contains a unique word or phrase. Also, Search takes you directly to the word you want to work with, not just to the general area.

The Search feature can also check for overused words. If you suspect that you are using a word too frequently, just use Search to find out. If your suspicions are confirmed, you can then use WordPerfect's Thesaurus, which you will learn about in another chapter, to find substitutes.

If you want to change the direction of the search by pressing ↑ or ↓, and there is already a search string present from your last search operation, then type the search string before pressing the arrow key.

I used Search to locate specific words and sections in this book that I had marked for revision. Positioning the cursor using the Search key saved me a lot of time as well as the eyestrain caused by searching the text visually as it scrolls by.

## *REVERSING THE SEARCH*

You have already learned that you can change the search direction by pressing ↑ or ↓. Another method of searching backward is by using the Reverse Search key, Shift-F2.

1. Press Home Home ↓ to move the cursor to the end of the file.

2. Press the Reverse Search key (Shift-F2).

This time the Search prompt will appear with an arrow pointing backward, as follows:

← Srch: F6

If you performed the exercise in the preceding section, the prompt will still have the *F6* search string next to it, since that was the last one you used. If not, type *F6*.

3. Press F2, Shift-F2, or Esc to proceed with the search, and watch as the cursor moves up to the last *F6* in the document.

4. Repeat the operation by pressing the Reverse Search key, Shift-F2, followed by F2 or Esc.

## *RESTRICTING THE SEARCH*

Searching for a string such as *F6* is uncomplicated because it's unlikely that it will ever be contained within another word. However, many commonly used words such as *to* are frequently found within other words such as in*to* and s*to*p. Let's see how WordPerfect handles these situations by searching for *the*.

1. Move the cursor to the beginning of the document (press Home Home ↑ or Page Up).

2. Press Forward Search (F2).

3. Type (in lowercase)

   **the**

   and press F2.

The cursor will stop at the *r* in the word *other,* which follows the first occurrence of the string *the.* Press F2 twice more and the cursor will stop at the *r* in the word *there,* which also contains *the.* As you can see, you have yet to find the word you were looking for! If you press F2 two more times, you will finally come to the word *the.* If you continue searching, you'll also stop on these words: *them, another,* and *then.*

To prevent this confusion, you can place a space before and after the search string, signaling that this is a separate word, not connected to or included within any other, but this is not a perfect solution to the problem. To try it:

4. Move the cursor back to the beginning of the file and press Forward Search (F2) again.

5. Press the Space bar, type

   **the**

   then press the Space bar again. Now your search string includes a blank space before and after the word *the.*

6. Press F2 again to begin the search.

The cursor should stop at the *d* in *default,* which follows the word *the.* (It stops at the *d* because you included a blank space in the search string, and Search always moves the cursor to the first position after the search string). If you continue searching by pressing F2 F2, you'll see that this method only locates the whole word, *the.*

When using a blank space in a search string, there is one problem that can arise: if there is a punctuation mark such as a period or comma immediately following the word or phrase, it won't be found if you surround the search string with blank spaces as described above. For example, if you were to search your document for the word *file,* you'd find it 14 times, and the cursor would stop on *file, files,* and *file.* (that is, *file* with a period at the end). If you were to press the Space bar to include a single space before and after the search string, you'd only find five occurrences of *file,* and you wouldn't find the one at the end of the first paragraph, with a period after it. To search for the word *file* where it appears at the end of a sentence, the search string would have to include the period that follows the word, as follows:

**[blank space]file.**

but this would skip all the other occurrences of the word *file*.

## SEARCHING WITH CTRL-X, THE WILD-CARD CHARACTER

The wild-card char-
acter can substitute
for any character on the
keyboard when you're
using Search or Search
and Replace, but it can-
not be the first one in
the string.

Ctrl-X functions as a *wild card* that can be used as a substitute for any character on the keyboard (except a blank space). You enter it by pressing Ctrl and holding it down while pressing *V*, then *X*. If you're unsure of the exact wording that was used in a phrase, the Ctrl-X combination can often help locate it. The only limitations are that a wild-card character cannot be the first one in the string, and that it cannot be used to locate a function code.

Your document identifies the List Files key as F5 one time and as F6 three others, so the only way you can locate all occurrences with a single search string is to use the wild card in place of the *5* or *6*. Let's try it.

1. Move the cursor to the top of the file by pressing Page Up.

2. Press the Forward Search key, F2.

3. In response to the Search prompt, type **F** then press Ctrl-V. You should see this prompt:

   Key =

   which is your signal to press Ctrl-X.

4. Press Ctrl-X.

5. Type

   )

   Your prompt should now appear as follows:

   → Srch:F ^ X)

6. Press F2 to begin the search. The cursor should stop at *F5,* the first occurrence of either *F5* or *F6* in the document.

7. Press F2 two more times, and the cursor moves to the first occurrence of *F6.*

If you continue to press F2, the program will find the other two *F6*'s in the paragraph.

Let's try another example. This time you'll use the wild card to locate a misspelled word. First, though, you'll have to change a word so that it's spelled incorrectly, then we'll search for the correct spelling to prove that the misspelled one will be skipped.

1. Use one of the Search keys (F2 for a forward search or Shift-F2 for a reverse one) to locate the word *retrieve* in the second sentence of the second paragraph, then change the spelling to *retreive.*

2. Press Page Up to move the cursor back to the top of the page.

3. Press Forward Search (F2).

4. In response to the Search prompt, enter the following string:

   **retrieve**

5. Press F2 again; notice how WordPerfect skips the misspelled version.

As you see, this procedure does not find the misspelled version of the word. To locate it, we'll use the wild card.

6. Move the cursor back to the top of the page.

7. Press F2 and enter the following string:

   **retr ^ X**

   (type *retr*, press Ctrl-V, then press Ctrl-X).

8. Press F2 again to begin the search.

This time, the cursor finds the misspelled version of the word *(retreive)*. If you continue to search by pressing F2 F2, it will also find *retrieve* in the third sentence of the paragraph and *retrieving* in the last sentence. Note that the same search string would also locate any other words in the document that began in *retr*, such as *retry* and *retribution*. The wild card also can be used with the Search and Replace feature, which you'll study next.

## SEARCHING AND REPLACING

Let's use Search and Replace to change the remaining *F6*'s to *F5*'s. As you'll soon see, this method is much more efficient than searching for each *F6,* then deleting and correcting each one individually.

There are two different ways to use Search and Replace. WordPerfect can pause each time it locates the search string and ask you to confirm that you want it replaced, or it can zip through the document and make all of the changes automatically with no further confirmation from you. The latter method should only be used when you are absolutely certain that you want the string replaced every time it occurs. In the exercise following this one, you'll see how risky this procedure can be. Let's try Search and Replace with confirmation.

1. Move the cursor back to the beginning of the first paragraph.
2. Press the Replace key (Alt-F2). You should see the following prompt:

   **w/Confirm? (Y/N) No**

If you respond with *Y,* each time *F6* is located WordPerfect will stop to ask if you wish to replace it. If you press *N* (or any other key, since WordPerfect assumes *No*), all of the changes will be made without your confirmation. In fact, you probably won't see them as they occur because Search and Replace works so fast. To be on the safe side, let's use the Confirm feature this time.

3. Press **Y**. The next message you will see is the familiar Search prompt.
4. Type (in either uppercase or lowercase)

   **F6**

   as the search string and press F2. You will then see this prompt:

   **Replace with:**

5. Since you want to change each occurrence of *F6* to *F5,* type (using uppercase)

   **F5**

   then press F2 (or Esc) to start Search and Replace.

For an instant, you'll see this message:

**\* Please Wait \***

and the cursor will move quickly to the first *F6*. Next, you'll see the following prompt:

Confirm? (Y/N) No

If you press any key other than *Y*, the replacement will not be made and the cursor will move to the next occurrence of the *F6* string. However, we are going to make the change each time, so you'll press *Y*.

6. Press **Y** and continue to do this each time you are asked.

When the Replace operation is completed, the cursor will be located on the *5* in the last *F5*. You can quickly move the cursor back to the position it was in before you used Search and Replace by pressing the Go To key (Ctrl-Home) twice. To try it, press Ctrl-Home Ctrl-Home.

Note that if you had typed a lowercase *f6* instead of the capitalized *F6* for your search string, the program still would have found them all. Also, if you had typed the text of the replacement string in lower-case (*f5* instead of *F5*), the *F6*'s would have been replaced with upper-case *F5*'s to match the case of the characters being replaced in the document.

Now let's see what happens when we repeat the operation without using the Confirm option. Be sure that the cursor is on the first word in the first paragraph before continuing.

1. Press Replace (Alt-F2).

2. Press **N** when asked "w/Confirm?"

3. For the search string, type **F5** then press F2.

4. For the replacement string, type **F6** (use uppercase) and press F2.

Happily, this was a straightforward procedure and the program replaced only the words you specified. Using Search and Replace without confirm can sometimes be dangerous, though, because it will often replace words you had not intended to change. The next example will illustrate this problem.

In this exercise, you are going to reword a phrase that appears in the third sentence of the first paragraph. The phrase *search the directory for files* will be replaced by *search the directory to find files,* so you are going to replace *for* with *to find*. To do this, follow these steps:

1. Move the cursor to the beginning of the first paragraph.
2. Press Alt-F2 (Replace).
3. Press **N** when asked "w/Confirm?"
4. Type the following search string:

   **for**

   and press F2.
5. Type this replacement string:

   **to find**
6. Press F2.

After the operation is completed, your file will resemble Figure 7.1.

As you can see, you've really made a mess! The cursor is on the last replacement, and it says *to find editing* instead of *for editing*. Other bloopers include the word *formatted* (in the second to last sentence of the first paragraph), which has been changed to *to findmatted,* the word *perform,* which has been changed to *perto findm* (in two separate places), and the word *forget,* which has been changed to *to findget.* Fortunately,

```
Unlike other word processors, with WordPerfect it is difficult,
if not impossible, to lose files when you run out of disk space.
If you try to save a file and receive a message indicating there
is not enough room on the default disk, don't worry. By pressing
the List Files key (F6), you can search the directory to find
files you don't need anymore and delete them to make more space
available. However, it is usually easier and always safer to
insert another to findmatted disk that has some room left on it
into the drive and then save the file.

The List Files key (F6) has many other functions. It can be used
to retrieve, delete, rename, print, or copy a file or perto findm
operations like print and delete on any number of files that you
have marked. If you to findget the name of a file you wish to
retrieve you can use the List Files key (F6) to perto findm a
word search, and the program will then find and list all files
containing a certain word or combination of words. You can also
use the List Files key (F6) to import a DOS text file into
WordPerfect, to change the default directory, or to look at a
file without retrieving it to find editing.
```

*Figure 7.1:* The paragraphs after replacing the word *for* with *to find*

the original paragraphs did not contain the words *to find,* so you could fix the mess by using the Replace key to reverse the operation and replace each *to find* with *for.* Reversing the damage will not always be this easy, though, so you can see why Search and Replace should be used with great care, preferably with the Confirm option set to *yes.* Although using Confirm is slower, you can clearly see that it has the potential to save you an enormous amount of clean-up work.

Search and Replace has many other interesting applications. For instance, it can be used when a proper name needs to be retyped throughout a lengthy document, as in a report that frequently mentions a client whose name has been changed or misspelled. If you find yourself frequently typing a long phrase in a document, you can save some time and aggravation by using Search and Replace to let the computer do the typing. Simply enter a few unique characters such as *X1* to represent the phrase and, when you are finished typing the document, use the Replace key to change *X1* to the correct phrase.

## FINDING AND DELETING CODES

WordPerfect's Macro feature, which you'll study in another chapter, can also be used to perform this task, and it has some additional benefits.

One of the most useful applications of Search and Replace is to locate and erase hidden codes that are disrupting your document's appearance. It's easy to accidentally insert extra codes such as underline, bold, and indent, since the same function keys that you use to implement them are used frequently for other operations too.

Extra codes can be left behind when you delete or move the text associated with them, and you may need to locate and erase these codes also. You normally initiate block operations by placing the cursor on the first character in the block you wish to highlight, but this procedure sometimes fails to include the invisible formatting codes that are located immediately before the first character. This is especially true when the effects of the code can't be seen on the Edit screen, such as page numbering. It helps to check the Reveal Codes screen before any block or move operations, but even then you'll probably only remember to look for codes such as bold and underline, whose effects on the text being deleted are quite obvious. If you leave an extra code behind and later suspect that something is wrong, the Search feature can be invaluable.

To try it out you'll need some codes to search for, so let's use the Format key to insert three different margin settings in your document, one at the beginning, one after the first paragraph, and one in the middle of the second paragraph.

1.  Place the cursor at the beginning of the first paragraph.

2.  Press the Format key, Shift-F8, and select **L** to get to the Format: Line menu.

3.  Select **M** for margins and change both the left and right margins to .5″ each, then press Exit (F7) to get back to the Edit screen.

4.  Move the cursor to the beginning of the second paragraph and repeat steps 2 and 3, but this time change the margins to 1.5″ each.

5.  Move the cursor to the beginning of the third sentence in the second paragraph and press ◄─┘ twice to make a third paragraph.

6.  Repeat steps 2 and 3 to change the margins to 1″ each.

Your document will be reformatted to fit into these margins. It may look ridiculous, but that doesn't matter since you're going to be deleting the margin settings right away using Search and Replace. Now you're ready to use the Search key to find them.

7.  Move the cursor to the beginning of the file. Press the Search key (F2). You should see the Search prompt (→ *Srch:*).

8.  To insert the margin code as your search string, press the Format key (Shift-F8). You'll see this prompt:

    1 Line; 2 Page; 3 Other: 0

9.  Select Line by pressing either **1** or **L**. Another prompt line appears, as shown in Figure 7.2.

10. Notice that option 6 is margins. Press **6** or **M** and you'll see a bracketed code for margin settings appear in the search string

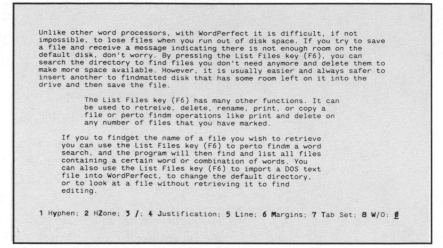

```
Unlike other word processors, with WordPerfect it is difficult, if not
impossible, to lose files when you run out of disk space. If you try to save
a file and receive a message indicating there is not enough room on the
default disk, don't worry. By pressing the List Files key (F6), you can
search the directory to find files you don't need anymore and delete them to
make more space available. However, it is usually easier and always safer to
insert another to findmatted disk that has some room left on it into the
drive and then save the file.

        The List Files key (F6) has many other functions. It can
        be used to retreive, delete, rename, print, or copy a
        file or perto findm operations like print and delete on
        any number of files that you have marked.

        If you to findget the name of a file you wish to retrieve
        you can use the List Files key (F6) to perto findm a word
        search, and the program will then find and list all files
        containing a certain word or combination of words. You
        can also use the List Files key (F6) to import a DOS text
        file into WordPerfect, to change the default directory,
        or to look at a file without retrieving it to find
        editing.

1 Hyphen; 2 HZone; 3 /; 4 Justification; 5 Line; 6 Margins; 7 Tab Set; 8 W/O: 0
```

*Figure 7.2:* The Format: Line prompt line after pressing Search

next to the prompt, as illustrated below:

→ Srch: [L/R Mar]

The Search prompt is now set to find all margin settings regardless of the different position numbers they may contain, such as 1 inch, 2 inches, or 1.5 inches. WordPerfect's Search feature works like this for all codes that contain a varying number. As another example, if you had pressed 5 for Line, then 3 for Line Spacing, it would have searched for all line spacing codes, regardless of whether they were for single spacing, double spacing, 1.5 spacing, etc.

11. Press F2 to begin searching. The cursor should move to the first margin setting. To verify this, you can look in Reveal Codes.

12. Press the Reveal Codes key (Alt-F3).

You should see the code with the margin setting you entered (it will appear to the left of the cursor). As you know, when the cursor is to the right of a code or character, you can delete it by pressing Backspace (but don't erase it yet). You could continue searching for and deleting the codes this way, but it's much easier to use Search and Replace, so we'll try that method next.

13. Exit the Reveal Codes screen by pressing the Reveal Codes key, Alt-F3.

14. Move the cursor to the top of the page again and press Replace (Alt-F2).

15. Press **N** in response to the *w/Confirm? (Y/N)* prompt.

16. Press F2 to accept your search string, the Margin Setting code (it will appear if you completed the previous exercise correctly, but if not press Shift-F8 L M, then press F2).

The next prompt will ask for the string you want to replace it with. If you leave this blank by pressing F2 again, all the margin codes will be erased, since they will be replaced, literally, by nothing.

17. Press F2 to leave the replacement string blank and start the search and replace action.

You will see the immediate effects of this procedure because the document will be reformatted to fit into WordPerfect's default margin settings, 1 inch each. If you can't tell by looking at the text, move the cursor back to the top.

Search and Replace can be used to replace certain formatting codes and to add features such as bold and underline to specific text in your document. For instance, you could use it to locate and underline all occurrences of the phrase *List Files key* in your paragraphs. Let's try it.

1. Move the cursor to the beginning of the first paragraph.

2. Press the Replace key, Alt-F2.

3. Type **N** in response to the *Confirm? (Y/N)* prompt.

4. For the search string, type the following exactly as shown (except that *L* and *F* can be either uppercase or lowercase):

   **List Files key**

   then press F2.

5. For the replacement string, press the Underline key, F8, then type the following exactly as shown:

   **List Files key**

Press F8 again to insert the second code that will turn off underlining. Your replacement string will look like this:

[UND]List Files key[und]

6. Press F2 to begin the replacement procedure.

If you followed the instructions carefully, all occurrences of the phrase *List Files key* should now be underlined. You could repeat the steps and try it again if you wanted to boldface the phrase, using the Bold key (F6) instead of the Underline key.

As mentioned earlier, one limitation to using Search and Replace with codes is that codes for features such as tab settings and line spacing can be located and erased, but you cannot change their specific settings. To understand why, look at the prompt that appears after you press the Search key (F2) followed by the Line option on the Format key (Shift-F8, L). As you can see, Tab Set is option 7 and Line (spacing) is option 5 followed by 3; there is no way to signify that you want to search for double spacing or triple spacing, or for a particular tab setting.

## *HOW TO DO AN EXTENDED SEARCH*

You'll learn about headers and footers in Chap. 6; Chap. 11 discusses footnotes and endnotes.

You can extend Search or Search and Replace so that headers, footers, footnotes, and endnotes are also checked for the word or phrase in the search string. You'll study these features in upcoming chapters, so don't worry if the terms are unfamiliar to you. What is significant about all of them, for purposes of this chapter, is that the text in them can't be seen on the Edit screen, and they only appear when printed (or in the Print key preview feature, View Document). Since they aren't part of the regular text, you have to use Extended Search to find search strings inside them. To do an extended search, you press the Home key before you press one of the three Search keys (Forward Search, Reverse Search, or Search/Replace). When you do, this prompt appears:

Extended srch:

If you're using the Replace key (Alt-F2), the prompt doesn't appear until after you choose *N* or *Y* in response to the *Confirm? (Y/N)* prompt.

You then type the search string and proceed as usual. If you are using Forward Search (F2) or Reverse Search (Shift-F2), when the word is found inside a header, footer, footnote, or endnote the cursor stops inside the appropriate Header, Footer, Footnote, or Endnote screen and you can then edit it. When you're ready to continue, you press Home F2 F2 for a forward search or Home Shift-F2 F2 for a reverse search. If you're using Search and Replace with confirm (Alt-F2 Y), the cursor stops in the appropriate screen, waits for you to enter *Y* or *N,* then moves to the next occurrence of the search string, which can be either in one of the special screens (that you'll learn about) or in the regular text. If you're using Search and Replace without confirm (Alt-F2 N), WordPerfect automatically changes the text in the Header/Footer and Footnote/Endnote screens, but you won't see the cursor stop inside these screens.

## *SEARCHING AND REPLACING IN A BLOCK*

In Chapter 5 you studied WordPerfect's Block key (Alt-F4) and learned that it could be used with many other keys, including any of the Search keys (Forward Search, Reverse Search, or Search/Replace). To use it, you simply highlight the block, press one of the Search keys, then proceed as usual to enter a search string and begin the search. Let's try it by blocking the first paragraph, then replacing the word *disk* with *diskette.*

1. Place the cursor at the beginning of the first paragraph.

2. Press the Block key, Alt-F4. You should see the *Block on* message in the lower left corner of the screen.

3. Press ⏎ to highlight the entire paragraph.

4. Press the Replace key (Alt-F2) then **N** at the *Confirm? (Y/N)* prompt.

5. For the search string, type

   **disk**

   then press F2.

6. For the replacement string, type

   **diskette**

   then press F2 to begin the procedure.

As you'll see, all three occurrences of the word *disk* in the first paragraph have been changed to *diskette,* and the highlighting has disappeared.

## THE BEEP WHEN SEARCH FAILS OPTION

Since the * *Not found* * message happens so fast that you may not see it unless you watch carefully, WordPerfect has provided another option to let you know when a search (or replace) has failed. Using WordPerfect's Setup key (Shift-F1), you can have WordPerfect make a loud (some say obnoxious!) beep to let you know when it can't find any more occurrences of the search string in the text. Here's how you set WordPerfect to make the beep:

1. Press the Setup key, Shift-F1.

2. Press either **5** or **I** for Initial Settings.

3. Press either **1** or **B** to select Beep Options.

4. Press either **3** or **S** to select Beep on Search Failure.

5. Press **Y** to set it to Yes.

6. Press Exit (F7) to get back to the Edit screen.

From now on, you'll hear a loud beep whenever WordPerfect displays the * *Not found* * message on the status line, indicating that it can't find the search string or that it is finished replacing all occurrences of the search string.

## SUMMARY

As you have seen, Search and Search and Replace are valuable features that can improve your productivity enormously. Their applications are limited only by your imagination. Some other uses for Search that you'll study in other chapters are to locate headings and subheadings in order to mark them for your table of contents, to locate words or phrases and mark them for an index, and to find a special word you have entered as a marker in your text so you can jump around in the document and always find the last area you worked on. Since the Search keys are often the quickest and easiest way to move the cursor to a particular location, I use them for cursor movement more than anything else.

# ADVANCED FORMATTING FEATURES

# FAST TRACK

**To enter a hard hyphen**                                                215

(one that remains in the document regardless of where the word is placed on the line), press the hyphen key alone. If a hyphenated word or an expression that contains a minus sign should not be split between two lines, press Home followed by the hyphen key.

**To enter a soft hyphen**                                                214

(one that will not appear if subsequent changes move the word away from the right margin), press Ctrl-hyphen or use WordPerfect's Hyphenation feature (as explained in Chapter 4).

**To align columns of text against or around a specified character**      220

(known as the alignment character) such as period, press the Tab Align key (Ctrl-F6). Characters that you type will then be inserted to the left of the cursor until you enter the chosen alignment character, after which they will be inserted normally.

**To prevent the separation of two words or a group of numbers,**         226

enter the spaces between them as hard spaces by pressing Home followed by the Space bar instead of the Space bar alone.

**To insert the date**                                                    228

from your computer's memory into a document, select Date Text from the Date/Outline key (Shift-F5). If you want the current date to be inserted every time you retrieve the document or send it to the printer, press Shift-F5 and select Date Code. To customize the appearance of the date and/or to insert the time of day, press Shift-F5 and select Date Format.

**To enter superscripted or subscripted characters,**        232

press the Font key (Ctrl-F8), select Size, then choose Suprscpt or Subscpt, then type the characters. To turn off superscripting or subscripting, press → once. To superscript or subscript existing characters, first mark them with the Block key (Alt-F4), then press Ctrl-F8, select Size, then select Suprscpt or Subscpt.

**To print text a specified distance**        234

up, down, left, or right from the current printing position, use the Advance feature by pressing the Format key (Shift-F8), selecting Other (*4* or *O*) and choosing the Advance option (*1* or *A*). Select the direction, type the distance (in inches), press F7 twice, type the text to be affected, and then enter an Advance command in the opposite direction to return to normal printing.

**To print two or more characters in the same position,**        239

as in some foreign words, press the Format key (Shift-F8), select Other (*4* or *O*), choose the Overstrike option (*5* or *O*), select Create (*1* or *C*), type the affected characters, and press ↵ three times to return to the Edit screen and finish typing the word.

**To produce certain accented characters and special symbols,**        241

press the Compose key (Ctrl-2) and either type the two characters that should appear in the same position (as with Overstrike) or enter the key sequence for a special symbol, as shown in the CHARACTER.DOC file supplied with WordPerfect.

**Set left, right, center, or decimal tabs**        217

by pressing Shift-F8, selecting Line, and then selecting Tab Set. Type the number (in inches) where you want to position a tab; then press ↵ and type R, C, or D if you want to change from a left tab to a right, center, or decimal tab.

THIS CHAPTER WILL INTRODUCE SEVERAL NEW FOR-matting features such as subscripts and superscripts, hard spaces, hanging paragraphs, overstrike, the Compose key, hard and soft hyphens, the alignment character, tabs (left, right, center, and decimal), redline, strikeout, and line numbering. It will also further explore some other features that have been mentioned only briefly in earlier chapters. Among these are the Hyphenation zone and the Date/Outline key. Finally, you will learn about a new and important feature of WordPerfect 5.0, Styles.

Many who use word processors do not bother to learn the more advanced formatting features unless required to, because none of them is absolutely essential, and many of them seem to be esoteric and difficult to learn. If you think of yourself as this type of user, you are still encouraged to skim this chapter and familiarize yourself with the advanced features so that if you are ever in a situation where one of them could help, you'll at least be able to recognize it and go back to find out how to use it. It is not an exaggeration to say that features such as hard space and hard hyphen can save you a lot of frustration and an enormous amount of time and energy.

## *HYPHENATION*

To turn on automatic hyphenation, press the Format key (Shift-F8), select Line, then select Hyphenation and choose Auto.

You have already worked with WordPerfect's Hyphenation feature in Chapter 4 and have been briefly introduced to the Hyphenation zone. To refresh your memory, it is the area on each line between two positions called the Left Hyphenation zone and the Right Hyphenation zone. By default, the Right Hyphenation zone is preset to 4% and the left one is set to 10%, so on a normal line of 6.5 inches, the left one is .65″ and the right one is .26″ (.04 × 6.5).

If the Hyphenation feature is on, whenever a word begins before or at the Left Hyphenation zone and extends past the Right Hyphenation zone, the following prompt will appear asking you where to split the word:

Position hyphen; Press ESC

By contrast, word wrap takes over if a word begins *after* the Left Hyphenation zone and extends past the Right Hyphenation zone, automatically pushing the whole word to the next line.

Like most other settings in WordPerfect, the hyphenation zone can easily be changed. If you make it smaller, you will be asked to hyphenate more frequently; if it is larger, less hyphenation will be called for and more words will be word wrapped to the next line in their entirety. You will learn how to alter the hyphenation zone later in this section.

When you see the hyphenation prompt and you prefer not to hyphenate the word, you can press Cancel (F1) and the entire word will be wrapped to the following line. If you do this, the Reveal Codes screen will display a slash (/) in front of the word. This is called the Cancel Hyphenation code; it will always be found in front of a word that you declined to hyphenate (after the hyphenation message asked you to). If you later change your mind and decide you do want to hyphenate it, you can delete the slash. WordPerfect's Search feature can be used to locate Cancel Hyphenation codes. Just press one of the Search keys (F2 or Shift-F2), followed by the Format key (Shift-F8), then select option 1, Line, and option 3, /, and press F2 or Esc. Once you delete the slash by pressing Backspace, you can press ↑ once, then ↓ to see the *Position hyphen; Press Esc* prompt again asking you to hyphenate that word.

## SOFT HYPHENS

The hyphen that WordPerfect inserts when you are using the Hyphenation feature is called a *soft hyphen*. It is important that you understand the meaning of this term, so let's review it. If you add or delete text near a word that contains a soft hyphen and the document is then reformatted so that the word is moved away from the right margin, WordPerfect will remove the hyphen from your editing screen (and from the printed version) but will retain it as a code that you can see using the Reveal Codes key (Alt-F3). The code appears as a bold hyphen, and you can see one in Figure 8.1 in the word *WordPerfect*. This word was originally hyphenated until the word *then* was inserted to the left of it, causing *WordPerfect* to be wrapped to the following line.

## OTHER HYPHENS

You can insert a Soft Hyphen code yourself, without prompting from the program, by pressing the Ctrl key and holding it while pressing the hyphen key. This hyphen will only appear on the screen if the word is moved to a position at the right margin where hyphenation or word wrap would be required.

A *hard hyphen* that you insert using the hyphen key alone, without any prompting from WordPerfect (and without pressing Ctrl first), will appear on screen and in print wherever the word appears on a line, so if the word is moved to the middle of a line as you add or delete, the hyphen will still be visible on the Edit screen. If the word has to be split between two lines, WordPerfect will use your hard hyphen for the break.

If you wish to prevent a hyphenated word from being split between two lines under any circumstances, press Home before pressing the hyphen key. WordPerfect calls this the *hyphen character* and treats the two words that it splits as though they were one word. This type of

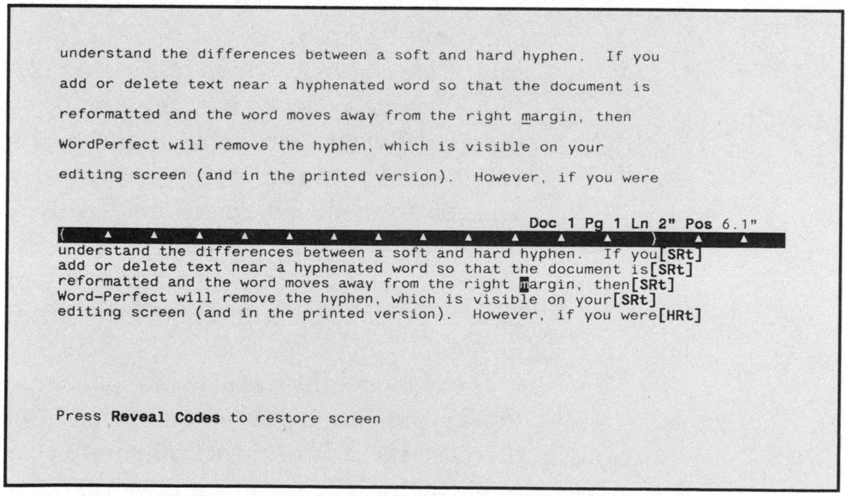

```
    understand the differences between a soft and hard hyphen.  If you

    add or delete text near a hyphenated word so that the document is

    reformatted and the word moves away from the right margin, then

    WordPerfect will remove the hyphen, which is visible on your

    editing screen (and in the printed version).  However, if you were




                                            Doc 1 Pg 1 Ln 2" Pos 6.1"
    understand the differences between a soft and hard hyphen.  If you[SRt]
    add or delete text near a hyphenated word so that the document is[SRt]
    reformatted and the word moves away from the right margin, then[SRt]
    Word-Perfect will remove the hyphen, which is visible on your[SRt]
    editing screen (and in the printed version).  However, if you were[HRt]




    Press Reveal Codes to restore screen
```

*Figure 8.1:* The soft hyphen in the Reveal Codes screen

hyphen should also be used to represent a minus sign in a numeric equation such as 15–5 = 10. If it is not, WordPerfect considers the sign to be a hard hyphen, and may split the equation into two lines against your intentions. Finally, to create a *dash* between two words, you must use the double hyphen (press Home hyphen hyphen). WordPerfect keeps the two hyphens that make up a dash together at the end of a line.

In the Reveal Codes screen, the hard hyphen created by pressing the hyphen key alone appears as follows:

[–]

The soft hyphen, created by WordPerfect's Hyphenation feature or by pressing Ctrl-hyphen, appears as a bold hyphen as shown in Figure 8.1. The dash (double hyphen) appears like this:

– [–]

Finally, the hyphen created with Home and the hyphen key (minus), used to keep text from being split at the hyphen, appears as a plain hyphen (like the soft hyphen but without the bold).

## CHANGING THE HYPHENATION ZONE

To change the settings for the Hyphenation zone, press the Format key (Shift-F8) followed by *1* or *L* for Line. You will then see the Format: Line screen as shown in Figure 8.2. Next, you select option 2, Hyphenation Zone, by pressing *2* or *Z* and enter the new settings for the left and right zones, following each entry with ⏎. For instance, if you wanted a smaller hyphenation zone so that WordPerfect would ask you to hyphenate more frequently, you could change the left hyphenation zone to 8% by typing **8** and pressing ⏎, then change the right one to 3% by typing **3** and pressing ⏎. Note that you don't have to type the percent sign (%) because WordPerfect will supply it for you.

If you reduce the size of the Hyphenation zone, you will encounter the Hyphenation prompt more frequently. Conversely, if you increase the size of the Hyphenation zone, you will be asked to hyphenate less frequently, and more words will be wrapped to the following line. With right justification off, a small Hyphenation zone

```
Format: Line

    1 - Hyphenation                        Off

    2 - Hyphenation Zone - Left            10%
                           Right           4%

    3 - Justification                      Yes

    4 - Line Height                        Auto

    5 - Line Numbering                     No

    6 - Line Spacing                       1

    7 - Margins - Left                     1"
                  Right                    1"

    8 - Tab Set                            0", every 0.5"

    9 - Widow/Orphan Protection            Yes


Selection: 0
```

*Figure 8.2:* The Format: Line menu showing the Hyphenation Zone option

will produce a more even (less ragged) right margin, and with right justification on, it helps reduce the extra blank space between words that is used to create an even right margin.

## *LEFT, CENTER, RIGHT, AND DECIMAL TABS*

In Chapter 4 you were introduced to the subject of left justified tabs and were promised further explanation of the other types of tabs: center, right, and decimal. As you may recall, left tabs are the standard type of tab used for aligning text. When you press the Tab key and type a word, the first letter of the word is actually in the same position as the tab stop and the remaining characters in the word are entered to the right of the tab stop as shown below:

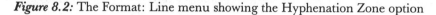

```
L   L   L   L   L   L   L   L   L   L   L   L
|   ^   |   ^   |   ^   |   ^   |   ^   |   ^
2"      3"      4"      5"      6"      7"
Dear
```

In the above case, left tabs are set every ½ inch (WordPerfect's default) and the word *Dear* was typed after pressing Tab twice. Left tabs are set for every ½ inch up to the end of the page size form you are using (8½ inches for the standard paper size of 8½″ × 11″) unless you change the tab settings using the Format key (Shift-F8 1 8 or Shift-F8 L T).

Center tabs are used primarily to center a heading over a column of text or numbers. The previous example looks like this when a center tab is used:

```
C    L    L    L    L    L    L    L    L    L    L
|    ^    |    ^    |    ^    |    ^    |    ^    |    ^
2″        3″        4″        5″        6″        7″
Dear
```

Decimal tabs are used to align a column of numbers around the decimal point, as shown below. Note that the decimal points are all directly under the tab stop position at the 2″ mark; this happens automatically when you press the Tab key after setting a decimal tab.

```
D    L    L    L    L    L    L    L    L    L    L
|    ^    |    ^    |    ^    |    ^    |    ^    |    ^
2″        3″        4″        5″        6″        7″
199.99
99.99
1999.99
```

Right-aligned tabs are used for numbers when they do not include decimal points. As shown below, the blank space following the last digit (0) in each number is aligned under the tab stop. For instance, when you round off the numbers shown above (let's hear it for truth in advertising!) and use a right tab instead of a center tab, they look like this:

```
R    L    L    L    L    L    L    L    L    L    L
|    ^    |    ^    |    ^    |    ^    |    ^    |    ^
2″        3″        4″        5″        6″        7″
200
100
2000
```

Incidentally, there are other methods for aligning decimal points under the Tab position, including the Tab Align key (Ctrl-F6) and WordPerfect's Math feature (Alt-F7). You will study Tab Align in the next section, and Math in Chapter 17.

In Chapter 4 you learned how to change tab stops. To refresh your memory, you press the Format key (Shift-F8), select Line by typing *1* or *L,* then select the Tab Set option by pressing *8* or *T.* Press Home ← or 0 ← to move the cursor to the beginning of the page, and delete all default tab stops by pressing Ctrl-End (the Delete EOL key). Next, either type the number (in inches) of the tab stop (such as *1* for 1″) and press ←, or set evenly spaced tabs by typing the starting tab number, a comma, and the interval number. For example, to set tabs every ½ inch starting at 1½ inches, you would enter

    1.5,.5 ←

Both of these methods insert left tab stops. To change the type of tab to right, center, or decimal (and in this example to insert tabs every ½ inch starting at 1½ inches) you vary the procedure slightly. After using Ctrl-End to clear the existing tabs, you press → until the cursor is on the 1½-inch mark on the ruler (½-inch increments are displayed by the use of the ^ —caret symbol), and type the letter corresponding to the type of tab you want to set (*R, C,* or *D*). Next type

    1.5,.5

and press ←.

To change individual tab settings, use the ← or → key or the Space bar to position the cursor over the tab stop, then press either *L, R, C,* or *D.* To delete individual tab settings, position the cursor over the tab stop and press the Delete key.

A word of warning: Whenever you change tab stops, you must use the Exit key (F7) to leave the Tab menu (Figure 8.3) and register the changes you just made. Do not try to exit by pressing the Cancel key (F1) or you will cancel the new tab stops.

## LEADER CHARACTERS

Selecting a leader character in the Tab menu fills the space between the tabs with a line of dots, as shown below:

```
RENT ................................................................................1000.00
UTILITIES .........................................................................46.66
SUPPLIES.........................................................................39.75
```

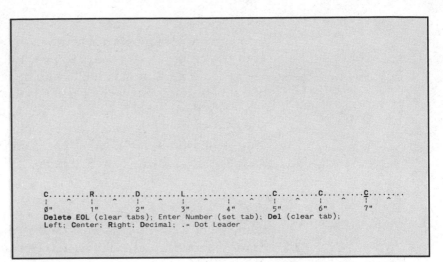

*Figure 8.3:* The Tab menu with left, center, right, and decimal tabs

In this example, the decimal tab was used to align the numbers. To set the leader character, you simply type a period over the *L, R, C,* or *D* when setting tab positions in the Tab menu. A bright box appears over the character, indicating that the text at that tab position will be preceded by a dot leader.

In the example shown above, I set a decimal tab with a dot leader at 5 inches. After typing each heading (RENT, UTLITIES, SUP-PLIES), I pressed the Tab key to move the cursor to 5 inches and typed the number, as shown in Figure 8.4. As I typed, the cursor remained stationary at the tab stop and the numbers were pushed to the left until the decimal point (period) was pressed.

## THE ALIGNMENT CHARACTER

The Alignment Character feature works in conjunction with the Tab Align key (Ctrl-F6), to create and align columns against or around a character such as a decimal point, asterisk, or blank space that is inserted using the Space bar. Although more commonly used with WordPerfect's Math feature, the Alignment Character can also be used to establish columns of text. You will learn about Math columns in Chapter 17, so this section will be limited to exploring text columns.

Using Tab Align with text columns is similar to using the Flush Right key to align text against the right margin, except that the Alignment Character replaces the right margin as the position against which the text will be lined up. Characters that are typed after pressing Tab Align are inserted to the left of the cursor, and the cursor remains stationary at the tab stop until the Alignment Character is entered. For example, in Figure 8.5, an excerpt from a legal document, the text in the last three lines is aligned against the dollar sign ($).

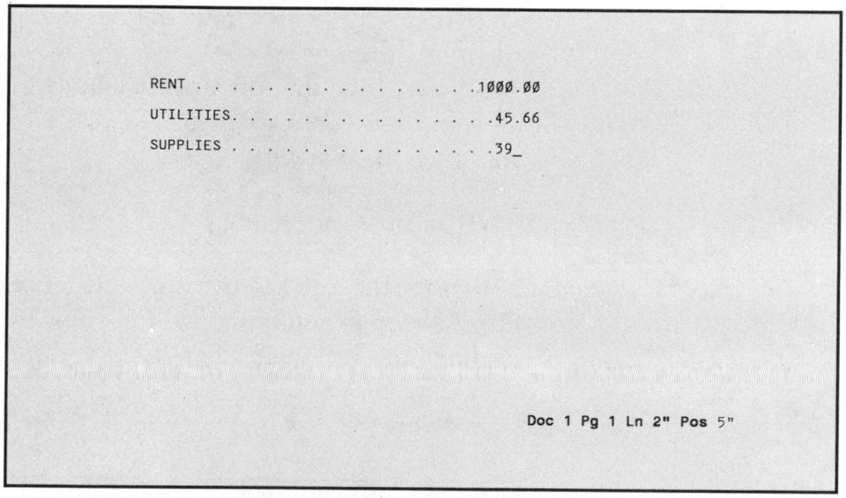

```
          RENT . . . . . . . . . . . . . .1000.00
          UTILITIES. . . . . . . . . . . .45.66
          SUPPLIES . . . . . . . . . . . .39_




                                        Doc 1 Pg 1 Ln 2" Pos 5"
```

*Figure 8.4:* Using a decimal tab with dot leaders

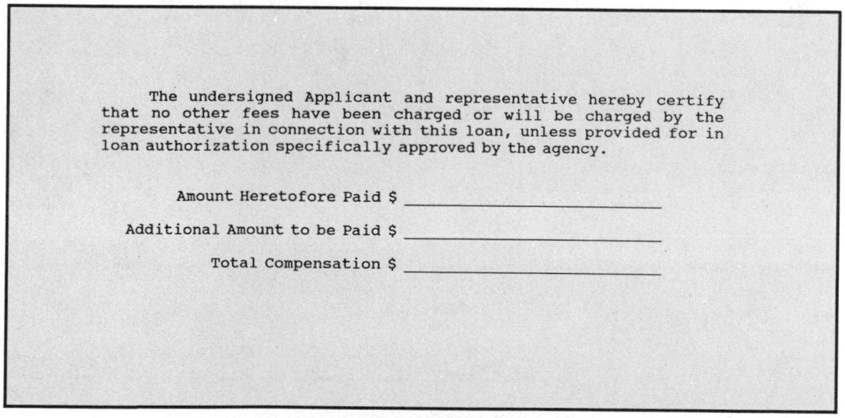

```
          The undersigned Applicant and representative hereby certify
       that no other fees have been charged or will be charged by the
       representative in connection with this loan, unless provided for in
       loan authorization specifically approved by the agency.


              Amount Heretofore Paid $ _____

          Additional Amount to be Paid $ _____

               Total Compensation $ _____
```

*Figure 8.5:* Text aligned against the dollar sign

The procedure that was used to align these sentences is simple, and certainly is easier than trying to align them visually. The first step is to designate the Alignment Character, in this case the dollar sign. Since the period (decimal point) is used so often for mathematical and financial typing, it serves as the default value for the Alignment Character. To change the Alignment Character, press the Format key (Shift-F8) and choose option 4 or O, *Other.* You will then see the *Other* menu options shown in Figure 8.6. To change the Alignment Character, you select the Decimal Character option by typing *3* or *D,* then type the dollar sign (*$*), which erases the period. You can leave the comma as the thousands separator by just pressing ◄—┘.

To verify that the Alignment Character has been changed to a dollar sign, you can look in the Reveal Codes screen (Alt-F3) where you'll see the following code:

**[Decml/Algn Char:$,,]**

Now press the Tab key five times, then press the Tab Align key (Ctrl-F6). As soon as you press Ctrl-F6, you will see this prompt on the status line, and it remains there until you press the $ key:

**Align char = $**

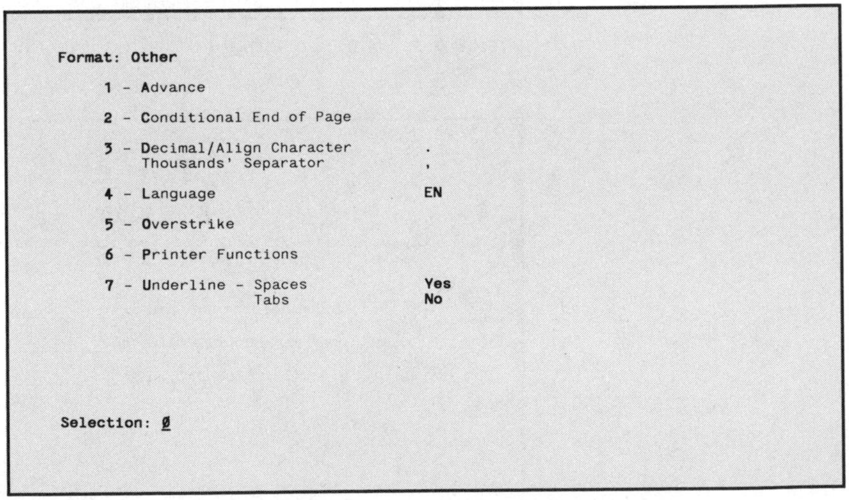

```
Format: Other

        1 - Advance

        2 - Conditional End of Page

        3 - Decimal/Align Character            .
            Thousands' Separator                ,

        4 - Language                          EN

        5 - Overstrike

        6 - Printer Functions

        7 - Underline - Spaces                Yes
                        Tabs                  No




    Selection: 0
```

*Figure 8.6:* The Format: Other menu showing the Decimal Character option

Next, type the first sentence:

Amount Heretofore Paid $

As soon as you typed the dollar sign, the prompt disappeared. This indicates that the alignment feature has been turned off, and whatever you type next will be entered in the usual manner (with the cursor moving to the right as you type).

When using tab alignment, you must be sure to leave enough space for all the characters in your sentence, which is why you were instructed to press Tab five times before pressing Tab Align. It is apparent that there are more than five characters in each of the sentences in this example, so if you had pressed the Tab Alignment key only once, without inserting extra tabs, the words would have been pushed all the way to the left margin. Once you had typed more than 15 characters, the *Align* prompt would have disappeared and you would no longer have been in Alignment mode.

The reason for this is not complicated. As you typed the first five characters, they would move to the left of the cursor (which would remain at the tab stop at position 1.5″) until the first character was at position 1″, the left margin. The next nine characters you typed would release the margin and continue to move to the left until the first character appeared at position 0″. At that point, if you were to enter one more character, they could go no further; with no more room at the left edge, tab alignment would end and any other characters you typed from that point on would be entered in the standard method, with the cursor moving to the right of each character after it is typed.

Now add the line to the right of the dollar sign by typing 27 underlines (using Shift with the underline key on the right of the top row), or by using the Esc key in the convenient method described below.

As you learned in Chapter 3, the Esc key can be used to repeat a function or character any number of times. To try it, press Esc and you will see the following prompt:

Repeat Value = 8

The *8* represents the number of times your action will be repeated. Eight is the default, so type *27* to replace the *8* with *27* (but don't press ⏎ yet). Next, type an underline and voilà, your line appears

The position numbers may be different on your screen because they vary according to the printer you are using and have installed in WordPerfect.

instantly! Esc can also be used in the same manner to move the cursor up, down, right or left a specified number of lines or positions, to delete several lines or characters following the cursor, and much more. To learn more about these applications, you can use Help (press F3, then Esc) or turn to the section in Chapter 3 that describes this key more thoroughly.

## *EDITING TEXT THAT HAS BEEN ALIGNED*

There is one hazard to watch out for when you use the Tab Align feature: if you try to edit the words that were aligned, the cursor will behave in a bizarre and unpredictable manner unless it is correctly positioned. Even worse, new text that you enter may not appear on the screen at all. This is not a flaw in WordPerfect (which appears to be nearly free of such problems). To learn why this occurs, look at the Reveal Codes screen to understand how the Alignment codes have been placed.

Do this now by pressing the Reveal Codes key (Alt-F3). You will see a pair of Alignment codes, [Align] and [C/A/Flrt], surrounding *Amount Heretofore Paid*. The screen will resemble Figure 8.7.

The Alignment codes always appear in pairs with the first one, [Align], signaling the beginning of the text being aligned, and the

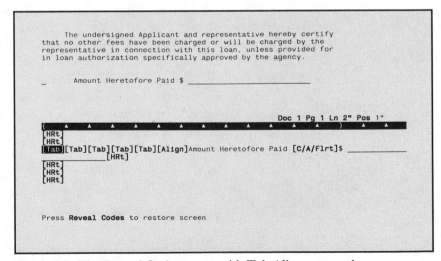

*Figure 8.7:* The Reveal Codes screen with Tab Alignment codes

second, [C/A/Flrt], signaling the end. The problem arises when you try to edit the text without checking the cursor location. Since the codes are invisible on the editing screen, it's easy to accidentally place the cursor in the wrong position when you are trying to edit the aligned text. Also, unless you use the Reveal Codes screen, it will seem as though the cursor refuses to stop at the first character of aligned text.

Use the Reveal Codes screen to help you move the cursor to the position following the first Alignment code, [Align] (on the *A*). Next, press Alt-F3 again to exit to the editing screen. Notice that it appears as though your cursor is positioned on the first character of the sentence (the *A* in *Amount*). Now type the following:

**This represents the**

Press the Space bar after you've finished typing the word *the* but don't press any other keys yet.

Did you see how the words were entered as you typed them? As you typed *This represents*, these two words were pushed to the left by the alignment character, but when you typed the *t* in *the*, the first Tab code in your sentence bumped into position 0 and could be pushed no further to the left. Next, you typed the *h* and saw the characters *This represents t* disappear altogether. After you typed the *e* and pressed the Space bar, your line appeared like this:

**he Amount Heretofore Paid $** _____

If you press the ↓ key at this point, the line will be reformatted, moving the underline characters down to the following line (assuming you pressed ↵ at the end of the line). It will then appear as follows:

**This represents the Amount Heretofore Paid$**

Look at the Reveal Codes screen shown in Figure 8.8, and you'll see what has happened. The line contains five Tab codes followed by [Align] and the words *This represents*. The [C/A/Flrt] code, which ends tab alignment, appears next, meaning that the rest of the phrase is no longer being affected by the Alignment Character. In fact, WordPerfect shifted the Alignment code immediately after you typed

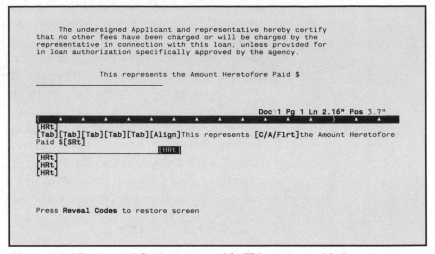

*Figure 8.8:* The Reveal Codes screen with *This represents* added

the *t* in *the* because at that point, the first of the five Tab codes hit position 0, and alignment ended. If you had inserted a few more tabs in front of the original sentence and shortened the line of underline characters, this problem would have been avoided.

Now you understand why you have to be so careful when using the Tab Alignment feature! It can be extremely confusing, especially when words disappear from your editing screen, or the cursor jumps around unpredictably as you try to edit. If this ever happens, it is likely that the new text has disappeared between a set of alignment codes ([Align] and [C/A/Flrt]), or that the cursor was accidentally placed in the wrong position before editing. To correct the problem, you must check the Reveal Codes screen and position the cursor properly before you try to edit.

## HARD SPACES

You already have been introduced to the concepts of hard and soft hyphens, so you should have little trouble understanding hard spaces. You use hard spaces to prevent the program from splitting words between two lines. This is often necessary with a mathematical formula, a date, or a name such as Henry VIII. To see why, look at the paragraph in Figure 8.9.

The date, November 23, and the address, 54 Main Street, would be much easier to read if they had remained unbroken; your eyes tend to read each of them as a unit and your reading slows down considerably when the words are separated. To prove this, read the revised version in Figure 8.10, in which hard spaces were used to keep the name and date on the same lines.

To insert a hard space, you press the Home key first, then press the Space bar, rather than the Space bar alone. For example, to use a hard space between *November* and *23* in Figure 8.9, you would delete the space that separates them now, then press Home followed by the Space bar. As you would expect, this action inserts a formatting code that is visible on your Reveal Codes screen. It is a space surrounded by brackets, and on the Edit screen it appears between the words instead of a normal space, but looks like a normal one.

If you use hard spaces, you may sometimes end up with excessive blank space at the end of a line when you add or delete text, just as with any long, unbroken word that word wraps. If this happens, you can delete the hard spaces using the Reveal Codes screen. Another problem with hard spaces occurs when you are using WordPerfect's Hyphenation feature. Since WordPerfect considers words separated

When you use Home-Space bar to create a hard space separating two words, Word-Perfect treats the two words as though they were a single word. Therefore, if you insert text on the same line and there is no longer enough room for both words at the right margin, Word Perfect will word-wrap them together to the next line.

```
        The bone-chilling event occurred on the night of November
23, long after Halloween's raucousness had faded into memory and
the town had taken on a prim demeanor for the new holiday.   The
slovenly house whose old remains barely covered the site at 54
Main Street had been empty for years .
```

*Figure 8.9:* A paragraph that needs hard spaces

```
        The bone-chilling event occurred on the night of
November 23, long after Halloween's raucousness had faded into
memory and the town had taken on a prim demeanor for the new
holiday.   The slovenly house whose old remains barely covered the
site at 54 Main Street had been empty for years .
```

*Figure 8.10:* The paragraph with hard spaces added

by hard spaces to be one word, it may ask you to place an inappropriate hyphen between them if they appear at or near the right margin. To prevent hyphenation in these cases, simply press the Cancel key (F1).

# THE DATE/OUTLINE KEY

You have already learned that pressing the Date/Outline key (Shift-F5) and selecting option 1 or T (Date Text) places the current date (based on the computer's clock or the entries you make at startup time) at the cursor location. In this section, you will learn about the remaining two date options on the Date/Outline key: Date Code and Date Format. Date Format allows you to customize the appearance of the date and can also be used to include the time of day. Date Code allows you to insert the date as a function code (although it will appear in your document as text, as in option 1), so that in the future it will always show the current date and/or time when you print the document or bring it from the disk to the screen for editing.

## DATE FORMAT

Let's experiment with the formats. Press the Date/Outline key (Shift-F5). Select the Date format option by pressing *3* or *F,* and you will see the screen shown in Figure 8.11.

Notice the boldfaced prompt line that displays the default format in the lower part of the screen:

**Date format: 3 1, 4**

Two columns are visible on the Date Format screen, one with characters and one that explains their meanings. To change the date format, you must enter one or more of these numbers in the prompt line, then press ←. For instance, if you want the date to appear as all numbers with hyphens but no spaces between the numbers, as in 3–12–89, you type the following:

**2-1-5**

and press ←. Note that *2* represents the month number, *1* represents the day, and *5* represents the last two digits of the year.

```
Date Format

     Character   Meaning
        1        Day of the Month
        2        Month (number)
        3        Month (word)
        4        Year (all four digits)
        5        Year (last two digits)
        6        Day of the Week (word)
        7        Hour (24-hour clock)
        8        Hour (12-hour clock)
        9        Minute
        Ø        am / pm
        %        Used before a number, will:
                    Pad numbers less than 1Ø with a leading zero
                    Output only 3 letters for the month or day of the week


     Examples:  3 1, 4      = December 25, 1984
                %6 %3 1, 4  = Tue Dec 25, 1984
                %2/%1/5 (6) = Ø1/Ø1/85 (Tuesday)
                8:9Ø        = 1Ø:55am

Date format: 3 1, 4
```

*Figure 8.11:* The Date Format screen

You will then see the Date/Outline key prompt again, and if you select either the Date Text option (*1* or *T*) or the Date Code option (*2* or *C*), the date will be placed at the current cursor position in your new format. For example, if the date in your computer is January 9, 1989, it will appear as follows:

**1-9-89**

Table 8.1 shows what each of the numbers would insert in your document on Monday, January 9, 1989, at 8:45 p.m.

When you use these numbers to change the date format, you can also include any other symbols or characters such as slashes, hyphens, spaces, or commas. You have already used hyphens in the first exercise, and can probably think of applications for the others. For example, it is standard practice to insert a colon between the hour and minute, so typing

**8:9 0**

(be sure to separate *9* from *0* with a space) will return the current time in the correct format when you select Date Text or Date Code from the Date/Outline key, as follows:

**8:45 pm**

*Table 8.1:* Date and Time Options

| NUMBER | MEANING | EXAMPLE |
|--------|---------|---------|
| 1 | Day of the month (number) | 9 |
| 2 | Month (number) | 1 |
| 3 | Month (text) | January |
| 4 | Year (4 digits) | 1989 |
| 5 | Year (last 2 digits) | 89 |
| 6 | Day of the week (text) | Monday |
| 7 | Hour (24-hour clock) | 20 |
| 8 | Hour (12-hour clock) | 8 |
| 9 | Minute | 45 |
| 0 | a.m. / p.m. | pm |
| % | Leading zero before numbers, or 3 letters for name of the month or day of the week | 01-09-89 Mon Jan 9, 1989 |

The only restriction in your date format pattern is that the total number of characters cannot exceed 29.

Each time you start WordPerfect, the default format, *3 1, 4,* will automatically appear when you select the Date Format option from the Date/Outline key, and this style will be used if you insert the date using Date Text or Date Code. However, once you change it, the new format will continue to appear each time you press Shift-F5 3 or insert the date using Date Text or Date Code, and it will be the same until you exit from the program or change it once again. Unlike most other features in WordPerfect, changing the date format does not insert a special code into your document (you won't see any indication on your Reveal Codes screen that this has been done). However, if you use the Date Code option (Shift-F5 2 or C) to insert the date into your document as a code, your Reveal Codes screen will display the new format, such as: [Date: 8:9 0].

Use WordPerfect's Setup key (Shift-F1) to customize the default date format. Press Shift-F1, select Initial Settings (*5* or *I*), then choose Date Format (*2* or *D*). You will see a Date Format screen like the one shown in Figure 8.11, and you can use it to change the appearance of the date and/or to include the time.

## *DATE CODE*

The Date Code option inserts a date that appears to be just like any other text in your document, but is actually a code. This date will change to match the one that is in your computer at the time you print the document or retrieve it from disk to be edited.

To use this feature, simply press *2* or *C* after pressing the Date/ Outline key (Shift-F5). The date in your computer's memory when you make this selection will be inserted into your text, using the default format. If you have changed the format since you started this session with WordPerfect, the date will conform to the most recent format used. I find this feature to be of great value and I use it often. For instance, while writing this book I have been saving each chapter as a separate file and inserting the Date code at the end to tell me the date and time. By doing this, I can always tell how long I have been working in each session (that is, since I last retrieved the file from the disk) by comparing it to the time on my watch. (It helps me maintain self-discipline!) I also use it in a footer on printed drafts of the chapters so I'll know which of several printouts is the most recent revision. I use this format:

6, 3 1, 4  8:9 0

It shows up as follows:

Monday, February 15, 1988   9:00 pm

This date function appears on the Reveal Codes screen as follows:

[Date:6, 3 1, 4  8:9 0]

## *HANGING PARAGRAPHS USING THE MARGIN RELEASE*

A hanging paragraph is one in which the entire paragraph is indented one or more tab stops to the right, except for the first line, which hangs out from the rest of the text at the left side because the indented margin has been released. This is especially useful in numbered outlines, so that the numbers or letters that are used to label each paragraph or section are set off from the body of text that follows.

Figure 8.12 shows three journal entries that are to be recorded in a general ledger with the date listed to the left of the transaction for emphasis. Each of the transactions is a hanging paragraph.

You create a hanging paragraph by following these steps:

1.  Press the Indent key (F4) one or more times.

2.  Press the Margin Release key (Shift-Tab) to release the temporary margin (just created with the Indent key) and move the first line one or more tab stops to the left.

3.  Type your paragraph. Pressing ◀━┘ at the end of the paragraph terminates automatic indentation and ends the paragraph. Note that in the example shown in Figure 8.12, the Indent key was pressed twice so that the sentences begin at the 2-inch position, and the Margin Release key (Shift-Tab) was pressed twice so that the date begins in the regular left margin at the 1-inch position.

This feature is also useful when you are typing lists of instructions, such as the ones in this book.

```
August 3: Spent $20,000 in cash to purchase computer equipment.

August 6: Paid by check the amount of $633.45, for invoice #4020
          from the phone company for the July bill.

August 9: Received a check for $5,455 from clients Smith, Jones and
          Brown for work performed from July 1 through July 9,
          billed on invoice #1355.
```

*Figure 8.12:* Hanging paragraphs

## SUPERSCRIPT AND SUBSCRIPT

Superscripted characters are ones that are printed in a position slightly above the standard line, as in the number

$1.05^2$

Subscripted characters appear in a position slightly below the standard line, as in the chemical formula for copper sulfate:

$Cu_2SO_4$

According to the WordPerfect manual, superscripted and subscripted characters are supposed to be printed one third of a line above or below the rest of the text on the line on which they are placed, but this placement can vary with the printer. In addition, not all printers can produce subscripts and superscripts, so you may want to test your printer before trying to use this feature. For details about printer installation and testing, please refer to Chapter 9.

You can place a Superscript or Subscript code in front of a character (or characters) before typing it or you can designate a block of characters that have been marked with the Block key (Alt-F4) to be superscripted or subscripted. To insert the code, press the Font key (Ctrl-F8). The following menu appears:

**1 Size; 2 Appearance; 3 Normal; 4 Base Font; 5 Print Color: 0**

The Superscript and Subscript options are on the Size menu. To access this menu, type *1* or *S*. When you do, the following options become available:

**1 Suprscpt; 2 Subscpt; 3 Fine; 4 Small; 5 Large; 6 Vry Large; 7 Ext Large: 0**

To superscript text, press *1* or *P* for Superscript and then type the character or characters to be superscripted. To turn off superscripting, repeat the command (Ctrl-F8 1 1 or Ctrl-F8 S P) or press the → key once to move the cursor past the Superscript code. To subscript text, press Ctrl-F8, select Size, press *2* or *B* for Subscript, and then type the character or characters to be subscripted. To turn off subscripting, repeat the command (Ctrl-F8 1 2 or Ctrl-F8 S B) or press the → key once, as you do to turn off superscripting.

If your monitor is not equipped with a special graphics adapter, your subscripted or superscripted characters do not appear to be different on screen (except that they appear in a different color on color screens), since these features only alter the printed version of your work. To verify that you have inserted the code correctly, you can check the Reveal Codes screen (Alt-F3). To superscript or subscript text, WordPerfect encloses the affected characters in a pair of formatting codes, just as it does when you boldface or underline text in the document. For example, if you entered $A^2$, the codes for superscripting the *2* in the text would appear in the Reveal Codes screen as

A[SUPRSCRPT]2[suprscrpt]

The pair of formatting codes for subscripting text is very similar. For instance, a subscripted *2* in $H_2O$ would appear in the Reveal Codes screen as

H[SUBSCPT]2[subscpt]O

Note that you can also superscript and subscript existing text in the document. To do this, mark the characters to be superscripted or subscripted with the Block key (Alt-F4) and cursor movement keys, then press the Font key (Ctrl-F8). When you press the Font key with the Block key on, you see this prompt:

**Attribute: 1 Size; 2 Appearance: 0**

Select option 1 from this menu by typing either *1* or *S*. You will then see the Size menu (shown earlier). Select *1* or *P* from this menu to superscript the blocked text, or select *2* or *B* to subscript it.

## *THE ADVANCE FEATURE*

If Subscript and Superscript don't work correctly with your printer, or if you want to move a character or phrase up or down the page in different increments, you can use WordPerfect's Advance feature. It is accessible from the Format key (Shift-F8) on the *Other* menu. You use it to print text a specified distance up, down, left, or right from the current printing position, or to print on a specific line or position.

Advance is very much like using the Subscript and Superscript features, primarily because it too must be turned on in front of the text you want altered and turned off immediately afterward. As with the Subscript and Superscript features, not all printers can take advantage of this feature, so it's helpful to test your printer before using it.

To use Advance, press the Format key (Shift-F8), select the *Other* option (*4* or *0*), and then the Advance option (*1* or *A*). This will bring up a prompt with the following options:

**Advance: 1 Up; 2 Down; 3 Line; 4 Left; 5 Right; 6 Position: 0**

From this menu, you select the direction in which you want to advance the printing position. After you select the direction (*1* or *U* for Up, *2* or *D* for Down, *4* or *L* for Left, *5* or *R* for Right), you see a prompt like this one for Up:

**Adv. up 0″**

Type the distance you want the printing position advanced, press ←┘ then press F7 to return to your document and type the text to be affected. When you are finished, you should enter an Advance command in the opposite direction (Down if you used Up, Left if you used Right, and so on) using the same distance. The cursor will not move when you use Advance, but you can watch the status line to tell where it will be printed. Also, the View Document option on the Print key (Shift-F8) shows the correct position for advanced text.

Figure 8.13 shows the Reveal Codes screen for a line of text that has been advanced. The bracketed code representing Advance Up [Adv Up: 0.25″] appears at the beginning of the line, indicating that the words *IT'S FUN UP HERE* have been advanced up by one fourth of an inch. The Advance Down code follows this phrase, and turns the feature off by advancing down the same distance. The code representing Advance Down appears again after the word *BUT,* indicating that the words that follow, *IT'S NO FUN AT ALL DOWN HERE,* have been advanced down by one fourth of an inch. At the end of the sentence, another code for Advance Up appears, which serves to turn the feature off once again by advancing up the same distance.

Although this sentence was started on line 1.25″, the only word that will appear on line 1.25″ of the printed text is the word *BUT,* which was unaffected by the codes. If you type this sentence (including the Advance codes) and then move your cursor to the word *UP,*

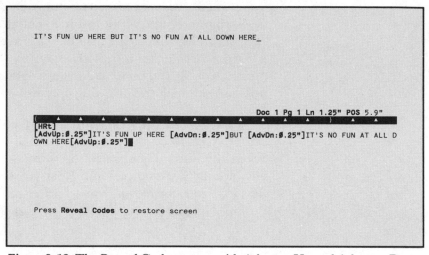

*Figure 8.13:* The Reveal Codes screen with Advance Up and Advance Down
codes

the line indicator on the status line shows that the cursor is on line 1″.
If you move your cursor to the word *DOWN*, the line indicator
reveals that the cursor is on line 1.5″.

You can also advance the printing position to the left or right using
the Advance Left or Right option (Shift-F8 O A L or R). The distance entered for the Left and Right Advance is relative to the cursor's position. For instance, if you are using the standard 1-inch
margin and the first thing you do before typing a line of text is enter
an Advance Left .5″ code, the line of text will begin ½ inch to the left
of the margin in the printed version and in View Document (Shift-F7
V). If you enter an Advance Right code of .5″, the line will be
indented ½ inch.

## ADVANCING BY LINES OR TO A POSITION

Option 3 on the Advance menu allows you to advance the printed
text up or down one or more whole lines. It can be used to insert blank
space on a printed page, without the blank lines appearing on the monitor. It's also useful to draw boxes around text so that you can type the
text, then draw boxes below it and move them back up in the printed
version only. Figure 8.14 shows an example. Since the fonts used for the
text could not produce line drawing, Line Advance was necessary to

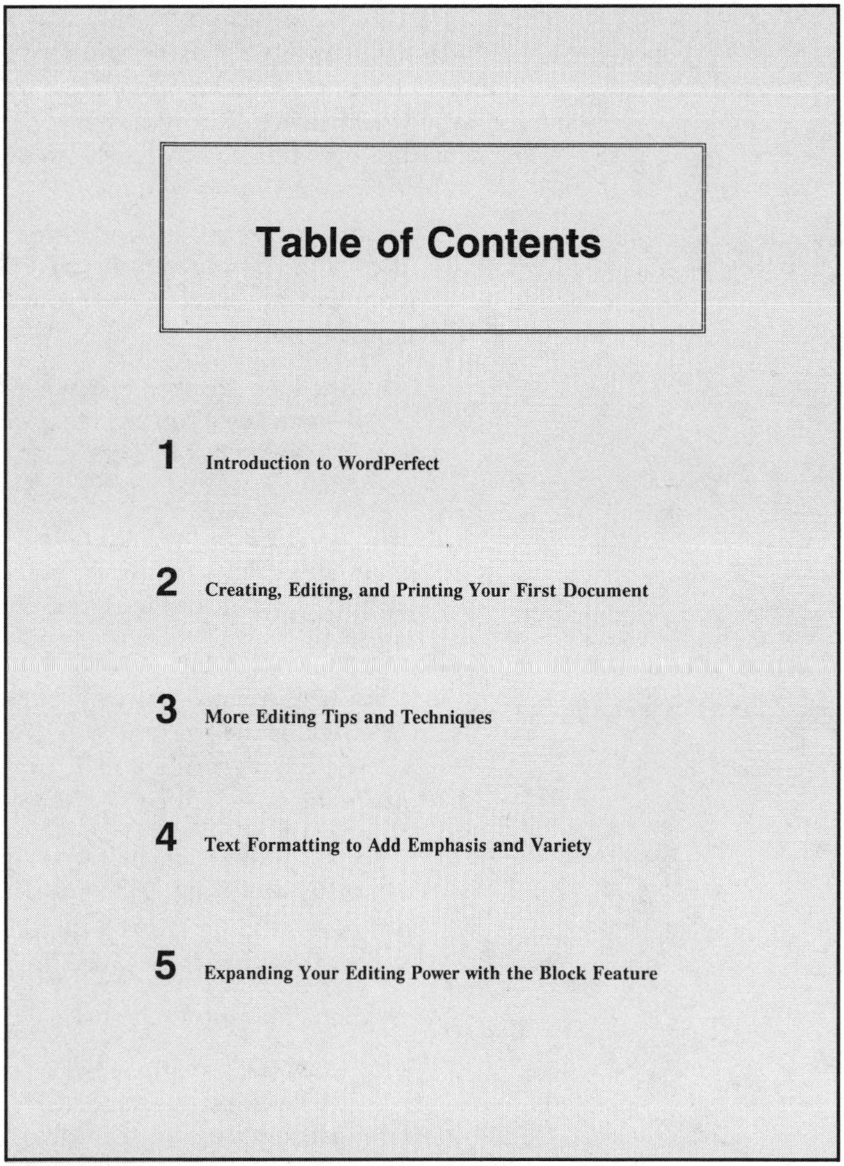

## Table of Contents

**1** Introduction to WordPerfect

**2** Creating, Editing, and Printing Your First Document

**3** More Editing Tips and Techniques

**4** Text Formatting to Add Emphasis and Variety

**5** Expanding Your Editing Power with the Block Feature

***Figure 8.14:*** Using Line Advance to draw boxes and mix fonts

switch to the Courier font and print the box, moving it back up to the *Table of Contents* heading. (Fonts are covered in Chapters 9 and 14; Line Drawing is covered in Chapter 13.) If you use this feature, you have to rely on the line indicator to tell you which line you are currently typing on. The distance you indicate (in inches, unless you have changed the default unit of measure with the Setup key) corresponds to the line indicator on the status line. For instance, if you wanted to advance to line 2″, you would have to enter 2 inches.

Since this option is slightly harder to understand unless you try it, do so now by following these steps:

1. Start at the first line in the page and type the following sentence without pressing ← (your line breaks may differ from those below):

   **The Line Advance option can be used instead of the Return key if you want to eliminate all the blank spaces on the monitor that are inserted by pressing the Return key.**

2. Check the status line and note the number of the line where your cursor is located when you finish. If you started typing at line 1″ (as instructed), the cursor should now be on line 1.33″.

3. Press ← and make sure the cursor is positioned on line 1.5″ by checking the line indicator. Next, press Shift-F8 O A, then select Line by typing **3** or **I**. You will see the prompt *Adv. to line* in the lower left corner of the screen.

4. Type **2** to move ½ inch down from the top of the page, to line 2″, then press Exit (F7). The line indicator will show that you are now on line 2″, even though you do not see any blank space on the screen between lines 1.33″ and 2″.

5. Type the following sentence (without pressing ←):

   **However, just remember when using Line Advance that what you see on screen will not be the same as what you get on paper.**

   When you're finished, the line indicator will show that the cursor is on line 2.16″, though only five lines will be visible on the screen.

The printed version of this page will resemble Figure 8.15, with several blank lines appearing between lines 1.33″ and 2″. You can also use the View Document option on the Print key (Shift-F7) to preview it.

The Position Advance option is very similar to the Line Advance feature. The distance that you specify represents the absolute distance of the column (in inches) from the left margin. You can use this feature to ensure that proportionally spaced text in a table always remains aligned even though you've used different fonts.

```
The Line Advance option can be used instead of the Return key if
you want to eliminate all the blank spaces on the monitor that are
inserted by pressing the Return key.



However, just remember when using Line Advance that what you
see on screen will not be the same as what you get on paper.
```

*Figure 8.15:* The printed version of two paragraphs that have been separated by Line Advance

## OVERSTRIKE

Overstrike, option 5 on the *Other* menu of the Format key (Shift-F8), allows you to print two or more characters in the same position, if your printer is capable of this. This feature can be used to print certain foreign characters such as the accents and circumflexes that are often placed over vowels to clarify pronunciation. For example, many French words include an accent over the *e*, as in that most famous street, the Champs Elysée, and in the original version of the word *résumé*.

To use Overstrike, place the cursor at the position where you want to type two or more characters, press the Format key (Shift-F8), select the *Other* option by typing *4* or *O,* then the Overstrike option by typing *5* or *O.* This brings up this prompt at the bottom of the Format: Other screen:

**1 Create; 2 Edit: 0**

Select the Create option by typing *1* or *C.* In response to the [Ovrstk] prompt, type the characters to be affected, such as the first *e* and the acute accent mark ( ´ ) in the word *résumé.* Next, press ⏎ three times to return to the Edit screen and finish typing the word. On the Edit screen, you will only see the last character, such as the acute accent mark ( ´ ) in our example, which will appear to replace the original character (*e*). However, when you use the Reveal Codes key (Alt-F3) you will see that both characters are still in your document, inside the formatting code [Ovrstk:e´], as shown in Figure 8.16. If your printer is capable, when you print this word both the *e* and the ´ will appear.

Once you have created a combination of characters to be overstruck, you can go back and make changes to it anytime. To edit a pair, position the cursor on the second overstruck character (the one you can see on the editing screen). Next, press the Format key (Shift-F8), select the *Other* option, then select Overstrike, and, finally, press *2* or *E* to select

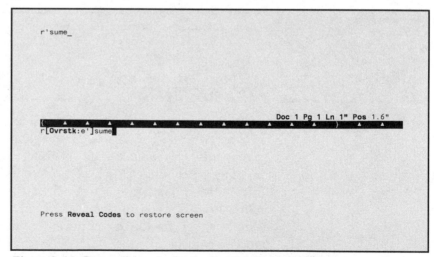

*Figure 8.16:* Overstrike codes in the Reveal Codes screen

Edit. This puts the cursor on the first character of the pair. After you have made your changes to the combination, press ◄—┘ then Exit (F7) to return to your document. Remember that you can verify your changes by using the Reveal Codes key (Alt-F3) and looking at the characters that are inside the bracketed Overstrike code.

## *COMPOSE*

Another method of creating special characters is to use the Compose key (Ctrl-2 or Ctrl-V). You can produce digraphs (combinations of two letters to represent one sound as in æ—in printing often referred to as *ligatures*) or diacriticals (accent marks added to letters to show how they are pronounced, like each é in *résumé*). For example, to produce the first *e* with an acute accent in résumé using the Compose key, you type *r*, press Ctrl-2 (nothing will appear to have happened), then type *e* followed by ´ (or another character that you use to represent the accent), and the properly accented é will appear on your screen. When entering the two characters with the Compose key, you can type them in any order and the results will be the same. (In other words, in our example, you could type *e* then ´ or ´ then *e*.)

When using the Compose key to produce special symbols and characters, you must make sure that your printer is capable of producing the character you have created on the screen. The Compose key can also be used to enter a special character that has already been defined in one of the WordPerfect character sets. You can see what characters are available in these sets by retrieving the file named CHARACTR.DOC. (To do this, use the regular retrieve methods: F5 1 or Shift-F10.) This file shows you the sequence of numbers used with the Compose key to produce each character as well as how the character will appear on your screen. If all you see is a solid box where the character should be, it means that your printer is incapable of producing the character.

The predefined character sets range from multinational ones that provide characters from Spanish, French, and German, such as the A diaeresis (Ä), C cedilla (Ç), and a grave (à), to those that use other alphabets, including Greek, Russian, Hebrew, and Japanese (Hiragana or Katakana). There are also character sets that include typographical symbols (for example, the paragraph sign, yen, pound/sterling, copyright sign, and en dash), mathematical and scientific symbols ( $\pm$ , $\leqslant \div$ , and $\Sigma$ ), and icon symbols (heart, happy

Do not confuse the Compose key, which is the Ctrl key together with the number 2 on the top row of the keyboard—not on the numeric keypad—with the Spell key, which is Ctrl together with the function key F2.

face, musical notes). To produce one of these characters, you press the Compose key (Ctrl-2) and type the number that corresponds to it (as shown in the *character.doc* file). For instance, if you are doing legal typing and need to produce the section symbol (§) in a document, you can use the Compose key to produce it. Look in the Typographic Symbol set, as shown in the *character.doc* file, and you will find that this symbol is produced by entering the sequence 4,6. To enter it into your document, you press the Compose key (Ctrl-2), type *4,6* (be sure to include the comma between the numbers), and press ←┘. As soon as you press ←┘, the section symbol will be displayed on your screen. Note that when you enter a special symbol or character (either with the Compose sequence or by entering two characters in succession), WordPerfect does not place any special formatting code in your document. In other words, if you view the character in the Reveal Codes screen, it will appear just as it does in the regular Edit screen. Therefore, to remove any characters or symbols entered with the Compose key, you simply delete them as you would any other character(s).

## REDLINE AND STRIKEOUT

Redline and Strikeout are two special formatting features used to designate editing changes. Strikeout is often used in legal documents to mark text that is to be deleted, by placing a line through the characters that will be removed. Redline has the opposite function; it is used to mark text that is being added to the document. Redline appears differently on various printers. On some, a vertical bar appears in the left margin next to each line that will be added. On color printers, the text appears in red. On laser printers such as the HP LaserJet Series II, Redline appears as a shadowed box around the text. Figure 8.17 shows the printed version of a line of text marked with Redline, and one marked by Strikeout (on an HP LaserJet printer).

This sentence is marked with redline.

This sentence is marked with strikeout.

*Figure 8.17:* Redline and Strikeout

To use Redline, press the Font key (Ctrl-F8) and select the Appearance option by typing *2* or *A*. The prompt shown below will appear:

**1 Bold; 2 Undrln; 3 Dbl Und; 4 Italc; 5 Outln; 6 Shadw; 7 Sm Cap; 8 Redln; 9 Stkout: 0**

Select option 8, Redln, by typing *8* or *R,* and begin typing the text that is to be marked with Redline. On color monitors, the text will actually be red. When you have finished entering this text, you must move the cursor outside of the pair of Redline formatting codes that WordPerfect uses (just as when boldfacing or underlining text). To turn off Redline, you have three alternatives: press → once to move beyond the second Redline code (the easiest method), press the Font key (Ctrl-F8) and select the Normal option (*3* or *N*), or repeat the key sequence that turned on redlining (Ctrl-F8 2 8).

If you want to redline text that has already been typed, you mark it using the Block key (Alt-F4), then press the Font key (Ctrl-F8), select Appearance (*2* or *A*), then Redln (*8* or *R*).

You can verify that your text is redlined by looking at the Reveal Codes screen (Alt-F3). When you do, your text will be surrounded by two formatting codes, [REDLN] just before the first character that was redlined, and [redln] after the last one.

You can change how the redline marking will appear on the printed page using the Format key. To do this, press the Format key (Shift-F8), select Document (*3* or *D*), then select Redline Method (*4* or *R*). The following menu appears at the bottom of the Format: Document screen:

**Redline Method: 1 Printer Dependent; 2 Left; 3 Alternating: 1**

The Printer Dependent option is the default; it marks redlining according to the instructions in your printer definition file. To find out what character is used by your printer, print the PRINTER.TST file (look for it in the List Files screen, move the cursor to it, and press the Print option). Options 2 and 3 determine where the Redline character appears on the page; you can also use these options to assign a new Redline character (the default may be a vertical bar, a box, or some other character, depending on the type of printer you selected. When you select option 2 or 3 on this menu, you see this prompt:

Redline character:

and the cursor is located under the current Redline character. To assign a new character, simply type it over the current one.

When you choose the Alternating option, WordPerfect marks red-lined text with the selected Redline character in the left margin on even-numbered pages and in the right margin on odd-numbered pages (useful when the pages are to be reproduced on both sides of the paper). When you choose the Left option, the selected Redline character is placed in the left margin on every page.

Strikeout works much like Redline. To turn on Strikeout, press the Font key (Ctrl-F8), select Appearance (*2* or *A*), select Stkout (*9* or *S*), then type the text. To turn off Strikeout, press either the → key once to move beyond the second formatting code [stkout] or the Font key and select Normal (*3* or *N*).

To use Strikeout with existing text, mark your text using Block (Alt-F4) and cursor movement keys, then press the Font key (Ctrl-F8), select the Appearance option (*2* or *A*), and then Stkout (*9* or *S*). The highlight-ing disappears and you can continue typing without having to turn off Strikeout (it won't affect the text you type afterward). In the Reveal Codes screen, you'll see a pair of Strikeout codes surrounding the text to be affected: [STKOUT] and [stkout].

After marking the text with one of these features, you can use the Mark Text key (Alt-F5) at any time to erase the Redline markings (not the text that's been redlined) and add the text to your document, and delete the Strikeout text. To do this, press Alt-F5 and select the Generate option by typing *6* or *G.* You'll see the Mark Text: Generate menu. The first option is *Remove Redline Markings and Strikeout Text from Document.* When you choose this option by typing *1* or *R,* the following prompt appears:

Delete redline markings and strikeout text? (Y/N) No

When you press *Y,* WordPerfect searches the entire document, deleting all text marked by Strikeout and erasing all markings used to Redline text.

# LINE NUMBERING

WordPerfect includes a Line Numbering feature that you can use to print line numbers in the left margin, as used in documents such as legal briefs. Line numbers are printed for the body of the document, as well as for all footnotes and endnotes. Although the numbers do not appear on the Edit screen, they can be viewed using the View Document feature—Shift-F7 6 or V. (See Chapter 9 for more information on using View Document.)

Several options are available when you use this feature: you can print numbers on every line or eliminate numbering from blank lines (except the blank lines generated by changing line spacing); use continuous numbering or restart numbering on each page; print numbers every *n* lines starting with the number *n;* and change the position where the numbers will be printed. You can turn numbering on and off as often as you wish in a dcoument. When you do, numbering restarts with the number 1.

To use Line Numbering, move the cursor to the top of the document (or wherever you want the numbers to begin) and press the Format key (Shift-F8). Select Line (*1* or *L*), then select Line Numbering (*5* or *N*) and type *Y* to set Line Numbering to Yes. The Format: Line Numbering screen illustrated in Figure 8.18 will appear. Select any options you wish to use from this menu (as described below), then press ◄—┘ twice to return to the document.

## THE LINE NUMBERING OPTIONS

Option 1, Count Blank Lines, is set to No. If you change it to Yes, the program will number every line in the document as long as it ends in a hard or soft return. Note that blank lines generated when you use double spacing (or any spacing other than single) do not end in a soft or hard return, so they are not counted regardless of your answer to the *Count Blank Lines* question. For example, Figure 8.19 shows a page from a legal brief that was formatted with double spacing, and for which the Count Blank Lines option was set to No. If you set the Count Blank Lines option to Yes, the results would be identical.

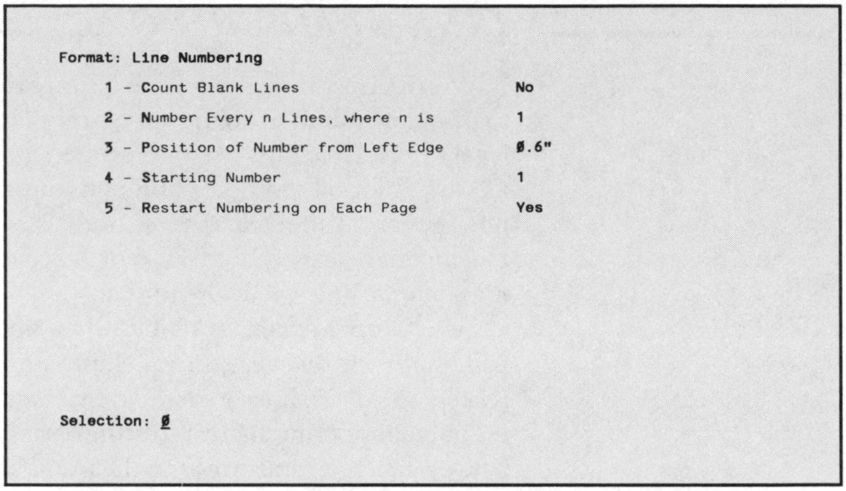

```
Format: Line Numbering

    1 - Count Blank Lines                        No

    2 - Number Every n Lines, where n is         1

    3 - Position of Number from Left Edge         0.6"

    4 - Starting Number                          1

    5 - Restart Numbering on Each Page           Yes




    Selection: 0
```

*Figure 8.18:* The Format: Line Numbering screen

Selecting Yes to count blank lines guarantees evenly placed numbering as long as line spacing is not mixed on a page. If a page includes varied spacing such as single spacing for the first ten lines and double
spacing for the rest, the numbers cannot be evenly placed.

Option 2, *Number Every n Lines, where n is,* can be used to change the
interval at which numbers are printed in the margin. For example, if
you change *n* to *2,* numbering will start with line 2 and only lines 2, 4, 6,
8, 10, 12, etc. will have a number next to them, as shown in the View
Document screen illustrated in Figure 8.20. Note that although the odd-
numbered lines are counted, the numbers themselves are not printed.

Option 3, *Position of Number from Left Edge,* allows you to change the
position where the number will be printed. The default is six tenths of
an inch. To change it, select *3* or *P* and type the distance from the left
edge of the paper (.5 for ½ inch, .7 for seven tenths of an inch, and so
on). Do not place them in a position where they coincide with text at
the margin. In other words, if your left margin is 1″ (the default), use
any number that is less than 1 inch.

Option 4, *Starting Number*, is used to begin line numbering with a
number other than the default, which is 1. To use it, just select the
option and enter the number that you want to use as the first number.
Note that you can use 0 as the starting number, but you cannot use
numbers with decimals (such as .5 or 1.5). When you make this change,
the cursor position determines where the new numbering will begin, so

```
 1   the ambiguity or uncertainty must be resolved in favor of
 2   apportionment, Smithfield, supra. at page 803.
 3        These rules of construction apply equally to determine
 4   whether the burden of California inheritance tax should be
 5   shifted from one transferee to others, Estate of Brown, 90 C.A.
 6   3d 582, 589 (1979).
 7        Finally, it is a judicial function to interpret written
 8   instruments unless the interpretations depends on the
 9   credibility of extrinsic evidence, Estate of Callahan, 6 C 3d
10   311,318 (1971). In this case, there was no testimony as to the
11   decedent's intentions, and the only extrinsic evidence
12   presented was the decedent's 1975 will, various uncontested
13   affidavits, and a stipulation that the decedent's attorney had
14   been in practice since 1923. Under these circumstances, the
15   interpretation of the relevant documents is a question of law,
16   Estate of Johnson, supra., at p 801, and it is the task of this
17   Court to medio at an independent interpretation of the
18   decedent's trust, Estate of Callahan, supra., at p. 602,
19   Estate of Jones, supra, at p. 534.
20        In the next section, Appellant will show that the
21   decedent's expressed intention regarding payment of the death
22   taxes equitably attributable to Respondent's accumulated
23   income is not clear and unambiguous, and the extrinsic
24   evidence which is available does not provide the necessary
25   clear and unambiguous intention. As a result, the death taxes
26   equitably attributable to Respondent's accumulated income must
```

*Figure 8.19:* A double-spaced page with line numbering

if you wish to alter the printed line numbers for the entire page, make sure that the cursor is at the top of that page before you press the Format key to turn on line numbering and select this option.

Option 5, *Restart Numbering on Each Page,* is set to Yes, meaning that the printed numbers on each page will always begin with the number

```
  2    apportionment, Smithfield, supra. at page 803.

            These rules ofconstruction apply equally todetermine whether
  4    the burden ofCalifornia inheritance tax should beshifted from one
       transferee to others, Estate of Brown, 90 C.A.3d 582, 589 (1979).
  6            Finally, it is a judicial function to interpret written
       instruments unless the interpretations depends on the credibility
  8    of extrinsic evidence, Estate of Callahan, 6 C 3d 311,318 (1971).
       In this case, there was no testimony as to the decedent's inten-
 10    tions, and theonly extrinsic evidence presentedwas the decedent's
       1975 will, various uncontested affidavits, and a stipulation that
 12    the decedent's attorney had been in practice since 1923. Under
       these circumstances, the interpretation of the relevant documents_
 14    been in practice since 1923. Under these circumstances, the
       interpretation of the relevant documents is a question of law,
 16    Estate of Johnson, supra., at p 801, and it is the task of this
       Court to arrive at an independent interpretation of the
 18    decedent's trust, Estate of Callahan, supra., at p. 602,
       Estate of Jones, supra, at p. 534.
 20        In the next section, Appellant will show that the
       decedent's expressed intention regarding payment of the death
 22    taxes equitably attributable to Respondent's accumulated
       income is not clear and unambiguous, and the extrinsic
 24    evidence which is available does not provide the necessary
       clear and unambiguous intention. As a result, the death taxes
 26    equitably attributable to Respondent's accumulated income must
```

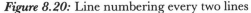

*Figure 8.20:* Line numbering every two lines

1. If you change it to No, numbering will start with *1* and be continuous on consecutive pages until the end of the document or until you turn Line Numbering off.

To turn Line Numbering off before the end of the document, press the Format key (Shift-F8), select Line, select Line Numbering (*5* or *N*), and type *N* to change Yes to No. Turning the feature on and off inserts the following codes in your document, visible only in the Reveal Codes screen:

[LnNum:On]                                                   [LnNum:Off]

# USING STYLES

Styles are a new and important feature of WordPerfect 5.0. You use styles to name and save sets of formatting codes that you use repeatedly for a particular type of application, such as margins, line spacing, fonts, and tab settings. For instance, if you type lists of instructions frequently, you can create styles to format the headings as centered and boldfaced, the first level of instructions with a hanging indent of 1/2 inch and line spacing of 1 1/2 lines, regular text as double spaced and right justified, and so forth. You can also include text in a style.

Styles are automatically saved with the document you created them in, but you can also save them as a separate file so that you can use them with any document you type. The real benefit of using styles is that if you change your mind about a particular formatting style in a document, you don't have to search through the document to erase all the pertinent codes and then insert new ones. Instead, you just change the code in the style, and the formatting in your document will change automatically.

## CREATING STYLES

To see how styles work, type the following list of instructions exactly as shown, without using any formatting (such as double spacing, tabs, or indents). You will then create several styles and apply them to your document so that it looks like the one shown in Figure 8.26.

EXERCISE 5: TABS
Tab stops are set for every 1/2 inch in WordPerfect 5.0. Press the Tab key several times to verify this fact. In this exercise, you will practice changing the tab stop settings.

1. Press the Format key (Shift-F8) and select Line, then Tab Set. The tab settings are marked with an L for left tab.
a. Press the Delete EOL key (Ctrl-End) to erase all tab settings.
b. Press 0 Return. Notice the two tab settings before the left

margin at 0 and 1/2 inch; these are used for the margin release
feature (Shift-Tab).

c. Set a tab stop at the 3 inch position by typing 3 then pressing
Return. Press Delete to erase it.

d. Use the right arrow key to move the cursor to the 4 inch
position, then press D to set a decimal tab.

e. Set tab stops every inch starting at 1 inch by typing 1,1 then
pressing Return.

2. Press Exit (F7) twice.

3. Press Reveal Codes (Alt-F3) to see the code for your new tab
settings.

When you finish typing, press the Save key (F10) and save the document under the name *Ex5tabs*.

Now you'll use the Style key, Alt-F8, to create four styles that you
can use to format your document. You will create a style for the heading *EXERCISE 5: TABS,* one for regular text, one for the level 1
instructions (1, 2, and 3) and one for the level 2 instructions (a, b, c,
d, and e).

1. Press the Style key, Alt-F8. You will see the Styles screen as
displayed in Figure 8.21.

2. Select Create (**3** or **C**) from the menu and you will see the
Styles: Edit menu as shown in Figure 8.22.

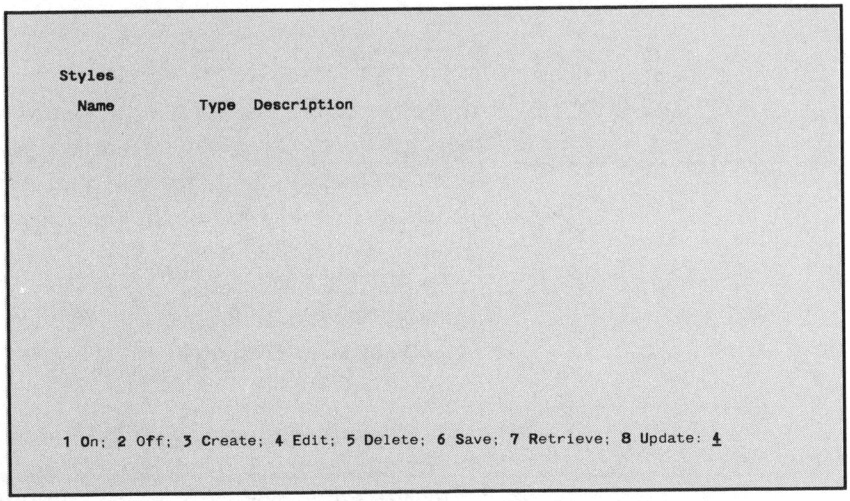

```
Styles
   Name          Type  Description




  1 On; 2 Off; 3 Create; 4 Edit; 5 Delete; 6 Save; 7 Retrieve; 8 Update: 4
```

*Figure 8.21:* The Styles screen

```
Styles: Edit

      1 - Name

      2 - Type              Paired

      3 - Description

      4 - Codes

      5 - Enter             HRt




Selection: 0
```

*Figure 8.22:* The Styles: Edit menu

3.  Enter a name for this style by selecting Name (**1** or **N**). For the name, type (in uppercase so it will stand out)

    **HEADINGS**

    and press ◄━┘.

      WordPerfect provides two choices for the Type option: paired and open. A *paired* style is used to surround a block of text, and you can turn it on and off so that it has a definite beginning and end. An *open* style is one that does not have an end, so you can only turn it on, and when you do it affects the rest of the document. The only open style you will create is the one for regular text, so leave the default of paired for the HEADINGS style.

4.  Select Description (**3** or **D**) to type a brief description of this style, with a maximum of 54 characters. Type

    **Center and boldface**

    and press ◄━┘.

5.  The next step is to insert the formatting codes for centering and bold. Select Codes (**4** or **C**) and you will see the screen in Figure 8.23.

      Notice that this screen is like the Reveal Codes screen except for the boxed document comment at the top that tells

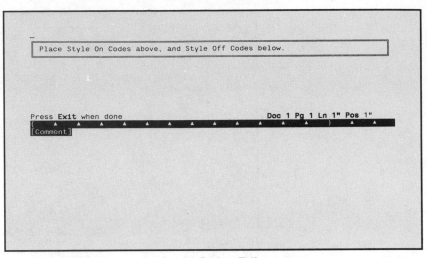

*Figure 8.23:* Selecting codes for the Styles: Edit menu

you where to place the Style On and Off codes. Since this is a paired style, you place the formatting codes you want to use with this style before (above) the [Comment] code, then place the codes to turn them off after (below) the [Comment] code. For instance, codes like Bold have to be turned on and off, so you would place the first Bold code before the comment and the second one after the comment.

6. To insert a Centering code, press the Center key (Shift-F6).

7. To insert a Bold code, press the Bold key (F6). This inserts a [BOLD] code in this screen, and will turn on boldfacing when you use the style.

8. Press → until the cursor is to the right of the Comment code, then press Bold (F6) again. This inserts a [bold] code and will turn off boldfacing at the end of the style when you apply it.

9. Press ←┘ to insert a [HRt] code. This will place an extra blank line after any paragraph formatted with this style.

10. The last step in creating this style is to press the Exit key (F7) twice. This returns you to the Styles menu, where you'll see the name, type, and description for your first style.

Now let's go back to your document and see how easy it is to apply this style to your heading.

1. Press the Exit key (F7) twice.

2. Place the cursor at the beginning of the document, on the *E* in *EXERCISE.*

3. Press the Block key (Alt-F4) then the End key to highlight the entire heading.

4. Press the Style key (Alt-F8). Use the arrow keys to highlight the HEADINGS style, then select On (**1** or **O**).

You will then be returned to your document, where you can see that your heading is now boldfaced and centered, and has an extra blank line following it. Wasn't that easy?

Now let's create the other three styles.

1. Press the Style key (Alt-F8) and select Create (**3** or **C**).

2. Select Name (**1** or **N**) and type (in uppercase)

    NORMAL TEXT

    Press ⏎.

3. Select Type (**2** or **T**) and change the type to Open (**2** or **O**).

4. Select Description (**3** or **D**) and type

    1 inch margins, tabs every 1/2″, double space

    Press ⏎.

5. Select Codes (**4** or **C**). Insert the formatting codes for margins, line spacing, and tabs by pressing Shift-F8 L M 1 ⏎ 1 ⏎ S 2 ⏎ T .5,.5 ⏎ F7 F7 F7. Since you are finished defining this style, press F7 again.

6. Select Create (**3** or **C**).

7. Select Name (**1** or **N**) and type (in uppercase)

    LIST LEV 1

    Press ⏎.

    This will be a paired style, so leave the default for option 2 (paired).

8. Select Description (**3** or **D**) and type

    Hanging indent, 1/2 inch

    Press ⏎.

9. Select Codes (**4** or **C**). Press F4 Shift-Tab to insert the formatting codes for a hanging indent. Press → to move the cursor beyond the [Comment] code, then press ◀── to insert a [HRt] code. Press F7.

The last option on this menu is Enter, and you can use it to change the function of the Enter key (◀──) when you are using a paired style. Pressing ◀── can insert a regular Hard Return code (the default), turn the style off, or turn the style off then turn it back on again. The third option is useful for styles such as this one, which includes formatting codes that affect the first line of each paragraph (the Indent and Margin Release codes), because it would allow you to turn the style on before you start typing, type as many paragraphs as you want using this style, then turn it off again. If you left the default, you would have to turn the style on and off before and after typing each paragraph.

10. Select Enter (**5** or **E**) and you will see this prompt at the bottom of the screen:

    **Enter: 1 Hrt; 2 Off; 3 Off/On: 0**

11. Select Off/On (**3** or **O**), then press Exit (F7).

12. Select Create (**3** or **C**), then Name (**1** or **N**), and type (in uppercase)

    **LIST LEV 2**

    Press ◀──.

    This will be a paired style, so leave the default for option 2 (paired).

13. Select Description (**3** or **D**) and type

    **Hanging indent, 1 inch**

    Press ◀──.

14. Select Codes (**4** or **C**). Press F4 F4 Shift-Tab to insert the formatting codes for a 1-inch hanging indent. Press → to move the cursor beyond the [Comment] code, press ◀── to insert a [HRt] code, then press F7.

15. Select Enter (**5** or **E**), select Off/On (**3** or **O**), then press F7.

You should now have four styles that you can apply to your document, and your screen should resemble Figure 8.24. Let's save these

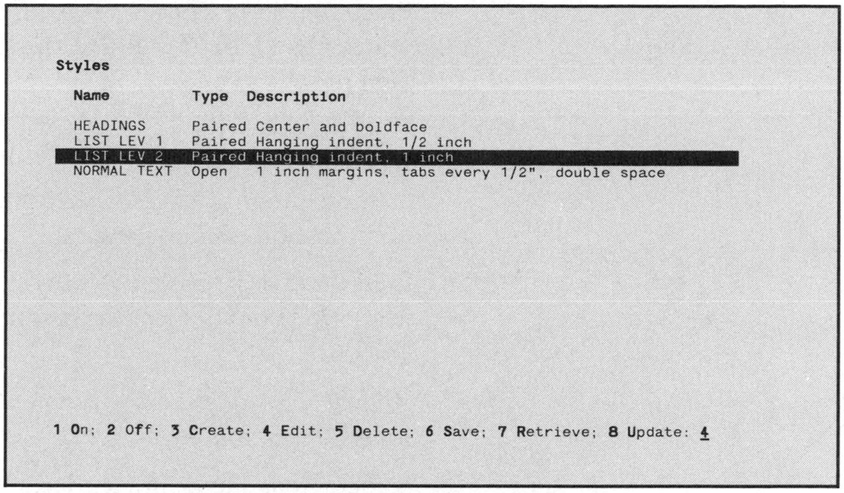

```
Styles

  Name          Type  Description

  HEADINGS      Paired Center and boldface
  LIST LEV 1    Paired Hanging indent, 1/2 inch
  LIST LEV 2    Paired Hanging indent, 1 inch
  NORMAL TEXT   Open  1 inch margins, tabs every 1/2", double space




  1 On; 2 Off; 3 Create; 4 Edit; 5 Delete; 6 Save; 7 Retrieve; 8 Update: 4
```

*Figure 8.24:* The Style screen after creating four styles

styles as a separate file so that you can use them again with other documents you type. To do this, you'll use the Save option from the Styles menu.

16. Select Save (**6** or **S**) and type this name:

> LISTS.STY

then press ◄━━┛.

## APPLYING STYLES TO A DOCUMENT

Now let's apply the new styles to the rest of your document. Remember, if you don't like the results, you can always change the formatting of the styles themselves in order to change the document.

1. Press Exit (F7) to return to your document. Place the cursor at the beginning of the first paragraph (on the *T* in *Tab*) where you'll apply the NORMAL TEXT style.

2. Press the Style key (Alt-F8), use ↓ to highlight the NORMAL TEXT style, then select On (**1** or **O**). You should see the effect on your document immediately, as the rest of the text changes to double spaced.

3. Block the next paragraph (instruction 1) by placing the cursor on the *1* and pressing Alt-F4 ◄━━┛ then ← once.

4. Press the Style key (Alt-F8), highlight *LIST LEV 1,* then select On (**1** or **O**). Place the cursor on the *P* in *Press,* then press Tab once to align *Press* with the indented position of the second line.

5. Block the next paragraph (instruction a) by placing the cursor on the *a,* pressing Alt-F4, then using the cursor movement keys to highlight the entire paragraph.

6. Press the Style key (Alt-F8), use ↓ to highlight *LIST LEV 2,* then select On (**1** or **O**). Place the cursor on the *P* in *Press,* then press Tab once.

7. Repeat steps 5 and 6 for the next four paragraphs (instructions b, c, d, and e).

8. Repeat steps 3 and 4 for the last two paragraphs (instructions 2 and 3).

Your document should now resemble Figure 8.25.

9. Save the document again by pressing F10 ↵ Y.

## *EDITING STYLES*

Now let's make some changes to your list of instructions. Suppose, for example, that you wanted to change the line spacing in the instructions to 1.5, and to add an extra indent to both levels. To do this, you just edit the styles for LIST LEV 1 and LIST LEV 2. Let's try it.

1. Press the Style key (Alt-F8) and use the arrow keys to highlight *LIST LEV 1.*

2. Select Edit (**4** or **E**).

3. Select Codes (**4** or **C**) then use the following keys to add another Indent code and then change the line spacing to 1.5: F4 Shift-F8 L S 1.5 ↵ F7 F7 F7.

4. Use the arrow keys to highlight *LIST LEV 2.*

5. Select Edit (**4** or **E**).

**EXERCISE 5: TABS**

Tab stops are set for every 1/2 inch in WordPerfect 5.0. Press the Tab key several times to verify this fact. In this exercise, you will practice changing the tab stop settings.

1. Press the Format key (Shift-F8) and select Line, then Tab Set. The tab settings are marked with an L for left tab.

   a. Press the Delete EOL key (Ctrl-End) to erase all tab settings.

   b. Press 0, Return. Notice the two tab settings before the left margin at 0 and 1/2 inch; these are used for the margin release feature (Shift-Tab).

   c. Set a tab stop at the 2 inch position by typing 2, then pressing Return. Press Delete to erase it.

   d. Use the right arrow key to move the cursor to the 4 inch position, then press D to set a decimal tab.

   e. Set tab stops every inch starting at 1 inch by typing 1,1 then pressing Return.

2. Press Exit (F7) twice.

3. Press Reveal Codes (Alt-F3) to see the code for your new tab settings.

*Figure 8.25:* Sample instructions after applying styles

6. Select Codes (**4** or **C**) then use the following keys to add another Indent code and to change the line spacing to 1.5: F4 Shift-F8 L S 1.5 ◄─┘ F7 F7 F7.

7. Press Exit (F7) to return to your document; you should immediately see the effects of the extra indent in both levels. You can't see 1.5 spacing on the screen, but you can move the cursor through the text and observe the line number indicator on the status line to tell that the spacing has been changed.

You could also try adding underlining to your HEADINGS style, or changing the NORMAL TEXT style back to single spacing. Here are the steps:

1. Press the Style key (Alt-F8), use the arrow keys to highlight *HEADINGS,* and select Edit (**4** or **E**).

2. Select Codes (**4** or **C**) then press the Underline key (F8) once. Use → to move the cursor to the right of the [Comment] code, then press F8 again to turn underlining off.

3. Press F7 twice.

4. Use the arrow keys to highlight *NORMAL TEXT,* then select Edit (**4** or **E**).

5. Select Codes (**4** or **C**) then place the cursor on the [Ln Spacing:2] code and press Delete.

6. Press Exit (F7) three times to return to your document and see how it has changed.

7. If you want to save the changes you just made to the styles in your LISTS.STY file, press the Style key (Alt-F8), select Save, and type **lists.sty** in response to the *Filename:* prompt.

***CHANGING FONTS***   If you are using a laser printer or a dot-matrix printer that can print in a variety of fonts, you could easily change the look of your document by including Font Change codes in your styles. For example, I changed the NORMAL TEXT style to a 12-point Times Roman font, the HEADINGS style to a 14-point

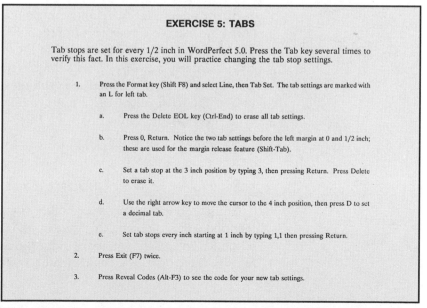

For more information about fonts, see Chapters 9 and 14.

Helvetica bold font (and removed the underline codes), and LIST LEV 1 and LIST LEV 2 to a 10-point Times Roman font. The results are shown in Figure 8.26.

Here are the steps you can use to change fonts. I use an HP Laser-Jet Series II printer with HP soft fonts for Times Roman and Helvetica, but the specific fonts available to you may differ.

1. Press the Style key (Alt-F8) and use the arrow keys to highlight *HEADINGS,* then select Edit (**4** or **E**).

2. Select Codes (**4** or **C**) then press the Font key (Ctrl-F8) and select Base Font (**4** or **F**) to see the list of fonts you have selected for use with your printer.

3. Use the arrow keys to highlight the font you want to use for your headings, then press **1** or **S** for Select.

4. Press F7 twice.

5. Repeat steps 1 through 4 for each style you wish to change.

6. Press Exit (F7) to return to your document and see how it has changed. Print your document or use View Document to see the font changes.

---

**EXERCISE 5: TABS**

Tab stops are set for every 1/2 inch in WordPerfect 5.0. Press the Tab key several times to verify this fact. In this exercise, you will practice changing the tab stop settings.

1. Press the Format key (Shift F8) and select Line, then Tab Set. The tab settings are marked with an L for left tab.

   a. Press the Delete EOL key (Ctrl-End) to erase all tab settings.

   b. Press 0, Return. Notice the two tab settings before the left margin at 0 and 1/2 inch; these are used for the margin release feature (Shift-Tab).

   c. Set a tab stop at the 3 inch position by typing 3, then pressing Return. Press Delete to erase it.

   d. Use the right arrow key to move the cursor to the 4 inch position, then press D to set a decimal tab.

   e. Set tab stops every inch starting at 1 inch by typing 1,1 then pressing Return.

2. Press Exit (F7) twice.

3. Press Reveal Codes (Alt-F3) to see the code for your new tab settings.

*Figure 8.26:* Sample instructions after changing fonts in the styles

7. If you want to save the changes you just made to the styles in your LISTS.STY file, press the Style key (Alt-F8), select Save, and type **lists.sty** in response to the *Filename:* prompt.

## USING STYLES WHILE TYPING TEXT

So far you have only learned how to apply styles after your text was typed. However, you can also use them as you are typing, turning them on before you enter text and, if you are using a paired style, turning them off again after you finish typing.

To use an open style before you begin typing, just press the Style key (Alt-F8), use the arrow keys to highlight the style name, and select On (*1* or *O*). Remember, open styles stay on and change the rest of the document. However, if you turn on another style after that, formatting codes in the open style can be overriden. For example, if you turn on the NORMAL TEXT style and type a paragraph, then turn on the LIST LEV 1 style and type a second paragraph, the spacing of 1.5 in the LIST LEV 1 style will override the double spacing from the NORMAL TEXT style and affect the second paragraph. When you turn off LIST LEV 1 style, text you type after that will be affected by the NORMAL TEXT style, so it will be double spaced.

To use a paired style before typing a paragraph, press the Style key (Alt-F8), use the arrow keys to highlight the style name, then select On (*1* or *O*). When you finish typing the text, press the Style key (Alt-F8) again, use the arrow keys to highlight the style name, then select Off (*2* or *F*). If your paired style changes the function of the ⏎ key to On/Off (as in your LIST LEV 1 and LIST LEV 2 styles), you can type several paragraphs in a row, then press Alt-F8 2 to turn it off when you're done using it.

## CREATING A STYLE FROM EXISTING CODES

You can create styles from codes in existing text by blocking the text and codes, pressing the Style key (Alt-F8), and selecting Create. The style will include all codes in the blocked section, but will exclude text. For example, you could create a style from the quotation shown in Figure 8.27. This paragraph was typed using an italic font (Ctrl-F8 A I), left and right indents (Shift-F4), and single spacing (Shift-F8 L S 1 ◄— F7 F7).

To try creating a style from existing codes, you can either type the paragraph shown in Figure 8.27 using the suggested formatting or find one of yours that already includes several formatting codes that you use often.

1. Press Reveal Codes (Alt-F3) and place the cursor at the beginning of the paragraph.

2. Press the Block key (Alt-F4), then press ◄— to highlight the entire paragraph, making sure all codes are included in your block.

3. Press the Style key (Alt-F8) and choose Create (**3** or **C**).

4. Select Codes (**4** or **C**) and you will see the codes from your paragraph (mine were left/right indent, italics, and single spacing). Notice that the text is not included. At this point, you can make changes if you want, then press F7 when you are done.

5. Select Name and assign a name to your style (I used *QUOTATIONS*).

6. Select Description and assign a description (I used *Italics, left/ right indent, single spaced*).

7. Press F7 twice. If you wish to save this style, remember to use the Save option from the Style menu before exiting from the document.

---

*Personally I'm always ready to learn, although I do not always like being taught.*

- Winston Churchill

---

*Figure 8.27:* A sample paragraph

## *RETRIEVING STYLES*

Since you saved your styles as a separate file under the name LISTS.STY, you can retrieve it and use it with any other document you create, or with any document you retrieve from the disk. However, you should not use the regular retrieval methods to retrieve it (the Retrieve option on the Lists Files key, F5, or the Retrieve Text key, Shift-F10). Instead, you press the Style key (Alt-F8) and select the Retrieve option (*7* or *R*) from the Styles menu. You will see a Filename prompt asking for the name of your style file, then you type its name and press ◄─┘. The styles you defined in the file will appear, and you can then press Exit (F7) to return to the Edit screen and apply them as though you had just defined them.

## *CREATING AND USING A STYLE LIBRARY*

You can ask WordPerfect to use a default set of styles called a *style library* by defining and saving the styles in a file, then using the Setup key to tell WordPerfect the file name and path. When you do this, WordPerfect will automatically retrieve the styles for use with any new document that you create, and they will be saved with the new document. If you retrieve a document that was created earlier without any styles, the default list of styles will be available for use with that document as well. If you created a document earlier and saved a separate set of styles with it, the default styles will not be available when you retrieve that document (but you can retrieve it and add it to your other list of styles by selecting the Update option in the Styles menu).

To use this feature, press the Setup key (Shift-F1) and select Location of Auxiliary Files (*7* or *L*). Next, select Style Library Filename (*6* or *L*), type the path and name of the file that contains your default styles, then press ◄─┘. Press Exit (F7) when you finish.

Once you have done this, you will find that when you start with a clear screen and press the Style key (Alt-F8), the default styles will already be available to you. Also, if you retrieve a document that you created earlier without any styles, you will find these styles available. If you want to use a different list of styles, use the Retrieve option on the Styles menu and both sets of styles will be available.

## *SUMMARY*

This chapter has given you some new tools and provided you with a more advanced understanding of a few of the old ones.

You've learned about the hyphenation zone and the various types of hyphens you can use in WordPerfect; the difference between left, right, center, and decimal tabs; how to insert and delete tabs and create automatic dot leaders to fill the space between tab stops, the Alignment Character features, and the Tab Align key; hard spaces; two new uses of the Date/Outline Key; how to format hanging paragraphs; super- and subscript characters; overstrike; redline and strikeout; how to use the Advance feature; how to create special characters such as scientific symbols, accent marks, and typographical symbols with the Compose Key; how to print line numbers in the left margin (as used in legal briefs); and how to use styles to standardize and facilitate formatting.

Now that you've read this far, you have practically mastered all of WordPerfect's formatting features. The remaining chapters cover the WordPerfect extras, those techniques that really set this program apart from the profusion of word processors on the market.

# GETTING THE MOST FROM
# YOUR PRINTER

# FAST TRACK

**To print the entire document that is on your editing screen,**     268
press the Print key (Shift-F7), then *1* or *F*.

**To print only the page on which the cursor is located,**     268
press the Print key (Shift-F7), then *2* or *P.*

**To print a document that is on disk,**     269
press the Print key (Shift-F7), then press *3* or *D*. At the *Document name:* prompt, type the name of the document to be printed, then press ◀━┘. WordPerfect then asks which pages you want to print. To print the entire document, press ◀━┘. To print a specific page or pages, enter the page numbers, separated by a comma, or a range of pages, separated by a dash.

**To print a document on disk using the List Files key,**     270
press F5, then ◀━┘ to see a list of all the files in the current directory. Use the arrow keys to move the cursor bar to the file you want to print, then press *4* or *P.* In response to the *Pages* prompt, enter the page numbers or press ◀━┘ to print all pages. Press the Space bar to exit from the List Files screen.

**To print a section of a document,**     272
move the cursor to the beginning of the section you want printed and press the Block key (Alt-F4). Move the cursor to the end of the section you want to print, then press the Print key (Shift-F7). At the *Print block?* message, press *Y.*

**To print the text that is currently visible on your screen,**     272
press the Print Screen key (Shift-PrtSc). Note that the status line and any prompt lines on the screen will also be printed.

**To stop or cancel a print job,**                                           274

> press the Print key (Shift-F7), select *4* or *C* (Control Printer),
> then press *5* or *S* to stop printing. To resume printing, press *G*.
> To cancel a print job, press *1* or *C* at the Control Printer menu
> and then press ← to cancel the current job or ← *Y* to cancel
> all jobs.

**To preview the way a page will look when printed,**                        277

> use the View Document option by pressing Shift-F7, then *6* or
> *V*. If your monitor has graphics capabilities, you will see a
> screen that shows the full page in small text; enlarge the text so
> you can read it (but view only part of the page) by pressing
> option *1* (100%) or *2* (200%), or press *4* to see two facing pages
> at once, such as pages 2 and 3.

**Install your printer**                                                     285

> by pressing the Print key (Shift-F7), then *S* for Select Printer. If
> your printer is not on the list, press *2* or *A* to see a list of
> printers; move the cursor bar onto your printer's name and
> press *1* or *S*, then ←. You will then see a Printer Helps and
> Hints screen that tells you about your printer. When you've
> read this screen, press Exit (F7) and you will see the Select
> Printer: Edit screen. You now can customize the printer set-
> tings. When you have finished, press Exit (F7) and you will see
> the Print: Select Printer screen. Select your printer from the list
> by moving the cursor onto the printer's name and pressing *1* or
> *S*. You will then be returned to the main Print menu.

WORDPERFECT'S PRINTING OPERATIONS ARE COMprehensive, flexible, and varied. For example, the Print key can be used to print an entire document or a single page, to select one or more documents from the disk and place them in a queue (waiting list) to be printed in turn, or to emulate a typewriter, typing text immediately onto a sheet of paper in the printer as you enter it. You can also use the Print key to select a new printer or preview the printout on the screen. In addition, you can use the Block key to print a marked section of a document, the List Files key to print a document from a directory listing without retrieving it for editing, and the Print Screen key to make a quick copy of the text on your screen. As you can see, you have many choices, so read carefully!

This chapter will describe the various printing methods, explain the terminology, and examine WordPerfect's printer control options. You will find out how to install a new printer and make use of all of its capabilities in WordPerfect, and you will learn to use the Font key to determine the size, style, enhancements, and color of the printed text. By the end of the chapter, you should have a clear understanding of WordPerfect's printing operations, which are, after all, among the most important functions of a word processor.

## THE PRINTING METHODS

The first thing you should learn is how to print your documents; WordPerfect provides you with many different methods. The two you will probably use most often—printing the full document and printing the current page—are found on the Print key (Shift-F7). When you press it you will see the menu shown in Figure 9.1.

```
Print

     1 - Full Document
     2 - Page
     3 - Document on Disk
     4 - Control Printer
     5 - Type Through
     6 - View Document
     7 - Initialize Printer

Options

     S - Select Printer            HP LaserJet Series II
     B - Binding                   Ø"
     N - Number of Copies          1
     G - Graphics Quality          Medium
     T - Text Quality              High




     Selection: Ø
```

**Figure 9.1:** The Print menu

## THE FULL DOCUMENT AND
## PAGE PRINTING OPTIONS ON THE PRINT KEY

By selecting the Full Document option (*1* or *F*), you can print the entire document that is currently on your editing screen. When you select the Page option (*2* or *P*), only the page on which the cursor is located will be printed. The Page method prints the entire page, not just the part visible on your screen, and will do this regardless of where the cursor is placed on the page.

Both of these methods create a temporary copy of the file in RAM or, if there is not enough room in your computer's memory, on the default disk. If you're printing a lengthy document and the disk does not have enough room for another copy, you will see a *disk full* error message on your screen. If you encounter this problem, you'll have to use one of the two methods of printing from the existing disk file, as described in the next section.

## TWO METHODS
## OF PRINTING A DOCUMENT ON DISK

WordPerfect includes two methods of printing a document from the disk: the Document on Disk option on the Print key (Shift-F7) and the Print option on the List Files key (F5). Bear in mind that when you print the document on disk using one of these two methods, you are printing the document as you last saved it (that is, as the file exists on the disk). If you have retrieved the document and made changes since last saving it, use the Save Text key (F10) to save the file before issuing the Print command. If you don't, the changes will not appear in the printed version.

You should also be aware of how the Fast Save option on the Setup key (Shift-F1) will affect these printing methods. With Fast Save set to Yes, WordPerfect saves your document without formatting it, reducing the time it takes to save it. However, the two methods of printing from disk may not work if you use Fast Save. In fact, the only way you can print a document from disk that was saved this way is if you had pressed Home Home ↓ just before you saved it. If you did not, you'll see this error message when you try to print through the List Files method or the Document on Disk method:

ERROR: Document was Fast Saved – Must be retrieved to print

If this happens, you have two options. You can retrieve the file and print it using the Full Document or Page option on the Print key (Shift-F7), or you can retrieve the file, press Home Home ↓, then save it and print it from disk using the Document on Disk or List Files option.

You can prevent this problem altogether by changing the Fast Save option to No. To do this, you press the Setup key (Shift-F1), select Fast Save (*4* or *F*), and type *N* to change it to No. Once you change it, this setting will remain in effect each time you start Word-Perfect (unless you later return to the Setup menu and change it back to Yes). Although it will take slightly longer to save your files with Fast Save set to No, this will enable you to use the Document on Disk and List Files print methods for any new documents that you create.

***THE DOCUMENT ON DISK OPTION***  The first method of printing a document from the disk is to use the Document on Disk option (3 or D) on the Print key (Shift-F7). When you select this option, this prompt appears at the bottom of the Print menu screen:

Document name:

Refer to Chapter 15 for information about paths and directories.

Here, you type the name of the document to be printed, then press ↵. If the document is not located in the current directory, be sure to enter its path as part of the file name, such as \\*WP*\\*filename*. As soon as you press ↵, WordPerfect tries to find the file on the disk. If it can't locate the file, it responds with this prompt:

**ERROR: File not found**

and redisplays the *Document name:* prompt, waiting for you to type a different file name. If this happens, you can either type another name or press Cancel (F1) twice then use the List Files key (F5) to help you find the file and print it (as described below).

If WordPerfect does find the file, you see this prompt:

**Page(s): (All)**

If you press ↵ at this point, WordPerfect prints the entire document. If you want to restrict printing to specific pages, you can enter individual page numbers separated by commas, such as *5,7,9* or a range of pages separated by a dash, such as *2–12,* or you can mix both a range of numbers and individual page numbers such as *1–5,12,15.* Typing a page number followed by a dash (such as *6–*) prints everything from that page through the last one in the document, and typing a page number preceded by a dash (*–6*) prints everything from the first page through (and including) that page.

If you want to print more than one document (and are using continuous paper or a cut-sheet feeder), you can continue selecting documents using this method, and they will be printed in the order you select them. WordPerfect assigns each document a job number and places it in the print job list (often called the *print queue*). If you forget the sequence, the Job List section of the Print: Control Printer screen displays the name of each document and a job number corresponding to it. To view this screen, you select Control Printer (*4* or *C*) on the Print key (Shift-F7). The information provided on this list will be explored in depth later in this chapter, in the section on printer control.

***PRINTING THROUGH THE LIST FILES KEY***   If you forget the exact name of a file you want to print and receive an error message when you try to use the Document on Disk option from the Print key, use the second method of printing from disk, the Print option on the List Files key (F5). When you press F5, you see the DOS directory command, DIR, followed by the letter corresponding to your default drive, the name of your current directory (if you are using a hard disk), and the wild-card characters *.*. For example, if your current directory is on drive C and is named *WP,* the prompt will appear like this:

Dir C:\WP\*.*

The asterisks are called *wild cards,* and if you press ◂──┘ they will produce a list of all files in the current directory. You can restrict the list to specific files using criteria such as file names that start with a certain letter or that end in a three-character extension such as .LTR. You can also type a different drive and/or directory name to view the list of files it contains.

Once you see the list of files, use the arrow keys to move the cursor bar onto the file you want to print, as shown in Figure 9.2, then press *4* or *P* to select the Print option. If you want to print more than one file from the List Files screen, move the cursor bar to each one individually and mark it by pressing the asterisk key. This places an asterisk after the file size statistic in the third column. Once you've marked all the files you want to print, press *4* or *P* to select the Print option. This prompt will appear:

Print marked files? (Y/N) No

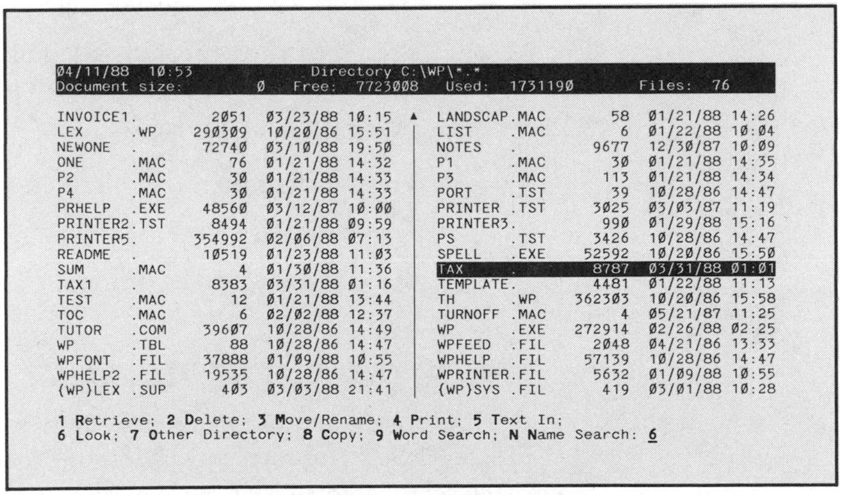

> If you are unfamiliar with the DIR command and the List Files key, see Chapter 15 for more help.

```
04/11/88  10:53              Directory C:\WP\*.*
Document size:        0   Free:   7723008   Used:   1731190      Files:  76

INVOICE1.           2051  03/23/88 10:15 ▲  LANDSCAP .MAC         58  01/21/88 14:26
LEX      .WP      290309  10/20/86 15:51     LIST     .MAC          6  01/22/88 10:04
NEWONE   .         72740  03/10/88 19:50     NOTES    .          9677  12/30/87 10:09
ONE      .MAC         76  01/21/88 14:32     P1       .MAC         30  01/21/88 14:35
P2       .MAC         30  01/21/88 14:33     P3       .MAC        113  01/21/88 14:34
P4       .MAC         30  01/21/88 14:33     PORT     .TST         39  10/28/86 14:47
PRHELP   .EXE      48560  03/12/87 10:00     PRINTER  .TST       3025  03/03/87 11:19
PRINTER2 .TST       8494  01/21/88 09:59     PRINTER3 .           990  01/29/88 15:16
PRINTER5 .        354992  02/06/88 07:13     PS       .TST       3426  10/20/86 14:47
README   .         10519  01/23/88 11:03     SPELL    .EXE      52592  10/20/86 15:50
SUM      .MAC          4  01/30/88 11:36     TAX      .          8787  03/31/88 01:01
TAX1     .          8383  03/31/88 01:16     TEMPLATE .          4481  01/22/88 11:13
TEST     .MAC         12  01/21/88 13:44     TH       .WP      362303  10/20/86 15:58
TOC      .MAC          6  02/02/88 12:37     TURNOFF  .MAC          4  05/21/87 11:25
TUTOR    .COM      39007  10/28/86 14:49     WP       .EXE     272914  02/26/88 02:25
WP       .TBL         88  10/28/86 14:47     WPFEED   .FIL       2048  04/21/86 13:33
WPFONT   .FIL      37888  01/09/88 10:55     WPHELP   .FIL      57139  10/28/86 14:47
WPHELP2  .FIL      19535  10/28/86 14:47     WPRINTER .FIL       5632  01/09/88 10:55
(WP)LEX  .SUP        403  03/03/88 21:41     (WP)SYS  .FIL        419  03/01/88 10:28

1 Retrieve; 2 Delete; 3 Move/Rename; 4 Print; 5 Text In;
6 Look; 7 Other Directory; 8 Copy; 9 Word Search; N Name Search: 6
```

*Figure 9.2:* Choosing a file from the List Files screen

If you type *Y*, the marked documents will be printed in the order in which you selected them. When you finish selecting files to print, press the Space bar to exit from the List files screen.

## PRINTING USING THE BLOCK FEATURE

What can you do if you want to print only a small section of the document? As you learned above, the Full Document and Page options on the Print menu (Shift-F7) allow you to print an individual page or an entire document from the Edit screen, but nothing in between, and the two methods of printing from disk can only print the entire document or a range of pages that you specify. When you want to print a portion of a document that does not fit into page units, neither of these methods works. Instead, you have to retrieve the file, use the Block key to mark the section you want to print, then print it. Since we've already covered this subject in Chapter 5, we'll limit this discussion to a brief review.

To print a block, follow these steps:

1. Move the cursor to the beginning of the section you want printed and press the Block key (Alt-F4). A *Block on* message will appear in the lower left corner of the screen.

2. Move the cursor to the end of the section you wish to print. The entire block will appear highlighted on the screen and the Block on message will still be visible.

3. Press the Print key (Shift-F7). This prompt will appear on the status line, asking if you wish to print the highlighted block:

   Print block? (Y/N) No

4. Press **Y**. This message will briefly appear on the status line:

   * Please wait *

   then the block will be printed.

## PRINTING WITH THE PRINT SCREEN KEY

If you want a "quick and dirty" printout, use the Print Screen key (Shift-PrtSc). This method will print the text that is currently visible on your screen as though it were taking a picture of it and sending it to your printer. Note that the status line and any prompt lines that may be on your screen when you press these keys will also be printed, which may be acceptable for rough drafts, but not for your final work.

## CONTROLLING THE PRINTER

When you ask WordPerfect to print a document using any of the methods described above (except the Print Screen key method), it assigns a job number to the task and places it in the print job list (often called the print queue). If you ask to print more than one document, WordPerfect assigns sequential numbers to them, and lines them up to await their turn at the printer. The number of print jobs that can be added to this list depends on the amount of free disk space you have and the size of each file you are printing. You can view the job list by pressing the Print key (Shift-F7), then pressing *4* or *C* to select Control Printer. When you do, you'll see the Print: Control Printer screen shown in Figure 9.3. The description of each print job will remain visible on this screen until the document has been printed, so you'll always know what your printer is doing (or is supposed to be doing). As you can see, this menu also provides several options that you can use to manage the printer, including stopping or canceling print jobs, rushing a print job, and displaying additional jobs if you asked WordPerfect to print more than three documents.

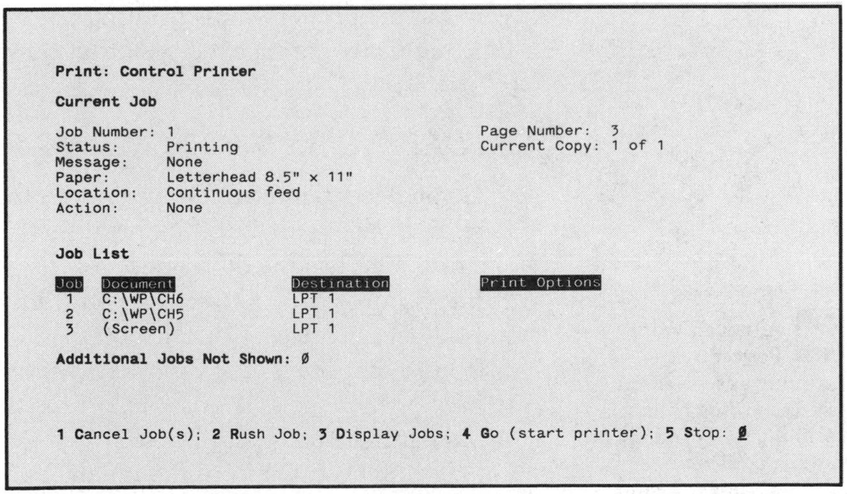

```
Print: Control Printer

Current Job

Job Number: 1                              Page Number:  3
Status:     Printing                       Current Copy: 1 of 1
Message:    None
Paper:      Letterhead 8.5" x 11"
Location:   Continuous feed
Action:     None


Job List

Job  Document                 Destination           Print Options
 1   C:\WP\CH6                LPT 1
 2   C:\WP\CH5                LPT 1
 3   (Screen)                 LPT 1

Additional Jobs Not Shown: 0



1 Cancel Job(s); 2 Rush Job; 3 Display Jobs; 4 Go (start printer); 5 Stop: 0
```

***Figure 9.3:*** The Print: Control Printer screen with three documents in the job list

## THE PRINT JOB LIST

Once you ask WordPerfect to print a document, it is placed on the job list and you can continue to edit it or another document while the printer is working (although the changes you make will not appear in the printed version). However, your printer may slow down or stop while you are performing operations that access the disk, such as moving the cursor to the top of a long document or saving a document.

Figure 9.3 shows a Print: Control Printer screen with three jobs on the list. As you can see from the Job Number and Job Status messages, Job 1 is currently printing. The Document column of the Job List section indicates that Job 1 is the file named CH6. After Job 1 has been printed, Job 2 will begin and the file named CH5 will be printed. When this is done, Job 3 will be printed.

Notice that Job 3 is described as *screen;* this means that it is the document currently on the Edit screen. This document was sent to the printer by pressing the Print key (Shift-F7) and selecting the Full Document option from the Print menu.

Look again at the Current Job section at the top of the screen. The message line is reserved for error messages; you'll see an example in the next section. The Paper message tells you what type of form you are using, such as letterhead 8.5″ × 11″ paper. The Location message tells you how the paper is fed into the printer, such as continuous or manual feed. The Page Number message on the right side informs you that the printer is now printing page 3 of the document, and the Current Copy message tells you that only one copy will be printed.

## STOPPING AND CANCELING PRINT JOBS

If you need to interrupt the printer temporarily because of a problem like a paper jam, but want printing to continue once you've fixed the problem, use the Stop option on the menu at the bottom of the Print: Control Printer screen. If you want to cancel one or more print jobs altogether, select Cancel Job(s).

To use Stop, press the Print key (Shift-F7), select Control Printer (*4* or *C*), then press *5* or *S*. Selecting this option should stop the printer immediately and cause it to pause until you select the Go (start printer) option from the menu, but printing may continue for awhile if your printer has a large memory buffer.

Although Word-Perfect tries to stop printing as soon as you select the Stop option, printing may continue for awhile until your printer's buffer is empty.

When you select Stop, the Job Status line in the Current Job section indicates that the printer is stopped and the Message line explains what to do:

> Adjust paper (press FORM FEED or advance paper to top of page). Press "G" to restart, "C" to cancel

The *Reset top of form* message is a reminder that you have to adjust the printer so that the printhead is at the beginning of a new sheet of paper before continuing (by pressing *G*). (This does not apply to laser printers.) This is because when you start the printer again by selecting the Go (start printer) option, the printer will start printing the document from the beginning, but will not advance the paper to a new page.

If you wish to cancel one or more print jobs, select the Cancel Job(s) option from the menu at the bottom of the screen by pressing *1* or *C*. You will then see this message at the bottom of the screen:

> Cancel which job? (* = All Jobs) 1

(where *1* is the number of the job currently being printed). At this point, you can either press ⏎ to cancel the current job, type a different job number to cancel another job, or type an asterisk to cancel all printing. If you enter an asterisk, you'll see this prompt (shown in Figure 9.4):

> Cancel all print jobs? (Y/N) No

Press *Y* to cancel all printing.

## RUSHING A PRINT JOB

The Rush Job option (2 or R) can be used to send a job to the beginning of the list and print it immediately. This is helpful when you are printing a long list of documents and suddenly discover that one is urgently needed. Rather than cancel all the print jobs and start over, you can use the Rush Job feature to print it immediately.

When you press *2* or *R*, a prompt will appear asking which job to rush (if there are multiple print jobs on the list). After you enter the

```
Print: Control Printer

Current Job

Job Number:  1                          Page Number:  3
Status:      Printing                   Current Copy:  1 of 1
Message:     None
Paper:       Letterhead 8.5" x 11"
Location:    Continuous feed
Action:      None


Job List

Job  Document              Destination          Print Options
 1   C:\WP\CH6             LPT 1
 2   C:\WP\CH5             LPT 1
 3   (Screen)             LPT 1

Additional Jobs Not Shown: Ø



Cancel all print jobs? (Y/N) No
```

*Figure 9.4:* The current job listing after interrupting the printer

number from the job list, another prompt will appear asking if you wish to interrupt the current job. If you type *Y* and press ◄─┘, you will see this prompt on the Action line:

### Completing page, press R to rush job immediately

Press *R* and the printer will stop printing the current document and start printing the rush job, resuming the current one after that. When the rush job is finished, the interrupted job will begin again at the top of the page that was being printed when you interrupted it. If you type *N,* the printer will not print the rush job until the current document is finished.

## THE DISPLAY JOBS OPTION

Since the Job List can only display three print jobs, the Display Job option (3 or D) allows you to view the others, if there are any. Notice the message at the bottom of the Print: Control Printer screen in Figure 9.4:

### Additional Jobs Not Shown: 0

If a number other than 0 appears here, use the Display Jobs option to see the list of remaining jobs. When you do, you'll see a screen resembling Figure 9.5. When you finish viewing it, press any key to return to the Control Printer screen.

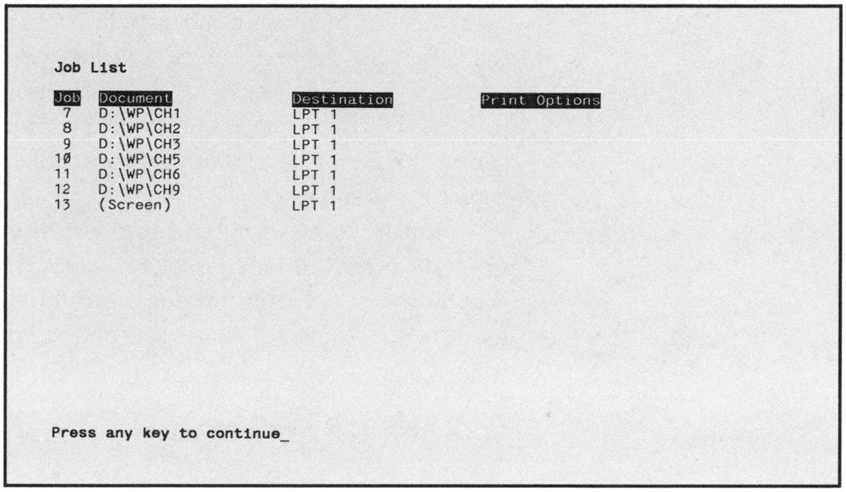

```
Job List

Job   Document              Destination       Print Options
  7   D:\WP\CH1             LPT 1
  8   D:\WP\CH2             LPT 1
  9   D:\WP\CH3             LPT 1
 10   D:\WP\CH5             LPT 1
 11   D:\WP\CH6             LPT 1
 12   D:\WP\CH9             LPT 1
 13   (Screen)             LPT 1




Press any key to continue_
```

*Figure 9.5:* The Additional Job List screen

## PREVIEWING THE PRINTOUT ON SCREEN

As you know, some WordPerfect features cannot be viewed on screen and appear only when printed. Among them are italics; line height; graphics; fonts in different point sizes; right justification; proportional spacing; left, right, top, and bottom margins; headers and footers; endnotes and footnotes; page numbers; and subscripts and superscripts. However, by using the View Document option on the Print key (Shift-F7), you can obtain a display that is much closer to the printed version, and save yourself some time and paper by previewing the way the document will look when printed. Not only will the margins be accurately portrayed in the View Document screen, but headers, footers, page numbers, footnotes, and endnotes will be included and various font sizes can be seen. Right justification is also shown. If you have a monitor with graphics capability, you can see graphics as well. Although you will be able to scroll through the document you are viewing using the regular cursor movement keys, you won't be able to make any editing changes until you press the Exit key (F7) and return to the Edit screen.

The View Document feature is extremely useful when you are working with complex layouts such as those that use multiple columns or that mix text and graphics. It also helps when you use features such as page numbers and headers and footers, so that you can tell if they are correct before sending the document to the printer.

When you select the View Document option by pressing Shift-F7 V (or Shift-F7 6), the page that the cursor is currently on will appear in a special screen. Its actual appearance will vary according to the type of monitor you have.

If you have a color monitor or a monochrome monitor with a graphics interface (such as a Hercules monochrome card), you will see the layout of the entire page, but the text will be too small to read, as shown in Figure 9.6. At the bottom of the screen, you'll see this menu:

**1 100%  2 200%  3 Full Page  4 Facing Pages: 3**

The Full Page option is in effect initially. You can use the first two options, 100% and 200%, to enlarge the page to actual size or twice actual size (respectively) as shown in Figures 9.7 and 9.8.

For more information about how you can use the View Document option to help with desktop publishing applications such as form layout or newsletters, see Chapter 14.

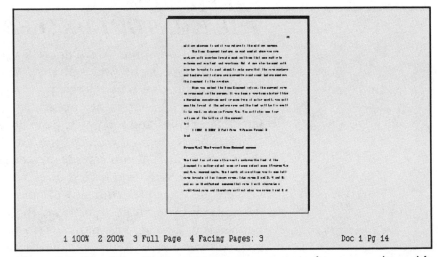

*Figure 9.6:* The View Document screen on a monochrome monitor with graphics capabilities

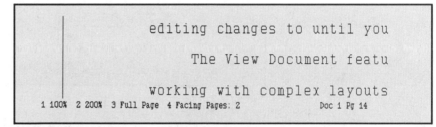

```
                                                                    14

         editing changes to until you return to the editing screen.
              The View Document feature is most useful when you are
         working with complex layouts such as those that use multiple
         columns and mix text and graphics. But it can also be used with
         simpler layouts to just check to make sure that the page numbers
         and headers and footers are correctly positioned before sending
         the document to the printer.
              When you select the View Document option, the current page
         is previewed on the screen. If you have a graphics adapter (like
         a Hercules monochrome card or some type of color card), you will
    1 100%  2 200%  3 Full Page  4 Facing Pages: 1              Doc 1 Pg 14
```

*Figure 9.7:* The document in the View Document screen at 100%

```
                     editing changes to until you

                        The View Document featu

                     working with complex layouts
    1 100%  2 200%  3 Full Page  4 Facing Pages: 2              Doc 1 Pg 14
```

*Figure 9.8:* The document in the View Document screen at 200%

The fourth option, Facing Pages, allows you to view full-page layouts of two facing pages, such as pages 2 and 3 or pages 4 and 5, as shown in Figure 9.9. Note that WordPerfect assumes that page 1 will always be a right-hand page and will not show you pages 1 and 2 of your document when you use this option.

If you have a color monitor, you can use the Setup key to change the View Document screen so that it is displayed in black and white instead of in color. To do this, press Setup (Shift-F1) and select Display, and then select View Document in Black & White. Type **Y**, then press Exit (F7). When you look at the View Document screen, if you find that the background is black and text is white, you can press Switch (Shift-F3) to reverse it.

If you have a monochrome monitor without graphics capabilities, you won't be able to blow up the page or display facing pages when you use View Document (Figure 9.10). Instead, you will see a screen very similar to the regular Edit screen except that the status line will be different (it will only show the document and page number indicators), and you'll see the top and left margins immediately. You'll also be able to see any features such as page numbers, headers, footers, footnotes, or endnotes that you've used, and if you used right

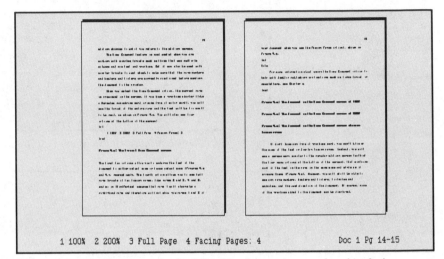

1 100%   2 200%   3 Full Page   4 Facing Pages: 4          Doc 1 Pg 14-15

***Figure 9.9:*** The document in the View Document screen showing facing pages

April 15, 1988

Mr. Raymond Vaughn
Western District Sales Manager
2134 Main Street
San Ramon, California 90122

Dear Ray:

     We sure are proud of you!  Once again you'veoutdone everyone

in the district  with phenomenal sales figures.  In  fact, if you

close the deal with Johnson next week, you'll probably  set a new

national sales record, unprecedented forthe month of January.Keep

**Doc 1 Pg 1_**

***Figure 9.10:*** The View Document screen on a monochrome monitor with no graphics capabilities

justification, your right margin will appear even instead of ragged as it does on the Edit screen.

### MOVING THE CURSOR
### IN THE VIEW DOCUMENT SCREEN

Cursor movement techniques are covered in Chapters 1 and 3.

When previewing a document with the View Document option, you can use any of the regular cursor movement keys such as ↑, ↓, ←, and → to scroll new sections of text into view. If you have more than one page in your document, you can use keys like Page Up and Page Down, Screen Up and Screen Down, and the Go To Page keys (Ctrl-Home and page number) to go directly to a specific page in the document. Remember, you cannot make editing changes in the View Document screen. You can return to the Edit screen anytime by pressing the Exit key (F7).

### DOWNLOADING
### SOFT FONTS INTO YOUR PRINTER

The Initialize Printer option (7 or I) on the Print menu (Shift-F7) allows you to load soft fonts into your printer's memory from within WordPerfect before you print, a process called *downloading*. When you use this option by pressing the Print key (Shift-F7), then 7 or I, WordPerfect downloads the fonts you have selected for use with your printer through the Select Printer: Cartridges and Fonts menu (which is explained later in this chapter). Note that the fonts must have been marked with an asterisk in this menu, to signify that they are to be present when the print job begins. Also, Initialize Printer will only work if you have used option 7 on the Select Printer: Edit screen (Shift-F7 S E) to specify the path where the downloadable fonts are located. On certain printers, such as the HP LaserJet Series II, selecting the Initialize Printer option will also clear the printer's memory buffer, removing all other fonts or codes that are currently in the printer's memory buffer. For more information about soft fonts, see "Selecting Fonts for Your Printer" later in this chapter.

# USING YOUR COMPUTER AND PRINTER AS A TYPEWRITER

Even though the typical business office is well stocked with word processors, that old white elephant known as the typewriter can still be found on many desks, where it is occasionally used for odd jobs such as envelopes, loan applications, and other printed forms that do not lend themselves well to a standard word processor. However, WordPerfect's Type Through feature may convince you to abandon this quaint mechanism once and for all, because Type Through effectively converts your computer and printer into a typewriter and prints text immediately onto a sheet of paper while you are typing it. Type Through can be used to type character-by-character or line-by-line. Either way, it's a convenient and readily accessible feature.

Type Through has no effect on the document on your Edit screen, so you can use it to type an envelope or form anytime, even if you're typing something else on one or both of your Edit screens (Doc 1 and Doc 2). Whatever text you enter in Type Through will only affect the sheet of paper in your printer, and will not appear on the Edit screen.

Some printers cannot use Type Through, including the Canon Laser printer and the Hewlett-Packard LaserJet printers. Others can use it, but are limited to the line-by-line typing method. If your printer is not able to take advantage of this feature, you'll see this message when you select the Type Through option:

**Feature not available on this printer**

## LINE TYPE THROUGH

To use Line Type Through, press Print (Shift-F7), then press *5* or *Y.* This prompt appears, asking you to select one of the two methods:

**Type Through by: 1 Line; 2 Character**

If you press *1* or *L,* Line, you will see the screen shown in Figure 9.11.

The next step is to position your paper in the printer so that the printhead is placed on the first line to be printed, just as you would in a typewriter, then type the first line of text. If you want the text printed to the right, as in addressing an envelope, press the Space bar to move the cursor over before typing the text. As soon as you press

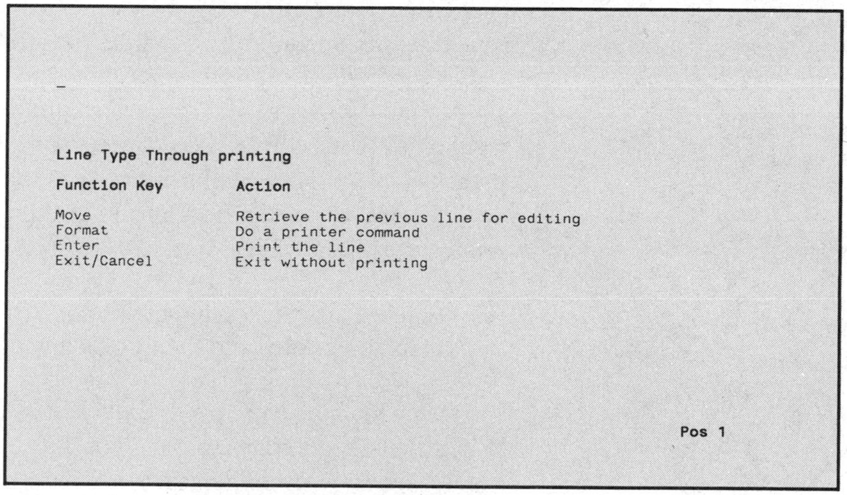

```
—

Line Type Through printing

Function Key        Action

Move                Retrieve the previous line for editing
Format              Do a printer command
Enter               Print the line
Exit/Cancel         Exit without printing




                                                              Pos 1
```

*Figure 9.11:* The Line Type Through screen

◄—, the line will be printed and a carriage return signal will be sent to the printer, moving the printhead to the next line.

If you make a mistake before you press ◄—, you can move the cursor back and fix it, but cursor movement methods are limited compared to those in normal Edit mode. The arrow keys on the numeric keypad can be used to move the cursor right or left one position at a time, and Home → or Home ← can be used to move to the beginning or end of a line. Press ◄— when you are done editing to print the line; the cursor does not have to be at the end of the line. According to the WordPerfect manual, if you press ↑ or ↓ the printhead will move up or down a line on your sheet of paper (don't press ◄—), but on some printers, ↑ does not work. Pressing ◄— by itself will also move the paper down by a line.

As the screen indicates under the headings *Function Key* and *Action*, certain WordPerfect function keys can be used in Type Through. For example, the Move key (Ctrl-F4) can be used to place a copy of the previous line on the current line, so that you can use it over again, either without change or in an edited form. The Format key can be used to send a special command to your printer in order to change the print style. For instance, you may want to switch your dot matrix printer to condensed mode in order to fit more characters on the line. To do this, find the appropriate code in your printer manual, press the Format key (Shift-F8), then in response to the *Command:* prompt, type the appropriate printer code and press ←.

Using Type Through, you can type up to 250 characters on a single line. The text will not word wrap; the screen just "pans" to the right on the same line to keep the cursor in view. However, when you press ←, the printer will print only as much as it can fit on a line (on a wide printer this can be a large number). If it runs out of space you see this error message:

**Printer is not accepting characters. Press EXIT or Cancel to quit or fix the printer and then press any other key to continue.**

When this happens, press Exit (F7) or Cancel (F1) and start over. When the screen starts to pan, you have typed 80 characters. If you are unsure how many characters will fit on a line on your form, just try it out. If you don't want to waste a form, measure it with a ruler and draw a line of the same width on a piece of scratch paper, then practice by typing on the scratch paper and counting the characters.

## CHARACTER TYPE THROUGH

Line Type Through has one important advantage over the character-by-character method: you have a chance to correct any typing errors on screen before you press the ← key and send the line to the printer. By contrast, the Character Type Through method sends each character to the printer as soon as it is typed, so if you make a mistake it can ruin your form. On the other hand, you do get immediate feedback on paper and more of a typewriter feel.

To use Character Type Through, follow the same steps outlined above, except that you press *2* or *C,* Character, after pressing Shift-F7 5 or Y. A screen similar to the Line Type Through screen shown in Figure 9.11 will appear.

As soon as you type a character, it will be printed on the paper at the printhead position (assuming your printer is capable of using this feature). Remember that you will not be able to change it after typing it. After printing one or more characters, you can clear them from the screen by using the Delete EOP key (Ctrl-PgDn). If you are finished typing, press either Cancel (F1) or Exit (F7).

## *PRINT OPTIONS*

The Options section of the Print menu (Shift-F7) has several functions. You use it to install your printer; to select a different printer if you have more than one; to edit printer settings such as the type of sheet feeder, available fonts, and forms; to specify extra binding width in opposite margins if your document will be bound; to specify the number of copies to be printed; and to adjust the resolution of printed text and graphics. Notice that you select each of these options by pressing the first letter of the option name, such as *S* for Select Printer or *B* for Binding.

### *INSTALLING A PRINTER WITH THE SELECT PRINTER OPTION*

To install your printer(s) for use with WordPerfect, you use the Select Printer option on the Print key (Shift-F7 S). When you do this, WordPerfect copies specific instructions for that printer (called a *printer definition*) from the appropriate printer disk and creates a new file in your WordPerfect directory (or WordPerfect system disk if you are using only floppy drives). The new file name corresponds to the printer name and has the extension *PRS*. For instance, if you install the HP LaserJet Series II printer, WordPerfect will create a file named *HPLASEII.PRS*. and if you install an Epson FX-80 it will create a file named *EPFX80.PRS*.

If you've never installed a printer, WordPerfect will give you an error message when you ask it to print a document. For this reason, you need to define the printer or printers you will be using through the installation process described below.

Installing a printer is not difficult. The first step is to press the Print key (Shift-F7) and choose the Select Printer option by pressing *S*. You will then see the Print: Select Printer menu shown in Figure 9.12.

If you haven't installed a printer yet, your screen will be very similar to Figure 9.12. If one or more printers have already been installed on your system, you will see their names in a list at the top of the screen. At the bottom of the screen, you will see six options, as shown in Figure 9.12.

```
Print: Select Printer




















    1 Select; 2 Additional Printers; 3 Edit; 4 Copy; 5 Delete; 6 Help: 1
```

*Figure 9.12:* The Print: Select Printer menu

 WordPerfect stores printer definitions in files with names like WPRINT1.ALL, WPRINT2.ALL, and so forth. Together, they require more than one megabyte of disk space (1000K). You don't have to waste precious disk space storing all these files on your hard disk, since you only need the one(s) for your printer. If you don't copy all of them onto your hard disk, use the Other Disk option to tell WordPerfect where to find your file during the printer installation process.

The next step is to select the Additional Printers option by pressing *2* or *A*. If you then see an alphabetical list of printers similar to the one shown in Figure 9.13, skip the next section and move ahead to the one called "Selecting a Printer from the List." However, if you see the *Printer files not found* screen shown in Figure 9.14, it means that WordPerfect can't find your printer files and you'll have to select Other Disk (*2* or *O*) to tell the program where they are located. If you have a floppy-based system (no hard disk), you will definitely see this screen; if you have a hard disk and you see it, this means either that your printer files are in a different directory or that they have not been copied onto the hard disk (an optional step).

Once you install a printer or printers, you can use this option to switch to a different printer (if you have more than one) or to edit certain printer characteristics such as the name of the sheet feeder, the form definitions (discussed in Chapter 6), and the cartridges or fonts you are using.

## LOCATING AND LOADING THE PRINTER FILES

Users of 3½-inch disks will have fewer printer disks than those who use 5¼-inch disks.

Among the disks that you received with WordPerfect are printer disks with names like Printer 1, Printer 2, and so forth. Depending on the date you purchased WordPerfect 5.0, you may have from four to fourteen of these disks. They contain the printer definition files for

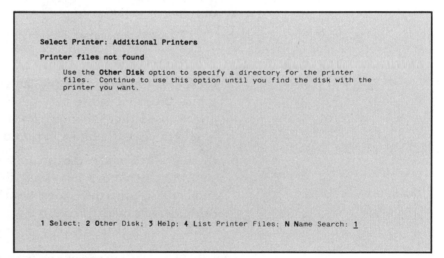

**Figure 9.13:** A list of printers on the Select Printer: Additional Printers screen

```
Select Printer: Additional Printers

Printer files not found

    Use the Other Disk option to specify a directory for the printer
    files.  Continue to use this option until you find the disk with the
    printer you want.




















1 Select; 2 Other Disk; 3 Help; 4 List Printer Files; N Name Search: 1
```

**Figure 9.14:** The *Printer files not found* screen

a wide variety of printers, as well as their fonts and sheet feeder
options. If you are using a floppy-based system, locate these disks
and proceed with the installation steps below. If you have a hard
disk and the files were copied into a different directory, you just have
to figure out the directory name and path, and enter it in response to
the *Directory for printer files:* prompt that appears when you select the
Other Disk option. If you find they were not copied onto your hard

disk, find the printer disks and use the steps described below for floppy-based systems.

You can use the List Files key (F5) to help you locate your printer files if they are in another directory. To do this, press F5 ↵ and look for directory names in the list (they end in <DIR>). By moving the cursor bar onto a directory name and pressing ↵ twice, you can see the names of the files it contains. The printer files you need to find have names such as WPRINT1.ALL, WPRINT2.ALL, and so forth.

1. First determine which of the many printer disks contains the information for your printer; this information is called a *printer driver.* Do this by printing the file named README from the Printer 1 disk. This document lists all printer drivers currently available, and which disks they are on. If your printer has an asterisk next to it, the disk containing that driver was not shipped with the WordPerfect program; you can request it by calling WordPerfect Corporation at 1-800-222-9409.

2. Once you have determined which printer disk contains your printer driver, place it in drive B.

3. Press **2** or **O** to choose the Other Disk option.

4. In response to this prompt:

   **Directory for printer files:**

   type **B:** as the directory (don't forget the colon).

5. Press ↵. You should then see an alphabetical list of printers similar to the one shown in Figure 9.13. If you don't see your printer, use Home ↓ to move down a screenful at a time, and ↑ and ↓ to place the cursor bar onto it.

6. If you get to the end of the list and find that your printer is not on it, you can remove the printer disk from drive B and insert another one, press the Cancel key (F1), then press **2** or **A** for Additional Printers.

WordPerfect Corporation is always creating new printer drivers, so if yours is not on the list you can telephone their Information Services Department at (801) 225-5000 to see if a driver has been written for your printer since you purchased the Word-Perfect program.

## *SELECTING A PRINTER FROM THE LIST*

Once you've located your printer in the list, move the cursor bar onto it and press *1* or *S* to choose the Select option. (If you don't see it, scroll through the list using cursor movement keys like ↑, ↓, and Home ↓.) You will then see a prompt displaying the file name of the printer you just selected. For example, if you are installing the HP LaserJet Series II, it will look like this:

**Printer filename: HPLASEII.PRS**

You can create a
separate directory
for your printer files and
tell WordPerfect where to
find them using the Setup
key (Shift-F1). To do
this, press Shift-F1, select
*Location of Files* (*7* or *L*),
select *Printer Files* (*5* or *P*),
then enter the directory
name and path.

If the prompt shows the correct file name for your printer, press ◄—┘
to accept it (otherwise press F1 and try again). WordPerfect will then
copy the file onto your disk. If you are using a floppy-based system, it
will be copied to the WordPerfect program disk in drive A. If you are
using a hard disk, it will be copied into the directory that contains
your WordPerfect program files or, if you changed it, to the directory
you entered under *Printer Files* in the Location of Files option on the
Setup key (Shift-F1).

After copying the printer file, WordPerfect displays a Printer Helps
and Hints screen that provides specific information about the printer
you've selected. (Incidentally, once a printer is installed you can view
this Help screen anytime by selecting the Help option (*6* or *H*) on the
Print: Select Printer menu, Shift-F7 S H.) You can print this screen by
pressing the Print Screen key (Shift-PrtSc). When you finish reading the
Printer Helps and Hints screen, press the Exit key (F7).

You will then see the Select Printer: Edit screen, similar to the one
shown in Figure 9.15 for the HP LaserJet II. You can use this screen
to customize settings such as initial fonts and the forms used with
your printer (you'll learn how in the following section). When you
finish making necessary changes and verifying that the information is
correct, press the Exit key (F7). A word of warning: Do not press the
Cancel key (F1) or WordPerfect will not add this printer definition to
your disk and you'll have to begin the installation process again!

```
Select Printer: Edit

           Filename              HPLASEII.PRS

    1 - Name                     HP LaserJet Series II

    2 - Port                     LPT1:

    3 - Sheet Feeder             None

    4 - Forms

    5 - Cartridges and Fonts

    6 - Initial Font             Courier 10 pitch (Roman-8)

    7 - Path for Downloadable
            Fonts and Printer
            Command Files



 Selection: 0
```

*Figure 9.15:* The Select Printer: Edit screen for the HP LaserJet Series II

Once you press the Exit key, you are returned to the Print: Select Printer screen, where you will see your printer's name added to the list of printers at the top. Note that the printer whose name is preceded by an asterisk (∗) on this screen is the currently selected printer (meaning it will be used the next time you print), so you have one last step before you can use the new printer definition: select your printer from the list by moving the cursor bar onto it and pressing *1* or *S*.

WordPerfect then returns you to the main Print menu, where you'll see your printer name on the S - Select Printer line. This tells you that your printer is currently selected and will be used the next time you issue a print command.

## INSTALLING AND USING MULTIPLE PRINTERS

If you have more than one printer, repeat the installation procedure described above to install the others. Once you have installed all of them, switching among them is easy. To select a different printer, just press the Print key (Shift-F7), choose the Select Printer option by pressing *S,* move the cursor bar onto the printer you want, then press *1* or *S*. WordPerfect will use the printer you selected for all subsequent print jobs until you repeat this procedure and select a new printer from the list.

## EDITING AND CUSTOMIZING YOUR PRINTER SETTINGS

As mentioned earlier, you can use the Select Printer: Edit screen shown in Figure 9.15 to customize the settings for a particular printer in a variety of ways, including selecting different fonts, changing initial fonts, and adding new forms that can be used with your printer. Since this screen is displayed during the installation process, you've already seen it, but you can return to it anytime after you have installed a printer by pressing the Print key (F7), choosing the Select Printer option (*S*), then selecting Edit (*3* or *E*). Notice that the Select Printer: Edit menu has seven options.

### CHANGING THE PRINTER NAME

You can use the first option, Name, to change the printer name and enter a new one of up to 36 characters. This name will always appear on the main Print menu that you see when you press Shift-F7. This is useful if you change your printer settings frequently. For example, if you use Courier as your initial font about as often as you use Times Roman, you can install the printer twice and assign a different name to one of the printers. That way, whenever you want to switch initial fonts you can save a few keystrokes by selecting the other printer name instead of going all the way into the Select Printer: Edit screen to make the change. (You'll study fonts later in this chapter.)

## SPECIFYING THE PRINTER PORT

The Port option tells WordPerfect the port (interface) that your printer is connected to on your computer, and it is filled in automatically when you install the printer. You shouldn't need to change this setting unless you add another printer and want to connect both of your printers at once via separate cables and interfaces to the computer. When you select this option, WordPerfect displays these menu choices all on one line:

**Port 1** LPT 1; **2** LPT 2; **3** LPT 3; **4** COM 1; **5** COM 2; **6** COM 3; **7** COM 4; **8 Other: 0**

The first three options, LPT 1, LPT 2, and LPT 3, refer to *parallel ports* that you use to connect printers that require a parallel (sometimes called *centronics*) interface to the computer. The parallel method has been the standard since IBM originally introduced the PC in 1981, so most printers use this method. The exceptions are certain laser printers (such as the original HP LaserJet, but not the HP LaserJet Series II) and older letter-quality printers (such as early Diablo models) that use the serial interface method. (Actually, most laser printers can be connected using either parallel or serial ports, but they are generally easier to connect through the parallel port.) If you have only one printer and it uses the parallel method, select option 1, LPT 1. If you have a second printer that connects via a parallel interface, it will be LPT 2. (In case you're curious, LPT means *line printer.*)

The next four options, COM 1, COM 2, COM 3, and COM 4, are used to connect serial printers and graphics devices such as a mouse or modem that require a serial interface. Again, if you have only one printer and it uses a serial interface, select the first COM option, COM 1.

ASCII is a standard format that can be used to exchange information between programs or computers. WordPerfect calls a file saved in this format a *DOS text file*.

You can use the last selection on the Port option, Other, to make a special type of file that will allow you to print a document on another computer, even though you don't have WordPerfect running on the other computer. It does this by "printing" the document to disk and saving it as an ASCII text file containing all the formatting codes required by the printer; you print it on the other computer using the DOS command PRINT. (If the other computer uses a different type of printer, you must install and select that printer before issuing the WordPerfect print command.) When you select the option, this prompt appears:

**Device or Filename:**

You type the name of the file that the document is to be printed to (and saved in), then press ◄───┘. When this option is selected, the next time you use one of the regular print methods to print a file, it will be printed to a disk file under the name you entered in response to the prompt (and will not be printed on your printer). To print this on the other computer, copy it to a disk, insert that disk in the other computer, and type *PRINT* followed by the file name. Press ◄───┘ when asked the name of the list device.

## USING THE SHEET FEEDER AND FORMS OPTIONS

Use the Sheet Feeder option from the Edit menu if you use a sheet feeder with your printer. When you select this option, WordPerfect displays a list of sheet feeders that are compatible with your printer. To select the appropriate sheet feeder model, move the cursor bar to it and press *1* or *S*.

The Forms option (4 or F) is used to add or edit form definitions such as letterhead, labels, and envelopes. Once you have used this option to define a form for your printer, you can use the form anytime through the Paper Size and Type option on the Format: Page menu (Shift-F8 P). This feature was covered in Chapter 6. If you need to review the procedures for defining and using forms, refer to that chapter.

## *SELECTING FONTS FOR YOUR PRINTER*

The last three options on the Select Printer: Edit menu pertain to the fonts that you will be using with your printer. In WordPerfect, a *font* represents a set of characters in a particular typeface, size, and weight (style), and the character set usually includes letters, numbers, punctuation, and certain special symbols. Commonly used typefaces are Helvetica, Times Roman, and Courier, in sizes such as 10- or 12-point, and weights such as light, regular, medium, bold, bold condensed, and medium italic. Fonts will be covered in more detail in Chapter 14.

You use the Cartridge and Fonts option (5 or C) on the Select Printer: Edit menu to install the cartridge and soft fonts (disk-based fonts) that you will be using, and to indicate whether they will be present when the print job begins or will be loaded during the job.

The type of printer you are using determines which fonts you can select in WordPerfect. Some printers come with a variety of built-in fonts, but don't have any external ones. For example, if you have an Okidata ML 192+ printer, WordPerfect can use all of the internal fonts shown on the Select Printer: Initial Font screen in Figure 9.16, but if you select the Cartridge and Fonts option, you'll receive this message indicating that there are no others available:

**This printer has no other cartridges or fonts**

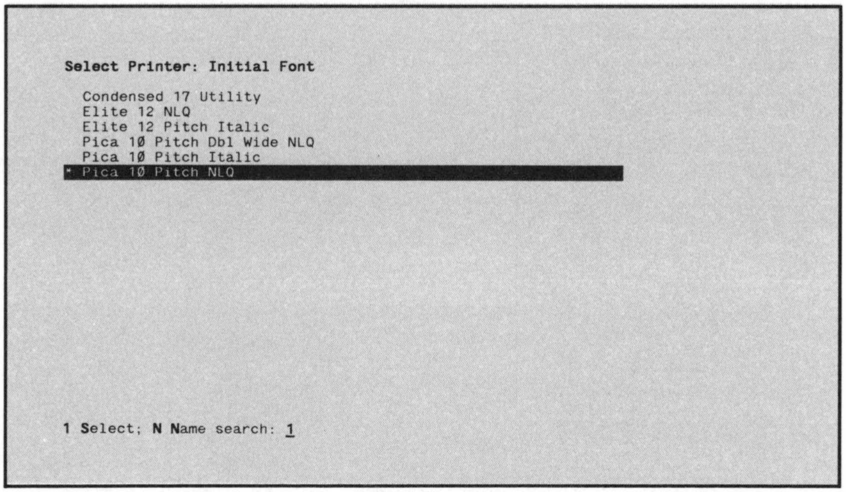

```
Select Printer: Initial Font

    Condensed 17 Utility
    Elite 12 NLQ
    Elite 12 Pitch Italic
    Pica 10 Pitch Dbl Wide NLQ
    Pica 10 Pitch Italic
  * Pica 10 Pitch NLQ




1 Select; N Name search: 1
```

*Figure 9.16:* The Select Printer: Initial Font screen for an Okidata ML 192+ printer

For some dot-matrix and letter-quality printers and nearly all laser printers, you can purchase a variety of fonts on cartridges that plug into slots on the printer. For example, the HP LaserJet Series II printer has two slots under the paper tray in the front to accommodate cartridge-based fonts. Soft fonts, which come on floppy disks, can also be purchased for most laser printers and many popular dot-matrix models. You download (copy) these fonts into the printer's memory prior to printing.

If your printer has optional cartridge or soft fonts available, when you select the Cartridges and Fonts option on the Select Printer: Edit menu, you see a screen similar to the one shown in Figure 9.17 for the HP LaserJet Series II.

Under the *Quantity* column at the upper right side of this screen, it tells you that this printer has two slots for font cartridges, and 350K of available memory (in the printer) for soft fonts. At the bottom of the screen, you see these options: Select Fonts, Name Search, and Change Quantity.

If you have equipped your laser printer with optional extra memory, you should tell WordPerfect by using the Change Quantity option to indicate the total amount of memory. To do this, press *2* or *Q* and in response to the Quantity prompt, type the number of kilobytes that it has, then press ←⏎. For example, if your printer has a total of 1 megabyte of memory, enter *1000* for the quantity (1000 kilobytes is roughly equal to 1 megabyte).

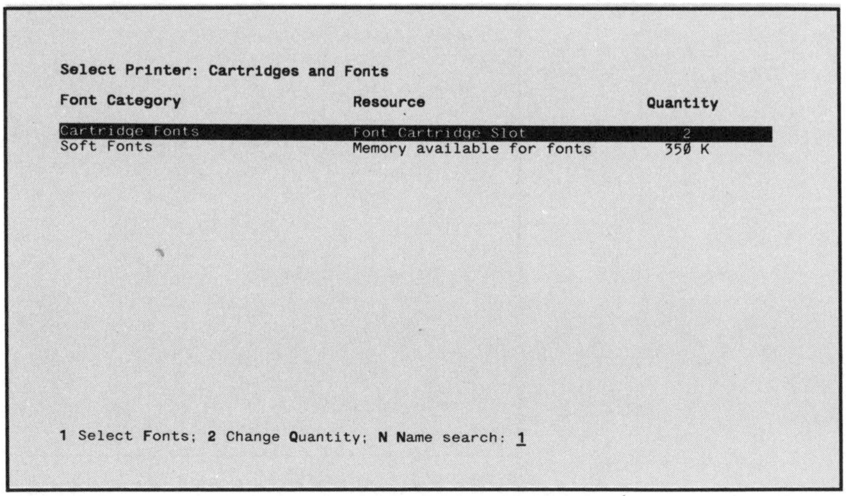

```
Select Printer: Cartridges and Fonts

Font Category              Resource                    Quantity

Cartridge Fonts            Font Cartridge Slot              2
Soft Fonts                 Memory available for fonts     350 K














1 Select Fonts; 2 Change Quantity; N Name search: 1
```

*Figure 9.17:* Cartridges and fonts for the HP LaserJet Series II

***INSTALLING CARTRIDGE FONTS***    Use the Select Fonts option to tell WordPerfect which fonts you will be using. To select cartridges, place the cursor bar on the Cartridge Fonts line before choosing the option; to select soft fonts, place the cursor bar on the Soft Fonts line. Figure 9.18 shows the screen that appears when you select the Cartridge Font option for an HP LaserJet Series II printer.

To select a cartridge from the list, use the arrow keys to move the cursor bar onto the cartridge name, then type an asterisk (*). The asterisk will appear to the left of the name to indicate that it is selected. If you change your mind, you can deselect the cartridge by placing the cursor bar on it and pressing the asterisk key again; the asterisk will disappear. After marking the cartridge font(s) you want to use, press the Exit key (F7) so that WordPerfect will update the printer definition file with the font selections you have just made.

***INSTALLING SOFT FONTS***    The process of selecting soft fonts is very similar to selecting cartridge fonts. Place the cursor bar on the Soft Fonts line in the Select Printer: Cartridges and Fonts screen, then choose the Select Fonts option (*1* or *F*). Figure 9.19 shows you the first screen that appears when selecting soft fonts for the HP LaserJet Series II (there are several).

This screen lists the font names in alphabetical order and according to point size, and also shows the amount of printer memory that

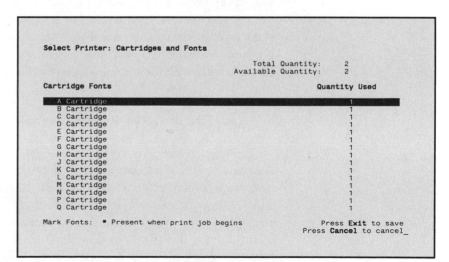

*Figure 9.18:* Selecting cartridge fonts for the HP LaserJet Series II

```
 Select Printer: Cartridges and Fonts

                                        Total Quantity:   350 K
                                    Available Quantity:   170 K

 Soft Fonts                                           Quantity Used

   (AC) Helv 06pt                                         8 K
   (AC) Helv 06pt (Land)                                  8 K
   (AC) Helv 06pt Bold                                    8 K
   (AC) Helv 06pt Bold (Land)                             8 K
   (AC) Helv 06pt Italic                                  8 K
   (AC) Helv 06pt Italic (Land)                           8 K
   (AC) Helv 08pt                                         9 K
   (AC) Helv 08pt (Land)                                  9 K
   (AC) Helv 08pt Bold                                   11 K
   (AC) Helv 08pt Bold (Land)                            11 K
   (AC) Helv 08pt Italic                                 10 K
   (AC) Helv 08pt Italic (Land)                          10 K
   (AC) Helv 10pt                                        13 K
   (AC) Helv 10pt (Land)                                 13 K
   (AC) Helv 10pt Bold                                   13 K

 Mark Fonts:  * Present when print job begins          Press Exit to save
              + Can be loaded during print job        Press Cancel to cancel_
```

***Figure 9.19:*** Selecting soft fonts for the HP LaserJet Series II

is required to load each font (the larger the point size, the more memory required). At the top of the screen, WordPerfect tells you the total amount of (printer) memory available and will reduce this number as you select fonts so you'll know how much is left during the installation process.

Notice in Figure 9.19 that you can only see the Helvetica fonts. To see more fonts, scroll through the list using the arrow keys, the Screen Down key (Home ↓), or Page Down. To go directly to a specific font name, you can use Name Search by pressing the Search key (F2) then typing the first letters of the name, such as *(AC)T* for Times Roman. WordPerfect will take you directly to the first font whose name begins with the letters which (for the HP LaserJet II) happens to be

### (AC) Tms Rmn 06pt (Roman-8) (Land)

To select a font, you type an asterisk if the font will be present (downloaded) before the print job begins, or type a plus sign ( + ) if you want WordPerfect to download it during the print job. If you mark a font with an asterisk to signify that it will be present when the print job begins, you can use the Initialize Printer option on the main Print menu (Shift-F7 7) to download it. Note that Initialize Printer will only work if you have used option 7 on the Select Printer: Edit screen (Shift-F7 S E) to specify the path where the downloadable fonts are located. If you choose to download the font during the print job by marking it with a plus sign, WordPerfect will download the font when you ask it to print the document if you have specified the path using option 7 on the Select Printer: Edit menu. After the print job is finished, fonts marked with a plus sign will be cleared from the printer's memory. After you have marked all the soft fonts you want to use, press the Exit key (F7) twice to have your printer definition file updated. You will see a brief message informing you that WordPerfect is updating the fonts, then you'll be returned to the Select Printer: Edit screen.

The Print key method of changing the initial font affects all new documents you create. However, this method does not alter documents that have already been created and saved. If you wish to change the font in an existing document, retrieve it and use either the Base font option on the Font key (Ctrl-F8 F), or the Initial Font option on the Format key (Shift-F8 D F).

**SELECTING THE INITIAL FONT**   Once you are back at the Select Printer: Edit menu, you should verify that the font listed as the Initial Font (option 6) is the one you want to use by default. If it's not, you can change it by selecting the Initial Font option (*6* or *I*). This brings up a list of all the fonts that you have installed for use with this printer, similar to the one shown in Figure 9.20. Use the arrow keys to move the cursor bar onto the desired font, then press *1* or *S* to choose the Select option. You will then be returned to the Select Printer: Edit screen, where you'll see the font name you just selected next to the Initial Font option (such as the Courier 10-pitch font shown in Figure 9.15). This font will be used for any new documents

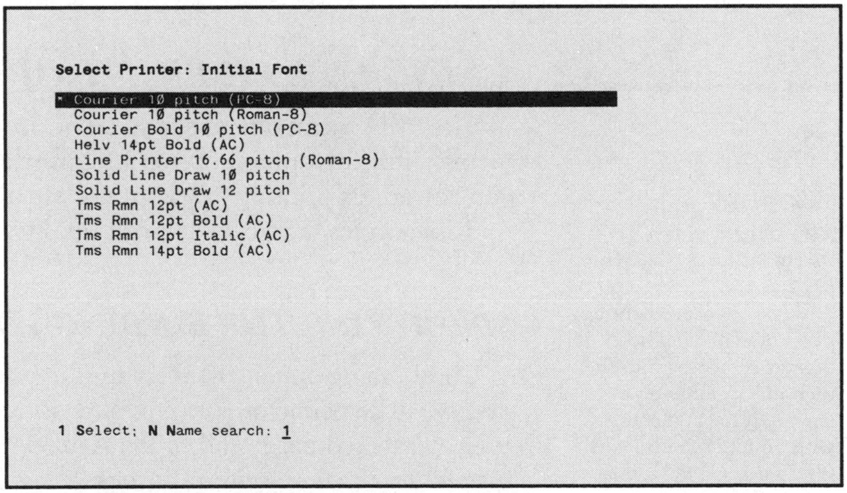

```
Select Printer: Initial Font

  Courier 10 pitch (PC-8)
  Courier 10 pitch (Roman-8)
  Courier Bold 10 pitch (PC-8)
  Helv 14pt Bold (AC)
  Line Printer 16.66 pitch (Roman-8)
  Solid Line Draw 10 pitch
  Solid Line Draw 12 pitch
  Tms Rmn 12pt (AC)
  Tms Rmn 12pt Bold (AC)
  Tms Rmn 12pt Italic (AC)
  Tms Rmn 14pt Bold (AC)




  1 Select; N Name search: 1
```

*Figure 9.20:* Selecting a new initial font

you create, unless you change the base font using the Font key (see Chapter 14) or you repeat these steps to select another initial font. Press the Exit key (F7) three times to return to the Edit screen and update the printer definition file. If you change the initial font while you have a document on the Edit screen, you may notice that it has been reformatted to a new line length, as dictated by the size and the type of the new initial font.

**USING THE DOWNLOADABLE FONTS AND PRINTER COMMAND FILES OPTION**   The last option on the Select Printer: Edit menu is Path for Downloadable Fonts and Printer Command Files (7 or D). Use this option if you have selected soft fonts that will be loaded into the printer's memory before or during the print job (indicated by marking with a plus sign or an asterisk when selecting the soft fonts, as described above) to tell WordPerfect where to find them. After selecting this option (by pressing *7* or *D*), type the drive letter or path name of the directory that contains the soft font files (and the printer command file that downloads them, as described in the ''Printer Commands'' section at the end of this chapter). Press the Exit key (F7) twice to update this and any other changes you've made on the Select Printer: Edit menu. You will then see the Print menu and can press F7 again to return to the Edit screen.

## USING OTHER PRINT OPTIONS

The Print menu offers several other useful options that enable you to take full advantage of your printer's capabilities. With them you can adjust printing to accommodate binding requirements, print multiple copies, and control print quality.

### SPECIFYING THE BINDING WIDTH

The Binding option (B) is useful for printing two-sided documents that are to be bound or hole-punched, for it shifts the text to the left on even-numbered pages and to the right on odd-numbered pages. You specify the binding width in inches (assuming inches are your default unit of measurement on the Setup key), so if you want WordPerfect to add 1 extra inch for binding, press Shift-F7 B 1 ◄─┘ F7. If the document

To change the default unit of measurement, press the Setup key (Shift-F1) and select Units of Measurement by pressing *8* or *U*. The default is inches (with the inch mark), but you can change it to (1) inches with an *i*; (2) centimeters; (3) points; (4) the units used in WordPerfect 4.2 (pitch and lines); or (5) 1200ths of an inch.

is to be printed on one side only, you don't need to use this option; instead, add an extra inch to the left margin (Shift-F8 L M).

Unlike most formatting changes, changing the binding width does not insert a code into your document. Also, binding width is a toggle, so the change you make will stay in effect and alter all the documents you print from that point forward until you repeat the steps to change it again or exit from WordPerfect.

### SPECIFYING THE NUMBER OF COPIES

Use the Number of Copies option on the Print menu (Shift-F7) to produce multiple copies of a document with a single print command. To use it, just press *N*, enter the number of copies you want to print, then press ◄—. Like the binding width, the new number of copies will remain in effect unless you change it again or exit from WordPerfect, and it does not insert a code into your document.

### CONTROLLING PRINT QUALITY WITH THE GRAPHICS AND TEXT QUALITY OPTIONS

You can use the Graphics Quality (G) and Text Quality (T) options on the Print menu (Shift-F7) to control print quality as well as to print the graphics separately from the text in a document. The second feature is useful if your printer doesn't have enough memory to print text and graphics in the same print job. First you select the Do Not Print feature from the Graphics Quality option to print the text without the graphics, then you print your document, reinsert the paper, select Do Not Print from the Text Quality option, turn the graphics back on, and print the job again, omitting the text. The graphics and text are printed in the same position in your document as though you had printed them at the same time.

To omit graphics or to change graphics resolution, select the Graphics Quality option from the Print menu by pressing Shift-F7 G. You will see this menu at the bottom of the screen:

**Graphics Quality: 1 Do Not Print; 2 Draft; 3 Medium; 4 High: 3**

Notice that the default is 3, Medium. To omit graphics and print only text, select the Do Not Print option by pressing *1* or *N*. To

You can use Word-Perfect's Setup key to change the defaults for the print options covered in this section: Binding Width, Number of Copies, Graphics Quality, and Text Quality. To do this, press Setup (Shift-F1), select Initial Settings, select Print Options, make any changes you wish, and then press Exit (F7). Changes made through Setup stay in effect (even if you exit WordPerfect) until you use the same method to change them.

change the graphics resolution, choose either Draft (*2* or *D*), Medium (*3* or *M*), or High (*4* or *H*). The higher the quality (resolution), the longer it will take to print your document. You may want to consult the Printer Helps and Hints screen for your printer to see what effect, if any, changing the resolution will have on your printout. You can do this by choosing Select (*S*) from the Print key (Shift-F7), then Help (*6* or *H*).

To omit text and print only graphics or to change the resolution of printed text, select the Text Quality option on the Print menu by pressing Shift-F7 T. When you do, you'll see this menu at the bottom of the screen:

**Text Quality: 1 Do Not Print; 2 Draft; 3 Medium; 4 High: 4**

Notice that the default is 4, High. To print only the graphics and omit text, select the Do Not Print option (*1* or *N*). To change the resolution of the printout, select either Draft (*2* or *D*), Medium (*3* or *M*), or High (*4* or *H*). Again, what effect, if any, changing the quality has on your printing is determined by the type and brand of printer you use. If you are using a laser printer, changing this setting will probably have no effect on print speed and quality. However, if you are using a dot-matrix printer, choosing between Draft and Medium or High quality will influence both the resolution of the printout and the printing speed. Choosing Draft mode will print the fastest but produce the worst print quality. The selections you make under Graphics Quality and Text Quality will only stay in effect until you exit WordPerfect.

## PRINTER COMMANDS

The Printer Command option on the Format key's *Other* menu (Shift-F8 O) allows you to send special codes to your printer to take advantage of your printer's special functions, if WordPerfect can't otherwise access them. This feature is especially useful with dot-matrix and laser printers, which usually accept a wide variety of codes to take advantage of such features as enlarged print, condensed print, and graphics characters. The codes are listed in your printer manual; take a moment to look at them so you'll be aware of all your printer's capabilities. You can insert them one at a time in a document, or you can create a whole file of codes and have WordPerfect send the file to the printer when the document is printed.

To enter a single command into your document, press the Format key (Shift-F8), select Other (*4* or *O*), select Printer Functions (*6* or *P*), then select Printer Command (*2* or *P*). You will see this menu at the bottom of the screen:

**1 Command; 2 Filename: 0**

When you select the Command option (*1* or *C*), you will see this message on the prompt line:

**Command:**

Command codes that are less than 32 decimal or greater than 126 must be entered in angle brackets. 27 is the decimal equivalent for Esc, a command used frequently with other letters to control printers.

You can then enter the printer command you want to use, as found in your printer manual. For example, to produce Elite type on an Epson printer, you enter the code Esc M in response to the *Command:* prompt. Since Esc is always represented by <27> in WordPerfect, you type it like this:

**<27>M**

The Filename option is useful if you've created a file of codes to send to the printer while printing the document. For example, if you have a laser printer, you could use this feature to download soft fonts whenever you need to print with them. When you select Filename (*2* or *F*), you'll see this prompt:

**Document name:**

Type the name of the file that contains the printer commands you want to insert at that point in the document. You may remember from an earlier section of this chapter that you can specify the path name for these types of files by using the Path for Downloadable Fonts and Printer Command Files option on the Select Printer: Edit menu (Shift-F7 S E 7).

The WordPerfect formatting code that will appear on your Reveal Codes screen after you insert a special printer command or file will resemble this one:

[Ptr Cmnd:n]

where *n* is your specific printer code or the name of the file that contains the printer commands to be executed.

## *PROPORTIONALLY SPACED VS. MONOSPACED FONTS*

As mentioned earlier, fonts are defined according to their typeface, size, and weight, but they are also characterized as either *monospaced* or *proportionally spaced.* One of the most commonly used monospaced fonts is the Courier type, which almost all typewriters produce (in fact, it is built into most printers, including laser printers), and one of the most commonly used proportional fonts is Times Roman. Courier is classified as a monospaced font because each character uses the same amount of horizontal space on the page, and if you were to draw a box around each character, the boxes would all be the same size. In proportionally spaced fonts, the characters use different amounts of horizontal space when printed, and if you were to draw boxes around certain characters, their sizes would vary. For example, a box drawn around an uppercase *W* would be much wider than one drawn around a lowercase *l*.

Almost all published material is printed in proportionally spaced fonts, including this book. The type that you are reading now is a proportionally spaced font called Baskerville. Look at the word ''minute'' in this sentence. Notice how much wider the *m* is than the *i* next to it and that the *i* takes about the same space as the *t*. Most printers are capable of proportional spacing, but the fonts aren't necessarily sold with the printer and usually are purchased as options.

Because characters produced with monospaced fonts are all the same width, it is convenient to describe their size by the number of characters used to produce one horizontal inch of type; this is called the *pitch.* Pica and Courier, for example, are 10 pitch because they print 10 characters per inch, while Elite (also a monospaced font) is

Monospaced fonts use a fixed pitch, which means that the number of characters per inch is always the same (as in 10 for Courier). When you use a proportional font, the number of characters per inch is variable, and depends entirely on the combination of characters that you type.

The ASCII charac-
ter set includes the
letters, numbers, and
punctuation available on
your keyboard, and other
symbols and graphics
characters that are available using the Alt key and
numeric keypad. Many
symbols are not included
in this set, including right
and left quotation marks,
the copyright symbol,
and accented European
characters. Some
Hewlett-Packard fonts
use the Roman-8 and
Roman-Ext (Roman
extended) character sets.
The Roman-Ext symbol
set includes accented
letters and special sym-
bols used to represent
currency, and the
Roman-8 character set
includes all of the characters available in both the
USASCII and Roman-
Ext character sets.

12 pitch because it prints 12 characters per inch. However, this system doesn't work when applied to proportionally spaced fonts
because of the variable character spacing that characterizes proportional fonts. An inch of type may include 10, 15, or even 22 characters, and is completely dependent upon which characters you type in
that inch. Therefore, these fonts are categorized according to a vertical measurement called the *point* size, which identifies the height.
There are approximately 72 points per inch, so one point equals
about 1/72 inch. Common point sizes are 10 and 12 for regular text,
and 14 for headings. This sentence, for example, is printed in 10 point.

Monospaced fonts can be described by both their point size and
their pitch. When selecting fonts, you will find that WordPerfect
sometimes lists monospaced fonts by both measurements. For
example, on the Select Printer: Cartridges and Fonts menu for the
HP LaserJet Series II printer, one of the Prestige Elite fonts is
described as *(EA) Prestige Elite 10pt 12 pitch,* but the Courier font that
you see on the Select Printer: Initial Font menu (because this font is
built into the printer) is described as *Courier 10 pitch (PC-8).* This tells
you that the Prestige Elite font is 10 points high, and that it prints 12
characters per inch. Note that *PC-8* is the name of the character set
that comes with the Courier font. A character set (sometimes called
symbol set) is the set of letters, numbers, and symbols that can produced with a font; the most commonly used character set is ASCII.
PC-8 (as used by Hewlett-Packard) includes both ASCII and
another set that they call Roman Extended. The (EA) designation for
the Prestige Elite font is used by Hewlett-Packard to identify their
Prestige Elite set of soft fonts. Other designations they use include
AC and AD for Helvetica fonts; the AC fonts use a different character set (USACII) than the AD fonts (Roman-8).

When referring to a proportionally spaced font, WordPerfect only
lists the point size. For instance, on the Select Printer: Cartridges and
Fonts menu for soft fonts (for the HP LaserJet Series II Printer), the
10-point Helvetica font is shown as *(AC) Helv 10 pt,* and the landscape
version, which prints sideways, is shown as *(AC) Helv 10 pt (Land).*

## THE FONT KEY

The Font key (Ctrl-F8) is used primarily for stylistic changes that
affect the size, style, enhancements, and color of the printed text.

These commands insert formatting codes that are visible on the Reveal Codes screen. Also, if you have a color monitor or a monochrome one with graphics capabilities, you can see most of these changes in the View Document option (Shift-F7 V).

When you press the Font key (Ctrl-F8), you see the following menu:

**1 Size; 2 Appearance; 3 Normal; 4 Base Font; 5 Print Color: 0**

Use the Size option to change the font size within the document, and to subscript or superscript text. Use the Appearance option to change font attributes such as bold, underline, double underline, redline, strikeout, shadow, outline, small caps (as used in A.M. and P.M. designations) and italics. Use the Normal option to return to the default size and style for the font you are using. Use the Base Font option to change the basic text font used for this document. If your printer can print in different colors, you can use the Print Color option to change the text color on the printed page.

Before using any of these options in your documents, you should test your printer to determine which features it can produce with WordPerfect. To do this, you can use the Printer.tst file, supplied on the WordPerfect Conversion disk. This file includes special features such as superscripts and subscripts, underlining, redline and strikeout, tab aligning and columns, advance up and down, and a figure containing a graphic. To print it, use Shift-F10 to retrieve the file (PRINTER.TST) to the Edit screen, then use the Full Document option on the Print key (Shift-F7 1). You could also print it using the Print option on the List Files key (F5 4). You should try printing the PRINTER.TST document with each of the printers you have installed for WordPerfect. Also, if you switch to a different base font, the results may be different, so try switching fonts if you find you can't print a certain feature.

## *BASE FONT*

The Base Font option on the Font key menu allows you to select a different font for use in the document on your Edit screen, overriding the Initial Font that you selected in the Select Printer: Edit menu

(Shift-F7 S E). Like other formatting changes, changing the base font inserts a code into your document and takes effect at the cursor position. It will remain in effect through the end of the document, or until you make another change to the base font.

The base font determines the size and style of the basic text, as well as the other fonts WordPerfect will use when you select certain font size and style options from the Size and Appearance menus of the Font key. For example, if you select 10-point Times Roman as the base font, WordPerfect will use 10-point Times Roman bold when you select Bold from the Appearance menu (or by pressing the Bold key), and 10-point Times Roman italic when you select Italic from the Appearance menu. If you select the Large option on the Size menu, the program will automatically use a large Times Roman font for this attribute, choosing from among the sizes that you have selected through the Select Printer: Cartridges and Fonts menu (Shift-F7 S E C). WordPerfect also makes automatic font-size selections for your printer when you use the Fine, Small, Vry Large, and Ext Large options on the Size menu. Be aware that if your printer doesn't support a bold typeface in the same style as the base font you have selected, WordPerfect will produce this attribute by double-striking the text. If an italics font is not available, WordPerfect will underline your text.

To select a new base font, move the cursor to the place in the document where you want the font change to begin, press the Font key (Ctrl-F8) and select the Base Font option (*4* or *F*). You will then see the Base Font screen, which lists all the fonts you have previously selected for your printer through the Select Printer: Cartridges and Fonts menu (Shift-F7 S E C). This screen is almost identical to the Initial Font screen that you see when you select the default font through the Print key (Shift-F7 S E I), except that this one says *Base Font* at the top. To choose one of the fonts, move the cursor bar until it highlights the font you want to use, then press *1, S,* or ↵ to use the Select option. You will then be returned to the document you are editing.

To verify that a font change has been made, you can use the Reveal Codes key (Alt-F3) to locate the Font code that WordPerfect inserted. For instance, if you select 12-point Times Roman as the new base font (for your HP LaserJet printer), you will see the code

[Font:Tms Rmn 12pt (AC)

You can use the Base Font option on the Font menu to continue changing fonts as you need, but most printers limit the total number of different fonts that you can use.

## SELECTING FONT SIZE

You use the Size option on the Font key to change the size of the font in the printed version of your document. When you select Size (Ctrl-F8 1), this menu appears:

**1 S**uprscpt; **2 S**ubscpt; **3 F**ine; **4 S**mall; **5 L**arge; **6 V**ry Large;
**7 E**xt Large: 0

If you read Chapter 8, you are already familiar with the Superscript and Subscript options. The last five options in the Size menu are used to change the size of the text. As explained in the previous section, the actual font size that WordPerfect uses when you select one of these options depends on the base font that is currently selected.

The Fine, Small, Large, Vry Large, and Ext Large options work very much like the Bold (F6) and Underline keys (F8), inserting a pair of codes into your document (to designate the beginning and end of the size change) and placing the cursor between the codes so that everything you type after that will be affected by the change until you turn it off. To do this, you have to move the cursor past the second code, either by pressing the → key once, or by selecting the Normal option on the Font menu (Ctrl-F8 3 or N). You can also use the Size menu to change the size of existing text in the document. Again, the procedure is exactly like underlining or boldfacing text that has already been typed. You mark the text with the Block (Alt-F4) and cursor movement keys, press the Font key (Ctrl-F8) and select the Size option (*1* or *S*), then select the number or letter next to the size you want to use.

## DETERMINING
## THE APPEARANCE OF THE FONT

The Appearance option on the Font key lets you select features like bold, underline, italics, outline, and shadow. When you select it by

If you use the HP LaserJet Series II printer, you can only select up to 32 soft fonts for use with the printer (through the Select Printer: Cartridges and Fonts menu), even if your printer has more available memory. Also, you can only mix up to 16 different fonts on a page.

pressing Ctrl-F8 2 or Ctrl-F8 A, the following menu appears:

**1 B**old; **2 U**ndrln; **3 D**bl Und; **4 I**talc; **5 O**utln; **6 S**hadw; **7 S**m **C**ap;
**8 R**edln; **9 S**tkout: **0**

The first two options, Bold and Undrln, are like the Bold and Underline keys, F6 and F8. The other options work like bold and underline also, inserting a pair of codes into your document and placing the cursor between the codes so that everything you type after that will be affected by the change until you turn it off. For instance, when you select italics, WordPerfect creates a pair of codes, [ITALC] and [italc], and positions the cursor between them. When you are finished entering the text that is to be italicized, move the cursor beyond the second code by pressing the Font key (Ctrl-F8) and selecting the Normal option (*3* or *N*), or by pressing the → key once. To use one of the enhancements on the Appearance menu on existing text, use the Block (Alt-F4) and cursor movement keys to mark the text, press the Font key (Ctrl-F8), select Appearance (*2* or *A*), then choose the number or letter of the enhancement you want to apply to the marked text.

## CHOOSING THE PRINT COLOR

The Print Color option (*5* or *C*) on the Font menu allows you to select a different color for your printed text if you are using a color printer. When you select this option, you see the Print Color menu shown in Figure 9.21. To choose a new color for printing, press the number or letter of the desired color, such as *5* or *B* for blue or *3* or *R* for red, then press Exit (F7). Note that the percentage amounts shown in the Current Color row indicate the intensity level of the primary colors (red, green, and blue) in the color you selected. You can create a print color yourself and vary the intensity of red, green, and blue in it by selecting the *Other* option from this menu.

When you select a new color, WordPerfect inserts a code into the text at the cursor position, visible only in the Reveal Codes screen (Alt-F3). For example, if you select Red (*3* or *R*) from the Print Color menu, the program inserts this code into the document:

[Color:Red]

```
Print Color

                              Primary Color Mixture
                           Red      Green      Blue

        1 - Black          0%        0%        0%
        2 - White          100%      100%      100%
        3 - Red            67%       0%        0%
        4 - Green          0%        67%       0%
        5 - Blue           0%        0%        67%
        6 - Yellow         67%       67%       0%
        7 - Magenta        67%       0%        67%
        8 - Cyan           0%        67%       67%
        9 - Orange         67%       25%       0%
        A - Gray           50%       50%       50%
        N - Brown          67%       33%       0%
        O - Other

        Current Color      0%        0%        0%




   Selection: 0
```

*Figure 9.21:* The Print Color menu

To turn off a color in the text, select the Print Color option on the Font menu and select Black (*1* or *K*).

## SUMMARY

As you have learned, WordPerfect's printing operations are complex and powerful. You can choose from among several different methods of printing and can vary many features. You can send a list of documents to the printer, interrupt or change their order, or cancel one or more jobs. Printing does not tie up your computer, and you can proceed to work on any document almost immediately after issuing a print command. You can use a variety of fonts with WordPerfect that will affect the printed version of your document. These fonts determine the size, style, enhancements, and color of your text. You will learn more about printing with a font in Chapter 14.

# 10.

## AUTOMATING YOUR INDEXES, TABLES OF CONTENTS, AND OTHER REFERENCE AIDS

**Mark an entry for a list**      314

by highlighting it with the Block (Alt-F4) and cursor movement keys. With Block still on, press the Mark Text key (Alt-F5) and press *2* or *L*, then at the *List Number:* prompt, type in the number you want to assign to your list. Repeat the procedure for each item you want in the list. Next, define the numbering style and generate the list.

**Define the numbering style for a list**      316

by pressing the Mark Text key (Alt-F5). Select *5* or *D,* then at the Mark Text: Define menu, press *2* or *L.* At the next prompt, type in the number of the list. You then will see a screen showing you five numbering styles; select the style you want to use.

**Mark an entry for a table of contents**      323

by highlighting the entry with the Block (Alt-F4) and cursor movement keys. With Block still on, press the Mark Text key (Alt-F5) and select *1* or *C.* At the *ToC Level:* prompt, enter the level number (1-5) of the entry. Repeat the procedure for each item you want in the table of contents. Next, define the numbering style and generate the table.

**Define the numbering style for a table of contents**      324

by pressing the Mark Text key (Alt-F5). Select *5* or *D,* and at the Mark Text: Define menu, select *1* or *C.* At the next screen, select the Number of Levels option and type in the total number of levels you will use in the table, then press *3* or *P* and select the numbering style you want for each level. When you have finished, press Exit (F7).

**Mark an entry for an index as you are typing**                              329

by placing the cursor on the word and pressing Mark Text (Alt-F5) if the entry is one word; for entries of more than one word, press Block (Alt-F4), use the cursor movement keys to highlight the phrase, then press Alt-F5. At the menu, press *3* or *I*. At the *Index heading:* and *Subheading:* prompts, type in the text and press ←, or press ← to accept the text WordPerfect suggests. Repeat the procedure for each item you want in the index. Next, define the numbering style and generate the index.

**Define the numbering style for an index**                                   331

by pressing the Mark Text key (Alt-F5). Select *5* or *D,* then *3* or *I.* If you are using a concordance file, type in the file name at the next prompt; if you are not using one, press ←. At the next screen, select the numbering style you want to use.

**Generate a list, table of contents or authorities, or an index**           319

by pressing the Mark Text key (Alt-F5), then selecting *6* or *G,* then *5* or *G,* then *Y* to replace any existing ones. WordPerfect will then generate your list, table of contents or authorities, or index, and you will see it on the screen.

**To create an outline,**                                                     342

press the Date/Outline key (Shift-F5) and select *4* or *0.* Press ← and a Roman numeral I will be inserted into your document for the first paragraph level of your outline. Type in the text next to the Roman numeral and press ←, and WordPerfect will insert a Roman numeral II into your document. Each time you press the Space bar or type text and press ←, another paragraph level is added to your outline. Each time you press the Tab key after a paragraph number (a Roman numeral), the paragraph number will change to the next level.

WORDPERFECT ENJOYS GREAT POPULARITY AMONG professional writers, for it is a virtual toolbox that can simplify a variety of projects. This chapter will cover several of its most important techniques, including those used for creating outlines, lists, indexes, tables of contents, automatic references, master documents, and tables of authorities.

Even though you may not be a professional writer, you'll want to know about the features covered in this chapter. Although they are most commonly used in books, dissertations, and other lengthy reports, they can also serve as a wonderful method of organizing ideas and thoughts. In fact, once you find out how easy it is to use these features, they may become your favorite tools.

The procedures used to create a list, index, or table of contents are similar and require these main steps:

- Marking text in your document for inclusion in your list, index, or table of contents
- Defining the numbering style
- Generating the list, index, and/or table of contents

Text can be marked anytime, either as you create the document or after it is written and thoroughly edited. Either way, the process is not entirely automatic and requires some careful planning.

## LISTS

This book includes numerous illustrations, designed to clarify step-by-step instructions and exemplify major problems and issues. The illustrations were created and incorporated into the chapters as they were written, but once the editing process began, figures were added, changed, or deleted. These changes made it necessary to reorganize and renumber the figures, so WordPerfect's List feature became indispensable. By providing a list of illustrations and their page locations that could be easily updated each time changes were made, it spared me hours of work.

WordPerfect permits you to keep as many as nine different lists in a document, so you can have separate lists for figures, graphs, maps, charts, and whatever else you want to enumerate. However, you can include a given word or phrase in only one list, so all of the nine potential lists must be mutually exclusive. You can get around this restriction by creating separate copies of the document and using different copies to mark and generate different lists. There is no limit on the length of the words or phrases that can be included.

If your document includes graphics figure boxes with captions, WordPerfect will automatically mark the captions for list 6. If you have table boxes with captions, WordPerfect will automatically designate the captions for list 7. If your document has text boxes with captions, WordPerfect will mark them for list 8. If you created user-defined boxes for the document, WordPerfect will automatically include them in list 9.

The lists of figures that I kept while working on this book were created after completing the manuscript of each chapter. Since the chapters were quite long, I used WordPerfect's Search feature to locate each illustration in the text. If you're more organized than I am, you can mark your items for inclusion in the list as you write. The following section provides step-by-step instructions explaining how I created my list of figures, and I encourage you to practice this procedure using one of your own documents.

See Chapter 14 for more information about graphics boxes, including user-defined boxes and boxes that enclose figures, tables, or text.

## CREATING A LIST

To create one or more lists, you mark each word or phrase in your document using the Block (Alt-F4) and Mark Text keys (Alt-F5), then use the Mark Text key to define the style and generate the list.

***MARKING THE ITEMS***    The first step is to mark all the items you want in your list. To do this, make sure that the document is on the Edit screen, then follow these steps:

1. If you are marking entries for your list after typing the document, the first step is to locate each word or phrase that you want to include in the list. To do this, I started with the cursor at the top of the document and used the Forward Search key (F2), searching for all occurrences of the word *Figure.* If you are marking entries for the list as you type the document, skip this step.

2. At each occurrence, use the Block key (Alt-F4) and the cursor movement keys to highlight all the text you want to include in this entry. I blocked the number and title of each illustration, as shown in Figure 10.1.

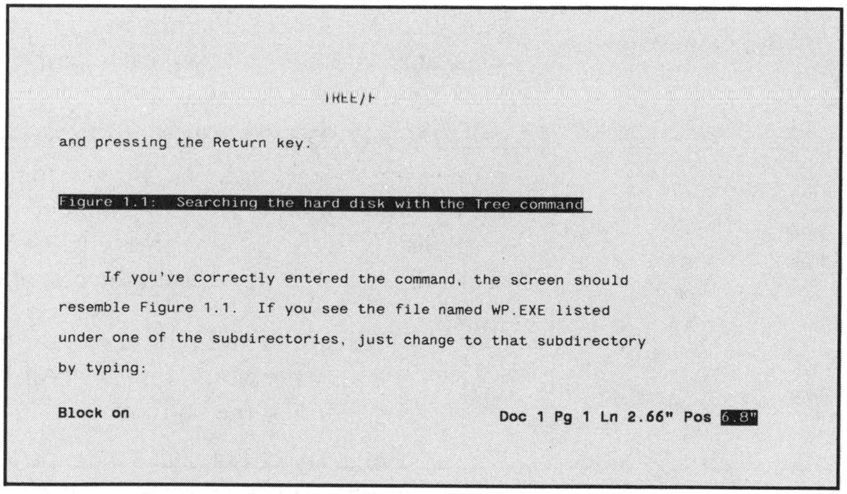

```
                                    IREE/F


and pressing the Return key.


Figure 1.1:   Searching the hard disk with the Tree command



     If you've correctly entered the command, the screen should
resemble Figure 1.1.  If you see the file named WP.EXE listed
under one of the subdirectories, just change to that subdirectory
by typing:

Block on                              Doc 1 Pg 1 Ln 2.66" Pos 6.8"
```

***Figure 10.1:*** Blocking text for a list

Note that this procedure may include formatting codes such as Center, Bold, and Underline in your block, because you cannot tell from the Edit screen where they are located. If you don't want such codes appearing in your list, before you mark the text be sure to check the Reveal Codes screen (Alt-F3) and move the cursor past the codes.

3. With Block still on, press the Mark Text key (Alt-F5). The following menu appears on the prompt line:

**Mark for 1 ToC; 2 List; 3 Index; 4 ToA: 0**

4. Select List (**2** or **L**) and this prompt will appear:

List Number:

Since this was to be my first list, I entered the number

1

5. To verify that the text was correctly marked, you can check the Reveal Codes screen by pressing Alt-F3. Each marked phrase will be surrounded by a pair of formatting codes, designating the beginning and end of the marked block, as shown below:

**[Mark:List,1]**Figure 1.2: The Function keys**[EndMark:List,1]**

Note that the *1* inside the brackets refers to list 1. Repeat these five steps until you have marked each item you want in your list.

***DEFINING THE STYLE*** The second step is to define the numbering style for your list. Be sure to move the cursor to the end of the document first, to guarantee that all marked text will be included in the list. You should also press Ctrl-⏎ to insert a hard page break that will set the list apart from the rest of the text.

1. With the cursor at the end of the document, define the list by pressing the Mark Text key (Alt-F5). You will see the following menu at the bottom:

**1 Auto Ref; 2 Subdoc; 3 Index; 4 ToA Short Form; 5 Define; 6 Generate: 0**

Note that the Mark Text menu differs when you press it alone instead of with Block on. (With Block on, the only options are table of contents, list, index, and table of authorities, as shown earlier.)

2. Select Define (**5** or **D**). You will see the Mark Text: Define menu illustrated in Figure 10.2.

3. Select Define List (**2** or **L**). You will then see this prompt:

**List Number (1-9):**

Type **1** to define list number 1. After you have selected the list number, the screen illustrated in Figure 10.3 will appear so that you can select one of the five numbering styles.

```
Mark Text: Define

        1 - Define Table of Contents

        2 - Define List

        3 - Define Index

        4 - Define Table of Authorities

        5 - Edit Table of Authorities Full Form




    Selection: 0
```

*Figure 10.2:* The Mark Text: Define menu

```
List 1 Definition

        1 - No Page Numbers

        2 - Page Numbers Follow Entries

        3 - (Page Numbers) Follow Entries

        4 - Flush Right Page Numbers

        5 - Flush Right Page Numbers with Leaders




    Selection: 0
```

*Figure 10.3:* The List 1 Definition screen

```
CHAPTER 1 ILLUSTRATIONS: STYLE 1

Figure 1.1: The Shift, Alt, and Ctrl Keys
Figure 1.2: The function keys
Figure 1.3: The result of pressing Shift-F8
Figure 1.4: The Return, Caps Lock, and Num Lock keys
Figure 1.5: The Del, Backspace, and Left Arrow keys
Figure 1.6: The Ins (Insert) and Cancel Keys
Figure 1.7: The arrow keys on the numeric keypad
Figure 1.8: The Home, Page Up, Page Down, Screen Up, Screen
Down, and End Keys
Figure 1.9: The Help screen
Figure 1.10: The Help screen for the letter S
Figure 1.11: The Exit Key Help screen


CHAPTER 1 ILLUSTRATIONS: STYLE 2

Figure 1.1: The Shift, Alt, and Ctrl keys    8
Figure 1.2: The function keys  9
Figure 1.3: The result of pressing Shift-F8   10
Figure 1.4: The Return, Caps Lock, and Num Lock keys   12
Figure 1.5: The Del, Backspace, and Left Arrow keys   16
Figure 1.6: The Ins (Insert) and Cancel Keys   17
Figure 1.7: The arrow keys on the numeric keypad  21
Figure 1.8: The Home, Page Up, Page Down, Screen Up, Screen
Down, and End Keys     22
Figure 1.9: The Help screen  25
Figure 1.10: The Help screen for the letter S   26
Figure 1.11: The Exit Key Help screen  27


CHAPTER 1 ILLUSTRATIONS: STYLE 3

Figure 1.1: The Shift, Alt, and Ctrl keys  (8)
Figure 1.2: The function keys (9)
Figure 1.3: The result of pressing Shift-F8 (10)
Figure 1.4: The Return, Caps Lock, and Num Lock keys (12)
Figure 1.5: The Del, Backspace, and Left Arrow keys (16)
Figure 1.6: The Ins (Insert) and Cancel Keys (17)
Figure 1.7: The arrow keys on the numeric keypad (21)
Figure 1.8: The Home, Page Up, Page Down, Screen Up, Screen
Down, and End Keys      (22)
Figure 1.9: The Help screen (25)
Figure 1.10: The Help screen for the letter S (26)
Figure 1.11: The Exit Key Help screen (27)


CHAPTER 1 ILLUSTRATIONS: STYLE 4

Figure 1.1: The Shift, Alt, and Ctrl keys                8
Figure 1.2: The function keys                            9
Figure 1.3: The result of pressing Shift-F8             10
Figure 1.4: The Return, Caps Lock, and Num Lock keys    12
Figure 1.5: The Del, Backspace, and Left Arrow keys     16
Figure 1.6: The Ins (Insert) and Cancel Keys            17
Figure 1.7: The arrow keys on the numeric keypad        21
Figure 1.8: The Home, Page Up, Page Down, Screen Up, Screen
Down, and End Keys                                       22
Figure 1.9: The Help screen                             25
Figure 1.10: The Help screen for the letter S           26
Figure 1.11: The Exit Key Help screen                   27


CHAPTER 1 ILLUSTRATIONS: STYLE 5

Figure 1.1: The Shift, Alt, and Ctrl keys . . . . . . . . .    8
Figure 1.2: The function keys . . . . . . . . . . . . . .      9
Figure 1.3: The result of pressing Shift-F8 . . . . . . . .   10
Figure 1.4: The Return, Caps Lock, and Num Lock keys . . . .  12
Figure 1.5: The Del, Backspace, and Left Arrow keys . . . .   16
Figure 1.6: The Ins (Insert) and Cancel Keys . . . . . . .    17
Figure 1.7: The arrow keys on the numeric keypad . . . . . .  21
Figure 1.8: The Home, Page Up, Page Down, Screen Up, Screen
Down, and End Keys   . . . . . . . . . . . . . . . . . . . .   22
Figure 1.9: The Help screen . . . . . . . . . . . . . . .     25
Figure 1.10: The Help screen for the letter S . . . . . . .   26
Figure 1.11: The Exit Key Help screen . . . . . . . . . . .   27
```

*Figure 10.4:* The output: five different versions of the list of illustrations in Chapter 1

Figure 10.4 shows five copies of the list of figures in Chapter 1, each using a different numbering style. (Incidentally, the page numbers and headings in the word-processed manuscript are different from those in the printed book.) I usually use the Flush Right Page Numbers with Leaders option, which places the corresponding page number at the right margin preceded by a row of dots called *leaders* (because they lead the eye from the item on the left to the matching page number on the right).

4. Select the numbering style that you want to use by pressing the letter or number of the option. After you complete this step, the Reveal Codes screen should include this code:

   [DefMark:List,1:5]

   where *1* is the list number that you selected in step 3 and *5* is page numbering style. This code marks the position in your document where the list will appear when it is generated.

**GENERATING THE LIST**   The final step is to have WordPerfect make, or *generate,* the list. To do this, press the Mark Text (Alt-F5) key, select Generate (*6* or *G*), then select *Generate Tables, Indexes, Automatic References, etc.* (*5* or *G*) from the next menu. The following message will appear:

   Existing tables, lists, and indexes will be replaced.
   Continue? (Y/N) Yes

Since this is the first list you have created, the appropriate response is Yes, so type *Y* or press ◄┘ to accept the Yes that WordPerfect assumes. As the list is being generated, this message will appear:

   Generation in progress. Pass: *n*, Page: *n*

where *n* represents the pass and page numbers WordPerfect is working on at the moment.

   The process will take a few minutes, depending on the total number of items that have been marked for inclusion. After the list is generated, this code will be added to your document, after the list:

   [EndDef]

The cursor will appear at the top of your list.

***CHANGING A PREVIOUSLY GENERATED LIST, INDEX, OR TABLE OF CONTENTS*** Your document may already include one or more lists or an index or table of contents that was previously generated. If you want to change the list, index, or table—either because you edited the document and the marked text now differs from that in the generated list, index, or table, or because you want to redefine the numbering style—follow these instructions.

If you have changed the text in your document, the first step is to locate the old entries and mark them again with the Block (Alt-F4) and Mark Text (Alt-F5) keys. The easiest way to locate them is to use the Search key (F2) and look for each occurrence of a Mark Text code. To do this, place the cursor on the first line of the document, press the Search key (F2), then press the Mark Text key (Alt-F5) in response to the *Srch* prompt. You will see this menu:

**1 ToC/List; 2 EndMark; 3 Index; 4 ToA; 5 Defs and Refs; 6 Subdocs: 0**

The first option, ToC/List, will locate the codes that mark text for a list or table of contents. Press *1* to select it, then your search prompt on the status line will appear as follows:

**→ Srch: [Mark]**

Press F2 or Esc to begin the search. When the cursor stops, press the Reveal Codes key (Alt-F3) to see the code, which will appear to the left of the cursor. An entry for list 1 will be surrounded by a pair of codes:

**[Mark:List,1]**

and

**[EndMark:List,1]**

An entry for a table of contents will be surrounded by these codes:

**[Mark:ToC,1]**

and

**[EndMark:ToC,1]**

If the edited text that you want to include is located between the codes, you will not have to mark it again. When the new list or table is generated, everything that appears between the pair of codes will be included. If you do need to mark the text again or just want to exclude it from your new list or table of contents, first delete the codes with the Backspace or Del key. If you are remarking the text, the next step is to press the Block (Alt-F4) key, highlight the text with the cursor movement keys, then press the Mark Text key (Alt-F5) and select the appropriate options (as described earlier).

Once you have finished locating and changing the entries and/or adding any new entries you want to include, move the cursor to the end of the document and select the *Generate Tables, Indexes, Automatic References, etc.* option from the Mark Text key (Alt-F5 6 5). As the next prompt indicates, this procedure will replace any existing table, lists, and index. However, the codes that define them remain intact during the procedure, so if your document already includes one or more lists, an index, or a table, they will be correctly regenerated along with the altered one whether or not any changes have been made to them. Enter *Y* or press ← to begin generating.

Your revised list, table, or index, and any existing ones, will then be generated, completely replacing the old ones. Since the original definition codes are still in effect, they will use the same page numbering style and appear in the same location as the old ones.

***CHANGING THE PAGE NUMBER POSITION*** If you have not altered the text but just want to change the definition for page number position before regenerating, follow these instructions. As you know, a list, index, or table of contents is set off from the rest of the document by a [DefMark] code at the beginning and an [EndMark] code at the end. When you are generating a list, index, or table, you instruct WordPerfect to delete your old list, index, or table of contents by pressing *Y* when this prompt appears:

**Existing tables, lists, and indexes will be replaced.
Continue? (Y/N): Yes**

The program regenerates the existing table, list, and/or index using the [DefMark] code you inserted when you defined it. Thus, if you want to change the page numbering style, you have to delete the original [DefMark] code and create a new one. A word of warning: If you create another list, index, or table of contents but don't delete the original, WordPerfect will create an extra.

The easiest way to find the original code is to use WordPerfect's Search feature. To do this, place the cursor at the top of the document, press the Forward Search key (F2), then the Mark Text key (Alt-F5). Next, select the Defs and Refs option (5 D or R) then choose the DefMark option (1 or D) from the next menu. Press F2 to start the search. When the cursor stops, delete the DefMark code by pressing the Backspace key (because Search always places the cursor one position to the right of the search string). When you press Backspace, you will see a prompt like this one for a List 1 definition code:

> See Chapter 7 for more information about WordPerfect's Search and Search and Replace features.

Delete [DefMark:List,1:4]? (Y/N) N

Press *Y* to delete it. Next, use the Define option from the Mark Text key (Alt-F5 D) to select a new page numbering style, then use the Generate option (Alt-F5 G G) to generate it again using your new page numbering style.

## *TABLES OF CONTENTS*

Creating a table of contents is similar to creating a list, for it involves moving the cursor to each occurrence of the text you want included, highlighting it with the Block key, and marking it with the Mark Text key. However, you can only create one table of contents per document, so the process of marking the entries is a bit different. Instead of being asked which list to include the text in, you are asked to select the *table of contents level* for each entry.

A table of contents can have up to five levels of entries; each level will be indented one tab stop to the right of the last one when you generate the table. For example, Figure 10.5 displays an excerpt from a table of contents with three levels. The first entry on level 1 is *Starting WordPerfect,* and the first entry on level 2 is *Starting WordPerfect on a Two Floppy Disk System.* There are several level 3 entries in the table: *The Default Drive, The Document Indicator, The Page Indicator, The Line Indicator,* and *The Position Indicator.*

It's important to decide which level each entry should appear on before you begin marking them or you may end up deleting and

**TABLE OF CONTENTS**

***Figure 10.5:*** An excerpt from a table of contents

reentering codes and regenerating the table several times. You can mark the entries as you type the document or you can wait until it is completed. Some writers feel they have a better overview after the text is complete; others prefer to specify the structure as they write. Whichever method you choose, the process is identical.

The five numbering styles that can be used in a table of contents are the same as in a list: no page numbers, page numbers that follow the entries, page numbers in parentheses that follow the entries, flush right page numbers, and flush right page numbers with leaders. Each level can have a different numbering style, as you will see.

## CREATING A TABLE OF CONTENTS

To create a table of contents, you use the Block and Mark Text keys to mark each word or phrase in your document that you want to include in the table, then use the Mark Text key to define the style and generate the list.

***MARKING ITEMS FOR THE TABLE OF CONTENTS*** To mark the words you want to appear in the table of contents, follow these steps:

1. Find each word or phrase that you want to include in the table of contents. You can use the Forward Search key (F2) to help.

2. When you locate one, place the cursor on the first character, then press the Block key (Alt-F4) and use the cursor movement keys to highlight the entire entry.

3. With Block on, press the Mark Text key (Alt-F5). You will see this menu at the bottom of the screen:

**Mark for: 1 ToC; 2 List; 3 Index; 4 ToA: 0**

4. Select **1** or **C** for Table of Contents. A prompt will then appear, asking you to type the level number for this particular entry, as shown below:

**ToC Level:**

Enter the level number (1-5). Repeat these steps until all entries have been marked.

***DEFINING THE STYLE***   To define the style for your table of contents, follow these steps:

1. Move the cursor to the end of the document and press Ctrl-⏎ to create a new page that will separate the table of contents from the rest of the document. You may wish to type a heading at the top of the page, such as the phrase *TABLE OF CONTENTS*.

2. Press the Mark Text key (Alt-F5) and select Define (**5** or **D**), then select Define Table of Contents (**1** or **C**) from the Mark Text: Define menu shown in Figure 10.2. The Table of Contents Definition menu will appear, as shown in Figure 10.6.

Use this screen to specify the total number of levels for the table and the page numbering style for each level. Since I used three levels in my table, my next step was to select the Number of Levels option and enter *3*.

3. Select the Number of Levels option and enter the number of levels you want in your table of contents.

Notice that the second option, Display Last Level in Wrapped Format, is set to No. *Wrapped format* means that entries in the last level of your table will be displayed next to each other, separated only by a semicolon, as shown in the partial table in Figure 10.7.

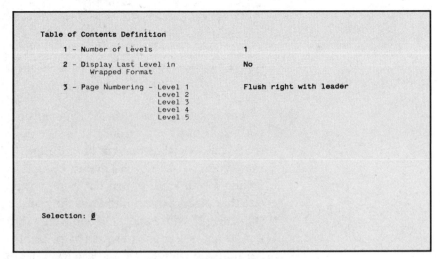

*Figure 10.6:* The Table of Contents Definition menu

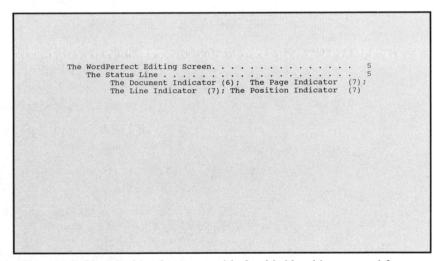

*Figure 10.7:* Partial table of contents with the third level in wrapped format

In this example, the last level is level 3, and it begins with the words *The Document Indicator* and ends with *The Position Indicator.* Note that I selected option 3, (Pg#) Follows Entry, for Page Numbering on this level, so the page numbers are in parentheses and come right after the entries. When the last level is displayed in wrapped format like they are in this example, WordPerfect only lets you use option 1, 2, or 3 for Page Numbering. Note that this illustration is part of the

table of contents shown in Figure 10.5, where wrapped format was
not used.

4.  Unless you want to use the wrapped format, leave option 2 as
    it is (set to No).

The next step is to select the page number style for each level. Unless
you are using wrapped format, you can choose from among the five
styles that were illustrated in Figure 10.4. If you are using wrapped format, your last level will have to be option 1, 2, or 3. WordPerfect's
default for all levels (when not using wrapped format) is option 5, the
one that places page numbers at the right and connects them with dots
(Flush Right with Leader). If you want to use this style, leave option 3 as
it is. If not, select another style by pressing *3* and typing the style number that you want to use for each level. Remember that a different style
can be used for each level. As you can see from the table of contents displayed in Figure 10.5, three levels were specified, and each level used
the default page number style.

5.  Unless you want to use a different numbering style for one or
    more levels, leave the default for page numbering, which is
    Flush Right with Leader for each level. To change the num-
    bering style, press **3** and in response to the prompt

    **1 None; 2 Pg# Follows; 3 (Pg #) Follows; 4 Flush Rt;
    5 Flush Rt with Leader**

    select the number you want for each level. Press Exit (F7)
    when you are finished.

6.  After you have selected the page number position, press Exit
    (F7) twice.

The Table of Contents Definition screen disappears and you are
returned to the Edit screen. You can then check the Reveal Codes
screen for the following code:

**[DefMark:ToC,*n*:5,5,5]**

where *n* corresponds to the number of levels you have selected: 1, 2,
3, 4, or 5, and the 5's represent the page numbering style.

***GENERATING THE TABLE OF CONTENTS*** Now you're ready to produce the table of contents. To do this, press the Mark Text key (Alt-F5), select Generate (*6* or *G*), then select *Generate Tables, Indexes, Automatic References, etc.* (*5* or *G*). The following message will appear:

Existing tables, lists, and indexes will be replaced.
Continue? (Y/N): Yes

See Chapter 3 for more information about using the Switch key to maintain two documents in memory simultaneously.

Press *Y* or ←. (If there is insufficient RAM in your computer, you may see a message at this point asking you to clear the screen used for Doc 2. If this happens, use the Switch key, Shift-F3, to move to Doc 2, and use F7 to exit from it.)

WordPerfect will then generate your table of contents, and this message will appear while the program is working:

Generation in progress. Pass: *n*, Page: *n*

where *n* represents the pass and page numbers WordPerfect is working on. The process will take a second or two, after which the table will appear. If you used the same options as I did, it will resemble Figure 10.5.

## *INDEXES*

As with lists and tables of contents, creating an index is not entirely an automatic process. Unless you use a concordance file (a list of words and phrases that you want to index on), you must individually mark every occurrence of each entry you want in the index. (Concordance files are explained later in this section.) Although this sounds like an enormous amount of work, it does not have to be, if you plan carefully. For one thing, you can mark entries as you type them. For another, you won't have to use the Block key except to mark phrases (more than one word). If you wait until after the document is completed to mark them, WordPerfect's Macro feature can be used to expedite the task.

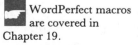 WordPerfect macros are covered in Chapter 19.

Headings and subheadings are both permitted in an index, and each entry can include as many as 73 characters. Unlike lists and tables of contents, you do not have to use the exact words or phrases being marked in your document, but can type the entries separately, rewording them just for the index. Headings are automatically capitalized, unless you type them in lowercase (instead of using the wording in the document). Subheadings appear in lowercase, unless you type them separately in capital letters.

I strongly recommend that you spend time analyzing your document and carefully consider which words or phrases will be used as headings and subheadings before you start marking them. If a word or phrase is not spelled exactly the same way each time it is marked, it will appear as a new entry, rather than as an additional page number next to the same entry. For example, Figure 10.8 shows two distinct headings, *Function key* and *Function keys,* that were obviously intended to be one heading. One way to avoid this duplication is to switch to the Doc 2 area (using Shift-F3), create a list of the correct spelling for each heading and subheading (a *style sheet*), and refer to it before you mark the entries.

```
Carriage Return key 11
Ctrl key    9
Cursor   6
Default Drive 3
Delete
      from cursor to end of line   28
      to the end of a page   28
      word   28
Document Indicator  6
Enter key   12
Exit Key   27, 28
Function   10
Function key   9, 10
Function keys   9
Function-key template 11
Help key   25
Line Indicator   7
Num Lock key   13
      and the position indicator   15
      with Shift keys   14
Overflow files   28
Page Down key   22
Page Indicator   7
Page Up key   22
```

*Figure 10.8:* A poorly planned index

## CREATING AN INDEX

To create an index, you use the Block and Mark Text keys to mark each phrase, and the Mark Text key alone to mark individual words, then define and generate the index. To simplify the process, you can also create a concordance file to designate words and phrases that you want indexed.

***MARKING TEXT FOR AN INDEX*** Follow these steps to indicate the words and phrases you want to appear in an index:

1. To designate a one-word entry for your index as you are typing the document, place the cursor anywhere in the word (or on the blank space following it) and press the Mark Text key (Alt-F5). The following menu will appear:

   **1 Auto Ref; 2 Subdoc; 3 Index; 4 ToA Short Form; 5 Define; 6 Generate: 0**

   To index a section of text that includes more than one word, mark it first with the Block key (Alt-F4), then press the Mark Text key (Alt-F5). This menu will appear:

   **Mark for: 1 ToC; 2 List; 3 Index; 4 ToA: 0**

2. Whichever method you are using, select Index (**3** or **I**). You will then see a prompt that asks for the index heading, followed by the word or phrase that you blocked or that you indicated with the cursor. WordPerfect assumes this is what you wish to mark, so it is the default. For example, when I blocked the phrase *Function keys* and selected the Index option from the Mark Text key, the prompt appeared as follows:

   **Index heading: Function keys**

3. If this is actually the wording that you want for this heading, press ◄─┘. Otherwise, type a different heading for this entry, then press ◄─┘.

4. Next you will be asked to type a subheading with this prompt:

   **Subheading:**

   If you accepted the default word or phrase as the heading in step 2 (such as *Function keys* in the example), nothing will appear after this prompt and you can simply type a subheading of your own choosing or press ◄─┘ to leave it blank if you don't want to create a subheading. However, if you typed something different (rather than accepting the text WordPerfect suggested for the heading), WordPerfect will assume that you now want to use the blocked text as a subheading. You then have three choices: accept it by pressing ◄─┘; press Ctrl-End to delete the suggested subheading if you don't want a subheading at all, then press ◀—┘; or type a different subheading (pressing any character will erase the old subheading).

5. Repeat the four steps above until you have marked each item you want in the index. If you check the Reveal Codes screen by pressing Alt-F3, you will see that each heading or subheading is marked with a code resembling this one:

[Index:Function keys]

where *Function keys* is the actual entry. If you included a subheading, it will resemble this:

[Index:Function keys;template]

where *template* is the subheading.

**USING A CONCORDANCE FILE**    The Concordance feature was designed to simplify the process of building an index. Rather than locating and marking each word or phrase individually throughout the document you are indexing, you can use this feature to type a list of commonly used words and phrases, save the list as a separate file, then instruct WordPerfect to use this concordance file when generating the index. When the index is completed, it will include entries individually marked (using the procedures described above), as well as entries from the concordance file that WordPerfect finds in your document. Entries from the concordance file that are not located in the document will not appear in the index. Incidentally, you can create an index using only a concordance file and do not have to mark individual entries in the document at all.

To sort your concordance file when it is on the Edit screen, press the Merge/Sort key (Ctrl-F9), select Sort, then press ◀—┘ twice. When the Sort by Line screen appears, if key 1 is not *field 1, word 1,* select Keys and press A 1 ◀—┘ 1 ◀—┘ F7. The last step is to select Perform Action. For more information about the Sort by Line feature, see Chapter 18.

To create a concordance file, you simply clear the screen, type the list of common entries, then save the file. Although an entry can exceed one line, each separate entry must be followed by an [HRt] code (pressing ◀—┘ inserts this code). Although it is optional, you should sort the file alphabetically using WordPerfect's Line Sort feature because this speeds up the process of index generation. Since WordPerfect ignores case when matching the entries in the concordance file to text in your document, you can use all uppercase (or all lowercase) when typing the list.

A word of warning: You may not be able to use this feature if your concordance file is very large and the amount of RAM in your system is limited. If your concordance file is too large, you'll know because when you generate the index you will be warned that there is not enough memory to use the entire file and you can choose to stop the index generation process. If you do not stop it, your final index will only contain entries located up to the point where the warning was issued.

While typing the concordance file, if you want the wording in your final index to differ from the wording of an entry in the concordance file, mark the entry using the Block key (Alt-F4) and Mark Text key (Alt-F5), then choose Index and assign a different expression to it (as described in the previous section). Note that when you generate the index, WordPerfect will search for a match based on the actual entry in the Index code (as seen in the Reveal Codes screen), not the entry visible on the Edit screen.

To create subheadings in a concordance file, you have no choice but to mark your entries using the Mark Text key. For example, Figure 10.9 shows part of a concordance file that I created. Note that three of the entries, *Retrieve, Return key,* and *Reveal Codes key,* have subheadings; I had to block and mark each subheading using the Block and Mark Text keys.

Figure 10.10 shows the subheading *in column mode* being marked with the index heading *Reveal Codes key.* After I typed the heading *Reveal Codes key* and pressed ←, WordPerfect suggested the blocked text *in column mode* for the subheading entry, as shown in Figure 10.11. To accept it, I pressed ←.

Note that you can have more than one index mark for an entry in your concordance file, if you want the reference to appear under more than one index heading.

After typing, marking, and sorting your concordance file, be sure to save it as a separate file.

***DEFINING THE STYLE***   The next step in creating an index is to define a numbering style, and it works almost exactly the same as when you create a list or a table of contents. Before you begin, move the cursor to the end of the document and insert a hard page break

```
           Ragged right margin
           RAM
           Realign
           Records
           Rectangle
           Redirecting overflow files, buffers, and temporary macros
           Redline
           Reformatting text
           Release left margin
           Relocating text
           Remove redline, and strikeout text
           Rename files
           Renumbering pages
           Repeating a macro
           Repeating a command
           Replace Key (Alt-F2)
           Required hyphen
           Required space
           Required page break
           Restoring deleted text
           Retrieve
            blocked text
            column
            files
            rectangle
           Retrieve Text Key
           Return key
            block mode
            code
            outline mode
           Reveal Codes Key
            in column mode
            line draw
            math
           Reverse Search Key
           Right justification
           Run merge
           Rush print job
```

*Figure 10.9:* A partial concordance file

```
       Move
       Newspaper columns
       Page Length
       Paragraph Sort
       Place markers
       Position indicator
       Print
       Realign
       Replace
       Retrieve
        blocked text
        column
        files
        rectangle
       Return key
       ------------------------------------------------------------
        block mode
        code
        outline mode
       Reveal Codes Key
        in column mode
        line draw
        math
       Reverse Search key
       Index heading: Reveal Codes key_
```

*Figure 10.10:* Marking a subheading in a concordance file

```
Replace
Retrieve
 blocked text
 column
 files
 rectangle
Return key
------------------------------------------------------------
 block mode
 code
 outline mode
Reveal Codes Key
 in column mode
 line draw
 math
Reverse Search key
Right justification
Ruler Line
Save
Search
Select
Sort
Speller
Switch
Subheading: in column mode
```

*Figure 10.11:* The suggested subheading

(by pressing Ctrl-◄┘) to isolate the index from the rest of the text. You may also wish to type a title for the index page.

1. Define the index by pressing the Mark Text key (Alt-F5) and selecting Define (**5** or **D**), then Define Index (**3** or **I**).

2. A prompt will appear asking you to enter the name of the concordance file:

   **Concordance Filename (Enter = none):**

   If you are not using a concordance file, just press ◄┘ to continue. Otherwise, type the name of your concordance file, then press ◄┘. The Index Definition screen will then appear, as shown in Figure 10.12. Note that this screen is nearly the same as the List Definition screen (Figure 10.3).

3. Select one of the five page numbering styles that are illustrated in Figure 10.4. Note that the index shown in Figure 10.8 uses the second option, Page Numbers Follow Entries.

After you complete step 3, the Reveal Codes screen should include a code like this (where *5* is the numbering style; yours may vary):

   **[DefMark:Index,5]**

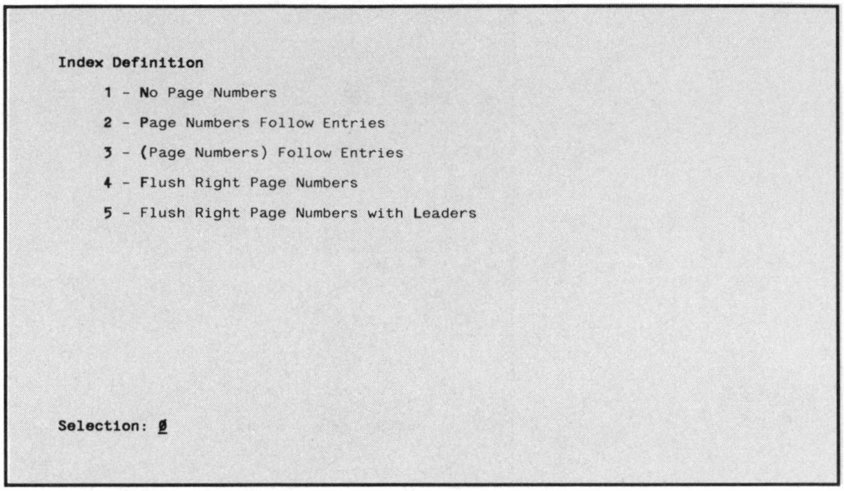

```
Index Definition
     1 - No Page Numbers
     2 - Page Numbers Follow Entries
     3 - (Page Numbers) Follow Entries
     4 - Flush Right Page Numbers
     5 - Flush Right Page Numbers with Leaders




Selection: 0
```

***Figure 10.12:*** The Index Definition screen

If you used a concordance file, the code will look like this:

    **[DefMark:Index,5;*filename*]**

where *filename* is the name you assigned to your concordance file when you saved it. Note that when you generate the index, it will appear at the code position.

***GENERATING THE INDEX***   To generate the index, select Generate from the Mark Text key (Alt-F5 G), then select *Generate Tables, Indexes, Automatic References, etc.* (*5* or *G*). The following message will appear:

    **Existing tables, lists, and indexes will be replaced.**
    **Continue? (Y/N): Yes**

Press *Y* or ←┘. WordPerfect will then begin generating your index and this message will appear while it is working:

    **Generation in progress. Pass: *n*, Page: *n***

A few minutes will elapse, then the index will appear. Note that an [EndDef] code will be inserted at the end, to mark the boundary of the defined index.

## TABLES OF AUTHORITIES

A *table of authorities* is a list of statutes, cases, rules of court, treaties, regulations, and other authorities that are cited in a legal brief. It is generally divided into sections such as statutes, cases, and rules of court, or federal, state, and local regulations. WordPerfect permits as many as sixteen different sections, and the formatting style can vary for each section. Each citation can include references to multiple page numbers. Individual sections are sorted alphanumerically, as shown in Figure 10.13, which displays a table containing three sections: statutes, cases, and rules of court.

## CREATING A TABLE OF AUTHORITIES

The procedure for marking entries for a table of authorities is similar to marking index entries in that you block and mark each entry with the Mark Text key, then edit the entry so that it appears exactly the way you want it in the table. However, you are then asked to enter a *short form*, which is an abbreviated version of the entry. If the reference appears more than once in the document, marking the others is easy because you can omit the lengthy initial step of blocking the text and typing the entry and instead simply type the abbreviated short form. The next step is to define the table of authorities, designating the order, location, and formatting style for each section of the table; this is followed by typing section headings. Generating the table is the last, and easiest, step.

### MARKING THE CITATIONS TO BE INCLUDED IN THE TABLE OF AUTHORITIES

You use the Block (Alt-F4) and Mark Text keys (Alt-F5) to mark each reference. The first time you mark a citation (or if there is only one occurrence) it must be designated as the full form. If there are multiple occurrences, be sure that you mark the *first* one in the document as the full form. Before marking anything, be sure you have planned the sections so you'll know which section number to enter for

TABLE OF AUTHORITIES

STATUES                                                      PAGE NUMBER

California Civil Code Section 930.03 (b) . . . . . . . . . . 16

California Civil Code Section 990.04 (d) . . . . . . . . . . 16

California Probate Code Section 1338.6 . . . . . . . . . . . 22

California Probate Code Section 1811.1 . . . . . . . . . . 3, 5

California Probate Code Sections 970-977 . . . . . . . . . . 10

California Revenue and Taxation Code Sections 12401-12443 . . . . 9

United States Internal Revenue Code Section 2061, 2063-2075 . 9


CASES

California First Bank v. Jones 99 CA 2D 415 . . . . . . . . 11

Estate of Gary 94 CA 3d 582 (1965) . . . . . . . . . . . 12, 19

Estate of Kensington 491 CA 3d 402 (1979) . . . . . . . . . 11

Estate of Lawrence 87 C 2d 976 (1958) . . . . . . . . . . . 9

Estate of Ramirez 11 CA 3d 605 (1971) . . . . . . . . . . . 12

Estate of Randolph 196 CA 2d 987 (1986) . . . . . . . . . . 10

Estate of Walsh 528 CA 3d 247 (1965) . . . . . . . . . . . 22

Estate of White 210 CA 2d 29 (1978) . . . . . . . . . . 10, 19

First National Trust Assn. v. Smith 125 CA 5D (1983). . . . . 9

Jones v. Browning 437 US 95 . . . . . . . . . . . . . . . . 9


RULES OF COURT

2(a) . . . . . . . . . . . . . . . . . . . . . . . . . . . . 7

3(b) . . . . . . . . . . . . . . . . . . . . . . . . . . . . 7

*Figure 10.13:* A sample table of authorities

each reference. Follow these steps to mark an item as the full form:

1. Highlight the citation using the Block key (Alt-F4) and the regular cursor movement keys, then press the Mark Text key (Alt-F5). This menu will appear:

**Mark for: 1 ToC; 2 List; 3 Index; 4 ToA: 0**

2. Select option 4, ToA.

3. You will see this prompt asking for the section number:

   **ToA Section Number (Press Enter for Short Form only):**

   Type the appropriate section number, then press ←. (Do not press ← alone because it designates the entry as a short form, which is incorrect.)

The blocked entry then appears on a special screen, similar to the one shown in Figure 10.14, where you can edit the entry to enhance the reference that will actually appear in the table of authorities (without changing it in the body of the document). For example, you can expand it to include up to 30 lines, designate formatting changes such as underline, bold, and italics, and indent the second and following lines if it is a multiple line entry.

4. Edit your entry if you need to, and press F7 when you are finished. If you don't want to make any changes to the entry, simply press F7 without editing.

   Next, you are asked to enter the short form for this citation. WordPerfect prompts you with the first 40 characters of the full form, as shown below:

   **Short Form: Estate of Kensington 491 CA 3d 402 (1979**

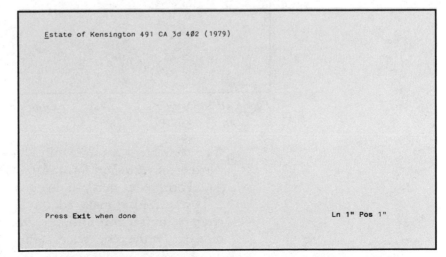

```
Estate of Kensington 491 CA 3d 402 (1979)




















Press Exit when done                                          Ln 1" Pos 1"
```

*Figure 10.14:* Editing the full form entry

The short form must be unique, since it is used to identify this particular citation wherever it occurs in your document. If it is not unique, you will see an error message later on, when you generate the table of authorities.

5. Use ← and → to move through the prompt and edit it if you want, then press ↵. If you want to use an entirely different short form, use Ctrl-End to delete the whole prompt, then type your entry. If you want the short form to match the full form, just press F7.

    In this example, you could change the short form to *Estate of Kensington* by pressing → until the cursor is on the *4*, then pressing Ctrl-End to erase the rest of the citation.

6. Check the Reveal Codes screen (Alt-F3) to see the Table of Authorities code, as shown in Figure 10.15.

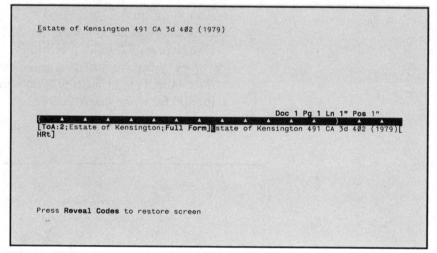

*Figure 10.15:* Viewing the Table of Authorities code in the Reveal Codes screen

The characters *ToA:2;* signify that this is a section 2 entry. Next comes the short form, *Estate of Kensington,* then the code Full Form. Note that you do not see the text of the full form.

If you need to make editing changes to the full form or change the section number, you must place the cursor directly *after* the code, select Define from the Mark Text key

(Alt-F5 5), then select Edit Table of Authorities Full Form (**5** or **E**). This will place the cursor in the special screen shown in Figure 10.14, where you can edit the citation using the regular editing keys. When you finish, press Exit (F7). WordPerfect will ask for the section number, prompting you with the original one. Either press ◄─┘ to accept the original section number, or type the one you want.

7. If there are any other occurrences of the citation, use the Short Form option from the Mark Text key to include them in your table of authorities. To do this, highlight the citation using the Block (Alt-F4) and cursor movement keys, press the Mark Text key (Alt-F5), and select **4**, ToA. Press ◄─┘ when you see this prompt:

     ToA Section Number (Press Enter for Short Form only):

The highlighted text appears in the prompt, as shown below:

     Short Form: Estate of Kensington

Next, you can either press ◄─┘ to accept the contents of the prompt as the short form, edit it as described in step 5, or erase it and type another short form. In this example, it must match the one you entered in step 5 for this citation, so you may need to edit it or type it again. In the Reveal Codes screen, the code for the short form is as follows:

     [ToA:;Estate of Kensington;]

where *Estate of Kensington* is the short form.

***KEEPING A LIST OF SHORT FORMS***    If your document is long and contains many frequently repeated citations, you may wish to use the Doc 2 work area to keep a separate list of the short forms so that you can refer back to it if you forget the exact text of a short form. To do this, after marking each full form press the Switch key (Shift-F3) and type the short form in the Doc 2 area, then press Switch again to get back to the document you are marking (in Doc 1). When you have finished marking all citations in the brief, save the list using a new file name, in case you need it for future reference.

***USING SEARCH TO MARK CITATIONS***   If you are marking the entries after your document has been typed, you can simplify your task by using WordPerfect's Extended Search feature to help you locate and mark each citation. To do this, begin at the top of the document and mark the first occurrence of a citation. Next, use Home F2 to search for the remaining occurrences using a unique word. For instance, in the above example you could search for the *Estate of Kensington* citation by entering *Kensington* as the search string (see Chapter 7 if you need to refresh your memory). Next, mark the citation by selecting the Short Form option from the Mark Text key (Alt-F5 4). WordPerfect prompts you with the short form you selected when marking the last full form, and you can simply press ⏎ to accept it.

## DEFINING THE STYLE

To define the style for your table of authorities, you type the section headings, use the Mark Text key to enter definition codes for each one, then for each section specify whether you want dot leaders, underlining, and/or blank lines separating each citation. A table of authorities usually appears at the beginning of a brief, so you should define the table at the top of the document.

1. Move the cursor to the top of page 1 (press Home Home ↑) and press Ctrl-⏎ to force a page break.

2. Change the page number of the first page of text, which has now become page 2, back to page 1. To do this, press the Format key (Shift-F8), select Page, select New Page Number, enter **1** as the new page number, and press ⏎ F7. Note that if you do not change the page number in this manner, you will get an error message when the table is generated, and the page numbers listed in the table of authorities may be incorrect.

3. Press Page Up to move the cursor to the top of the document. You may want to give the document a title, such as *TABLE OF AUTHORITIES*.

4. Type the heading for the first section, such as *STATUTES*. As you can see in Figure 10.13, my next step was to press the

Flush Right key (Alt-F6) and type *PAGE NUMBER,* but this is optional.

5. Press ◄┘ twice to leave a few blank lines between the section heading and the entries. Although you aren't required to leave the blank lines, the entries will begin immediately after the code so it is advisable to leave at least one.

6. To enter the definition code for the first section, press the Mark Text key (Alt-F5) and select Define, then select Define Table of Authorities. You will see this prompt:

> **Section Number (1-16):**

Since this is the first section, type **1**, then press ◄┘. You will then see the screen illustrated in Figure 10.16. Note the *1* at the top (*Definition for Table of Authorities 1*), indicating that you are defining the first section.

By default, dot leaders appear between each entry and its corresponding page number(s) at the right margin, as shown in Figure 10.13. If you prefer flush right numbers without the leading dots, select option 1 and press **N**.

The second selection, Underlining Allowed, is set to No. If you want to include underlining in the table, press **2** then **Y** to change it. Note that I set it to Yes in my example, since it is common practice to underline case citations.

You can use the Setup key (Shift-F1) to change the Table of Authority defaults for Dot Leaders, Underlining Allowed, or Blank Line Between Authorities. Press Shift-F1, select Initial Settings (*5* or *I*), then choose Table of Authorities (*6* or *A*). You will see the Setup: Table of Authorities screen, which you can use to change the defaults. The changes you make in this screen will be permanent, unless you use Setup to change them again.

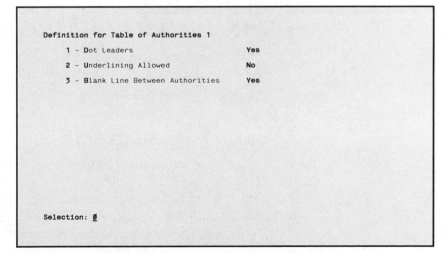

*Figure 10.16:* The Definition for Table of Authorities screen

The third selection, Blank Line Between Authorities, is set to Yes, meaning that when the table is generated, each citation will automatically be separated from the next one by a blank line. In my example, I left this setting at Yes. Press ◄─┘ when you finish making your choices, and you will be returned to the Edit screen.

7. For each remaining section in your table, follow the steps described above to enter a heading and define the style.

### GENERATING THE TABLE OF AUTHORITIES

The last step is the easiest one. After marking each citation and defining the sections, you press the Mark Text key (Alt-F5) and select Generate (*6* or *G*), then select *Generate Tables, Indexes, Automatic References, etc.* (*5* or *G*). Note that the cursor can be anywhere in the document when you do this. When you do, you will see this prompt:

Existing tables, lists, and indexes will be replaced.
Continue? (Y/N): Yes

Press ◄─┘ or *Y* to begin the process. After a few minutes, the table will appear with the cursor at the end of it.

## OUTLINES AND PARAGRAPH NUMBERING

Very few word processors can be used to create outlines and numbered lists automatically. WordPerfect includes both these features, and as you'll soon see, they are very useful.

### CREATING AN OUTLINE

To create an outline, you use the Date/Outline key (Shift-F5). When you work in Outline mode, the ◄─┘ and Tab keys function quite differently from how they work in Edit mode, so you'll have to practice until you get used to their new functions. As you'll find out, ◄─┘ creates a number, and Tab moves it to the next level. Follow these steps to see how they work:

1. Turn on Outline mode by pressing the Date/Outline key (Shift-F5) and selecting the Outline option (**4** or **O**). To verify that Outline is on, this message appears in the lower left corner of the screen:

   **Outline**

2. The next step is to press ◄┘. As you can see, this inserts a number into your document that designates the first paragraph level of your outline, Roman numeral *I*.

3. Press the Space bar (or type one or more characters), then press ◄┘ again. The Roman numeral *II* will appear underneath the *I*.

4. Repeat this action five more times, so that your screen appears as follows:

   I.
   II.
   III.
   IV.
   V.
   VI.
   VII.

As you have learned, pressing ◄┘ adds a paragraph number to your outline. However, you may have also discovered that if you do not press the Space bar or type at least one character before pressing ◄┘, the paragraph number will just move down a line and a blank line will be inserted above it.

Look in the Reveal Codes screen (Alt-F3) to see the code that WordPerfect inserted when you pressed ◄┘ to create a number:

[Par Num:Auto]

As you can see, the "numbers" are really just codes that appear as characters on the Edit screen. The word *Auto* inside the brackets indicates that WordPerfect automatically inserted this number for you, and it will change automatically as you add, delete, or move other numbered paragraphs around it. For instance, if you move the cursor onto the Roman numeral II and press the Delete key (you can do this while in Reveal Codes), you will see that what used to be *III* will be changed into *II,* what used to be *IV* will become *III,* and so forth.

5. Now delete all the paragraph numbers except the first so that you can start over. To delete a number, move the cursor to the right of it and press Backspace once, or place the cursor on the number and press Delete.

6. To begin creating the outline shown in Figure 10.17, position the cursor after the Roman numeral I and type the following text:

**Alternative Solutions**

7. Press ⟵ and the Roman numeral II will appear.

```
I.   Problem Definition

     Due to poor cost control, insufficient growth, sloppy
     staffing practices and lax product evaluation, the company
     has had a $3 million loss in the last quarter.  The Board of
     Directors has issued a mandatory order to lay off 15% of all
     managers, and 20% of all other workers.

     Issues and guidelines are needed to formulate reduction
     plans.

II.  Alternative Solutions

     A. Early retirement for senior personnel

        1. Advantages:

           a.   Less harsh feelings; optional early
                retirement may be welcomed by older workers

        2. Disadvantages:

           a.   May lose the best, most experienced employees
           b.   This action alone will not meet reduction
                targets

        3. Issues:

           a.   Guidelines won't allow this option
```

*Figure 10.17:* Outline for the XYZ Plastics, Inc. case (continued on next page)

```
   B.  Performance and ability will be used as criteria to lay
       off/and or fire

       1. Advantages:

           a.  Potential benefits to the company to get rid
               of the deadwood
           b.  Improve morale of better workers
           c.  Fair policy

       2. Disadvantages:

           a.  A rating system has never been devised since
               the company has never fired or laid off an
               employee
           b.  Possible union activity

       3. Issues

           a.  Expense of creating job review system

   C.  Offer all employees pay cuts so that nobody will be
       fired or laid off.

       1. Advantages:

           a.  Maintains company's paternalistic image
           b.  Morale booster: everyone pitches in and works
               hard to get wages back up, prevent their
               friends from being laid off.

       2. Disadvantages:

           a.  ⟨illegible⟩
               to support the deadwood
           b.  Chaotic, hard to implement

       3. Issues:

           a.  Possible legal action

   D.  Seniority

       1.  Advantages:

       2.  Disadvantages:

       3.  Issues:

III. Recommended Solution
```

*Figure 10.17:* Outline for the XYZ Plastics, Inc. case  (continued)

8. With the cursor positioned right after the *II*, press Tab. The *II* is moved one tab stop to the right and converted into an *A*. If you press Tab once more, the *A* will change into the Arabic numeral *1;* pressing it again will change the *1* into lowercase *a.* Pressing Shift-Tab moves it back to the previous level. This process can continue for eight levels. However, if you type any characters or press the Space bar after the number,

then the Tab key will work the regular way, indenting the cursor to the next tab stop.

As you've just found out, when you work in Outline mode, pressing the Tab key right after a paragraph number changes the paragraph number to the next level, which is level A in our example. The first level (I) is at the margin, the second level (A) is at the first tab stop, the third level is at the second tab stop, and so forth.

For the numbers 1 through 5, this is this order:

Level 1: I. II. III. IV. V.

Level 2: A. B. C. D. E.

Level 3: 1. 2. 3. 4. 5.

Level 4: a. b. c. d. e.

Level 5: (1) (2) (3) (4) (5)

Level 6: (a) (b) (c) (d) (e)

Level 7: i) ii) iii) iv) v)

Level 8: a) b) c) d) e)

Figure 10.18 shows how these levels actually look in an outline. Note that if the last level is reached, and you indent yet another tab stop, WordPerfect will continue to use the last style.

In Outline mode, when you want to move the cursor one or more tab stops to the right without adding or changing a paragraph number, you can use the Indent key (F4) or press the Space bar once followed by Tab. The Indent key will function just as it does in Edit mode, moving all text to the next tab stop until the ⏎ key is pressed.

9. Press Indent (F4) and type this entry for level A:

   **Early retirement for senior personnel**

10. Press ⏎, which inserts the Roman numeral *II,* and press Tab again to change it to *B.*

11. Press Indent (F4) again and type

    **Performance and ability will be used as criteria to lay off and/or fire**

```
I.    Introduction
II.   Background
III.  Problem definition
IV.   Principal issues
V.    Alternative solutions
      A.
      B.
      C.
      D.
      E.
          1.
          2.
          3.
          4.
          5.
              a.
              b.
              c.
              d.
              e.
                  (1)
                  (2)
                  (3)
                  (4)
                  (5)
                      (a)
                      (b)
                      (c)
                      (d)
                      (e)
                          i)
                          ii)
                          iii)
                          iv)
                          v)
                              a)
                              |||
                              c)
                              d)
                              e)
```

*Figure 10.18:* Outline numbering

12. Press ⏎ again, inserting a *II,* then press Tab to convert the *II* to *C.* Press F4 to indent, then type this sentence as the third alternative:

    **Offer all employees pay cuts so that nobody will be fired or laid off**

Now your document is beginning to look like a useful outline! However, a few paragraphs to explain the problems these alternative solutions are supposed to solve might be helpful, so you should insert another level 1 entry, *Problem Definition,* before *Alternative Solutions.*

13. Move the cursor to the beginning of the document by pressing Home Home ↑. Press ⏎ and the Roman numeral I will be inserted. Did you see the number in front of the entry *Alternative Solutions* turn into a II? If you press the Space bar

and press ← once more, a new II will be added and the old II will turn into a III. This happens because of WordPerfect's automatic renumbering of outline entries. Now press the Backspace key to delete the extra II (if you tried it).

14.  Type this entry after the *I*:

**Problem Definition**

Your outline should now appear like the one in Figure 10.19.

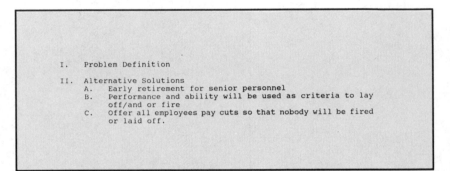

```
I.    Problem Definition

II.   Alternative Solutions
      A.   Early retirement for senior personnel
      B.   Performance and ability will be used as criteria to lay
           off/and or fire
      C.   Offer all employees pay cuts so that nobody will be fired
           or laid off.
```

*Figure 10.19:* The partial outline

15.  To complete the outline at IIA, *Early retirement for senior personel,* position the cursor after the word *personnel,* press ←, press the Tab key twice, press the Space bar once, and type

**Advantages**

16.  Press ←, then press Tab twice, press the Space bar once, and type

**Disadvantages**

17.  Press ←, then press the Tab key twice, press the Space bar once, and type

**Issues**

Remember, if you press ← too often and find you have added a number you don't want, you can delete it by pressing either the Backspace key (if the cursor is to the right of it) or the Delete key (if the cursor is on it). This will delete the extra Tab code and renumber your entry correctly. If you press Tab and accidentally move a paragraph number and change it to the next level, you can press Shift-Tab to convert it back to the previous level.

Figure 10.17 shows the completed outline; you can continue exploring WordPerfect's Outline feature by typing the rest of the entries.

***NUMBERING AND PUNCTUATION STYLE***   You are now familiar with the default numbering style, called *outline style,* as shown in Figure 10.17. If you prefer another style, you can use the Define option on the Date/Outline key (Shift-F5) to change it. You can select from among three other styles supplied by WordPerfect, or you can customize the numbering style using your own characters or symbols.

When you select this option by pressing Shift-F5 6, you'll see the Paragraph Number Definition menu shown in Figure 10.20.

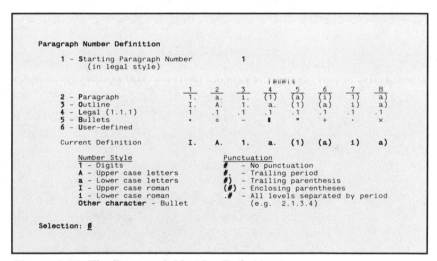

*Figure 10.20:* The Paragraph Number Definition menu

As you can see from this screen, the three other styles WordPerfect provides are paragraph, legal, and bullet style. For the numbers 1 to 5, paragraph style is as follows:

Level 1: 1.  2.  3.  4.  5.

Level 2: a.  b.  c.  d.  e.

Level 3: i.  ii.  iii.  iv.  v.

Level 4: (1)  (2)  (3)  (4)  (5)

Level 5: (a)  (b)  (c)  (d)  (e)

Level 6: (i)  (ii)  (iii)  (iv)  (v)

Level 7: 1)  2)  3)  4)  5)

Level 8: a)  b)  c)  d)  e)

and legal style is as follows:

Level 1: 1  2  3  4  5

Level 2: 1.1.  1.2.  1.3.  1.4.  1.5.

Level 3: 1.1.1.  1.1.2.  1.1.3.  1.1.4.  1.1.5.

Level 4: 1.1.1.1.  1.1.1.2.  1.1.1.3.  1.1.1.4.  1.1.1.5.

Level 5: 1.1.1.1.1.  1.1.1.1.2.  1.1.1.1.3.  1.1.1.1.4.  1.1.1.1.5.

Level 6: 1.1.1.1.1.1.  1.1.1.1.1.2.  1.1.1.1.1.3.  1.1.1.1.1.4. 1.1.1.1.1.5.

Level 7: 1.1.1.1.1.1.1.  1.1.1.1.1.1.2.  1.1.1.1.1.1.3. 1.1.1.1.1.1.4.  1.1.1.1.1.1.5.

Level 8: 1.1.1.1.1.1.1.1.  1.1.1.1.1.1.1.2.  1.1.1.1.1.1.1.3. 1.1.1.1.1.1.1.4.  1.1.1.1.1.1.1.5.

Figure 10.21 shows the screen version of the outline you saw in Figure 10.17, as it looks when you select the bullets style.

You can test these styles on your practice outline by moving the cursor to the top of the file, selecting Define from the Date/Outline key (Shift-F5 6), then selecting *2* or *P* for Paragraph style, *4* or *L* for Legal, or *5* or *B* for Bullets. Press Exit (F7) twice, then Home Home ↓ to reformat the text and update the numbers in your outline.

The sixth option on the Paragraph Number Definition menu is *User-defined;* as the name implies, you can use it to make up your own numbering style. To do this, press *6* or *U,* then select a style for each of the eight levels from among the number and punctuation styles shown on the menu such as *1* for digits, *A* for uppercase letters, *#* for no punctuation, and *#.* for a trailing period.

You can use the first option on the Paragraph Number Definition menu, Starting Paragraph Number, to select a number other than *1* for the first paragraph in your outline, regardless of which numbering style

```
    •     Alternative Solutions

          ○ Early retirement for senior personnel

                - Advantages:

                      ■     Less harsh feelings; optional early
                            retirement may be welcomed by older workers

                - Disadvantages:

                      ■     May lose the best, most experienced employees
                      ■     This action alone will not meet reduction
                            targets

                - Issues:

                      ■     Guidelines won't allow this option


          ○    Performance and ability will be used as criteria to lay
               off/and or fire

    -                                          Doc 1 Pg 1 Ln 5" Pos 1"
```

*Figure 10.21:* Outline numbering with bullets

you use. To do this, just press *1* or *S* then type the number you wish to start with. If you want the entire document to be altered, be sure the cursor is at the top of the document before you select this option.

Whenever you use the Paragraph Number Definition screen to select a new starting paragraph number or use a different numbering style, WordPerfect inserts this code into your document:

[Par Num Def]

Like all formatting codes, it takes effect from that point forward in the document.

When you have finished your outline, position the cursor where you want Outline mode to end and turn it off by pressing the Date/Outline key (Shift-F5) and selecting Outline again (*4* or *O*).

## NUMBERING PARAGRAPHS

WordPerfect's Paragraph Numbering feature works very much like the Outline feature, but it's easier to use because you insert the paragraph numbers one at a time by selecting an option on the Date/Outline key. Also, the ◄┘ key works the same as it does in Edit mode, and the Tab key does not automatically change the number to the next level unless you position the cursor on or in front of the number before you press it. As with Outline mode, when you add, move, or delete paragraphs (and their automatic numbers), WordPerfect automatically renumbers them and all the following paragraphs that were numbered automatically.

To use this feature, you select Para Num from the Date/Outline key (Shift-F5 5). When you do, this prompt will appear, providing two options:

**Paragraph Level (Press Enter for Automatic):**

If you press ⏎, WordPerfect inserts the code for an automatic paragraph number, [Par Num:Auto], and a number appears on your screen. Note that this is the same code that WordPerfect inserts when you press ⏎ in Outline mode, and the code works the same way.

Instead of pressing ⏎ in response to the Paragraph Level prompt that you see after pressing Shift-F5 5, you can type a number between 1 and 8 for the level. This is called a *fixed number*. The disadvantage to using this method is that these numbers will not automatically change if you press Tab to move them to the right, so you should only use them if you want all paragraph levels lined up against the left margin or the same tab stop. If you do insert a fixed number, the code you'll see in Reveal Codes will differ. The *Auto* inside the brackets will be replaced by the number you type, such as

**[Par Num:1]**

where *1* was the number that was typed in response to the Paragraph Level prompt.

To create a short outline using paragraph numbering, follow these steps:

1. Press Shift-F5 5 ⏎. This will insert the Roman numeral I for your first level.

2. Press Tab to indent one tab stop and type

   **Introduction and Overview**

   Press ⏎.

3. Repeat this procedure twice, so that you add II and III to your outline. Type these entries for them:

 II. Historical Background
 III. Principal Issues

Press ←┘.

4. Press Tab, then press Shift-F5 5 ←┘ Tab, then type

 Fair employment practices

5. Press ←┘ and repeat this procedure twice so that you have *B* and *C,* and type these entries for them:

 B. Union activity
 C. Employee morale and impact on profits

6. Move the cursor to a blank line and repeat step 1, typing this entry at IV:

 Alternatives

When you finish, your outline should look exactly like this:

 I. Introduction and Overview
 II. Historical Background
 III. Principal Issues
    A. Fair employment practices
    B. Union activity
    C. Employee morale and impact on profits
 IV. Alternatives

If you add another paragraph number between the existing ones, the numbers that follow will change. For example, if you press ←┘ after *Introduction and Overview,* then press Shift-F5 5 ←┘, you'll create a new II. Press Home Home ↓ to realign the text and the numbers that follow will change to III, IV, and V. If you delete one of the paragraphs, this will also cause the numbers that follow to change.

# *AUTOMATIC REFERENCE*

The Automatic Reference feature is not available in versions of WordPerfect earlier than 5.0.

WordPerfect's Automatic Reference feature is a valuable tool that you can use to cross-reference your documents in a variety of ways. You can tell the reader to seek additional information on a specific page number, paragraph/outline number, footnote, endnote, or graphics box number. The information you reference is called the *target,* and the number that WordPerfect inserts to tell you where it is (such as a page number) is called the *reference.*

For example, if you were writing an annual report and wanted the reader to be aware of a section about the company's newest product line, you might type a note like this:

**(See Latest Developments, page 22.)**

By using the Automatic Reference feature instead of typing the page number (22), you can have WordPerfect enter the page number for you (the reference) and change this number if the page number of the section called "Latest Developments" (the target) changes after you add, delete, or move text. You can have multiple references which could, for example, direct the reader to see both a page number and a footnote. You can also have multiple page numbers in one reference. For instance, you could direct the reader to see pages 23, 34, and 55 for more information about the latest developments. Let's see how easy it is to use Automatic Reference.

To create a reference number that will direct the reader to a specific page, place the cursor in the blank space that follows the reference item (such as *See Latest Developments, page*   ), then press the Mark Text key (Alt-F5). You will see this prompt:

**1 Auto Ref;  2 Subdoc; 3 Index; 4 ToA Short Form; 5 Define; 6 Generate: 0**

Select Auto Ref by pressing *1* or *R.* You will see the Mark Text: Automatic Reference screen illustrated in Figure 10.22.

Select the third option, Mark Both Reference and Target. You will then see the screen that is illustrated in Figure 10.23.

Select the Page Number option for the target. Next, you will see this prompt directing you to move the cursor to the target and press ⬅ (Enter):

**Press Enter to select page.**

Move the cursor to the item that you want to reference (such as the beginning of the section "Latest Developments"), then press ⬅.

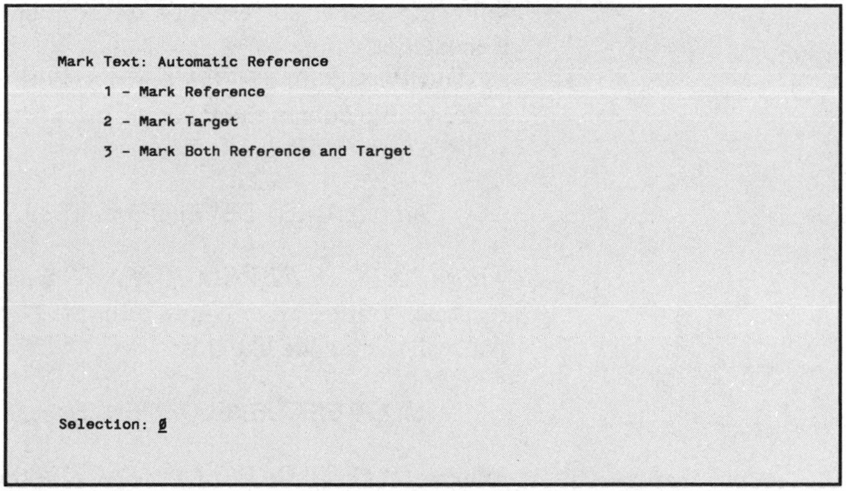

```
Mark Text: Automatic Reference

    1 - Mark Reference

    2 - Mark Target

    3 - Mark Both Reference and Target




Selection: 0
```

*Figure 10.22:* The Mark Text: Automatic Reference screen

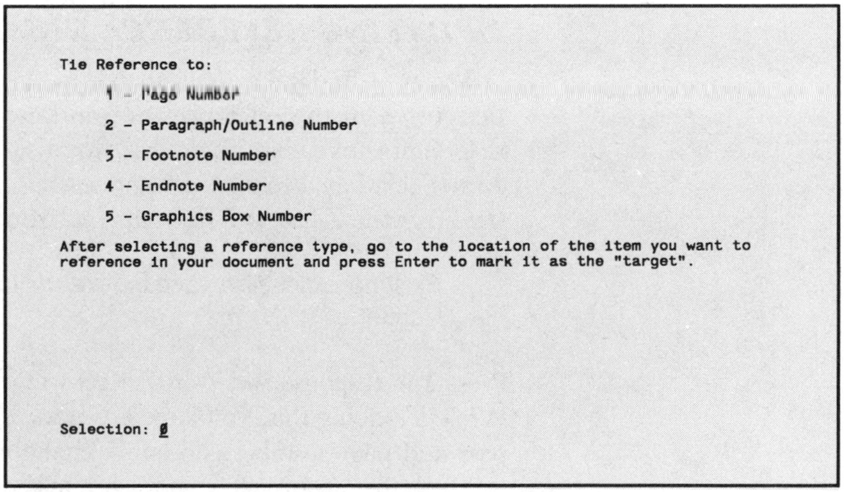

```
Tie Reference to:

    1 - Page Number

    2 - Paragraph/Outline Number

    3 - Footnote Number

    4 - Endnote Number

    5 - Graphics Box Number

After selecting a reference type, go to the location of the item you want to
reference in your document and press Enter to mark it as the "target".




Selection: 0
```

*Figure 10.23:* The *Tie Reference to:* screen

You will see this prompt:

**Target Name:**

This may already be filled in for you. If not, type a name that will tie it to the reference, such as *Latest Developments,* then press ←⏎. The cursor will return to the reference position, and you will see a number following it that corresponds to the page number where the target is located.

WordPerfect inserts codes next to both your target and your reference, visible only in the Reveal Codes screen. Next to the target, you will see a code similar to this:

**[Target(LATEST DEVELOPMENTS)]**

where *LATEST DEVELOPMENTS* was the target name typed in response to the Target Name prompt. Next to the reference number, you will see a code like this:

**[Ref(LATEST DEVELOPMENTS):Pg 34]**

Where *LATEST DEVELOPMENTS* is the target name and *Pg 34* is the page number where the target is located.

## UPDATING REFERENCE NUMBERS

You may find it necessary to update the references if the page numbers listed in the references are no longer accurate after you add, delete, or move text. To do this, you use the Generate option on the Mark Text key. Press Alt-F5 and select Generate, then select *Generate Tables, Indexes, Automatic References, etc.* You will then see this prompt:

**Existing tables, lists, and indexes will be replaced.**
**Continue? (Y/N) Yes**

Press *Y* in response and WordPerfect will update the numbers for you. While it's doing this, you'll see a *Generation in progress* prompt, with the pass and page number constantly changing. When the generation is finished, the cursor will be at the top of the document and you can use the Search key to locate each reference number and verify that it is correct. To do this, press F2, press Alt-F5 in response to the *Srch* prompt, select Defs and Refs, then select Ref. You will see the code for references and the Search prompt will look like this:

**Srch: [Ref]**

Press F2 or Esc and WordPerfect will find the first one. Verify the number, then press F2 F2 to look for the next one.

# *LINKING DOCUMENTS WITH THE MASTER DOCUMENT FEATURE*

Master Document is a feature that enables you to link several lengthy documents, even though they are contained in separate files on disk. You do this by creating a *master document* that names each file you want included as a *subdocument*. You can then use the master document to generate a table of contents, index, list, and so forth that will include marked text from each subdocument as though they were all contained in one file. For example, if you were writing a book you could save each chapter as a separate file, then create a short master document that would allow you to generate a table of contents and index for the entire book.

A master document can consist of nothing but subdocument names, or it can contain text such as a book introduction or table of contents. You can expand the master document to include the text from all your subdocuments, or condense it to include only the subdocument file names. There is no limit on the number of subdocuments you can include in a master document. You can even use a master document as a subdocument in a different master document.

## *CREATING A MASTER DOCUMENT*

Here are the steps I used to create a master document that links the first five chapters of *Mastering WordPerfect 5*. If you want to try it with files of your own, be sure you start with a clear screen.

1. To insert the first chapter, I pressed Mark Text (Alt-F5) and selected Subdocument (**2** or **S**).

2. This prompt appears:

   **Subdoc Filename:**

3. I then typed the file name of the first chapter, **CH1**, and pressed ⏎. WordPerfect displays a box with a *Subdoc: CH1* prompt inside, as shown in Figure 10.24.

4. Press ⏎ to insert a blank line and repeat steps 1 through 3 for each file to be included in the master document (Chapters 2 through 5 in my case).

```
┌─────────────────────────────────────────────────────────────┐
│                                                             │
│   ┌───────────────────────────────────────────────────┐     │
│   │ Subdoc: CH1                                        │     │
│   └───────────────────────────────────────────────────┘     │
│   _                                                         │
│                                                             │
│                                                             │
│                                                             │
│                                                             │
│                                                             │
│                                                             │
│                                                             │
│                                     Doc 1 Pg 1 Ln 1" Pos 1" │
│                                                             │
└─────────────────────────────────────────────────────────────┘
```

*Figure 10.24:* Creating a master document

5.  Use the Save Text key (F10) to save the document. I named my file *bkmaster.pt1*.

I then used the master document to create a table of contents and index for the five chapters, using these steps.

1.  Move the cursor to the end of the document and force a page break by pressing Ctrl-←.

2.  Define the table of contents in the usual way by pressing the Mark Text key (Alt-F5), selecting Define, then selecting Define Table of Contents. I used three levels for my table, and left the default page number position for each level, *Flush right with leader.*

3.  Press Ctrl-← to insert another forced page break that will separate the table of contents from the index.

4.  Define the index in the usual way by pressing the Mark Text key (Alt-F5), selecting Define, then selecting Define Index. I used a concordance file for my index, and chose *Flush right page numbers with leaders* for the page numbering style.

5. The last step is to select the Generate option from the Mark Text key. To do this, press Alt-F5 6 5 Y. Before generating, WordPerfect will automatically expand the master document to include all text from each of the subdocuments.

6. After generating, WordPerfect will automatically condense the master document again by deleting the subdocuments, and after a few minutes this prompt will appear, asking if you want to update the subdocument files before they are deleted (assuming you did not expand the master document yourself, but let WordPerfect do it automatically as described in the previous step):

**Update Subdocs? (Y/N) No**

If you press *Y*, WordPerfect will save all the subdocuments to disk before deleting them. If you press *N*, WordPerfect will delete the subdocuments from the master document without saving them.

You will be left with a master document that includes a table of contents and index for all of the subdocument files. The pages in the table of contents will be numbered consecutively, unless you used the New Page Number option from the Format key (Shift-F8 2 6) to change the starting page number of any of your subdocuments. To ensure that all pages will be numbered correctly, you should avoid using New Page Number. Also, if you want numbers printed on your pages, you can place your page numbering code in the master document instead of in the subdocuments.

## EXPANDING AND CONDENSING A MASTER DOCUMENT

If you want to print the entire master document, you have to expand it to include all text from each subdocument, replacing each subdocument code with the actual subdocument text. After expanding and printing a master document, you may wish to condense it again, deleting all text and replacing it with subdocument code(s).

To expand a master document, follow these steps:

1. Press the Mark Text key (Alt-F5) and select Generate (**6** or **G**).

2. Select Expand Master Document (**3** or **E**) from the Mark Text:
   Generate screen.

After WordPerfect finishes expanding the master document, you will
see boxes before and after the text from each subdocument. The box at
the beginning of each subdocument will include a *Subdoc Start:* prompt
and the file name of the subdocument. The box at the end will include a
*Subdoc End:* prompt and the subdocument file name.

To condense a master document that has been expanded, follow
these steps:

1. Press the Mark Text key (Alt-F5) and select Generate (**6** or **G**).

2. Select Condense Master Document (**4** or **O**) from the Mark
   Text: Generate screen. You will then see this prompt asking if
   you want to save the subdocuments:

**Save Subdocs? (Y/N) Yes**

If you press *Y,* WordPerfect will save all your subdocuments before
erasing them from the master document. If you press *N,* WordPerfect will erase all subdocuments from the master document without
saving them to disk. If you made editing changes while the master
document was expanded and you wish to keep them in
the subdocument(s), the appropriate response is *Yes.*

If you select *Yes* and WordPerfect finds that a file with the same
name as one of your subdocument files already exists on disk, you
will see this prompt:

**Replace *filename*? 1 Yes; 2 No; 3 Replace All Remaining: 0**

If you press *Y,* WordPerfect erases the file of the same name on the
disk and replaces it with the one being deleted from the master document. If you choose Replace All Remaining, WordPerfect automatically erases all remaining disk files with identical names and replaces
them with the subdocuments being deleted from the master document; you won't see this prompt again if WordPerfect finds another
file with the same name as one of your subdocuments. If you press *N,*
you can assign a different name to the subdocument.

## *COMPARING SCREEN AND DISK VERSIONS OF DOCUMENTS*

You can use Document Compare to compare the document on your screen with the disk version as you last saved it, to see what changes you have made since retrieving it. WordPerfect compares the two documents on a phrase-by-phrase basis, looking for phrase markers such as periods, commas, question marks, colons, semi-colons, exclamation points, hard returns, and hard page breaks. When a phrase on screen is not found in the disk version of the document, the phrase is redlined. (On color monitors, the text will actually appear red.) When a phrase in the disk version is not found on screen, the phrase will be marked with strikeout codes (strikeout text is also a different color on color monitors). If a phrase has been moved, you will see the message *The Following Text was Moved* before the phrase, and this message after it: *The Preceding Text was Moved.* The two messages are displayed as strikeout text.

Document Compare is easy to use. The steps are outlined below; they assume you have a document on screen that you have altered since retrieving it from disk (but that you have not yet saved it again).

1. Press the Mark Text key (Alt-F5) and select the Generate option (**6** or **G**).

2. Select *Compare Screen and Disk Documents and Add Redline and Strikeout* (**2** or **C**). You will see this prompt:

   **Other Document:**

3. Type the name of the file that you are comparing with the screen version, then press ←. If the file name already appears next to the prompt, just press ←.

A * *Please wait* * message will appear briefly while WordPerfect is comparing the two documents, then the screen will change to show you in redline or strikeout the phrases that have been added, deleted, or moved, as described above.

After you compare the documents, you can change back to the edited screen version by asking WordPerfect to remove the redline markings and strikeout text. To do this, follow these steps:

1. Press the Mark Text key (Alt-F5) and select the Generate option (**6** or **G**).

2. Select *Delete Redline Markings and Strikeout Text from Document* (**1** or **R**), then press **Y** in response to this prompt:

**Delete redline markings and strikeout text? (Y/N) No**

Your document on screen should now match the edited screen version before you used Document Compare.

## SUMMARY

You can use WordPerfect to create a variety of reference tools, including an index, table of contents, table of authorities, lists, outlines, numbered paragraphs, automatic references, and master documents. The principal steps used to create a list, index, or table of contents are similar: mark the text to be included, define the numbering style for the page numbers, and generate the structure. After you edit your document, any of these structures can be easily updated by regenerating it. Marking the text is not an automatic process, for you must move the cursor to each item in the document and mark it separately. However, WordPerfect's Search and Macro features—you'll learn about Macros in Chapter 19—can be used to expedite the process. There are five numbering styles to choose from: no page numbers, page numbers that follow the entries, page numbers in parentheses that follow the entries, flush right page numbers, and flush right page numbers with leaders.

You can use WordPerfect's Outline and Paragraph Numbering features to create outlines and numbered lists with as many as eight paragraph levels. Paragraph numbering is slightly easier to work with than outlining, because Outline mode alters the functions of the ↵ and Tab keys. Other than that, the procedures used are quite similar. WordPerfect provides four predefined numbering styles: paragraph, outline, legal, and bullet. If these aren't acceptable, you can customize the settings to create your own style.

The Master Document feature links several documents together, even if they are on separate files on disk, so you can generate a table of contents, index, list, and so on, from the marked text of each linked document. Document Compare is another useful feature that compares the document on screen with the disk version as you last saved it. This enables you to see the changes you have made since you retrieved it.

11.

# FOOTNOTES AND ENDNOTES
# MADE EASY

# *Fast Track*

**To create a footnote or endnote,**                               367

position the cursor next to the text you would like to reference with a footnote, then press the Footnote key (Ctrl-F7). At the prompt, select either Footnote or Endnote, then select the Create option at the next prompt; the note number will automatically appear to the left of the cursor. Type the text of your note (leaving a space between the number and the note), then press the Exit key (F7). Though you can't see the note text on the editing screen, you can view it in the Reveal Codes screen or by using the View Document option on the Print key (Shift-F7 V).

**To edit a footnote or endnote,**                                 367

press the Footnote key (Ctrl-F7), select either Footnote or Endnote, choose the Edit option at the next prompt, then type the number of the note you wish to edit and press ⏎. When you've finished editing the note, press the Exit key (F7) to return to the Edit screen.

**Change the footnote and endnote options**                        370

by pressing the Footnote key (Ctrl-F7), selecting either Footnote or Endnote, then selecting Options at the next prompt. The Footnote and Endnote Options menus list several features that can be changed, such as spacing within and between notes, the numbering method, and the amount of note to keep together on a page. To change the defaults shown, press the number of the option you wish to change, then enter the new setting.

### Delete footnotes and endnotes

by placing the cursor on the number or character that identifies the note in the document, then pressing the Del key. At the *Delete [Footnote:1]* or *Delete [Endnote:1]* prompt, type *Y* to delete the note. All notes following the one deleted will be renumbered automatically (it happens instantly).

378

### To move a footnote or endnote,

place the cursor on the number or character that identifies the note in the document, then press the Del key. At the *Delete [Footnote]* prompt, press *Y* to delete the note, then move the cursor to the new position for the note and use the Restore option on the Cancel key (F1 1) to retrieve it.

378

### To change a footnote or endnote number,

place the cursor just left of it, press the Footnote key (Ctrl-F7), select either the Footnote or the Endnote option, then choose the *New number* option at the next prompt. At the *Footnote number?* or *Endnote Number?* prompt, type the new number for the next footnote and press ←. Any notes following the one with the new number will be renumbered as the text is reformatted.

378

### To view footnote and endnote text before printing,

use the View Document feature. Press the Print key (Shift-F7), then choose the View Document option. If you have a monochrome monitor, scroll through the document to find the note. If you have a graphics monitor, select *100%* from the menu, then scroll through the page and view the notes. Press the Exit key (F7) to return to the Edit screen.

380

FOOTNOTES AND ENDNOTES ARE USED IN ACADEMIC work, books, articles, and research reports. The difference between footnotes and endnotes is that footnotes usually appear on the page to which they refer, whereas endnotes are grouped together at the end of the document. WordPerfect permits both types of notes in a single document, and numbers them separately. When you create footnotes or endnotes, the program automatically inserts the appropriate numbers into your document and changes them as you add or delete notes, so you only type the text itself. As you'll see, WordPerfect's Footnote and Endnote features are very flexible.

WordPerfect prints all footnotes at the bottom of the page to which they refer if there is enough room. They are separated from the text by one blank line and a solid two-inch line, and from each other by a single blank line. These blank lines and the lines used by the footnotes themselves are subtracted from the total number of text lines on the page.

Although you can't see footnotes or endnotes in the Edit screen, you can preview them using the View Document option on the Print key (Shift-F7 V).

## CREATING AND EDITING FOOTNOTES

Creating footnotes is a simple process. You just position the cursor next to the text that will have a footnote, then press the Footnote key (Ctrl-F7). You'll see this prompt:

**1** Footnote;  **2** Endnote;  **3** Endnote Placement: 0

Select option 1, Footnote, by pressing either *1* or *F*. Next you'll see this prompt:

**Footnote: 1** Create;  **2** Edit;  **3** New Number;  **4** Options: 0

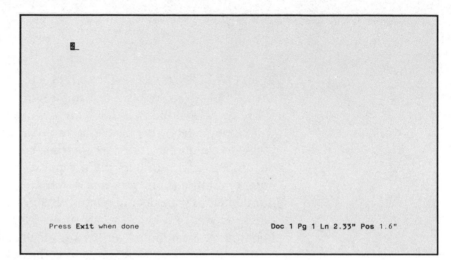

*Figure 11.1:* The Footnote screen

Select the Create Footnote option by pressing either *1* or *C*. You will then see the screen illustrated in Figure 11.1. Notice that it resembles the Edit screen, except for this message in the lower left corner:

**Press EXIT when done**

and the footnote number to the left of the cursor.

Press the Space bar to leave a blank space between the number and the text of your note, then type the text of your note.

When you finish typing the footnote, press the Exit key (F7). As you can see, the program automatically enters the footnote number into your document, and it will be printed in superscript if your printer is capable.

If you want to see the contents of a footnote, approximately the first 40 characters are visible in the Reveal Codes screen, so you can press Alt-F3 to see them. When you do, you'll see the note number and text, as shown in Figure 11.2, and any codes such as [TAB] or [UND] that you may have placed in the footnote text.

If a footnote is longer than 40 characters, you can view and edit it using the Footnote Edit option. To select it, you press the Footnote key (Ctrl-F7), type either *1* or *F* for Footnote, type either *2* or *E* for Edit, then type the number of the note you wish to edit. The cursor

I often use the Indent key (F4) instead of the Space bar to leave a blank space between the number and text of the note in the Footnote screen, because if a note is longer than one line, I prefer to indent the entire note. There is almost no limit to the length of the footnote, except common sense.

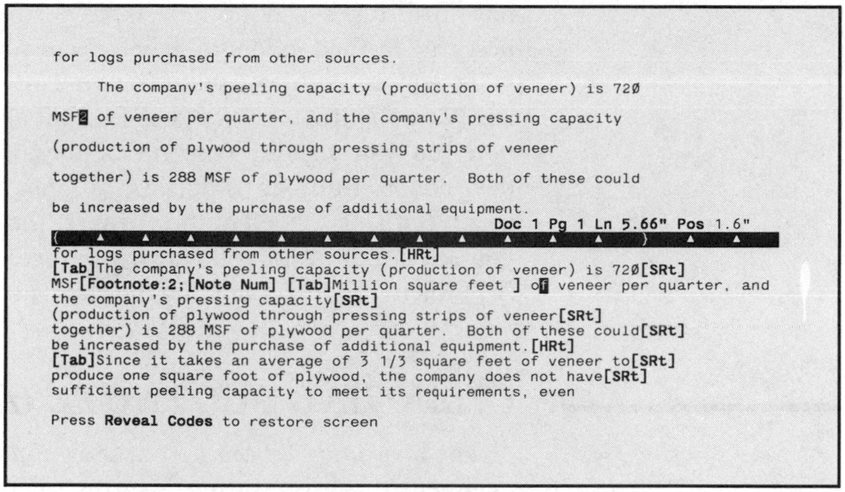

```
    for logs purchased from other sources.

        The company's peeling capacity (production of veneer) is 72Ø
    MSF█ of veneer per quarter, and the company's pressing capacity

    (production of plywood through pressing strips of veneer

    together) is 288 MSF of plywood per quarter.  Both of these could

    be increased by the purchase of additional equipment.
                                          Doc 1 Pg 1 Ln 5.66" Pos 1.6"
    for logs purchased from other sources.[HRt]
    [Tab]The company's peeling capacity (production of veneer) is 72Ø[SRt]
    MSF[Footnote:2;[Note Num] [Tab]Million square feet ] of█ veneer per quarter, and
    the company's pressing capacity[SRt]
    (production of plywood through pressing strips of veneer[SRt]
    together) is 288 MSF of plywood per quarter.  Both of these could[SRt]
    be increased by the purchase of additional equipment.[HRt]
    [Tab]Since it takes an average of 3 1/3 square feet of veneer to[SRt]
    produce one square foot of plywood, the company does not have[SRt]
    sufficient peeling capacity to meet its requirements, even

    Press Reveal Codes to restore screen
```

*Figure 11.2:* Viewing a footnote in the Reveal Codes screen

can be anywhere in the document when you select this option. However it's easier if the cursor is just left of the note number you want to edit, because the number will automatically appear when you press the keystrokes to choose Footnote Edit, and you can just press ◄─┘ to edit it.

When you edit a footnote, you see the same screen illustrated in Figure 11.1, and you can use all of the familiar WordPerfect commands to insert or delete text. If you accidentally erase a footnote number while in this screen, press the Footnote key (Ctrl-F7) to restore it. If you erased it using Delete or Backspace, you can also use the Undelete feature of the Cancel key, F1, to restore it. When you finish editing or viewing a footnote, press the Exit key (F7) to get back to Edit mode.

After you finish editing a footnote and press Exit, the cursor will be positioned next to the footnote reference number in your text. You can move the cursor back to where it was before you edited the note by pressing the Go To key (Ctrl-Home) twice.

## CREATING AND EDITING ENDNOTES

Creating and editing endnotes is almost identical to creating and editing footnotes, except that you select option 2, Endnote, from the Footnote key instead of option 1, Footnote. The remaining steps are identical. You press the Footnote key (Ctrl-F7), select *2* or *E* for Endnote, press *1* or *C* for Create, type the text, then press the Exit key (F7). Endnotes are numbered separately from footnotes, so you can have both types of notes in a single document. Like footnotes, endnotes are limited in length only by common sense.

To edit an endnote, select option 2, Endnote, from the Footnote key (Ctrl-F7), then press *2* or *E* for Edit and enter the number of the note you want to edit. Your cursor does not have to be positioned on the endnote number to do this, but can be anywhere in the document. If it is to the left of the number, the number will appear when you select Edit, and you can simply press ◄─┘ to edit it. Press Exit (F7) when you finish making the changes.

## CHANGING FOOTNOTE OPTIONS

The Footnote Options menu, shown in Figure 11.3, allows you to change several formatting features such as the spacing within or between footnotes, the numbering mode, and the type of line separating the text of your document from the footnotes. To guarantee that all footnote references will be changed, you should move the cursor to the top of the document before making any changes. Press the Footnote key, Ctrl-F7, select *1* or *F* for Footnotes, then select *4* or *O* for Options. The screen shown in Figure 11.3 will appear.

```
Footnote Options

     1 - Spacing Within Footnotes          1
               Between Footnotes           Ø.16"

     2 - Amount of Note to Keep Together    Ø.5"

     3 - Style for Number in Text           [SUPRSCPT][Note Num][suprscpt]

     4 - Style for Number in Note                   [SUPRSCPT][Note Num][suprscp

     5 - Footnote Numbering Method          Numbers

     6 - Start Footnote Numbers each Page   No

     7 - Line Separating Text and Footnotes 2-inch Line

     8 - Print Continued Message            No

     9 - Footnotes at Bottom of Page        Yes


  Selection: Ø
```

*Figure 11.3:* The Footnote Options menu

Option 1 on the Footnote Options menu is *Spacing within footnotes* and *Spacing between footnotes*. As you can see from the screen, the default for *Spacing within footnotes* is single spacing, meaning that the text in the footnotes is single spaced. You can change it to 2 for double spacing, 1.5 for 1½-line spacing, or whatever you want as long as your printer can print it. The default for *Spacing between footnotes* is .16″, so footnotes are separated from each other by .16 inches. Be aware that if you increase these numbers it reduces the number of lines available for regular text on the page (not the 1-inch bottom margin) and the results are sometimes unattractive. To change either of these options, press *1* or *S*, then enter the new number that you want to use. For the *Spacing between footnotes* option, WordPerfect automatically inserts the inches sign unless you had previously changed the default unit of measurement.

The second option, *Amount of footnote to keep together*, allows you to change the number of lines that will remain together on the page in case the footnote is very long and needs to be split between two pages. The default is ½ inch, meaning that if you have a note of 1 inch (which is usually six lines, but this depends on your printer), at least half of it will remain on the same page as the reference number in the text. If there isn't enough room for at least ½ inch, the entire note and number will be moved to the next page. To change this number, press either *2* or *A*, then type a new number. Like the *Spacing between footnotes* option, the number you type will automatically be converted to inches, unless you had previously changed the default unit of measurement.

You can use options 3 and 4 to change the appearance of the footnote numbers. Footnotes as well as their references in the text are designated by a superscripted number such as [1] or [2]. Like underline, bold, and center codes, superscript codes come in pairs. Press *3* or *T* and you'll see this default string for footnote reference numbers in text:

[SUPRSCPT][Note Num][suprscpt]

The string for the numbers in the notes themselves is almost the same, except that the notes are indented five spaces, as you can see in the Footnote Options menu shown in Figure 11.3. Once you select option 4, you see the entire prompt:

**Replace with:**               [SUPRSCPT][Note Num][suprscpt]

You can change the style for footnote numbers in text and notes to include characters and/or font attributes such as underline, italics, bold, and shadow. The process is the same for both options, 3 and 4.

To insert a code such as [UND] for underline, you have to press the key that generates the code. To add underlining to the above prompt, though, you would want to use the cursor movement keys to edit it so that you wouldn't have to enter the other codes again. Here's how: Select option 3, which calls up the following prompt:

Replace with: [SUPRSCPT][Note Num][suprscpt]

Press → once so that you can edit the prompt without erasing the existing codes, then press ← to move the cursor back to the beginning. Press the Underline key, F8, which inserts the [UND] code to turn on underlining. Next, press → three times and press F8 again to insert the code that turns off underlining, [und]. Here's what the prompt will look like when you finish:

[UND][SUPRSCPT][Note Num][suprscpt][und]

Press ← to accept it.

You can also edit the prompt using keys such as Delete and Backspace. For instance, to change the numbering style so that the number denoting the note reference will appear without superscript, press 4 or *N* to select the option, press → until the cursor is on the [supsrscpt] code at the end, then press Delete once to erase it. Use ← to move the cursor back onto the first superscript code (they come in pairs), then press Delete to erase it. When you're done, the prompt will look like this:

Replace with:        [Note Num]

Press ← to enter it.

You can use option 5, Footnote Numbering Method, to change the numbering style, which is set to numbers by default. You can change it to letters or characters. Letters are the lowercase alphabetical characters, *a* through *z*. Characters can be anything you want, and you can select as many as five. When you select this option by pressing *5* or *M,* you see this prompt on the status line:

**1 Number  2 Letters  3 Characters: 0**

To change to letters, you press *L* or *2*. To change to characters, press *3* or *C*; the cursor then moves up next to option 5 and you just type the character(s). For instance, you could designate a symbol such as the plus sign to mark each footnote. If you did, the first footnote would be marked by a single plus sign, the second by two plus signs, the third by three, and so on. If you designate two characters such as an asterisk and a dollar sign, the first footnote would be marked by an asterisk, the second by a dollar sign, the third by two asterisks, the fourth by two dollar signs, etc.

You can use option 6, *Start footnote numbers each page*, to number the footnotes on each page separately. As you see on the Footnote Options menu, the default is No. If you change it to Yes, the first footnote on each page will be number 1. To use this method, just select the option by pressing *6* or *P,* then type *Y.*

You can use option 7, *Line separating text and footnotes*, to change the line that separates the footnotes from the text. As you can see in Figure 11.4, the default is a 2-inch line. You can change it to no line, or a line across the entire page. When you press *7* or *L* to select this option, you see this prompt:

**1 No Line;  2 2-inch line;  3 Margin to Margin: 0**

Select *1* or *N* to change it to No line, or *3* or *M* to change it to Margin to Margin, which means WordPerfect will print a line across the entire page.

Option 8, Print Continued Message, is set to No. If you change it to Yes by pressing *8* or *C* then typing *Y,* whenever a footnote is so long that it has to be split between two pages, WordPerfect will print *(continued...)* on the last line of the footnote on the page to which it refers, and on the first line of the same footnote on the next page. Figure 11.5 shows an example.

Option 9, *Footnotes at bottom of page*, insures that footnotes are always placed all the way at the bottom of the page, even if the page contains only a few lines of text. The default is Yes, so if you do type a footnote

The plywood manufacturing process is moderately complex. Logs are peeled into thin strips of veneer, dried in an oven, then pressed and glued into varying thicknesses of plywood. By-products of the peeling process, lumber cores and wood chips, are shipped to the company's beam mill and paper mill, respectively.

The process involves several important decision variables. One is the mixture of logs used in the peeling (veneer producing) process. The company uses their own logs as well as logs purchased on the outside. Currently, this mixture is half of each. Another important variable is the cost of logs. Currently, this cost is $45.00 per MBF[1] for its own logs, and $55.00 per MBF for logs purchased from other sources.

The company's peeling capacity (production of veneer through the peeling process) is 720 MSF[2] of veneer per quarter, and the company's pressing capacity (production of plywood through pressing strips of veneer together) is 288 MSF of plywood per quarter. Both of these could be increased by the purchase of additional equipment.

Since it takes an average of 3 1/3 square feet of veneer to produce one square foot of plywood, the company does not have sufficient peeling capacity to meet its requirements, even

---

[1] Thousand board feet

[2] Million square feet

*Figure 11.4:* A 2-inch line separating text and footnotes

on a page that contains only a few lines of text, WordPerfect inserts enough blank lines between the text and footnotes to start the footnotes in the usual position, near the bottom of the page. When you change it by pressing *9* or *B* and typing *N,* the footnotes will begin two lines below the text.

4.  Move the cursor to the left of the word "Congratulations" in the first paragraph and change to double spacing. Press the Format key (Shift F8), select Line, then select Line Spacing. Change line spacing to 2 (double spacing) by typing 2. Press Return then press Exit (F7).[1]

5.  Place the cursor on the Y in Yours truly and change back to single spacing.[2] Note that line spacing changes take place from the cursor position forward so the text between "Congratulations" and "Yours truly" is still double spaced.

6.  Press PgUp to move the cursor to the top of the document. Try changing the entire document back to single spacing by pressing Shift-F8 L S 1 and pressing Return F7. It does not work! This is because there is a double spacing code at the beginning of the first paragraph of the letter, before the word "Congratulations." To remove the double spacing, you must find and delete the code. Use the Reveal Codes Key (Alt F3) and cursor movement keys to find the code: [Ln Spacing: 2]. Place the cursor on it, then delete it using either the Delete or the Backspace key.

7.  Save the letter (using F10 or F7) using this name: WINNER.LTR [3]

8.  Practice additional cursor movement methods using the Esc key and the GoTo key, as instructed in class.[4]

---

[1]  Use *Mastering WordPerfect* page 59 for more information.

[2]  To single space, press Shift-F8, select Line, select Spacing, type 1, press ~CR, then press F7.

[3]  F10 is the Save Text key and you use it when you want to save and remain in the document. F7 is the Exit key and you use it when you want to save the document and clear the screen to type another document or exit from WordPerfect.

[4]  The Esc key is used to repeat other keys such as cursor movement keys a certain number of times. When you press it, you will see a prompt that says "Repeat Value = " followed by a number, usually 8 (unless the default number has been changed on your computer). For instance, pressing Esc followed by up arrow moves the cursor up 8 lines, while pressing Esc followed by right arrow moves the cursor to the right 8 positions. You can also use Esc to draw a line of characters such as asterisks. As you'll learn in Lesson 10, Esc is also very useful with Line Draw. The GoTo key is Ctrl-Home, and it has many important functions in WordPerfect. When you press it, you see this message: Go to. If you want to go to a specific page, you then type the page number. If you want to go to a specific character, you type the character (it is case-sensitive). If you want to go to the
(continued...)

*Figure 11.5:* The Continued string (continued on next page)

9.  **Print** the letter (Shift F7,1). Notice the smooth right margins. WordPerfect documents appear this way when printed because right justification is on. You can turn it off by pressing Ctrl F8, 3. Right justification is not shown on the screen.

10. Use **typeover** and the **Del** key to change the letter so that it includes the misspellings shown below, then use the Speller (Ctrl F2,3) to correct them.

**Typeover:**      Replace old text with new text by pressing the **Ins** key and typing. Pressing Ins turns off insert mode and places the **Typeover** message in the lower left corner of the screen. Notice that when the **typeover** message appears, you erase existing text by typing something else over it. When you press the Ins key a second time, it will turn off the typeover message and put you back into **insert** mode. This means that as you type you will find existing characters are pushed to the right, making room for the new ones. WordPerfect normally operates in insert mode unless you press the Ins key and see the Typeover message in the lower left corner of the screen.

| CHANGE: | TO: |
|---|---|
| Congratulations | Congradulations |
| winner | weiner |
| Sweepstakes | Swepstakes |
| phone | fone |
| inform | informm |
| Administrator | Administrater |

**THE BLOCK KEY: ALT F4**

1.  Place the cursor at the top of the document, on line 1 (press Home, Home, justification.

    **Right justification** is WordPerfect's default - when you print a document, the right margins are even (but text always appears uneven on screen). It achieves this affect by adding extra spaces between words. However, it often leaves large empty spaces between the words that are unattractive.

---

[4](...continued)
     bottom of the current page, you press down arrow. For more information, see <u>Mastering WordPerfect</u> pages 14-16, 112, 134-5, and 417.

*Figure 11.5:* The Continued string (continued)

# *CHANGING ENDNOTE OPTIONS*

To change endnote options, you press the Footnote key (Ctrl-F7) and select Endnotes (*2* or *E*), then press *4* or *O* for Options. The menu shown in Figure 11.6 appears.

As you can see, there are only five options on this menu, and they are exactly the same as the first five options on the Footnote Options menu discussed in the previous section.

Option 1 lets you change the spacing within or between endnotes. It is set for single spacing within endnotes, and you can change to double spacing, 1½-line spacing, or whatever you want (as long as your printer can print it). Between endnotes, the spacing is set to .16″, so they are separated from each other by .16″. Option 2 can be used to change the number of lines that will remain together on the page in case the endnote is very long and needs to be split between two pages, and it's set to ½ inch. Options 3 and 4 are used to change the appearance of the endnote numbers. Endnotes as well as their references in the text are designated by a superscripted number such as $^1$ or $^2$, and you can change the style for endnote numbers in text and notes to include characters and/or font attributes such as underline, italics, bold, and shadow. Option 5 is used to change the numbering method for endnotes, which is set to numbers by default. You can change it to letters (the lowercase alphabetical characters, *a* through *z*) or any other characters you want.

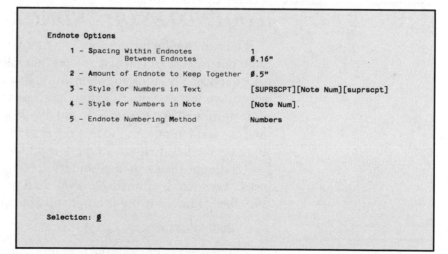

```
Endnote Options

     1 - Spacing Within Endnotes              1
               Between Endnotes               Ø.16"

     2 - Amount of Endnote to Keep Together   Ø.5"

     3 - Style for Numbers in Text            [SUPRSCPT][Note Num][suprscpt]

     4 - Style for Numbers in Note            [Note Num].

     5 - Endnote Numbering Method             Numbers




     Selection: Ø
```

*Figure 11.6:* The Endnote Options menu

For specific details on how to change these options, refer to the previous section, "Changing Footnote Options."

## DELETING AND MOVING FOOTNOTES OR ENDNOTES

To delete a footnote or endnote, you have to delete the code that generates it. To do this, position the cursor on the number or character that identifies your note in the document and press the Delete key. You will see a message like this (where *1* is the number of the note being deleted):

    Delete [Footnote:1]? (Y/N)  No

or, for endnotes

    Delete [Endnote:1]? (Y/N)  No

Press *Y* to delete it. The notes that follow the deleted one will be renumbered automatically.

To move a footnote or endnote, delete it using the steps described above, then move the cursor to the new position and use the Restore option on the Cancel key (F1 1).

## RENUMBERING FOOTNOTES OR ENDNOTES

You can change the number of a footnote or endnote anywhere in your document, and all of the notes that follow it will be renumbered in sequence. This is useful when you split a large file into two or more separate ones, yet wish to retain the same sequential footnote or endnote numbers. For example, if you divide a 50-page file into two files and the last footnote in the first file is #11, you could use this feature to make the first footnote in the second file #12 instead of #1.

To change the footnote number, press the Footnote key (Ctrl-F7), select Footnote by pressing *1* or *F,* then press *3* or *N* to choose New Number. The following prompt will appear:

    Footnote number?

Type the new number for the next footnote, and press ←⅃. When the document is reformatted as you move the cursor through it, the

numbers will be reordered, and any new footnotes you type after that
will begin with the new numbering scheme. To speed up the reformatting process, press the Screen key, Ctrl-F3, then *0* or ◄─┘ to select
the Rewrite Screen option.

To change the endnote starting number, you follow the same procedures described above, except that you select Endnote instead of
Footnote from the Footnote key (Ctrl-F7) by pressing *2* or *E.*

## *DETERMINING ENDNOTE PLACEMENT*

WordPerfect normally begins printing endnotes on the last page of
the document, but you can change this default using the Endnote
Placement option on the Footnote key. For instance, if you wanted
all the endnotes cited on pages 1 through 5 of a 20-page document to
be printed after page 5, you could use this option to place them at the
end of page 5 (of the printed version).

To use it, you move the cursor to the position where you want the
endnotes generated (but it can't be in the middle of a paragraph,
because WordPerfect will create a hard page break there). Next,
press the Footnote key (Ctrl-F7) and press *3* or *P* to select Endnote
Placement. You'll see this prompt:

**Restart endnote numbering? (Y/N)  Yes**

WordPerfect is asking if you would like all the endnotes that follow
this section to begin with 1. Press *Y* or *N.* You'll see a double line of
dashes signifying a hard page break (so don't do this in the middle of
a paragraph), and a message box. If you look in the Reveal Codes
screen (Alt-F3), you'll see these codes:

**[Endnote Placement][HPg]**

If you pressed *Y* in response to the *Restart endnote numbering* prompt,
you'll also see the code:

**[New End Num: 1]**

In the printed version of your document, all the endnotes that
appear before the Endnote Placement code will start printing at the
code position. All the endnotes that follow will be placed at the end of

the document (or after the next endnote placement code, if you inserted another one). Remember, you can use the View Document option on the Print key (Shift-F7 V) to preview the endnotes before printing your document.

## *PREVIEWING FOOTNOTES AND ENDNOTES BEFORE PRINTING*

If your monitor has graphics capabilities, View Document lets you enlarge or reduce the page views. You also can view facing pages. You cannot edit your document while in the View Document screen.

Although you can't see footnotes or endnotes in the Edit screen, you can preview them before printing using the View Document option on the Print key. To do it, you press the Print key (Shift-F7), then press *6* or *V* to choose View Document. If you have a monochrome monitor, you can press ↓ or Page Down to scroll through the document and look for the footnotes or endnotes. If you have a color monitor or one with graphics capabilities, the View Document option works differently. You'll see the entire page (assuming you haven't changed the default option, which is *Full page*) but the characters will be too small to read. To enlarge the text, select 100% or 200% from the menu at the bottom of the screen by pressing *1* for 100% or *2* for 200%. You can then press ↓ to scroll through the page and view the footnotes at the bottom. Press Exit (F7) when you finish.

## *SUMMARY*

In this chapter, you have learned how easily WordPerfect creates and numbers footnotes and endnotes, and automatically renumbers them as notes are inserted or deleted. The two types of notes are numbered separately, so both can be used in the same document. Whenever possible, footnotes are printed at the bottom of the page to which they refer, whereas endnotes are all placed in sequential order at the end of the document. These features are very flexible. The Footnote and Endnote options can be used to further customize the appearance of your footnotes and endnotes, by changing formatting features such as the spacing within or between notes, the numbering mode, the amount of footnote or endnote that should remain together on a page if the note is very long, and the type of line that separates the footnotes from the text.

# PRODUCING POLISHED
# DOCUMENTS WITH
# MULTICOLUMN LAYOUTS

# FAST TRACK

**To define newspaper columns,** 386

press the Math/Columns key (Alt-F7), then press *4* for Column Def. At the next prompt, press *1* for Type, then choose Newspaper columns from the next menu. Select *2* for Number of Columns, then enter the number of columns you want to use (from 2 to 24) and press ⏎. You may also change the distance between columns and the right and left margins for each of your columns if you don't want to use WordPerfect's defaults. Press Exit (F7) when you are finished.

**To turn on columns and type text in columns,** 391

press the Math/Columns key (Alt-F7), then select *3* for Column On/Off. You then can type text in columns according to the format you have defined, just as you would in regular text mode.

**Convert a document into newspaper column format** 394

before defining the columns by retrieving the file with the Retrieve Text key (Shift-F10), placing the cursor at the top, defining the columns, then pressing *3* to turn on Column mode.

**Convert a noncolumnar document after columns are defined** 394

and Column mode is on by retrieving the file into columns that have already been defined with the Retrieve Text key (Shift-F10).

**Erase column formatting**                                          395

by pressing Alt-F3 to see the Reveal Code screen, then locating the [Col On] code. Move the cursor onto the code and press Delete, then press Alt-F3 to exit Reveal Codes. The text will be reformatted instantly.

**To change column definitions,**                                    395

go to the Reveal Codes screen (Alt-F3). Place the cursor between the [Col Def] and [Col On] codes (or on the [Col On] code if they are right next to each other), press the Math/Columns key (Alt-F7), and redefine your columns using the Column Def option.

**When moving the cursor in Column mode,**                           396

remember that each column is considered a separate page. To move the cursor from column to column, use the Go To key (Ctrl-Home), followed by → or ←.

**To define parallel columns,**                                      400

press the Math/Columns key (Alt-F7) and select Column Def. At the next prompt, select Type, then choose Parallel or Parallel with Block Protect. Next, choose the number of columns by pressing *2*, then enter the number of columns you want. Choose the distance between columns by pressing *3*, then entering the distance. Press ← to exit the screen.

THE ABILITY TO PRODUCE TEXT COLUMNS IS AMONG WordPerfect's most exciting features, and it has many applications. You can create two basic types of text columns, newspaper and parallel. Use *newspaper columns* for ''snaking'' text that flows up and down from one column to another, and *parallel columns* for short blocks of text that you read across the page. WordPerfect permits as many as 24 columns per page, and the columns appear next to each other both on the screen and in your printed version.

Creating text columns involves four basic steps:

- Defining the columns
- Turning columns on
- Typing the text into each column
- Turning columns off

Most WordPerfect features work the usual way in newspaper and parallel columns, but there are a few that can't be used at all. Among them are Footnotes and Sorting. Also, once you have defined columns and turned them on, you won't be allowed to change margins. To move or delete text, you can use the Block and Move keys, but not their options for cutting, copying, or retrieving tabular columns.

## CREATING NEWSPAPER COLUMNS

As the name implies, newspaper columns are for documents such as newsletters or magazine articles, where the text is in two or more columns and flows up and down through the columns. You read the text down the columns, not across as in parallel columns. These are the easiest type of columns to create and use.

## *DEFINING NEWSPAPER COLUMNS*

To define newspaper columns, you specify *Newspaper* as the type of column, then enter the number of columns you want on each page, the amount of blank space that will separate the columns, and the column margins. To try it, follow these steps:

1. Press the Math/Columns key (Alt-F7). You should see this menu:

   **1 M**ath On; **2** Math D**e**f; **3 C**olumn On/Off;
   **4** Column D**e**f: **0**

2. Select Column Def by pressing **4** or **D**. You will then see the Text Column Definition screen, as illustrated in Figure 12.1.

The first option on the Text Column Definition screen is Type, and you use it to specify which type of columns you want to use: Newspaper, Extended Parallel, or Parallel with Block Protect. Since Newspaper is the default, it will probably already be selected.

3. Select Type by pressing **T** and this menu will appear:

   Column Type: **1** Newspaper;  **2 P**arallel;
   **3** Parallel with **B**lock Protect: **0**

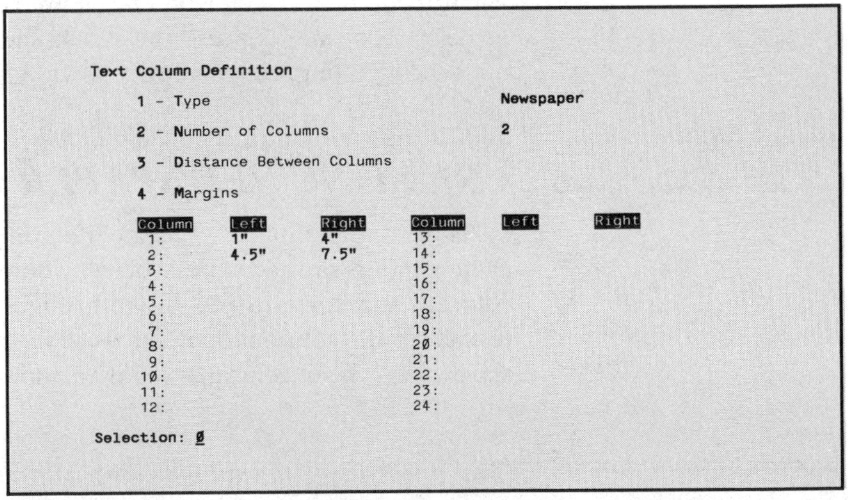

```
Text Column Definition

  1 - Type                              Newspaper

  2 - Number of Columns                 2

  3 - Distance Between Columns

  4 - Margins

 Column    Left      Right    Column    Left      Right
   1:       1"        4"        13:
   2:       4.5"      7.5"      14:
   3:                           15:
   4:                           16:
   5:                           17:
   6:                           18:
   7:                           19:
   8:                           20:
   9:                           21:
  10:                           22:
  11:                           23:
  12:                           24:

Selection: 0
```

*Figure 12.1:* The Text Column Definition screen

4. If another column type appears next to the Type option at the top of the screen, select Newspaper by pressing **N**, then press ⏎.

You use option 2, Number of Columns, to select the total number of columns that you want to use, from 2 to 24. Be careful with this, because if you use too many columns the results will be unattractive. For example, the glossary shown in Figure 12.2 has two columns, and Figure 12.3 shows the same glossary split into five columns. As you can see, there is only enough room in each column for a few words and it looks terrible.

5. Select Number of Columns by pressing **N**, then enter the number of columns you want to use and press ⏎.

Option 3, Distance Between Columns, lets you change the amount of blank space that separates columns; it's set to .5 inch, as you'll see when you press *D* to select the option. Be careful with this option too, because it can dramatically affect the appearance of your columns. For example, Figures 12.2 and 12.4 show two versions of the two-column glossary that was created with the Newspaper Column feature. In the original version (Figure 12.2), .5 inch separates the two columns, and in the second one (Figure 12.4), 1 inch separates them. As you can see, there is a lot of wasted paper in Figure 12.4. In fact, it may have looked even better if the distance between columns had been reduced to .3 inch.

6. Select Distance Between Columns by pressing **D**, then enter *.5*. WordPerfect will automatically add the inch symbol for you as soon as you press ⏎.

The final step is to enter the left and right margins for each of your columns using the Margins option. Unless you changed the margin settings in your document before pressing the Math/Columns key to define your columns, the total space available for all your columns will be 6.5 inches, equal to the difference between the default margins of 1 inch and 7.5 inches. WordPerfect automatically calculates the margins for you, using the assumption that you want columns of equal width. For instance, if you define two columns with .5 inch separating them, the program will enter the left and right margins

## GLOSSARY OF COMPUTER TERMS

**Alphanumeric** Containing both alphabetic and numeric characters

**ASCII** American Standard Code for Information Interchange; a standard format for encoding the alphabet, numbers, symbols and functions used by computers. Many word processing programs, for example, read text and data in ASCII format so that they can exchange files with other programs.

**Backup** A duplicate copy of a database or program stored on separate disk(s) or on tape, as a precaution in case of loss or damage to the original.

**Bit** Binary digIT, either a "0" or a "1". Bits represent the smallest unit of information used in a computer, and are combined into units including groups of 4 called a "nibble," groups of 8 called a "byte," and groups of 16 called a "word."

**Boot** In data processing, the term is used to describe turning on a computer.

**Byte** A set of eight bits, usually used to represent one character or number.

**Character set** The characters which can be displayed or used for processing on a specific computer, printer, plotter or other peripheral.

**Chip** A small piece of silicon or other semiconductor material which has been etched with a microscopic pattern of circuits. It is mounted in a package with electrical connections.

**Command** A directive or instruction such as the "save" command which saves a file from RAM onto a storage disk.

**CPU** The Central Processing Unit of a computer; it is the brains of the system, controlling all operations such as retrieving, decoding, and executing program instructions. The CPU of a microcomputer is normally contained on a single chip, such as the Intel 8088 in the IBM PC and compatibles.

**Crash** In data processing, to stop functioning. When a computer system crashes, it can be because of a power loss or other hardware problem or because of a bug in the program.

**CRT** Cathode Ray Tube; a picture tube used in a video monitor. It is often used to describe the computer display unit which resembles a television screen.

**Cursor** An electronic marker on the video display screen indicating the position where the next character will be inserted or deleted. It is usually a blinking character such as a rectangle or a flashing underline symbol.

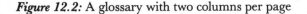

*Figure 12.2:* A glossary with two columns per page

shown in Figure 12.1: 1 and 4 for column 1, 4.5 and 7.5 for column 2. Notice that each column is 3 inches wide, and that they are separated from each other by .5 inch, since you selected .5 in the Distance Between Columns option.

## GLOSSARY OF COMPUTER TERMS

**Alphanumeric** Containing both alphabetic and numeric characters

**ASCII** American Standard Code for Information Interchange; a standard format for encoding the alphabet, numbers, symbols and functions used by computers. Many word processing programs, for example, read text and data in ASCII format so that they can exchange files with other programs.

**Backup** A duplicate copy of a database or program stored on separate disk(s) or on tape, as a precaution in case of loss or damage to the original.

**Bit** Binary digIT, either a "0" or a "1". Bits represent the smallest unit of information used in a computer, and are combined into units including groups of 4 called a "nibble," groups of 8 called a "byte," and groups of 16 called a "word"

**Boot** In data processing, the term is used to describe turning on a computer.

**Byte** A set of eight bits, usually used to represent one character or number.

**Character set** The characters which can be displayed or used for processing on a specific computer, printer, plotter or other peripheral.

**Chip** A small piece of silicon or other semiconductor material which has been etched with a microscopic pattern of circuits. It is mounted in a package with electrical connections.

**Command** A directive or instruction such as the "save" command which saves a file from RAM onto a storage disk.

**CPU** The Central Processing Unit of a computer; of the system, controlling all operations such as retrieving, decoding, and executing program instructions. The CPU of a microcomputer is normally contained on a single chip, such as the Intel 8088 in the IBM PC and compatibles.

**Crash** In data processing, to stop functioning. When a computer system crashes, it can be because of a power loss or other hardware problem or because of a bug in the program.

**CRT** Cathode Ray Tube; a picture tube used in a video monitor. It is often used to describe the computer display unit which television screen.

**Cursor** An electronic marker on the video display screen indicating the position where the next character will be inserted or deleted. It is usually a blinking character such as a rectangle or a flashing underline symbol.

*Figure 12.3:* The glossary with five columns per page

If WordPerfect's automatic settings are unacceptable or you choose to use columns that are not evenly spaced, you can override them by selecting the Margins option and typing new ones. Remember to leave several blank spaces between columns. For instance, to create a narrow column of 1.5 inch and a wide one of 4.5 inch with ½ inch separating them, you would enter these settings:

| *COLUMN MARGINS* | *LEFT* | *RIGHT* |
|---|---|---|
| Column 1: | 1 | 2.5 |
| Column 2: | 3 | 7.5 |

## GLOSSARY OF COMPUTER TERMS

**Alphanumeric**  Containing both alphabetic and numeric characters

**ASCII**  American Standard Code for Information Interchange; a standard format for encoding the alphabet, numbers, symbols and functions used by computers.  Many word processing programs, for example, read text and data in ASCII format so that they can exchange files with other programs.

**Backup**  A duplicate copy of a database or program stored on separate disk(s) or on tape, as a precaution in case of loss or damage to the original.

**Bit**  Binary digIT, either a "0" or a "1". Bits represent the smallest unit of information used in a computer, and are combined into units including groups of 4 called a "nibble," groups of 8 called a "byte," and groups of 16 called a "word."

**Boot**  In data processing, the term is used to describe turning on a computer.

**Byte**  A set of eight bits, usually used to represent one character or number.

**Character set**  The characters which can be displayed or used for processing on a specific computer, printer, plotter or other peripheral.

**Chip**  A small piece of silicon or other semiconductor material which has been etched with a microscopic pattern of circuits. It is mounted in a package with electrical connections.

**Command**  A directive or instruction such as the "save" command which saves a file from RAM onto a storage disk.

**CPU** The Central Processing Unit of a computer; it is the brains of the system, controlling all operations such as retrieving, decoding, and executing program instructions.  The CPU of a microcomputer is normally contained on a single chip, such as the Intel 8088 in the IBM PC and compatibles.

**Crash**  In data processing, to stop functioning.  When a computer system crashes, it can be because of a power loss or other hardware problem or because of a bug in the program.

**CRT**  Cathode Ray Tube; a picture tube used in a video monitor.It is often used to describe the computer display unit which resembles a television screen.

**Cursor**  An electronic marker on the video display screen indicating the position where the next character will be inserted or deleted.  It is usually a blinking character such as a rectangle or a flashing underline symbol.

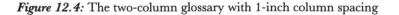

*Figure 12.4:* The two-column glossary with 1-inch column spacing

7. If you want to change the margins that WordPerfect has calculated for you, select Margins by pressing **M** then enter the margins you want to use. Press ◄┘ twice when you're finished. For the example shown in Figure 12.2, leave the default margins.

As you have just seen, all the options on the Text Column Definition screen have defaults, so if you want to define two evenly spaced newspaper columns separated by ½ inch, you really only have to press the Math/Columns key (Alt-F7), press *D* to select the Column Def option, then press ◄┘.

After the columns have been defined, a [Col Def] code with your specifications will be inserted into your document; press the Reveal Codes key (Alt-F3) to see it. The code for the definition shown in Figure 12.2 appears as follows:

[Col Def:2,1″,4″,4.5″,7.5″]

The first number after *Col Def* represents the total number of columns that have been defined, two in this example. The remaining numbers represent the left and right margin settings for each of your columns: 1 and 4, 4.5 and 7.5.

## TURNING THE COLUMNS FEATURE ON

It isn't necessary to begin using columns as soon as they are defined; you can turn the Columns feature on whenever you want. When you're ready to start entering text into columns, select the Column On/Off option from the Math/Columns key (Alt-F7). You'd typically do this right after defining the columns, since exiting the Text Column Definition screen returns you to the Math/Columns menu and you can just press *3* or *C* to turn columns on. Notice that Column On/Off is a toggle key. Once you are done working with columns, you repeat the same steps to turn it off again (but if the rest of the document will be in column format, you don't have to turn it off).

To turn on the newspaper columns, you select the Column On/Off option from the Math/Columns key (Alt-F7) by pressing *C*.

Once you turn columns on, a column number indicator is added to the status line to let you know which column the cursor is in. If the cursor is in column 1, for instance, the status line will be similar to this:

Col 1 Doc 1 Pg 1 Ln 1″ Pos 1″

Also, a [Col On] code is added to your document, visible only in the Reveal Codes screen. When you turn columns off, a [Col Off] code is inserted.

## ENTERING TEXT IN NEWSPAPER COLUMNS

As you type in a newspaper column, your text will be automatically formatted to fit within the boundaries of the first column. When the cursor reaches the end of the column, it will automatically move to the top of the second column on that page (possibly taking the word you were typing with it) and text will be entered there as you continue to type. This process continues until all columns on the first page are full, at which point the cursor moves to the first column on the second page, along with any text that would have exceeded the page length limit, and the process continues.

It's important that you understand how page breaks work in your columns. WordPerfect treats each column as an independent page, automatically inserting a Soft Page code at the bottom of each column after you fill it, and moving the cursor into the next one. You can force a column to end before the last line of the page by pressing the Hard Page Break key, Ctrl-←. This immediately moves the cursor into the next column or, if you press it with the cursor in the last column on the page, into the first column of the next page. If you look into the Reveal Codes screen (Alt-F3) after creating your columns, you'll see Soft Page codes, [SPg], at the bottom of each column (or Hard Page codes, [HPg], if you used Ctrl- ← to end any of the columns).

Because WordPerfect considers each column a separate page, the Reveal Codes screen will appear differently in Column mode. For instance, in Figure 12.5 the cursor was positioned on line 2″ of the second column, as the status line indicates. However, in the Reveal Codes screen the second column is displayed on the left side and the first column is not visible at all. While this can be confusing, it is

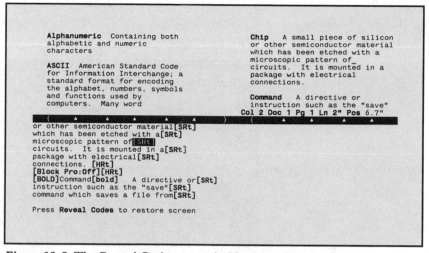

*Figure 12.5:* The Reveal Codes screen in Newspaper Column mode

inconsequential since the columns on your editing screen and printed document will be correctly aligned.

## INSERTING AND DELETING TEXT

Inserting and deleting text in Columns mode is really no different from regular text mode, except that features such as Delete, Backspace, Block Delete, and Move operate on a column-by-column basis. For instance, WordPerfect's Delete to End of Line function (Ctrl-End) will only delete lines within a column. However, as you delete them, the entire document will be reformatted, just as it would be in noncolumn mode, so the text in other columns on the page will be shifted up or down within the columns. When you type words (in Insert mode), it may appear as though the text in columns to the right is being pushed aside, but as soon you press ↓ to reformat the text, the columns will be realigned correctly. For example, in Figure 12.6 it looks as though column 2 (the CPU paragraph) is being disrupted by the insertion of the phrase *as a precaution in case of loss or damage to the* (in the Backup paragraph in column 1), since *damage to the* seems to have moved into column 2. However, as soon as the ↓ key is pressed, the columns realign and look like Figure 12.2 again.

```
      standard format for encoding        connections.
      the alphabet, numbers, symbols
      and functions used by               Command   A directive or
      computers.  Many word               instruction such as the "save"
      processing programs, for            command which saves a file from
      example, read text and data in      RAM onto a storage disk.
      ASCII format so that they can
      exchange files with other           CPU The Central Processing Unit
      programs.                           of a computer; it is the brains
                                          of the system, controlling all
      Backup A duplicate copy of a        operations such as retrieving,
      database or program stored on       decoding, and executing program
      separate disk(s) or on tape, as     instructions.  The CPU of a
      a precaution in case of loss or damage to the
                                          contained on a single chip,
      Bit   Binary digIT, either a "0"    such as the Intel 8088 in the
      or a "1".  Bits represent the       IBM PC and compatibles.
      smallest unit of information
      used in a computer, and are         Crash   In data processing, to
      combined into units including       stop functioning.  When a
      groups of 4 called a "nibble,"      computer system crashes, it can
      groups of 8 called a "byte,"        be because of a power loss or
      and groups of 16 called a           other hardware problem or
      "word."                             because of a bug in the
                                               Col 1 Doc 1 Pg 1 Ln 4.66" Pos 4.2"
```

*Figure 12.6:* Inserting text in a newspaper column

## CONVERTING AN EXISTING DOCUMENT INTO NEWSPAPER COLUMNS

Converting a noncolumnar document into newspaper column format is easy. You can retrieve the file either before or after defining the columns and turning on Column mode. A file can be retrieved into a column by using the Retrieve Text key (Shift-F10) or the Retrieve option on the List Files key (F5), or by blocking and copying a section of text from a file in the Doc 2 area and retrieving it into the columns in Doc 1.

To retrieve a file after defining and turning on columns, check the Reveal Codes screen to be sure the cursor is positioned after the [Col On] code, then retrieve the file or marked block using one of the methods mentioned above. As you move the cursor through the text, WordPerfect will align the text correctly into the newspaper columns that you've defined.

Alternatively, you can retrieve a file, place the cursor at the top, define the columns, then turn on Column mode. As you scroll down through the text, the document will be realigned to fit into the columns. To speed up the reformatting process, use the Rewrite option on the Screen key (Ctrl-F3 0).

See Chapter 5 for more information about how to copy text between two documents in memory using the Switch key along with the Block and Move keys.

## ERASING COLUMN FORMATTING

It's equally easy to remove newspaper column formatting from a document; all you have to do is find and erase the [Col On] code. You can use the Reveal Codes screen (Alt-F3) to help you find it, then move the cursor onto it and press Delete. Alternatively, you can use the Replace key (Alt-F2) to locate and erase it. To do this, press Alt-F2, select *N* (for Confirm), then press Alt-F7 C to insert the [Col On] code into the search string, then press F2 twice. Once you delete the [Col On] code, the text will be reformatted instantly, and the integrity of your work will be maintained. In other words, column 2 will move under column 1, and column 3 will move under column 2. For instance, Figure 12.7 shows the glossary after the [Col On] code was deleted. If you compare it to Figure 12.2, you'll see that it's still in correct alphabetical order, since the text of column 2 (which began with *Chip*) was moved underneath column 1 (which ended with the *Character set* paragraph).

## CHANGING THE COLUMN DEFINITION

To change your column definition, you have to place the cursor between the [Col Def] and [Col On] codes. If the cursor is after the [Col On] code, you won't be able to select any of the options on the Text Column Definition screen; if you try, you'll just be returned to the Math/Columns key menu. If the cursor is before the [Col Def] code, you'll be able to define columns, but the change will have no effect since the original code will follow it and WordPerfect will find and use that one instead.

The first step in changing the column definition is to use either the Reveal Codes screen (Alt-F3) or the Search key (F2) to position the cursor after the [Col Def] code. If the [Col On] code is right next to the [Col Def] code, place the cursor on the [Col On] code (although the cursor will be on the [Col On] code, it will not be in effect at that point). You can then press the Math/Columns key (Alt-F7) and redefine your columns using the steps described earlier. When you exit from the Text Column Definition screen, your text will be realigned to fit into your new column definition.

### GLOSSARY OF COMPUTER TERMS

**Alphanumeric**  Containing both alphabetic and numeric characters

**ASCII**  American Standard Code for Information Interchange; a standard format for encoding the alphabet, numbers, symbols and functions used by computers.  Many word processing programs, for example, read text and data in ASCII format so that they can exchange files with other programs.

**Backup**  A duplicate copy of a database or program stored on separate disk(s) or on tape, as a precaution in case of loss or damage to the original.

**Bit**  Binary digIT, either a "0" or a "1".  Bits represent the smallest unit of information used in a computer, and are combined into units including groups of 4 called a "nibble," groups of 8 called a "byte," and groups of 16 called a "word."

**Boot**  In data processing, the term is used to describe turning on a computer.

**Byte**  A set of eight bits, usually used to represent one character or number.

**Character set**  The characters which can be displayed or used for processing on a specific computer, printer, plotter or other peripheral.

**Chip**  A small piece of silicon or other semiconductor material which has been etched with a microscopic pattern of circuits.  It is mounted in a package with electrical connections.

**Command**  A directive or instruction such as the "save" command which saves a file from RAM onto a storage disk.

**CPU**  The Central Processing Unit of a computer; it is the brains of the system, controlling all operations such as retrieving, decoding, and executing program instructions.  The CPU of a microcomputer is normally contained on a single chip, such as the Intel 8088 in the IBM PC and compatibles.

**Crash**  In data processing, to stop functioning.  When a computer system crashes, it can be because of a power loss or other hardware problem or because of a bug in the program.

**CRT**  Cathode Ray Tube; a picture tube used in a video monitor.It is often used to describe the computer display unit which resembles a television screen.

**Cursor**  An electronic marker on the video display screen indicating the position where the next character will be inserted or deleted.  It is usually a blinking character such as a rectangle or a flashing underline symbol.

*Figure 12.7:* The glossary after the [Col on] code has been deleted

## CURSOR MOVEMENT WITHIN COLUMNS

Cursor movement in parallel and newspaper columns—you'll learn about parallel columns soon—is basically the same as in Edit mode, as long as you remember that each column is considered a separate page. If you press Home → or End, for example, the cursor moves to the end of the line in the column you're in, not to the end of the last column on the page. If the cursor is on the last character in the column, pressing ↓ wraps it down to the next line in the same column, and pressing → moves it to the first character at the top of the next column. To move the cursor horizontally into the next column from any other position, you have to use the Go To key (Ctrl-Home). When you press Ctrl-Home, the *Go to* prompt appears in the lower left corner of the screen, then you press ← or → to move left or right one column. For example, if the cursor is in column 1 and you want to move it to column 2, press Ctrl-Home →. If it's in column 2 and you want to move it to column 1, press Ctrl-Home ←. In either case, the cursor moves horizontally to the same line in the next column. If you have more than two columns, you can use Ctrl-Home Home followed by → or ← to move to the last or first column. If the cursor is in column 3, for example, you can press Ctrl-Home Home ← to move it into column 1.

If the cursor is located on the last character of a column, pressing → will reposition it to the first character of the next column, but if you press ↓ instead of →, the cursor will move straight down to the same column on the following page. If the cursor is located on the first character of a column, pressing ← will move it to the last character of the previous one. If text (or blank lines) has not yet been entered into a column, you will not be able to move the cursor to it at all.

Other applications for the Go To key are covered thoroughly in Chapter 3.

## USING BLOCK FEATURES WITH COLUMNS

Block and Move key operations, such as move, copy, and delete, work normally in parallel and newspaper columns, except that you cannot use the Tabular Columns option on the Move key (with Block on), since this option is used to move or copy a different type of column (one created using Tab, Indent, or Tab Align). Instead, you must use either the Block option from the Block and Move key combination, or the Sentence, Paragraph, or Page option from the Move key. If you use Move to cut or copy a page, all columns on the page will be included. Other functions such as printing and saving by block work normally also.

Chapter 5 provides more information about the Move, Copy, Delete, and Append options on the Block and Move keys, and it tells you how to print and save blocks of text.

When defining a block in Column mode, if you reach the bottom of a column, do not press ↓ because it will immediately block the remaining columns on the page. Instead, use →, which will move the cursor to the top of the next column. Also, be extremely careful with the hidden codes when you define a block. For example, if you accidentally include a [Col On] code in the block you are moving or deleting, you could remove column formatting altogether. To prevent this, I highly recommend that you press the Reveal Codes key (Alt-F3) and leave it on while you are defining the block. Although it takes some getting used to, it can prevent some disastrous results!

To keep text from being split between two newspaper columns, you can place Block Protect codes around it, just as you would if you wanted to prevent the text from being split between pages in noncolumn mode. For instance, in the glossary shown in Figure 12.2, Block Protect codes were placed around the *Chip* paragraph to keep it together. Otherwise, the first two lines would have remained in the first column and the rest of it would have been at the top of column 2. To use block protection, you start at the beginning of the section you want to keep together, turn Block mode on by pressing Alt-F4, use the cursor movement keys to highlight the section, then press Shift-F8 and type *Y* in response to the *Protect block* prompt.

See Chapter 5 for more information about WordPerfect's Block Protect feature.

## *USING HYPHENS IN COLUMNS*

Hyphenation is introduced in Chapter 4, and the hyphenation zone is discussed more thoroughly in Chapter 8.

In most cases, you will be using right justification in your columns, so you should always use hyphens to help reduce the extra blank space that WordPerfect inserts between words to create even right margins. To do this, you can either use WordPerfect's built-in Hyphenation feature or type the hyphens yourself using the soft hyphen key, Ctrl-hyphen. Both methods create *soft hyphens,* the type that disappears if the word moves away from the right margin when you add or delete text near it. Figure 12.8 shows a hyphenated version of the familiar glossary, and if you compare it to Figure 12.2 you'll see much less blank space between words.

To type hyphens yourself, just press Ctrl and the hyphen (minus) key each time you want to hyphenate a word. To use WordPerfect's built-in method, move the cursor to the top of the document, press the Format key (Shift-F8), select Line, select Hyphenation from the

Format: Line screen, then specify whether you want to use the manual or automatic method. The automatic method zips through your document and hyphenates all appropriate words automatically. The manual option stops at each word that could be hyphenated and suggests a location for the hyphen, but lets you change the location or eliminate the hyphen altogether from that word. You can turn on

## GLOSSARY OF COMPUTER TERMS

**Alphanumeric** Containing both alphabetic and numeric characters

**ASCII** American Standard Code for Information Interchange; a standard format for encoding the alphabet, numbers, symbols and functions used by computers. Many word processing programs, for example, read text and data in ASCII format so that they can exchange files with other programs.

**Backup** A duplicate copy of a data file or program stored on separate disk(s) or on tape, as a precaution in case of loss or damage to the original.

**Bit** Binary digIT, either a "0" or a "1". Bits represent the smallest unit of information used in a computer, and are combined into units including groups of 4 called a "nibble," groups of 8 called a "byte," and groups of 16 called a "word."

**Boot** In data processing, the term is used to describe turning on a computer.

**Byte** A set of eight bits, usually used to represent one character or number.

**Character set** The characters which can be displayed or used for processing on a specific computer, printer, plotter or other peripheral.

**Chip** A small piece of silicon or other semiconductor material which has been etched with a microscopic pattern of circuits. It is mounted in a package with electrical connections.

**Command** A directive or instruction such as the "save" command which saves a file from RAM onto a storage disk.

**CPU** The Central Processing Unit of a computer; it is the "brains" of the system controlling all operations such as retrieving, decoding, and executing program instructions. The CPU of a microcomputer is normally contained on a single chip, such as the Intel 8088 in the IBM PC and compatibles.

**Crash** In data processing, to stop functioning. When a computer system crashes, it can be because of a power loss or other hardware problem or because of a bug in the program.

**CRT** Cathode Ray Tube; a picture tube used in a video monitor.It is often used to describe the computer display unit which resembles a television screen.

**Cursor** An electronic marker on the video display screen indicating the position where the next character will be inserted or deleted. It is usually a blinking character such as a rectangle or a flashing underline symbol.

*Figure 12.8:* Using hyphens in columns

automatic or manual hyphenation either before or after typing your text. If you use one of the built-in methods, you can also benefit by reducing the left hyphenation zone to 8% or 7% so that you will be asked to hyphenate more words.

## SPEEDING UP REFORMATTING AND CURSOR MOVEMENT

You may have noticed that as the cursor moves through text that is formatted into columns (by using ↑ or ↓, Screen Up or Screen Down, PgUp or PgDn, etc.), it moves a little slower. Also, when you add or delete text, automatic reformatting is not as fast as when you're working in noncolumnar mode. You can avoid these inconveniences by using WordPerfect's Setup key (Shift-F1) to turn off side-by-side column display. This will alter the appearance of both newspaper and parallel columns so that each column appears to be on a separate page. For instance, if you're using two columns, the first column will be displayed on the left side of the first page and the second column will be displayed on the right side of the following page. Although the columns *appear* to be on separate pages with page break indicators separating them, if you look at the page number indicator on the status line as you move from the first to the second column, it will show you that they are actually on the same page. In any case, they will be printed side by side even if you leave Column Display set to No.

To do this, press the Setup key (Shift-F1), press *D* for Display, press *S* for Side-by-side Columns Display, then change it to No by pressing *N*. Note that Column Display will remain set to No until you repeat the procedure and change it to Yes, even if you exit from WordPerfect.

## CREATING PARALLEL COLUMNS

Parallel columns are short blocks of text that always remain next to each other (parallel) so that you can read across the pages, as in a side-by-side translation. You can use them to create short charts, tables, scripts, or class descriptions, or whenever you want to type columns of text and retain the benefits of word wrap within the column. If you create columns using Tab or Indent, word wrap does not operate within the columns as you add or delete text because you have to press ⬅ to end each line.

You use the first type of parallel columns, Parallel with Block Protect, on a page-by-page basis, when the parallel blocks are short enough to remain on one page. You use Extended Parallel Columns whenever one or more of the columns extends into a second page, so that the text from each column flows into the corresponding column on the next page. This is different from text in newspaper columns, which flows up and down through the columns until it fills all the columns on a page, then starts in column 1 of the following page.

To create parallel columns, you follow the same basic steps you did to create newspaper columns, except that under the Type option, you select either Parallel or Parallel with Block Protect. The following sections will teach you how.

## PARALLEL COLUMNS WITH BLOCK PROTECT

When you use Parallel with Block Protect, side-by-side blocks of text are kept together by WordPerfect's Block Protection feature. For example, Figure 12.9 shows an advertisement with three columns. The first three paragraphs, about the Honda, Chevy, and Volvo, are surrounded with Block Protect codes, and so are the last three (Chevy Blazer, Ford Bronco, and Jeep Cherokee).

Here's how it works: When you turn on Parallel Columns with Block Protect, WordPerfect inserts a [BlockPro:On] code to begin block protection, then a [Col On] code to begin columns. You type the first paragraph (about the Honda, in our example) then press Ctrl-⬅. This inserts a Hard Page code [HPg] into your document and moves the cursor to the next column. Type the next one (Chevy Citation), and press Ctrl-⬅ again to insert another [HPg] code and move the cursor into column 3. Type the last one (Volvo), then press Ctrl-⬅. This inserts an [HRt] code, a [BlockPro:Off] code to end block protection, and a [Col Off] code, then another [BlockPro:On] code and [Col On] code to start the second block. It also moves the cursor back to column 1, where you type the fourth paragraph (Chevy Blazer). As with all WordPerfect features, you'll understand it better if you try doing it.

Before you begin, I want to issue a warning about cursor movement: once you have created the columns and entered text, use the Go To key

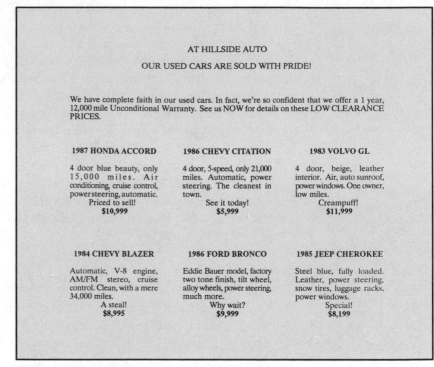

AT HILLSIDE AUTO

OUR USED CARS ARE SOLD WITH PRIDE!

We have complete faith in our used cars. In fact, we're so confident that we offer a 1 year, 12,000 mile Unconditional Warranty. See us NOW for details on these LOW CLEARANCE PRICES.

**1987 HONDA ACCORD**

4 door blue beauty, only 15,000 miles. Air conditioning, cruise control, power steering, automatic.
Priced to sell!
**$10,999**

**1986 CHEVY CITATION**

4 door, 5-speed, only 21,000 miles. Automatic, power steering. The cleanest in town.
See it today!
**$5,999**

**1983 VOLVO GL**

4 door, beige, leather interior. Air, auto sunroof, power windows. One owner, low miles.
Creampuff!
**$11,999**

**1984 CHEVY BLAZER**

Automatic, V-8 engine, AM/FM stereo, cruise control. Clean, with a mere 34,000 miles.
A steal!
**$8,995**

**1986 FORD BRONCO**

Eddie Bauer model, factory two tone finish, tilt wheel, alloy wheels, power steering, much more.
Why wait?
**$9,999**

**1985 JEEP CHEROKEE**

Steel blue, fully loaded. Leather, power steering, snow tires, luggage racks, power windows.
Special!
**$8,199**

*Figure 12.9:* Parallel columns

(Ctrl-Home) followed by the → or ← key to move the cursor from column to column (as described above under "Cursor Movement within Columns"). *Do not* use Ctrl-⏎ to move the cursor into the next column. If you do, you'll create another new column and disrupt the column(s) that follow. To illustrate this, I placed the cursor on the dollar sign (*$*) in column 1 of my example, then pressed Ctrl-⏎. The results appear in Figure 12.10. Notice that the dollar sign and price moved into column 2, but that the second column (Chevy Citation) moved into column 3, on top of the Volvo description. It's difficult to recover from a mistake like this, so remember my advice!

Follow the instructions below to create the columns shown in Figure 12.9. You will be defining three parallel columns of equal size, separated by ½ inch.

1. Center and type the heading, then type the first paragraph.

2. To define the columns, press the Math/Columns key (Alt-F7) and select Column Def by pressing **D**.

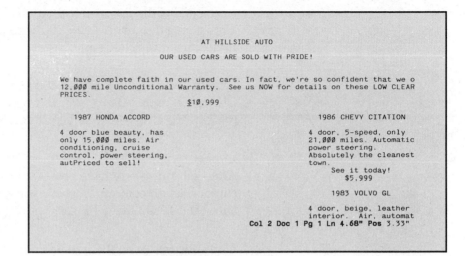

*Figure 12.10:* Using Ctrl-◄┘ for cursor movement disrupts the columns

3. Press **T** to change the type of column, then press **B** to select Parallel with Block Protect.

4. To change Number of Columns, press **N** then type **3** for the number of columns.

5. Press **D** to select Distance Between Columns. It should be .5 inch; if not, type **.5** and press ◄┘.

As soon as you enter the distance between columns, WordPerfect automatically recalculates the margin settings, so you don't have to change them.

6. Press ◄┘ to exit the Text Column Definition screen.

7. Turn columns on by pressing **C**, Column On/Off. Note the Col 1 indicator on the status line.

8. Press the Center key (Shift-F6), then type the first heading **(1987 HONDA ACCORD)**. As you can see, it is centered over the first column, not the entire page.

9. Press ◄┘ twice to leave a blank line, then type the rest of the description. Note that I pressed ◄┘ after *automatic.* and *Priced to sell!*, and used the Center key (Shift-F6) to center the last two lines (*Priced to sell!* and *$10,999*).

10. At the end of the paragraph about the Honda, press Ctrl-←. This places the cursor at the top of column 2. Note the Col 2 indicator on the status line.

11. Repeat steps 8 and 9 to type the next paragraph, about the Chevy Citation. After you finish typing the description and price, press Ctrl-← to move the cursor into column 3.

12. Repeat steps 8 and 9 again to type the Volvo description. After you finish typing it, press Ctrl-←. This will move the cursor back to column 1, where you can type the paragraph about the 1984 Chevy Blazer.

13. Continue following these steps until you've finished entering the last two paragraphs, then press Save (F10) and save the file under the name *Car.ad*.

Now you're free to experiment with your columns. Use Ctrl-Home → or ← to move from column to column. Try adding and deleting text in each column, and watch what happens. If the text in the next column seems to be disrupted, press ↓ to realign it. Remember, you can't ruin the alignment of your columns unless you press Ctrl-←, which you are only meant to do when you originally create the columns and type the text into them.

## EXTENDED PARALLEL COLUMNS

Extended parallel columns are very similar to the other type of parallel columns, except that they don't have the block protection. As a result, text in individual columns can extend across a page break. When text does extend to the next page, it flows into the same column. Thus, text in column 1 of page 1 continues in column 1 of page 2, text in column 2 of page 1 continues in column 2, and so forth. By contrast, groups of text in block-protected parallel columns must remain on a single page. For example, if text was inserted above the descriptions of the last three cars in Figure 12.9 (Blazer, Bronco, and Cherokee) and they approached the end of the page, WordPerfect would move the entire group as a unit to the next page, not just the last few lines.

To create extended parallel columns, you follow the same procedures described above for parallel columns with Block Protect except that in step 3, you select Parallel (*P*) for the type of column. The other steps are the same. You type the first section of text, press Ctrl-◄┘ to create the next column and move the cursor there, type that one, then press Ctrl-◄┘ again. Each time you press Ctrl-◄┘, WordPerfect inserts a [HPg] code into your document, except after the last section in a parallel group (such as the Volvo description in Figure 12.9). At that point, WordPerfect turns off columns, then turns them back on again, inserting [Col Off], [HRt], and [Col On] codes simultaneously (in that order). The cursor stops after the [Col On] code, waiting for you to type the next group.

In all three types of columns—extended parallel, newspaper, and block-protected parallel—Ctrl-◄┘ has a special function: it operates to create a new column, not a new page. You must be careful not to use it once you have created your columns and entered text, because it will ruin the alignment of your columns. Instead, to move the cursor into the next column, use the Go To key (Ctrl-Home) followed by the → or ← key.

## SUMMARY

As you have seen, WordPerfect's text columns are powerful and valuable tools. You can create three types: newspaper, extended parallel, and parallel with Block Protect. Newspaper columns are useful for text in which the words flow up and down the page from column to column, as in a newspaper. Parallel columns with Block Protect are useful for short blocks of text that must remain next to each other on a single page, such as side-by-side translations. Extended parallel columns are similar to parallel without the block protection. You use them if one or more of the columns extends into a second page, so that the text from each column flows into the same column on the next page.

You can have as many as 24 columns of text on a page, and you can define the margins for each column individually so that they can be uneven in width. Since WordPerfect treats each column as though it were a separate page, editing changes within one column do not affect text on the same line in the adjacent column. Columns appear next to each other both on screen and in the printed document.

Chapter 14 will cover more advanced aspects of column layout and design, and you'll see an improved version of the parallel column example shown in Figure 12.9.

# 13.

## CREATING BOXES, GRAPHS, CHARTS, AND OTHER ILLUSTRATIONS

# FAST TRACK

**To use Line Draw,**                                                                411

press the Screen key (Ctrl-F3) and select Line Draw (option 2 or L). At the next prompt, choose the type of character you want to draw with—single line (1), double line (2), or asterisk (3)—then use the arrow keys to draw. Press Exit (F7) or Cancel (F1) to end a line drawing.

**To draw with a different character,**                                              416

press the Screen key (Ctrl-F3) and select Line Draw (*2* or *L*), then choose the Change option (4). You will see eight additional characters to choose from. Press the number of the character you want to use. This character will replace the asterisk on the Line Draw menu next to option 3, and you can press an arrow key to start drawing with it.

**To draw with any ASCII character in the extended character set,**                   417

press the Screen key (Ctrl-F3), select Line Draw (*2* or *L*), select the Change option, then the Other option. In response to the *Solid character:* prompt, enter the ASCII code for that character by pressing Alt and typing the decimal code. Press any arrow key to draw with it.

**To move or copy a line drawing,**                                                  420

exit from Line Draw by pressing F1 or F7 and place the cursor at the upper left corner of the drawing. Press Block (Alt-F4), then use ↓ and → to place the cursor at the opposite corner. Press Move (Ctrl-F4) and select the Rectangle option, then select Move or Copy. You'll see the *Move Cursor; press Enter to retrieve* prompt. Move the cursor to the place you want to retrieve the drawing and press ↵.

**To print your drawing,** 420

first test your printer to find out if it is capable of producing the graphics characters you have used. Draw a few of the characters, then use the Print key (Shift-F7 P) to print the page.

LINE DRAW IS A USEFUL FEATURE THAT ALLOWS YOU to draw lines, boxes, graphs, borders, and simple illustrations such as flowcharts and organization charts. The drawings can be seen on both monochrome and color monitors, but a printer with graphics capability (such as many of the dot matrix and laser printers) is required to print them as they appear on the screen. If you ever used an Etch-a-Sketch when you were a kid, you'll have just as much fun with this feature!

## USING LINE DRAW

ASCII stands for American Standard Code for Information Interchange

You can choose from among 11 different characters to draw with, including single or double lines and asterisks, or you can change the asterisk character to one of the decimal equivalents of ASCII characters or any other graphics character your printer will print. Every character on your keyboard has a standard decimal value called an ASCII code, and there are also ASCII codes for symbols and characters that are not on the keyboard, such as foreign language characters (ñ), the section symbol (§), numeric symbols (½) scientific symbols (∞), and graphic characters ( ■ ). The numbers for these symbols range from 1 to 31, and 128 to 255, and are generally referred to as the *IBM Extended Character Set*. Appendix B shows a chart of the ASCII characters and their decimal equivalents. Although all these characters you draw with can be seen on all monitors, many printers are incapable of printing them. The "Printing Your Drawing" section of this chapter gives instructions on how to test your printer's ability to print graphics characters.

Line Draw works in Typeover mode, replacing other characters on the screen as you draw (if you draw over existing characters). To add text after creating a drawing, you must be in Typeover mode, as you'll soon see. Also, you can't press the ⬅ key on a line that includes a drawing or you will disfigure the drawing (although pressing Backspace realigns it). WordPerfect automatically inserts a hard return when you press ↓ to draw a corner, and inserts spaces to fill up blank areas.

To learn how this feature works, let's start by drawing a small box. Begin with a clear screen to make sure no formatting codes such as tabs or margins have been entered (use the Exit key, F7, to clear the screen), and start with the cursor at the beginning of line 1.

1. Press the Screen key (Ctrl-F3), and select the Line Draw option by pressing either **L** or **2**. You should see the prompt illustrated in Figure 13.1.

Notice that the status line in this screen shows only the line and position indicators, not the page and document indicators that you see in Edit mode.

There are three standard characters you can draw with: a single line, a double line, and an asterisk. Option 1, a single line, is the default; as you can see, it's the last character in the prompt line so it will be used unless you select another. You change the line drawing character by selecting option 2 for a double line, or 3 for asterisks. WordPerfect also has a fourth drawing option, Change, that lets you use other characters; you'll study this shortly. Note that asterisks can

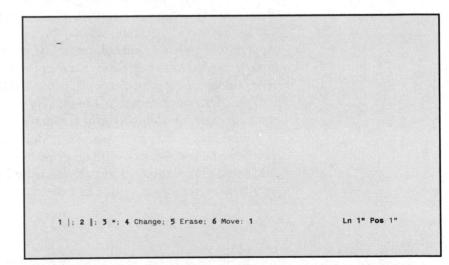

*Figure 13.1:* The Line Draw prompt

be printed by most printers, including letter-quality ones, but that many can't print the lines.

2.  Select option 2 for a double line.

3.  Press → 30 times, and a horizontal double line will appear.

4.  Press ↓ 20 times. Now you've completed two sides of the box (Figure 13.2).

As you can see from Figure 13.2 and your screen, you are starting to create a rectangle. Moving the cursor 30 positions vertically is not the equivalent of moving 30 positions horizontally, so you were only instructed to move the cursor 20 times vertically.

5.  To complete the rectangle, press ← 30 times, then press ↑ 20 times.

6.  Press Exit (F7) or Cancel (F1) to end line drawing, then press ↵ to move the rectangle down a line.

7.  Press ↑ once to move the cursor onto the blank line.

Now take a look at the Reveal Codes screen (press Alt-F3) to see what WordPerfect has actually done. (Make sure the cursor is on line 1, outside of the rectangle.) As you can see, there is a Hard Return

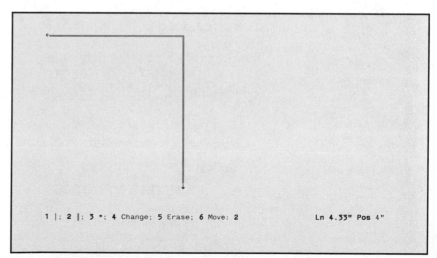

*Figure 13.2:* Drawing a box with Line Draw

code at the end of each line; the program inserted it automatically when you pressed ↓. If you tried to draw a line in Edit mode (using the hyphen key, for example), you would also have to press ↵ at the corner and then insert several blank spaces on line 2 until you reached the position where the first vertical character would be entered.

Now let's see what happens when we try to type some text into the box. Press Alt-F3 to exit Reveal Codes.

1. Move the cursor down a few lines, then use → to move it inside the rectangle.

2. Type

   **IMPORTANT NOTICE**

Notice that the character that forms the right border on line 6 has been pushed to the right several spaces. Now you're beginning to understand why you must use Typeover when you type text inside a rectangle: since WordPerfect was in Insert mode, everything was pushed to the right to make room for the new text as you typed. Don't worry, though, because you can easily fix the border using the Backspace key.

3. Press Backspace until you've deleted the words IMPOR-TANT NOTICE, and the border will move back to the correct position.

Now let's try doing it the right way. We'll turn on Typeover mode, then type IMPORTANT NOTICE again. If you make a mistake while typing, use the Space bar to erase it, not Delete or Backspace.

4. Press the Ins key. You should see the Typeover prompt in the lower left corner of the screen.

5. Type

   **IMPORTANT NOTICE**

This time the border remains in the correct position, as you can see in Figure 13.3. As you've seen, you must be in Typeover mode if you want to type inside a line drawing. You can also draw around text that has already been entered, but the text can't begin at the left margin or the line will erase the first character, and it can't exceed the right margin or you'll erase the last character as you draw. Let's try drawing around preexisting text.

1. Press the Exit key (F7 N N) to clear the screen without saving.

2. Press ⏎ twice.

3. Press the Space bar twice so that your text is indented a few positions.

4. Type

   **WARNING!**

5. Move the cursor to the blank line above the text.

6. Turn Line Drawing on by pressing the Screen key (Ctrl-F3) then pressing **L** or **2**.

7. To draw a small rectangle, press → 10 times, press ↓ 5 times, press ← 10 times, then press ↑ 5 times.

8. Press F7 to exit Line Draw mode.

That was easy! However, if you hadn't pressed the Space bar twice in step 3 to indent the word, the first character *(W)* would have been erased by the double line.

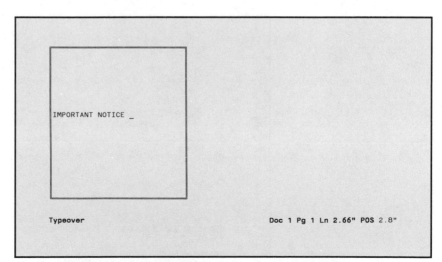

*Figure 13.3:* Text typed inside the box

## USING THE ESCAPE KEY TO SPEED UP DRAWING

As you learned in Chapter 3, you can use the Escape key to repeat a keystroke as many times as you want. This can really speed up line drawing. To try it, clear the screen, select Line Draw from the Screen key (Ctrl-F3 2 or Ctrl-F3 L), then select option 1 to draw a single line. Press Esc and you'll see the following prompt:

Repeat Value = 8

This number tells you the number of times your action will be repeated, and 8 is the default. Type *35* in its place, then press →. A line of 35 characters will automatically be drawn for you.

Notice that if you press Esc again, you will see the original prompt, *Repeat Value = 8*. To replace the default number of 8, you can type the number you want to use, such as 35, then press ←. The next time you press Esc, that number will appear.

## USING THE CHANGE OPTION TO SPECIFY DIFFERENT DRAWING CHARACTERS

The Change option (4) on the Line Draw menu gives you additional characters with which you can draw (Figure 13.4). This option

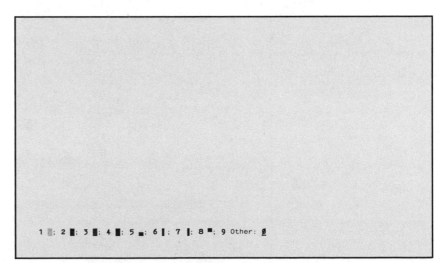

*Figure 13.4:* The Change option on the Line Draw menu

works by changing the asterisk (option 3) to one of the eight other characters on this menu or to any ASCII character you select.

As you can see, options 1 through 8 are characters, and they can be used to draw the lines shown in Figure 13.5. You select one of the eight characters by pressing the number next to it. As soon as you type one of the numbers, you'll be returned to the main Line Draw menu and the character you selected will have replaced the asterisk next to option 3. To draw with it, press any arrow key.

If you want to use an ASCII character that is not on this list, select option 4, Change, then option 9, Other. Next, type any character on the keyboard or press the Alt key and hold it down while typing the decimal code for the ASCII character you want to use. Note that you

See Appendix B for an ASCII table with decimal codes.

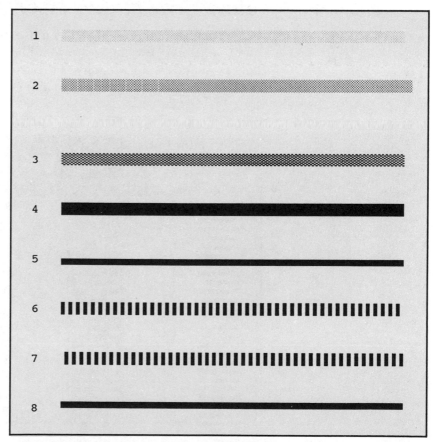

*Figure 13.5:* A line drawn with each of the eight characters on the Change menu

must use the numeric keypad to enter the numbers that represent ASCII characters. For instance, pressing Alt-1 will produce a smiling face, and Alt-3 will produce a heart. After you release the Alt and number keys, you'll see the character next to option 3 in the prompt line, and you can press any arrow key to draw it. If you like to doodle, you can really have fun with these characters, as I did in Figure 13.6.

On a more serious note, I drew the keyboard shown in Figure 13.7 to help my students identify certain unmarked keys on the IBM PC keyboard, and I drew the hard disk organization chart shown in Figure 13.8 to help them understand directories and subdirectories.

## MOVING THE CURSOR IN A LINE DRAWING

You can use option 6, Move, to move the cursor without drawing new characters or erasing any of your line drawing. To use it, press *6* then move the cursor with any of the arrow keys. Select option 1, 2, or 3 when you're ready to draw again.

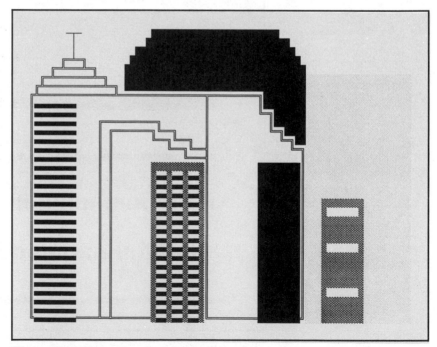

*Figure 13.6:* Abstract art?

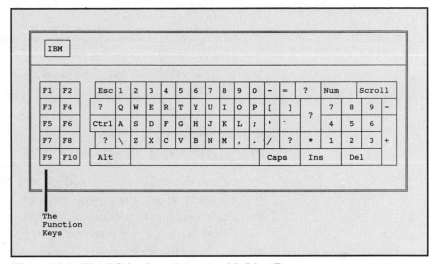

*Figure 13.7:* The PC keyboard drawn with Line Draw

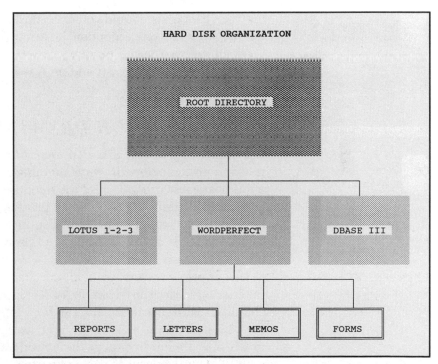

*Figure 13.8:* A chart showing hard disk organization drawn with Line Draw

### ERASING A LINE

Option 5, Erase, allows you to erase a line that has been drawn. To use it, move the cursor to the position where you want to start erasing and press 5. As you move the cursor with any of the arrow keys, the line will be deleted.

### CUTTING, COPYING, OR MOVING A LINE DRAWING

You can use WordPerfect's Block and Move keys to cut, copy, or move a line drawing; the process is the same as moving text except that you mark two opposite corners and use the Rectangle option on the Move key. To try it, be sure you've exited Line Drawing by pressing either Cancel (F1), or Exit (F7). The first step is to place the cursor at the upper left side of the drawing, then press the Block key (Alt-F4). To mark the section as a rectangle, press ↓ until you reach the bottom of the drawing, then press → until you reach the lower right edge. Next, press Move (Ctrl-F4) and select option 3, Rectangle. Choose either Move or Copy in response to the prompt, then move the cursor to the place where you want to retrieve it and press ↵.

See Chapter 5 for more information about how to cut, copy, and paste text.

## PRINTING YOUR DRAWING

Printing your drawings may present problems. In fact, you should test your printer before drawing anything elaborate. To do this, draw a few characters using each of the options on the Line Draw menu, then use the Print key (Shift-F7) to print the page. You may also try using different printer definitions. For instance, I was able to print all of the characters after redefining my Epson printer, which is actually an RX-80, as an FX-85.

If your printer cannot print all the characters you want to use, the manual suggests using Search and Replace to redefine the graphics characters with characters that can be printed by all printers, such as the plus and minus signs. However, this alters the appearance so much that it's hardly worth the considerable effort involved. You have to enter the decimal value of each ASCII graphics character in the search string, by pressing the Alt key along with the decimal number from the numeric keypad.

WordPerfect includes a printer test file that you can retrieve and print to check some of your printer's graphics capabilities. To do this, retrieve the file PRINTER.TST and press Shift-F7 F to print it.

## SUMMARY

Line drawing is another of WordPerfect's many extras. Use it to enhance the appearance of your documents by adding charts, boxes, and similar figures. You can choose from eleven different characters, or change the characters using the decimal equivalents of ASCII characters. As you've learned, Line Drawing is easy to use as long as you remember that it works in Typeover mode. Also, you should be careful not to insert extra hard returns, since WordPerfect automatically inserts them at the end of each line when you draw with ↓.

**14.**

# USING DESKTOP PUBLISHING
# TECHNIQUES FOR A
# PROFESSIONAL LOOK

# FAST TRACK

**Create a box**

    by pressing the Graphics key (Alt-F9). Select the type of box by pressing *1*, *2*, *3*, or *4*, then press *1* or *C* for Create. This will place you in the Definition menu where you can change the position of the box on the page, change its size, enter a text caption, and more. Press Exit (F7) when you finish.

**To retrieve a graphic file into WordPerfect**

    that was created using one of the graphics programs that the program supports, press the Graphics key (Alt-F9) and create a box (see the procedure above). Next, tell WordPerfect the name of the graphic file by pressing *1* or *F* for Filename, typing the drive and/or directory (if the file is not in the current directory or disk drive) and file name, then pressing ◄─┘. WordPerfect then determines the format of the file and retrieves the image into the box. If the file was not created in a program that is supported by WordPerfect, you will see an error message instead.

**Edit the graphic image inside a box**

    by pressing the Graphics key (Alt-F9) and selecting the type of box. Next, choose the Edit option (*2* or *E* ), enter the number, and press ◄─┘. You'll see the Definition menu. Select Edit (*8* or *E* ) from this menu and (if your monitor is capable) you will see the image inside the box and a menu with options that allows you to move, scale, rotate, or invert the image inside the box.

**Add a caption to an existing box**

    by pressing the Graphics key (Alt-F9) and selecting the type of box. Next, choose the Edit option (*2* or *E* ) and enter the number of the box you want to edit, then press ◄─┘ . Select Caption (*2* or *C* ) from the Definition menu that appears, and you will see the default caption, which is the figure number. Press EXIT

(F7) to accept it as the default, or Backspace to erase it and type your own caption in its place. Press Exit (F7) when finished.

**To move a box,** 436

press Graphics (Alt-F9) and select the type of box. Choose Edit (*2* or *E*), type the number, then press ←┘. You then will see the Definition menu. To change the position of the box on the page, use the Vertical Position and Horizontal Position options on this menu.

**To change the height and width of an existing box,** 438

press Graphics (Alt-F9) and select the type of box. Choose Edit (*2* or *E*), type the figure number, then press ←┘. Select the Size option (*6* or *S*) from the Definition menu, select Width, Height, or Both Width and Height, then type in the width and/ or height in inches, then press ←┘. Press Exit (F7) when finished.

**Use the Options menu to make changes to a box** 439

such as selecting a different border style, increasing or decreasing the space around the outside or inside of the box, adding gray shading, changing the caption style, or changing the caption position. To do this, press Graphics (Alt-F9), enter the type of box, then select Options (*4* or *O*).

**Create a rule (a vertical or horizontal line)** 455

by pressing Graphics (Alt-F9), selecting Line (*5* or *L*), then selecting Create Line: Horizontal (*1* or *H*) or Vertical (*2* or *V*). A menu will appear that you can use to change the line's horizontal or vertical position, its length or width, and the gray shading.

DESKTOP PUBLISHING IS ESSENTIALLY THE APPLICA-
tion of personal computers to the process of creating material such as
newsletters, flyers, brochures, advertisements, catalogs, and manuals, and it involves layout, design, and the integration of graphics to
create the appearance of a professionally published document. Using
a computer to do this work can save you an enormous amount of time
and money, so desktop publishing software has become quite popular in the last few years. Ventura Publisher and PageMaker are the
best known programs in this category, and they are used exclusively
for desktop publishing. When you use one of them, you type your
text in a word processing program, then retrieve it into the desktop
publishing program for formatting and layout. This means that you
have to use two separate programs to produce your documents, and
the desktop publishing programs, while powerful, are quite complex
and difficult to master.

WordPerfect 5 includes many of the important features that you
need to create attractive documents. You can easily incorporate
drawings and illustrations from other graphics programs such as PC
Paintbrush, Freelance, Windows Paint, PC Paint Plus, Dr. Halo II,
Publisher's Paintbrush, and GEM Paint, and from popular programs such as PlanPerfect and Lotus 1-2-3. You can also incorporate
files created using a scanner, such as logos, graphics, and even digitized photographs. You can manipulate a graphic image to change its
size or horizontal or vertical position on the page, and can scale,
rotate, move, or invert it. You can draw boxes, horizontal and vertical rules, tables, shaded boxes, text boxes, and more.

If your monitor is capable of producing graphics, you can use
WordPerfect's preview mode, View Document, to see the text and
graphics on screen as they will appear when printed; you can also see
features such as type size, line height, subscript, superscript, shadow,
small caps, and italics, and can zoom in and view a page at close
range or look at two facing pages of text simultaneously.

Important features such as leading, kerning, and word and letter spacing are also available. You can mix a large variety of fonts, and are no longer limited to eight of them, as in earlier versions of the program. If your printer is capable, you can even print in color. You can use WordPerfect's Styles feature to help standardize your formatting, and to easily change formatting characteristics throughout the document with just a few keystrokes, giving you the ability to see quickly how a document will look if you change fonts or other formatting.

To use WordPerfect's desktop publishing features, you should have a monitor that is capable of displaying graphics, such as a color monitor or a monochrome monitor with an interface such as the Hercules card, but you can get by with a monochrome screen without graphics capabilities. To produce the most attractive and professional looking output, you should use a laser printer and have a variety of fonts, but again this is not a requirement. You may want to invest in a scanner to convert logos, graphs, photographs, and other printed images into computer files, but if you live in or near a large city, you probably can find a copy center that will charge you a reasonable fee to scan an image and turn it into a file.

This chapter will teach you how to use many of WordPerfect's new graphics features, including horizontal and vertical rules, text boxes, figures with captions, and table boxes, and how to use features like Line Height to improve the appearance of your document. In the process, you will create a two-column newsletter that incorporates graphic images from two external files, a clip-art image of a map (supplied with WordPerfect), and a Lotus 1-2-3 graph (but don't worry if you don't have Lotus 1-2-3, because you can use one of the graphs that WordPerfect supplies). You will also work through other examples, including a test form and an advertisement. WordPerfect's desktop publishing features are significant, so keep in mind that this is only an introduction.

## USING GRAPHICS WITH WORDPERFECT

WordPerfect's Graphics key allows you to create boxes and incorporate graphic images from other programs into them. WordPerfect can automatically incorporate graphics created in the following formats: Lotus PIC files, PC Paintbrush, AutoCAD, GEM SCAN, Macintosh Paint, Picture Pak, Professional Plan, Symphony, Windows Paint, TIFF files (from scanners), HPGL plotter files, PC Paint Plus, Dr. Halo II, Publisher's Paintbrush, GEM Paint, and PlanPerfect graphs. Also, WordPerfect supplies a screen utility that you can use to capture a graphics screen image from any graphics program. For specific information on this procedure, see the next section, ''Creating a Box and Retrieving a Graphic Image into It.''

Other graphics abilities include drawing horizontal lines, vertical lines, and shaded rectangles. You can create four different types of boxes: figure boxes for graphic images, diagrams, and charts; table boxes for numeric tables, maps, and statistical data; text boxes for quotations, sidebars, and other text that you want to set off from the rest of the document; and user-defined boxes for anything else.

You can change the location and size of the box in your document and rotate, scale, move, or invert the graphic image inside of the box. You won't be able to see the graphics on your Edit screen, but you will see an outline of the box and the figure number, and the rest of the text on the page will wrap around it. WordPerfect will also place a code representing the figure into your document, visible in the Reveal Codes screen. If you have a color monitor or one with graphics capabilities, you can use the View Document option on the Print key (Shift-F7 V) to see both the box and its contents. If not, you'll have to wait until you print it.

## CREATING A BOX AND RETRIEVING A GRAPHIC IMAGE INTO IT

Creating a box and incorporating a graphics file into it is actually quite easy. The procedure to incorporate a graphics file of any type supported by WordPerfect is the same. As you'll see in step 4 of the following exercise, you only need to supply the file name; if the file is in a different disk or directory, you will also need to give the drive name and/or path. WordPerfect will then convert it into its own format. To help you use this feature, several clip-art files created by Marketing Graphics, Inc. have been included with the WordPerfect disks. You can easily identify them because the file names all end in

*.WPG*. We'll use one called USAMAP.WPG. Be sure you start with a clear screen (use F7 to clear it if necessary).

1. Press the Graphics key (Alt-F9) and you'll see this menu:

   **1 Figure; 2 Table; 3 Text Box; 4 User-defined Box; 5 Line: 0**

2. Select Figure (**1** or **F**). You will then see this menu:

   **Figure: 1 Create; 2 Edit; 3 New Number; 4 Options: 0**

3. Select Create (**1** or **C**). You will see the Definition: Figure menu shown in Figure 14.1.

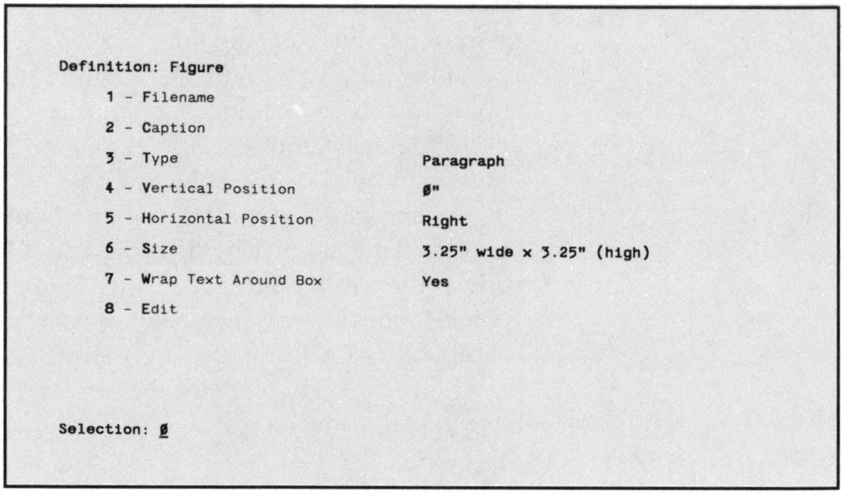

```
Definition: Figure
        1 - Filename
        2 - Caption
        3 - Type                    Paragraph
        4 - Vertical Position       0"
        5 - Horizontal Position     Right
        6 - Size                    3.25" wide x 3.25" (high)
        7 - Wrap Text Around Box    Yes
        8 - Edit




Selection: 0
```

*Figure 14.1:* The Definition: Figure menu

4. To retrieve the USAMAP.WPG file, select the Filename option (**1** or **F**) then type **usamap.wpg** and press ◄┘. If you have a system with only floppy disk drives, you may need to type the drive name before the file name, as in *b:usamap.wpg* if the file is on the disk in drive B. A brief *\*Please wait\** message will appear, then you will see the name USAMAP.WPG next to the Filename option at the top of the screen.

Let's look next at the Type option on the Definition: Figure menu. You use it to select the type of graphics box—paragraph, page, or character—and its importance lies in the way the box relates to the text in your document. If you select a paragraph-type box, a code is inserted at the beginning of the paragraph that the cursor is in, and the graphics box will stay with the text that surrounds it, moving as the paragraph moves on the page. If you select a page-type box, WordPerfect inserts a code at the cursor location and the graphics box will stay at that fixed position on the page. If you use the page type, be sure to select it before entering or retrieving any text on the page or WordPerfect will move the box to the next page when you type or retrieve text. If you select a character-type box, WordPerfect treats it as though it were a single character, and if the text containing it is wrapped to the next line, the next line will start below the box. Character boxes are the only type that can be used in footnotes and endnotes.

For this exercise, you will be creating a paragraph type, which is WordPerfect's default. If you do not see *Paragraph* next to the Type option, change it before continuing.

5. If Type is not set to Paragraph, select Type (**3** or **T**) then select Paragraph (**1** or **P**) in response to this prompt:

**Type: 1 Paragraph; 2 Page; 3 Character: 0**

## EDITING A GRAPHIC IMAGE

At this point you can use the Edit option to view the image and make changes such as moving, scaling, rotating, or inverting it. Note that if your monitor does not have graphics capabilities, you won't be able to see the graphic image as you experiment with these features. However, you will see a text representation (a rough representation of the graphic that is composed of dots or symbols) of it and you will see the menu options on the screen.

1. Select the Edit option (**8** or **E**) and the screen shown in Figure 14.2 will appear (if your monitor is capable). As you can see, the map graphic is surrounded by a box, and there is a menu at the bottom of the screen with these options: Move, Scale, Rotate, and Invert.

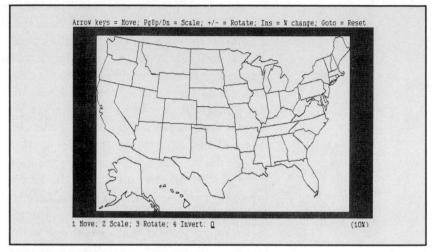

*Figure 14.2:* Editing a graphic image

Notice the following line at the top of the screen, which tells you how specific keys work in Graphics Edit mode:

> Arrow keys = Move; PgUp/Dn = Scale; + / - = Rotate;
> Ins = % change; Go to = Reset

Finally, look in the lower right corner of the screen for this message:

> (10%)

This tells you the percentage of change that will occur if you select Move, Scale, or Rotate; you'll learn more about this in the next section. Let's look first at a couple of ways to move the map around inside the box.

***MOVING A GRAPHIC WITHIN A BOX***   In this exercise, you'll move the graphic first using the arrow keys, then you'll use another method—the Move option.

As the prompt at the top of the screen indicates, the arrow keys move the map around inside the box each time you press one of them; ↑ pushes the map up, ↓ pushes the map down, → pushes it to the right, and ← pushes it to the left. The amount of distance that the map moves depends on the *percent of change* figure that is in effect. For example, if you use the default of 10%, pressing ↑ once will move the map up 10%, and pressing → will move it to the right 10%. The percent can be changed using the Insert (Ins) key. Note that the box itself does not move when you press an arrow key, only the graphic image (in this case, the map) inside it.

2.  Press ↑ once to move the map up, then ↓ to bring the map back to its original position. Press ← to move the map to the left, then → to move it back.

The Insert key changes the percentage figure to 5%, 1%, or 25%. The first time you press it, it changes to 5%, the second time you press it, it changes to 1%, and the third time you press it, it becomes 25%.

3.  Press Insert once, then press ↑ to move the map up 5%. Press ↓ to bring it back. Press Insert again to change the percentage to 1%, then press ↑ and ↓.

You can also use the Move option on the menu to move the map horizontally or vertically within the box. With this method, you type (in inches) the amount you want to move the graphic. Let's try it.

4.  To move 2 inches horizontally, press **1** or **M** and you'll see this prompt:

    Horizontal: 0″

    Type **2**, then press ←. Press ← again to leave 0″ for the vertical movement. Return the map to the original position by selecting Move again, then entering **0** for both horizontal and vertical movement, or by pressing Ctrl-Home (GoTo).

***CHANGING THE SIZE OF THE IMAGE***   The Page Up and Page Down keys serve to increase and decrease the size of the graphic image within the box, scaling it according to the percentage figure in the lower right corner.

5.  Press Insert once to change the percentage to 25%, then press Page Up three times to enlarge the map. Press Page Down three times to return it to the original size.

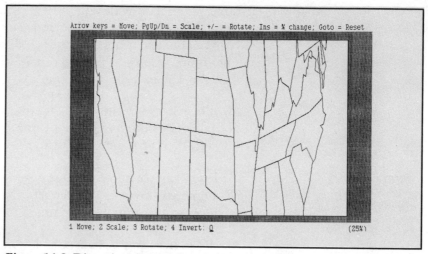

*Figure 14.3:* Distorting the map by changing the Y-axis

You can also use the Scale option (2) on the menu to change the size of the map by altering the X- and Y-axis scales. The X-axis is a horizontal axis, and changing the percentage affects the width of your image. The Y-axis is a vertical one, and changing its percentage affects the height of your image. In most cases you should change them equally to avoid distortion. For example, if you were to leave the X-axis at 100, and change the Y-axis to 300, the map would stretch out vertically and become very thin, as shown in Figure 14.3.

In this exercise, you will scale and move the map so that only the Western states are visible in the box. Let's try it.

6. Press **2** or **S** to select Scale and you'll see this prompt asking for the percent change of the X-axis:

   Scale X: 100

   Type **200**, then press ◄─┘. Next you'll see a prompt asking for the percent change of the Y-axis:

   Scale Y: 100

   Type **200** again, then press ◄─┘.

7. Press Insert three times to change the percentage to 25%, then press → twelve times to move the map until California is visible. Press ↓ a few times to see Oregon (above California). Now change the map back to the original size and position by

pressing the Go To key (Ctrl-Home), which resets your image to the original version.

***ROTATING THE GRAPHIC***   You can use the plus and minus keys on the numeric keypad to rotate the image inside the box, as long as it is not a bitmapped image. For example, if percent change is set to 10% and you press the plus key five times, the map will be upside down because you rotated the image 50%. You can also use the Rotate option on the menu to do this.

8.  Press **3** or **R** for Rotate and you'll see this prompt:

    **Enter number of degrees (0-360): 0**

    Type **180** then press **◄──┘**. You will see this prompt:

    **Mirror image? (Y/N) No**

A mirror image changes the dots in the image to display the graphic from right to left instead of left to right. Selecting Yes in our map example would be inappropriate because Florida would then appear to the left of California, which is inaccurate. However, the Mirror Image option is useful for graphics such as the one in Figure 14.4, which depicts a man reading a proclamation (this is the clip-art file named ANNOUNCE.WPG that came with your WordPerfect disks). Selecting Yes for Mirror Image would turn him around so that he faces left instead of right, as shown in the image in the lower half of the figure. Note that I left the number of degrees at 0 in this graphic in order to keep the image the same size in both pictures.

A bitmapped image is a file created using a paint program such as PC Paintbrush, Dr. Halo, or GEM Paint, or by using a scanner. The image consists of a collection of tiny dots called *pixels*.

***Figure 14.4:*** A mirror image

9. Press **N** or ← to rotate the image 180 degrees and the map will be upside down. To return it to the original upright position, select Rotate and enter **0** ← for the number of degrees and **N** in response to the *Mirror image* prompt.

Keep this example on your screen, because you will use it in a moment to learn how to change the appearance of a graphic on the page.

***INVERTING IMAGES***   The Invert option is used with bitmapped images to change the color of each dot, so that black becomes white and white becomes black. It will have no effect on line drawing graphics such as the .WPG files that come with WordPerfect (including the map). Figure 14.5 shows two versions of a logo that was turned into a computer file *(digitized)* through a scanner. The Invert option was used to change the lettering in the logo from white to black, and the logo itself from black to white. The image on the right shows the inverted logo.

## CHANGING THE APPEARANCE OF A GRAPHIC ON THE PAGE

Now that you've experimented with the editing options in the Graphics screen, let's take a look at how the map will appear in your document. You'll learn how to change options such as the style of the box that surrounds the graphic, the amount of space that separates the graphics box from the text in your document, and the caption that appears above or below the box. To view the map as it now appears on the page, we'll use the View Document option on the Print key; remember that this won't work if your monitor does not have graphics capabilities.

Since you'll be using View Document frequently, you may want to create a macro to view this screen. Here are the keystrokes: Press Ctrl-F10, type *ALTV*, press ← twice, press Shift-F7 V, then press Ctrl-F10. To use this macro, press Alt and hold it down while pressing *V*. Macros are discussed in Chapter 19.

1. If you're still looking at the map in the Graphics Edit screen, press Exit twice (F7) to return to document edit mode.

2. Press the Print key (Shift-F7) and select View Document (**6** or **V**). You should see the map in the upper right corner of the page (you may have to select the Full Page option if you were using View Document earlier and changed it).

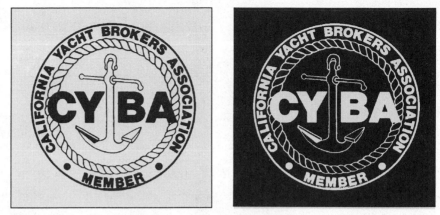

*Figure 14.5:* Using the Invert option

3. When you finish looking at it, press Exit (F7) to return to document edit mode.

Now let's type some text near the graphic image.

4. Use Reveal Codes (Alt-F3) to position the cursor to the right of the [Figure:1;USAMAP.WPG;] code that WordPerfect inserted to represent your graphic image, then type this paragraph:

> 1988: Another banner year for the yachting industry! According to James Kelly, President of the California Yacht Brokers Council, recreational boat sales in the United States were the best since 1979. Retail sales of new and used power yachts outperformed 1987 sales by 31%, while gross profits were up an astounding 29% over the 1987 figures.

5. Use the View Document option (Shift-F7 V) and select 100% (**1**) to see how the text looks; it should resemble Figure 14.6. Notice that each line wraps to the next line before it reaches the border, so that the text does not spill into the box. Press Exit (F7) when you're finished looking at it.

**CREATING A CAPTION FOR A GRAPHIC**   The map will be more meaningful if we add a caption to the graphics box. To do this, we'll use the Definition: Figure menu.

*Figure 14.6:* The map with text

1. Press the Graphics key (Alt-F9). Select Figure (**1** or **F**), select Edit (**2** or **E**), then press **1** ◄┘ at the *Figure number?* prompt. You will then see the Definition: Figure menu that you used previously (shown in Figure 14.1). We'll use the Caption option to add a caption below the box.

2. Select Caption (**2** or **C**) and you will see the default caption

   **Figure 1**

3. Press Backspace once to erase it, then type

   **North American Yachting News**

4. Press Exit (F7) once.

***CHANGING THE POSITION OF A GRAPHICS BOX*** You can use the Vertical and Horizontal Position options to change the location of the box on the page so that it is at the left or right margin, centered on the page, or farther down in the paragraph. Let's use them to move the box from the right side of the page to the left.

1. You should still be in the Definition: Figure menu; if not, press Alt-F9 1 2 1 ◄┘. Select Horizontal Position (**5** or **H**)

and you will see this menu at the bottom of the screen:

**Horizontal Position: 1 Left; 2 Right; 3 Center; 4 Both
Left & Right: 0**

2.  The graphics box is currently on the right side of the text. Move it to the left side by pressing **1** or **L**. Next, press Exit (F7) and use View Document (Shift-F7 V) to see the difference. The map should be on the left side now, with the text to its right. You can also see the caption *North American Yachting News* under the box. Press Exit (F7) when you're finished looking at it.

When you created the box there was no text on the screen, but once you typed the text, WordPerfect automatically placed the box next to the first line of the paragraph. Let's change the Vertical Position to move the box ¼ inch down in the paragraph.

3.  Press Alt-F9 F E 1 ⏎ to see the Definition: Figure menu again, then select Vertical Position (**4** or **V**). You will see this prompt at the bottom of the screen:

**Offset from top of paragraph: 0″**

4.  Type **.25** for a ¼-inch offset, then press ⏎ twice. Use View Document (Shift-F7 V) to see the results. Notice that the first line now is above the box and has expanded to fit between the left and right margins, but that the rest of the text wraps around the box, as shown in Figure 14.7. Press Exit (F7) when you finish looking at it.

***CHANGING THE BOX SIZE***   You can use the Size option on the Definition: Figure menu to change the width, height, or both width and height of the graphics box on the page. This differs from the Scale option in graphics edit mode that you used earlier to change the size of the image itself (the map) *inside* the box. When you select Size, you see this menu:

**1 Width (auto height); 2 Height (auto width); 3 Both Width and
Height: 0**

If you select the first option, Width, WordPerfect will automatically calculate the correct height for you, retaining the original shape of

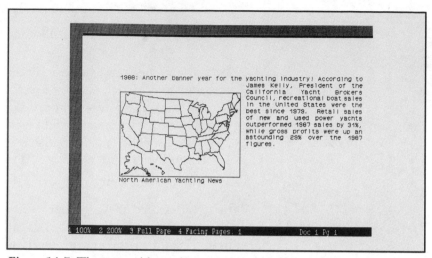

*Figure 14.7:* The map with caption and text after changing its horizontal and
vertical positions

the graphic image. If you select Height, WordPerfect will calculate the correct width, retaining the original shape. If you select Both,
you can enter both width and height yourself. Let's try changing the
height. The current size of the box is 3.25″ wide by 2.86″ high. Let's
make it smaller by entering 1.5″ for the height.

1. Press the Graphics key (Alt-F9), select Figure (**1** or **F**), select
   Edit (**2** or **E**), then press **1** (for Figure Number) followed by
   ↵. Select Size (**6** or **S**), then Height (**2** or **H**).

2. Type **1.5** in response to the Height prompt, then press ↵.
   You'll see that WordPerfect has calculated the corresponding
   width, 2.26″.

3. Press Exit (F7) then use View Document (Shift-F7 V) to see
   the new size. As you can see from Figure 14.8, the box is now
   much smaller. Press Exit (F7) when you're finished looking
   at it.

***WRAPPING TEXT AROUND THE GRAPHICS BOX***    Option 7
on the Definition: Figure menu shown in Figure 14.1 is Wrap Text
Around Box. It is set to Yes by default. If you change it to No, your
text will wrap in the regular way, from margin to margin, ignoring

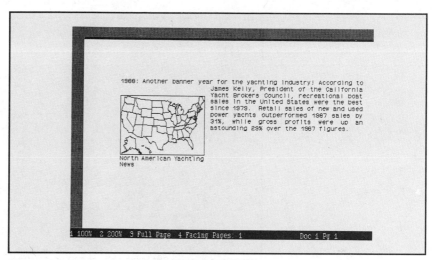

*Figure 14.8:* The map after changing the box size

the box. This would be inappropriate for a box such as ours with a graphic image inside it, because the text would be typed right over the graphic.

## USING THE FIGURE OPTIONS
## TO CHANGE YOUR GRAPHIC

WordPerfect has provided several other graphics options that you can use to change the border style, the outside and inside border space, numbering methods, caption numbering style, position of the caption, minimum offset from paragraph, and gray shading.

1. Before you experiment with these options, you must make sure that the cursor is on or to the left of the code that Word-Perfect inserted when you created the graphic or your changes will not take effect. Press Reveal Codes (Alt-F3) and you'll see this code for your graphic image:

   [Figure:1;USAMAP.WPG;North American Yachting News]

   Notice that since you changed the caption, it was inserted in the code. Use the arrow keys to position the cursor on the code, then press Alt-F3 to exit Reveal Codes.

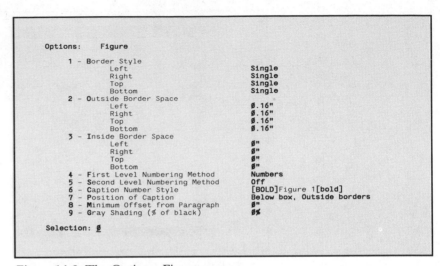

***Figure 14.9:*** The Options: Figure menu

2. Now press the Graphics key (Alt-F9) and select Figure (**1** or **F**), then Options (**4** or **O**). You will see the Options: Figure menu illustrated in Figure 14.9.

***CHANGING THE BORDER STYLE***  The first option on the menu is Border Style, and you can use it to select a different style for each side of the border that surrounds your graphic. The border around the map is currently a single line on all four sides. Let's experiment with the border style.

3. Select Border style (**1** or **B**) and you'll see these options at the bottom of the screen:

   **1** None; **2** **S**ingle; **3** **D**ouble; **4** **D**ashed; **5** **D**otted; **6** **T**hick; **7** **E**xtra Thick: **0**

Selecting None would eliminate the border altogether, so the map would appear without the box around it. Single is the default choice; as you saw in the View Document screen, it draws a box with a single line. Double creates a box with a double line. You can also create a border with dashed, dotted, thick, or extra thick lines or you can mix different styles for different sides of the border.

4. Press **N** four times to select None for the left, right, top, and bottom border styles, then press F7 and use View Document (Shift-F7 V) to see how this has changed your graphic. Press F7 when you are finished looking at it.

You may wish to repeat these steps and try some of the other border styles such as Double or Thick, or choose one style for left and right and another for top and bottom, then see how they look in View Document.

5. Change the border back to a single line by deleting the [Fig Opt] code that WordPerfect inserted when you selected the option for no border. To do this, press Reveal Codes (Alt-F3), position the cursor on the [Fig Opt] code, then press the Delete key.

***CHANGING THE OUTSIDE BORDER SPACE***    The second choice on the Options: Figure menu is Outside Border Space, and it refers to the amount of space that separates each border from the text around the box. When you used the View Document option (Shift-F7 V) earlier, you may have noticed that there was some blank space between the text and the right border of the box, as shown in Figure 14.8. The default for this outside border space is .16 (about one sixth of an inch) and we'll change it to 1 inch in the next step.

1. Use Reveal Codes (Alt-F3) and the arrow keys to position the cursor on the [Figure:1;USAMAP.WPG;North America] code.

2. Press the Graphics key (Alt-F9), select Figure (**1** or **F**) then Options (**4** or **O**), then select Outside Border Space (**2** or **O**). Change the left, right, top, and bottom outside border space to 1 inch each by pressing **1** ↵ four times, then press Exit (F7).

3. Use View Document (Shift-F7 V) to view the box, and you'll see that the text is now separated from the box by more blank space (when printed, it will equal 1 inch). Press Exit (F7) when you're finished looking at it.

4. Change the outside border space back to .16 inch by pressing Reveal Codes (Alt-F3), placing the cursor on the [Fig Opt] code, then pressing the Delete key.

***CHANGING THE INSIDE BORDER SPACE*** Inside Border Space measures the amount of space that separates the graphic image inside the box from the borders around it. The default is 0″; let's change it to ½ inch.

1. Use Reveal Codes (Alt-F3) and the arrow keys to position the cursor on the [Figure:1;USAMAP.WPG;North America] code.

2. Press the Graphics key (Alt-F9), select Figure (**1** or **F**) then Options (**4** or **O**), then select Inside Border Space (**3** or **I**). Change the left, right, top, and bottom outside border space to ½ inch each by pressing *.5* ⏎ four times, then press the Exit key (F7).

3. Use View Document (Shift-F7 V) to view the box, and you'll see that there is more blank space separating the map from the borders. In fact, the map inside the box has become tiny because of the extra space used for the inside border. Press Exit (F7) when you finish looking.

4. Delete the code and change the inside border space back to 0″ by pressing Reveal Codes (Alt-F3), placing the cursor on the [Fig Opt] code, then pressing the Delete key (or pressing the Backspace key followed by **Y**).

***CHOOSING A CAPTION NUMBERING STYLE*** In this exercise you will use the First and Second Level Numbering Method options to define a numbering style for the caption, but this will only change the number that appears on the Edit screen. You have to use the Caption Number Style option, as described in the next section, to change the appearance in the printed version (and in View Document). By default, WordPerfect labels the first level with numbers, so on the Edit screen you see *FIG 1* on the top border of the box. The second level is not numbered. You can change them to numbers, letters, or Roman numerals. For instance, if you change the second level to letters, your first figure will be numbered FIG 1a, the second will be FIG 1b, and so forth. Let's try it. Your first step will be to change the caption back to *Figure 1,* since you changed it to *North American Yachting News* earlier.

1. Press the Graphics key (Alt-F9), select Figure (**1** or **F**), select Edit (**2** or **E**), then press **1** ↵ at the *Figure Number?* prompt.

2. Select Caption (**2** or **C**) and you'll see *North American Yachting News*.

3. Press Ctrl-End (twice if necessary) to erase it, then press Exit (F7).

4. Select Caption again (**2** or **C** ) and you'll see that WordPerfect has inserted *Figure 1* for you. Press Exit (F7) twice.

Now change the second level numbering method.

5. Press Reveal Codes (Alt-F3) and notice that the figure code has changed to [Figure:1;USAMAP.WPG;[Box Num]], since you erased the North America caption and replaced it with the figure number (box number). Use the arrow keys to position the cursor on the [Figure:1;USAMAP.WPG;[Box Num]] code, then press Alt-F3 to exit Reveal Codes.

6. Press the Graphics key (Alt-F9), select Figure (**1** or **F**) then Options (**4** or **O**).

7. Select Second Level Numbering Method (**5** or **S**) and you'll see this menu at the bottom of the screen:

**1 Off; 2 Numbers; 3 Letters; 4 Roman Numerals: 0**

8. Select Letters (**3** or **L**). Do not press Exit yet, because you have a few more options to change.

***CHANGING THE CAPTION STYLE IN PRINT***   The next step is to use the Caption Number Style option to change the appearance of the caption in the printed version and in View Document. By default, captions are printed in boldface. You can use other attributes such as italics or underlining, or change the numbering to include the two levels. For instance, if you set the second level of numbering to letters, as described above, you can display the levels in the printed version. Let's try it.

9. Select Caption Numbering Style (**6** or **C**) and you will see this prompt:

**Replace with: [BOLD]Figure 1[bold]**

10. Press → several times until the cursor is just after the 1, then type **-2** so that your prompt says: *Figure 1-2.* Note that *1* stands for level 1, and *2* stands for level 2. Since you chose Letters for the second level numbering method in the previous step, the first caption will be *Figure 1-a,* and if you had a second box, it would be labelled *Figure 1-b.* Press ← when you finish. Do not exit the Options: Figure menu yet, since you have one last change to make, which is the position of the caption.

***CHANGING THE POSITION OF THE CAPTION*** Use the Position of Caption option to specify where you want the caption to appear. By default, it is placed below the box, outside of the border. You can choose to place it below the box inside the border, above the box outside the border, or above the box inside the border.

11. Select the Position of Caption option (**7** or **P** ) and this prompt appears:

**Caption Position: 1 Below Box; 2 Above Box: 1**

12. Select Above Box (**2** or **A**) for the position, and this prompt appears:

**Caption: 1 Outside of Border; 2 Inside of Border: 1**

13. Choose Outside of Border (**1** or **O**), then press Exit (F7) and use View Document (Shift-F7 V) to see the change. Your caption should now be *Figure 1-a* and should be placed above the box. You may have to select 200% to be able to read the caption. Press Exit (F7) when you finish looking at it. You will see that the figure number on the Edit screen has also been changed to *FIG 1a.*

14. At this point you should save your document, since it has taken so much work to get to this stage! Press F10 and enter **newsletr** in response to the *Document to be saved* prompt.

***GRAY SHADING*** The last option on the Options: Figure menu is Gray Shading, and you can use it to create a shaded box. Although it often is not applicable when your box has a graphic image inside (as in our example), gray shading can be used to create many interesting effects. To use this option, you specify the shading intensity level as a percentage, such as 10%, 25%, or 50%. The higher the percentage, the darker the box will be. If you enter 100%, the box will be completely black. Shaded boxes can also be created using a different method, which you'll learn in the next section.

## CREATING A SHADED BOX AND FILLING IT WITH TEXT

The next exercise will show you how to add a shaded box and title to your document, as seen in Figure 14.10. You will create this type of box using the Line option on the Graphics key (the shaded box is actually a thick line), then type the title and move it into the box using WordPerfect's Advance feature on the Format: Other menu. You'll begin by moving the paragraph of text underneath the box so that you can place the shaded box and title in its place.

### CREATING AND SHADING THE BOX

If your version of WordPerfect was released prior to January 3, 1989, the prompt line you see when you press Graphics (Alt-F9) and select the Line option will not include the two Edit Line options shown in step 2. You can determine the creation date by pressing Help (F3) once and looking at the date in the upper-right corner of the screen.

1. Use Reveal Codes to position the cursor on the *1* in *1988* in the first sentence, then press ⏎ 15 times (or as needed) until the paragraph is below the box. Move the cursor back up so that it is three lines under the top border of the box.

2. Press the Graphics key (Alt-F9), select Line (**5** or **L**), and you'll see this menu:

   **Create Line: 1 Horizontal; 2 Vertical;**
   **Edit Line: 3 Horizontal; 4 Vertical: 0**

3. Select Create Line: Horizontal (**1** or **H**) and you will see the Graphics: Horizontal Line menu shown in Figure 14.11.

4. Select Horizontal Position (**1** or **H**) and you will see this menu at the bottom of the screen:

   **Horizontal Pos: 1 Left; 2 Right; 3 Center; 4 Both Left & Right; 5 Set Position: 0**

We want the line to start at a fixed position on the page, a few spaces after the border of the graphic image (the map), so you'll use the Set Position option to place it there.

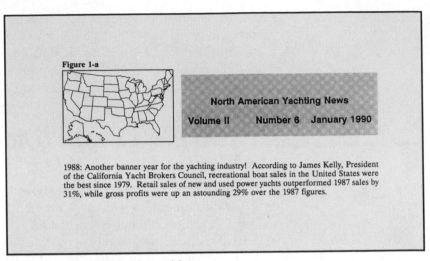

*Figure 14.10:* A shaded box with text

```
Graphics: Horizontal Line
      1 - Horizontal Position              Left & Right
      2 - Length of Line
      3 - Width of Line                    0.01"
      4 - Gray Shading (% of black)        100%




   Selection: 0
```

*Figure 14.11:* The Graphics: Horizontal Line menu

5. Select Set Position (**5** or **S**) and you will see that WordPerfect has already supplied the current cursor position, which should be about 3 inches from the left side of the page. My prompt looked like this:

   **Offset from left of page: 3.43″**

   Press ↵.

6. WordPerfect then fills in the Length of Line option for you, assuming that you want the horizontal line to stretch across the rest of the page. If you want it to be shorter, you can select Length of Line and enter a smaller number.

The next step is to change the width of your line in order to create a box instead of a line. The width is now set to .01″; to create a box, you'll have to make it much wider.

7. Select Width of Line (**3** or **W**) and change it to 1.3 inches by typing **1.3** and pressing ◄─┘.

The last step in creating the box is to add the shading. You will choose shading that is lighter than WordPerfect's default of 100% so that the title, which you will add later, can be easily read.

8. To create the shaded effect, select Gray Shading (**4** or **G**). Notice that gray shading is now 100%, which means that the box will be black unless you change it. Type **10** ◄─┘ for 10%.

9. Press Exit (F7) then use the View Document option at 100% (Shift-F7 V 1) to see the shaded line, which appears to be a box of dots. If it appears to be higher than the graphics box, you'll have to exit View Document and press ◄─┘ a few times above the horizontal line to push it down. To do this, press Exit (F7) then use Reveal Codes (Alt-F3) to place the cursor on the code that WordPerfect created for the line:

[HLine:3.43″,4.06″,1.3″,10%]

Press ◄─┘ once to move it down. Check View Document again to determine its position, and repeat this step if it is still too high.

## USING WORDPERFECT'S ADVANCE FEATURE TO PLACE TEXT IN A BOX

Now you're ready to type the text that appears inside the box. To move the text into the box in the printed version (and in View Document), you'll use WordPerfect's Advance feature.

1.  Move the cursor to the last line next to the graphics box; it should be near position 3.43″ and line 3.13. Press the Format key (Shift-F8) and select Other (**4** or **O**), then select Advance (**1** or **A**). You will see this menu at the bottom of the screen:

    **Advance: 1 U**p; **2 D**own; **3 Line; 4 Left; 5 R**ight; **6 Position: 0**

2.  Select Up (**1** or **U**), and you'll see this prompt:

    **Adv. up 0″**

3.  Type **.8** then press ⮐ three times.

4.  Press the Center key (Shift-F6), then type

    **North American Yachting News**

5.  Use ↓ to move the cursor down a few lines and type the second line. Press the Space bar twice, then type

    **Volume II**

    then press Center (Shift-F6) and type

    **Number 6**

    Press Flush Right (Alt-F6) and type

    **January 1990**

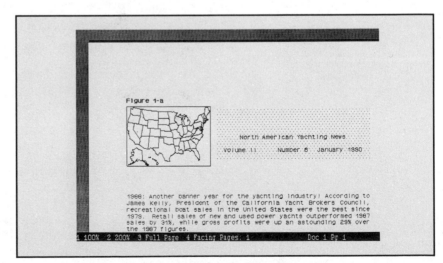

*Figure 14.12:* The shaded box and text in View Document

Press the Space bar twice.

6. Use View Document at 100% (Shift-F7 V 1) to see the shaded box with the text in it. It should resemble Figure 14.12. Press Exit (F7) when you finish looking at it.

You may need to move the text paragraph below the box back down into the correct position. The easiest way is to place the cursor on it and press ← repeatedly.

7. If necessary, move the cursor onto the *1* in *1988* and press ← several times until the paragraph has moved back below the map.

8. Save your document again by pressing F10 ← Y.

## *INTEGRATING NEWSPAPER COLUMNS AND GRAPHICS*

Now the document is starting to get interesting! In fact, why don't we turn it into a newsletter by creating newspaper columns and filling them with text, then bring in a bar graph from Lotus 1-2-3 and insert it between the two columns so that the columnar text wraps around it.

1. Position the cursor on the *1* in *1988* (in the sentence *1988: Another banner year*), then press the Math/Columns key (Alt-F7). Select Column Def (**4** or **D**), and you'll see the Text Column Definition screen.

2. Number of Columns should be *2*. If not, select Number of Columns (**2** or **N**), then press **2** ← to create two newspaper columns.

3. Select Distance Between Columns (**3** or **D**), then enter *.3* and press ←.

4. Press Exit (F7), then turn Columns on by selecting Column On/Off (**3** or **C**).

The creation and use of newspaper columns is covered in Chapter 12. Figure 12.1 shows the Text Column Definition screen.

### *PLACING A GRAPHIC IN THE NEWSLETTER*

The next enhancement we'll make to the newsletter is to insert a graph created in Lotus 1-2-3, then type and let the columns of text wrap around it. The instructions here apply to a graph created in Lotus 1-2-3 (such graph files always end in *PIC* and are created using the Lotus 1-2-3 Graph Save command), but if you don't have that program, you can use a similar graph that you created in a different program, or use one of the graphics files supplied with WordPerfect—the GRAPH.WPG file on the Learning diskette is a good choice. (It's not important what the graph looks like, just that you understand how to retrieve it and wrap text around it.) This graph will be a page-type figure, so it will stay at a fixed position on the page, as opposed to the map graphic, which is a paragraph figure and thus moves around as the paragraph it belongs to moves.

1. Place the cursor on the *1* in *1988* (in the sentence *1988: Another banner year*). Press the Graphics key (Alt-F9) and select Figure (**1** or **F**).

2. Select Create (**1** or **C**). You will again see the Definition: Figure menu shown in Figure 14.1.

3. To retrieve the Lotus file, select the Filename option (**1** or **F**) then type the file name, preceded by a directory or drive if it is in a different one (mine was YACHT.PIC), and press ←⎯.

4. Select Type (**3** or **T**) then select Page (**2** or **A**).

5. Next, select Horizontal Position (**5** or **H**), then select Set Position (**3** or **S**).

6. In response to the *Offset from left of page* prompt, type **3** for 3″, then press ←⎯.

7. Select Vertical Position (**4** or **V**), then Set Position (**5** or **S**). In response to the *Offset from top of page* prompt, type **7** for 7″, then press ←⎯. This will place the graph near the bottom of the page.

8. Select Size (**6** or **S**), then Height (**2** or **H**), and enter **2** followed by ←⎯ to change the height of the graphic to 2 inches. Notice that WordPerfect has automatically calculated the corresponding width (2.68″ on my screen).

9. Press Exit (F7) to get back to Edit mode.

Now take a moment to use View Document (Shift-F7 V) to see your work; select Full Page to see the entire page. Notice the border lines around the Lotus graph. Let's change the border style to remove the lines from Figures 1a and 1b. Press Exit (F7) when you finish looking at the graphic.

10. Press Page Up, then use Reveal Codes (Alt-F3) to move the cursor onto the [Figure:1a;USAMAP.WPG;[Box Num]] code. Press the Graphics key (Alt-F9) and select Figure (**1** or **F**), then Options (**4** or **O**).

11. Select Border Style (**1** or **B**), then press **N** four times to select None for the left, right, top, and bottom border styles. Press F7 when you're done.

## TYPING OR RETRIEVING TEXT INTO THE COLUMNS

In this section you will place text into the document. You will be typing the text you see in Figure 14.13, and it will be automatically formatted into the columns you just created. Type the text in the columns, as illustrated in Figure 14.13, or you could save time by finding a practice file and retrieving it into your columns. If you use a practice file, make sure that it is not in columnar format already, and use one of the regular methods to retrieve it (Shift-F10 or F5 1) at the current cursor position.

When you finish, use View Document (Shift-F7 V) to see your document and observe how the text in the two columns automatically wraps around the box that has the Lotus graph inside (and is missing borders). Now use Shift-F7 1 to print the document.

If you discover that your printer cannot print both the text and the graphics in the document, your printer may not have enough memory to print both text and graphics at once, so the next section, "Printing Text and Graphics Separately," explains what to do.

Once you've printed and examined the document, you'll see that a few more changes could be made to improve its appearance. For instance, before printing the version shown in Figure 14.13, I reduced the top margin to ½ inch, changed the Base Font to 14-point Helvetica for the heading, and to 12-point Times Roman for the rest of the text, eliminated the caption above the map, and changed the Hyphenation zone and turned on hyphenation to reduce the blank

To move the cursor between your columns after the text has been entered, use the Go To key (Ctrl-Home), followed by ← or →.

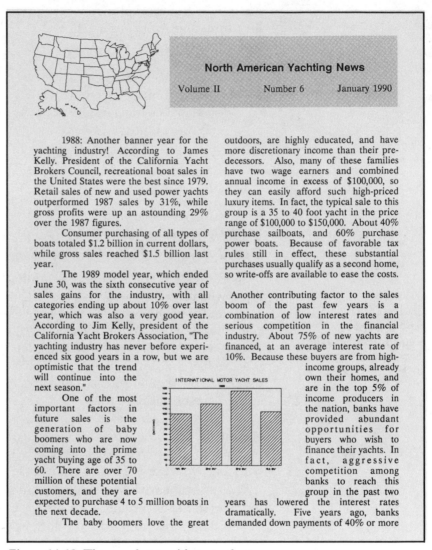

*Figure 14.13:* The newsletter with text columns

space between words. If you wish to make these changes to your newsletter, follow these steps:

1. To reduce the top margin to ½ inch, place the cursor at the top of the document and use Reveal Codes (Alt-F3) to help

you position it before any other codes. Press Format (Shift-F8), select Page (**2** or **P**), select Margins (**5** or **M**), then type **.5** ↵ ↵ ↵. You should remain in the Format menu for the next step.

2. To turn on hyphenation and reduce the size of the Hyphenation zone so you will be asked to hyphenate more frequently, select Line (**1** or **L**), select Zone (**2** or **Z**), then type **8** (for the left zone) ↵ ↵. Next, select Hyphenation (**1** or **Y**), select Manual (**2** or **M**), then press ↵ ↵. Press Home Home ↓ and WordPerfect will ask you to hyphenate several words; in each case, use the arrow keys to move the hyphen to the appropriate position and press Esc to hyphenate, or press Cancel (F1) if you do not want a specific word hyphenated.

3. To change the font size for the heading, place the cursor on the *N* in *North,* then press Reveal Codes (Alt-F3) and ← to position the cursor before the [Cntr] code. Press Ctrl-F8 and select Base Font (**4** or **F**), then select a larger font from the list by using the arrow keys to highlight it and pressing **1** for Select. I used an HP LaserJet Series II printer with soft fonts, and I selected Helvetica 14-point bold from the list. Next, move the cursor past the date (January 1990) and repeat the steps to select a regular-size font. I chose 12-point Times Roman from the list.

4. To eliminate the caption from the printed version of the map figure, press the Graphics key (Alt-F9), select Figure (**1** or **F**), select Edit (**2** or **E**), and type **1** followed by ↵. Select Caption (**2** or **C**) then press Ctrl-End to erase the caption. Press Exit (F7) twice, then use View Document (Shift-F7 V) to check your newsletter and Full Document (Shift-F7 F) to print it again.

## PRINTING TEXT AND GRAPHICS SEPARATELY

You can use the Graphics Quality and Text Quality options on the Print menu (Shift-F7) to print the graphics separately from the text in a document in case your printer cannot print both simultaneously. To do this, you first print your document with the text only. Next, you reinsert the paper and print the document again, printing the graphics. The graphics and text are printed in the same position in your document as though you had printed them at the same time. Here are the steps to print your text first, then graphics. For more detail, see the section in Chapter 9, "Controlling Print Quality with the Graphics and Text Quality Options."

1. Select the Graphics Quality option from the Print menu by pressing Shift-F7 G. Select the Do Not Print option (**1** or **N**).

2. Select Full Document (**1** or **F**) to print the text. When the printer finishes, reinsert the paper into your printer.

3. Select the Text Quality (**T**) option on the Print menu. To print only the graphics, select the Do Not Print option (**1** or **N**). Select the Graphics Quality option (**G**) from the Print menu and change it to Medium (or High if you wish).

4. Select Full Document (**1** or **F**) to print the graphic.

## CREATING A BANNER HEADLINE

In the previous exercise, you created a shaded box then used WordPerfect's Advance feature to place text inside it. This section will teach you another method of placing text into a box; you may find this method easier. Using the Text Box feature, you will create a banner headline that could be used with a newsletter like the one shown previously. To place text inside it, you use the Graphics key to edit the box itself, then you type inside it. Use Exit (F7) to clear the screen before you begin.

1. Change the left and right margins to 0″ each so that the text box will cover the entire width of the page. To do this, press Shift-F8 L M 0 ⟵ 0 ⟵ F7.

2. Press the Graphics key (Alt-F9) and select Text Box (**3** or **B**), then select Create (**1** or **C**).

3. Select Horizontal Position (**5** or **H**), then select Both Left & Right (**4** or **B**). This will place the box across the entire page.

4. Select Size (**6** or **S**), select Height (**2** or **H**) and type **1.5** for 1.5″, then press ⟵.

5. Select Edit (**8** or **E**), then press ⏎ twice to vertically center the text that you will type inside the box. Change the font to a larger one such as 24-point by pressing Ctrl-F8 F, then highlighting the font and pressing ⏎.

6. Press Center (Shift-F6) and type

   **North American Yacht Brokers Association**

   Press Exit (F7) twice.

Now you can print the headline or view it using Shift-F7V, and the results should be similar to Figure 14.14.

## *PRODUCING ATTRACTIVELY DESIGNED FORMS*

The next exercise will show you how to create the test form shown in Figure 14.15. You will combine fonts, draw horizontal lines to create the rules, and use the Text Box feature of the Graphics key to create the shaded boxes for the answers. Although it takes some planning and experimenting to design such a form, the results are interesting and easy to read.

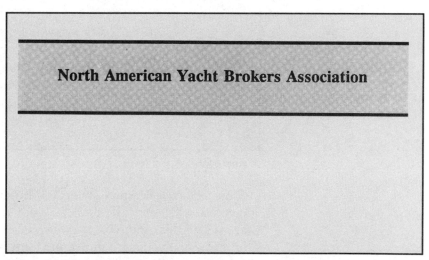

*Figure 14:14:* A banner headline

## WordPerfect  Test

**1**  **The End key is used to:**                              Your answers:

    a.     Move the cursor to the end of the page
    b.     Move the cursor to the end of the line
    c.     End WordPerfect
    d.     None of the above

**2**  **Pressing the Insert key (Ins) more than once:**

    a.     Turns insert mode on and off
    b.     Inserts previously deleted text
    c.     Inserts a blank line
    d.     Both a and c

**3**  **The List Files key (F5) can be used to:**

    a.     Delete a file
    b.     Rename a file
    c.     Copy a file
    d.     All of the above

**4**  **The Status line at the bottom of the Edit screen tells you:**

    a.     The status of the disk
    b.     The amount of available memory
    c.     The current position of the cursor
    d.     The names of all your files on disk

***Figure 14.15:*** A test form

This form was designed for an HP LaserJet Series II printer using Helvetica soft fonts. The fonts for your printer may not match the ones used in this example, but you can use fonts that are close in size. Don't worry if you can't match the fonts in the form exactly.

The first step is to set the top margin to .5 so that the first rule (horizontal line) and heading *(WordPerfect Test)* will be closer to the top of the page. After that, you'll expand the left and right margins so that the rules can stretch across the entire width of the page.

1. Press the Format key (Shift-F8) and select Page (**2** or **P**), then Margins (**5** or **M**). Type **.5** ◄┘ for the top margin, press ◄┘ once to leave 1 inch for the bottom margin, then press ◄┘. This should place you back in the main Format menu.

2. Select Line (**1** or **L**), then Margins (**7** or **M**) and set both left and right margins to 0. Press Exit (F7) to return to the Edit screen.

3. At this point I changed the Base Font, selecting 12-point Helvetica. If you don't have that font, you can use any font in 12-point size such as Courier or Pica. To change the font, press the Font key (Ctrl-F8), select Base Font (**4** or **F**), then move the cursor bar onto the font you want to use and press **1** or **S**.

Now you're ready to create the first rule, using the Line feature on the Graphics key.

4. Press Graphics (Alt-F9) and select Line (**5** or **L**), then select Create Line: Horizontal (**1** or **H**). You'll see the Graphics: Horizontal Line menu shown previously in Figure 14.11.

5. Select Horizontal Position (**1** or **H**) then select Left (**1** or **L**) to start the rule at the left margin (now set to 0″).

6. Select Length of Line (**2** or **L**) and type **8.5** followed by ◄┘ so that the rule will stretch across the entire page.

7. Select Width of Line (**3** or **W**) and type **.1** followed by ◄┘ to make the rule wider, then press Exit (F7).

8. Press ◄┘ three times to leave three blank lines.

Before typing *WordPerfect Test*, I changed the Base Font to 30-point bold Helvetica. If you don't have that font, you can use any large font (size 14, 18, 24, 30, etc).

9. To change the font, press the Font key (Ctrl-F8), select Base Font (**4** or **F**), then move the cursor bar onto the font you want to use and press **1** or **S**.

10. Press the Center key (Shift-F6) then type **WordPerfect Test**. After that, change the Base Font back to the 12-point font you used in step 3. Press ⏎ twice.

The next step is to create another horizontal line for the rule underneath *WordPerfect Test*. To do this, you can either repeat steps 4 through 7, or you can use the Delete key to copy the code that Word-Perfect inserted when you made the first rule in steps 4 through 7. The next instruction teaches you how to copy the code.

11. Press Reveal Codes (Alt-F3) and move the cursor onto the Horizontal Line code [HLine:Left,8.5",0.1",100%]. Press Delete to erase it, then press Cancel (F1) and select Restore (**1** or **R**) to copy it back at the original position. Next, move the cursor to the end of the document (after the two [HRt] codes you created in step 10). Press Cancel (F1) again and select Restore (**1** or **R**) to make another copy of it. Press ⏎ three times.

At this point, you may wish to check View Document (Shift-F7 V) to see if the rules and title are correct. After that, you will change the left and right margins back to 1 inch each, change the font size to 30, type the number *1*, change the font size to 14, and type the text for the first question.

12. Change the left and right margins to 1 inch each by pressing the Format key (Shift-F8), selecting Line (**1** or **L**), then Margins (**7** or **M**). Enter **1** for both the left and right margins, then press Exit (F7).

13. Change the font to the large one you used in step 9. (I used 30-point bold Helvetica.)

14. Press the Tab key once, then type **1**. Next, change the font to a 14-point size if you have one (see step 9). I used a 14-point bold Helvetica.

15. Press Tab then type the first question:

    **The End key is used to:**

16. Press the Flush Right key (Alt-F6) then type

    **Your answers:**

17. Change the font to the one you used in step 3. (I used 12-point Helvetica.) Press ⏎ twice.

Now type the a, b, c, and d choices for the first question.

18. Press Tab twice then type **a.**, then press Tab again and type **Move the cursor to the end of the page**. Press ⏎ and repeat this step for b, c, and d. Press ⏎ one extra time after typing the text for d.

## CREATING A TEXT BOX

The next procedure will be to use the Graphics key to create a text box. Text boxes are generally used to enclose any text that you want to set off from the rest of the document, such as sidebars and quotations, but in this situation, it is also an easy way to create the small shaded box next to each question. You will then complete the first test form question by drawing a rule under the question.

1. Move the cursor onto the line with the first answer choice (a), and place it at the left margin.

2. Press the Graphics key (Alt-F9) and select Text Box (**3** or **B**), then select Create (**1** or **C**). You will see the Definition: Text Box menu, which is almost the same as the Definition: Figure menu shown in Figure 14.1. (The only difference is the title at the top.)

3. Select Size (**6** or **S**), then Both Width and Height (**3** or **B**) and enter **.7** for both the width and the height. Press Exit (F7) when done.

Now you need to use the Options menu to remove the border that would otherwise appear above and below the box. Use View Document at 200% (Shift-F7 V 2) to see the borders. (You may have to press → several times to see the right side of the page.) Press Exit (F7) when you are done.

4. Use Reveal Codes (Alt-F3) to place the cursor on the [Text Box:1;;] code. Press the Graphics key (Alt-F9) and select Text Box (**3** or **B**), then select Options (**4** or **O**). You will then see the Options: Text Box menu shown in Figure 14.16.

```
Options:     Text Box

      1 - Border Style
            Left                              None
            Right                             None
            Top                               Thick
            Bottom                            Thick
      2 - Outside Border Space
            Left                              0.16"
            Right                             0.16"
            Top                               0.16"
            Bottom                            0.16"
      3 - Inside Border Space
            Left                              0.16"
            Right                             0.16"
            Top                               0.16"
            Bottom                            0.16"
      4 - First Level Numbering Method        Numbers
      5 - Second Level Numbering Method       Off
      6 - Caption Number Style                [BOLD]1[bold]
      7 - Position of Caption                 Below box, Outside borders
      8 - Minimum Offset from Paragraph       0"
      9 - Gray Shading (% of black)           10%

   Selection: 0
```

*Figure 14.16:* The Options: Text Box menu

Notice that this menu provides the same options as the Options: Figure menu shown in Figure 14.9, but several options have different defaults. For example, Border Style is a thick line above and below the box, whereas in the Options: Figure menu, Border Style is a single line on all four sides of the box. Other defaults that are different are the Inside Border Space and the percentage figure in the Gray Shading option.

5.  Select Border Style (**1** or **B**) and press **N** four times to select None for all four borders. Press Exit (F7) when done.

Next, create the horizontal rule under the first question.

6.  Move the cursor down and place it two lines under the last answer (d). Press Graphics (Alt-F9) and select Line (**5** or **L**), then select Create Line: Horizontal (**1** or **H**). Select Horizontal Position (**1** or **H**) then select Set Position (**5** or **S**) and type **1.5** followed by ⏎ for the offset.

7.  Select Length of Line (**2** or **L**) and type **7** followed by ⏎, then select Width of Line (**3** or **W**) and type **.02** followed by ⏎. Press Exit (F7) when done, then use View Document (Shift-F7 V) to see your work.

Now you've created all the elements for the test; all you have to do to complete the form is to repeat the steps above for each of the other answers. Remember, you can use the method described in step 11 of the previous section to copy the codes for the fonts, rules, and text boxes. Alternatively, you could use the Block (Alt-F4) and Move (Ctrl-F4) keys to make three copies of the question-and-answer section that starts with number 1 and ends with the rule, and then change the text.

## *WORKING WITH COLUMNS AND GRAPHICS*

The next exercise will be familiar if you read Chapter 12, for it is an improved version of the parallel columns shown in Figure 12.9; the new version will resemble Figure 14.17. The desktop publishing features that I used to create it include Line Height, Horizontal and Vertical Lines, and the Table option. The large gray box at the top is a Horizontal Line, and the thick line that surrounds it is a Table. The text was moved inside the box and the thick line was moved around it using Advance Up. I created the two horizontal lines around the car descriptions using the Horizontal Line feature of the Graphics key, and the two vertical ones using the Vertical Line feature. I used the Between Columns option to place the vertical lines between the columns. To narrow the blank space separating the automobile names from the text below, and to slightly increase the blank space separating the italicized lines and prices from the descriptive text above, I used Line Height. I also used Styles to help standardize the formatting. I used a mixture of Helvetica fonts, including 12-point italic, 30-point bold, 14-point bold, and 12-point regular.

If you did not complete the exercise in Chapter 12, you can either type it before beginning this exercise or use one of your own documents that is in columnar format. The instructions below make the following assumptions about the position of your text: the first line of text, *AT HILLSIDE AUTO,* begins on line 3; *OUR USED CARS* starts on line 5; *We have complete faith* starts on line 12; *1987 HONDA ACCORD* is on line 23; *4-door blue beauty* is on line 25; *1984 CHEVY BLAZER* is on line 39; and *Automatic, V-8* is on line 41.

*Figure 14.17:* The used car advertisement enhanced with desktop publishing features

## CREATING A SHADED BOX

The first step is to retrieve the file to the Edit screen, then create the large shaded box and type the text inside it. The method is similar to the one you used earlier in this chapter.

1. Use List Files (F5) or Retrieve Text (Shift-F10) to retrieve the file you created in Chapter 12. You were instructed to name it *car.ad*. If you don't have it, retrieve another document you created with three parallel columns. Place the cursor on the first position of line 1.

Use the following steps to create the large shaded box. It will be a horizontal line 6.5 inches long and 2 inches wide, centered between the margins. The gray shading will be reduced to ten percent.

2. Press Graphics (Alt-F9), select Line (**5** or **L**), then select Create Line: Horizontal (**1** or **H**). Select Horizontal Position (**1** or **H**) and choose Center (**3** or **C**). Next, select Length of Line (**2** or **L**) and type **6.5**, followed by ◄─┘, then select Width of Line (**3** or **W**) and type **2** followed by ◄─┘. Select the Gray Shading option (**4** or **G**) and type **10**, followed by ◄─┘, then press ◄─┘ to exit from the menu.

3. Place the cursor on the *AT HILLSIDE AUTO* line. Press Home Home Home ◄── to be sure the cursor is at the left margin, before any codes.

4. Use Advance to move this and the next line up 1.5 inches so they will be inside the box when printed. Press the Format key (Shift-F8), select Other (**4** or **O**), select Advance (**1** or **A**), then select Up (**1** or **U**) and enter **1.5**, followed by ◄─┘F7.

## CHANGING FONTS

The next step is to change the fonts. I used Helvetica 30-point bold for the heading *AT HILLSIDE AUTO,* Helvetica 14-point bold for the second line, and Helvetica 12-point for the paragraph that follows, except for *Unconditional Warranty,* which is in Helvetica 12-point italics. The automobile names are in 12-point Helvetica bold. The lines above the prices, such as *See it today!,* are in Helvetica 12-point italic, and the prices are in Helvetica 12-point bold. If you don't have these fonts for your printer, you can approximate the look by using fonts in the same size and weight (bold, italics). You may want to use Styles to help you with this process, as explained in Chapter 8 and in the "Using Styles to Format Your Text" section later in this chapter.

To change fonts, press Font (Ctrl-F8), select Base Font (**4** or **F**), then move the cursor bar onto the font you want to use and press **1** to select it.

## CREATING HORIZONTAL RULES

Next, you'll create the two horizontal rules above and in the middle of the automobile descriptions. The method you'll use is the same as the one you used earlier in this chapter when you created the test form.

1. Place the cursor three lines above *1987 Honda Accord*. Press Graphics (Alt-F9), select Line (**5** or **L**), and select Create Line: Horizontal (**1** or **H**). From the Graphics: Horizontal Line menu, select Horizontal Position (**1** or **H**) and choose Left (**1** or **L**), then select Length of Line (**2** or **L**) and type **6.5** followed by ←. Next, select Width of Line (**3** or **W**) and type **.04** followed by ←. Press ← to exit from the menu.

2. Place the cursor three lines above *1984 Chevy Blazer* and repeat step 1 to create the second horizontal line. Use View Document (Shift-F7 V) to see the lines.

## CREATING VERTICAL RULES

Next, you'll create the two vertical lines between the columns. This will be a new procedure for you, but it's similar to creating the horizontal rules. When you use this option, you can place the line against the top or bottom margin, centered between the top and bottom margins, or at a fixed position that is measured from the top of the form. Your line will begin at a fixed position, the position where you created the first horizontal line (above *1987 HONDA ACCORD*). However, you won't be able to create the vertical line between the columns unless you place the cursor after the column definition code, which is a few lines below the horizontal line. As a result, when you start at the position below the horizontal line and select Fixed Position from the Graphics: Vertical Line menu, WordPerfect will enter the current cursor position for you, which will be incorrect. The easiest way I have found to figure out where the vertical line should begin is to use the Reveal Codes screen to locate the Horizontal Line code and determine its position by looking at the line indicator on the status line. After that, you move the cursor down and create the vertical line in the correct location (after the [Col On] code).

1. Use the Reveal Codes key (Alt-F3) to help you locate the code for the horizontal line that you created earlier: [HLine:Left,6.5″,0.04″,100%].

2. Place the cursor on the code and write down the line position (Ln on the status line) so you'll remember it.

Now you can create the first vertical line, on the *1987 HONDA ACCORD* line. You will use the Between Columns option to place the line between columns 1 and 2.

3. Place the cursor at the beginning of the *HONDA ACCORD* line, where you will create the first vertical line.

4. Press Graphics (Alt-F9), select Line (**5** or **L**), then select Create Line: Vertical (**2** or **V**).

5. Select Horizontal Position (**1** or **H**), then Between Columns (**3** or **B**). You will see this prompt asking which column to place the line next to:

    **Place line to right of column: 1**

6. Type **1** followed by ⏎ to place it after the first column (or just press ⏎ if *1* is already entered).

7. Select Vertical Position (**2** or **V**), then Set Position (**5** or **S**). The current cursor position, which was 4.97 in my example, will be entered for you. Since you do not want the line to start at this position, change it to match the number you determined in step 3 (representing the position of the horizontal line above the car descriptions); mine was 4.59. Press ⏎ and WordPerfect will automatically calculate Length of Line for you.

8. Select Width of Line (**4** or **W**) and type .04 followed by ⏎. Press ⏎ to return to Edit mode.

9. Repeat steps 5 through 9 to create the second vertical line; in step 7, you must type **2** to place the line correctly.

Unfortunately, if your version of WordPerfect was released prior to January 1989, you cannot edit vertical or horizontal lines once you've created them. If you make a mistake, you have to locate and erase the code, and then create it all over again.

At this point, you should use View Document (Shift-F7 V) at 100% or 200% to check your work. Your horizontal and vertical rules may not be exactly the same as mine since the original document you typed may be a little different (such as having more hard returns). If you find that your lines are incorrect, you can use the Edit Line option on the Graphics key (press Alt-F9, select Line, then select Horizontal or Vertical) to change any of the other options: the position, length, width, or gray shading. If you find that the vertical rule went up too far, select Vertical Position and use a larger number for Fixed Position (since this represents the position from the top of the page).

## USING THE TABLE OPTION TO CREATE LINES AROUND A BOX

Now move the cursor to the end of the document and use the Table option on the Graphics key to create the thick lines around the shaded box. You won't be able to draw the lines around the entire box unless you change the left and right margins to 0, so that will be your first step. After that, you'll need to use Advance to move the table you are going to create back up to the top of the page.

1. Press Home Home ↓ to move the cursor to the end of the document. The cursor must be on page 1 or Advance will not work, so if it has moved to page 2, move it back up near the end of page 1.

2. Press Format (Shift-F8) and select Line (**1** or **L**) then Margins (**7** or **M**). Type **0** for both margins, then press ↵ to return to the main Format menu.

3. From the Format menu, select Other (**4** or **O**), then Advance (**1** or **A**), then Up (**1** or **U**). Type **9** then ↵ to advance up 9 inches, then press Exit (F7).

4. Press Graphics (Alt-F9) and select Table (**2** or **T**), then Create (**1** or **C**). You will see the Definition: Table menu shown in Figure 14.18.

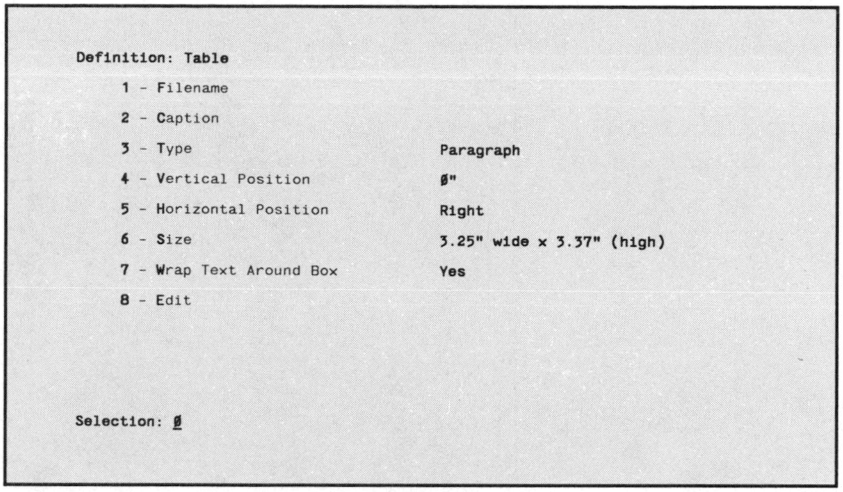

```
Definition: Table
    1 - Filename
    2 - Caption
    3 - Type                    Paragraph
    4 - Vertical Position       0"
    5 - Horizontal Position     Right
    6 - Size                    3.25" wide x 3.37" (high)
    7 - Wrap Text Around Box    Yes
    8 - Edit



Selection: 0
```

*Figure 14.18:* The Definition: Table menu

5. Select Type (**3** or **T**) and change the type to Page (**2** or **A**).

6. Select Horizontal Position (**5** or **H**), then Set Position (**3** or **S**). Enter **1** followed by ◄──┘ in response to the *Offset from left of page* prompt so the box will begin at the left margin.

7. Select Size (**6** or **S**), then Both Width and Height (**3** or **B**). To duplicate the dimensions of the shaded box, type **6.5** for width, followed by ◄──┘, and type **2** ◄──┘ for height. The prompt should now read

    6.5″ wide x 2″ high

    Press ◄──┘.

Now use the Options: Table menu to change the border of the table—currently set to a thick line above and below the box—to a thick line all the way around it. You may wish to view the border before changing it by using View Document (Shift-F7 V).

8. Press Reveal Codes (Alt-F3) and place the cursor on the [Table:I;;] code, since this procedure will not work if the cursor is to the right of the Table code. (Remember, all formatting changes in WordPerfect take place from the cursor position forward.)

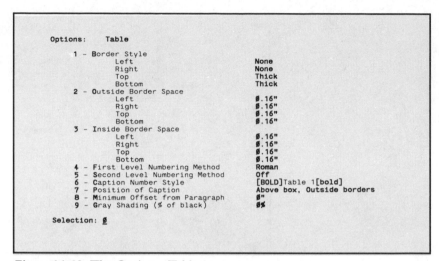

*Figure 14.19:* The Options: Table menu

9. Press Graphics (Alt-F9), select Table (**2** or **T**), then Options (**4** or **O**). You should see the Options: Table menu shown in Figure 14.19. Notice the default border style, None for left and right and Thick for top and bottom.

10. Change the left and right borders to Thick by selecting Border Style (**1** or **B**), pressing **T** four times, then pressing ←.

Use View Document (Shift-F7 V) to see your work, then print it (Shift-F7 F). When you see the printed version, you'll notice two areas that will require line spacing adjustments. In the next section you'll learn to make these changes.

## USING LINE HEIGHT TO CHANGE THE SPACING BETWEEN LINES

Notice in the printed version how much blank space separates the car names from the first line of the description. One extra line is more than is necessary, and if your printer is capable, you can use Word-Perfect's Line Height feature to reduce the blank space. You can also use it to slightly increase the blank space that separates the last two lines, such as before *Priced to sell!* and *$10,999* in the Honda Accord box. Although WordPerfect calls this feature *Line Height,* it is also frequently referred to as *leading.* The term leading originated with hot-metal typesetters, who placed strips of lead between lines of text to create blank space in printed documents.

1. Place the cursor after the *D* in *HONDA ACCORD,* where you'll make your first change.

2. Press Format (Shift-F8), select Line (**1** or **L**), then Height (**4** or **H**). Select Fixed (**2** or **F**). Notice the default, which will vary with your printer; mine was .17, or about one sixth of an inch. Reduce it by typing **.12**, then press ◄━┘ and Exit (F7).

3. Place the cursor on the *4* in the first line of the description *(4-door blue beauty)* and change the Line Height back to automatic. Press Format (Shift-F8), select Line (**1** or **L**), then Height (**4** or **H**). Select Auto (**1** or **A**), then press ◄━┘ and Exit (F7). Repeat these steps five more times, once for each car name, or skip to the next section, which shows you how to use Styles to make the procedure easier.

I also changed the leading after the last line of the description in each box, so that the italicized line and price were separated by slightly more blank space, ¼ inch. To do this, repeat steps 2 and 3, entering .25 for the amount of fixed space in step 2, then change back to Automatic Line Height after the price.

## USING STYLES TO FORMAT YOUR TEXT

You can simplify tasks such as the one in the previous exercise by creating a style and applying it to each of the remaining car names. Using Styles will reduce the number of keystrokes you need to use and make your work easier, but there is another significant advantage to this method: if you change your mind after creating and applying a style, you can easily change it everywhere that you used the style in your document. To do this, you just change the formatting in the style itself. For instance, suppose you create and apply a style for .12 line height, as explained below, then print it and decide you'd like to try a different line height or return to automatic line height. All you have to do is use the Style key to edit the line height style and change its formatting.

Here are the steps to create and use a style for this application.

Styles are covered in Chapter 8.

1. Press the Style key (Alt-F8) and select Create (**3** or **C**). This will be a paired style that you'll use with the Block key.

2. Select Type (**2** or **T**), then Paired (**1** or **P**).

3. Select Name (**1** or **N**) and type **leading .12**, then press ←⏎.

4. Select Description (**3** or **D**) and type **.12 inch blank space**, then press ←⏎.

5. Select Codes (**4** or **C**) and you will be in a screen similar to the Reveal Codes screen. If it contains any codes, erase them by placing the cursor on the code and pressing Delete (but do not delete the [Comment] code). Insert the codes for line height by pressing Format (Shift-F8), selecting Line (**1** or **L**), selecting Height (**4** or **H**), then Fixed (**2** or **F**). Type **.12**, then press ←⏎ and Exit (F7).

6. Press → to move the cursor past the [Comment] code and change the Line Height back to automatic. Press Format (Shift-F8), select Line (**1** or **L**), select Height (**4** or **H**), select Auto (**1** or **A**), then press ←⏎ and Exit (F7). The Reveal Codes section of the screen should now look like this:

   [Ln Height:0.12″][Comment][Ln Height:Auto]

7. Press Exit (F7) twice. You may wish to use the Save option on the Styles menu to save the styles as a separate file. When you finish, press Exit (F7) to return to Edit mode.

8. To apply your style, place the cursor after the *N* in *CHEVY CITATION,* press Block (Alt-F4), then press ↓ twice to move the cursor onto the *4* in the first description line. Press Style (Alt-F8), move the cursor bar onto the *leading .12* style, then select On (**1** or **O**). If you look in Reveal Codes (Alt-F3) you'll see the Style On and Style Off codes. Repeat this procedure for the four other car names, then print the document.

That should simplify the procedure a bit; if you were using the style before typing the text, it would be even easier because you would turn on the style before typing it, then turn it off again by pressing → when you finished. Now let's see how easy it is to change the meaning of your style, and reduce the line height in all five of the blocks that you applied it to. We'll reduce line height to .08.

9. Press the Style key (Alt-F8), use the arrow keys to highlight the *leading .12* style, then select Edit (**4** or **E**).

10. Select Codes (**4** or **C**) from the Style: Edit menu, then move the cursor onto the [Ln Height:0.12″] code and press Delete to erase it.

11. To reduce line height to .08, press Format (Shift-F8), select Line (**1** or **L**), select Height (**4** or **H**), select Fixed (**2** or **F**), type **.08**, then press ←.

12. Press Exit (F7) four times to return to Edit mode.

Now you can use View Document (Shift-F7 V) to see the effect of this change on your document. Enlarge it to 200% by pressing *2*, and it should be even more obvious. You may wish to try a few other line heights in your style; feel free to experiment.

## MORE DESKTOP PUBLISHING IDEAS

Another application of WordPerfect's columns and desktop publishing features is to enhance the appearance of documents such as those in Figures 14.20 and 14.21. If you've studied the previous examples in this chapter, you've covered all the features used to create both of these documents.

## SUMMARY

This chapter has explored many of WordPerfect's desktop publishing capabilities, and has given you a solid introduction to these powerful new features. You have learned how to incorporate graphic images from other programs into your documents and how to manipulate them in many ways, including how to rotate, scale, invert, and

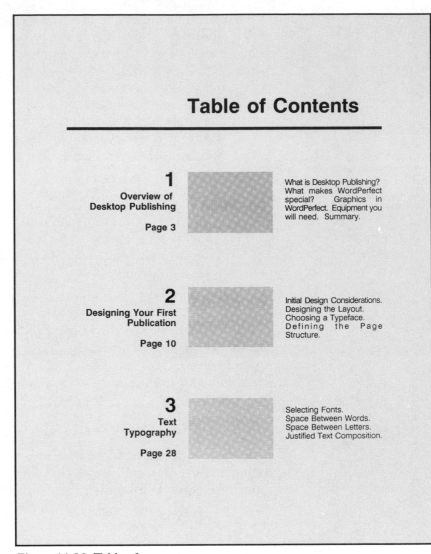

*Figure 14:20:* Table of contents

move them, and how to change the borders, captions, and gray shading. You also learned how to draw boxes and add shading and text to them, and how to create horizontal and vertical rules, including vertical rules between columns of text. You can use these features to

**Lesson 1:**
**Typing and Editing**

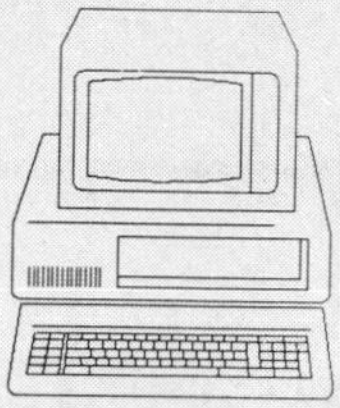

**What you will study:**

- The Status Line
- Word wrap
- Erasing text with the Delete and Backspace keys
- How to save a document
- Basic cursor movement

**Practice document 1**

WordPerfect is one of the most powerful and comprehensive word processing programs available. It is fast, efficient, and a genuine pleasure to use. However, the program is better known for an abundance of helpful features and the fact that WordPerfect Corporation keeps adding more to each version.

All of the fundamental word processing functions are available, such as automatic word wrap which creates a new line when the cursor reaches the right margin and moves the cursor down to the new line; automatic rewrite, which automatically reformats your paragraphs after any editing changes such as adding or deleting text; and search and replace, which can be used to locate and/or change a word or phrase.

WordPerfect's abilities extend way beyond the basics, though, to include such special features as a spelling checker, thesaurus, automatic footnotes, windows, newspaper columns, alphabetical and numeric sorting, line drawing, merge, macros, and mathematical functions such as addition, subtraction, multiplication, division, and averaging.

***Figure 14:21:*** A page from a workbook

create attractive, professional-looking documents such as newsletters, flyers, brochures, advertisements, report covers, tables, catalogs, manuals, and more, without having to learn a complex program such as Ventura Publisher or PageMaker.

**III.**

# PART III

## SUPPLEMENTAL FEATURES

**15.**

# *GETTING ORGANIZED: FILE MANAGEMENT TOOLS*

# FAST TRACK

**To retrieve a file with the List Files key,**        **484**

    press F5 ←, move the cursor to the file you want to retrieve, then press *1*.

**To delete a file with the List Files key,**        **484**

    press F5 ←, move the cursor to the file you want to delete, then press *2*, then *Y* at the next prompt.

**To rename a file,**        **485**

    press the List Files key (F5) ←, move the cursor to the file you want to rename, then press *3*. At the *New name:* prompt, type in the new name and press ←.

**To copy a file to another directory on your hard disk,**        **490**

    press F5 ←, move the cursor to the file and press *8*, type \ and the name of the directory, and press ←.

**Create a document summary before first saving the document**        **494**

    by pressing the Format key (Shift-F8), selecting Document, then selecting Summary. At the Document Summary menu, select *1* to assign a descriptive name to the document, select *2* to describe the subject of the document, select *3* or *4* to enter the initials or names of the author or typist, or *5* (for Comments) to type up to 780 characters describing the document. WordPerfect will automatically enter the first 400 characters of your document in the Comments area; you can add any additional comments before this text by pressing ← to add blank lines. Press F7 when you finish.

**To convert a WordPerfect file to ASCII**      498

(called a DOS text file) so that it can be used in other programs, place the file on the Edit screen, then press Ctrl-F5 1 1. At the prompt, enter the name you want the DOS text file saved under, then press ←⏎.

**Protect your files with a password**      502

by pressing Ctrl-F5, then *2*, then *1*. Enter your password, up to 75 characters (the characters will not be visible on the screen as you type), then press ←⏎. Another prompt asks you to enter the password a second time, and you must type it exactly as you first entered it. Next, press F10 and type a file name (not password) to save the document with the password you have just entered. To retrieve this file using either F5 or Shift-F10, you must enter the password as it was defined when prompted.

**To exit to DOS temporarily**,      508

press the Shell key (Ctrl-F1) and select *1* or *G*, the *Go to DOS* option. To return to WordPerfect, type *exit* (don't press F7) and press ←⏎.

**To work with two documents on two full-size editing screens**,      509

press the Switch key (Shift-F3). You will then have a new Edit screen to work on. You can then retrieve a file, create a file, or transfer data to and from both documents. Press Switch (Shift-F3) to move back and forth between the documents.

YOU HAVE ALREADY USED MANY OF WORDPERFECT'S
file management features to save, retrieve, and print files, but you've
only scratched the surface of the program's sophisticated filing operations. In addition to being able to run many DOS functions from within
WordPerfect, such as deleting, renaming and copying files, and checking the directories and file allocation tables, you can also use WordPerfect to search all files for a word or phrase, convert files to and from
ASCII, lock and save documents with a password, temporarily exit to
DOS and run another program, split the screen in two, and much
more. Users with hard disks will especially appreciate commands that
allow you to change default directories, search other directories for files
to work with, create a new directory, or delete an empty directory. Since
the WordPerfect commands are menu-driven, they are much easier to
work with than the equivalent DOS commands.

## THE LIST FILES KEY

The List Files key (F5) is the major file management key. It can be
used to retrieve, delete, move, rename, print, or copy a file, to
retrieve a DOS text file, to view the contents of a file without retrieving it, to change the default directory or make a new directory, and to
perform a word search. When you press F5 ←⏎, a screen similar to
the one in Figure 15.1 appears.

At the top of the screen, in the highlighted section, you see the current
date and time, the name of the default disk and the path to the directory
you are working in, the available space on the default disk (free disk
space), the amount of used space, and, if you have a document on the
editing screen, the size of that document and the number of files in the
directory. Underneath is an alphabetical list of all files in the directory,
showing their size and the time and date they were last saved. Notice

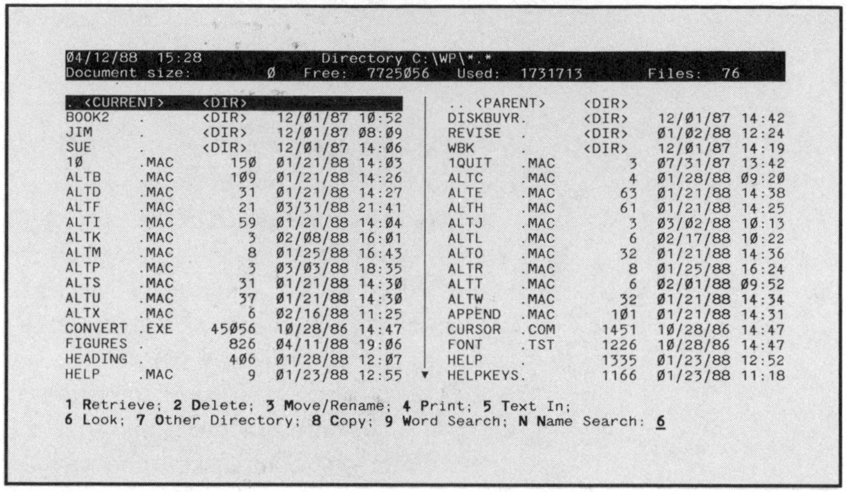

```
04/12/88  15:28              Directory C:\WP\*.*
Document size:      0  Free:  7725056   Used:  1731713        Files:  76

. <CURRENT>    <DIR>                   .. <PARENT>    <DIR>
BOOK2    .     <DIR>   12/01/87 10:52  DISKBUYR.     <DIR>   12/01/87 14:42
JIM      .     <DIR>   12/01/87 08:09  REVISE   .    <DIR>   01/02/88 12:24
SUE      .     <DIR>   12/01/87 14:06  WBK      .    <DIR>   12/01/87 14:19
10       .MAC    150   01/21/88 14:03  1QUIT    .MAC    3    07/31/87 13:42
ALTB     .MAC    109   01/21/88 14:26  ALTC     .MAC    4    01/28/88 09:20
ALTD     .MAC     31   01/21/88 14:27  ALTE     .MAC   63    01/21/88 14:38
ALTF     .MAC     21   03/31/88 21:41  ALTH     .MAC   61    01/21/88 14:25
ALTI     .MAC     59   01/21/88 14:04  ALTJ     .MAC    3    03/02/88 10:13
ALTK     .MAC      3   02/08/88 16:01  ALTL     .MAC    6    02/17/88 10:22
ALTM     .MAC      8   01/25/88 16:43  ALTO     .MAC   32    01/21/88 14:36
ALTP     .MAC      3   03/03/88 18:35  ALTR     .MAC    8    01/25/88 16:24
ALTS     .MAC     31   01/21/88 14:30  ALTT     .MAC    6    02/01/88 09:52
ALTU     .MAC     37   01/21/88 14:30  ALTW     .MAC   32    01/21/88 14:34
ALTX     .MAC      6   02/16/88 11:25  APPEND   .MAC  101    01/21/88 14:31
CONVERT  .EXE  45056   10/28/86 14:47  CURSOR   .COM 1451    10/28/86 14:47
FIGURES  .       826   04/11/88 19:06  FONT     .TST 1226    10/28/86 14:47
HEADING  .       406   01/28/88 12:07  HELP     .     1335   01/23/88 12:52
HELP     .MAC      9   01/23/88 12:55 ▼ HELPKEYS.     1166   01/23/88 11:18

1 Retrieve; 2 Delete; 3 Move/Rename; 4 Print; 5 Text In;
6 Look; 7 Other Directory; 8 Copy; 9 Word Search; N Name Search: 6
```

*Figure 15.1:* The List Files screen

that it resembles the listing you see when you use the DOS command
DIR, except that the file names are listed in two columns. You can
obtain a printed version of this file list by pressing the Print key
(Shift-F7).

If you use a hard disk, you can obtain a list of the files in a different
directory by placing the cursor on *<CURRENT DIR>*, pressing
◄┘, and typing the name (and path if necessary) of that directory,
preceded by the DOS backslash symbol (\) if necessary. If the name
of the directory is shown on the List Files screen (indicated by
<DIR> where the file size normally appears), you can view the files
in that directory by moving the highlighted bar to the name of the
directory and pressing ◄┘ twice (the first time to select the directory
and the second time to get a list of the contents of that directory).

## CURSOR MOVEMENT
## IN THE LIST FILES SCREEN

The highlighted bar at the top left side of the list represents the cursor. To move this cursor bar, press any of the arrow keys on the
numeric keypad or the Screen Up or Screen Down key. The Home
Home ↑ (or ↓) combination moves the cursor to the first (or last) file in
the list. When the list of files extends beyond the limits of the screen,
WordPerfect lets you know by adding an arrow to the line that

divides the list into two columns. If the file list extends below the screen view, the arrow points downward (as in Figure 15.1). If the file list extends above the screen view, the arrow points upward. If the file list extends in both directions, there will be arrows pointing in both directions.

***CURSOR MOVEMENT WITH NAME SEARCH*** WordPerfect's Name Search option is the most efficient method of moving the cursor onto the file name of your choice. To use the Name Search option, either type *N* or press the Search key (F2). The List Files menu at the bottom of the screen disappears and you see this prompt in the lower right corner:

(Name Search; Enter or arrows to Exit)

Next, you press the first letter of the file name you're searching for, and the cursor moves to the first file in the list that begins with that letter. If there is more than one file that begins with the same letter, you can narrow the search by typing the second and third letters of the file name, as shown in Figure 15.2. If there are no files that begin with the letter, the cursor will move to the first file beginning with the next letter in the alphabet. For example, if you type *b* and there are no file names in the list that start with *b,* the cursor will move to the first name that begins with *c,* if there is one (if not, it will move to a file

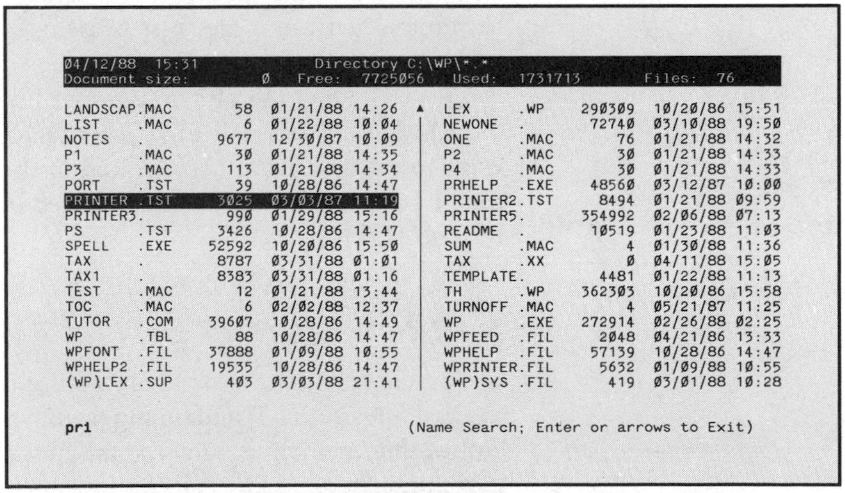

*Figure 15.2:* Highlighting a specific file with the Name Search option

name that starts with *d* ). Once the cursor has moved onto the file you want to use, press ← or one of the four arrow keys to get the List Files menu back. You can then use one of the menu options like Retrieve or Print. When you want to return to the editing screen, press the Cancel key (F1), the Space bar, Exit (F7), or *0*.

## SELECTING MULTIPLE FILES

To perform operations such as Delete, Print, or Copy, on a group of files, move the cursor to each file you want to include and mark it by pressing the asterisk key (*). When you do, an asterisk will appear next to the file-size statistic in the third column. Note that a directory name such as *<PARENT> <DIR>* cannot be marked. Next, select an option such as Delete or Copy from the List Files menu. You will see a prompt indicating that all of the marked files will be affected and asking for your approval. For instance, if you select option 2 to delete several marked files, this prompt will appear:

**Delete marked files? (Y/N) No**

Notice that *No* is the default, so pressing any key other than *Y* will remove the prompt and cancel the action (of deleting multiple files), and you will then be asked if you want to delete the individual file that the cursor bar is highlighting. Press *N* to cancel this action and the List Files menu will return. The asterisk mark is a toggle; if you want to remove it from a file, just press it again. Exiting the List Files screen removes all asterisks.

To mark all of the files on the List Files screen at one time, press the Mark Text key (Alt-F5). (This feature is very handy when you want to make backup copies of all of the files in a particular directory.) To deselect all of the files marked in this fashion, just press Alt-F5 a second time.

## NARROWING THE DISPLAY WITH WILD CARDS

You can restrict the directory listing to a specific file by pressing the List Files key (F5) and typing the file name after the DIR prompt. Notice that as soon as you type the first character, the default directory name, such as C:\WP, disappears.

If you have forgotten the exact name, or if you want to look up a group of files with similar names, you can use the question mark, which functions as a wild-card character representing any single character. For instance, the page numbers of all examples used in this book are stored in files with names that begin with *Page*, such as Page103, Page110, Page131, etc. To look them up all at once, I type the following in response to the DIR prompt:

**page???**

and my list appears as in Figure 15.3.

You will often find it helpful to list a group of files with a common pattern such as the same extension (the three character identifier that follows the file name, such as .LTR). To do this, you can use another wild-card character, the asterisk, which represents the character in the position it is located on, plus any remaining characters in the file name or extension. For example, to look up the names of all files ending in *.LTR*, press F5 and type this sequence: *.LTR* so that the prompt line looks like this:

**Dir *.LTR**

Once you press ←┘, you'd see a list of all files that end in *.LTR*.

> The Directory prompt on the first line of the screen indicates that the directory listing is limited to all files on drive A that begin with the word *page* and include 1 to 3 more characters in the first part of the name.

```
04/12/88  15:34                     Directory A:\PAGE???.*
Document size:         0     Free:    106496    Used:     46993          Files:  42

  . <CURRENT>   <DIR>                    .. <PARENT>    <DIR>
PAGE103 .         1185   07/25/87 17:36   PAGE110 .        1128   07/25/87 17:45
PAGE131 .          171   07/30/87 08:53   PAGE133 .         451   07/25/87 17:57
PAGE138 .          404   07/25/87 18:01   PAGE142 .         488   07/25/87 18:06
PAGE145 .           58   07/25/87 18:07   PAGE147 .         302   07/25/87 18:11
PAGE148 .           10   07/30/87 08:56   PAGE149 .          84   07/25/87 18:14
PAGE152 .         1637   07/30/87 09:00   PAGE153 .        1637   07/30/87 09:01
PAGE210 .         1081   07/30/87 09:19   PAGE221 .        2472   08/01/87 10:07
PAGE232 .         2434   08/01/87 10:13   PAGE233 .        2350   08/01/87 10:14
PAGE235 .         2124   08/01/87 10:14   PAGE240 .        2516   08/01/87 10:15
PAGE243 .         1426   08/01/87 10:16   PAGE253 .        1426   07/31/87 09:14
PAGE29  .          385   07/25/87 14:06   PAGE293 .         742   07/31/87 09:16
PAGE301 .          563   07/31/87 09:46   PAGE31  .         532   07/31/87 14:08
PAGE311 .          368   07/31/87 10:25   PAGE313 .         460   07/31/87 10:27
PAGE314 .          567   07/31/87 10:59   PAGE320 .         872   07/31/87 10:35
PAGE325 .          819   07/31/87 10:36   PAGE330 .         253   07/31/87 12:07
PAGE333 .          702   07/31/87 12:08   PAGE337 .         392   07/31/87 12:12
PAGE338 .         1883   07/31/87 12:14   PAGE369 .        6202   07/31/87 12:39
PAGE370 .         4791   07/31/87 12:46 ▼ PAGE371 .         430   07/31/87 12:48

1 Retrieve; 2 Delete; 3 Move/Rename; 4 Print; 5 Text In;
6 Look; 7 Other Directory; 8 Copy; 9 Word Search; N Name Search: 6
```

*Figure 15.3:* Using the wild card *?* in a directory listing

## RETRIEVING FILES

You have already used the Retrieve Text key (Shift-F10) to retrieve a copy of a file from disk to the Edit screen. Option 1 on the List Files key is another method of doing the same thing. To use it, move the cursor until it highlights the file you want to retrieve and press *1.* The List Files screen will disappear and the file will appear on the editing screen.

Always be sure you have cleared any document on the Edit screen before you use the List Files method to retrieve a new document. If you are uncertain, exit the List Files screen by pressing Cancel (F1) or Exit (F7) and see if there is any text on the Edit screen. If so, use Exit (F7) to clear it. If there is already another document on the screen when you use List Files to retrieve, the one you are retrieving will be added to it in front of it, at the cursor position. You will receive a warning, though, because when you press 1 or R to retrieve a file and there already is one on your Edit screen, you see this prompt:

**Retrieve into current document? (Y/N) No**

If you press any key other than Y or y, the retrieve action is cancelled. Pressing Y is fine if your intention is to join two documents together. However, it is confusing if this is done unintentionally. Another way you may be able to tell if your Edit screen is empty is to look in line 2 of the List Files screen and observe the number next to the *Document size:* prompt, which refers to the size of the document currently on your Edit screen. If it is not 0, you need to exit and clear the screen.

## DELETING FILES

To delete a file from the disk, press the List Files key (F5), then ←┘, highlight the file with the cursor, and select option 2, Delete. This prompt will appear on the status line, double-checking to make sure you really want to delete the file:

**Delete (*filename*)? (Y/N) No**

Needless to say, once you press *Y,* the file is permanently erased from the disk, so be careful with this one. As mentioned above, you can delete several files at once by marking them with asterisks before selecting this option.

## MOVING OR RENAMING FILES

You can use the Move/Rename option on the List Files key to move a file or change its name. To rename a file, move the cursor to the file you want to rename and press *3;* the following prompt will appear:

New name:(filename)

It is followed by the current name so that you can use the regular cursor movement keys to change the name. As soon as you type the new name (and press ⬅), it replaces the old one and appears in the highlighted bar on your screen. However, if another file by the same name already exists, you will see a message like this one:

Replace (filename)? (Y/N) No

This is a warning that there is already a file by the same name in your current directory, so if you press *Y* you will erase it and replace it with the contents of the file that the cursor is highlighting. Unless you really want to erase the other file, you should press *N*, then press *3* or *M* again and type a different file name.

If you want to move a file into another directory or disk and erase it from the current one, highlight the file with the cursor bar, select Move/Rename (*3* or *M*), type the disk name or directory name, then type the file name. After you press ⬅, the file will be moved into the other directory or disk and its name will disappear from the current directory listing.

## PRINTING FILES

As you learned in Chapter 9, you can print one or more files by selecting option 4, Print, from the List Files menu. When you highlight a file and press *4*, you will be asked to enter the page numbers; type individual numbers or just press ⬅ if you want to print the entire document. To print a group of files, highlight each one and press the asterisk key to mark them, then press *4* and type *Y* in response to the *Print marked files* prompt. The file or files you select will be sent to WordPerfect's print queue and listed on the Printer Control screen. If you get an error message such as this when you try to print a file using the Print option on the List Files key:

ERROR: Document was Fast Saved — Must be retrieved to print

it means that the document cannot be printed using this method. This happens because you are using WordPerfect's Fast Save option. This speeds up the saving process by saving your document without formatting. However, a document cannot be printed from disk if it has been saved this way unless you press Home Home ↓ just before saving it. To print it, retrieve it first, then press Shift-F7 F or P. You can remove Fast Save using option 4 on the Setup menu (Shift-F1).

## IMPORTING ASCII FILES

When you want to use a file that has been saved as an ASCII file from another program (other than files created under specific programs that can be converted with the WordPerfect Convert utility, such as WordStar, MailMerge, and MultiMate), do not use the Retrieve Text key or the Retrieve option on the List Files key. Instead, move the cursor bar to highlight the name of the ASCII file and then select option 5, Text In, on the List Files menu. The manual suggests resetting the WordPerfect margins before retrieving a file this way, to preserve its format (since WordPerfect's margins begin at the 1-inch position, while many other programs' margins begin at position 0″). You can also use the Text In/Out key (Ctrl-F5) to import and revise ASCII files (also known as DOS files) created from the keyboard, such as batch files created using the DOS command COPY. If you are retrieving text from an ASCII file created using a different word processor, select the DOS Text option from the Text In/Out key, then select option 3, *Retrieve (CR/LF to [SRt] in HZone)*. This will maintain the soft returns found at the end of each line within your paragraphs, and will place hard returns at the end of each paragraph (or wherever two or more carriage return line feed codes are found). You will learn about the Text In/Out key and its uses later on in this chapter.

## *LOOKING AT FILES*

The Look option on the List Files screen is a wonderful utility that you can use to view the contents of any file in the directory listing or to view a listing of all files in another directory. It is helpful when you've forgotten what's in a file and want to take a quick look at its contents without retrieving it to the Edit screen. To use it, move the cursor to the file you want to look at and press *6, L,* or ←. The file will appear on screen, but it won't display certain formatting features such as line spacing.

The file name, path, and size are displayed in the highlighted bar at the top of the screen, as shown in Figure 15.4. Note that you will not be able to edit the document, but you can use all the regular cursor movement keys such as ↓ and ↑, Screen Up and Screen Down, or Page Up and Page Down to scroll through it and view sections that are not visible on the screen. To return to the List Files screen after looking at the text of a document, press the Exit key (F7), as the prompt on the last line tells you.

To view a list of the files in another directory, move the cursor to the directory name and press ← twice (or press *6* or *L* to select the Look option, then press ←). Directory names always end in <DIR> and appear like this in the List Files screen:

<PARENT> <DIR>

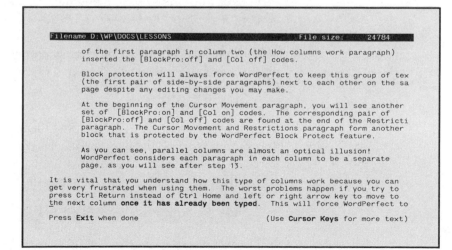

*Figure 15.4:* Viewing a file with the Look option

Once you see the list of file names in that directory, you can select any of the List Files options from the menu at the bottom of the screen, or press F7 or F1 to return to the Edit screen.

If the cursor bar is highlighting *<CURRENT> <DIR>* and you keep pressing ◄┘, you can get yourself into an endless loop looking at the same list of files over and over again. Notice that the Look option is the default choice, since the cursor is under *6* at the end of the menu (in Figure 15.1), so by pressing ◄┘ twice, you are selecting the Look option and looking at <CURRENT> <DIR>. However, <CURRENT> <DIR> means the directory you are already in, so you just keep viewing the same files.

## CHANGING, CREATING, AND DELETING A DIRECTORY

You can use option 7 on the List Files key to change the default directory if you are using a hard disk, or to switch from one disk drive to another. To use option 7, just press *7* or *O,* then type the directory name (and path, if needed) in response to the *New directory* = prompt. To switch drives, type the drive designator (*a* or *b*) followed by a colon. When you press ◄┘, you will be switched to that directory, subdirectory, or disk drive (it will become the default). Pressing ◄┘ a second time will obtain a listing of the directory just selected. Alternatively, you can move the cursor (the highlighted bar) to the subdirectory name and press *7* (or *O*), and the name will appear after the *New directory* = prompt. Press ◄┘ to switch it, then press ◄┘ once more to see the list of files in the new directory.

For example, I have a subdirectory named SCREEN that appears on my List Files screen as follows:

SCREEN . <DIR>

(The *<DIR>* appears in place of the file-size statistic.) To switch to that subdirectory, I highlight it with the cursor bar, and select Other Directory (*7* or *O*). (Note that my WordPerfect directory name is *WP5.*) The status line prompt changes to

New directory = C:\WP5\SCREEN

and I can press ◄┘ twice to obtain a directory listing.

Once you have changed to a different disk, directory, or subdirectory, you can also use option 7 (or O) on the List Files menu to go back to the parent directory, the one that is one level above the current directory. To do this, look for *<PARENT> <DIR>* on the List Files screen, move the cursor bar onto it, press *7* or *O*, then press ◄─┘ twice. In my example, WP5 is the parent directory. To switch back to it, I press the List Files key (F5), press ◄─┘, then look for a file in the list named

.. <PARENT> <DIR>

Next, I move the cursor bar to highlight *<PARENT> <DIR>*, then press *7* or *O.* This prompt appears on the status line:

New directory = C:\WP5

Pressing ◄─┘ completes the change. The prompt *DIR C:\WP5\ \*.\** will then appear, and I can either press ◄─┘ to get a directory listing, or press the Cancel key (F1) twice to get back to the Edit screen.

Another way to change the default directory is by pressing the List Files key (F5) and typing an equal sign ( = ), followed by the name of the directory you want to use. Instead of retyping the name from scratch, you can edit it by using the arrow keys to move the cursor to the place in the prompt where you need to add or delete characters from the directory name. For example, to switch to the SCREEN subdirectory from the parent directory (WP5), I press F5 and then type the equal sign ( = ). The prompt

New directory = C:\WP5

appears at the bottom of the screen. Next, I press the → key several times to move to the end of the directory name, then I type \\*SCREEN* so that the entire prompt reads

New directory = C:\WP5\SCREEN

and then I press ◄─┘ to make this subdirectory the new default. After that, I can press ◄─┘ to see the List Files screen for the Screen subdirectory, or F1 to return to Edit mode. To change back to my Word-Perfect subdirectory, I reverse this action by pressing F5, typing an equal sign ( = ), pressing → to get to the end of the prompt, then using the Backspace key to delete \\*SCREEN* before pressing ◄─┘.

You can also use this method to create a new directory. To do this, press F5 = and type or edit the name (path) for the new directory when you see this prompt:

**New directory =**

then press ◄┘. If the directory does not yet exist, you will receive a prompt that asks if you wish to create this directory, and you should type *Y*. You can also create a new directory by using the Other Directory option (7 or O) from the List Files menu and typing a new name.

If you do not enter a path (using \), WordPerfect assumes this will be a subdirectory one level under the directory you are presently using, and will enter the path for you. The directory name will show up at the top of your file list on the List Files screen.

You can use the Delete option on the List Files menu to delete a directory, but it must be empty of all files before you can delete it. To do this, press F5 ◄┘ and move the cursor bar to highlight the directory name. Next, select the delete option by pressing *2*, and type *Y* in response to the Delete prompt. If the directory contains any files, you will get the following message:

**ERROR: Directory not empty**

If this happens, you must erase all the files in that directory before proceeding (if you still want to delete the directory). To be on the safe side, you should follow the procedures outlined above to change to that directory, and use option 6 to look at the files and make sure that you really want to delete them. You then can use option 2 to delete them or the Copy or Move option to copy or move them into a different directory before deleting them. Next, switch back to the parent directory and select option 2 to complete the process of deleting the directory.

## COPYING FILES

You can use the Copy option on the List Files key to copy one or more files to another disk drive or directory. Unlike the Move/ Rename option, this one makes an additional copy of the file in the new directory or disk and leaves the original intact. To copy a file to another disk, move the cursor to the file and type either *8* or *C* to select Copy. The following prompt will appear:

Copy this file to:

Next, type the name of the disk drive (*a, b, c*) followed by a colon. Notice that you do not have to type the file name if you want the copy to have the same name as the original. When you press ←┘, it will be copied. If there is another file with the same name on that disk, you will be asked if you want to replace that file. Enter *Y* only if you are certain you want to replace it.

To copy the file to another directory on your hard disk, press *8* or *C*, and in response to the *Copy this file to*: prompt, type the name (path) of the directory (following the DOS rule of preceding it by \ if necessary), and press ←┘.

You can also use this option to make an extra copy of a file by assigning a new name to it at this prompt:

Copy this file to:

By giving it a different name, you ensure that the copy will not replace the original.

To make copies of several files on the List Files screen in one operation, mark all of the files to be copied with an asterisk (*) before selecting option 8. When you type *8* or *C*, you will see this prompt:

Copy marked files? (Y/N) No

Type *Y* for Yes and then indicate the letter of the drive or directory path that the files are to be copied to. Remember that you can mark all of the files on the List Files screen for copying by pressing Alt-F5 before you select option 8.

## SEARCHING ALL FILES FOR A WORD OR PHRASE

Option 9, Word Search, is another practical utility, one that allows you to locate any file or group of files that contains a particular word or phrase, or to search for all files created between a certain range of dates. You can use it to search all of the files on the List Files screen or to restrict the search to those that match a particular pattern.

To use the Word Search utility, press the List Files key (F5), press ←┘, then mark all of the files that you want searched with an asterisk

(\*). If you want to search all files on the current directory or disk, leave them unmarked. Next, type *9* or *W* to select Word Search. The Word Search menu will appear at the bottom of the List Files screen:

**Search: 1 Doc Summary; 2 First Page; 3 Entire Doc; 4 Conditions: 0**

If you select option 1, the word search is restricted to the document summaries that you have added to the files (you will learn about document summaries in the next section). If you select option 2, the word search is restricted to the first 4,000 characters of the document or to the first page, whichever occurs first. If you select option 3, the program searches the entire document for the word or phrase you enter. You'll study option 4 shortly.

After you select one of these three options, WordPerfect prompts you for the word pattern. Here, you can type as many as 39 characters, including the wild-card characters *?* and *\**, which you read about earlier in this chapter, to tell WordPerfect what you're searching for. The program does not distinguish between uppercase and lowercase during the word search, so the search string can be typed either way. If your phrase includes a single quotation mark, you must use double quotes around the entire phrase. After entering the word pattern, press ◄┘ to begin the search.

You can fine tune the word pattern with the use of semicolons, blank spaces, or commas, which serve as *logical operators.* A semicolon or a single blank space between two words stands for AND; it means that you want the program to locate only those files that contain both of the words. A comma between two words stands for OR; it means that you want the program to locate files that contain either one or both of the words.

WordPerfect will search all of the marked files or, if none have been marked, all of the files, indicating its progress with a *Searching file* prompt that counts the files as they are being searched. If you have included any password-protected files in the search, the program will stop and prompt you to enter the password and you'll see the file name of the protected file in the prompt. If you don't know the password, press ◄┘ to have it bypass this file and continue the search.

When WordPerfect finishes searching, it places an asterisk next to all files that contain the word or phrase you typed in response to the *Word pattern* prompt. You can then press the Tab key to go forward from one

If WordPerfect doesn't begin the word search when you press ◄┘, select the Word Search option again, then select 4, Conditions. Next, select option 1, *Perform Search on,* from this menu to begin the search. The word pattern you entered will appear next to the appropriate heading in this screen: 5 – First Page, 6 – Entire Doc, or 7 – Document Summary.

selected file to the next. To back up to a previously selected file, you press Shift-Tab. To help verify which one of the selected documents is the one you are looking for, check each selected file by moving the cursor bar onto each one individually and selecting the Look option.

If the word or phrase you entered as the word pattern is not found in any of the files searched, you will receive the message

**\* Not found \***

and none of the files will be selected with an asterisk.

You can expand or restrict the search by using option 4, Conditions, on the Word Search menu. When you select this option, the screen shown in Figure 15.5 appears.

From this menu, you can search for those documents whose file dates (recorded by DOS when you save the file) are within a certain range by selecting the File Date option. For example, if you want to locate all of the files created or updated between August 30, 1989, and November 23, 1989, you select the File Date option (by typing *4* or *D*). This changes the No to the right of File Date to Yes. Next, press ◄—┘ and enter the *From* date, such as

**8/30/89**

Press ◄—┘, then enter the *To* date, such as

**11/23/89**

and press ◄—┘.

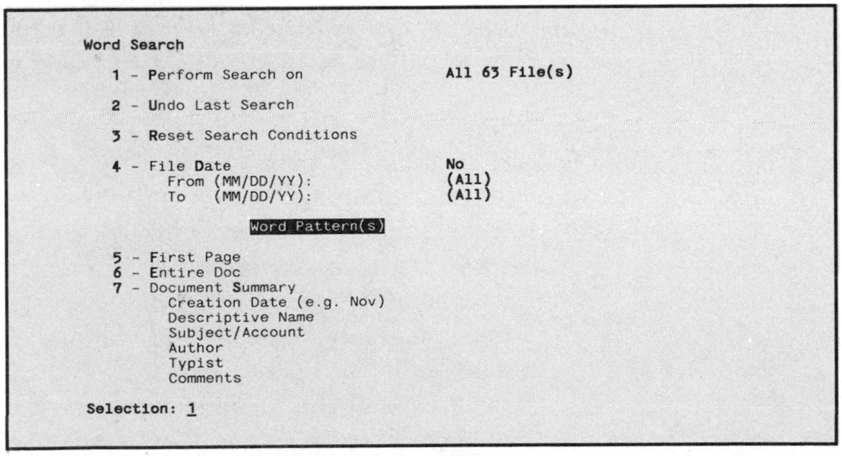

```
Word Search

    1 - Perform Search on            All 63 File(s)

    2 - Undo Last Search

    3 - Reset Search Conditions

    4 - File Date                     No
        From (MM/DD/YY):              (All)
        To   (MM/DD/YY):              (All)
                        Word Pattern(s)

    5 - First Page
    6 - Entire Doc
    7 - Document Summary
        Creation Date (e.g. Nov)
        Descriptive Name
        Subject/Account
        Author
        Typist
        Comments

    Selection: 1
```

*Figure 15.5:* The Word Search Conditions menu

This returns the cursor to the bottom of the screen, next to *Selection*. Notice that the default is option 1, *Perform Search on*. This means that if you press ←⎯, the search will begin. If you entered a word pattern, WordPerfect will find and mark all those documents that have file dates between the dates specified, and that contain the word pattern you entered. If you want to search for all files saved between a certain range of dates, do not include a word pattern next to option 5, 6, or 7.

When searching by file dates, you don't have to specify the complete date. For example, to search for documents with file dates between February 1 and March 31, 1989, you would enter *2//89* as the *From* date and *4//89* as the *To* date. To restrict the search to years only, you enter the last two digits of the year preceded by two slashes. For instance, to locate all documents saved in 1989 and 1990 (between January 1, 1989, and December 31, 1990), enter *//89* as the *From* date and *//91* as the *To* date.

After WordPerfect performs a word search, the statistic next to the *Perform Search on* option is updated to indicate the number of marked files that contain the search string and/or date specified, and you can see it by pressing *9* or *W*, then *4*. If you want to perform another word search using a new search string, use the Undo Last Search option (2 or U) to change the files that will be searched back to the ones you had selected before performing this search. For example, if you had selected all files, the prompt *Perform Search on* will change to reflect this.

To reset all search conditions, erasing any search strings next to options 4 through 7 (File Date, First Page, Entire Doc, Document Summary), select the Reset Search Conditions option by pressing *3* or *R* on the Word Search menu. After you do, you can enter another word pattern or range of file dates, and perform a different search.

## DOCUMENT SUMMARY

You can use the Document Summary feature in WordPerfect to create a brief description of a file, including information about the subject, author, or typist, and comments that you can use to describe its contents or special formatting characteristics. As part of the document summary, WordPerfect automatically includes the name and date of the document's creation. You can create a document summary anytime the document is on the Edit screen, even after the file has been saved.

One important reason to create document summaries is to view them with the Look option on the List Files menu (F5) so that you can get a quick overview of the file's content. When you use Look to view your file, the summary is always visible at the top, as shown in Figure 15.6. You can also perform a Word Search on any part of the information contained in the document summary, as explained in the previous section.

Consistent and logical use of this feature can be invaluable in keeping track of your files, particularly if you use a hard disk. In fact, I recommend that you use WordPerfect's Setup key (Shift-F1) to make it mandatory, so that the Document Summary screen will appear automatically the first time you save the file. The advantages to doing this include the fact that you'll never forget to make a document summary for your file, and that the *Date of Creation* message shown on the Document Summary screen will always match the original creation date of your file, not the date you decided to add a summary.

To make the Document Summary screen mandatory, press the Setup key (Shift-F1), select Initial Settings (*5* or *I*), select Document Summary (*3* or *S*), then select *Create on Save/Exit* (1). Type *Y* to answer Yes, then press the Exit key (F7) to return to your document. From then on, whenever you save a document, the Document Summary screen will appear as soon as you press one of the keys that saves text (F7 or F10). If you don't want to create a summary, just press Cancel (F1) when the Document Summary screen appears.

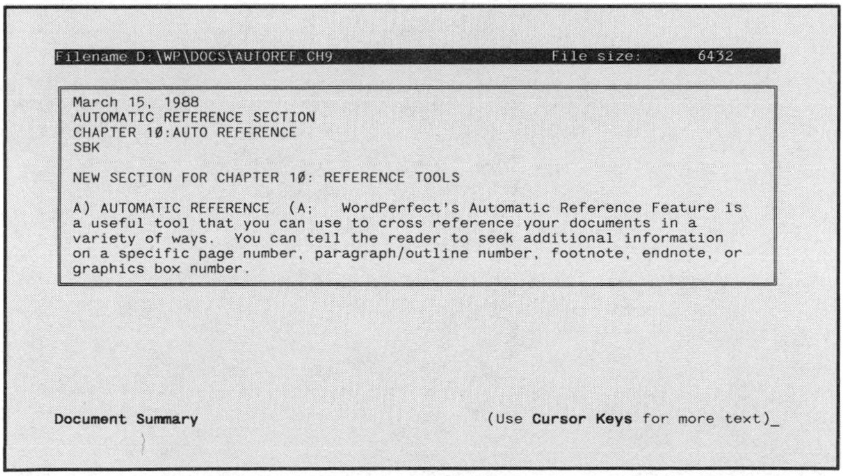

*Figure 15.6:* The document summary viewed with the Look option on the List Files key

If you have not used the Setup key to make the document summary mandatory, you can still create a document summary by pressing the Format key (Shift-F8) and selecting Document (*3* or *D*), then Summary (*4* or *S*). The Document Summary screen shown in Figure 15.7 will then appear and you can fill it out. You can also use this option to edit the summary after it has been created.

You can use the Descriptive Filename option from the Document Summary screen to assign a longer file name to the document, with a maximum of 40 characters (DOS limits system file names to 11 characters). If you have not yet assigned a name to your document (by saving it), you will see this prompt next to *System Filename* at the top of the screen:

**(Not named yet)**

If this is this case and you enter a descriptive file name using option 1, the first 11 characters you type there will become the system file name (the first eight are assigned to the file name and the next three to the file name extension). Later, when you save the document by pressing F7 or F10, the system file name from the Document Summary screen will automatically be supplied as the suggested name for your document. You can either press ◄─┘ to accept it, or type a different one.

Use the Subject/Account option on the Document Summary screen to describe the document's subject or account. This will be filled in automatically if your document includes the word *RE:* within

```
Document Summary

        System Filename            (Not named yet)

        Date of Creation           April 12, 1988

   1 -  Descriptive Filename

   2 -  Subject/Account

   3 -  Author

   4 -  Typist

   5 -  Comments



Selection: 0
```

*Figure 15.7:* Creating a document summary

the first 400 characters. *RE:* is called the *subject search text,* a term that refers to the character(s) that WordPerfect uses to automatically find the subject and enter it on this screen (next to *Subject/Account*). Since *RE:* is commonly used in business letters and memos, it is the default. You can change or erase the subject search text through the Setup key. To do this, press Setup (Shift-F1), press *5* or *I* to choose Initial Settings, press *3* or *S* to choose Document Summary, then press *2* or *S* to choose Subject Search Text. Next, either type in the new subject search text (up to 19 characters) or press Ctrl-End to erase the old one and leave it blank. Press ⏎ when you finish, then Exit (F7) to return to Edit mode.

Use options 3 and 4 to enter the initials or names of the author and typist of the document. Option 5, Comments, allows you to enter comments describing the document, with a maximum of 780 characters. Notice that the first 400 characters of the text of your document are automatically inserted in this area for you. When you select option 5, the cursor moves to the first character in the Comments box and you can type other comments that won't be printed as part of the document. Unless you are using Typeover mode, your new comments will push the other comments aside as you type. The comments you enter here will not become a part of your document. Instead, they will only be visible when you view the document summary using Shift-F8 D S or using the Look option on the List Files menu.

## BLOCK FILE COMMANDS

You can use two file commands when working with WordPerfect's Block feature—Save (F10) and the Append option on the Block menu.

### SAVE

In Chapter 5 you learned how to save a copy of a block of text as a separate file on disk. To review briefly, you use the Block key (Alt-F4) and cursor movement keys to mark the text, press the Save key (F10), then type a name for the new file in response to the prompt

**Block name:**

After you press ⏎, WordPerfect saves the block of text as a new file. If you want the block saved to a disk in a drive or directory other than the current one, be sure to add the drive letter and/or path name as part of the file name.

## *APPEND*

Instead of saving a block of text in a new file, you can use the Append feature to add it to the end of an existing disk file. To do this, highlight the text with the Block key (Alt-F4), press the Move key (Ctrl-F4), select the Block option by pressing *1* or *B*, then select the Append option by pressing *4* or *A*. You will see this prompt:

**Append to:**

Type the name of the file to which you wish to add the block. The block will still be highlighted as it's being saved, but it will disappear once the block has been appended.

# *THE TEXT IN/OUT KEY*

WordPerfect's Text In/Out key (Ctrl-F5) is very versatile. You can use it to import and export ASCII files, to save a document in the WordPerfect version 4.2 format, to add password protection to a file so that unauthorized users cannot read, print, or edit it, or to create or edit a document comment.

## *CONVERTING A WORDPERFECT FILE TO ASCII*

Option 1, DOS Text, can be used to create a DOS text file from a WordPerfect document, or to retrieve a DOS text file so that you can edit and print it in WordPerfect. You create a DOS text file so that it can be read by other programs. This action removes all the formatting codes that appear on the Reveal Codes screen, such as line spacing, margin settings, and headers and footers, and also replaces all Soft Return codes (found at the end of each line within a paragraph if word wrap was used) with hard returns.

When you press the Text In/Out key (Ctrl-F5) and type *1* or *T* to select the DOS Text option, the following menu appears:

**1 Save; 2 Retrieve (CR/LF to [HRt]); 3 Retrieve (CR/LF to [Srt] in HZone): 0**

Option 1, Save, is used to save a file as a DOS text file (in ASCII). When you select the Save option from this menu, you'll see this prompt asking for the name you want to assign to the DOS text version:

Document to be saved (DOS Text):

If the document on your editing screen has already been named (using the Save Text or Exit key), its name will automatically be supplied next to the prompt. If you want to retain a WordPerfect version of the document you are about to convert to ASCII, you must change the file name before proceeding. I usually assign the extension .*TXT* to my DOS text files so that I can easily distinguish between Word-Perfect files and DOS text files on the List Files screen. If you add such a file name extension, you need not modify the rest of the file name, just edit it to add .*TXT* to the end. Of course, you could completely rename the ASCII version of the document, if you prefer.

If you don't change the file name, the program assumes you want to replace the WordPerfect version of the file with the ASCII version you are about to create. When you press ←⏎, you will be asked to confirm that you do want to replace the WordPerfect version of the file with an ASCII version (this prompt won't appear if a new name is used). Press *Y* and the conversion will then take place. While this is happening, a message will indicate that it is being saved. A word of warning: Do not try to retrieve an ASCII (DOS text) file back into WordPerfect unless you use the Retrieve option from the DOS Text option on the Text In/Out key, as described below in the section called "Retrieving ASCII Files into WordPerfect."

## *CREATING A DOS BATCH FILE TO START WORDPERFECT*

If you are using WordPerfect on a computer with a hard disk drive and you don't have the WordPerfect Library or a DOS menu system from which you can start WordPerfect, you have to start WordPerfect by using the DOS command CD (Change Directory) to make the WordPerfect directory current, then typing *WP* (the WordPerfect startup command). To facilitate this procedure, you may want to create a DOS batch file that executes these commands for you. To do this, you can create the file in WordPerfect and then save it as a DOS text file.

Here are the steps for creating this batch file:

1. First, make sure that the Edit screen is clear. Use the Exit key (F7) to clear it if necessary.

On the first line of the document, you will enter the CD command with the path to your WordPerfect directory. To do this, you must know the name of the directory that contains the WordPerfect program files, which is usually WP or WP5. However, if your computer still has WordPerfect 4.2 on it, this directory may be called WP5.

2. With your cursor at the beginning of the first line, type

   **CD\WP**

   and press ← (be sure to add the name of *your* directory after *CD\* if it is not *WP*). When you use the batch file, this command will switch you to the WordPerfect directory.

3. Type

   **WP**

   and press ←. This command will start WordPerfect when you use the batch file.

4. Next, type

   **CD\**

   and press ←. In the batch file, this command will take you back to the root directory of your hard disk after you exit WordPerfect. Now you're ready to save the file.

5. Press the Text In/Out key (Ctrl-F5) and select the DOS Text option by typing **1** or **T,** then pressing **1** or **S** to select Save.

6. In response to the *Document to be saved* prompt, enter the file name

   **C:\WP.BAT**

   and press ←. Note that the file name must include the *.BAT* extension (which means *batch file*) in order to work properly.

   If you already have a WP.BAT file in the root directory of your hard disk, WordPerfect will ask you if you want to replace the disk file with this version. To be safe, answer No by typing **N** or pressing ◄┘, then type a different name with the .BAT extension (such as C:\WP5.BAT).

To try out your new batch file, you need to exit WordPerfect and get the DOS prompt back.

7. Press the Exit key (F7). WordPerfect will ask if you want to save the file. (Note that this file has never been saved as a WordPerfect file, only as a DOS text file, but you don't need a WordPerfect version of the batch file since it can only be executed as a DOS text file.) Answer **N** to the save prompt and **Y** to the *Exit WP* prompt that follows it.

8. At the DOS prompt, type

    **CD\**

    and press ◄┘. This takes you to the root directory that now contains your WordPerfect batch file. This is the directory you will be in when you first turn on your computer.

9. Now test out your batch file by typing

    **WP**

    (or *WP5* if you named your file WP5.BAT) and pressing ◄┘. In a few moments, you will see the WordPerfect startup screen and then be back in the WordPerfect editing screen. When you exit, the batch file will switch you back to the root directory.

Notice that you didn't have to type the entire batch file name (including the .BAT extension) to use the WP batch file that runs the DOS commands to start WordPerfect. From now on, when you start your computer and want to run WordPerfect, you only have to type *WP* from the DOS prompt (*C>*) and the batch file will do the rest.

## RETRIEVING ASCII FILES INTO WORDPERFECT

You can use the Text In/Out key to retrieve a file from other programs that create ASCII files (or that can convert their files to ASCII) or to retrieve and revise files like the batch file outlined above. To retrieve a DOS text (ASCII) file into WordPerfect, you press Ctrl-F5 and select option 1, DOS Text. When you do, the following menu appears:

**1 Save; 2 Retrieve (CR/LF to [HRt]); 3 Retrieve (CR/LF to [Srt] in HZone): 0**

You can use option 2 or option 3 to retrieve an ASCII file into Word-Perfect. The difference between them is that option 3 converts the hard returns at the end of each line into soft returns within paragraphs, so that you can use word wrap and insert and delete text as usual; option 2 leaves hard returns at the end of each line. The *CR/LF* refers to ASCII codes that the DOS text file contains. *CR* stands for a carriage return character and *LF* stands for a line feed character; these move the cursor to the beginning of the next line (when you press ←⏎, the hard return you create incorporates both these codes). As you can see from the descriptions of options 2 and 3, WordPerfect can convert these codes to either hard returns ([HRt]) or soft returns ([SRt]) when you retrieve a DOS text file into WordPerfect.

If you intend to save the DOS text file as a WordPerfect document file and want to be able to edit the text file as you would any other WordPerfect document, use option 3 to convert the CR/LF codes to soft returns when they fall within the Hyphenation zone. If these codes occur outside of the Hyphenation zone, WordPerfect will eliminate them during the conversion.

Option 2 on the DOS Text menu of the Text In/Out key, *Retrieve (CR/LF to [HRt])*, is the same as option 5, Text In, on the List Files key (F5).

If you are retrieving the DOS text file to edit it and intend to save it afterward as a DOS text file (using option 1 on this menu), you will want to use option 2 so that all of the CR/LF codes are converted into hard returns. This is the option you would use if you needed to make editing changes to the WP.BAT file outlined above. After making your changes, you would then save the batch file as a DOS text file using option 1, Save.

## *PASSWORD PROTECTION*

The Password option (2 or P) on the Text In/Out key lets you save a file with a password so that nobody else can use it. Once you do this, you will never be able to retrieve it again or even use the Look option on the List Files key to view its contents unless you remember the password, so be very careful with this option. The easiest way to remember your password is to be consistent; if you always use the same one, chances are you'll never forget it. Otherwise, I strongly recommend that you keep a written record of the passwords you have used for each document. There's nothing worse than losing an important document because you can't remember a password you created six months ago.

To protect a document, press Ctrl-F5, then select the Password option by typing *2* or *P*. The following menu will appear:

**Password: 1 Add/Change; 2 Remove: 0**

Select the Add option by typing *1* or *A*. You will then see this prompt:

**Enter Password:**

Enter a password containing as many as 25 characters. For extra security, the password is not visible on the screen as you type it. When you press ◄—, WordPerfect prompts you to enter the password a second time with this prompt:

**Re-Enter Password:**

At this point, you must enter the password *exactly* as you did the first time. Again, you will not be able to see the characters as you type them on the screen. If you alter the password in any way you will receive this message:

**ERROR: Incorrect Password**

WordPerfect will then return you to the first password prompt and you will have to start the process all over again.

After typing the password the same way twice, you must use the Save Text key (F10) or the Exit key (F7) to save the document and lock it with the password you just assigned. Thereafter, to retrieve the locked file (either with the Retrieve Text key or with the Retrieve option on the List Files key), you will have to type the password exactly the same way you typed it originally. When you press the Retrieve Text key (Shift-F10) or List Files key (F5) to retrieve a password-protected file, this prompt appears: *Enter Password* followed by the file name. If you can't reproduce the password correctly when the *Enter Password* prompt appears, WordPerfect will not retrieve the document and you will see this message: *Error: File is locked*. Also, if you forget the password you won't be able to print the document using any of the methods that print from disk, including the Document on Disk option on the Print key (Shift-F7) and the Print option on the List Files key (F5), and you won't be able to look at its contents using the Look option on the List Files key.

One important warning: Be sure to have a completely clear screen before you retrieve a file that has a password. If you retrieve a file to a screen that is not clear, then edit and save it again under the same name, it will no longer have the password protection.

To remove password protection from a file, retrieve the document in the usual way using the password, press the Text In/Out key (Ctrl-F5), select the password option by typing *2* or *P*, then select option 2, Remove, on the Password menu by typing *2* or *R*. Next, use F7 or F10 to save your document, and it will be saved without the password. The next time you retrieve it, you will not see the Enter Password prompt.

## SAVING A DOCUMENT IN A GENERIC WORD PROCESSOR FORMAT

Option 3 on the Text In/Out menu allows you to save your document in a generic word processing format that can be used with other text editors and word processing programs. The converted file is saved without any of WordPerfect's special formatting codes such as [Tab] and [CNTR]. However, the basic look of the document is maintained during the conversion. Hard returns marking the end of paragraphs are replaced by CR/LF codes. Soft returns, centering, indenting, and flush right are replaced by spaces. Tabs in the document are replaced by the ASCII tab character code.

Use this option only when you want to export a WordPerfect document to a word processor or text editor whose format is not supported by the Convert utility. To retain a copy of the file in the WordPerfect format, enter a different name when you use this method to save the file so that the original remains intact.

## DOCUMENT COMMENTS

Document comments are nonprinting comments that you can create anywhere in the document. When the on-screen display of comments is on, they appear on the screen where you create them, surrounded by a box. To create a comment at the cursor position, press the Text In/Out key (Ctrl-F5) and select the Comment option by typing *5* or *C*. When you do, the following menu options appear:

**Comment: 1 Create; 2 Edit; 3 Convert to Text: 0**

Select the Create option by pressing *1* or *C*, and the screen shown in Figure 15.8 will appear. Type the text of your comment in the box, then press the Exit key (F7). You can type a maximum of 1,024 characters. As you type, you can use boldface or underline to enhance your text, but since the Block key (Alt-F4) doesn't work in the comment box, you can't add these enhancements after you've entered the text.

If the Display Comments feature is set to Yes (as described below) and you create the comment in the middle of a line of text, the comment appears to split the text, as shown in Figure 15.9. In reality, the text starts again immediately after the comment, so check the status line to determine the actual position of the text. If your cursor is at the end of the line, press → to jump over the box to the next word.

***DISPLAYING COMMENTS*** WordPerfect displays comments on the Edit screen by default, but you can turn off the display through

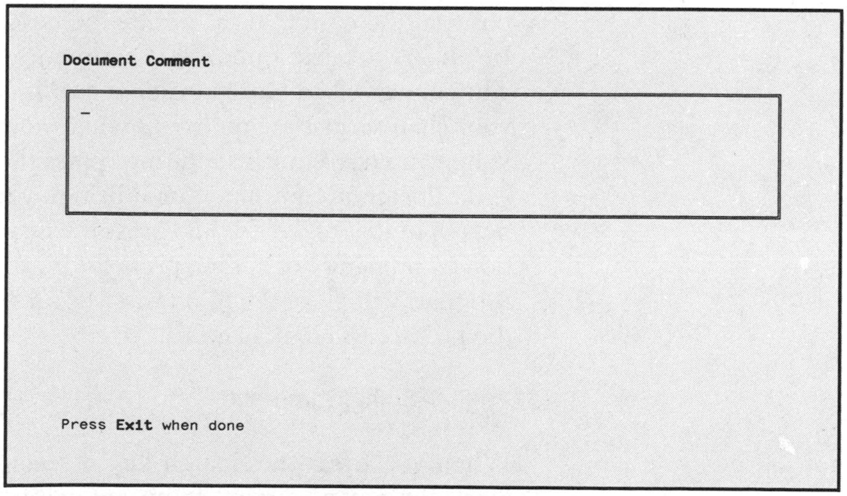

*Figure 15.8:* The Document Comment screen

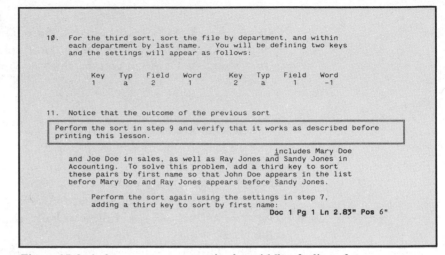

```
1Ø.  For the third sort, sort the file by department, and within
     each department by last name.  You will be defining two keys
     and the settings will appear as follows:


          Key  Typ  Field  Word      Key  Typ  Field  Word
           1    a     2      1         2    a     1     -1


11.  Notice that the outcome of the previous sort
     ┌────────────────────────────────────────────────────────────┐
     │ Perform the sort in step 9 and verify that it works as described before │
     │ printing this lesson.                                        │
     └────────────────────────────────────────────────────────────┘
                                            includes Mary Doe
     and Joe Doe in sales, as well as Ray Jones and Sandy Jones in
     Accounting.  To solve this problem, add a third key to sort
     these pairs by first name so that John Doe appears in the list
     before Mary Doe and Ray Jones appears before Sandy Jones.

          Perform the sort again using the settings in step 7,
          adding a third key to sort by first name:
                                      Doc 1 Pg 1 Ln 2.83" Pos 6"
```

*Figure 15.9:* A document comment in the middle of a line of text

the Setup key. To do this, press Shift-F1, select Display by pressing *3* or *D*, then select Display Document Comments by pressing *3* or *D* and change the answer to No by pressing *N*. The Comments display stays off permanently and you can only see Comments again by going back to the Setup key and selecting Yes for the Display Document Comments option.

***EDITING COMMENTS*** To modify the text of a comment, position the cursor right under the comment box, press the Text In/Out key, select option 5, Comment, then select option 2, Edit. The cursor will be placed inside the comment box and you can make your changes just as you would when editing regular document text. When you have finished editing, press the Exit key (F7).

To locate a comment for editing, you can use WordPerfect's Search function. To do this, press the Search key (F2), select a direction by pressing ↑ or ↓, then press the Text In/Out key (Ctrl-F5). The program will place the [Comment] code into your search string and the prompt will look like this:

->Srch: [Comment]

When you press the Search key a second time, WordPerfect will locate the next document comment in the direction of the search, and the cursor stops right after it. You can then proceed to edit the comment by pressing the Text In/Out key (Ctrl-F5), pressing *5* or *C* for Comment, then *2* or *E* for Edit.

To delete a comment, use Search as described above to position the cursor right after its code, then press Backspace. You will receive the message

>Delete [Comment]? Y/N No

To proceed with the deletion, type *Y* to answer Yes.

***CONVERTING COMMENTS INTO TEXT***   Comments are never seen in the printed document, regardless of whether they are displayed or not. However, if you want to print them, you can convert them into text so that they become part of the actual document. To do this, position the cursor somewhere *after* the comment you want to convert. Press the Text In/Out key (Ctrl-F5), select the Comment option by pressing *5* or *C* , then choose the Convert to Text option by pressing *3* or *T*. The text of the first comment that is located above the cursor will be converted to document text whether Comment Display is turned on or off.

***CONVERTING TEXT TO A DOCUMENT COMMENT***   You can convert a block of text into a document comment by highlighting it with the Block (Alt-F4) and cursor movement keys, then pressing the Text In/Out key (Ctrl-F5). You will see this prompt:

>Create a comment? (Y/N) No

Press *Y* and the text will be converted, and you'll see it in a box above the cursor (if you have the Display Document Comments option on the Setup key set to Yes).

## *EXCHANGING DOCUMENTS BETWEEN WORDPERFECT 4.2 AND WORDPERFECT 5.0*

Before you can retrieve a document created with WordPerfect 5.0 into WordPerfect 4.2, you must convert it into 4.2 format. To do this, be sure you have the document on your Edit screen, then select the *Save WP 4.2* option on the Text In/Out menu by pressing Ctrl-F5 and typing *4* or *W*, then type the file name and press ◀─┘ in response to the *Document to be saved* prompt.

WordPerfect 5.0 automatically converts 4.2 documents to the new format when you use the regular methods to retrieve them (either the Retrieve Text key, Shift-F10, or the List Files key, F5 1), so you don't have to perform any special conversion. When you use Retrieve Text or List Files to retrieve a 4.2 file, you will see the message *Document conversion in progress* as WordPerfect 5.0 converts it.

## TEMPORARILY EXITING TO DOS: THE SHELL KEY

If your computer contains enough memory, you can use the Shell key to exit to DOS in order to run commands such as FORMAT, DISKCOPY, or DISKCOMP (if you have them on your disk), or to load and run another program. To use this feature, press the Shell key (Ctrl-F1) and select the *Go to DOS* option by typing *1* or *G*. You will see a screen like the one illustrated in Figure 15.10, which shows the DOS logo and version number and tells you to enter EXIT when you're ready to return to WordPerfect.

```
Microsoft(R) MS-DOS(R)  Version 3.30
          (C)Copyright Microsoft Corp 1981-1987

Enter 'EXIT' to return to WordPerfect
D>_
```

*Figure 15.10:* The *Go to DOS* screen

Since you have a DOS prompt (C> or B>), you can then use DOS commands or run another program if you have enough RAM.

If you are running WordPerfect under the control of the WordPerfect Library when you press Ctrl-F1, you will see different menu options:

**1 Go** to Shell; **2 Retrieve Clipboard: 0**

Select option 1 to return to the Library's shell, then press 1 to select *Go to DOS*. The screen will be slightly different from Figure 15.10, but you'll still have a DOS prompt.

When you are ready to return to WordPerfect, just type the letters *exit* (don't press the Exit key—F7!) and press ◄┘. If you are using the Shell key, press ◄┘ again to get back to WordPerfect. The *Enter 'EXIT'* prompt shown in Figure 15.6 will always reappear on the screen after you have run another program or DOS command, such as *DIR*, but if you forget and try to return by typing *WP,* you will receive this error message indicating that the program is too large to fit in memory:

**Program too big to fit in memory**

You should never turn off the computer until you have returned to WordPerfect by typing *exit*, and have pressed F7 to exit from WordPerfect and close all files.

## WORKING WITH TWO DOCUMENTS IN RAM

WordPerfect provides two methods of maintaining separate documents in your computer's memory, the Switch feature and the Window feature. The main difference is that Switch provides two full editing screens to work with, whereas Window splits a single editing screen into two smaller ones.

To use the first feature, press the Switch key (Shift-F3). The document indicator on the status line will change from Doc 1 to Doc 2, and you will have a new Edit screen to work on. You can then retrieve a file from the disk, create a new file, or use the Move or Block and Move keys to transfer data between the two documents in memory. Press the Switch key (Shift-F3) to move back and forth between the documents. I use this feature constantly to test program features without ruining my manuscript by forgetting to remove formatting codes.

To use the Window feature, press the Screen key (Ctrl-F3) and select the Window option by pressing *1* or *W*. You will then see a prompt asking how many lines you want in this window. The screen has 24 lines available, so if you want to split it exactly in half, type *12* ←┘. Alternatively, you can select the number of lines by pressing the ↑ or ↓ key. As soon as you press one of the arrow keys, you will see the Tab Ruler, which you are familiar with from the Reveal Codes screen. Keep pressing ↑ or ↓ until the Tab Ruler reaches the location where you want to split the screen, then press ←┘. If you were working on a document in the Doc 1 area, it will appear in the top window and you will see the Tab Ruler between the windows.

To move the cursor to the second window, press the Switch key (Shift-F3). Notice how the tab marks on the ruler line change direction when you do this, pointing downward to indicate that you are working in the lower window. You will also see two separate status lines, one at the bottom of the screen and one just above the Tab Ruler. Notice that the document number indicators (Doc *n*) are different. You can now retrieve another file into the second window by using the Retrieve key (Shift-F10), or option 1 on the List Files key (F5), or use the screen to create a new document. Figure 15.11 shows a screen split in half, with different documents on each half.

To return to a single screen, select the Window option again (by pressing Ctrl-F3 1 or W) and enter *25* or any number that exceeds the total number of lines on your screen (*0* also works), or press ↑ or ↓ until the Tab Ruler disappears, then press ←┘. If you do this from the lower window, you will find yourself in document 2, and will have to press the Switch key (Shift-F3) again to return to the first document.

If you like having the Tab Ruler on your screen, you can use the Window option to place it there permanently. To position the ruler at the top of the screen, start with blank edit screens in both Doc 1 and Doc 2 and place the cursor in Doc 1. Press Ctrl-F3 W to select the Window option and enter *2* as the number of lines you want to keep in the window. Next, use the Switch key to move to the lower window, and use that window as the editing screen. To place the ruler at the bottom, enter *22* in response to the *Number of lines in this window* prompt.

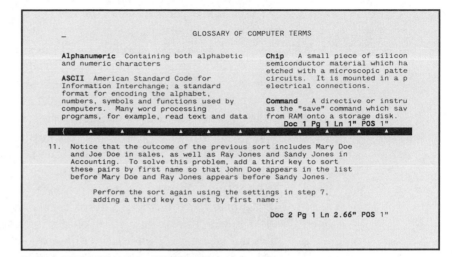

```
                        GLOSSARY OF COMPUTER TERMS

  Alphanumeric   Containing both alphabetic        Chip   A small piece of silicon
  and numeric characters                           semiconductor material which ha
                                                   etched with a microscopic patte
  ASCII   American Standard Code for               circuits.  It is mounted in a p
  Information Interchange; a standard              electrical connections.
  format for encoding the alphabet,
  numbers, symbols and functions used by           Command   A directive or instru
  computers.  Many word processing                 as the "save" command which sav
  programs, for example, read text and data        from RAM onto a storage disk.
                                                 Doc 1 Pg 1 Ln 1" POS 1"
```

```
  11.   Notice that the outcome of the previous sort includes Mary Doe
        and Joe Doe in sales, as well as Ray Jones and Sandy Jones in
        Accounting.  To solve this problem, add a third key to sort
        these pairs by first name so that John Doe appears in the list
        before Mary Doe and Ray Jones appears before Sandy Jones.

            Perform the sort again using the settings in step 7,
            adding a third key to sort by first name:

                                                 Doc 2 Pg 1 Ln 2.66" POS 1"
```

*Figure 15.11:* Using the Window feature

# MAKING AUTOMATIC BACKUPS

WordPerfect has two methods of making automatic backups, the Timed Backup feature and the Original Backup feature. The Timed Backup feature enables you to recover data that might otherwise be lost due to a power failure, computer failure, or any other problem that forces you to leave WordPerfect without saving your work. The other method makes an extra copy of the disk version of the file before it is replaced by saving an edited version, and this copy is permanent.

When you use the Timed Backup feature, you specify how often you want a backup copy of the file on your editing screen saved, and the program interrupts and saves the file at these intervals under the name WP {WP}.BK1, or WP{WP}.BK2. (If you are working with two document screens, it will only save the one currently on your screen.) When you leave WordPerfect via the Exit key (F7), these backup files are closed and erased. However, if there is a power failure or you shut off the computer while WordPerfect is still running, the files will remain on disk and you can use them by renaming and then retrieving them. If you start WordPerfect without either renaming or deleting them (and continue to use the Timed Backup feature), you will see this message when the program tries to make a new backup copy:

Old backup file exists: 1 Rename; 2 Delete

At that point, you can select option 2 to delete the old backup file or option 1 to rename it.

The Original Backup feature creates a permanent copy on the default disk using the same name but changing the three-character extension to BK!. As you know, when you retrieve a file for editing, you are actually using a copy of it, and after you have made editing changes and saved the document, the copy on screen replaces the version on the disk. If Original Backup is being used, the original (disk) version will be saved in a separate file with the same name but a different extension (.BK!), instead of being erased by the copy on the Edit screen. However, if you choose to save the extra copy on the same disk, you still should make extra backup copies on separate disks in case of disk failure. If you are in the habit of saving different files under the same name with different extensions, such as *sample.1, sample.2,* and *sample.3,* this procedure will only make a backup of the most recently edited document, naming it *sample.bk!*. To retrieve one of these files, you must rename it first, using characters other than BK! for the extension.

To implement either or both of these features, press the Setup key (Shift-F1) and select the Backup option by pressing *1* or *B*. You will see the screen illustrated in Figure 15.12.

```
Setup: Backup

        Timed backup files are deleted when you exit WP normally.  If you
        have a power or machine failure, you will find the backup file in the
        backup directory indicated in Setup: Location of Auxiliary Files.

        Backup Directory

    1 - Timed Document Backup                    No
        Minutes Between Backups                  30

        Original backup will save the original document with a .BK! extension
        whenever you replace it during a Save or Exit.

    2 - Original Document Backup                 No




Selection: 0
```

*Figure 15.12:* Setting the Backup options

Select Timed Document Backup by typing *1* or *T.* Type *Y* to turn on the automatic timed backup (*No* is the default when you install WordPerfect). Next, enter the number of minutes between backups and press ←⏎.

To use Original Document Backup, type *2* or *O,* then type *Y* to change the setting to Yes. Next, press the Exit key (F7) to return to the editing screen. Once you select these options, they will always be loaded when you start the program unless you press the Setup key and choose Backup to change them again. You can change the location of the backup files that are created by the Timed Backup option so that WordPerfect saves them in a different disk or directory by using the Location of Auxiliary Files option on the Setup key. To do this, press Shift-F1, *7* or *L, 1* or *B,* then type the drive or directory.

## *SUMMARY*

As you have seen, WordPerfect's file management features are comprehensive and powerful, and the program provides much more than the typical DOS-based commands such as COPY, DEL, and RENAME. Furthermore, they are menu-driven and are easier to use than the equivalent DOS commands. Several helpful features accommodate users with hard disks, including commands that allow you to change default directories, search other directories for files to work with, create a new directory, or delete an empty directory. Other interesting features you have explored in this chapter include Word Search, which can search all files for a word or phrase; the Text In/Out key, which can convert files to and from ASCII and lock and save documents with a password; the Shell key, which you can use to temporarily exit to DOS and run another program; and the Window feature, which can split the screen in two so that you can view two documents at once.

# 16.

## CREATING FORM LETTERS, MAILING LABELS, AND LISTS WITH THE MERGE FEATURE

# FAST TRACK

**Create a form letter using WordPerfect's Merge feature**      **518**

to combine a primary and secondary file. Type the letter, using the Merge Codes key (Shift-F9) to insert the field codes (such as F1, F2, etc.) that represent variable data (such as name, address, and salutation). Place the codes at each place in the letter where this data is to be substituted. Store this letter as a primary file by assigning a name with the extension *pf*, then clear the screen (F7). Create the secondary file by typing a list of all the actual variable data, separating the fields with an ^R code by pressing F9. Separate each record with an ^E code (press Shift-F9 E). Save this file as a secondary file, naming it with the extension *sf*. Next, merge the two files to create your form letters (Ctrl-F9-1).

**Merge a primary and secondary file**      **523**

by clearing the screen (F7) and pressing the Merge/Sort key (Ctrl-F9). At the prompt, select the Merge option. At the *Primary file:* prompt, enter the name of your primary file and press ←, then at the *Secondary file:* prompt, enter the name of your secondary file and press ←. The merge process then begins, and when it is complete you will see one or more letters that result from the merged primary and secondary files.

**To produce mailing labels and envelopes from a secondary file,**      **530**

use the Format key to select the correct paper size and paper type (Shift-F8 P 8), then use option 5 on the same menu to adjust the top and bottom margins. Next, use the Merge Codes key (Shift-F9) to create a new primary file that contains only the fields that represent data to be printed on the labels or envelopes, such as name and address. Press Exit to save the new primary file, using the *pf* extension. Begin merging this file with your secondary file by clearing the screen, pressing Ctrl-F9, selecting Merge, and entering the names of your new primary file and your secondary file. The merge begins, and WordPerfect inserts a page break after each label or envelope.

**Merge a primary and secondary file directly to the printer**  525
(in case you don't have enough memory in your computer) by creating a primary file with the following codes at the bottom: ^T ^N ^P ^P. To do this, press the Merge Codes key (Shift-F9) and type the letter *T*, then press it again and type *N*, press it again and type *P*, then press it again and type *P*. Save the revised file under a different name, using the *pf* extension. Merge the new file and your original secondary file by first clearing the screen (F7), then pressing Ctrl-F9 1. Enter the names of your new primary file and secondary file. The merged document will be sent directly to the printer; you will not see it on the screen.

**Merge data from a primary file with data from the keyboard**  526
(bypassing the creation of a secondary file), by creating a primary file in which variable data (such as name and address) is represented by ^C codes. To insert the ^C codes, press Shift-F9 C. Save the file under a new name, using the *pf* extension, and clear the screen (F7). Begin the merge by pressing Ctrl-F9 1. At the prompt, enter the name of the new primary file and press ◄—┘ twice to leave the secondary file name blank when asked for the name of the secondary file. The merge will begin, and the cursor will stop at the first ^ C code. Type in the variable information at that point, then press F9 to resume the merge. Repeat this process until you have entered all the variable information at each ^C code.

WORDPERFECT'S MERGE FEATURE IS POWERFUL AND versatile, with 14 merge commands that you can combine to generate form letters, reports, lists, mailing labels, contracts, and much more. The easiest and most common application is to create form letters that appear to be personalized. You type the letter only once, inserting special codes in place of data that differs for each letter, such as the name, address, phone number, and salutation, and store this letter in a file called the *primary file*. The variable data (name, address, salutation) is typed in a list that is stored in a file called the *secondary file*. When they are combined in the merge operation, one letter is produced for each set of variable data.

If you don't need to save the variable data for future use, you have the option of typing it at the keyboard as each letter is assembled. You can insert messages in the letter to remind yourself what information is needed at each point. (The messages are only visible on screen when you merge; they won't be printed.) The letters can be produced on screen and saved in a file or sent directly to the printer. If you store your variable data in a secondary file, you can use it to produce other lists, such as a list of each name and phone number, or to produce mailing labels that exclude phone numbers, salutations, and other extraneous information. A secondary file can also be created using another program such as dBASE and imported to WordPerfect's merge format through the Convert program.

You can further automate the merge process by using WordPerfect's Sort, Select, and Macro features. In Chapter 18 you will learn, for example, how to use sorting to organize your mailing labels by ZIP code in order to take advantage of lower postal rates, and in Chapter 19 you will learn how to simplify your word processing by using macros with merges.

# CREATING FORM
# LETTERS WITH MERGE

Suppose the administrator of a national sweepstakes wants to send a letter informing all winners of their prizes and verifying their phone numbers. Rather than type each recipient's letter individually, he sets up a form letter with codes for the following variable data: the date, the recipient's name, address, and phone number, and the dollar amount of the prize he or she has won. He then merges it with a secondary file containing the specific data for each winner. Figure 16.1 shows the final letter for one of the million-dollar winners.

## CREATING THE PRIMARY FILE

The first step is to create the form letter, using merge codes that direct the program to insert variable data during the merge. Notice that the first variable is the date. Although you can use the Date key to insert a date function, there is also a merge code for this purpose. To enter it, use the Merge Codes key (Shift-F9).

```
April 15, 1989

Ms. Colleen McDuffy
54 Prince Lane
Salem, GA 32255


Dear Ms. Colleen McDuffy,

Congratulations!  You are a winner in the $20,000,000 National
Sweepstakes and are soon to be the recipient of a check for
$1,000,000, less the appropriate amount of tax required by the
Federal Government.  We will be contacting you soon to determine
this amount.

Our records show your phone number to be (513) 222-0000.  If this
has changed, please inform us immediately by calling this toll-free
number: (800) 445-0000.

Please keep this letter for your records.



Yours truly,



Irwin Kronsky

Sweepstakes Administrator
```

*Figure 16.1:* The sweepstakes letter

1.  Press the Merge Codes key (Shift-F9). The prompt line will list thirteen of the special merge codes, as shown below:

    **^ C; ^ D; ^ E; ^ F; ^ G; ^ N; ^ O; ^ P; ^ Q; ^ S; ^ T; ^ U; ^ V:**

    Most of these codes are mnemonic, and correspond to the first letter of a command. For instance, ^ U updates the screen, ^ N means next record, ^ F means field, and ^ D stands for date.

2.  To insert the Date code, type

    **D**

    and press ◄─┘. Notice that this inserts the code with a caret ( ^ ) in front of the letter.

The next step is to insert codes for the recipient's name and address. This information is divided into distinct parts called *fields* and the collection of all the fields for one recipient is called a *record.* There is no limit to the number of fields a record can contain, but they must be used consistently so that the fields designated by the same number in each record contain the same type of information. For example, in each record in our example file, field 6 must always contain the check amount. You will learn why later in this chapter.

In this letter there are seven fields per record: the name, street address, city, state, ZIP code, check amount, and phone number. Although several of these fields could have been combined into a single field, such as the street address, state, and ZIP code, it is advantageous to place data into separate fields. This way you can sort it by any of these categories, or use individual fields separately in a different merge operation.

The first field that appears in the letter is called *F1,* for field 1. The remaining fields are numbered sequentially in the order they appear. In your letter, field 1 will be the name; field 2 will be the street address; field 3 will be the city; field 4, the state; field 5, the ZIP code; field 6, the check amount; and field 7, the phone number.

To enter the first field:

3.  Press ◄─┘ three times to add two blank lines, then press the Merge Codes key (Shift-F9).

4. Type

F

You will see this prompt:

**Field:**

5. Next, type

1

and press ⏎ twice, once to enter the ^ F1 ^ and once to move to the next line for the address. The code will appear as

^ F1 ^

on your screen. (The carets are inserted for you by WordPerfect.)

6. Repeat this process for fields 2, 3, 4, and 5. Fields 3, 4, and 5 will be on the same line, so be sure to type a comma and enter a blank space after entering ^ F3 ^ in order to separate fields 3 and 4 (the city and state) and be sure to leave a blank space between fields 4 and 5 (the state and ZIP code).

Since fields 3, 4, and 5 appear on the same line, the only time you press ⏎ twice consecutively on this line is after entering field 5, ZIP code. (You press it just once after 3 and 4.)

7. Next, press ⏎ twice to add a few blank lines between the inside address and the saluation. Now type the salutation:

**Dear**

and enter the name field code, ^ F1 ^ , once again. (Be sure to insert a space after *Dear* and a comma after the field code.)

As you can see, a field number can be used more than once in the same primary file. In fact, there is no limit to the number of times it can be used.

When you have entered the first seven codes, your primary file will appear as follows:

^ D


^ F1 ^
^ F2 ^

^ F3 ^ , ^ F4 ^ ^ F5 ^

Dear ^ F1 ^ ,

8. Type the rest of the letter, inserting the codes for fields 6 (F6) and 7 (F7) in place of the check amount and phone number. It will appear as follows:

Congratulations! You are a winner in the $20,000,000 National Sweepstakes and are soon to be the recipient of a check for ^F6^, less the appropriate amount of tax required by the Federal Government. We will be contacting you soon to determine this amount.

Our records show your phone number to be ^F7^. If this has changed, please inform us immediately by calling this toll-free number: (800) 445-0000.

Please keep this letter for your records.

Yours truly,

Irwin Kronsky
Sweepstakes Administrator

9. Save the file under the name *letter1.pf* and clear the screen.

The extension PF stands for *primary file* (it serves to identify this as a primary merge file) and although it is a good habit to use such an extension, it is optional. That's all there is to creating a primary file. As you will see, this letter can be used over and over with different variable data to produce a limitless number of form letters.

## CREATING THE SECONDARY FILE

The next step is to create the secondary file, which consists of a record for each recipient, with each record containing seven fields of variable data separated by merge codes that mark the end of each field and the end of the record. For instance, the record for Colleen McDuffy, which was used to create the letter shown in Figure 16.1, appears as follows:

Ms. Colleen McDuffy ^ R
54 Prince Lane ^ R
Salem ^ R
GA ^ R
32255 ^ R
$1,000,000 ^ R
(513) 222-0000 ^ R
^ E

= = = = = = = = = = = = = = = = = = = = = = = = = = = = =

Note the ^ R and ^ E codes and hard page break (double line of dashes). The ^ R codes mean this is the end of a field and the ^ E code means this is the end of the record. After typing each field, you press the Merge Return key (F9), which inserts the ^ R code. Since this action also adds a hard return, do not press ◄─┘ at the end of each line. When you reach the end of a record (after typing the phone number, which is the last field in each letter), press the Merge Codes key (Shift-F9) and type *E*. This inserts the ^ E code and a hard page break, which marks the end of one form.

1. Begin your new secondary file by entering the record shown above. Be very careful not to add any spaces before the ^ R and ^ E codes as you enter this record, because the spaces will show up in the merged letter. Also, do not use the ◄─┘ key at all or you will insert extra lines into the merged letter. For example, if you were to press ◄─┘ after typing the state field, the ZIP code would appear on its own line instead of on the one with the city and state.

2. Next, enter the second record as follows:

   Mr. James Browder ^ R
   100 Main St. ^ R
   Mt. Hood ^ R
   WA ^ R
   81233 ^ R
   $10,000 ^ R

(802) 331-0000 ^ R
^ E

= = = = = = = = = = = = = = = = = = = = =

3. Finally, add a third record to your secondary file:

Mrs. Rhonda Flamestein ^ R
233 12th Ave. ^ R
San Francisco ^ R
CA ^ R
91212 ^ R
$50,000 ^ R
(415) 444-0000 ^ R
^ E

= = = = = = = = = = = = = = = = = = = = =

4. Save the file under the name *Winners.sf.* (SF stands for *second-ary file.* )

## MERGING THE PRIMARY AND SECONDARY FILES

The final step, merging the files and creating the three letters, is the easiest one.

1. Clear the screen with the Exit key (F7) and press the Merge/Sort key (Ctrl-F9). As you see, the prompt provides the following choices:

   **1 M**erge; **2 S**ort; **3** Sort Order: **0**

2. Select option 1, Merge, by typing either **1** or **M**.

3. The next prompt asks you for the name of the primary file, and you enter

   **LETTER1.PF**

   then press ◄┘.

4.  The last prompt asks you for the name of the secondary file; you enter

    **WINNERS.SF**

    press ← and the merge process begins. During the merge, this message will appear in the lower left corner:

    **\* Merging \***

When the merge is complete, you will have three letters on screen, separated by hard page breaks, and you will be looking at the last letter generated (the one to Mrs. Flamestein). Scroll up through the letters to verify that the correct data was entered in each field (use Page Up). You can then print the letters using the Print key (Shift-F7) or save them to disk to be printed later.

Notice the salutations (Dear Mrs. Rhonda Flamestein, etc.). You could have added a separate field for the salutation in the primary and secondary files so that it would have read *Dear Mrs. Flamestein* instead. If you'd like to try it, clear the screen, retrieve the secondary file *(winners.sf)*, and add a field 8 to the end of each record, above the ^ E code. The field should consist of the individual's title (such as Mr. or Ms.) and last name, followed by the merge R code ( ^ R). Next, save the file, clear the screen, and retrieve the primary file *(winners.pf)*. Erase the ^ F1 ^ code after the word *Dear* and replace it with this code: ^ F8 ^ . Use steps 1 through 4 to run the merge again, and the salutations will be correct.

## *STOPPING A MERGE*

A merge can be stopped anytime by pressing the Cancel key (F1). If you know in advance where you want to end a merge, you can include the merge code ^ Q (for *quit*) inside the secondary file. This is especially useful if you are using a secondary file with a large number of records, and don't need to print forms for all of the records. Without the ^ Q code, you would have to either create an extra secondary file consisting of just those records to be merged in the current operation or else delete the ones you don't need. To insert the code in the secondary file, place it on the line following the last field (after the ^ R code) in the last record you want to include.

## UPDATING THE SCREEN

By including the merge code ^U *(update)* in your primary file, you can watch each form letter as it is generated. Whenever WordPerfect encounters this code, it rewrites the screen to show the letter with the new set of data and displays it for you. To use it, press the Merge Codes key (Shift-F9) and select *U.* Be careful where you place the code in the document. In the form letter you just created, if you place the ^U at the beginning, you will see the merge codes, not the variable data, as the letters are generated, because at that point the program has not yet performed the merge. If you place it at the end, you will only see the bottom half of each form letter. The best place to put it is after the phone number, which is the last field in the form.

## MERGING TO THE PRINTER

As you have seen, the merged letters are created on the screen and are not printed until you issue a print command. If your secondary file is very large, you may not have enough memory in your computer to hold all of the letters being created, and the process will stop. Furthermore, you may not want to review them on the screen or save all of them to disk, so WordPerfect provides the option of merging directly to the printer.

To try it:

> You can also enter merge codes by pressing the Ctrl key and then typing the letter. However, be sure that you don't use the circumflex character (the shifted 6 on the top row) to produce the caret in the merge code—use only the Ctrl key. Although the result would *look* the same on your screen, WordPerfect interprets a caret-letter combination as a merge code only if the caret is produced by the Ctrl key or with the Merge Codes key.

1. Retrieve your primary file, *letter1.pf,* and insert these codes at the end of the document, using the Merge Codes key (Shift-F9):

   ^T^N^P^P

The ^T means *type,* and it causes the program to print (that is, type on the printer) everything that has been merged to that point (one letter), then erase it from memory (RAM). This action occurs after each letter has been merged, which means that none of the letters will appear on screen. The ^N means *next,* and it causes WordPerfect to find the next record in the secondary file. If there are no more records, it ends the merge. The two ^P codes mean *primary,* and they cause the program to look for a primary file and start the merge process all over again. The file name is normally entered between the two ^ P codes, but when it is left out, as in this case, the most recently used primary file is automatically used.

2. Save the revised letter as *letter2.pf*.

The final step is to perform the merge. You follow the same process you used to send merged letters to the screen, except that the name of the altered primary file is different. Be sure the printer is turned on and supplied with paper, and clear the screen.

3. Press the Exit key (F7 N N) to clear the screen.

4. Press the Merge/Sort key (Ctrl-F9) and select option **1** or **M**, Merge, to start the merge.

5. Enter

   **LETTER2.PF**

   when you are asked for the name of the primary file, and press ◄┘.

6. Now enter the name of the secondary file:

   **WINNERS.SF**

   and press ◄┘.

As you see, the three letters are sent directly to the printer, and you do not see them on the screen.

## *MERGING FROM THE KEYBOARD*

When you don't have to save the variable data for future use, you can simply enter it from the keyboard, eliminating the lengthy step of creating a secondary file. To do this, you have to change the primary file to eliminate the field codes ( ^ F1 ^ through ^ F7 ^ ) and replace them with another code, ^ C, which tells WordPerfect to stop so that you can type the names, addresses, and other variable data for each letter as it is created. ( ^ C stands for *console,* which means input from the keyboard.)

To try merging from the keyboard, follow these steps:

1. Retrieve the *letter1.pf* file.

2. Next you could either move the cursor to each ^ F code, erase it, and enter a ^ C code in its place, or use Search and Replace to automate the process. Since the Search and Replace method is faster, let's use it here.

3. Press the Replace key (Alt-F2), press ⏎ (that is, answer No) when asked if you want to use Confirm, then press the Merge Codes key (Shift-F9). The prompt line will appear as follows:

   ^ C; ^ D; ^ E; ^ F; ^ G; ^ N; ^ O; ^ P; ^ Q; ^ S;
   ^ T; ^ U; ^ V:

4. To select the ^ F code, type **F**. Each of the codes in your primary file has a different number (1 through 7), but you don't have to repeat the operation for each code if you use the wildcard character ^ X as a substitute for the numbers. This will locate all of the field numbers in one operation.

5. To use the wild card, press Ctrl-V and at the prompt *KEY* = press Ctrl-X.

6. Press Ctrl-V Ctrl-X once again to include the second caret sign, which you want to delete since the ^ C code is not followed by a caret as the ^ F ^ code is. The prompt line will appear as follows:

   → Srch: ^ F ^ X ^ X

7. Press F2 and you will be asked what to replace it with.

8. Press the Merge Codes key (Shift-F9) again and type **C**, (the ^ C code does not require a number). You will see the *Replace with:* ^ C prompt.

9. Press F2 once more to begin the search and replace action. When it is completed, the pertinent sections of your form letter will appear as follows:

   ^ C
   ^ C
   ^ C, ^ C ^ C

   Dear ^ C,

Congratulations! You are a winner in the $20,000,000 National Sweepstakes and are soon to be the recipient of a check for ^ C, less the appropriate amount of tax required by the Federal Government. We will be contacting you soon to determine this amount.

Our records show your phone number to be ^ C.

10.  Since you are not saving the variable data, reduce the five codes of the address to a single ^ C code by erasing the four extra ^ C's on lines 3 and 4. When the program pauses at this point during the merge, you will enter the entire address: name, street address, city, state, and ZIP code, pressing ←— as necessary to separate the lines.

11.  Save the file under the name *letter3.pf* and clear the screen.

12.  Press the Merge/Sort Key (Ctrl-F9) and select the Merge option, **1** or **M**, to begin the merge.

13.  Enter **letter3.pf** as your primary file and press ←—.

14.  Press ←— again at the *Secondary file:* prompt to leave it blank (since there is no secondary file in this type of merge). When the merge begins, the first ^ C disappears and the cursor is now positioned where the ^ C had been.

15.  Go ahead and type your name here.

16.  Press ←— to move to the next line and type in your street address.

17.  Press ←— again and type the city, state, and ZIP code on the following line.

18.  Press the Merge R key, F9 (also called the Merge Return key since it inserts a hard return), to move to the next field, which is the name in the salutation (after *Dear*).

19.  The second ^ C disappears and you type your name in the salutation.

20.  Press F9 again to move to the check amount field and type **$500,000**.

21.  Press F9 again and the cursor will stop on the phone number field. Type your phone number, then press F9 one last time. WordPerfect needs to search the rest of the document for ^ C

codes, so if you don't press F9 one last time, the *Merging* prompt will remain on the status line, even if you press Exit to clear the screen. After you press F9, the cursor will move to the end of the letter to signify that you are finished.

Now that you have entered data in each field, the first form letter is complete and you can print it. To start over with a new record, either clear the screen or insert a hard page break (by pressing Ctrl-←), then press Ctrl-F9 again and repeat the process.

## INSERTING REMINDERS IN YOUR PRIMARY FILE

If you set up a merge operation that will be used by others, they may need help understanding what should be entered in each field where a ^ C appears. WordPerfect has a special merge code, ^ O, which means *output* a message to the screen. By typing an explanation between a pair of ^ O's, you can inform the user exactly what to type at each point in the document. Clear the screen before you begin (F7 N N).

To try this:

1. Retrieve the file named *letter3.pf* and position the cursor on the caret next to the first ^ C code.

2. Press the Merge Codes key (Shift-F9) and type

   O

3. Next, type this message:

   Type the recipient's name and address

4. Press Shift-F9 and type **O** to insert another ^ *O*, and the completed sentence will look like this:

   ^ OType the recipient's name and address ^ O ^ C

Don't forget to save the file. When you merge this file (using the keyboard for variable data input), this message will appear as a highlighted prompt in the lower left corner of the screen, as shown in Figure 16.2. You can insert similar messages for each field in the primary file.

May 13, 1988

Dear ^C,

Congratulations!  You are a winner in the $20,000,000 National
Sweepstakes and are soon to be the recipient of a check for $^C,
less the appropriate amount of tax required by the Federal
Government.  We will be contacting you soon to determine this
amount.

Our records show your phone number to be ^C.  If this has changed,
please inform us immediately by calling this toll-free number:
(800) 445-0000.

Please keep this letter for your records.


Yours truly,

Irwin Kronsky
**Type the recipient's name and address**                Doc 1 Pg 1 Ln 1.33" Pos 1"

*Figure 16.2:* The customized message

# PRODUCING LABELS AND ENVELOPES FROM A SECONDARY FILE

Creating a list from your secondary file (*winners.sf*) that can be used to print mailing labels or envelopes is a simple process that requires running another merge. First, you create a new primary file to merge with the *winners.sf* file, making use of only five of the original seven fields: name, street address, city, state, and ZIP code. Your output from this merge must go to the screen; it will consist of three short forms containing the name and address of each recipient, as shown in Figure 16.3. Next, you change the form setting, top margin, and left and right margins to fit your labels, and then you're ready to print.

> See Chapter 6 for more information about formatting labels and envelopes.

1. First, create a new primary file containing fields F1 through F5, arranged in this order:

   ^ F1 ^
   ^ F2 ^
   ^ F3 ^, ^ F4 ^  ^ F5 ^

   Use the Merge Codes key (Shift-F9) to do this, as described earlier.

```
Ms. Colleen McDuffy
54 Prince Lane
Salem, GA 32255
==============================================================================
Mr. James Browder
100 Main St.
Mt. Hood, WA 81233
==============================================================================
Mrs. Rhonda Flamestein
233 12th Ave.
San Francisco, CA 91222




                                                  Doc 1 Pg 3 Ln 0.83" Pos 2.9"
```

*Figure 16.3:* The mailing label forms

Next, you need to change the top and bottom margins. If you don't, WordPerfect won't let you change the paper size for your labels to 2 inches in length, since the top and bottom margins are 1 inch each and there would be no room left for text!

2. Move the cursor to the top of the document first, press the Format key (Shift-F8), then select Page. Select Margins by typing **5** or **M**.

3. Enter **.5** as the top margin, press ◄─┘, enter **0** as the bottom margin, press ◄─┘, then press Exit (F7).

4. The next step is to change the paper size through the Format key. However, you must be certain that a corresponding form type for labels has been defined for your printer in the Select Printer: Forms screen. You can check by pressing Shift-F7 S E F. If you do not see a Labels form in the first column, create it before continuing. Press **A** for Add, **4** for Labels, **S** for Size, **O** for Other, then enter **4** for Width and **2** for Length. Press Exit (F7) five times.

5. Now, change the paper size using the Format key. Press Shift-F8, select Page, then select Paper Size by typing **8** or **S**.

6. Select Other by typing **O**.

7. Enter **4** at the Width prompt and press ⬅.

8. Enter **2** at the Height prompt and press ⬅.

9. Select Labels as the Paper type by typing **4** or **L**, then press Exit (F7).

10. Save the file under the name **labels.pf** and clear the screen.

11. Begin the merge process by pressing the Merge/Sort key (Ctrl-F9), pressing **M** or **1**, and entering **labels.pf** as your primary file and **winners.sf** as your secondary file.

The results are shown in Figure 16.3. Note that each form is considered a separate page, and a page break has been inserted after each one.

The next step is to print your labels. To do this, place them in the printer so that the top of the first one is under the print head, and use the Print key to print the entire file from the screen (press Shift-F7 1).

For legal-size envelopes that will be inserted manually, you would create another primary file containing fields 1 through 5, as described in steps 1 through 11 above. However, in steps 2 through 9 you'll use these steps to enter the settings for envelopes:

1. Press Shift-F8 P S E E.

2. Press M 0 then ⬅ three times.

3. Press L M 4 ⬅ 2, followed by ⬅ three times.

To print the envelopes, place the first one in the printer and line it up at the exact spot where you want the first line printed. Next, press the Print key (Shift-F7) and select the Page option (*2* or *P*). Press Page Down to move to the second envelope. Repeat this process for each envelope.

## ACCOMMODATING MISSING DATA

If data for any of the fields in the secondary file is unavailable, it is imperative that you leave a blank field in its place by pressing the Merge R key (F9). For example, if a ZIP code is missing in the first record and you do not leave a blank field, you will end up with this label:

>     Mr. James Browder
>     100 Main St.
>     Mt. Hood, WA  $10,000

ZIP code is the fifth field in the primary file (*labels.pf*) that creates the labels, and when it is missing, the program assumes that the next field is field 5, and inserts it in place of a ZIP code. The secondary file that produced this label is shown below:

>     Mr. James Browder ^ R
>     100 Main St. ^ R
>     Mt. Hood ^ R
>     WA ^ R
>     $10,000 ^ R
>     (802) 331-0000 ^ R
>     ^ E

Notice that it only has six ^ R codes, so there are only six fields.

To prevent this, you would retrieve the secondary file, place the cursor on the $ in the field with the amount won, and press the Merge R key (F9) after the state field. This would leave a blank field between the state and the check amount, and the secondary file would appear as

>     Mr. James Browder ^ R
>     100 Main St. ^ R
>     Mt. Hood ^ R
>     WA ^ R
>      ^ R
>     $10,000 ^ R
>     (802) 331-0000 ^ R
>     ^ E

When the ZIP code is missing, if you leave an empty field in the secondary file with just a Merge Return code ( ^ R) (as shown above), a blank space appears in the mailing labels where the ZIP code would have been. In this case, it is not a problem. However, in other cases when data is missing, it would leave a blank line that you would want to eliminate. For example, if we were to modify our secondary field to include titles and company names, and Rhonda

Flamestein's title were missing, the first two labels would look like this:

Mr. James Browder
President
Big Computers, Inc.
100 Main St.
Mt. Hood, WA 81233

Mrs. Rhonda Flamestein
ABC Parts, Inc.

233 12th Ave.
San Francisco, CA 91222

To prevent this, you would modify the primary file to include a question mark inside of any field number that may be missing data, as shown below:

^ F2? ^

To do this, you could either place your cursor on the second ^ and type the question mark, or type the question mark after pressing Shift-F9 F and typing the Field number, so that the prompt is similar to this: *Field: 2?* before you press ⏎ to enter it. Note that a field with a question mark must be alone on a line because WordPerfect will delete the rest of the line if the data is missing. Thus, both in our original letter (*letter1.pf*) and in our label file (*labels.pf*), we would have to include the question mark inside the field containing the title. Rhonda Flamestein's mailing label would look like this after a merge operation:

Mrs. Rhonda Flamestein
ABC Parts, Inc.
233 12th Ave.
San Francisco, CA 91222

## *CREATING LISTS FROM A SECONDARY FILE*

Another useful application for WordPerfect's Merge feature is to create lists from your secondary files that include one or more fields on the same line (or multiple lines). For example, you could produce a list from the *winners.sf* secondary file that would place each winner's name, amount won, and telephone number on a single line, as shown below.

| | | |
|---|---|---|
| Mr. James Browder | $10,000 | (802) 331-0000 |
| Mrs. Rhonda Flamestein | $50,000 | (415) 444-0000 |
| Ms. Colleen McDuffy | $1,000,000 | (513) 222-0000 |

To do this, you create another primary file consisting of the fields you want to include in the list, and three merge codes at the end that direct WordPerfect to find the next record and insert it at that point without making a page break. Here are the steps you would use to create the list shown above:

1. Clear the screen and use the Format key to clear all tab stops and set two new ones at 4″ and 5.5″ (Shift-F8 L T 0 ◄┘ Ctrl-End 4 ◄┘ 5.5 ◄┘ F7 F7).

2. Use the Merge Codes key (Shift-F9) to insert fields 1, 6, and 7 in your file, placing them all on one line and separating them with tabs, as shown below:

   ^F1^ ^F6^    ^F7^

   Press ◄┘.

3. On the second line, use the Merge Codes key (Shift-F9) to insert the codes ^N ^P ^P (note that you'll press Shift-F9 three times, once for each code). The ^N code directs Word-Perfect to find the next record in the secondary file, and the ^P codes tell WordPerfect which primary file to use with the next record from the secondary file. When a primary file name is not included between the pair, as in this case, Word-Perfect continues using the same one.

4. Save the file (F7 Y) under the name *winlist.pf,* then press **N** to clear the screen.

5. To produce the list, press the Merge/Sort key (Ctrl-F9) and select the Merge option. Type **winlist.pf** for the name of the primary file, press ◄┘ and type **winners.sf** as the name of the secondary file, then press ◄┘. The resulting list should resemble the one shown above.

## SUMMARY

WordPerfect's Merge feature can be used to automate repetitious tasks such as form letters, reports, lists, mailing labels, and contracts. Merged documents can be created on screen and saved in a file to be printed later, or they can be sent directly to the printer.

Form letters are the most common merge application, and they are created in three steps. You type the letter once, inserting special codes that represent variable data (data that changes in each letter). This master letter is stored in a file called the primary file. Next, you type a list of the variable data and save it in a file called the secondary file. (Instead of creating a secondary file, you have the option of typing the variable data at the keyboard as each letter is assembled. This is useful if you do not want to save and reuse the data.) The final step is to initiate the merge operation, which produces one letter for each set (record) of variable data.

You also can use Merge to extract names and addresses from a secondary file in order to print them on envelopes or mailing labels. To do this, you create a new primary file that includes only the name and address fields from each record, then clear the screen and run the merge. The last step is to adjust the left, right, top and bottom margins as well as page size and paper type to match the labels or envelopes.

WordPerfect's Sort, Select, and Macro features can help you simplify your merges and rearrange the data. These subjects are covered in the Sort and Select and Macros chapters, so be sure to read through those sections.

# 17.

## USING WORDPERFECT'S
## BUILT-IN CALCULATOR

# *F*AST *T*RACK

**To total and subtotal numbers down a column,**
> press the Math/Columns key (Alt-F7) and press *1* or *M* to turn Math on. Press Tab and enter the numbers you want calculated in each column, separating them with tabs. When you have finished entering the numbers, press ◄┘, tab to the column, then press Shift + (plus sign) to enter a subtotal; do this for each column of numbers. Next, press the Math key (Alt-F7) and press *2* or *A* to calculate the numbers. The subtotals will appear next to the + sign. When you finish, press Alt-F7 then *1* or *M* to turn off Math so that the Tab key functions normally again.

**Use Math Columns to designate four types of columns:**
> Numeric, Text, Calculation, or Total. You can use mathematical formulas to add, subtract, divide, or multiply in the Calculation columns, and can add or average numbers in the Total columns. Columns are defined as data separated by tabs, so you should always set appropriate tab stops before defining columns with the Math key.

**Define math columns**
> by pressing the Math/Columns key (Alt-F7), then selecting *2* or *E* to reach the Math Definition screen. You'll see a screen with three options for each column: type, negative numbers, and number of digits to the right. Choose *0* for a calculation column, then type a formula to add, subtract, divide, or multiply. Press Exit (F7) then turn Math on by pressing *1* or *M*.

**To enter data in defined math columns,**
> press the Tab key so that the *Align char* prompt appears before you type a number that will become part of a calculation.

**Create a separate Total column** 555

by pressing Alt-F7 2 to reach the Math Definition screen. In the Type row, press *3* to define a column as a Total column. Press F7 twice to return to the Edit screen.

**Rearrange a math or text column** 557

by placing the cursor on the first character of the column you want to move, then pressing the Block key (Alt-F4). Move the cursor to any character in the last row of the column, press Move (Ctrl-F4), then press *2* or *C* to highlight only the column you want to move. Select *1* or *M* from the next menu and you'll see a message prompting you to move the cursor. Place the cursor on the first character of the column where you want to insert the cut column and press ◄─┘ to retrieve it.

**To calculate averages,** 559

first define the Math columns (Alt-F7 2). In the column where you want the average calculated, press *0* for a calculation type, then type in the calculation formula for averaging ( + /) and press ◄─┘. Press Exit (F7) to leave the Math definition screen, then type *1* to turn Math on. Type in the column headings and the numbers you want averaged, separating them with tabs. When you have entered all the numbers, press the Math/ Columns key (Alt-F7) and select *2* or *A*.

MATHEMATICAL OPERATIONS ARE VITAL IN BUSI-ness, and it's unrealistic to confine them to the realm of the spreadsheet. Although WordPerfect does not purport to replace this type of software for complex analytical operations, its Math feature is adequate to handle common calculations so that you can incorporate them into your documents. Like a basic calculator, the program can add, subtract, multiply, and divide, as well as calculate subtotals, totals, grand totals, and averages. You can also create formulas to perform operations such as multiplying the numbers in two columns, and you can use parentheses to change the order of calculation in a formula.

Subtotals, totals, and grand totals can be easily computed by turning on Math and adding down columns. More complex calculations require the use of formulas that you enter in structured columnar format, with columns located at each tab stop. You can define up to 24 columns containing either text, numbers, calculations, or totals, but only four of them can contain calculation formulas. In the Calculation columns you can create formulas using fixed numbers, numbers in the same row in other columns, or a combination of the two. You can also define Total columns for subtotals, totals, or grand totals so that the figures appear in the column to the right rather than at the bottom of the column of numbers being added. When you use math columns, calculations are performed across the rows.

## TOTALLING NUMBERS DOWN A COLUMN

The simplest method of performing mathematical operations is to total numbers down a column, without predefining the column. You must change the tab settings before doing this, because the default settings (every ½ inch) are so close together that the numbers you enter may overlap, in which case your calculations will not be accurate. You can use four operators: the plus sign ( + ) for subtotals, the equals sign ( = ) for totals, the asterisk (*) for grand totals, and *N* for subtraction. The next exercise will teach you how. You will be entering the left side of a balance sheet, as shown in Figure 17.1.

Begin this exercise by changing the tab settings so that the first tab setting is at 4.5 inches and others are placed every 2 inches, then turn the Math feature on.

1. Press the Format key (Shift-F8), select Line by pressing **1** or **L**, then select Tab Set by pressing **8** or **T**. To clear all existing tabs, press

   0 ↵ Ctrl-End

   For the new tab stops enter

   4.5, 2

   press ↵, then press Exit (F7) twice.

2. Press the Math/Columns key (Alt-F7) and you'll see this menu:

   **1 M**ath On; **2** Math Def; **3 C**olumn On/Off; **4** Column Def: **0**

3. Select Math On by pressing either **1** or **M**.

The following indicator will appear in the lower left corner of your screen to tell you that Math is now on:

   Math

It will remain there until you turn Math off by pressing the Math key (Alt-F7) and selecting option 1, Math Off (don't do it yet though). Turning Math on and off inserts a pair of codes into your document ([Math On] and [Math Off ]) that you can only see in the Reveal Codes screen. Whenever you move the cursor into the area between these codes, the Math prompt appears on the status line.

4. The next step is to type the first heading. Type

   Cash

5. Press the Tab key once. You should see this message in the

```
Cash                      10,000.55
Accounts receivable       40,300.00
Inventory                 51,000.67
   Total current assets  101,301.22+

Equipment                 20,400.00
Property                  15,300.00
Other fixed assets        12,240.23

                          47,940.23+

   Total assets          149,241.45=



-


Math                                        Doc 1 Pg 1 Ln 4" Pos 1"
```

*Figure 17.1:* The asset side of a balance sheet

lower left corner of the screen:

### Align char = . Math

When Math is turned on, the Tab key always invokes this *Align char* prompt. The alignment character serves to automatically line up numbers at the tab setting, against or around a character such as a decimal point, an asterisk, or a blank space inserted using the Space bar. The default is the decimal point, as shown in the prompt, but you can change it anytime. Chapter 8 includes a detailed section about the alignment character as it is used with text columns, and that information is relevant to this chapter. To summarize it, after you press the Tab key, the *Align char* prompt appears; as you type numbers, they are inserted to the left of the cursor with the cursor remaining stationary on the tab stop. Once you press the alignment character (a decimal point), the prompt disappears and the cursor moves normally again, advancing to the right of the remaining digits as you type them. As a result, columns of numbers are evenly aligned around their decimal points even though they may not have the same number of digits, as in this example:

199.99

5999.99

39.99

One warning: Never enter numbers that are to be calculated unless you see the *Align char* prompt. This means that numbers to be used in calculations cannot be entered at the left margin. Also, if you press Tab then accidentally press some other keys that make the prompt disappear, you must erase the alignment codes, move the cursor back to the position it was in before you pressed Tab, and start again. To do this, you would press the Backspace key until you saw this message in the lower left corner of the screen:

Delete [C/A/Flrt]? (Y/N) No

This code represents three formatting changes: center *(c)*, alignment character *(a)*, and flush right *(flrt)*, and in this example it refers to the tab alignment character that was inserted when you pressed Tab and saw the *Align char* prompt. At this point, you would press *Y* to delete it, then the cursor would move back to the position before the tab stop at the left. Next, you would press Tab again so the *Align char* prompt would appear, then type the number.

   6. Enter this number, including the comma:

       **10,000.55**

       Did you see how the *Align char* prompt disappeared as soon as you pressed the decimal point? Also, the cursor moved normally (to the right) after that.

   7. Press ⏎ to skip a line, then type **Accounts receivable**.

   8. Press Tab, then type **40,300.00**.

   9. Press ⏎ to skip a line, then type **Inventory**.

   10. Press Tab, type **51,000.67**, then press ⏎.

The first calculation in your column will be the subtotal, *Total current assets*. As you can see in Figure 17.1, the column description has been indented a few spaces.

   11. Press the Space bar twice to indent it, then type **Total current assets**.

Next you will enter the Subtotal operator, which is a plus sign ( + ).

When you perform the calculation a number will appear, representing the sum of the first three numbers above it.

12. Press the Tab key to move the cursor to the Math column.

13. Be sure that the *Align char* message appears on the status line, then press Shift and the plus ( + ) key. Remember, if you accidentally pressed plus without Shift and the *Align char* message disappeared, you'd have to delete the Tab Align codes and type it ( + ) again.

14. Press ⏎, then press the Math/Columns key (Alt-F7). You should see this menu on the status line:

    **1 Math Off; 2 Calculate; 3 Column On/Off;
    4 Column Def: 0**

Notice how the menu differs when Math is turned on; before you turned it on in step 3, option 1 was Math On and option 2 was Math Def.

15. Select the Calculate option by pressing 2 or **A**.

The correct subtotal, 101,301.22, should now appear in front of the plus sign. Although the plus sign remains on the screen, it will not appear in the printed document.

16. Now use the method described in steps 4 through 10 to type the next three headings and their numbers, as shown below:

    | | |
    |---|---|
    | Equipment | 20,400.00 |
    | Property | 15,300.00 |
    | Other fixed assets | 12,240.23 |

17. Skip a few more lines, press Tab and type

    +

    This plus sign will calculate the second subtotal (which will be 47,940.23 after you use the Calculate option). Press ⏎ twice.

The last entry, *Total assets,* will add the two subtotals created with the plus signs in steps 13 and 17. To add the subtotals, you use the total operator, which is the equal sign ( = ).

18. Press the Space bar twice, then type the heading **Total assets**.

19. Press Tab, watching for the *Align char* prompt, then type the equal sign ( = ).

20. Press the Math/Columns key (Alt-F7) then press **2** or **A** to select the Calculate option.

If you were going to type more text, your next step would be to turn Math off so that the Tab key could be used to insert text tabs again. However since you won't be typing anything else, this step is optional.

21. If you want to turn Math off, press the Math/Columns key (Alt-F7) then press **1** or **M** to select Math Off. Notice that the Math indicator on the status line is gone.

22. Use the Save Text key (F10) to save the file under the name *math.ex1.*

Now that the file is saved, feel free to experiment with the figures. For instance, you could change a few of the fixed numbers (but don't try to type over the calculated ones!) then use the Calculate option on the Math/Columns key to recalculate them. Be sure that the Math prompt is visible when you try to calculate, because if it's not, you won't see the Calculate option on the Math/Columns menu. If it's not, just move the cursor up or down until it is between the Math on/off codes and you see the prompt.

You could also try changing a figure to a negative number by entering a minus sign in front of it, surrounding it with parentheses, or typing *N* in front of it. These are the only methods of subtracting numbers down a column (although you can subtract across rows using math formulas, as described in the next section). For example, Figure 17.2 shows an income statement in which all of the expenses were entered in negative numbers. If they had been entered without parentheses, a minus sign, or *N,* they would have been added to the total income figure to produce an incorrect net income of $822,310.86. Once you have performed the calculation and are sure you won't need to recalculate it, you can erase the parentheses or minus signs so that it looks like a standard

```
 _
Sales                      $455,677.55
Interest Income               9,666.10

   Total Income             465,343.65+


Wages and salaries         (182,044.00)
Cost of goods sold          (95,233.45)
Supplies                    (37,889.76)
Depreciation                (22,300.00)
Interest expense            (19,500.00)

   Total Expenses          (356,967.21)+


Net Income                 $108,376.44=



Math                              Doc 1 Pg 1 Ln 1" Pos 1"
```

*Figure 17.2:* An income statement

income statement. If you use the *N* operator, you won't have to erase it because, like the subtotal and total operators ( + and = ), it will not show up on the printed version of your document.

The only operator you have not used in this exercise is the asterisk, which calculates grand totals. You use it to add two totals (i.e., the figures computed with an equal sign), and it works exactly the same way as the other operators.

## USING MATH COLUMNS

A more formal and flexible approach to mathematical operations is to define columns and set up formulas to do the calculations. You can create four types of columns: Numeric, Text, Calculation, and Total. Out of 24 possible columns, only four can be Calculation columns. The formulas in your Calculation columns can include operators for addition, subtraction, multiplication, and division, and there are four special operators to add or average numbers in Numeric columns ( + , +/ ) and add or average numbers in Total columns ( = , =/ ).

As always, the best way to learn these operations is through exercises, so let's begin with an easy one. You will be creating the table shown in Figure 17.3, which shows budgeted vs. actual expenditures and calculates the dollar variance and percentage variance.

```
                    Budgeted vs. actual expenses


                  Budgeted   Actual     Variance      %
   Expense A       1000.00   1555.25     555.25!     55.5!

   Expense B       2000.00   1900.75     -99.25!     -5.0!

   Expense C       3000.00   3500.50     500.50!     16.7!


                 6,000.00+ 6,956.50+    956.50!     15.9!




                                             Doc 1 Pg 1 Ln 1" Pos 1"
```

*Figure 17.3:* Budgeted vs. actual expenses

Before defining the columns, you'll type the title and headings, then change the tab settings to every 1 inch beginning at 3.5 inches. Clear the screen before proceeding (F7 N N).

1. Switch to double spacing by pressing the Format key (Shift-F8), selecting Line (**1** or **L**), selecting Spacing (**6** or **S**), then typing **2**. Press ←┘ three times.

2. Center and type the title:

   **Budgeted vs. actual expenses**

3. Press ←┘ a few times, then enter the column titles on the first row. Use the Tab key to enter **Budgeted** at position 3″, **Actual** at 4″, **Variance** at 5″, and % at 6.5″. Press ←┘ twice.

4. Press the Format key (Shift-F8), select Line (**1** or **L**), then select Tab Set (**8** or **T**).

5. Press **0** followed by ←┘, then press Ctrl-End to delete the old settings. For the new ones, type

   **3.5,1** ←┘

   then press Exit (F7) and ←┘ until you're back to Edit mode.

## *DEFINING THE COLUMNS*

Now you're ready to define the math columns. To do this, you'll use the Math/Columns key (Alt-F7).

1. Press the Math/Columns key (Alt-F7) and select Math Def by pressing either **2** or **E**. You should see the screen shown in Figure 17.4.

Notice the row descriptions on the left: *Columns, Type, Negative Numbers,* and *Number of Digits to the Right.* The first row, *Columns,* refers to columns of numbers or characters in your document that you define by pressing the Tab key. Columns are labelled *A* through *X;* in the example shown in Figure 17.3, the *Budgeted* column is A, *Actual* is B, *Variance* is C, and % is D. The row below that, *Type,* is full of 2's. You use it to specify the type of data each column will contain: *0* for a calculation, *1* for text, *2* for numeric, and *3* for a total. You use the third row, *Negative Numbers,* to define the symbol that will appear with negative numbers, either a minus sign ( − ) or a set of parentheses. As you can see, the default is parentheses. In the fourth row, *Number of Digits to the Right,* you specify how many numbers will appear after the decimal point, and the default is *2.*

```
Math Definition            Use arrow keys to position cursor

Columns                    A B C D E F G H I J K L M N O P Q R S T U V W X

Type                       2 2 2 2 2 2 2 2 2 2 2 2 2 2 2 2 2 2 2 2 2 2 2 2

Negative Numbers           ( ( ( ( ( ( ( ( ( ( ( ( ( ( ( ( ( ( ( ( ( ( ( (

Number of Digits to        2 2 2 2 2 2 2 2 2 2 2 2 2 2 2 2 2 2 2 2 2 2 2 2
  the Right (0-4)

Calculation      1
  Formulas       2
                 3
                 4

Type of Column:
     0 = Calculation    1 = Text     2 = Numeric     3 = Total

Negative Numbers
     ( = Parentheses (50.00)         - = Minus Sign  -50.00


Press Exit when done
```

*Figure 17.4:* The Math Definition screen

Since you'll be typing numbers in columns A and B, you'll leave the default type, Numeric, for both. Columns C and D will be formulas, so you'll change the type to Calculation, then enter the formulas.

2. Press → twice to accept the default type, Numeric, in columns A and B.

3. The cursor moves to column C, which will be the first calculation column. Type

    **0**

The cursor jumps to the calculation definition area in the middle of the screen. The letter C appears to the left of the cursor, to remind you that you are creating a formula for column C.

For each row in our example, the *Variance* column (C) will calculate the difference between the numbers in the column labelled *Actual* (column B) and the numbers in the column labelled *Budgeted* (column A), so the formula will be column B minus column A.

4. Enter this formula (you can use either lowercase or upper-case, but no spaces):

    **B – A**

    and press ←┘. After you press ←┘, the cursor will move back to the top row, under column D. This column will also be a formula: C/A*100. It calculates *Variance* divided by *Budgeted*, then multiplies by 100 to give a percent.

5. Press

    **0**

    to define a Calculation column and move the cursor back into the calculation definition area.

6. Enter this formula:

    **C/A*100**

    and press ←┘.

The next step is to change the symbol for negative numbers to a minus sign, so you have to move the cursor to the next row (the one with the parentheses).

7. Press ↓ to move the cursor to the next row, then press ← four times to move it to column A. Enter minus signs ( – ) in columns A through D.

The last step in the definition process is to move to column D and change the number of digits to the right of the decimal point to 1.

8. Press ↓ and ← to move the cursor to the last row under Column D, then enter **1** for the number of digits.

Your Math Definition screen should now resemble Figure 17.5.

9. Since you've finished defining the columns, press Exit (F7), which brings back the Math/Columns prompt.

10. Turn the math feature on by pressing **1** or **M** to select Math On. Notice the *Math* indicator in the lower left corner of your screen.

## ENTERING THE DATA

Now you're ready to enter the row headings and numbers.

1. Enter the first row title:

Expense A

```
Math Definition            Use arrow keys to position cursor

Columns                    A B C D E F G H I J K L M N O P Q R S T U V W X

Type                       2 2 Ø Ø 2 2 2 2 2 2 2 2 2 2 2 2 2 2 2 2 2 2 2 2

Negative Numbers           - - - - ( ( ( ( ( ( ( ( ( ( ( ( ( ( ( ( ( ( ( (

Number of Digits to        2 2 2 1 2 2 2 2 2 2 2 2 2 2 2 2 2 2 2 2 2 2 2 2
  the Right (Ø-4)

Calculation     1     C     B-A
  Formulas      2     D     C/A*1ØØ
                3
                4

Type of Column:
     Ø = Calculation     1 = Text     2 = Numeric     3 = Total

Negative Numbers
     ( = Parentheses (5Ø.ØØ)          - = Minus Sign  -5Ø.ØØ


Press Exit when done
```

*Figure 17.5:* The completed Math Definition screen

Never enter numbers that are to be calculated unless you see the *Align char* prompt. If the prompt disappears, press the Backspace key until you see *Delete [C/A/ Flrt]? (Y/N) No,* then press **Y**. Press Tab again and type the number with the *Align char* prompt showing.

2. Press the Tab key to move to the first column, and the *Align char* prompt will appear. Enter the budgeted amount for expense A:

   **1000.00**

3. Press the Tab key again and enter the amount in the *Actual* column:

   **1555.25**

4. Press the Tab key to move to column C, then press Tab again to move to column D. Exclamation points (*!*) will appear in both columns, as shown in Figure 17.6.

The exclamation points indicate that these are predefined Calculation columns, which will turn into numbers when you use the Calculate option on the Math/Columns key. Do not enter anything in these columns, because it will be disregarded when the program calculates the number.

5. Press ← to move to the next row.

6. To calculate the last two columns, press the Math/Columns key (Alt-F7) and select Calculate by pressing **2** or **A**. Under the *Variance* heading in row 1 you should see 555.25, and under % you should see 55.5. Although the exclamation points remain at the right of the numbers on the screen, they will not show up when the document is printed.

7. Repeat the steps outlined above to enter these headings and figures for the next two rows. Don't forget to press Tab twice to insert the two exclamation points after the *Actual* columns.

   | | | | | |
   |---|---|---|---|---|
   | Expense B | 2000.00 | 1900.75 | ! | ! |
   | Expense C | 3000.00 | 3500.50 | ! | ! |

8. Press ← a few times, then type

   **Total**

9. Press the Tab key and enter the Subtotal operator ( + ) in the *Budgeted* column.

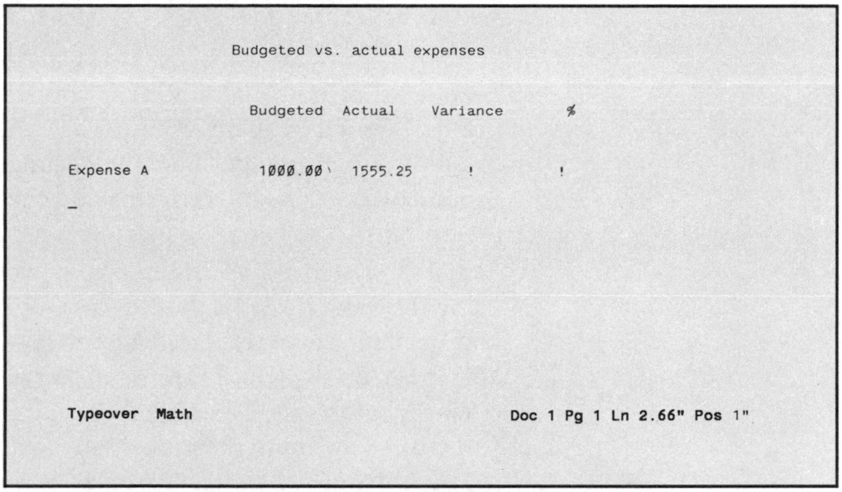

```
                        Budgeted vs. actual expenses

                        Budgeted   Actual    Variance      %

        Expense A         1000.00`  1555.25       !          !

        −





        Typeover  Math                          Doc 1 Pg 1 Ln 2.66" Pos 1"
```

*Figure 17.6:* Exclamation points in the Calculation columns

10. Press the Tab key and enter the Subtotal operator ( + ) for column B, *Actual*.

11. Press Tab twice to enter the exclamation points in columns Ĉ and D, then press ◄─┘.

When you are finished, the last row will contain no numbers, and it will look like this:

**Total**                              +      +     !    !

Now select the Calculate option from the Math/Columns key and your work will be complete.

12. Press the Math/Columns key (Alt-F7) and press **2** or **A** to calculate.

When you print your math document, it should look just like Figure 17.3. Note that the calculated variance and percent figures for Expense B in the second row will be negative after you've calculated them, as indicated by minus signs (shown in Figure 17.3).

## *CHANGING THE MATH DEFINITION*

You may not always be pleased with the appearance of your math document, or you may find that your formulas were incorrect and need to be entered again. For instance, the last column in Figure 17.3 contains only one digit after the decimal point, whereas the others contain two, so let's be consistent and change the % column to match the others.

The first step is to position the cursor on the [Math On] code, using the Search key or the Reveal Codes screen. This is important because if the cursor is placed after the [Math On] code, you won't be able to call up the Math Definition screen to make the changes. If the cursor is before the [Math Def] code, the new code you create when you change the math definition will have no effect! (When it is on the [Math On] code, Math is not on at that point.)

1. To use Search, press Page Up to move the cursor to the top of the page, then press the Search key (F2). For the search string, press Alt-F7 1 and you'll see the [Math Def] code next to the *Srch* prompt. Press F2 to begin the search. The cursor will stop right after the [Math Def] code (as you can verify by pressing the Reveal Codes key, Alt-F3). The cursor will be highlighting the [Math On] code.

   If you find it easier to use Reveal Codes, press Alt-F3 and use the cursor movement keys to place the cursor after the [Math Def] code. (The cursor will be highlighting the [Math On] code.)

2. Press the Math/Columns key (Alt-F7) and select Math Def by pressing either **2** or **E**.

3. Move the cursor to column D, row 3, and change the *1* to a *2*, then press F7 ◄┘ to exit.

4. Use ↓ to move the cursor until the Math indicator appears in the lower left corner of the screen. Recalculate the formulas by pressing the Math/Columns key (Alt-F7) and selecting Calculate (**2** or **A**). The result is that the fourth column now contains two digits after the decimals, just like the other three.

5. Save the file under the name *math.ex2*, then clear the screen.

See Chapter 7 for more information about using the Search and Search and Replace features to locate and erase hidden codes.

See Chapters 3 and 4 for more information about the Reveal Codes screen.

## CREATING COLUMNS FOR TOTALS

Instead of placing a subtotal, total, or grand total at the bottom of a column, you can set it apart by creating a Total column in the next column to the right. For instance, Figure 17.7 shows a balance sheet in which subtotals and totals for assets, liabilities, owners equity, and total equities are calculated in a separate column (column B).

This example will demonstrate one of the limitations of WordPerfect's Math feature when compared to a spreadsheet: the formulas in a column calculate *all* figures in a column, and cannot be used selectively to add figures such as the total liabilities and total owners' equity in this example. As a result, it was necessary to turn Math off after calculating the subtotal for total assets, then turn Math on again so that the last Total calculation, total equities, would include only the subtotals for total liabilities and total owners' equity. If Math had not been turned off and on again, the figure for total equities would equal the sum of assets, liabilities, and owners' equity, 13,312.00, and the balance sheet would appear to be out of balance! Follow these steps to see how it was done:

1. Set the tabs so that there are only two tab stops, at 4″ and 5.5″ (press Shift-F8 L T 0 ◄─┘ Ctrl-End 4 ◄─┘ 5.5 ◄─┘ F7 ◄─┘ ◄─┘).

2. Use the Math Definition screen (Alt-F7 2) to change column B to a Total column by pressing → once, then entering *3* for Type.

3. Press F7 to exit from the Math Definition screen, then turn Math on by pressing **1** or **M**.

4. Refer to Figure 17.7 to enter the headings and numbers for each of the assets: **Current, Other investments, Property,** and **Prepaid expenses.** Use the Tab key to align the numbers.

5. After you type the heading **TOTAL ASSETS**, press the Tab key twice and enter the subtotal operator ( + ) in column B.

6. Calculate the subtotal by pressing Alt-F7 2 or A.

7. Press ◄─┘, then turn Math off (Alt-F7 1 or M).

8. Press ◄─┘, then turn Math on again (Alt-F7 1 or M).

9. Type the headings and numbers for the liabilities and owners

```
ASSETS


Current                2432
Other investments       448
Property               3648
Prepaid expenses        128
                       ————

   TOTAL ASSETS                         6,656.00
                                       ═════════



EQUITIES


Current                1024
Long-term debt          576
                       ————

   Total liabilities                    1,600.00



Common stock           1024
Capital surplus         960
Retained earnings      2816
Reserves                256
                       ————

   Total owners equity                  5,056.00


TOTAL EQUITIES                          6,656.00
                                       ═════════
```

*Figure 17.7:* Using a Total column

equities, as shown in Figure 17.7 (type everything from *EQUITIES* through *Total owners equity*). Type the lines under the last entries in each group. Also, after typing the headings *Total liabilities* and *Total owners equity,* press Tab twice then type the subtotal operator (the plus sign).

10. Enter the last heading, *TOTAL EQUITIES,* then press the Tab key twice and enter the equal sign (the totals operator). Press ◄┘.

11. Select Calculate from the Math/Columns key (Alt-F7) by pressing **2** or **A**.

That's all there is to it! Save the file if you want, then clear the screen for the next exercise.

## COPYING, DELETING, AND MOVING MATH AND TEXT COLUMNS

In Chapter 5 you learned how to cut, copy and move blocks of text, but we saved the subject of rearranging columns for this chapter. The next exercise will teach you how to move a Math column. The same steps can be used to move any columns, whether they contain numbers or letters, as long as they have been defined by using the Tab, Tab Align, Indent, or Hard Return keys. Note that this procedure does not work for parallel or newspaper columns.

You will be using the table shown in Figure 17.3, *Budgeted vs. actual expenses,* and switching the *Budgeted* and *Actual* columns (you created it in a previous exercise and saved it as *math.ex2*). The process is similar to moving a block of text: you mark the column with the Block key (Alt-F4), select the Tabular Column option from the Move key (Ctrl-F4) to cut the column, select Move, move the cursor to the new location, then press ◄┘. The only difficult step is the first one, blocking the column.

1. Use the Retrieve Text key (Shift-F10) to retrieve the file, *math.ex2*.

The titles in the first row must have been positioned with the Tab key or this procedure will not work. You must also delete the extra blank line separating the Expense C row from the Total row. (To be sure, you can check the Reveal Codes screen for a [Tab] code in front of each title.) Also, you must begin this process with the cursor on the first row of the column to be moved.

2. To block and highlight the column, move the cursor to any character in the column title, *Budgeted,* and press the Block key (Alt-F4).

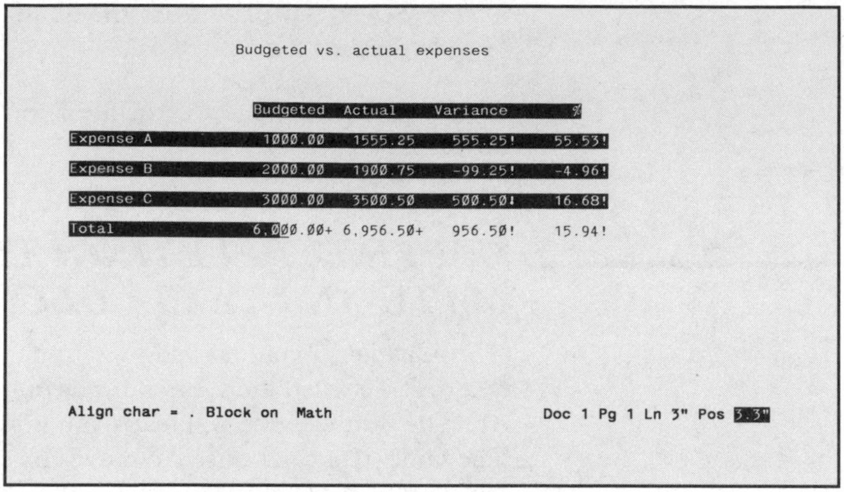

```
                    Budgeted vs. actual expenses


                    Budgeted   Actual     Variance         %
Expense A            1000.00   1555.25      555.25!      55.53!

Expense B            2000.00   1900.75      -99.25!      -4.96!

Expense C            3000.00   3500.50      500.50!      16.68!

Total              6,000.00+ 6,956.50+     956.50!      15.94!




Align char = . Block on  Math                    Doc 1 Pg 1 Ln 3" Pos 3.3"
```

*Figure 17.8:* The blocked columns

3. Move the cursor to the last row in the column, so that it is located anywhere on the number 6,000.00. At that point, all of the columns will be highlighted, as shown in Figure 17.8.

4. Press the Move key (Ctrl-F4) and press **2** or **C** to select Tabular Column. This will reduce the block so that only the column under the title *Budgeted* is highlighted, as shown in Figure 17.9.

5. Next, select Move from this prompt:

**1 Move; 2 Copy; 3 Delete; 4 Append: 0**

You'll see the message *Move cursor; press **Enter** to retrieve.*

6. Place the cursor on the *V* in the heading *Variance,* which is where you will be inserting the column you just cut. Press ⏎ to retrieve the column.

The results will be as follows:

|           | Actual   | Budgeted  | Variance  | %      |
|-----------|----------|-----------|-----------|--------|
| Expense A | 1555.25  | 1000.00   | 555.25!   | 55.53! |
| Expense B | 1900.75  | 2000.00   | -99.25!   | -4.96! |
| Expense C | 3500.50  | 3000.00   | 500.50!   | 16.68! |
| Total     | 6,956.50 | +6,000.00 | +956.50!  | 15.94! |

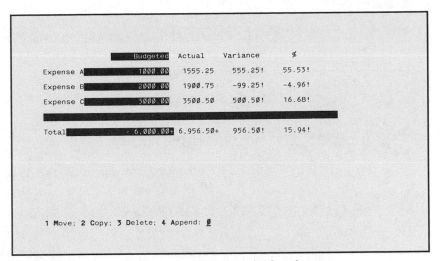

*Figure 17.9:* After narrowing the block to a single column

Note that the calculation is now reversed, so that the *Variance* column equals the budgeted figures minus the actual ones, instead of actual minus budgeted, and the percentage column is variance divided by actual. Let's recalculate the figures so they will be accurate.

7. Move the cursor down until you see the Math indicator. Press the Math/Columns key (Alt-F7) and press **2** or **A** to calculate.

The new results for the last two columns will be

|            | Variance   | %        |
|------------|-----------|----------|
| Expense A  | -555.25!  | -35.70!  |
| Expense B  | 99.25!    | 5.22!    |
| Expense C  | -500.50!  | -14.30!  |
|            |           |          |
| Total      | -956.50!  | -13.75!  |

## USING MATH COLUMNS TO CALCULATE AVERAGES

You can also use the Math Columns feature to calculate averages. For example, Figure 17.10 shows expenses A, B, and C for the years

1988 and 1989, with averages for the two years in the third column. The steps used in creating this chart are similar to the ones you used for the *Budgeted vs. actual expenses* chart (Figure 17.3), except that the formula in column 3 is as follows:

+/

To create the chart, clear the screen by pressing F7 N N, then follow these steps:

1. Enter the headings using the Tab key: **1988** at position 3″, **1989** at position 4″, and **Average** at position 5″.

2. Use the Format key to switch to double spacing: Shift-F8 L S 2 ← ← ←.

3. Press ← to add the blank lines, then change the tab settings to every 1 inch beginning at 3.5″ (Shift-F8 L T 0 ← Ctrl-End 3.5, 1 ← F7 ← ←).

4. Press Alt-F7 2 to define the Math columns. Press → twice to leave the default of *2* (for Numeric columns) in columns A and B, and enter **0** to create a calculation in column C.

5. The cursor will move down to the *Calculation formulas* area, where you type

+/

|           | 1988  | 1989  | Average |
|-----------|-------|-------|---------|
| Expense A | 2000  | 1500  | 1,750   |
| Expense B | 1000  | 1250  | 1,125   |
| Expense C | 3100  | 2400  | 2,750   |
| Total     | 6,100 | 5,150 | 5,625   |

*Figure 17.10:* Calculated averages for expenses A, B, and C

and press ←. Change the *Number of Digits to the Right* to *0* for columns A, B, and C. Press Exit (F7) to leave the Math Definition screen.

6. You will see the Math/Columns menu, so press **1** to turn Math on.

7. Type the first heading, **Expense A**.

8. Press Tab and type **2000**.

9. Press Tab and type **1500**.

10. Press Tab, which places an exclamation point in column C, then press ←.

11. Repeat steps 7 through 10, typing these headings and numbers for the next two rows, and pressing Tab to insert the exclamation points in the Calculation column.

```
Expense B    1000      1250        !
Expense C    3100      2400        !
```

12. Press ← twice and enter the heading **Total**.

13. Press Tab then type a plus sign ( + ) in column A, then repeat for column B.

14. Press Tab so an exclamation point (!) appears in column C, then press ←.

15. Press the Math/Columns key (Alt-F7) and select Calculate (**2** or **A**).

Your work should now resemble Figure 17.10. Remember, the plus signs and exclamation points will not be printed.

## SUMMARY

WordPerfect's Math feature can be used to calculate subtotals, totals, and grand totals, as well as to add, subtract, multiply, divide, and average in predefined columns of numbers. You can define up to 24 columns, using a maximum of 4 for calculations. To add numbers down a column (in subtotals, totals, and grand totals), you can skip the Math Definition step and just turn on the Math feature. This converts the Tab key into a Tab Alignment key, and lets you use three special operators in the columns: the plus sign ( + ) for subtotals, the equal sign ( = ) for totals, and the asterisk ( * ) for grand totals. The only method of subtracting down a column is to add negative numbers to positive ones.

To perform more complex mathematical operations, use the Math Definition option on the Math/Columns key. With it you can establish columns for text, numbers, calculations, or totals, and in the Calculation columns you can create formulas using fixed numbers, numbers in the same row in other columns, or a combination of the two. You can also define Total columns for subtotals, totals, or grand totals so that the figures appear in the column to the right rather than at the bottom of the column of numbers being added. When you use Math columns, calculations are performed across the rows.

Individual columns of numbers or text that have been defined using the Tab, Tab Align, Indent, or Hard Return keys can be cut, copied, or moved by marking them with the Block key, then pressing the Move key and selecting Tabular Column, then Move.

# MANIPULATING YOUR DATA
# WITH SORT AND SELECT

**Sort data that is formatted in rows and columns**     567

and is separated by tabs or indents by using a line sort. Press the Merge/Sort key (Ctrl-F9) and select Sort (*2* or *S*). At the prompt, enter the name of the file you want to sort or just press ⏎ to sort the file that is on screen. At the next prompt, type the name of the file that will contain the results of the sort—the output file—and press ⏎, or press ⏎ alone to have the output go to the screen. Press *7* or *T* and select Line (*2* or *L*) and you will see the Sort by Line screen and the Tab Ruler. Press *3* or *K* to specify the sort order. At the *Typ* heading, press ⏎ to sort alphanumerically (or enter *N* if you are sorting numbers), then enter the field number of your first sort key under the *field* heading and press ⏎. At the *Word* heading, specify which word you want to sort by, and press ⏎. Press Exit (F7), then press *1* or *P* to start the sort.

**Alphabetize paragraphs using a paragraph sort.**     581

Press the Merge/Sort key (Ctrl-F9) and select *2* or *S*. Press ⏎ or enter the name of the file you want to sort, then press ⏎ or enter a file name for the Sort output. Press *7* or *T*, then *3* or *P*; you then will see the Sort by Paragraph screen. Select *3* or *K*, then define the key with the options Type, Line, Field, and Word. Press Exit (F7), then press *1* or *P* to start the sort.

**Sort secondary merge files alphabetically or numerically**     583

with a merge sort. Press the Merge/Sort key (Ctrl-F9), and select *2* or *S*. Enter the name of the file you want to sort, then press ⏎, or just press ⏎ if the file you want to sort is already on screen. When prompted for the name of the output file, enter a file name to send the sort results to, or press ⏎ to sort to the screen. Select the Type option (*7* or *T*), then Merge (*1* or *M*); you will see the Sort Secondary Merge File screen. Press *3* or *K*, then define the key with the options Type, Line, Field, and Word. Press Exit (F7), then *1* or *P* to start the sort.

## To select certain records from a file                             587

that match your criteria, use the Select feature. Press the Merge/Sort key (Ctrl-F9) and select *2* or *S*. Press ◄─┘ if your file is on screen, or enter the file name to be sorted, then press ◄─┘ to send the output to the screen, or enter a new file name to send it to. Press *7* or *T*, then choose the appropriate type of sort—Line, Paragraph, or Merge. Select *3* or *K*, then define the keys with the options Field and Word. When you have finished, press Exit (F7), then *4* or *S* for Select. A prompt line will appear showing the operators you can use to establish selection conditions. To enter an operator, type the key number, the operator symbol, and the selection condition, such as *key 1 >  100*. Press ◄─┘ when you are finished. Press *1* or *P* for Perform Action to start the sort and select operation.

WORDPERFECT'S SORT AND SELECT FEATURES ARE easy, fast, and useful. You can perform a sort or select operation on an entire file, or you can mark a block and limit the sort or select to a specific area.

WordPerfect can perform three different types of sorts: *line sorts, paragraph sorts,* and *merge sorts.* If data is arranged in rows and columns, as in a spreadsheet, you use line sort. If data is arranged in paragraphs so that one or more paragraphs exceeds one line in length, you use paragraph sort. You use merge sort to sort data stored in secondary merge files. The sort direction can be either ascending or descending; the default is ascending order. If you're sorting numbers, this means that the smallest numbers will come first (0, 1, 2, 3, . . .) and if you're sorting letters, they will be arranged from A to Z.

The Select feature can be used alone or in conjunction with the Sort feature. You can use it to isolate records from a list that meet conditions you define, such as those of customers who live in California or who have a line of credit exceeding a specified amount. Operators such as *equals, greater than, less than,* and *greater than or equal to* help you define the selection conditions.

## *SORTING ROWS AND COLUMNS WITH LINE SORT*

Line sorts are the easiest sorts to perform in WordPerfect. To use line sort, the data must be arranged in rows and columns, as in a spreadsheet. Figure 18.1 shows a list of names that were entered in no particular order. The list consists of a single column containing a first and last name, with one person's name in each row. Each row constitutes one *record,* and each entry (in one column) in a record is called a *field.* Each field must contain the same type of data down the column.

For instance, if you were to create a second column for Social Security numbers, each entry in the new column would have to contain a Social Security number (or remain blank), but no other type of data. You would have to separate the two columns, name and Social Security number, by a single tab stop.

In the next exercise, you'll use a line sort to rearrange the list by last name. To try it, type the list as you see it in Figure 18.1, then use the Save Text key (F10) to save it under this file name: *NAMES.LST*. Be sure to press ⟵ after typing each name.

Now you'll see how fast and easy it is to sort this list. Your cursor can be located anywhere in the list when you begin.

1. Press the Merge/Sort key (Ctrl-F9).

2. Select Sort by pressing either **2** or **S**. You should see this prompt:

   **Input file to sort: (Screen)**

WordPerfect is asking for the name of the input file, the one you want to sort. Although the file to be sorted can be either on screen or on the disk when you begin (and if it's on the disk, the screen will be completely blank), WordPerfect assumes that the document is on screen so you see the *(Screen)* message next to the prompt. Since Screen is the default, it appears in the prompt even if you have an empty screen when you begin.

> After you press ⟵ in response to the prompt *Input file to sort: (Screen)*, you may get an error message such as *ERROR: not enough memory*. This means you don't have enough RAM to sort the file that is on the screen. If this happens, clear the screen (F7 N N) and begin again with a blank screen. When asked for the name of the input file to sort, type the name of the disk file, NAMES.LST.

JOHN BROWN
JANET SMITH
EILEEN FRANK
DANIEL BLAIR
SALLY COLEMAN
BARBARA ANDERSON
LAURA JEFFREYS
ROBERT JONES
SANDRA JACOBS
LOU ROBINSON
JOE FULLER

*Figure 18.1:* A list of names to be sorted

3. Press ◄─┘ to accept the default (Screen). You will then see this prompt:

**Output file for sort: (Screen)**

Here WordPerfect is asking where you want the results of the sort action, called the *output file*, to go—to the screen or to a new file on disk. As you can see, WordPerfect assumes that you want the output file to go to the screen. If you wanted to send it to a disk file, you could type a name at this point. If you sort to a disk file, your screen remains unchanged after the procedure and you have to retrieve the new file from the disk to see the sorted list.

4. Press ◄─┘ to accept the default (Screen).

Your screen should be split in half with the Tab Ruler in the middle and the Sort by Line screen below it, as illustrated in Figure 18.2.

If a different screen appears—either Sort Secondary Merge File or Sort by Paragraph—select Type from the menu by pressing either *7* or *T,* then select Line by pressing either *2* or *L.* Your screen should now match Figure 18.2.

The next step is to specify the sort order. To do this, you use option 3, Keys, and enter the number of the field (column) that you want to sort

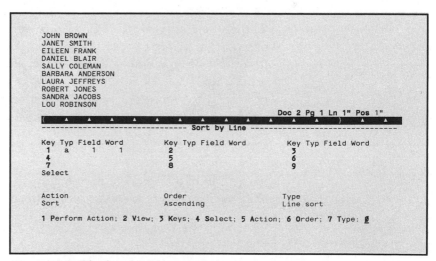

***Figure 18.2:*** The Sort by Line screen

on. Each field you choose to sort on is called a *key.* The first field you select (which will be first and last name in this example) will be the first sort order. In this example, you only have one field, first and last name, but if you had more you could sort on as many as nine. I'll explain how and why shortly.

    5.  Select option 3, Keys, by pressing either *3* or **K.**

The cursor will then move into position to select the first key, under the heading *Typ.* This is where you define the sort order (key).

    The first heading, *Typ,* is where you specify whether the key field is Alphanumeric *(a)* or Numeric *(n).* Alphanumeric fields can consist of letters or numbers, but the numbers must be equal in length, such as ZIP codes. Numeric fields contain only numbers, which may be of unequal length and may contain dollar signs, commas, and periods. Since your name field is alphanumeric, you'll leave the default, *a.*

    6.  Press ◄━━┘ to accept alphanumeric as the *Typ* (type of sort).

The cursor moves under the heading *Field,* which is where you specify the field number of your first sort key. Since you have only one field, you'll leave the default of *1.*

    7.  Press ◄━━┘ to accept *1* as the field.

The last heading is *Word.* If the field you are sorting by has more than one word in it, you can use this area to specify which word you want to sort by. Words within a field are separated by blank spaces, and are counted from left to right. In our example, if you leave the default of word 1, the sort order will be by first name. To sort by last name, you have to change the key word to word 2.

    8.  Type **2** to change the key word to *2,* then press ◄━━┘.

To get out of the key definition area, you have to press the Exit key (F7), as this prompt at the bottom of the screen tells you:

**Press EXIT when done**

9. Press Exit (F7) to return the cursor to the menu. Now you're ready to perform the sort.

10. Press **1** or **P** to select Perform Action.

You will see several messages (very briefly, since your file is so small) listing the number of records examined, records selected, and records transferred, and then the sorted file will appear. It should resemble the one below.

BARBARA ANDERSON
DANIEL BLAIR
JOHN BROWN
SALLY COLEMAN
EILEEN FRANK
JOE FULLER
SANDRA JACOBS
LAURA JEFFREYS
ROBERT JONES
LOU ROBINSON
JANET SMITH

What if your list had contained names with middle initials, as shown below? To find out, exit without saving (F7 N N) then retrieve the original file (NAMES.LST) and change three of the records to include the initials shown below:

JOHN R. BROWN
JANET SMITH
EILEEN B. FRANK
DANIEL BLAIR
SALLY COLEMAN
BARBARA ANDERSON
LAURA A. JEFFREYS
ROBERT JONES
SANDRA JACOBS
LOU ROBINSON
JOE FULLER

Now sort it again using the steps described above.

The results of your sort will be quite different this time, because *last name* is no longer word 2 in all the records. Here's what it should look like after you sort it:

```
LAURA A. JEFFREYS
BARBARA ANDERSON
EILEEN B. FRANK
DANIEL BLAIR
SALLY COLEMAN
JOE FULLER
SANDRA JACOBS
ROBERT JONES
JOHN R. BROWN
LOU ROBINSON
JANET SMITH
```

Do you remember that you defined the Sort key as word 2? Since the second word in LAURA A. JEFFREYS is the middle initial, *A,* her name appears first in the list instead of BARBARA ANDERSON. For the same reason, EILEEN B. FRANK and JOHN R. BROWN are in the wrong position.

To prevent this problem, you can count the words in reverse order when you select the key. If you had chosen  *– 1* as the key word to sort by, WordPerfect would have counted the words from right to left within the field instead of left to right, and the names would have been correctly sorted by last name. Let's try it.

1. Press the Merge/Sort key (Ctrl-F9).

2. Select Sort by pressing either **2** or **S**.

3. Press ⏎ twice to accept *(Screen)* as the input and output file.

4. Select option 3, Keys, by pressing either **3** or **K**.

5. Press ⏎ to accept an alphanumeric sort.

6. Press ⏎ to accept *1* as the field.

7. Type  **– 1** to change the key word to the last one in the field, last name.

8. Press ⏎, then Exit (F7) to return the cursor to the menu.

9. Press **1** or **P** to select Perform Action.

Now your list should look like this:

BARBARA ANDERSON
DANIEL BLAIR
JOHN R. BROWN
SALLY COLEMAN
EILEEN B. FRANK
JOE FULLER
SANDRA JACOBS
LAURA A. JEFFREYS
ROBERT JONES
LOU ROBINSON
JANET SMITH

If your list of names had included a third word such as Jr. or II, as shown below, even this procedure wouldn't have worked.

JOHN R. BROWN
JANET SMITH
EILEEN B. FRANK
DANIEL BLAIR JR.
SALLY COLEMAN
BARBARA ANDERSON
LAURA A. JEFFREYS
ROBERT JONES II
SANDRA JACOBS
LOU ROBINSON
JOE FULLER

Here's how the above list would have looked if you sorted it using  *– 1* as the key word:

BARBARA ANDERSON
JOHN R. BROWN
SALLY COLEMAN
EILEEN B. FRANK
JOE FULLER
ROBERT JONES II
SANDRA JACOBS
LAURA A. JEFFREYS
DANIEL BLAIR JR.
LOU ROBINSON
JANET SMITH

Hard spaces are discussed more thoroughly in Chapter 8.

WordPerfect would place ROBERT JONES II under the category of *I* instead of *J*, and DANIEL BLAIR JR. under *J* instead of *B*. To prevent this problem, you have to use hard spaces between the last name and the word that follows. That way, the program will consider JONES II to be a single word that begins with *J*, and BLAIR JR. to be one word that starts with *B*. To do this, you would erase the space separating JONES from II (and BLAIR from JR.) then insert a hard space by pressing Home followed by the Space bar. If you were to sort it again after changing the spaces to hard spaces, all the names would be in alphabetical order by last name: DANIEL BLAIR JR. would come after BARBARA ANDERSON and ROBERT JONES II would follow LAURA JEFFREYS.

## CHANGING THE SORT ORDER

You can use option 6 on the Sort by Line menu, Order, to change the sort order from Ascending to Descending. As you can see from Figure 18.2, the default (under the heading *Order*) is Ascending. When you sort a numeric field in ascending order, it is arranged with the lowest numbers at the beginning (1, 2, 3, 4, 5, and so on). When you sort an alphanumeric field in ascending order, it is arranged from A to Z (with A at the beginning).

To see how it works, sort the NAMES.LST file again in descending order by last name. Clear the screen and retrieve the file, then follow the steps below.

1. Press the Merge/Sort key (Ctrl-F9).

2. Select Sort by pressing either **2** or **S**.

3. Press ◄─┘ twice to accept *(Screen)* as the input and output file.

4. Select option 3, Keys, by pressing either **3** or **K**.

5. Press ◄─┘ to accept alphanumeric as the type of sort.

6. Press ◄─┘ to accept *1* as the field.

7. Type – 1 to change the key word to last name.

8. Press ◄─┘, then Exit (F7) to return the cursor to the menu.

9. Press **6** or **O** to select Order, then change it to Descending by pressing **2** or **D**.

10. Press **1** or **P** to select Perform Action.

The results will look like this:

JANET SMITH
LOU ROBINSON
ROBERT JONES
LAURA JEFFREYS
SANDRA JACOBS
JOE FULLER
EILEEN FRANK
SALLY COLEMAN
JOHN BROWN
DANIEL BLAIR
BARBARA ANDERSON

## *LINE SORTING A BLOCK*

If you don't want to sort the entire file that's on screen, use the Block key (Alt-F4) to designate the text you want sorted, then press Merge/Sort (Ctrl-F9) and proceed as usual. If you use this method, you'll also save a few keystrokes because you won't have to designate the input and output files at all. To try it, clear the screen and retrieve your original file, NAMES.LST. You may want to separate the first five names from the other six names with a blank line (press ↵ after SALLY COLEMAN) before you begin.

1. Place the cursor at the beginning of the first name in the list.

2. Press the Block key (Alt-F4) then press ↓ four times and Home → once to highlight the first five names in the list.

3. Press the Merge/Sort key, Ctrl-F9. The Sort by Line screen appears almost instantly.

4. To sort the records in first name order, change key 1 to *field 1, word 1*. Press **3** or **K** for Keys, then enter **1** under the heading *Field* and **1** under the heading *Word*. Press Exit (F7) when you are finished. Press **6** then **A** to change the order back to Ascending.

5. Press **1** or **P** to begin sorting.

When WordPerfect is finished sorting, the first five names will appear in alphabetical order by first name, as follows:

DANIEL BLAIR
EILEEN FRANK
JANET SMITH
JOHN BROWN
SALLY COLEMAN

I use the block sort method frequently, and I find it to be much easier. Often you'll find that you must use block sort, and the next exercise is a good example of why. In it you'll learn how to sort a list with three columns of data, and with the headings *Name, Department,* and *Level* at the top. If you don't use the block sort method to sort it, the headings will be sorted along with the data and will probably end up somewhere in the middle of the list!

## *SORTING WITH MULTIPLE FIELDS*

To perform a line sort that includes more than one field (column) of data, there should only be one tab stop separating your columns. WordPerfect defines fields in a line sort as being separated by a tab or indent, and each tab stop is considered a different field number. It's imperative that you always press the Tab or Indent key the same number of times before you begin typing data into a field (column). The example below will help you understand why.

Look at the list of employees shown in Figure 18.3. Field 1 is the name, field 2 is the department, and field 3 is the level. Note that field 1 starts at the left margin, field 2 starts at position 3″, and field 3 starts at position 5″. If you were to retain the default tab stop settings of every half inch while typing this list, you might have to press Tab three times to move the cursor to position 3″ after you typed a short name such as Joe Doe, but only twice after typing a longer name such as Michael Wright. If that were the case, Joe Doe's department would be in field 3, but Michael Wright's would be in field 4, so the sort would not work properly (if you sorted by department).

If you were to leave the original tab settings and sort the file by the department column, which is field 3 in some records and field 4 in

| Name | Department | Level |
|------|-----------|-------|
| Jane Smith | Accounting | A1 |
| Joe Doe | Sales | S1 |
| Mary Brown | Accounting | A2 |
| Michael Wright | Marketing | M2 |
| John Black | Accounting | A3 |
| Mary Doe | Sales | S2 |
| Ann Smith | Sales | S1 |
| Pam Brown | Administration | AD1 |
| Jim White | Sales | S3 |
| Sandy Jones | Accounting | A1 |
| Paul Smith | Marketing | M2 |
| Sally Coleman | Accounting | A1 |
| Larry Fuller | Administration | AD2 |
| Ray Jones | Accounting | A2 |
| Laura Jeffrey | Sales | S3 |
| Daniel Clair | Administration | AD2 |
| Jack Schmidt | Accounting | A3 |

*Figure 18.3:* A list with three fields

others, here's how it would look after you finished, if you selected 3 as the sort key.

| | | |
|------|-----------|-------|
| Pam Brown | Administration | AD1 |
| Mary Doe | Sales | S2 |
| Ray Jones | Accounting | A2 |
| Jim White | Sales | S3 |
| Joe Doe | Sales | S1 |
| Ann Smith | Sales | S1 |
| Sally Coleman | Accounting | A1 |
| Jack Schmidt | Accounting | A3 |
| Sandy Jones | Accounting | A1 |
| Jane Smith | Accounting | A1 |
| Mary Brown | Accounting | A2 |
| John Black | Accounting | A3 |
| Daniel Clair | Administration | AD2 |
| Larry Fuller | Administration | AD2 |
| Michael Wright | Marketing | M2 |
| Paul Smith | Marketing | M2 |
| Laura Jeffrey | Sales | S3 |

Here's what happened: Tabs are set for every ½ inch, at position 1.5″, 2″, 2.5″, 3″, 3.5″, 4″, 4.5″, 5″, etc. The first six names (Pam Brown through Ann Smith) end before position 2″ so the tab key had to be pressed three times to move the cursor to the middle column, position 3″. Since they are separated by three tabs from the department column, the department is field 4. In the records that follow (John Black through Laura Jeffrey), only two tabs separate the names from the departments, so field 3 is department, and the sort worked correctly.

Now let's try the exercise the right way!

1. Delete the old tab settings and set a tab stop every 2 inches beginning at 1 inch (Shift-F8 L T Ctrl-End 1, 2 ← F7 F7).

2. Type the list shown in Figure 18.3, separating the data in each column by pressing the Tab key once.

3. Save the file under the name *SORTTEST*.

4. You'll use the block sort method (so the column headings aren't sorted), so place the cursor on the *J* in Jane Smith and press the Block key (Alt-F4).

5. Press ↓ and → to include all the data through the last row, stopping after *A3*. Do not include the blank line below the last row.

6. Press the Merge/Sort key (Ctrl-F9).

7. You will be sorting by department, which is field 2. Select option 3 (Keys) and enter these settings for key 1:

   • Typ: **a**
   • Field: **2**
   • Word: **1**

8. Use Delete to erase any settings under Key 2, if you have them.

9. Press the Exit key (F7) when you are finished, then select **1** or **P** (Perform Action) to begin the sort.

The list will look like this when you're done:

| | | |
|---|---|---|
| Sally Coleman | Accounting | A1 |
| Ray Jones | Accounting | A2 |
| Jane Smith | Accounting | A1 |

| | | |
|---|---|---|
| Sandy Jones | Accounting | A1 |
| Jack Schmidt | Accounting | A3 |
| Mary Brown | Accounting | A2 |
| John Black | Accounting | A3 |
| Pam Brown | Administration | AD1 |
| Larry Fuller | Administration | AD2 |
| Daniel Clair | Administration | AD2 |
| Michael Wright | Marketing | M2 |
| Paul Smith | Marketing | M2 |
| Joe Doe | Sales | S1 |
| Laura Jeffrey | Sales | S3 |
| Mary Doe | Sales | S2 |
| Ann Smith | Sales | S1 |
| Jim White | Sales | S3 |

***USING TWO KEYS*** Notice that the departments are in order, but the individuals within each department are not alphabetized. Let's add a second key definition to sort each department's employees alphabetically by last name. You will be defining two keys, and the second key will be the last name, field 1, word – 1.

1. Place the cursor on the *S* in *Sally Coleman* and press the Block key (Alt-F4).

2. Press ↓ and → to include all the data through the last row, stopping after *S3*.

3. Press the Merge/Sort key (Ctrl-F9).

4. Select option 3 (Keys). Leave key 1 as it is by pressing ↵ three times, then add these settings for key 2: type a, field 1, word – 1.

5. Press the Exit key (F7), then press **1** or **P** to select Perform Action and begin the sort. The results of this sort are shown below.

| | | |
|---|---|---|
| John Black | Accounting | A3 |
| Mary Brown | Accounting | A2 |
| Sally Coleman | Accounting | A1 |
| Ray Jones | Accounting | A2 |
| Sandy Jones | Accounting | A1 |
| Jack Schmidt | Accounting | A3 |
| Jane Smith | Accounting | A1 |

| Pam Brown | Administration | AD1 |
| Daniel Clair | Administration | AD2 |
| Larry Fuller | Administration | AD2 |
| Paul Smith | Marketing | M2 |
| Michael Wright | Marketing | M2 |
| Mary Doe | Sales | S2 |
| Joe Doe | Sales | S1 |
| Laura Jeffrey | Sales | S3 |
| Ann Smith | Sales | S1 |
| Jim White | Sales | S3 |

***USING THREE KEYS*** Notice that the outcome includes Mary Doe and Joe Doe in Sales. They share the same key 1 and key 2, and appear in the same order as they did in the original file. In this situation, you could add first name as a third key to insure that individuals with identical departments and last names are sorted in first name order, so that John Doe would appear in the list before Mary Doe.

Perform the sort again, adding a third key so that individuals in the same department who have the same last name will be listed in alphabetical order by first name.

1. Place the cursor on the *J* in *John Black* and press the Block key (Alt-F4).

2. Press ↓ and → to include all the data through the last row, stopping after *S3*.

3. Press the Merge/Sort key (Ctrl-F9).

4. Select option 3 (Keys). Leave key 1 and key 2 as they are, and another key for first name. Key 3 will be type a, field 1, word 1.

5. Press the Exit key (F7), then select option 1 (Perform Action) to begin the sort. The results of this sort are shown below.

| John Black | Accounting | A3 |
| Mary Brown | Accounting | A2 |
| Sally Coleman | Accounting | A1 |
| Ray Jones | Accounting | A2 |
| Sandy Jones | Accounting | A1 |
| Jack Schmidt | Accounting | A3 |
| Jane Smith | Accounting | A1 |
| Pam Brown | Administration | AD1 |

| Daniel Clair | Administration | AD2 |
| Larry Fuller | Administration | AD2 |
| Paul Smith | Marketing | M2 |
| Michael Wright | Marketing | M2 |
| Joe Doe | Sales | S1 |
| Mary Doe | Sales | S2 |
| Laura Jeffrey | Sales | S3 |
| Ann Smith | Sales | S1 |
| Jim White | Sales | S3 |

## PARAGRAPH SORT

A paragraph sort is used for alphabetizing paragraphs by first word, as in a glossary. WordPerfect defines a paragraph as a group of text ending in two or more hard returns or a page break; each paragraph can be as small as a single line or as large as a page. Figure 18.4 shows the first page of a document describing the WordPerfect function keys and their various commands, arranged in ascending function-key order. Note that the longest paragraph is five lines, and that there is only one tab setting, at position 2″. After typing each key name, I pressed Indent (F4) so that the second and following lines in each paragraph could word-wrap to the indented position automatically. I used the Paragraph Sort feature to rearrange the document in alphabetical order by function key name (such as Block and Help key), using these steps:

1. Press The Merge/Sort key (Ctrl-F9) and select option 2, Sort, by pressing **2** or **S**.

2. Press ⏎ twice to accept the defaults for input and output to the screen.

3. Press **7** or **T** for Type to change to a paragraph sort.

4. Select option 3, Paragraph, for paragraph sort by pressing **3** or **P**.

You then will see the Sort by Paragraph screen illustrated in Figure 18.5. Note that there is a new option under key definition that you didn't see on the Sort By Line screen. Since paragraphs can include multiple lines, in addition to specifying the sort key type, field, and word, you are asked for the line number.

```
F1          Cancel Key: undelete when used alone; cancel when
            pressed after other key combinations

Alt-F1      Thesaurus Key: list synonyms and antonyms

Ctrl-F1     Shell Key: temporary exit to DOS

Shift-F1    Setup Key: change defaults for initial settings,
            display, fast save, auxiliary file locations, backup,
            keyboard, screen, and units of measure.

F2          Forward Search Key: search forward for characters or
            function codes

Alt-F2      Replace Key: search and replace

Ctrl-F2     Spell Key: Check spelling of current word, page or
            document; look up words phonetically; look up words
            that match a pattern; word count

Shift-F2    Reverse Search Key: search backwards for characters or
            function codes

F3          Help Key: provide alphabetical list of features; info
            on any key combination; keyboard template when pressed
            twice

Alt-F3      Reveal Codes Key: display a screen with hidden function
            codes

Ctrl-F3     Screen Key : 1) rewrite screen 2) split screen into
            windows 3) line draw

Shift-F3    Switch Key: switch to document 2; case conversion with
            Block Key on

F4          Indent Key: temporary left margin

Alt-F4      Block Key: define a block of text

Ctrl-F4     Move Key: copy or cut 1) sentence or  2) paragraph or
            3) page; 4) retrieve column  5) retrieve text 6)
            retrieve rectangle. When pressed after Alt-F4 (Block
            on): 1) cut block 2) copy block 3) append block; 4) cut
            or copy a column 5) cut or copy a rectangle

Shift-F4    Left/Right Indent Key: indent left and right margin one
            tab stop
```

*Figure 18.4:* The WordPerfect function keys

5.  Select option 3, Keys, to define the key. For Key 1 enter **a** for Typ, **1** for Line, **2** for Field, and **1** for Word. Be sure to delete any other keys that you defined in the previous exercise before continuing. (Press the Delete key until they're all gone.)

6.  Press F7 to exit.

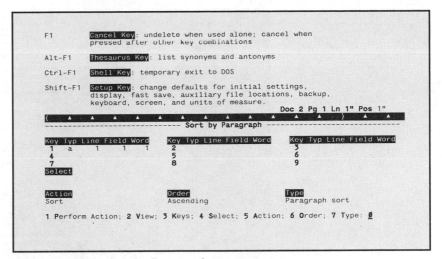

**Figure 18.5:** The Sort by Paragraph screen

7.  Press **1** or **P** for Perform Action.

The results of this sort are shown in Figure 18.6. Notice that the list is now ordered alphabetically by function key name.

## USING MERGE SORT FOR SECONDARY MERGE FILES

The Merge process is covered in detail in Chapter 16.

Once you have worked with WordPerfect's Merge feature, the merge sort operation is easy because you are already familiar with the concepts of field and record. To review, data that changes for each form (such as the recipient's name and address in a form letter) is divided into *fields,* and the collection of all fields for each form (such as each form letter) is called a *record.* The records are stored in a file called a *secondary file,* then merged with a master file called a *primary file.* The primary file contains codes such as *F1, F2,* and *F3* (where *F* means field), that tell WordPerfect where to place the actual data for these fields when it is merged with the secondary file.

You can use the merge sort to enhance your merge operations by sorting your merge records numerically, such as by ZIP code, or in alphabetical order, such as by last name. In this exercise, you are going to rearrange a file by last name.

```
Alt-F4       Block Key: define a block of text

F1           Cancel Key: undelete when used alone; cancel when pressed
             after other key combinations

F2           Forward Search Key: search forward for characters or
             function codes

F3           Help Key; provide alphabetical list of features; info on
             any key combination; keyboard template when pressed twice

F4           Indent Key: temporary left margin

Shift-F4     Left/Right Indent Key: indent left and right margin one
             tab stop

Ctrl-F4      Move Key: copy or cut 1) sentence or  2) paragraph or 3)
             page; 4) retrieve column  5) retrieve text 6) retrieve
             rectangle. When pressed after Alt-F4 (Block on): 1) cut
             block 2) copy block 3) append block; 4) cut or copy a
             column 5) cut or copy a rectangle

Alt-F2       Replace Key: search and replace

Alt-F3       Reveal Codes Key: display a screen with hidden function
             codes

Shift-F2     Reverse Search Key: search backwards for characters or
             function codes

Ctrl-F3      Screen Key : 1) rewrite screen 2) split screen into
             windows 3) line draw

Shift-F1     Setup Key: change defaults for initial settings, display,
             fast save, auxiliary file locations, backup, keyboard,
             screen, and units of measure.

Ctrl-F1      Shell Key: temporary exit to DOS

Ctrl-F2      Spell Key: Check spelling of current word, page or
             document; look up words phonetically; look up words that
             match a pattern; word count

Shift-F3     Switch Key: switch to document 2; case conversion with
             Block Key on

Alt-F1       Thesaurus Key: list synonyms and antonyms
```

*Figure 18.6:* The WordPerfect function keys list after paragraph sort

In Chapter 16 you created a secondary merge file named WIN-NERS.SF, with which you produced several form letters from a single primary file. If you still have it, use it for this exercise (but do not retrieve it from disk). If not, enter the names and addresses shown below and remember to press Merge R (F9) after each field to insert the ^ R, and Merge E (Shift-F9 E) after each record to insert the ^ E. Save the file under the name WINNERS.SF and clear the screen using the Exit key (F7).

```
Ms. Colleen McDuffy ^ R
54 Prince Lane ^ R
Salem ^ R
GA ^ R
32255 ^ R
$1,000,000 ^ R
(513) 222-0000 ^ R
 ^ E
= = = = = = = = = = = = = = = = = = = =
Mr. James Browder ^ R
100 Main St. ^ R
Mt. Hood ^ R
WA ^ R
81233 ^ R
$10,000 ^ R
(802) 331-0000 ^ R
 ^ E
- - - - - - - - - - - - - - - - - - - -
Mrs. Rhonda Flamestein ^ R
233 12th Ave. ^ R
San Francisco ^ R
CA ^ R
91222 ^ R
$50,000 ^ R
(415) 444-0000 ^ R
 ^ E
= = = = = = = = = = = = = = = = = = = =
```

In a merge sort, each field ends in ^ R, so each of the three records contains seven fields. Field 1 is the name, field 2 the street address, field 3 the city, field 4 the state, field 5 the ZIP code, field 6 the dollar amount, and field 7 the phone number.

1. Press Ctrl-F9 2 to begin the sort.

2. For the input file, enter

   **winners.sf**

3. For the output file, press ⏎ to accept the default, the screen.

One of the sort screens will then appear, and some of the records from your WINNERS.SF file will also appear above it. (The Sort by Paragraph screen will appear if you just completed the last exercise, and the Sort by Line screen will appear if you have not performed another type of sort since turning on the computer.) Be sure to delete any keys or selection conditions that may remain on the screen from previous exercises before you continue.

4. Use the Type option to select Merge (press either **7** or **T**, then **1** or **M**).

5. The screen illustrated in Figure 18.7 will appear.

Like the Sort by Paragraph screen, this screen is slightly different from the Sort by Line screen because the sort keys are defined by type, field, line, and word. (The Sort by Line screen does not include the line specification.)

The next step is to define the key WordPerfect will use to perform the sort. Since the records are to be sorted alphabetically by last name, the key field will be *1*. There is only one line within this field, so the key line will be *1*. Since you'll sort by last name, which is the third word in each record, the key word will be *3*.

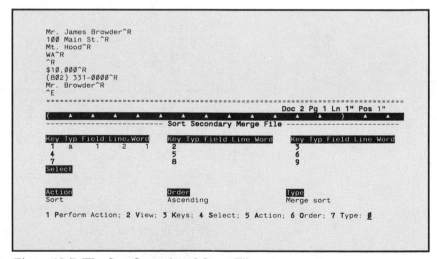

*Figure 18.7:* The Sort Secondary Merge File screen

6. Press **3** or **K** to select Keys, then change key 1 to field 1, line 1, word 3.

7. Press F7 after making these entries, then press **1** or **P** for Perform Action.

Your three records will then be rearranged (on screen) so that the record for Mr. James Browder is the first on the list, Mrs. Rhonda Flamestein is the second, and Ms. Colleen McDuffy is the last.

You may want to try it again using one of the numeric fields such as ZIP code or check amount as your key. To do this, just repeat the steps and replace key 1. To sort by ZIP code, for example, you would enter either *alphanumeric* or *numeric* as the type, *5* as the field, and *1* as the line and word. To sort by check amount, you would have to enter *N* for numeric type under key 1, since there is a dollar sign in the field and since the numbers are not even in length. Then enter field *6,* line *1,* and word *1* as the other options. Note that the list will be sorted in ascending order (unless you change this default), so the largest check amount ($1,000,000) will be at the bottom. To change to descending order so that the largest amount comes first, select Order from the Sort by Line screen by pressing *6* or *O,* then select Descending by pressing *2* or *D.*

## USING THE SELECT FEATURE

WordPerfect's Select feature is useful when you want to separate certain records from the rest of the file, such as all customers from New York, or all customers whose credit limit exceeds $5,000. You can use select alone, or along with the Sort feature so that the resulting list is also sorted.

Let's use the NAMES.LST file to perform a simple task, selecting those individuals whose last names begin with characters between *A* and *J.* To do this, clear the screen and retrieve the file NAMES.LST.

1. Press The Merge/Sort key (Ctrl-F9) and select option 2, Sort, by pressing **2** or **S**.

2. Press ⏎ twice to direct both input and output to the screen.

3. If you just completed the exercise in the last section, you'll have to select option 7, Type, and change the type of sort back to Sort by Line (press **2** or **L**).

4. Since you will be selecting based on the name field, change the field to *1* by pressing **K** or **3**, then entering **A** for Alphanumeric type, **1** for key line, **1** for the key field, and **2** for the key word. Press ◄─┘, then Exit (F7) when you have finished.

5. Choose Select by pressing either **4** or **S**.

The cursor will move under Select on the screen. This is where you specify the conditions that must be met for a record to be included in your new list. Notice that the prompt line has changed and appears as follows:

+(OR), *(AND), =, <>, >, <, >=, <=;
Press EXIT when done

These symbols are called *operators,* and they allow you to establish selection conditions. For example, using the NAMES.LST file, you could use *equal* to select only those whose ZIP codes are equal to 94920. You could use *+(OR)* to specify an *either/or* condition, such as last name equals either Anderson or Jones. You could use *\*(AND)* to specify two conditions, both of which must be met, such as those who both live in San Francisco and have the ZIP code 94112. (Daniel Blair would be the only San Francisco resident who would be excluded from the resulting list.) Table 18.1 below shows what each symbol means.

Our condition is going to be that the last name starts with a character between *A* and *J*. To enter it, you define a key, just like when you are using the Sort feature, then you use the key along with an operator to define the condition that must be met. Our key will be last name, which is field 1, word 2. Our operator and condition will be *less than or equal to JX* (< =JX).

6. For the selection condition, type (case is irrelevant)

Key1 < =JX

then press ◄─┘.

Because you typed *JX* instead of *J*, your resulting list will include all last names starting with *A* through *J* and with the second character between *A* and *X*. If you enter *Key1< =J*, names beginning in *J* would not be included unless that were the only letter in the last name. If you were to use *JE*, it would include *Jacobs* but not *Jeffreys*.

Your screen should now resemble Figure 18.8. Notice that the Action is *Select and Sort* and the Direction is *Ascending*.

***Table 18.1:*** Soft Operator Definitions

| SYMBOL | MEANING |
|--------|---------|
| + | or |
| * | and |
| = | equals |
| < > | does not equal |
| > | greater than |
| < | less than |
| > = | greater than or equal to |
| < = | less than or equal to |

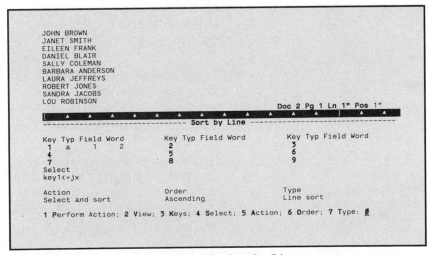

***Figure 18.8:*** Selection conditions on the Sort by Line screen

If you did not want the list to be sorted, you could use option 5, Action, to limit the action to select only. If you did, you would see this prompt:

> Action: 1 Select and Sort; 2 Select Only: 0

If you then selected option 2, the message under Action would change to

> Select

to verify that you were performing only a select.

However, since this will be a sort and select, do not change it. Now generate your sorted and selected list.

7. Press **1** or **P** to select option 1, Perform Action.

The results will be as follows:

> BARBARA ANDERSON
> DANIEL BLAIR
> JOHN BROWN
> SALLY COLEMAN
> EILEEN FRANK
> JOE FULLER
> SANDRA JACOBS
> LAURA JEFFREYS
> ROBERT JONES

As you can see, all the records that are left have last names that begin with a letter between *A* and *J*. The other records have disappeared from the screen. If you want to save this list, you should assign a different name from the original one so you retain the other names in that file (NAMES.LST).

Now let's try a sort with two conditions. You will need to set a single tab stop so that you can add a second field, *age,* to your original list.

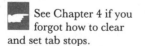
See Chapter 4 if you forgot how to clear and set tab stops.

1. Clear the screen, then retrieve the NAMES.LST file. Place the cursor at the top of the file and use the Format key (Shift-F8) to clear all the other tab stops and set one at 4 inches.

2. Enter the data shown below for the age field:

| | |
|---|---|
| JOHN BROWN | 32 |
| JANET SMITH | 20 |
| EILEEN FRANK | 45 |
| DANIEL BLAIR | 56 |
| SALLY COLEMAN | 29 |
| BARBARA ANDERSON | 31 |
| LAURA JEFFREYS | 52 |
| ROBERT JONES | 36 |
| SANDRA JACOBS | 37 |
| LOU ROBINSON | 24 |
| JOE FULLER | 30 |

3. Use the Save Text key (F10) to save the file under the name NAMEAGE.LST.

4. Press the Merge/Sort key (Ctrl-F9), select **2** for Sort, then press ← twice.

5. Press **3** or **K** to use the Keys option to add a second key for the age column. Press ← three times to get to key 2, then enter **2** for field and **1** for word. Note that the new key definition can be either alphanumeric or numeric. Press F7 to exit.

6. Use Select to restrict the list to those whose last names range between *A* and *JX* and who are over 30 years old (greater than 30). Press **4** or **S** and type this condition:

    Key1 < = JX * Key2 > 30

    Press ←.

7. Press **1** or **P** to use option 1, Perform Action.

Your results will be as follows:

| | |
|---|---|
| BARBARA ANDERSON | 31 |
| DANIEL BLAIR | 56 |

| JOHN BROWN | 32 |
| EILEEN FRANK | 45 |
| SANDRA JACOBS | 37 |
| LAURA JEFFREYS | 52 |
| ROBERT JONES | 36 |

Notice that Joe Fuller was excluded from the resulting list. Although his name comes before *JX* in the alphabet, he is not *over* 30 years old so he didn't meet both selection conditions.

## SUMMARY

WordPerfect's Sort and Select features are fast and powerful. There are three types of sorts: line sorts for data in rows and columns, paragraph sorts for paragraphs, and merge sorts for secondary merge files. Each type can rearrange alphanumeric or numeric data in ascending or descending order, using one to nine key words. The data to be sorted can be on screen or in a disk file, and the results can be directed to the screen or to a disk file. You can sort an entire file, or use the Block key to mark and sort just a section of it. With WordPerfect's Select feature, you can isolate information that meets the exact conditions you define with the help of operators such as *equals, greater than, less than or equal to,* and so on.

# SAVING TIME AND KEYSTROKES WITH MACROS

# FAST TRACK

**Create a macro**          **597**

by pressing the Macro Definition key (Ctrl-F10), then typing the name of your macro (up to eight characters) at the *Define macro:* prompt and pressing ◄┘. You then will see the *Description:* prompt. Type in a description of what the macro will do (up to 60 characters) and press ◄┘. You will see the *Macro Def* message telling you to record the macro. Type the exact keystrokes you want included, then press Ctrl-F10 to save your macro and turn off Macro Definition.

**To use a macro,**          **599**

press the Invoke Macro key (Alt-F10). At the *Macro:* prompt, type the macro name, then press ◄┘. WordPerfect will automatically type in the keystrokes you included when defining the macro.

**Create an Alt macro**          **605**

by pressing the Macro Definition key (Ctrl-F10), then naming the macro by pressing the Alt key and any letter key from A to Z, or by typing *alt* and a letter A to Z. At the *Description:* prompt, type in a description of what the macro will do, then press ◄┘. Record the macro by typing the exact keystrokes you want included, then press Ctrl-F10 to save your macro and turn off Macro Definition. To use an Alt macro, just press the Alt key and hold it down while pressing the letter key that you used to name the macro.

**Create a temporary macro**          **608**

that contains only text by pressing Ctrl-PgUp, typing a number 0 through 9 in response to the *Variable* prompt, and then typing your text in response to the *Value* prompt. When you press

←, macro definition ends. To use this type of macro, press Alt and the number that you typed. You can also create a temporary text macro by blocking text in your document using the Block (Alt-F4) and cursor movement keys, pressing Ctrl-PgUp, and typing the number (0 through 9). These macros will be deleted when you exit WordPerfect

**To edit a macro,**                                                        610

press the Define Macro key (Ctrl-F10), type the name of the macro you want to change, then press ←. At the prompt, press *2* or *E* and you will see a screen with a box that shows the keystrokes in the macro. Place the cursor in the box by pressing *2* or *A,* then edit the macro. Press Exit (F7) then ← to end macro editing.

A *MACRO* IS A SEQUENCE OF KEYSTROKES THAT IS saved in a special file so that you can use it again whenever you wish, just by pressing one or two keys and typing the file name. The macro can include text and/or WordPerfect commands, such as the keystrokes you use to change margins or tab stops or to print multiple copies of a document. Macros are one of WordPerfect's most useful features, and they are easy to set up and use. Anytime you find yourself repeatedly typing a sequence of commands or a word, phrase, or paragraph, consider recording the keystrokes in a macro file so that you can save yourself extra typing the next time you need them.

Macros can range from very short, simple entries to very elaborate chains. Some macros will save you a few keystrokes, others will save many. However, it is often the shortest ones that prove the most valuable because you use them the most often.

## CREATING AND USING MACROS TO SIMPLIFY YOUR WORK

WordPerfect's macros are easy to create. The process often has been compared to making a tape recording; you turn on the recorder, type the keystrokes that you want to record, then turn it off again. After that you can play them back anytime. The recording starts when you press the Macro Definition key (Ctrl-F10). Next you assign a name to your macro, enter a description of what it does (although this is optional), and type the appropriate keystrokes to record them in the file. The last step is to press Ctrl-F10 again, which saves the macro on the disk and turns off the recording.

### CREATING A SIMPLE MACRO

Let's try creating a simple macro to type a letter closing to see how easy it can be. We'll call it CLOSE because whenever you use it, the macro will type *Yours truly,* then skip three lines and type your name.

1. Press Ctrl-F10. You'll see this message on the status line in the lower left corner of the screen:

   **Define macro:**

2. Type this name for your first macro:

   **CLOSE**

   Press ⏎. Like other file names, macro names can consist of one to eight characters, but you cannot type a three-character extension because WordPerfect automatically adds the three-character extension *WPM*. Next, this prompt appears:

   **Description:**

   Here you can enter a short description of what this macro does, with a maximum of 60 characters. This description will be visible in a special screen that appears if you edit the macro after creating and saving it (which you'll do shortly).

> If you don't want to type a description for your macro, just press ⏎ when the *Description:* prompt appears.

3. For the description, type

   **closing for a letter**

   then press ⏎. You will then see this message on the status line, in the lower left corner:

   **Macro Def**

   When you see this message, it means that any keys you press from now until you turn off Macro Definition will be recorded as part of the macro, so be careful! For example, if you accidentally press a letter key such as *U* then press Backspace to erase it, your macro will also press *U* and Backspace whenever you use it.

4. Type the following:

   **Yours truly,**

   then press ⏎ three times and type your name.

5. Press Ctrl-F10 to turn off Macro Definition.

Pressing Ctrl-F10 in the last step saved your macro, so now you can use it anytime you want. WordPerfect automatically assigns the extension *.WPM* (for *WordPerfect Macro*) to all macros, so the file name is actually CLOSE.WPM, and you could see it if you looked in the List Files screen (F5). However, don't ever try to retrieve a macro file into WordPerfect using either the List Files key (F5) or the Retrieve Text key (Shift-F10) since it can't be done. Macros can be edited in WordPerfect 5.0 (earlier versions did not have this feature), but you use a different procedure that you'll study later in this chapter.

Notice that the contents of the macro (*Yours truly* and your name) remain on screen. This always happens, because when you create a macro, the keystrokes are executed in your document at the same time they are being recorded in the file. If you're in the middle of typing a document and you don't want to disrupt it by having the keystrokes take effect at the cursor position while you are creating a macro, press Shift-F3 to switch to the Doc 2 work area (if it's empty) before creating the macro. After you finish creating the macro, exit from Doc 2 without saving (press F7 N Y).

To clear *Yours truly* and your name from the screen, press F7 N N.

## USING MACROS

Now let's learn how to use the macro.

1. Press Alt-F10, the Invoke Macro key. This prompt will appear in the lower left corner of the screen:

   **Macro:**

2. Type the macro name, **CLOSE**, then press ←. The message

   **\* Please wait \***

   will appear very briefly (so quickly that you may miss it), then *Yours truly* and your name will appear on your screen at the cursor position.

## CREATING A MACRO TO DELETE A SENTENCE

Now let's create a different type of macro, one that performs a function instead of typing text. This one will delete a sentence, using the Move option on the Move key (Ctrl-F4). Incidentally, using the Move option is safer than using the Delete option, because if you change your mind after using the macro to erase a sentence, you can easily get it back by pressing Ctrl-F4 R B (until you use Block and Move or Move alone to move or copy another section of text). If you use the Delete option, you can bring back your sentence by pressing Cancel (F1) but this won't work if you've made three other deletions since using the macro, which is very easy to do (by pressing Delete, Backspace, Ctrl-Backspace, etc).

See Chapter 5 if you need to review the delete and undelete functions of the Move and Cancel keys.

1. Place the cursor anywhere on the line *Yours truly*.

2. Press the Macro Define key (Ctrl-F10).

3. In response to the *Define macro:* prompt, type **S** for the macro name, then press ⏎.

4. For the description, type

   **Deletes a sentence**

   then press ⏎.

5. Press the Move key (Ctrl-F4) and press **1** or **S** to select the Sentence option.

6. At the next prompt, press **1** or **M** for Move.

7. Press Cancel (F1) to get rid of the prompt *Move cursor; press **Enter** to retrieve*.

8. Press Ctrl-F10 to end Macro Definition.

To test your new macro, place the cursor anywhere on the line with your name and press Alt-F10 S ⏎. Remember, you can always retrieve the erased sentence by pressing either Ctrl-F4 R B or Shift-F10 ⏎.

This macro reduces what would have taken five keystrokes down to three; this doesn't sound like much, but it really does make the process easier because you don't have to look at all those menus and figure out which option to select. As I said at the beginning of the chapter, it's often the simplest macros that you use most frequently; I use this one all the time.

## CREATING A MACRO TO DELETE A LINE

Here's another macro that will delete a whole line for you, no matter where the cursor is positioned on the line when you use it. It works by moving the cursor to the left side of the line, then using Ctrl-End to erase it. To retrieve a line you've erased with this macro, you have to use the Undelete function on the Cancel key (F1). Here are the steps to create the macro:

1. Press Ctrl-F10 and name the macro **L**, then press ⏎.

2. For the description, type **deletes a line**, then press ⏎.

3. Press Home ← so that when you use the macro, the cursor will always start at the beginning of the line.

4. Press Ctrl-End to delete the line.

5. Press Ctrl-F10 to end Macro Definition.

If you want to test the macro, make sure you have a line of text to delete, then place the cursor on the line and press Alt-F10 L ⏎. Remember, to undelete it you can press F1 1.

## ORGANIZING YOUR MACROS

WordPerfect macros are automatically stored in the current directory or disk drive, which could become very confusing if you use multiple subdirectories because you'd have macro files all over the place. Fortunately, you can set up WordPerfect so that it will automatically save all macros in their own subdirectory or on the disk in drive B, allowing you to use a macro from any subdirectory or drive. I strongly recommend that you do it, especially if you have a hard disk.

### STORING MACROS ON A HARD DISK SYSTEM

The first step is to create a new directory for your macros; then you can use the Setup key to tell WordPerfect where to find them. I store my macros in a subdirectory called MACS; Figure 19.1 shows the List Files screen for my subdirectory.

Here's how to create a new subdirectory called MACROS.

1. Press the List Files key (F5), then ⏎.

2. Select the Other Directory option by pressing **7** or **O**. You'll see a prompt like this one:

   New directory = C:\WP

```
04/12/88  17:50              Directory D:\WP\MACS\*.*
Document size:        Ø   Free: 10305536   Used:     5667     Files:  51

. <CURRENT>      <DIR>                ..  <PARENT>    <DIR>
A        .WPM       69  03/14/88 15:06   ALTB    .WPM      82  02/29/88 12:31
ALTC     .WPM       74  02/11/88 20:21   ALTD    .WPM      93  03/20/88 18:31
ALTE     .WPM       82  03/11/88 23:18   ALTF    .WPM     107  03/17/88 12:04
ALTG     .WPM       59  03/28/88 10:10   ALTH    .WPM     120  03/11/88 17:03
ALTJ     .WPM       65  03/11/88 17:02   ALTK    .WPM      68  02/12/88 15:01
ALTL     .WPM       92  03/05/88 10:24   ALTM    .WPM     191  03/17/88 11:49
ALTN     .WPM       98  03/15/88 00:04   ALTO    .WPM      90  04/01/88 22:07
ALTP     .WPM       65  03/05/88 23:59   ALTQ    .WPM      81  02/27/88 10:32
ALTR     .WPM       93  03/17/88 12:01   ALTS    .WPM      73  03/11/88 16:06
ALTT     .WPM      119  03/23/88 11:07   ALTU    .WPM      91  02/14/88 14:13
ALTV     .WPM       75  03/21/88 14:22   ALTW *  .WPM      92  02/11/88 13:06
ALTX     .WPM       87  03/17/88 12:00   ALTZ    .WPM      77  03/28/88 10:06
C        .WPM       97  03/03/88 09:14   CAPS    .WPM     128  03/17/88 12:11
CHAIN    .WPM      164  03/11/88 16:12   CLOSE   .WPM     145  03/17/88 11:35
CONVERTS.WPM        57  03/01/88 18:43   D       .WPM     103  03/03/88 16:25
ENV      .WPM      131  03/17/88 13:01   ENVCOPY .WPM     103  03/17/88 13:03
FIRSTWOR.WPM        95  03/17/88 12:51   FIRSTWRD.WPM     129  03/01/88 23:44
FRSTWORD.WPM        93  03/04/88 00:26 ▼ KMERGE  .WPM      99  02/27/88 12:10

1 Retrieve; 2 Delete; 3 Move/Rename; 4 Print; 5 Text In;
6 Look; 7 Other Directory; 8 Copy; 9 Word Search; N Name Search: 6
```

*Figure 19.1:* Macro file names shown in the List Files screen

If it says something else after *WP*, press End, then Backspace until it matches the prompt line above (assuming that *WP* is the name of your main WordPerfect directory).

3. Press the End key to move the cursor to the end of the prompt line, then press the backslash key (\) and type the name for your new subdirectory: **MACROS.** Since MACROS will be a subdirectory of your main WordPerfect directory, you had to type its name *after* the WordPerfect directory name (to make it a subdirectory). The prompt should now look like this:

New directory = C:\WP\MACROS

4. Press ⏎ and you will see this prompt asking if you want to create the subdirectory:

Create C:\WP\MACROS? (Y/N) No

5. Press **Y.** WordPerfect creates the subdirectory, and in an instant you'll see its name near the top of your file list, like this:

MACROS .          <DIR>

Now press the Space bar to exit from the List Files screen, then you'll use the Setup key to tell WordPerfect where your macro files are located. Once you follow the steps to do this, all macros you create will automatically be saved there, and they can be used from any WordPerfect subdirectory you may be working in.

1. Press the Setup key (Shift-F1).

2. Select the Location of Auxiliary Files option by pressing either **7** or **L**.

3. Select the Keyboard/Macro Files option by pressing either *3* or **K**.

4. Type the drive and path leading to your macro subdirectory:

   C:\WP\MACROS

5. Press ◄─┘ three times to get back to Edit mode.

From now on, all the macros you create will automatically be saved in your new subdirectory (and you don't have to make it the current directory). I don't recommend you save any other files there, but this shouldn't be a problem because you never have to switch to the macro subdirectory in order to save or use your macros.

At this point you may wish to move your CLOSE macro into the macro subdirectory. If so, you can use the List Files key to accomplish the task easily. Press F5 ◄─┘, move the cursor bar onto the file name (CLOSE.WPM), then press *3* or *M* to select the Move option. At the *New name:* prompt, type the path to your macro subdirectory, \WP\MACROS, then press ◄─┘.

Although you can copy, move, and delete macros through the List Files screen, don't try to retrieve one into the WordPerfect editing screen (using either the Retrieve option on the List Files screen or the Retrieve Text key). If you try, you'll receive this error message: *ERROR: Incompatible file format.* Macros can be edited through a special method that you will learn shortly.

## STORING MACROS ON A FLOPPY DISK SYSTEM

If you are using a system with floppy drives, you may want to store all your macros on the disk in drive B because you could easily run out of space on the disk in drive A. When you press Alt-F10 to start a macro, WordPerfect searches both the A and the B drives even if you don't type the drive designator (*B:*) before the macro name. However, it will not automatically store them on drive B as you create them unless you use the Setup key to tell WordPerfect where to store them. Follow these steps to do it:

1. Press the Setup key (Shift-F1).

2. Select the Location of Auxiliary Files option by pressing either **7** or **L**.

3. Select the Keyboard/Macro Files option by pressing either **3** or **K**.

4. Type the drive designator: **B:**

5. Press ⏎ three times to get back to Edit mode.

Once you've done this, all the macros you create will automatically be saved on the disk in drive B. If you use this method, you may want to keep a master macro disk that contains your most frequently used macros and copy each macro you create onto it. That way, each time you format a new data disk you can copy all of the macros at once from the master onto the new data disk, and they'll always be available for you to use.

## *USING A MACRO WHEN YOU START WORDPERFECT*

You can ask WordPerfect to run a macro as soon as the program starts by using the */M* option upon startup. For instance, you may have a macro that changes several default formatting features, such as margins and fonts, that you always use when creating a certain type of document. If you were going to start WordPerfect and create that type of document, you could have WordPerfect run the macro as soon as the program is loaded by typing *WP/M-* followed by the macro name. For instance, if the macro was called REPORT, you would start WordPerfect by typing

**WP/M-REPORT**

WordPerfect would start and you'd see the familiar status line, then it would use the macro to make your formatting changes.

I used this technique frequently as I was writing this book, since I often spent several days writing and editing the same chapter. Each time

I started WordPerfect, I had it run a macro called GO which automatically changed subdirectories (each chapter was in a separate subdirectory) and retrieved the file for the chapter I was working on at the time. Whenever I finished a chapter, I edited the GO macro so that it would change to a different subdirectory and load the next chapter.

## ALT MACROS

As you can see, several of the macros in the directory listing shown in Figure 19.1 have names that start with *ALT.* These are macros that were assigned to an Alt key in combination with one of the letters A through Z. Using them is easier than using the other type of macros you've studied so far, because you only press two keys to do it: Alt along with the letter key. Since you do not have to press the Invoke Macro key (Alt-F10), type a name, then press ←, you can see how these Alt macros can be real time-savers. For example, the macro ALTW in my listing enters the word *WordPerfect,* which I had to type often while writing this book. The program does the typing with just two keystrokes, saving me a total of 11 keystrokes, including pressing the Shift key twice, every time I use it. The macro ALTU underlines a whole word at once, no matter what it's length (you'll create this macro later in the chapter). Since Alt macros are easy to invoke accidentally, you should not use them to perform such tasks as deleting text or clearing the screen, which may have a detrimental effect on your document if the macro is invoked unintentionally.

### CREATING A LINE-SPACING ALT MACRO

Two Alt macros that I use constantly change the line spacing to double or single by executing this series of commands: Shift-F8 to use the Format key, *L* to select the Format: Line menu, *S* for spacing, *1* or *2* for single or double spacing, then ← three times to get back to Edit mode. Try following these steps to create an Alt macro for double spacing. We'll call it ALTD.

1. Press Ctrl-F10 to define the macro.

2. To assign the name, press Alt and hold it down while pressing **D**.

3. For the description, type

   **Double spacing macro**

   then press ◄─┘.

4. Now enter the keystrokes that double-space. Type

   **Shift-F8 L S 2 ◄─┘ ◄─┘ ◄─┘**

5. Press Ctrl-F10 to end Macro Definition.

Now clear the screen (F7 N N), type a few lines, move the cursor back to the top, and press Alt-D to use the macro. Your text should be double spaced immediately. If you check the Reveal Codes screen (Alt-F3), next to the cursor you'll see the code for double spacing:

**[Ln Spacing:2]**

Wasn't that easier than working through all those ponderous menus?

You may want to try using the same steps to create another macro for single spacing, and name it ALTS in step 2. The only differences will be that in step 3 you enter a description like *single spacing macro,* and in step 4 you select *1* instead of *2* for the line spacing.

## CREATING A MACRO TO CONVERT A LETTER TO UPPERCASE

Here's another Alt macro you can try. This one will convert the first character of a word to uppercase, and it is useful when you rearrange a sentence in a way that causes the first word to be deleted or moved so that the new first word needs to be capitalized. Using this procedure to convert a character from lowercase to uppercase involves six keystrokes: pressing Alt-F4 to turn on Block mode, pressing → to highlight the character, then pressing the Switch key (Shift-F3) and selecting the Uppercase option. Let's name this macro ALTC (for capitals).

See Chapter 5 for a complete explanation of the Case Conversion option on the Switch key.

1. Type **a** then press ← to place the cursor on it.

2. Press Ctrl-F10.

3. Press Alt-C or type **ALTC** to name the macro ALTC, then press ◄─┘.

4. For the description, type

   **converts a letter to uppercase**

5. Enter these keystrokes:  Alt-F4 → Shift-F3 U.

6. Press Ctrl-F10 to end Macro Definition.

To use the macro, move the cursor onto another letter you want capitalized (or type one and move the cursor back onto it), then press Alt-C. If you watch the prompt line carefully, you may be able to see prompts like *Block on* as the macro does its work. The letter will be converted almost instantly.

The uppercase conversion macro can be expanded into a macro that will convert the first letter of the first word in each sentence of your document to uppercase, so that you could type the entire document in lowercase and fix it later. You'll learn how to create such a macro later in this chapter.

## *CREATING A MACRO TO UNDERLINE A WORD*

Here are the steps to create the ALTU macro, which underlines a word.

1. Type your first and last name on a blank line, then press ←⏎. Move the cursor onto the first letter of your first name.

2. Press Ctrl-F10.

3. Press Alt-U for the macro name, then enter this description:

   **underline word macro**

   Press ←⏎.

4. Enter these keystrokes to underline the word:

   **Alt-F4 Ctrl→ ← F8**

   Note that you press the Ctrl→ combination to highlight a whole word, regardless of its length, and that you must press ← after that so that you won't underline the blank space that follows it (since Ctrl→ pressed in Block mode moves the cursor into the space following the word).

5. Press Ctrl-F10 to end Macro Definition.

To test it, type another word, place the cursor on the first letter, and press Alt-U. Note that if your line does not end in a hard or soft return, the macro will not underline the last character if it is the last word on the line. This happens because you used ← in the macro to move the cursor back one position so that it would not underline the blank space that follows most words (except when the word is the last one on the line and there is no hard or soft return following it). This can be avoided if you press the Space bar at the end of such a word.

## CREATING TEMPORARY MACROS

The first two methods you studied create permanent macros, but WordPerfect also lets you establish temporary macros to use in just one editing session. Note that this method only allows you to enter text into your macro. Such a macro would be useful if you were typing a long name or phrase frequently in a document, but didn't anticipate using it again in your other work. Temporary macros are deleted when you exit from WordPerfect. The advantage is that they do not consume valuable space on your disk and clutter up your directory with macros you'll never use again.

To create a temporary macro, press the Macro Commands key (Ctrl-PgUp) then assign a number from 0 through 9 to the text. To run the Ctrl-PgUp macro, you press the Alt key and the number.

### CREATING TEMPORARY MACROS USING CTRL-PGUP

Let's create a temporary macro that will type *International Business Machines*. This would be useful if you had to type this name frequently in a report you were currently working on, but were not planning to use it again in other documents. There are actually two ways to create this type of macro. The first is to press Macro Commands (Ctrl-PgUp), type a number 0 through 9, then type your text and press ← to end Macro Definition. The second is to use the Block key (Alt-F4) and the cursor movement keys to highlight the text in your document, then press Macro Commands (Ctrl-PgUp) and type a number. Whichever method you use to create the macro, you use it by pressing Alt and holding it down while typing the number.

Remember that both types of temporary macros can only be used until you exit from WordPerfect.

***USING THE MACRO COMMANDS METHOD***    Let's use the first method for the *International Business Machines* macro, and assign the number 1 to it. Here are the steps to create it. Unlike other macros, the text will not be entered on your Edit screen as you record it in the macro.

1. Press Ctrl-PgUp. You will see this prompt:

   **Variable:**

2. Press **1**. Note that if you are using the numeric keypad, Num Lock must be turned on.

3. You will then see this prompt:

   **Value:**

   Warning: Do not press ◄─┘ at this point or you will end Macro Definition. Type

   **International Business Machines**

   then press ◄─┘ to end Macro Definition. Notice that the text in the macro *(International Business Machines)* is not on your Edit screen.

4. Now test the macro. To use it, just press Alt and hold it down while pressing **1** once. *International Business Machines* should appear on your screen.

You are limited to typing about 119 characters.

***CREATING MACROS WITH THE BLOCK AND MACRO COMMANDS METHOD***    Let's create a macro using the Block and Macro Commands method. This one will type your company name and address whenever you use it.

1. Begin by typing your company name and address.

2. Place the cursor on the first character of your company name, then press Block (Alt-F4) to turn on Block mode. Press ↓ until you've highlighted all the text.

3. Press Ctrl-PgUp. You will see the Variable prompt again. Type the number **2** for this macro. The *Block on* prompt disappears, and Macro Definition ends.

4. Now try using the macro. Place the cursor on a blank line, then press Alt-2. Your company name and address should appear at the cursor position.

## EDITING MACROS

The macro editor was not available in WordPerfect 4.2 and earlier versions, but it was included in the WordPerfect Library.

WordPerfect includes a macro editor that you can use to alter your macros. Suppose, for instance, that you wanted to change the CLOSE macro so that instead of typing *Yours truly* it types *Sincerely yours*. Instead of typing it all over again, you can use the macro editor to change it quickly and easily. Let's try it.

1. Press the Define Macro key (Ctrl-F10), type the name of your macro, **CLOSE**, then press ←┘. You should see this prompt at the bottom of the screen:

   **CLOSE.WPM is Already Defined.  1 Replace; 2 Edit; 0**

2. Press **2** or **E** to edit the macro. Your will see the macro editing screen shown in Figure 19.2.

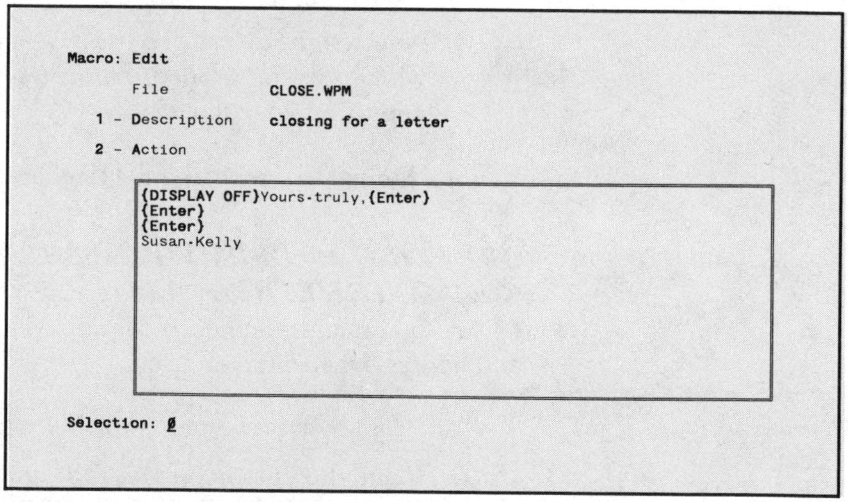

```
Macro: Edit

        File          CLOSE.WPM
  1 - Description      closing for a letter
  2 - Action

        ┌──────────────────────────────────────────┐
        │ {DISPLAY OFF}Yours·truly,{Enter}          │
        │ {Enter}                                   │
        │ {Enter}                                   │
        │ Susan·Kelly                               │
        │                                           │
        │                                           │
        │                                           │
        └──────────────────────────────────────────┘

  Selection: 0
```

*Figure 19.2:* The Macro Editing screen

The box in the middle shows the actual keystrokes of your macro. My keystrokes look like this:

```
{DISPLAY OFF} Yours·truly {Enter}
{Enter}
{Enter}
Susan·Kelly
```

The word in braces, {Enter}, represents the three times I pressed the ⏎ key to leave three blank lines between *Yours truly* and my name. WordPerfect places the {DISPLAY OFF} code in macros automatically, so you don't see them as they execute.

To change *Yours truly*, you have to get the cursor into the box, then delete it and type the new closing. To do this, you use the Action option.

3. Press **2** or **A** for Action. This places the cursor at the left side of the line.

4. Press → Ctrl-Backspace once, then Del, then Ctrl-Backspace to delete *Yours truly*, then type

    Sincerely yours,

    Don't worry if you make a mistake, because you can always press Cancel (F1) Y, then select Action to start over again.

5. Press Exit (F7) then ⏎ to end macro editing.

Now try using the macro again to see if you succeeded in making the change. Press Alt-F10, type the name *CLOSE*, then press ⏎. Wasn't that easy?

## REPEATING A MACRO

The Escape key (Esc), which you studied in Chapter 3, can be used to repeat a macro several times. For example, you could use it with the ALTC macro you created earlier so that instead of converting a single letter to uppercase, it will convert a word. To do this, you press Esc, type the number of times you want to repeat the macro, then start the macro. Let's try it.

1. Type **macro** in lowercase, then place the cursor on the first letter, *m.*

2. Press Esc. You should see this prompt:

   **Repeat Value = 8**

3. Type *5* for the number of times you want to repeat it, which is the total number of characters in the word. Do not press ←! The prompt should look like this:

   **Repeat Value = 5**

4. Press Alt-C.

Your entire word will then appear in capital letters. It's really fun to watch the cursor zip along as the macro is repeated.

## USER INPUT IN A MACRO

▶ You could have used the Pause command in the double-spacing macro that you created earlier to make the macro pause and allow you to enter the number for line spacing that you want to use each time, such as 1 or 2.

WordPerfect allows you to insert a pause in a macro while you're defining it so that you can enter data from the keyboard while the macro is being used. This feature has many applications. Among the most useful ones is to create a memo form that does most of the setup work for you, pausing to let you type data such as the sender, recipient, and subject. For instance, it could center and type the heading *MEMORANDUM,* press ← a few times, type *TO:,* pause until you type the recipient, press ← twice, type *FROM:,* pause until you type the sender, and so forth. To insert the pause while recording the macro keystrokes, you press Ctrl-PgUp, select the Pause option from the prompt line that appears, then press ←. Let's see how it works. After you use this macro, the results will be similar to Figure 19.3.

1. Press Ctrl-F10 and name the macro ALTM. Type

   **memo setup**

   for the description, and then press ←.

2. Change the tab settings so that there will only be two tab stops, one at 1″ and one at 5″. Press Format (Shift-F8) and type **L T**, then press Ctrl-End. Type **1,4** and press ←, then press Exit (F7) twice.

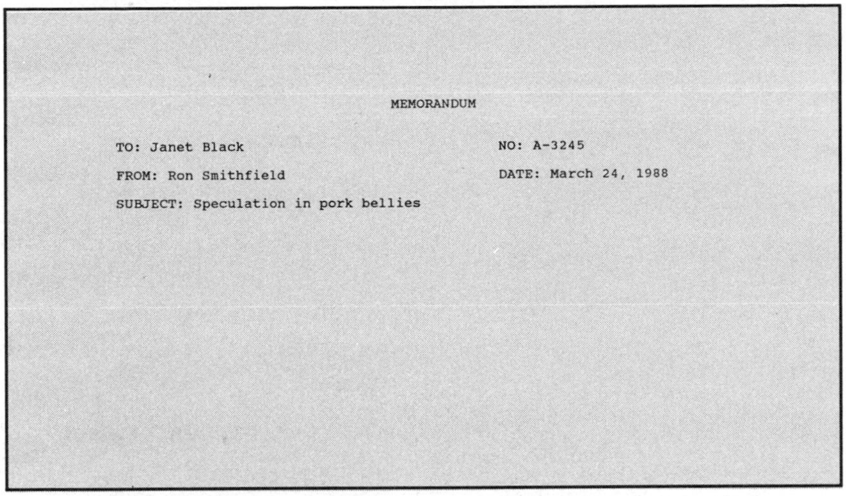

MEMORANDUM

TO: Janet Black NO: A-3245

FROM: Ron Smithfield DATE: March 24, 1988

SUBJECT: Speculation in pork bellies

***Figure 19.3:*** Using a macro to help type a memo

3. Press the Center key (Shift-F6) then type

   **MEMORANDUM**

4. Press ↵ three times, then type

   **TO:**

   Press the Space bar once.

5. Insert the first pause by pressing Ctrl-PgUp. You'll see this prompt:

   **1 Pause; 2 Display; 3 Assign; 4 Comment: 0**

   Select the Pause option by pressing **1** or **P**, then press ↵.

6. Press Tab once to move the cursor to position 5″. Type

   **NO:**

   Press the Space bar once.

7. Insert the next pause by pressing Ctrl-PgUp 1 ↵.

8. Press ↵ twice then type

   **FROM:**

   Press the Space bar once.

9. Insert the last pause by pressing Ctrl-PgUp 1 ↵.

10. Press Tab once so that the cursor is at position 5", under *NO:*
Type

   **DATE:**

then press the Space bar.

11. Insert the Date code, which will always turn into the current date (if your computer keeps the date accurately). Press the Date/Outline key (Shift-F5) and select the Date Code option by pressing **2** or **C**. Today's date will appear at the cursor position.

12. Press ↵ twice then type

   **SUBJECT:**

Press the Space bar once.

See Chapter 8 for a complete explanation of the Date key and its options.

13. Press Ctrl-F10 to end Macro Definition, then press F7 N N · to clear the screen.

Are you ready to try it? Before starting the macro, press the Ins key so that you see the Typeover prompt in the lower left corner. This will prevent *NO:* from being pushed out of alignment (over *DATE:*) as you type the recipient's name.

1. Press Alt-M.

2. *MEMORANDUM* and *TO:* will be entered, then the cursor will stop. Type the recipient's name, then press ↵ to continue.

3. *NO:* will be entered, then WordPerfect will stop again and wait for you to fill in the number. Type a number, then press ↵.

4. The cursor moves down and *FROM:* is entered. Type the sender's name, then press ↵.

5. The date is filled in, then the cursor stops after *SUBJECT:* Type the subject, then press ↵ and type the text of the memo.

If you want to keep the file, be sure to save it when you finish typing.
   Incidentally, this memo could also be set up as a keyboard merge, a topic that was covered in Chapter 16. I find it easier to use the macro.

# USING SPEED CONTROL
# TO MAKE A MACRO VISIBLE

As you've seen, macros run so fast that sometimes you can't tell what they are doing until they're finished. If this bothers you, you can use the Speed command and add a delay value to your macro, slowing it down so that you can watch the keystrokes as they are executed. To see how, let's edit the double-space macro (ALTD).

1. Press Ctrl-F10.

2. Enter the name by pressing Alt-D. You will see the prompt asking if you want to replace or edit the original macro. Select Edit by pressing **2** or **E**.

3. You should see the Macro: Edit screen. Press **A** to select Action and move the cursor inside the box.

4. Press Ctrl-PgUp. A pop-up menu of commands appears in a box at the right side of the screen, as shown in Figure 19.4.

5. Press **S** and the cursor highlights the macro programming command {*Speed*}*100ths* ˜ . Press ←┘. This inserts the Speed

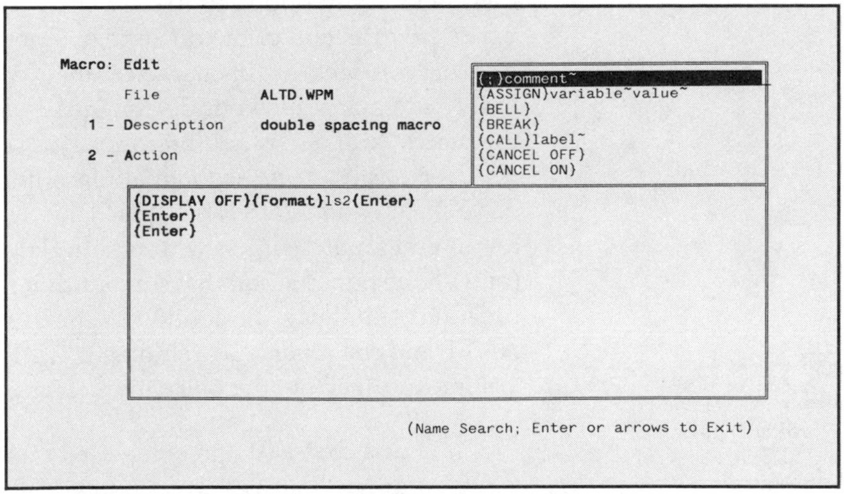

```
Macro: Edit                          {;}comment˜
                                     {ASSIGN}variable˜value˜
        File        ALTD.WPM         {BELL}
                                     {BREAK}
  1 - Description   double spacing macro  {CALL}label˜
                                     {CANCEL OFF}
  2 - Action                         {CANCEL ON}

        {DISPLAY OFF}{Format}1s2{Enter}
        {Enter}
        {Enter}




                        (Name Search; Enter or arrows to Exit)
```

*Figure 19.4:* The pop-up menu of macro commands

command into your macro, at the beginning. The first line will look like this:

**{SPEED}{DISPLAY OFF}{Format}**ls2**{Enter}**

6. The next step is to type a number for the delay value. Type **100**, then press the tilde key ( ~ ).Press Delete once to erase the {DISPLAY OFF} code so you'll be able to see the macro as it is being executed.

7. Press the Exit key (F7), then ↵.

Now start the macro by pressing Alt-D, and watch as it completes its task.

## USING MACROS WITH SEARCH AND REPLACE

When combined with other features such as Search and Replace, macros become especially powerful. For example, I have a macro that inserts a special place marker for me, and I have two other macros that locate it with forward and reverse searches. I use them when editing long documents so that I can jump around in the document and easily return to the last place I was working, which isn't necessarily the end of the document. For your place marker, use an unusual combination of characters that will never appear under normal circumstances in your documents. I use XXXXX, and I named the macro ALTX. By adding a number to the end after pressing Alt-X, I can easily create sequential place markers such as XXXXX1, XXXXX2, and XXXXX3. Since the Search feature does not look for an exact match unless you surround the search string with spaces (or with the punctuation that surrounds it in the document), the combination will always be found. I named the forward search macro ALTF and the reverse search macro ALTR.

First you'll create the place marker macro.

See Chapter 7 if you need to review WordPerfect's Search and Search and Replace features.

1. Press Ctrl-F10 and enter Alt-X for the macro name.

2. For the description, type

**Place marker macro**

then press ↵.

3. Type

   **XXXXX**

4. Press Ctrl-F10 to end the macro.

Now create the forward search macro.

1. Press Ctrl-F10 and enter Alt-F for the macro name.

2. For the description, type

   **Forward search macro**

   then press ◄──┘.

3. Press the Search key (F2) and enter **XXXXX** as the search string.

4. Press F2 to begin the search. (You may hear it beep and see the * *Not found* * prompt.)

5. Press Ctrl-F10 to end the macro.

Finally, create the reverse search macro by following these steps:

1. Press Ctrl-F10 and enter Alt-R for the macro name.

2. For the description, type

   **Reverse search macro**

   then press ◄──┘.

3. Press the Reverse Search key (Shift-F2) and enter **XXXXX** as the search string.

4. Press F2 to begin the search. You may hear a beep and see the * *Not found* * prompt.

5. Press Ctrl-F10 to end the macro.

Now use Alt-X to enter the place marker on lines 2″, 4″, 6″, and 8″, then press Home Home ↑ to move the cursor to the top of the document. Test your ALTF macro a few times, then test the ALTR macro. Note that the cursor always stops on the blank space after **XXXXX**.

Once you have used one of the search macros (ALTF or ALTR), you can repeat your search by starting the macro again (or pressing the appropriate Search key, either F2 F2 or Shift-F2 F2). However, in some situations you might want the macro to repeat itself until there are no more occurrences of the search string (XXXXX). To try it, we'll edit the ALTF macro, adding one more step that will cause the macro to start itself again each time it finds the search string. Here's how to do it:

1. Press the Macro Definition key (Ctrl-F10) and press Alt-F for the macro name.

2. You'll see the prompt telling you that ALTF.WPM is already defined and asking if you want to replace or edit it. Choose the Edit option by pressing **2** or **E**.

3. Press either **2** or **A** to choose Action. This moves the cursor into the macro editing box.

4. Press the End key to place the cursor after the last keystroke, which should be {Search}.

5. Press the Macro Definition key (Ctrl-F10) so that you can enter new keystrokes into your macro. This prompt appears under the box:

   **Press Macro Define to enable editing**

6. Press the Invoke Macro key (Alt-F10). You should see this keystroke added to your macro:

   {Macro}

   which means that you want WordPerfect to start running another macro when it reaches this point in the ALTF macro.

7. Type

   **ALTF**

   as the name of the macro you want to run, then press ⏎. The macro should now look like Figure 19.5.

8. Press Ctrl-F10 and the *Press **Macro Define*** prompt should disappear.

9. Press the Exit key (F7) twice.

```
Macro: Edit

       File           ALTF.WPM

  1 - Description     FORWARD SEARCH MACRO

  2 - Action

      ┌─────────────────────────────────────────────────────────────────┐
      │ {DISPLAY OFF}{Search}XXXXXX{Search}{Macro}ALTF{Enter}_            │
      │                                                                   │
      │                                                                   │
      │                                                                   │
      │                                                                   │
      │                                                                   │
      │                                                                   │
      └─────────────────────────────────────────────────────────────────┘

  Press Macro Define to enable editing
```

*Figure 19.5:* Editing a macro to start itself again

Now move the cursor to the top of the document and press Alt-F to run the macro again. Although the search string appears several times on your screen, the macro seems to ignore all but the last one. In reality, it stops at each occurrence of the search string but you don't see it because of the {DISPLAY OFF} code. To slow it down, you could edit it once again so that it will pause at each search string (XXXXX) and wait for you to press ⏎ before trying to find the next one. Here's how to do it:

1. Press the Macro Definition key (Ctrl-F10) and enter Alt-F for the macro name.

2. Select Edit in response to the *ALTF.WPM is Already Defined* prompt.

3. Choose Action to place the cursor into the macro editing box, then press Delete once to erase the {DISPLAY OFF} code.

4. Place the cursor on the left brace in {Macro}.

5. Press Ctrl-PgUp. You'll see the pop-up menu box appear in the upper right corner, as shown in Figure 19.4.

6. Press **P** so the cursor bar highlights the {Pause} command. Press ⏎. This inserts the {Pause} command into your macro.

7. Press F7 to end macro editing, then press ⏎.

Move the cursor to the top of the document, then press Alt-F again to start the macro. This time, you'll see that it stops at the first instance of the XXXXX search string, and you have to press ⏎ before the cursor will move to the next one. If you keep pressing ⏎, it will finally stop on the last one and you'll hear the beep and see the * *Not found* * prompt on the status line. If you find the one you want before reaching the last one, you can press the Cancel key (F1) to stop the macro and leave the cursor there.

## *MACRO CHAINING*

The macro you just finished running is called a *repeating chain*. As you have seen, this is not nearly as complex as it sounds. *Chained macros* are two macros strung together, with one macro invoking the other. When a search is included and a macro invokes itself, as in the example above, it is called a repeating chain. This type of macro ends when the search string can no longer be found, as you saw. You could use this technique to create a repeating chain macro that would capitalize the first character of each sentence, building on the ALTC macro you created earlier.

Follow these steps to create it:

1. Press Ctrl-F10 and name the macro CAPS.

2. For the description, type

    **capitalizes 1st letter of each sentence**

    then press ⏎.

3. Press the Search key (F2).

4. For the search string, type . (period) then press the Space bar twice. (This assumes that when you type, you always press the Space bar twice after pressing the period key to end a sentence. If you don't, be sure these keystrokes match your sequence.)

5. Press F2 (to start the search).

6. Press Alt-F4 (Block on).

7. Press → (to highlight a character when you use the macro).

8. Press Shift-F3 **1** or **U** (for uppercase conversion).

9. Press Alt-F10 and type the macro name, **CAPS**, then press ◄┘. This will cause the macro to repeat itself when you use it.

10. Press Ctrl-F10 to end Macro Definition.

Now test the macro by typing a few sentences (all in lowercase), moving the cursor to the beginning, pressing Alt-F10, then typing the macro name, *CAPS*. It capitalizes the first letter of each sentence that ends with a period and two spaces, then beeps and displays the * *Not found* * message after the last one has been converted.

You may have realized that there are a few flaws in this macro. First, it does not capitalize the first word in each paragraph because those characters don't follow the period and Space bar combination which is used to locate the first word of each sentence. Second, it does not convert the first character if the sentence before it ends in a question mark or exclamation point. To overcome the second flaw, you can create two more macros that are like the CAPS macro except that they search for a question mark or exclamation point instead of a period. To overcome the second problem, you can create a macro that will uppercase the first character of each paragraph. If each paragraph starts with a tab, for instance, you can just direct the macro to search for Tab codes, then follow the same steps as in the CAPS macro to block and convert the character to the right of the tab, and repeat the macro. Here are the steps:

1. Press Ctrl-F10 and name the macro FRSTWORD.

2. For the description, type

   **capitalizes 1st word in each paragraph**

   then press ◄┘.

3. Press the Search key (F2).

4. For the search string, press the Tab key. The prompt should now look like this:

   → Srch: [Tab]

5. Press F2 (to start the search).

6. Press Alt-F4 (Block on).

7. Press → (to highlight the character).

8. Press Shift-F3 **1** or **U** (for uppercase conversion).

9. Press Alt-F10 and type the macro name, **FRSTWORD**, then press ← to repeat the macro when you use it.

10. Press Ctrl-F10 (to end Macro Definition).

To try it, press Alt-F10 and type *FRSTWORD,* then press ←.

## USING MACROS WITH MERGES

Macros and merges can be combined in many ways. An especially useful macro is one that automatically creates mailing labels by running a merge that extracts the name and address fields from a secondary file. In this exercise you'll use two files that you created in Chapter 16, the primary file *labels.pf* and the secondary file *winners.sf.* Here are the steps:

1. Press Ctrl-F10 and name the macro **LABELS**.

2. For the description, type **mailing label generator**.

3. Press the keys to start the merge: Ctrl-F9 **M** or **1**.

4. When prompted for the primary file, type **labels.pf** and press ←.

5. When prompted for the secondary file, type **winners.sf**, then press ←.

Notice that you don't have to turn Macro Definition off, because when the merge starts, Macro Definition automatically ends. From now on, you can use this macro to create mailing labels from the *labels.pf* and *winners.sf* files. To make it more useful for you, you could edit it to erase the file names in steps 4 and 5, and add pauses so that you could enter the names of your own primary and secondary files.

### CREATING A MACRO TO PRINT ENVELOPES FROM MERGED LETTERS

Another macro that's useful with merge files enters the formatting codes to print addresses on legal-size envelopes, then starts another macro that extracts the inside addresses from your merged letters and places them in the Doc 2 area. It pauses twice in each letter, once so that you can place the cursor on the first letter of the inside address, and once so that you can block all the lines in the address (since this usually varies).

Clear the screen (F7 N N) then follow these steps to create the macros. The first macro will switch to Doc 2 and enter the formatting that is used for legal-size envelopes, then start another macro called ENVCOPY to copy the addresses.

1. Press the Macro Definition key (Ctrl-F10) and type **ENV** for your macro name, then press ←.

2. For the description, type **envelope address generator** then press ←.

3. Press the Switch key (Shift-F3).

4. Press the Format key (Shift-F8).

5. Press **2** or **P** to select Page.

6. Press **8** or **S** for Paper Size, **5** or **E** for Envelope.

7. Press **5** or **E** again for Envelope on the Paper Type screen.

8. Press ← twice.

9. Change the left and top margins by pressing

   Shift-F8 L M 4 ← ← ← P M 0 ← ← ← ←

10. Press the Switch key (Shift-F3) again.

11. Press the Invoke Macro key (Alt-F10) and type **ENVCOPY**, then press ← to start the macro that copies the addresses (when you use this macro).

12. Press Ctrl-F10 to end Macro Definition.

If you wish to verify that you performed all the steps correctly (and make any necessary changes), you can use the macro editor and compare it to the Macro: Edit screen shown in Figure 19.6. To do this, press Ctrl-F10, type the macro name (*ENV*), press ←, then select the Edit option.

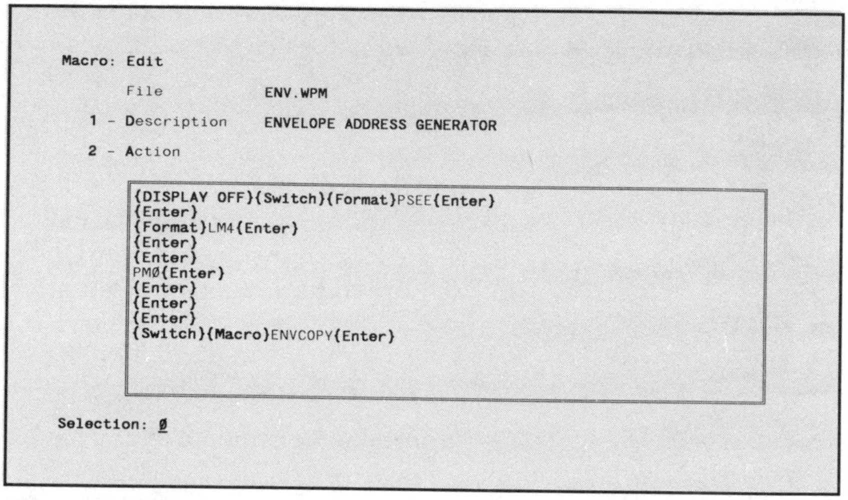

```
Macro: Edit

        File            ENV.WPM

1 - Description     ENVELOPE ADDRESS GENERATOR

2 - Action

    ┌─────────────────────────────────────────────────────────────┐
    │ {DISPLAY OFF}{Switch}{Format}PSEE{Enter}                      │
    │ {Enter}                                                       │
    │ {Format}LM4{Enter}                                            │
    │ {Enter}                                                       │
    │ {Enter}                                                       │
    │ PMØ{Enter}                                                    │
    │ {Enter}                                                       │
    │ {Enter}                                                       │
    │ {Enter}                                                       │
    │ {Switch}{Macro}ENVCOPY{Enter}                                 │
    │                                                               │
    │                                                               │
    └─────────────────────────────────────────────────────────────┘

Selection: Ø
```

*Figure 19.6:* The Macro: Edit screen for the completed ENV macro

The second macro will block and copy the addresses into the Doc 2 area. Here are the steps to create it:

1. Press the Macro Definition key (Ctrl-F10), type **ENVCOPY** for your macro name, then press ◄─┘.

2. For the description, type **envelope address generator, part 2** then press ◄─┘.

3. Enter the first pause, which in your macro will allow you to move the cursor to the first line in the inside address. Press Ctrl-PgUp 1 or P then press ◄─┘.

4. Press the Block key, Alt-F4.

5. Enter another pause so that in the macro you will be able to highlight all the lines of the inside address at this point. Press Ctrl-PgUp P ◄─┘ or Ctrl-PgUp 1 ◄─┘.

6. Press the Delete key and type **Y** in response to the Delete Block prompt. Press the Cancel key (F1) then **1** or **R** to bring back the deleted address (in the macro).

7. Press the Switch key (Shift-F3).

8. Press the Cancel key (F1), then **1** or **R**. In your macro, this will retrieve the address into Doc 2.

9. Press ←, then Ctrl-← to insert a hard page break.

10. Press the Switch key (Shift-F3) again.

11. Press the Invoke Macro key (Alt-F10) and type **ENVCOPY** so that the macro will start itself again and allow you to block and copy another address. Press ←.

12. Press Ctrl-F10 to end Macro Definition.

To use the macro, clear both the Doc 1 and Doc 2 screens, place the cursor in Doc1, and merge your *letter1.pf* and *winners.sf* files (or retrieve a few letters you have on disk). Press Home Home ↑, then start the macro by pressing Alt-F10, typing *ENV,* and pressing ←. When it pauses, move the cursor to the first character in the inside address of the first letter you want to make an envelope for, then press ←. Next, press ↓ until you've highlighted all the lines in the address, then press ←. When the macro stops again, move the cursor to the beginning of the next inside address, press ←, press ↓ to highlight it all, then press ←. Repeat until all the addresses you want have been copied into Doc 2.

When you want to stop this macro, press the Cancel key, F1. To print the addresses, switch to Doc 2 by pressing Shift-F3, insert an envelope into your printer, roll it up to the position where you want the address to begin printing, then use the Page option on the Print key (Shift-F7 P). Press Page Down to move to the next address and repeat the procedure for each envelope.

## STARTING A MACRO FROM WITHIN A MERGE

Creating a menu of macros is covered in Sybex's complete Word-Perfect reference, *The WordPerfect Desktop Companion,* by Greg Harvey and Kay Yarborough Nelson. It also explains the many macro programming commands that are not covered in this chapter.

WordPerfect has a special merge code, ^G, which starts a macro from within a merge as soon as the merge operation ends. To use it, you place the macro name at the end of the primary merge file, surrounded by a pair of ^G merge codes. This feature has many important applications. For example, you could use it to create a menu of macros. You could also use it with a primary merge file that gets its data from the keyboard (not a secondary file) so that after you use the merge to create the first letter, it will automatically save the file, clear the screen, then start the merge again; we'll try this one in the next exercise. You will be using the *letter3.pf* file that you created in Chapter 16.

1. Retrieve *letter3.pf* (if you don't have it, you can use any primary file that uses the keyboard merge method).

2. Place the cursor at the end by pressing Home Home ↓.

3. Press the Merge Codes key (Shift-F9) then type **G**. This enters the merge code ^ G.

4. Type the macro name, **SAVEIT**.

5. Press Shift-F9 G again. The macro name inside the merge codes should look like this:

   ^ GSAVEIT ^ G

6. Use the Exit key (F7) to save the file again and clear the screen (press F7 Y ↩ Y N).

See Chapter 16 for a complete explanation of the keyboard merge process.

The next step will be to create the SAVEIT macro. This macro will invoke the Save key, type *LTR* as the first characters of the file name, and pause for you to enter the remaining characters such as a number or a person's name. This will allow you to name your merge letters in sequence, such as *LTR1, LTR2, LTR3,* or to add the recipient's name such as *LTRSMITH, LTRJONES, LTRBROWN,* etc. Here are the steps:

1. Press Ctrl-F10 and name the macro **SAVEIT**. For the description, type

   saves merged letter, starts merge again

2. Press the Save Text key, F10.

3. Type **LTR**, but don't press ↩. Instead, enter a pause by pressing Ctrl-PgUp 1 ↩ or Ctrl-PgUp P ↩.

4. Press ↩ to begin the Save operation. (This will also save whatever is on your screen under the name LTR. You can delete the file later.)

5. Press F7 N N to clear the screen.

6. Press the keys to start the merge, Ctrl-F9 M, then type the name of your primary file, **letter3.pf**. Press ←⏎ twice. Since the keystrokes are actually working while you record them as a macro, the merge will begin.

7. Press F9 four times until the * *Merging* * message disappears.

8. When you see the *Document to be Saved* prompt, press Cancel (F1) twice.

Now clear the screen (F7 N N) and try merging the document so that you see how the macro works when the merge ends. To start the merge, use the usual method: press Ctrl-F9 1, then enter the primary file name (*letter3.pf*) and press ←⏎ twice. After you fill out all the information for your first letter, the macro will take over and ask for a file name. You'll see this prompt:

**Document to be saved: LTR**

Notice that the macro has entered the first part of the name, LTR, for you. Type a number such as *1* or *2*, or the recipient's name or initials, then press ←⏎. The document will be saved, the screen will be cleared, and the merge will begin again. When you want to stop the macro, press F7 N N then F9 to get rid of the * *Merging* * message.

## SUMMARY

As you've seen, WordPerfect's Macro feature is a powerful tool with innumerable applications. You can think of macros as shortcuts for entering frequently used data, commands, or combinations of the two; whatever you use them for, they certainly will save you a lot of time. I use macros constantly, and I have macros to do just about everything! For example, I use them to switch fonts: ALTI switches to italics, ALTB switches to a big (18-point) font, ALTH uses a Helvetica font, and ALTR switches back to my regular Times Roman font (12-point). My ALTE macro creates an endnote and places the cursor in the endnote screen so that I can type the text of the endnote. I have a macro that I use to create automatically numbered lists, using WordPerfect's Paragraph Numbering feature to insert a paragraph number into my document. My ALTS macro starts the spell checker and my ALTT macro saves the file then starts the Thesaurus. (I've had trouble with my hard disk when using the Thesaurus, so I save first!) My TOC macro blocks text and designates it for the table of contents, stopping to ask which level I want to use. I could go on for pages describing them all, but I'll spare you. I hope this chapter will help you to understand how to create and use macros, so that you will benefit from them as much as I have.

**20.**

# USING WORDPERFECT'S
# SPELLER AND THESAURUS

# FAST TRACK

**To check for spelling and typing errors,**        634

    use WordPerfect's spelling checker. If you have a floppy disk system, insert the Speller disk into drive B, then press the Spell key (Ctrl-F2). If you see a prompt indicating that the WP{WP}EN.LEX file was not found, select the *Enter Path* option and type *B:* ⬅. If you have a hard disk, just press the Spell key. A menu will appear, offering six options; choose *3* to check the entire document, *2* for the current page, or *1* for the word the cursor is on. When WordPerfect finds a word that it identifies as misspelled, it stops, highlights it, and provides a list of possible replacements if it finds any. You can replace the misspelled word in your document with one of these words by pressing the letter next to it, or select one of the two Skip options to ignore correctly spelled words, such as proper nouns.

**To find a synonym or antonym for a word,**        646

    use WordPerfect's Thesaurus feature. If you have a floppy disk system, insert the Thesaurus disk in drive B before pressing the Thesaurus key. The next step is the same for hard or floppy systems. Move the cursor to the word you want to look up, then press the Thesaurus key (Alt-F1). If the word is found, you will see a list of synonyms and antonyms. To use one of the words in the list, select the Replace Word option, then type the letter next to the word you want. It will replace the one in your document.

WORDPERFECT'S SPELLING CHECKER CONTAINS OVER 100,000 words, about as many as the average desktop dictionary. However, the Speller does much more than automatically find and correct your spelling mistakes. Think about how you use a dictionary: if you forget how to spell a word, you usually look it up before typing it, or else just after typing it. WordPerfect can do both. If you're really uncertain about how to spell a word, you can have the program check the dictionary for a pattern, and have it enter the correct word into your document. The program can also check a page, a block, or the entire document, provide you with a count of the total number of words, and catch double occurrences of a word. To customize the dictionary, you can direct the program to add words to the list as they are found, or you can add an entire file of your own words to the dictionary. The Speller is definitely one of WordPerfect's most valuable utilities, and one of the easiest to use.

The WordPerfect Speller comes with two dictionaries, a common word list and a main word list. A third one is created as you add words of your own, using one of the menu choices available while spell checking, and it's called the supplemental dictionary. The common word list contains about 1,500 of the most frequently used words in the language, and the Speller always checks these first. Since it's the smallest one, it's loaded into RAM when you start the Speller, and WordPerfect can check it very quickly. If the word is not found there, WordPerfect searches the supplemental list, if you have one; it's also loaded into RAM. The last list to be checked is the main one. If the word is not found in any of the three dictionaries, you can add it to the supplemental list for future reference. This list can later be incorporated into the main one using the Speller Utility.

The WordPerfect Thesaurus is another wonderful tool for writers, but it can be useful for everyday applications as well, especially if you aren't sure of the exact meaning of a word. If a word is found in the

Thesaurus, a list of synonyms and antonyms appears on the screen, classified into groups of nouns, adjectives, and verbs, and subdivided into groups with the same connotation. There are over 10,000 *headwords* in the Thesaurus, comparable to the average desktop version.

## SPELL CHECKING A WORD, PAGE, OR DOCUMENT

In Chapter 4 you learned how to check the entire document on your Edit screen for spelling mistakes, so this section should be a review for you. Remember that you can interrupt the operation anytime by pressing the Cancel key (F1).

Retrieve the file you want to check. If you are spell checking a file you just typed, the WordPerfect manual recommends that you save it before you begin checking it. If your system includes a hard disk, start the spell checker by pressing the Spell key (Ctrl-F2). If your computer has only floppy disk drives, insert the Speller disk into drive B and press the Spell key (Ctrl-F2); if you see the prompt *WP{WP}EN.LEX not found*, select option 1, Enter Path, and type *B:* ⏎ in response to the *Temporary dictionary path* prompt. The following menu will appear:

> Check: **1 W**ord; **2 P**age; **3 D**ocument; **4 N**ew Sup. Dictionary;
> **5 L**ook Up; **6 C**ount: 0

To check the entire document on your edit screen, press *3* or *D* to select Document. To limit the operation to the page where your cursor is located, press *2* or *P* to select Page. To check the word your cursor is located on, press *1* or *W* to select Word. If you use either the Page (2) or Document (3) option, the Speller will also check any headers, footers, footnotes, and endnotes in your document. After you select the option you want, you'll know that the Speller is looking for misspelled words because this prompt will appear on the status line:

> \* Please wait \*

(On some computers it happens so fast that you'll miss it.)

If you're checking a single word and the cursor moves to the next word after you've selected option 1, it means that the word is correctly spelled. You then have several options. For example, you

*If you see an error message after pressing the Spell key (Ctrl-F2), refer to the Setup menu (Shift-F1).*

could press a key such as ←⎯, the Space bar, or Cancel (F1) to exit from the Speller menu, or you could select option 1, 2, or 3 to continue spell checking another word, a page, or the entire document.

If the Speller locates a word that is not in one of WordPerfect's dictionaries, it will stop and highlight the word in reverse video or another color in your document. The screen will be divided by a dashed line, and you'll see this prompt on the status line at the bottom:

Not Found: **1** Skip once; **2** Skip; **3** Add Word; **4** Edit;
**5** Look Up: **0**

If WordPerfect finds some possible replacements for this word in its dictionaries, you'll see a list of them under the dashed line, like the one shown in Figure 20.1 for the word *aks*. If the list fills up the entire screen, press *0* to see more words, as the prompt suggests. To replace the misspelled word in your document with one of the suggestions, just type the letter appearing next to the correct one. Note that if the word in your document was capitalized, the replacement will also be capitalized. Also, if the document contains other identical misspellings of the word, they will also be replaced.

## SKIPPING OR ADDING A WORD

When you see the *Not Found* message on the status line, it does not necessarily mean that the word is misspelled, just that it was not found in one of the Speller's dictionaries. Although the dictionaries are extensive and contain over 100,000 words, you'll find that many correctly spelled words can't be found because they are proper nouns such as people's names, or industry-specific terminology such as the jargon and acronyms used in the computer industry (such as WSIWYG, download, asynchronous, OCR, VLSI, or VMOS). If a word is correctly spelled but not in the list of suggested replacements, you have two basic choices: *skip* or *add*.

If the Speller stops on a word you use frequently in your work, the best option would be to add it to your supplemental dictionary by selecting option 3, Add Word. If you do, the Speller will never again stop on that word. Be careful that the word is spelled correctly before you add it! The speller automatically names this supplemental dictionary WP{WP}EN.SUP.

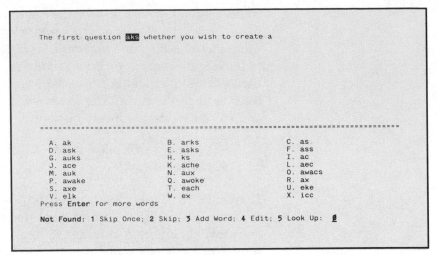

The first question `aks` whether you wish to create a

```
===================================================================
    A. ak               B. arks              C. as
    D. ask              E. asks              F. ass
    G. auks             H. ks                I. ac
    J. ace              K. ache              L. aec
    M. auk              N. aux               O. awacs
    P. awake            Q. awoke             R. ax
    S. axe              T. each              U. eke
    V. elk              W. ex                X. icc
Press Enter for more words

Not Found: 1 Skip Once; 2 Skip; 3 Add Word; 4 Edit; 5 Look Up: 0
```

*Figure 20.1:* Suggested replacements

It's a good idea to use the Setup key to tell WordPerfect the location of your supplemental dictionary files because if you don't, you may end up with different supplemental dictionaries in each directory that you use, and words that you thought you added previously may not be found. To do this, press Shift-F1, select Location of Auxiliary Files (*7* or *L*), then press *7* or *S* for Supplementary Dictionary(s). Type the drive and path where you want the supplementary dictionaries to be stored (but don't type the file name), press ◄┘, then press Exit (F7).

When you select the Add Word option, the words are temporarily stored in the computer's memory (RAM) but are not added to the supplemental dictionary until spell checking is finished. If you add a large number of words during one session, you may run out of room in your computer's memory (RAM), and you'll see this message:

### Dictionary Full

If this happens, you can exit from the Speller by pressing the Cancel key (F1), then ◄┘. WordPerfect then adds the words that are in RAM into the supplemental dictionary, and clears the memory so that you can resume spell checking. After that, you may wish to use the Block Spell method (reviewed later in this chapter) to check the rest of the document. To prevent this problem in the future, you should add the supplemental dictionary to the main dictionary using the method described in the Speller Utility section.

If the Speller stops on a word you do not plan to use often, such as an addressee to whom you are writing a one-time letter, you should choose one of the two Skip options. If you select option 1, Skip Once, the Speller will accept this occurrence of the word but if it finds it anywhere else (on the page if you are checking the page, or in the document if you are checking the document), it will stop again. If you select option 2, Skip, the Speller will accept the word wherever it is found, but only during this spell check session. Whichever Skip option you choose, the next time you run the Speller it will stop on the words that you skipped this time. If you want the Speller to skip this word any other time you use it, select the Add Word option instead.

## EDITING WHILE SPELL CHECKING

Option 4, Edit, allows you to leave the Not Found menu temporarily and enter the editing screen to revise the text yourself by using keys like Backspace, Delete, ←, →, and Insert, or just by typing missing letters. This option is useful when a word is so misspelled that it can't be located in the dictionary, or when two words run together and you need to insert a blank space to separate them. After you finish editing, you must press EXIT (F7) to get back to the Speller. While you're editing, you'll see this prompt to remind you:

**Press EXIT when done**

If the revised word is not found in the dictionary after you edit it and press Exit (F7), the *Not Found* prompt will reappear and you'll have to select another option, such as Skip or Add, to continue spell checking. Incidentally, whenever the *Not Found* prompt appears, you can press → or ← to begin editing, instead of pressing *4*.

## LOOKING UP A WORD

WordPerfect uses a phonetic method to look up words that otherwise can't be found. For instance, if you type *fone* instead of *phone,* the speller will list words like *fine, font, phone,* and *phoney* as possible replacements.

The Look Up option (5) on the Not Found menu allows you to look up a word that the Speller can't find in the dictionary. You can use this option to try a different spelling to locate the word, and you can use a question mark (?) and/or asterisk (*) as wild-card characters to help with the search. The question mark stands for any single letter, and an asterisk stands for a sequence of letters. For example, if you type *concientous,* a misspelling of the word *conscientious,* the Speller will not find any possible replacements, and no words will appear under the dashed line when the *Not Found* prompt appears. To find the correct word, try selecting option 5, Look Up. When you do, you'll see this prompt:

**Word or word pattern:**

Type this sequence:

**cons\***

Press ◄┘ and you'll see the list shown in Figure 20.2.

As you can see, the word next to the letter K is the correct one, so you could press *K* to insert it into your text. This message:

**Select word: 0**

which you can see in Figure 20.2, means that you can press *0* to view a list of additional words. When you've pressed *0* enough times to see the entire list, the *Word or word pattern* prompt will reappear. If the word you want is not on the list, you can either press Cancel (F1) or try typing another pattern.

Question marks are helpful to find the correct spelling for words such as *apparent,* which is often misspelled as *apparant.* To locate it, select the Look Up option and enter this sequence:

**app?r?nt**

You'll find that the correct spelling shows up with the letter A next to it. To substitute it into your document, press *A.*

## DOUBLE WORD OCCURRENCES

If the Speller locates a word that occurs twice in a row, it will stop and highlight both of them, as shown in Figure 20.3. Pressing option 3, Delete 2nd, will delete the second one.

If deleting the second word in the identical pair is not the solution, you can either skip it (using either option 1 or 2) or edit it (option 4). Option 5, Disable Double Word Checking, allows you to turn this feature off so that the Speller will not stop at double words (during this session only).

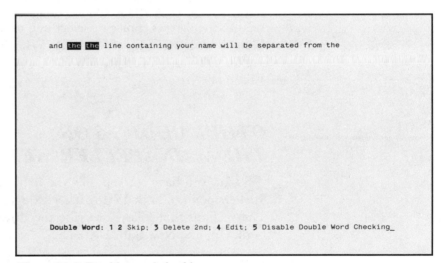

*Figure 20.2:* Looking up a word

*Figure 20.3:* Double word checking

## THE WORD COUNT DISPLAY

When the Speller is finished checking a page or document, it displays a count of the total number of words and this message:

Press any key to continue

To return to the document, you can press any key. Be sure to save it again if any corrections were made.

## SPELL CHECKING A BLOCK OF TEXT

Refer to the section in Chapter 5 called "Spell Checking a Block" if you need more information.

In Chapter 5 you learned how to spell check a highlighted block of text, so this will be a brief review. To limit spell checking to a section of text, mark it first by moving the cursor to the beginning of the section, pressing the Block key (Alt-F4), then moving the cursor to the end of the block. Next, press the Spell key (Ctrl-F2) and the Speller will immediately begin searching for misspellings (and unrecognized words). A *Please wait* prompt will appear on the status line as Word-Perfect searches. The rest of the process is identical to spell checking using option 3 (Document) on the main Speller menu. If any misspelled words are found, the Not Found menu will appear along with a list of suggested replacements, and you can either press the letter next to the correct choice or select one of these options: Skip Once, Skip, Add Word, Edit, or Look Up. When the Speller finishes, you'll see the *Word count* prompt, and you can press any key to get back to Edit mode.

## OTHER CHOICES ON THE MAIN SPELLER MENU

So far, you have studied only the first three options on the main Speller menu: Check Word, Check Page, and Check Document. The sections that follow describe the three other choices, Count, Look Up, and New Sup. Dictionary.

### THE COUNT OPTION

When the Speller is done checking your page or document, it always provides a count of the total number of words. You can also obtain a count of the total number of words in your document without spell checking by using the Count option from the main Speller

menu. To do this, press the Spell key (Ctrl-F2) then press either *6* or
*C.* If you have a floppy disk system (no hard disk), be sure to insert
the Speller disk into drive B before you press the Spell key. After a
few seconds, you will see a prompt at the bottom of the screen telling
you the total number of words, and reminding you to press any key
to continue.

## THE LOOK UP OPTION

The Look Up option on the main Speller menu (option 5) allows
you to look up a word in the dictionary and determine the correct
spelling before typing the word, but, unlike the equivalent choice on
the Not Found menu, it cannot be used to substitute the word into
your document. To use this option, you press the Spell key (Ctrl-F2),
press *5* or *L,* then type the word or word pattern using asterisks
and/or question marks. For example, when you use this method to
look up the pattern *lau\** from this menu, you see the screen illustrated
in Figure 20.4.

Note that there are letters next to the words, but you can't use them to
enter the word into your document. As the prompt *Press any key to continue*

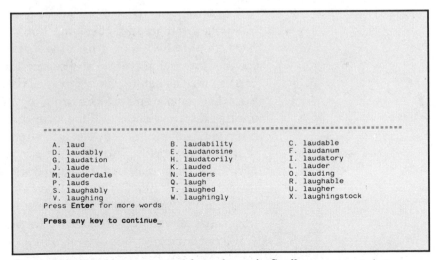

*Figure 20.4:* Looking up a word from the main Speller menu

suggests, as soon as you press a key, you see the next screenful of words in the dictionary. When you come to the last screenful that matches your word pattern, this prompt appears, asking you to enter another word or word pattern:

**Word or word pattern:**

Press ⏎ or Cancel (F1) to get back to the main Speller menu.

If you want to use the Look Up option to replace a word, type the word first (don't worry about the spelling) then place the cursor anywhere on it and select the Word option from the main Speller menu by pressing either *1* or *W*. Next, press *5* to select the Look Up option from the Not Found menu, type your word pattern, then press ⏎. Once you see the correct spelling in the list, press the letter next to it, and WordPerfect will replace the incorrect one in your document with the correct one from the list. To get back to Edit mode, press ⏎, Cancel (F1), or Exit (F7).

### THE NEW SUP. DICTIONARY OPTION

Use this option if you want to use a different supplemental dictionary when you are spell checking. You create a different supplemental dictionary by typing a list of words in alphabetical order (or by sorting it after you type it) and saving the list as a separate file. You can use this file before you begin spell checking by selecting the New Sup. Dictionary option. However, if your Setup menu references another directory or drive as the location of your supplemental dictionary, you will have to copy the new supplemental dictionary file into that directory before WordPerfect can use it (when you select the New Sup. Dictionary option on the Spell menu). To check this, press the Setup key (Shift-F1), select Location of Auxiliary Files (*7* or *L*), then select Supplementary Dictionary(s) (*7* or *S*). Look for the directory name next to the *Supplementary Dictionary(s)* prompt; this is where you'll need to copy your new dictionary before using it. You can use the Move/Rename option on the List Files key (F5) to move it into the correct directory (see Chapter 15).

## USING THE SPELLER UTILITY

The Speller Utility is an independent program that can be used to create a new dictionary, change dictionaries, add a list of words to the dictionary, delete words, display the common word list, check to see if a word is in the dictionary, or perform a look-up. Don't use this program casually, or you may end up erasing the WordPerfect dictionary. Also, it is not a practical method of adding or deleting a small number of words, since the process takes up to 20 minutes. After you add or delete words with this utility, the entire dictionary has to be sorted to place each word in the proper alphabetical order.

As you know, when you add words to the dictionary using the Add Word option (3) on the Not Found menu, they are added to a supplemental dictionary named WP{WP}EN.SUP. If this dictionary becomes very large, you may want to use the Speller Utility to add it to the main one. To do this, first use the Exit key (F7) to quit WordPerfect.

If you have a hard disk, you should still be in the WordPerfect subdirectory with a C prompt *(C>)* on the screen. Start the Speller Utility by typing

SPELL

If your system has only floppy drives, you should have a B prompt *(B>)* on the screen. Press A: ◄━┘ to get the A> prompt, then insert the Speller disk into drive A and type

SPELL

to start it.

You will see the Speller Utility's main menu (Figure 20.5). Select option 2, *Add words to dictionary,* from the menu. Next, select option 4, *Add to main word list (from a file).* Type the name of the supplemental file, WP{WP}EN.SUP, as shown in Figure 20.6 (be sure to include the braces), then press ◄━┘ and select option 5, Exit (F7).

You will then see a *Please Wait* prompt and a message indicating that the dictionary is being updated, as shown below:

**Updating dictionary**
**Writing the a's**

```
Spell -- WordPerfect Speller Utility                    wp{wp}en.lex

0 - Exit
1 - Change/Create dictionary
2 - Add words to dictionary
3 - Delete words from dictionary
4 - Optimize dictionary
5 - Display common word list
6 - Check location of a word
7 - Look up
8 - Phonetic look up
9 - Convert 4.2 Dictionary to 5.0

Selection: _
```

*Figure 20.5:* The Speller Utility's main menu

```
Spell -- Add Words                                      wp{wp}en.lex

0 - Cancel - do not add words
1 - Add to common word list (from keyboard)
2 - Add to common word list (from a file)
3 - Add to main word list (from keyboard)
4 - Add to main word list (from a file)
5 - Exit

Selection: 4
Enter file name: wp{wp}en.sup_
```

*Figure 20.6:* Using the Speller Utility to add words from the supplemental dictionary to the main dictionary

You can also use the
Delete option from
the List Files menu to
erase this file. See Chapter 15 if you need a
refresher.

This process can take several minutes, so be patient. When it's finished, the Main menu will reappear and you can press *0* to exit to DOS. You can then delete the supplemental dictionary from your disk, since it is no longer needed. You can do this from the DOS prompt by typing

**Erase WP{WP}EN.SUP**

If you get no feedback from DOS, you'll know it worked.

You can also use the Speller Utility to find out if a word is contained in one of the Speller dictionaries, and if so, whether it's in the common one or the main one. To check a word, select option 6 from the Speller Utility's main menu, Check Location of a Word. In response to the prompt

**Word to check:**

type your word. If it is found, you will see one of these messages:

**Found in main dictionary**

or

**Found in common word list**

If it is not found, you will see

**Not found**

In all cases, after a few seconds you'll be returned to the *Word to check* prompt and you can either enter another word or press ←, Exit (F7), or Cancel (F1) to return to the Speller Utility menu.

You can use option 5 on the Speller Utility's main menu, Display Common Word List, to display all the words in the common word list. When you do, the list will be displayed in alphabetical order, one screen at a time. You can exit from it anytime by pressing the Cancel key (F1) or Exit (F7).

Option 7, Look Up, works like the Look Up option on the main Speller menu.

## THE THESAURUS

The WordPerfect Thesaurus is useful as a supplement to the Speller and as an independent tool for writers. If you don't understand the exact meaning of a word, use the Thesaurus instead of the Speller.

To use it, move the cursor to the word you want to look up or the space following it and press the Thesaurus key (Alt-F1). If you don't have a hard disk, you'll have to insert the Thesaurus disk in drive B before pressing Alt-F1. If you see the prompt *ERROR: File not found --- WP{WP}EN.THS,* you will have to use the Setup menu to tell Word-Perfect where to find the Thesaurus file before you can use this feature. To do this, press Shift-F1 7 8 and type *B:* next to the Thesaurus prompt. Press ←┘, then Exit (F7), and proceed to look up a word by pressing the Thesaurus key (Alt-F1). If you get an error message telling you there's not enough memory, clear the Doc 2 work area and start over.

If the word that you were looking for is not found, you will see a *Word not found* prompt, which will soon change to this prompt:

**Word:**

This message indicates that WordPerfect is waiting for you to type another word. At this point, you can either press F1 (or F7 or ←┘) twice to cancel the Thesaurus, or enter another similar word to look up.

If the word you are looking up is found, three lines of your document (or two lines if it's double spaced) will remain at the top of the screen, and the synonyms and antonyms, which are called *references,* will appear in columns surrounded by boxes, as shown in Figure 20.7 for the word *top.*

Notice that the screen is divided into groups of nouns, adjectives, verbs, and antonyms, and that each group is separated by a solid line. The first twelve references (*A* through *L* in column 1) are nouns, and the next sixteen (*M* and *N* in column 1 and all of the second column) are adjectives. Observe the *(n)* next to the word *top* above the first group, and the *(a)* above the second group. The numbers to the left (such as *1, 2, 3,* and *4* in the first column) represent subgroups of words that have the same basic meaning, such as group 1: *crest, crown, peak, summit,* and *zenith.*

If you see an error message after pressing the Thesaurus key, refer to the Setup menu (Shift-F1).

## HEADWORDS

Notice that the word *top* is highlighted in the text, above the box surrounding the references, since it represents the word being looked up in the Thesaurus. Any word that can be found in the Thesaurus is called a *headword.* The references that are preceded by bullets (dots) are also headwords, and if you press the letter next to them, a list of their synonyms will replace whatever is in the next column. For instance, pressing *C* will yield a list of words under the headword *peak,* as shown in Figure 20.8.

If you see a headword that you want to look up and it's in a column that doesn't have letters next to the words, use → or ← to move the cursor to that column, and the letters will follow the cursor. The column of bolded letters is called the *Reference menu.* As you can see in Figure 20.8, another way to move the Reference menu to the next column is to press the letter next to a bulleted headword. However, this action fills the column(s) with synonyms for that particular headword. In the example shown, pressing *C* for *crown* would fill column 3, and many of the references that were in column 3 would no longer be visible, such as *crest, culminate, and bottom, as shown in Figure 20.8.* While they actually remain in column 2, they don't fit on the screen. To see them, you can move the Reference menu back to column 2 (using ←) then press the usual cursor movement keys like ↑, ↓, Page Up, Page Down, Screen Up, and Screen Down to scroll up or down through the column. If you press

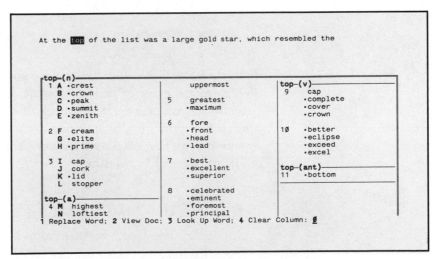

*Figure 20.7:* The Thesaurus screen

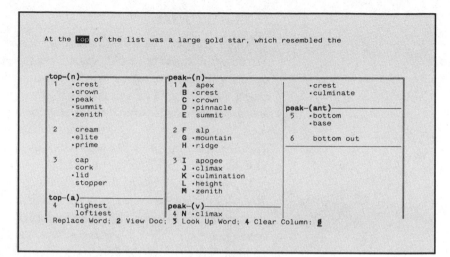

*Figure 20.8:* Looking up another headword

See Chapter 3 for more information about these and other cursor movement methods.

Home Home ↓, the cursor will move all the way to the last word, the antonym *bottom out* that was originally at the end of the third column.

## REPLACING A WORD

To replace the word in your text with one of the words in the list, select option 1, Replace Word. You'll see this prompt:

**Press letter for word**

Type the letter that's next to the word you want, and it will immediately replace the one in your document. If the cursor was on a blank space when you pressed Thesaurus, this action will insert the word into your document. If you decide not to replace the word, you can exit from the Thesaurus screen by pressing the Space bar, ←, Exit (F7), or Cancel (F1) two times.

## VIEWING YOUR DOCUMENT

Option 2, View Doc, can be used to leave the Thesaurus temporarily and move the cursor around in the document, or to move to another word and look it up. However, you cannot perform any editing tasks in this mode or type anything new. To return to the Thesaurus without looking up another word, press ←┘, Exit (F7), or Cancel (F1). To look up a different word, move the cursor onto it then press the Thesaurus key (Alt-F1). This will clear the original word and its references, and replace it with the one the cursor is on.

## LOOK UP WORD

If the word that you were looking for is not in the list of references, you can use option 3, Look Up Word, to look it up. If you select this option when all three columns are full, it won't replace the original word and its references in column 1, but will replace column 2 and/or 3. If you want to start with a clean slate, move the cursor into the first column (using ←) then select option 4, Clear Column, to erase the other columns before you choose the Look Up option. You may have to press 4 (Clear Column) more than once (if you had looked up headwords that are displayed in columns 2 and 3).

## CLEAR COLUMN

As mentioned above, the Clear Column option is useful when you want to clear one or more columns in order to look up another word. If you press it once after looking up a word that fills up all three columns with references (such as *top,* as shown in Figure 20.7), it will clear all three columns. If you look up the word *top* then press a letter next to one of the headwords to fill up columns 2 and 3, selecting option 4 clears columns 2 and 3 of those references, but they are immediately replaced with references from the word *top*. The screen ends up looking just like it did when you first pressed Alt-F2 to find references for *top*. When this happens, keep pressing 4 until all the columns have been cleared. You can also clear columns with the Backspace and Delete keys.

## SUMMARY

WordPerfect's spelling checker is comprehensive, consisting of two dictionaries with over 100,000 words. You can use it to look up individual words, or to check the spelling of a block, page, or document that is on the screen. Words can be found by matching patterns that include the wild-card characters * or ?. The Speller provides a count of all the words it checks; it can also perform this count without checking the spelling. If you use specialized terminology, as in the legal or medical profession, you can add words to the dictionary as the Speller finds them, or you can create a file with a list of the words you use most often and append it to the dictionary with the Speller Utility.

The Thesaurus is another helpful tool that you can use to find a list of synonyms and antonyms for approximately 10,000 different words. When a word is found, it is shown on screen with one or more columns of synonyms and antonyms, classified according to whether they are nouns, verbs, or adjectives, and subdivided into groups of words with the same connotations. Both the Thesaurus and the Speller are easy to use, and if you get into the habit of using them often, your writing should improve significantly.

# INSTALLING WORDPERFECT

WORDPERFECT 5 REQUIRES AN IBM OR COMPATIBLE computer with a minimum of 512K, either two double-sided disk drives, or one hard disk and one double-sided disk drive, and DOS 2.0 (or later version).

## *INSTALLING WORDPERFECT ON A 5¼-INCH FLOPPY DRIVE SYSTEM*

To install WordPerfect on a system with 5¼-inch floppy disk drives, you format 12 new disks to use as your working copies of the program (plus another disk to use as a data disk), then copy the files from the original WordPerfect disks onto the newly formatted disks. Label the diskettes so that they match the labels on the WordPerfect diskettes, then store the originals in a safe place.

Place the first new disk, WordPerfect System 1, in drive B and follow these steps to format it. A word of warning: This procedure completely destroys any data on the disk in drive B, so you must be sure that you are using a new disk (or one that contains nothing you want to keep). If you are unsure, check the disk for files by typing

DIR B:

and pressing ←⏎. If the disk is unformatted, you will be asked to abort, retry, or ignore. This means that the disk is new and can't be read, so it is safe to proceed with formatting. Type

A

(for abort). Place your DOS disk in drive A. With the *A* > prompt on the screen, enter

FORMAT B:

and press ◄┘. You will see a message telling you to insert a new disk into drive B and press any key to continue. Press ◄┘ at this point. It will take a minute or so to format the disk, and then you will be asked if you want to format another disk. Enter *Y*, then place the next disk in drive B and press ◄┘. Repeat this procedure until all your disks are formatted.

You must now place a file called *CONFIG.SYS* on your DOS system disk. This file will contain a command to set up your computer so that WordPerfect can operate properly. If you don't start the computer with this file present on the start-up disk, WordPerfect won't work. Let's create this file on the DOS disk in drive A, using the DOS command COPY. Type

```
COPY A:CONFIG.SYS + CON: A:CONFIG.SYS◄┘
FILES = 20◄┘
```

then press F6 ◄┘. You have now created your CONFIG.SYS file.

Now you must restart your computer, using the DOS disk with your CONFIG.SYS file. Restart your computer by holding down both Ctrl and Alt and pressing Del. From now on, you should always start the computer with this DOS disk in drive A so that the instructions in the CONFIG.SYS file are followed.

The next step is to copy the files from the original WordPerfect disks. Place the original WordPerfect 1 disk in drive A and the one you formatted and labeled to match it in drive B. To copy the files, type

```
COPY A:*.* B:
```

then press ◄┘. Repeat the process to make copies of the original versions of the remaining disks.

To start the program now, place the extra blank formatted disk in drive B (this will be your data disk) and your copy of the WordPerfect 1 disk in drive A. Log on to drive B by entering

```
B:
```

Then type

```
A:WP
```

and press ◄—┘ to start WordPerfect. The message

**Insert diskette labeled "WP 2" and press any key**

will appear. Remove the WordPerfect 1 disk, replace it with the WordPerfect 2 disk, and press ◄—┘. Refer to the instructions in Chapter 1 for more details on what to do once you've started WordPerfect.

## *INSTALLING WORDPERFECT ON A 3¹/₂-INCH MICRO FLOPPY SYSTEM*

To install WordPerfect on a system with micro floppy disk drives, you format seven new disks to use as your working copies of the program (plus another disk to use for a data disk), copy the DOS system files onto the disk that will be the working copy of the WordPerfect System disk, copy the files from the original WordPerfect disks onto the newly formatted disks, then store the originals in a safe place. The steps are as follows.

Label the first new disk *WordPerfect1/WordPerfect2* and place it in drive B. You will be formatting the disk and copying onto it certain DOS files that are needed to start your computer. A word of warning: This procedure completely destroys any data on the disk in drive B, so you must be sure that you are using a new disk (or one that contains nothing you want to keep). If you are unsure, check the disk for files by typing

**DIR  B:**

and pressing ◄—┘. If the disk is unformatted, you will be asked to abort, retry, or ignore. This means that the disk is new and you can safely proceed with formatting. Type

**A**

(for abort). Place your DOS disk in drive A. With the *A* > prompt on the screen, type

**FORMAT  B:/S**

and press ◄──. You will see a message telling you to insert a new disk into drive B and press any key to continue. Press ◄── at this point. It will take a minute or so to format the disk, then you will be asked if you want to format another disk. Enter *N*.

You must now place a file called *CONFIG.SYS* on your WordPerfect1/WordPerfect2 disk. This file will contain a command to configure your computer so that WordPerfect can operate properly. If you don't start the computer with this file present on the start-up disk, WordPerfect won't work. Let's create this file on the WordPerfect1/WordPerfect2 disk, so leave it in drive B and type

COPY CON: B:CONFIG.SYS◄──
FILES = 20◄──

then press F6 ◄──. You have now created your configuration file, CONFIG.SYS.

Now copy the WordPerfect system files onto the newly formatted disk. Place the WordPerfect1/WordPerfect2 disk in drive A and type

COPY A:*.* B:

and press ◄──.

Now you must restart your computer, using the WordPerfect1/WordPerfect2 disk with your new CONFIG.SYS file on it. Place the WordPerfect1/WordPerfect2 disk in drive A and hold down both Ctrl and Alt and press Del. This will restart your computer. (Or you can press the reset button if your computer has one.)

The next step is to place another new disk in drive B. This one will be formatted without the /S option, since the DOS files aren't needed on the remaining disks. Place your DOS disk back in the A drive and type

FORMAT B:

then press any key to begin the process. After the disk is formatted, you will be asked if you want to format another. This time, enter *Y*. You will then be asked to place a new disk in drive B, so insert another new one and press any key to begin formatting the next one. Repeat this procedure to format each of the remaining new disks.

The next step is to copy the files from the original WordPerfect disks onto your newly formatted disks. Place the original Speller/

Thesaurus disk in drive A and the one you labeled *Speller/Thesaurus* in drive B. To copy the files, at the *A>* prompt type

        COPY  A:*.*  B:

and press ◄─┘. Label the other two disks and repeat the copy process to make copies of the original versions of the Printer1/Printer2, Printer3/PTR Program, Printer4, Learning/Fonts/Graphics, and Conversion disks.

   To start WordPerfect now, place the extra blank formatted disk in drive B (this will be your data disk) and your copy of the WordPerfect System disk in drive A. Log on to drive B by typing

        B:

Press ◄─┘ then type

        A:WP

and press ◄─┘ again.

## *INSTALLING WORDPERFECT ON A HARD DISK SYSTEM*

   You may follow the instructions in this section or turn to the "Installing WordPerfect Using Automatic Installation" section if you prefer to use WordPerfect's Auto-Install program. If you have a hard disk, it is still a good idea to follow the steps outlined above to make backup copies of the original WordPerfect disks. However, this is not necessary for installation.

   First, you must make sure that there is a CONFIG.SYS file in your root directory and that it contains the statement

        FILES = 20

To verify this, turn on your computer, and with the *C>* prompt on your screen, enter

        TYPE  C:\CONFIG.SYS

and press ←. If this file exists, you will see the contents, which may look like this:

```
FILES = 10
BUFFERS = 15
```

If your CONFIG.SYS file does not contain the statement *FILES = 20* or has a different FILES statement, as shown above, you will have to change it using the following procedure.

1. Type

   ```
   COPY CONFIG.SYS + CON CONFIG.SYS
   ```

   then press ←.

2. Type

   ```
   FILES = 20 ←
   ```

3. Press F6 ←.

If you do not have a CONFIG.SYS file, you need to create it using the DOS command COPY, as described below. To create this file, type

```
COPY CON: C:\CONFIG.SYS←
FILES = 20←
```

then press F6 ←.

You must now restart your system for this change to take effect. Hold down Ctrl and Alt and press Del.

The next step is to make a new directory for your WordPerfect files. You can name the directory *WP*, or *WP5* if you already have a WP directory for an earlier version of WordPerfect. The main text of this book assumes you named the directory WP. To create a directory with the name WP from the root directory, enter

```
MD\WP
```

Next, switch to the WP subdirectory by entering

```
CD\WP
```

Now insert the original WordPerfect1 disk into drive A. With the *C>* prompt on your screen, enter

    COPY A:*.*

To avoid cluttering your hard disk, it's better to create a separate subdirectory for the Learn files if you want to copy them to your hard disk. *See* Chapter 15 for details on creating a subdirectory.

and press ◄─┘. This will copy all of the files from the original Word-Perfect disk onto your hard disk. When the files are all copied, a message will appear, telling you how many were copied. Repeat this process to copy the remaining disks (originals) onto your hard disk.

To start WordPerfect, enter

    **WP**

and press ◄─┘. You can also use several other start-up options to enter WordPerfect, as described in the next section.

# *OPTIONS FOR STARTING WORDPERFECT*

When you start WordPerfect, you can use one or more options to perform tasks such as immediately starting a macro, changing the screen size, configuring expanded memory, and more. You do this by entering the option(s) as part of the WP command that you use to start the program.

## *STARTING WORDPERFECT WITH A DOCUMENT FILE*

If you start the program by typing

    WP *filename*

the named file will be retrieved as soon as WordPerfect is loaded.

## *STARTING WORDPERFECT AND RUNNING A MACRO*

If you want to start a macro as soon as the program is loaded, enter

    WP/M-*macroname*

where *macroname* is one of your macros. If you want to start an Alt macro, just type *WP/M-AltN* (where *AltN* is the name of the macro).

## SPEEDING UP THE PROGRAM

If your computer has expanded memory, you can make WordPerfect run faster by starting it with this command:

**WP/R**

This loads menus, error messages, and overlays from the System disk into your computer's memory.

## USING TERMINATE-AND-STAY-RESIDENT PROGRAMS WITH WORDPERFECT

Some software programs, called *terminate-and-stay-resident programs,* stay in RAM while you run other programs and can interfere with WordPerfect. If you are using one of these programs and have trouble starting WordPerfect, you should start WordPerfect with

**WP/NC**

This will disable the WordPerfect Cursor Speed feature, which occasionally conflicts with these other programs.

## STARTING WORDPERFECT WITH AUTOMATIC BACKUP

If you want WordPerfect to back up your files at regular intervals, such as every 5 minutes, use the */B* option upon startup by typing

**WP/B-*n***

where *n* is the number of minutes. This will copy the document in your Doc 1 work area to a file named *WP{WP}.BK1.* If you are working in Doc 2, it will back up your document to a file named *WP{WP}.BK2.* The backup file will be deleted if you exit properly using the Exit key (F7), but if your computer is turned off before you exit WordPerfect due to a power failure or other problem, the backup files will remain on the disk and you can rename and use them. You can make this a permanent option by using the Setup menu, as described in the "Making Automatic Backups" section of Chapter 15.

# USING THE
# WORDPERFECT SETUP MENU

You can use WordPerfect's Setup menu to change many options permanently, including the defaults for line spacing, tabs, margins, and justification. You can also specify screen attributes such as underlining, specify locations for the dictionary and thesaurus, set the backup and beep options, and much more.

To display the Setup menu, start WordPerfect and press Shift-F1 (hold down the Shift key and press F1). You will then see a menu with the following eight selections:

1. Backup
2. Cursor Speed
3. Display
4. Fast Save (unformatted)
5. Initial Settings
6. Keyboard Layout
7. Location of Auxiliary Files
8. Units of Measure

Some of these options are discussed at various points in the book and will not be discussed here. Backup is discussed in Chapter 15 in the section "Making Automatic Backups," Fast Save and Units of Measure are explained in Chapter 9. The others are discussed in the following sections.

## CURSOR SPEED

You can use the Cursor Speed option on the Setup menu to increase or decrease the cursor speed, which is normally 10 characters per second. This means that if you press a key like → and hold it down, it will be repeated ten times in one second. You can increase this rate to 15, 20, 30, 40, or 50 characters per second. To change the speed, press Shift-F1, select Cursor Speed (*2* or *C*), then select the number next to the speed you want to use. Changing Cursor Speed may conflict with some memory-resident programs and compatible computers, so if you have problems, use the Normal option on the Cursor Speed menu to return to the normal speed for your keyboard.

## *THE DISPLAY OPTIONS*

You can use the Display options on the Setup key to change the defaults so that WordPerfect does not automatically rewrite the screen as you add or delete text; to change the screen colors, fonts, and attributes; to display document comments; to remove the file name display from the status line; to change the graphics screen type; to display a character every time you press ◄─┘; to change the appearance of the letters that appear on WordPerfect's menus; to turn off the display of side-by-side columns; and, if you have a color monitor, to change the screen that you see when you select the View Document option (on the Print key) so that it is displayed in black and white. Three of these options are discussed in other chapters: Display Document Comments is covered in Chapter 12, Side-by-Side Column Display is covered in Chapter 12, and View Document in Black & White is covered in Chapter 9. The remaining options are discussed below.

*AUTOMATICALLY FORMAT AND REWRITE*   WordPerfect automatically reformats your document as you type and edit, but you can save formatting time by turning off the automatic process so that the program only reformats as you scroll through the text with the cursor movement keys. To do this, press Setup (Shift-F1), select Display (*3* or *D*), select Automatically Format and Rewrite (*1* or *A*) from the Setup: Display menu, type *N*, then press Exit (F7).

*COLORS/FONTS/ATTRIBUTES*   The Colors/Fonts/Attributes option lets you change the appearance of various attributes on screen in order to take full advantage of your monitor. For example, if you have a color monitor, you can use the Screen Colors/Fonts menu to change the background and text colors for normal text, as well as the colors of 19 attributes including underline, boldface, italics, large print, fine print, redline, strikeout, subscript, and superscript. If your system includes an EGA or VGA color monitor and interface, you can change the "font" to italics, underline, small caps, or 512 characters. This reduces the number of foreground colors to eight, but lets you see italics, underline, small caps, or extra characters on the screen. If you have a monochrome monitor and display card, you can use the Colors/Fonts/Attributes option to select one of five display options for each attribute that can be seen on a monochrome screen: blink, bold, blocked, underlined, or normal. If you have a Hercules Graphics Card Plus or Hercules InColor Card with RamFont, you can display 6 fonts with 512 characters each or 12 fonts with 256 characters each so that you can see attributes such as italics, double underlining, strikeout, shadow, small caps, and outline.

The screen you see may differ, depending on the type of monitor and graphics card you are using

To change colors on a color monitor, press Shift-F1, select Display (*3* or *D*), select Colors/Fonts/Attributes (*2* or *C*), then Screen Colors (*1* or *S*). The Setup: Colors menu will appear, with the cursor in the first row of the *Foreground* column. This is where you select the color for your foreground, which is the normal text; you can select from among 16 colors. You switch colors by pressing the letter next to the one you want (*A* through *P*), and the *Sample* column shows you how the text will appear. When you're ready to select the background color, press → to move the cursor into the Background column, then press a letter *A* through *H*. Again, the *Sample* column will display the background text so you can get an idea of what it will look like. If you wish to change any of the other colors such as those for underlining or bold text, use ↓ to move the cursor into the corresponding row, then select the color. After that, you can either press Exit (F7) twice to return to Edit mode or change the colors for the Doc 2 screen.

If you wish to change colors for the Doc 2 screen, press the Switch key (Shift-F3) and repeat the selection process. I recommend using different foreground and background colors in Doc 2 so you can easily differentiate the two work areas, but if you wish to use the same colors, you can use the Move key to copy them. To do this, press Move (Ctrl-F4) and you'll see this prompt:

**Copy attributes from other document? (Y/N) No**

If you are in Doc 2, typing *Y* will copy the colors that you selected for the Doc 1 area. If you are in Doc 1, typing *Y* will copy the colors from the Doc 2 area. When you finish, press Exit (F7) twice to return to the Edit screen.

One important advantage of changing colors is that you can change the way codes appear in the Reveal Codes screen. For instance, I have my background color set to blue (B), my foreground (normal text) set to pale blue (L), and bold text set to pink (N). In Reveal Codes, the cursor, tab ruler, and all codes are pink, so it's much easier to distinguish them from the text.

To change attributes on a monochrome monitor, press Shift-F1, select Display (*3* or *D*), then select Colors/Fonts/Attributes (*2* or *C*). The Setup: Attributes menu will then appear, with the cursor in the *Normal* row. You can switch the display style for normal text or for any of the attributes such as bold text, blocked text, or underlined text, by moving the cursor with the arrow keys and pressing *Y* or *N* in the appropriate columns for blink, bold, blocked, underline, and normal. The *Sample* column shows you what each option will look like. After you finish, you can either press Exit (F7) twice to return to Edit mode, or use the Switch key (Shift-F3) then use the same procedure to change the display options for the Doc 2 screen. If you want the Doc 2 screen to be identical, you can use the Move key to copy the display options you selected for Doc 1. To do this, press Switch (Shift-F3) to get to Doc 2, then press Move (Ctrl-F4). You'll see this prompt:

Copy attributes from other document? (Y/N) No

Type *Y*, then press Exit (F7) twice to return to the Edit screen.

**FILENAME ON THE STATUS LINE**   You can use this option to remove the file name from the status line. The file name appears whenever you have retrieved a file to the Edit screen, or after you have saved a file and continue to edit it. In WordPerfect 4.1 and earlier versions, this message did not appear on the status line, and this option is for users who prefer not to see it. To turn off the file name display, press Shift-F1, select Display (*3* or *D*), select Filename on the Status Line (*4* or *F*), type *N*, then press Exit (F7).

***GRAPHICS SCREEN TYPE*** WordPerfect can be used with several different monitor and interface combinations, including color monitors using EGA, VGA, or Hercules InColor interface cards, and monochrome monitors using Hercules or IBM interface cards. The program automatically selects the correct type for your system, so you shouldn't have to use this option to change it. However, if you are using two monitors, you may need to use this option to change the graphics screen type. To do this, press Shift-F1, select Display (*3* or *D*), then select Graphics Screen Type (*5* or *G*). The Setup: Graphics Screen Type menu with a list of screen types will appear. Use the arrow keys to move the cursor bar onto the screen type you want to select, press *1* to select it, then press Exit (F7). If your graphics screen type is not on the list, you may need to copy the file from the Fonts/Graphics diskette into the directory where the WP.EXE file is located (in your main WordPerfect directory if you use a hard disk system, or on a disk if you are using a floppy disk system).

***HARD RETURN DISPLAY CHARACTER*** When you press ←, you insert a *hard return* into your document, represented by the [HRt] code in the Reveal Codes screen. You can use the Hard Return Display Character option to display a character on the Edit screen as well. This way, you'll know without looking in the Reveal Codes screen the difference between soft returns inserted by WordPerfect when the cursor reaches the right margin, and hard returns you inserted when you pressed ←. You can choose to display a character from the keyboard, such as an asterisk, or to display any symbol in the IBM extended character set.

To display a character for the hard return, press Shift-F1, select Display (*3* or *D*), then select Hard Return Display Character (*6* or *H*). Next, enter the character that you want to use. For instance, if you want to use the paragraph symbol, press Alt-20 (using the numeric keypad to type *20*), which is the ASCII code for this symbol. When you release the keys, the symbol will appear on the menu. Press Exit (F7) when you finish. If you change your mind and decide you don't want the hard return display character, press Shift-F1, select Display, select Hard Return Display Character, then press ← and Exit (F7).

***MENU LETTER DISPLAY*** You can use this option to change the appearance of the letter that you press to select options in the various WordPerfect menus. It is currently set to Bold, so that when you press a key like the Setup key, the letter you press to make a selection, such as *B* (Backup), *C* (Cursor Speed), or *D* (Display), is bolder than the rest of the text on a monochrome screen; on color monitors these letters appear in a different color. If your monitor is capable of displaying it, you can change the size of the letters so that they are fine, small, large, very large, extra large, subscripted, or superscripted. You also can change their appearance so that the letters are in underline, double underline, italics, outline, shadow, small caps, redline, or strikeout (this also depends on your monitor), or you can use the Normal option to change the letters to appear as normal text. When you press *7* or *M* for this option, you see three choices—Size, Appearance, and Normal. Appearance enables you to select a text attribute, such as bold or underline. Use Size if you want to change the size of the letter. If you leave the option at Normal, the letter will be the same size as the rest of the text, and it may be difficult to distinguish it from the other letters.

## *KEYBOARD LAYOUT*

You can use the Keyboard Layout option to change the function of any key on your keyboard by creating a new keyboard definition, or to use one of the alternative keyboard definitions that comes with WordPerfect. To create a keyboard definition, press Setup (Shift-F1), select Keyboard Layout (*6* or *K*), then select Create (*4* or *C*) from the Setup: Keyboard layout screen. In response to the *Keyboard Filename* prompt, type the file name you wish to assign to the new keyboard, then press ←. You will see the Keyboard: Edit menu. Select Create to begin defining the keys. Next, you can change a specific key by pressing the key (or key combination with Alt, Ctrl, etc.), then assigning a function using the regular function keys. For instance, if you want to change the F1 key to display the WordPerfect Help menus, press F1 and you will see the Key: Edit menu. Select Action (*2* or *A*), which places the cursor inside the box, then press the Delete key once to erase {Cancel}, the current meaning of the F1 key. Next, press F3 so that {Help} appears. Press F7 three times until you see the Setup: Keyboard Layout screen again, then use Select (*1* or *S*) to select this keyboard for use with WordPerfect. Press Exit (F7) to return to Edit mode, then press F1 to verify that it now brings up the Word-Perfect Help screens.

Once you have created a keyboard, you can use the Edit option from the Setup: Keyboard Layout screen (Shift-F1 6) to alter any of the key assignments. To do this, you press Shift-F1 6, move the cursor bar onto the file name of the keyboard definition you want to edit, then select Edit (*5* or *E*). Move the cursor onto the key that you wish to change, then select Edit (*1* or *E*). You will see the Key: Edit menu, and you can select Action (*2* or *A*) then make any changes you want. Press Exit (F7) when you finish.

## THE INITIAL SETTINGS OPTIONS

You can use the Initial Settings options on the Setup key to change the Beep Options, Date Format, Document Summary, Initial Codes, Repeat Value, Table of Authorities, and Print Options. Six of these options are discussed in the following chapters: Date Format, Chapter 8; Document Summary, Chapter 15; Initial Codes, Chapter 6; Repeat Value, Chapter 3; Table of Authorities, Chapter 10, and Print Options, Chapter 9. Beep Options is discussed below.

***BEEP OPTIONS*** You can use this option to force WordPerfect to beep when an error occurs, when you are asked to hyphenate a word, or when the Search or Search and Replace feature can find no more occurrences of a word. To change any of these, press Shift-F1, select Initial Settings (*5* or *I*), then select Beep Options (*1* or *B*). The first choice, Beep on Error, is set to No; if you change it to Yes, it will beep whenever an error message appears on the status line. The second choice, Beep on Hyphenation, is set to Yes, and it forces WordPerfect to beep whenever you see the *Position Hyphen; press ESC* prompt on the status line, indicating that the program is trying to hyphenate a word. The third option, on Search Failure, is set to No, and if you change it, the computer will beep whenever you are using Search or Search and Replace and see the *\*Not Found\** message on the status line.

## LOCATION OF FILES

This option lets you specify the drive and/or path where various files are located on your hard disk, including the files used by the

Speller, Thesaurus, and Automatic Hyphenation; Printer Definition files; Macro and Keyboard layout files; Backup files (if you use timed backup); and the name of the Style Library file (if you are using one).

By pressing *7* or *L*, you can specify the directories for your thesaurus (WP{WP}EN.THS), dictionary (WP{WP}EN.LEX), supplementary dictionary, macros, and other files. You will see a display listing all the different file locations you can set. To set the main dictionary location, press *4* or *M*. Next, enter the full path name, but not the file name itself. For example, if your WordPerfect system files are on drive C in a directory named WP and your WP{WP}EN.LEX file (the Speller dictionary) is located in a subdirectory named SPELL, you enter

C:\WP\SPELL

The new defaults will remain in effect until you change them by pressing Shift-F1. Press ⏎ to exit the Setup menu.

## *INSTALLING WORDPERFECT USING AUTOMATIC INSTALLATION*

Your set of WordPerfect disks includes an installation program that will automatically create two subdirectories on your hard disk, and copy all the WordPerfect files into them for you (it does not install your printer). The WordPerfect files will be copied into a subdirectory named WP50, and the tutorial files on the Learn diskette will be copied into a subdirectory named LEARN (LEARN will be a subdirectory of the WP50 file). Before you use the installation program, you should check to see if you have a CONFIG.SYS file in the computer's root directory and make a backup copy of it, because the installation program will alter this file, which could be a problem for you if it contains other commands your system requires. (Although it is supposed to rename your original CONFIG.SYS file and save it as CONFIG.OLD, it did not do this when I used it.)

To use the auto installation program, follow these steps.

1. Start the computer and load DOS, so that you have a C prompt on the screen.

2. To check for the existence of a CONFIG.SYS file, type

   type c:\config.sys

   and press ◄─┘. If you don't have such a file and see a *File not found* prompt, skip to step 3.

If this file exists, you'll see a message showing you the contents, which will look similar to this:

   FILES = 20
   BUFFERS = 15

If you do get such a message, use the following procedure to rename the file. Later, you'll have to check to make sure that the file WordPerfect creates for you when you run the installation program includes the commands you need from your original version. If you are uncomfortable with this procedure, I strongly recommend that you refrain from using the Automatic installation method, and instead refer to the section of this Appendix called "Installing Word-Perfect on a Hard Disk System" for instructions on how to install WordPerfect. However, if you wish to proceed (and if you have a CONFIG.SYS file), type

   rename config.sys config.bk

and press ◄─┘.
   This changes the file name from CONFIG.SYS to CONFIG.BK. Now it is safe to proceed with auto installation.

3. Place the Learn disk in drive A.

4. If you have a C prompt, switch to the A drive by typing

   A:

   and press ◄─┘.

5. Type **install** and press ◄─┘.

The install program will then begin running and will guide you through the process of installing WordPerfect. It will begin by asking if you have a hard disk, and you must answer *Y* or the program will stop. Next, it will display a screen that explains what it does (creates the two subdirectories, copies the files into them, and alters your CONFIG.SYS file) and will ask if you wish to continue. Press *Y* if you want to proceed. You will then be asked to verify that the Word-Perfect 1 disk is in the A drive, so remove the Learn disk and insert the disk labelled *WordPerfect 1*, then press any key to continue. The program will then copy all the files from that disk. When it is finished, you will be asked to verify that the WordPerfect 2 disk is in the A drive. Remove WordPerfect 1 and insert WordPerfect 2 in A, then press any key. This process will continue until you have inserted each of the remaining diskettes (in this order): Font/Graphics, Speller, Thesaurus, Ptr Program, and Learning. The copying process takes several minutes, and a prompt in the lower left corner of the screen keeps you informed of the file names it is copying. You may see an occasional error message telling you that a file was not copied, and asking if you wish to continue. When this happens, write down the file name and press *Y* (you can later copy those files individually using the DOS command COPY or the List Files key in Word-Perfect). When the process has been completed, you will see a C> prompt on the screen, and you will be in the WP50 subdirectory.

If you renamed your CONFIG.SYS file to CONFIG.BK, compare the two now. Type *CD\*, then check the CONFIG.SYS file by typing

    type c:\config.sys

Next, check the CONFIG.BK file by typing

    type c:\config.bk

If you find they are different, you must modify the CONFIG.SYS file so that it contains both commands. The easiest way to do this is from inside WordPerfect. You can retrieve the files using the DOS Text option on the Text In/Out key (Ctrl-F5 1 2), then modify and save them through the DOS Text key (Ctrl-F5 1 1). See chapter 15 for more information on how to do this.

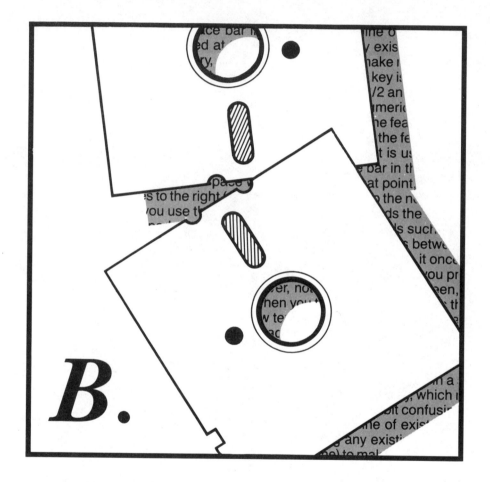

**B.**

*CURSOR MOVEMENT CHART*
*AND ASCII TABLE*

# CURSOR MOVEMENT

| KEY SEQUENCE | COMMAND |
|---|---|
| ↓ | Move one line down |
| ↑ | Move one line up |
| ← | Move one position left |
| → | Move one position right |
| Ctrl ← | Move one word left |
| Ctrl → | Move one word right |
| End | Move to end of the line |
| PgDn | Move one page down (top of next page) |
| PgUp | Move one page up (top of previous page) |
| + (numeric keypad) | Move one screen down |
| − (numeric keypad) | Move one screen up |
| Home ↓ | Move one screen down |
| Home ↑ | Move one screen up |
| Home Home ↑ | Move to beginning of file |
| Home Home ↓ | Move to end of file |
| Home Home Home ← | Move to left edge of screen before codes |
| Home Home Home → | Move to right edge of screen before codes |
| Home ← | Move to left edge of screen |
| Home → | Move to right edge of screen |
| *Go To Key: Ctrl-Home* | |
| Ctrl-Home ↑ | Move to top of current page |
| Ctrl-Home ↓ | Move to bottom of current page |
| Ctrl-Home *n* | Go to page *n* |

| KEY SEQUENCE | COMMAND |
|---|---|
| Ctrl-Home <*character*> | Go to next occurrence of character |
| *Esc key:* | |
| Esc <*n*> ↑ (or ↓) | Move up or down *n* lines |
| Esc <*n*> → (or ←) | Move right or left *n* spaces |
| Esc *n* <*command*> | Repeat *command n* number of times |

## ASCII TABLE

| ASCII VALUE | CHARACTER | CONTROL CHARACTER | ASCII VALUE | CHARACTER | CONTROL CHARACTER |
|---|---|---|---|---|---|
| 000 | (null) | NUL | 016 | ► | DLE |
| 001 | ☺ | SOH | 017 | ◄ | DC1 |
| 002 | ● | STX | 018 | ↕ | DC2 |
| 003 | ♥ | ETX | 019 | !! | DC3 |
| 004 | ♦ | EOT | 020 | ¶ | DC4 |
| 005 | ♣ | ENQ | 021 | § | NAK |
| 006 | ♠ | ACK | 022 | ▬ | SYN |
| 007 | (beep) | BEL | 023 | ↨ | ETB |
| 008 | ◘ | BS | 024 | ↑ | CAN |
| 009 | (tab) | HT | 025 | ↓ | EM |
| 010 | (line feed) | LF | 026 | → | SUB |
| 011 | (home) | VT | 027 | ← | ESC |
| 012 | (form feed) | FF | 028 | (cursor right) | FS |
| 013 | (carriage return) | CR | 029 | (cursor left) | GS |
| 014 | ♫ | SO | 030 | (cursor up) | RS |
| 015 | ☼ | SI | 031 | (cursor down) | US |

This table was reprinted by permission from *IBM PC Basic Manual* ©1984 by International Business Machines Corporation.

| ASCII VALUE | CHARACTER | ASCII VALUE | CHARACTER |
|---|---|---|---|
| 032 | (space) | 070 | F |
| 033 | ! | 071 | G |
| 034 | '' | 072 | H |
| 035 | # | 073 | I |
| 036 | $ | 074 | J |
| 037 | % | 075 | K |
| 038 | & | 076 | L |
| 039 | ' | 077 | M |
| 040 | ( | 078 | N |
| 041 | ) | 079 | O |
| 042 | * | 080 | P |
| 043 | + | 081 | Q |
| 044 | , | 082 | R |
| 045 | - | 083 | S |
| 046 | . | 084 | T |
| 047 | / | 085 | U |
| 048 | 0 | 086 | V |
| 049 | 1 | 087 | W |
| 050 | 2 | 088 | X |
| 051 | 3 | 089 | Y |
| 052 | 4 | 090 | Z |
| 053 | 5 | 091 | [ |
| 054 | 6 | 092 | \ |
| 055 | 7 | 093 | ] |
| 056 | 8 | 094 | ∧ |
| 057 | 9 | 095 | — |
| 058 | : | 096 | ` |
| 059 | ; | 097 | a |
| 060 | < | 098 | b |
| 061 | = | 099 | c |
| 062 | > | 100 | d |
| 063 | ? | 101 | e |
| 064 | @ | 102 | f |
| 065 | A | 103 | g |
| 066 | B | 104 | h |
| 067 | C | 105 | i |
| 068 | D | 106 | j |
| 069 | E | 107 | k |

| ASCII VALUE | CHARACTER | ASCII VALUE | CHARACTER |
|:---:|:---:|:---:|:---:|
| 108 | l | 146 | Æ |
| 109 | m | 147 | ô |
| 110 | n | 148 | ö |
| 111 | o | 149 | ò |
| 112 | p | 150 | û |
| 113 | q | 151 | ù |
| 114 | r | 152 | ÿ |
| 115 | s | 153 | Ö |
| 116 | t | 154 | Ü |
| 117 | u | 155 | ¢ |
| 118 | v | 156 | £ |
| 119 | w | 157 | ¥ |
| 120 | x | 158 | Pt |
| 121 | y | 159 | ƒ |
| 122 | z | 160 | á |
| 123 | { | 161 | í |
| 124 | ¦ | 162 | ó |
| 125 | } | 163 | ú |
| 126 | ~ | 164 | ñ |
| 127 | ⌂ | 165 | Ñ |
| 128 | Ç | 166 | ª |
| 129 | ü | 167 | º |
| 130 | é | 168 | ¿ |
| 131 | â | 169 | ⌐ |
| 132 | ä | 170 | ¬ |
| 133 | à | 171 | ½ |
| 134 | å | 172 | ¼ |
| 135 | ç | 173 | ¡ |
| 136 | ê | 174 | « |
| 137 | ë | 175 | » |
| 138 | è | 176 | ▒ |
| 139 | ï | 177 | ▒ |
| 140 | î | 178 | ▓ |
| 141 | ì | 179 | │ |
| 142 | Ä | 180 | ┤ |
| 143 | Å | 181 | ╡ |
| 144 | É | 182 | ╢ |
| 145 | æ | 183 | ╖ |

| ASCII VALUE | CHARACTER | ASCII VALUE | CHARACTER |
|:---:|:---:|:---:|:---:|
| 184 | ╕ | | ▬ |
| 185 | ╣ | | ▐ |
| 186 | ║ | | ▌ |
| 187 | ╗ | | ▬ |
| 188 | ╝ | 224 | α |
| 189 | ╜ | 225 | β |
| 190 | ╛ | 226 | Γ |
| 191 | ┐ | 227 | π |
| 192 | └ | 228 | Σ |
| 193 | ┴ | 229 | σ |
| 194 | ┬ | 230 | μ |
| 195 | ├ | 231 | τ |
| 196 | ─ | 232 | Φ |
| 197 | ┼ | 233 | φ |
| 198 | ╞ | 234 | Ω |
| 199 | ╟ | 235 | δ |
| 200 | ╚ | 236 | ∞ |
| 201 | ╔ | 237 | Ø |
| 202 | ╩ | 238 | ε |
| 203 | ╦ | 239 | ∩ |
| 204 | ╠ | 240 | ≡ |
| 205 | ═ | 241 | ± |
| 206 | ╬ | 242 | ≥ |
| 207 | ╧ | 243 | ≤ |
| 208 | ╨ | 244 | ⌠ |
| 209 | ╤ | 245 | ⌡ |
| 210 | ╥ | 246 | ÷ |
| 211 | ╙ | 247 | ≈ |
| 212 | ╘ | 248 | ° |
| 213 | ╒ | 249 | • |
| 214 | ╓ | 250 | · |
| 215 | ╫ | 251 | √ |
| 216 | ╪ | 252 | ⁿ |
| 217 | ┘ | 253 | ² |
| 218 | ┌ | 254 | ■ |
| 219 | █ | 255 | (blank 'FF') |

# C.

# *COMPANION PROGRAMS FOR WORDPERFECT*

THIS APPENDIX DESCRIBES ADDITIONAL SOFTWARE programs that may be of interest to WordPerfect users.

## *OTHER WORDPERFECT CORPORATION PROGRAMS*

WordPerfect is available in several foreign-language versions, including Danish, Dutch, Finnish, French, German, Icelandic, Norwegian, Spanish, Swedish, and UK English. A network version of WordPerfect is also available that is compatible with Novell NetWare, AST-PCnet, 3Com EthernetSeries, 3Com 3 + , NOKIA PC-Net, IBM PC Network, Torus Tapestry, and Fox 10-NET. WordPerfect is also being developed for IBM 370/VM mainframes and for computers that use the Unix operating system, including the AT&T 3B2 and NCR Tower computers. Separate versions of WordPerfect are available for the Apple Macintosh, Apple IIe and IIc, Apple IIGs, Atari ST, Amiga, Data General computers using the AOS/VS operating system, DEC VAX VT100 and VT300, and compatible terminals that use the VAX/VMS operating system.

WordPerfect Corporation also offers other programs that are compatible with WordPerfect, including WordPerfect Library, DataPerfect, PlanPerfect, Repeat Performance, Personal WordPerfect, Junior WordPerfect, and WordPerfect Executive. Personal WordPerfect offers home users a version with many of WordPerfect's features, and Junior WordPerfect offers new and younger users a version that is easier to learn. Both are completely compatible with WordPerfect, and they include rebates that can be applied to the price of WordPerfect. The next sections describe WordPerfect Corporation's other programs.

For more information about any of these programs, contact WordPerfect Corporation in Utah at (801) 225-5000 or at this address:

WordPerfect Corporation

288 West Center St.

Orem, UT 84057

## WORDPERFECT LIBRARY

WordPerfect Library is a collection of programs that supplement and integrate the company's other software. The Library includes a program manager, a calculator, an appointment calendar/alarm clock, a notebook, a file manager, a program editor, a macro editor, and a game called Beast. You can customize the program manager, called Shell, to integrate all your programs. It lists up to twenty applications programs such as WordPerfect, PlanPerfect, DataPerfect, Lotus 1-2-3, dBASE, and batch files, as well as any number of subordinate menus. Some or all of the programs on your menu can be loaded into memory (RAM) simultaneously, depending on the memory capacity of your system, so that you can switch between them without exiting. Switching back and forth between the programs on your menu requires a single keystroke, and you can easily transfer data between programs using the Clipboard feature.

The Calculator has mathematical, financial, scientific, programming, and statistical functions, and results can be displayed in decimal, octal, hexadecimal, scientific notation, or binary mode. It displays a ''tape'' on screen that you can save, print, or send to another program through the Clipboard.

You can use the Calendar to keep track of appointments, memos, and to-do lists, and to set an alarm. You can sort the to-do lists according to priority, and if you don't mark items as completed, they are carried forward to the next day's agenda. You can print lists or appointments, or use the Clipboard to send them to other programs. A Date Search feature lets you move quickly to a specific date, and a Word Search feature lets you find appointments, lists, or memos containing a certain word or words.

The Notebook is a list manager that stores records in rows and columns, and saves them in WordPerfect merge file format. You can use it to create fill-in form screens, and to sort and/or select your records with WordPerfect's Sort and Select features. If you have a modem, you can have the Notebook dial phone numbers for you.

The File Manager is an expanded version of the menu that appears when you press the WordPerfect List Files key. It includes List Files utilities such as delete, copy, look, change directory, word search, and rename. You can also use it to sort files by file name, extension, or date and time; to narrow the list to files that were modified before, on, or after a certain date; to lock files with a password; to find the directory in which a certain file is located; and to print the list of files.

You can use the Program Editor to create and edit ASCII files, batch files, object files, binary encoded files, and program files. It has many of the same features found in WordPerfect, including undelete for the last three deletions; search and replace in a forward or reverse direction with optional wild cards; cut, copy, and move by block; split-screen windows; and on-screen help. The Macro Editor is an extension of the Program Editor, and you can use it to create and edit macros that will run under any of the programs you have installed through your Shell menu.

## *PLANPERFECT*

PlanPerfect is WordPerfect Corporation's integrated spreadsheet program. It includes a spreadsheet of 8,192 rows by 256 columns, as well as graphics, word processing, and database functions. The program is completely compatible with WordPerfect, and many of the commands and function keys are the same for both programs. Also, it offers similar print functions such as bold and underline, and gives you the ability to change fonts (including proportionally spaced ones), specify pitch, vary line spacing and margins, add headers and footers, insert page numbers, print borders, and use the print queue to print several documents and print and edit simultaneously. Like WordPerfect, it offers a Preview option so you can view a spreadsheet before retrieving it.

You can build formulas, including arithmetic, financial, date, logic, text, and special functions, and you can create macros that are stored as separate files or with the worksheet. Other features include password protection; windows that let you view two separate documents simultaneously; sort, search, select, and locate capabilities; a transpose function to switch rows with columns; linking and overlaying of worksheets; single and multiple linear regression; what-if tables; text windows with word wrap; and document switching that lets you work with two worksheets in memory simultaneously and switch back and forth to exchange data between them. To document your worksheet, you can create your own help messages and attach them to individual cells in the worksheet. When the computer's memory is full, worksheet data are temporarily moved to the disk, freeing up RAM for cells that contain data. Files can be imported and exported in several formats, including WordPerfect, ASCII, dBASE, Lotus 1-2-3, DIF, and WordPerfect mail merge. A network version is available that supports Novell NetWare, AST-PCnet, AT&T StarLan, 3Com EthernetSeries, 3Com 3 +, NOKIA PC-Net, IBM PC Network, Torus (Tapestry) Network, and Fox 10-NET.

You can use PlanPerfect to create graphics such as bar graphs, stacked bar graphs, pie charts, line graphs, hi-lo graphs, and scatter charts. Graphs can be saved as text files so that you can use them with WordPerfect. The database features are powerful, and include automatic forms input for data entry, an automatic cursor-advance mode, and search and sorting features.

PlanPerfect is available in regular and network versions for the IBM PC and close compatibles, and for Data General computers.

## DATAPERFECT

DataPerfect is a menu-driven database program that can store over 16 million records and that requires no programming. The program displays information in panels, framing records on the screen. More than one panel can be viewed at once, so that you can look up related information in other records. Each record can contain up to 80 fields, and when you define fields, you can choose from among several formats. Variable-length text fields can contain up to 32,000 characters, and have editing features similar to WordPerfect. You can use formulas to initialize field values, calculate field values from other data, manipulate dates, and validate fields.

Built-in operations include addition, subtraction, multiplication, division, mod, and forced negation; nine logical operators for value comparison such as AND, NOT, and OR; and IF and CASE statements for conditional formulas. To cross-reference your data, you can create several indices using one or more fields per index. You can search for records using ranges, templates (with wild-card characters), AND/OR formulas in the search string, and conditional formulas with AND/OR. Single-level (flat file) or multiple-level data structures can be defined, and fields can be shared by source and destination files. A single-level structure displays all the information for each record in one panel, whereas a multilevel structure lets you link several panels together by a common field containing the same information.

The DataPerfect report generator lets you create customized reports to view on screen, print, save as a disk file, or append to an existing file. Reports can include headers and footers, and you can use previously designed reports as models for repeated use. The Sub-reports feature to combines information from two or more linked files and prints it in the same report.

DataPerfect is compatible with WordPerfect, the Library, and PlanPerfect. It supports field locking and can run under networks using Novell Netware, 3Com 3 + , 3Com EtherSeries, AST-PCnet, AT&T StarLan, Fox 10-NET, IBM PC Network, NOKIA PC-Net, and Torus Tapestry. You can import records in either delimited DOS text or WordPerfect merge format.

## WORDPERFECT EXECUTIVE

WordPerfect Executive is an integrated package that includes a word processor, spreadsheet, appointment calendar, calculator, note cards, and phone directory. Although it is available for IBM PC, XT, AT, PS/2, and many other full-sized computers, it was designed to be used by travelling executives on portable and laptop computers such as the ones offered by Zenith, NEC, and Toshiba. On these models, the entire program fits on a 3½-inch diskette.

Like the WordPerfect Library, the Executive runs under the Shell program, which keeps the other programs in memory so that you can move back and forth and exchange information among the programs through the Clipboard. The appointment calendar is similar to the one that comes with the WordPerfect Library. You can use it to keep track of appointments, make to-do lists, and set an alarm. The calculator has built-in functions for addition, subtraction, multiplication, division, square root, and percent, and includes a paper tape display, memory register, and fixed and floating decimal point. It does not include the more advanced statistical, scientific, programming, and financial functions of the Library calculator, but if you need them, you can copy the calculator program from the WordPerfect Library into the Executive Shell. You can use Note Cards to organize, store, and sort information by subject, description, or date, and to keep extensive notes about each subject. The Phone Directory enables you to store information, to sort your list, and to add a note about each individual in the list.

The spreadsheet is compatible with PlanPerfect and includes financial functions such as net present value, future value, present value, payment, periodic interest, and term; arithmetic functions such as absolute value, count, logarithm, square root, sum, and pi; logical functions such as IF, OR, NA, and FALSE; date functions such as day, month, year, time, and datevalue; and special functions such as *lookup, foreach, cell,* and *col.* You can also use it to sort data, and to create bar charts that you can either print or transfer into the word processor. You can easily convert spreadsheets to and from Lotus 1-2-3.

The Executive word processor is similar to WordPerfect, and is completely compatible with it. Since it uses many of the same cursor movement and function keys, it is easy for WordPerfect users to learn and use. The word processor includes features such as a spelling checker, merge, macros, and list files, as well as word processing functions such as cut, copy, move, bold, center, underline, tab and margin set, search and replace, right justification, indent, page numbering, flush right, and headers and footers. You can easily transfer documents to and from WordPerfect.

## WORDPERFECT OFFICE

WordPerfect Office is an integrated tool for networks that combines a Shell, Calendar, Scheduler, Calculator, File Manager, Macro Editor, Program Editor, Notebook, and Electronic Mail. It supports network printing, user management, and protected multi-user access to files. You can use the Mail program to send messages and files to other users on the network; the program features password protection and automatic deletion of expired messages. Recipients of mail receive a message on screen to inform them when a message has arrived. The Shell is similar to the Library Shell, and includes a work log feature to help you keep track of the time and keystrokes you spend on each project. The Notebook program is similar to the Library Notebook, and you can use it to organize information into records, sort your data individually or in groups, create WordPerfect merge files, and dial phone numbers if you have a modem. The Scheduler helps you schedule appointments for multiple users by searching the schedules of other users on the network, posting "open times," then posting the meeting on each user's calendar.

The File Manager, Calculator, Calendar, Macro Editor, and Program Editor are similar to those in the WordPerfect Library.

The WordPerfect Office runs on most networks that support the DOS file-locking feature. You require DOS 3.0 to use it.

### REPEAT PERFORMANCE

Repeat Performance is a keyboard enhancer featuring several utilities that you can use with WordPerfect, the Library, PlanPerfect, DataPerfect, and many other programs. One of Repeat Performance's most important functions is to change the speed at which the cursor moves on the screen; you can vary it between 11 and 1000 characters per second to match your typing skills. You can create a "panic button" that will temporarily increase key repeat speed to a preselected level, and assign it to any key you want. Fast typists can set the keyboard buffer to "remember" up to 10,000 keystrokes typed in advance. This is useful when you load WordPerfect from the DOS prompt and are anxious to start typing before the Edit screen appears. Another feature clears the keyboard buffer so that the auto-repeat feature is disabled as soon as you take your finger off a key. If you type with "heavy fingers," you can adjust the repeat delay so that as you press and hold a key, it doesn't repeat as often. You can also use Repeat Performance to disable the reverse Caps Lock on an IBM PC, so that if Caps Lock is turned on and you press the Shift key then type a letter, it will be entered in uppercase instead of lowercase.

### INTRODUCTION TO WORDPERFECT TRAINING VIDEO TAPE

WordPerfect Corporation and Video Projects offer a 35-minute introductory video training course designed for individuals who have never used a computer before. It covers basic WordPerfect features, and comes with a money-back guarantee.

## THE WORDPERFECT SUPPORT GROUP

The WordPerfect Support Group publishes a monthly newsletter called *The WordPerfectionist,* which is full of useful advice and information for users of WordPerfect Corporation's products. The group also runs a bulletin board on CompuServe, where members can exchange ideas and answer each other's questions. You can purchase past issues of the newsletter, diskettes containing monthly messages and software utilities from their bulletin board, and several other utilities and learning tools. You can join the group by writing to them at this address:

WordPerfect Support Group
P.O. Box 1577
Baltimore, MD 21203

or by calling them at 1-800-USA-GROUP. The WordPerfect Support Group is independent of WordPerfect Corporation.

## USEFUL SOFTWARE FROM OTHER MANUFACTURERS

This section describes programs that can make WordPerfect easier to use, enhance your printer's operation, aid in file management, teach you to use WordPerfect, and more.

### POINT-N-SHOOT POP-UP MENUS

Point-N-Shoot Pop-Up Menus are memory-resident pop-up menus that appear as soon as you click a mouse button, and they help you perform various functions faster and more easily by replacing typed commands and function keys. The menus that I've tested are a joy to use, and can be helpful both to the beginner and to advanced users. One of the main advantages to using Point-N-Shoot is that you can move the cursor around very quickly by moving the mouse on the pad. It also enables you to easily block text for cut-and-paste operations. The mouse buttons also call up the Point-N-Shoot menus, select a highlighted item from the menu, and invoke the WordPerfect Cancel key, Exit key, Escape key, and Switch key.

The main Point-N-Shoot menu includes options to temporarily exit to DOS using the Shell key then return to WordPerfect from DOS (through the Shell); a help screen for the Pop-up program; options to change cursor speed; and access to these other Point-N-Shoot menus: File, Edit, Format, Miscellaneous, Macros, Print, and Numbers. You can use the File menu to perform file management tasks. The Edit menu lets you turn Reveal Codes on and off; block and cut, copy, or delete text; copy text into another document; search and replace; add superscript, subscript, bold, or underline; insert tabs; center a line; sort; and more. The Format menu lets you set tabs, margins, line spacing, and access the Line Format, Page Format, and Print Format menus at the click of a button. The Miscellaneous menu includes options to split the screen into two windows; run the Speller or Thesaurus; and access many WordPerfect keys, including Footnote, Math/Columns, Merge/Sort, and Line Draw. The Print menu lets you print a page or a document; run print preview; change printers, number of copies, or binding width; access the Printer Control menu; and run Type-Thru. The Macros menu lists Alt-key macros A through R so that you can run one of your macros by pointing to it and clicking a button on the mouse. You can also use it to invoke the Macro Define key or Invoke Macro key. The Numbers menu provides the numbers 0 through 9 as well as Y, N, and A, so that when you call up one of WordPerfect's menus through a pop-up menu, you can use it to make a menu selection without pressing a number or letter on the keyboard.

Point N Shoot Pop-Up Menus comes with menus for several other popular programs, including Lotus 1-2-3, dBASE III Plus, MS-DOS, and the WordPerfect Library. The program can be used with the IBM PC, XT, AT, and compatibles, and requires a Mouse Systems or LogiTech mouse.

For more information about Point-N-Shoot Pop-Up Menus, contact Yolles Development at (408) 270-0934, or at this address:

Yolles Development
124-H Blossom Hill Rd. #3200
San Jose, CA 95123

### SOFTCRAFT FONTS

SoftCraft produces several font programs for laser printers and dot-matrix printers, including Laser Fonts, Fancy Font, the Fontware Installation Program, the Font Editor, Standard Series Fonts, Font Effects, and the Bitmap Font Library.

Fancy Font for WordPerfect supports the Epson FX, Epson MX, Epson LQ, Toshiba, and compatible printers, and uses those printers' high-resolution graphics mode to produce high-quality, proportionally spaced printing. On the Epson EX80 and JX80, the program can print in several colors. Fancy Font comes with 18 fonts that are licensed from Bitstream Inc., including Times Roman, Italic, Bold, Helvetica, Courier, Script, and Old English. They come in sizes from 8 to 24 points. A graphics command is also included that lets you incorporate graphs from other programs into your WordPerfect documents.

Laser Fonts works automatically with WordPerfect, and supports all of the WordPerfect formatting features. The fonts provided with Laser Fonts are licensed from Bitstream, Inc., and include Times Roman, Helvetica, Italic, Bold, Script, Old English, and Courier. They come in sizes ranging from 8 to 24 points, and in portrait or landscape mode. They also include a symbol set with foreign symbols, ligatures, fractions, mathematical characters, bullets, and more. The Courier font includes all the characters in the IBM graphics character set, and I have used it to print WordPerfect line drawings. You can also purchase extra fonts in a variety of typefaces. A conversion program is also included so that you can convert SoftCraft fonts to HP Soft Font format, and use programs designed for HP fonts. Laser Fonts lets you mix built-in fonts, cartridge fonts, and downloaded fonts. Laser Fonts runs on IBM PC computers and compatibles with Hewlett-Packard LaserJet Plus, LaserJet 500 +, and Series II printers, Canon LPB8A1 and 8A2 laser printers, NCR Laser Beam printers, and any compatible printers.

Font Editor, Standard Series Fonts, and Font Effects can enhance your printing even more. Use Font Editor to create new fonts and change existing ones, or to create special symbols, logos, or foreign-language characters. Font Effects is a special-effects program that you can use to create impressive effects such as drop shadows, outlines, contours, shades, boxed characters, and scaled or slanted characters. Standard Series Fonts are disk-based fonts that you can purchase in a large variety of type styles.

The Fontware Installation Program lets you use a font outline to create as many fonts as you want from it—in point sizes between 3 and 120 points—and also lets you use a variety of foreign and special characters. The font outlines are designed by Bitstream, and are purchased separately (from SoftCraft). Over 80 typefaces are available.

For more information, contact SoftCraft at (800) 351-0500 or

(608) 257-3300, or at this address:

SoftCraft, Inc.
16 N. Carroll St., Suite 500
Madison, WI 53703

### HERCULES RAMFONT

Hercules RamFont gives you the ability to view up to 3,072 characters on screen instead of the 256 characters of the IBM character set, and it is included with three of Hercules' new monitor interfaces: the Hercules Graphics Card Plus, In Color Card, and Network Card Plus. WordPerfect 5 completely supports RamFont, so that in Edit mode you can see attributes such as underline; double underline; redline; boldface; strikeout; superscript and subscript; fonts in fine, small, large, very large, and extra large sizes; italics; outline; small caps; and special characters. When you use one of these cards, you can either select 12 "fonts" of 256 characters each, or 6 "fonts" of 512 characters each.

For more information, contact Hercules Computer Technology at 1-800-532-0600, extension 909, or at this address:

Hercules Computer Technology
921 Parker St.
Berkeley, CA 94710

### POWERMAX

POWERMAX is a collection of over 115 macros in WordPerfect format that you can use to automate many tasks. It includes macros to delete a sentence, paragraph, or page with two keystrokes; delete a line from anywhere within the line; move the cursor sentence by sentence; delete the preceding word; transpose words; open or close a window; place the tab ruler at the bottom of the screen; move to the beginning or end of a sentence; transpose letters in a word; print a page; print an entire document; move the cursor and text to the top of the screen; change fonts; center text; find and display codes; delete a word or phrase throughout the document; delete bold or underline throughout your document; print an address from the screen to an envelope; turn right justification off or on; create headers and footers; create mailing list records; and much more.

POWERMAX is very useful for those who want to learn more about macros and discover the nearly endless possibilities that they provide to automate your work. It is available in 4.2 and 5.0 format for IBM and compatible computers. For more information, contact PowerMax at this address:

>PowerMax
>15840 Ventura Blvd., Suite 845
>Encino, CA 91436

or phone them at (818) 905-5919.

## *ZYINDEX*

ZYINDEX is a text retrieval program that you can use to find a file anywhere on your hard or floppy disk, and to index your files so that you can quickly locate all files containing any word, phrase, number, or combination of these. The program indexes every word in your files, and uses powerful search options like those used in mainframe text retrieval programs. You also can use it to search for words that are ''close together'' or related by logical operators such as AND, OR, NOT, and WITHIN, and you can use wild-card characters such as the asterisk. When the program finds files containing your search string, you can print or view them. When viewing them, you can use a function key to move to each occurrence of the search string, which is highlighted in the text. ZYINDEX does not change your files while reading them, or place any special marks on them, so it cannot corrupt your files.

ZYINDEX comes in three versions: Personal ZYINDEX, which can search up to 325 files; Professional ZYINDEX, which can search up to 5,000 files; and Plus ZYINDEX (for networks), which can search up to 15,000 files. Information can be located in a matter of seconds. You can use ZYINDEX to search through ASCII files (DOS text files); files created in a variety of word processors; public databases like Dow Jones and CompuServe; and popular programs such as Lotus 1-2-3.

The programs come with a 30-day money-back guarantee. For more information, contact ZYLAB Corporation at (312) 632-1100 or at this address:

ZYLAB Corporation
3105-T N. Frontage Rd.
Arlington Heights, IL 60004

## *TEACH YOURSELF WORDPERFECT*

Teach Yourself WordPerfect is a disk-based training program that includes novice and advanced training programs, and a user handbook that summarizes the lessons. The lessons include these topics: starting WordPerfect; entering text; saving; moving the cursor; editing; changing formatting features; printing; centering text; underlining and boldfacing; indenting; on-line help; search and replace; merge; columns; the spell checker; and table of contents and index.

The maker of Teach Yourself WordPerfect, American Training International, offers a guarantee that you may return it within ten days for a full refund if you are not satisfied. I tried several lessons and found them to be helpful. The split-screen format of the lessons is especially easy to follow because you can view a simulation of WordPerfect on the top half of the screen as you read the directions and explanations on the bottom half.

For more information, contact American Training International at 1-800-421-4827 or at this address:

American Training International
12638 Beatrice St.
Los Angeles, CA 90066

## *EXACT*

EXACT works with WordPerfect (and other word processors) to help you produce technical documents. It facilitates mathematical and statistical typing, and you can use it to create equations, formulas, and functions. Its features include superscripts and subscripts automatically raised or lowered by the correct amount; automatic spacing between lines that include extra-high or extra-low characters; and automatic creation of fractions and radicals. The program includes 20 font files with over 1000 graphic designs for characters and symbols, and if that's not enough, you can use the EXACT Font Editor to create more. EXACT stays in memory (RAM) until you need to use it. When you call it up, the program splits your screen in two so that you can see your expression as you create it, while remaining in WordPerfect.

For more information, contact Technical Support Software at (617) 734-4130 or at this address:

> Technical Support Software
> 72 Kent St.
> Brookline, MA 02146

## *WORD-LINK*

Word-Link is a program that you can use to convert files between WordPerfect and the following software programs: MultiMate; Microsoft Word; DisplayWrite 1, 2, 3, or 4; OfficeWriter; PFS:Professional Write; WordStar; and ASCII (DOS text files). Documents can be converted to and from any of these formats, for a total of 56 different conversion combinations. You can convert several documents in one session, or select all documents on a disk or subdirectory for conversion with a single keystroke. Files are converted directly to and from the disk. The program maintains formatting information through the conversion. You can use a defaults menu to specify how you want documents converted into WordPerfect, changing features such as the page length and number of text lines, top margin, pitch, and whether right justification should be on or off.

Word-Link is entirely menu driven, and various screens let you select the type of conversion (such as WordPerfect to MultiMate), the drive and path for the files you are converting, and the file names (it lists the files for you to select from). Information about which keys to press to select the various options is always displayed on screen, so that you may never have to read the manual. In fact, I was able to successfully convert three Microsoft Word files into WordPerfect format without ever opening the manual.

For more information, contact the M/H Group at (312) 443-1222 or at this address:

M/H Group
222 West Adams St.
Chicago, IL 60606

## *PERFECT EXCHANGE*

Perfect Exchange is a menu-driven program that you can use to convert files to and from WordPerfect and the following software: WordStar; WordStar 2000; MultiMate; Samna Word; Microsoft Word; DisplayWrite 2, 3, and 4; Wang PC (IWP); Volkswriter 3; DEC WPS PLUS (DX); and ASCII (DOS text files). The program transfers files directly from your disks, so you don't need to load them first. As many as 250 files can be placed in a conversion queue. The following functions are maintained during the conversion process: hard and soft carriage returns, regular and decimal tabs, bold, overstrike, superscript and subscript, line spacing, indenting, centering, underline, merge codes, required hyphens, required page ends, right and left margins, and headers and footers. Since Perfect Exchange is menu-driven, it is easy to use; I was able to convert a short Microsoft Word document into WordPerfect without referring to the manual.

Perfect Exchange runs on the IBM PC, XT, AT, and compatibles. For more information, contact Systems Compatibility Corporation at (312) 329-0700, or at this address:

Systems Compatibility Corporation
401 North Wabash
Chicago, IL 60611

# INDEX

*[handwritten annotation:]* SEE PFS FiRST ON MAIN MENU

# Selections from The SYBEX Library

## WORD PROCESSING

### The ABC's of WordPerfect (Second Edition)
**Alan R. Neibauer**
300pp. Ref. 504-2

This introduction explains the basics of desktop publishing with WordPerfect 5: editing, layout, formatting, printing, sorting, merging, and more. Readers are shown how to use WordPerfect 5's new features to produce great-looking reports.

### The ABC's of WordPerfect
**Alan R. Neibauer**
239pp. Ref. 425-9

This basic introduction to WordPefect consists of short, step-by-step lessons— for new users who want to get going fast. Topics range from simple editing and formatting, to merging, sorting, macros, and more. Includes version 4.2

### Mastering WordPerfect
**Susan Baake Kelly**
435pp. Ref. 332-5

Step-by-step training from startup to mastery, featuring practical uses (form letters, newsletters and more), plus advanced topics such as document security and macro creation, sorting and columnar math. Includes Version 4.2.

### Advanced Techniques in WordPerfect 5
**Kay Yarborough Nelson**
500pp. Ref. 511-5

Now updated for Version 5, this invaluable guide to the advanced features of WordPerfect provides step-by-step instructions and practical examples covering those specialized techniques which have most perplexed users – indexing, outlining, foreign-language typing, mathematical functions, and more.

### Advanced Techniques in WordPerfect
**Kay Yarborough Nelson**
400pp. Ref. 431-3

Exact details are presented on how to accomplish complex tasks including special sorts, layered indexing, and statistical typing. Includes details on laser printing operations.

### WordPerfect Desktop Companion
### SYBEX Ready Reference Series
**Greg Harvey/Kay Yarbourough Nelson**
663pp. Ref. 507-7

This compact encyclopedia offers detailed, cross-referenced entries on every software feature, organized for fast, convenient on-the-job help. Includes self-contained enrichment material with tips, techniques and macros. Special information is included about laser printing using WordPerfect that is not available elsewhere. For Version 4.2.

### WordPerfect 5 Desktop Companion
### SYBEX Ready Reference Series
**Greg Harvey/Kay Yarborough Nelson**
700pp. Ref. 522-0

Desktop publishing features have been added to this compact encyclopedia. This title offers more detailed, cross-referenced entries on every software features including page formatting and layout, laser printing and word processing macros. New users of WordPerfect, and those new to Version 5 and desktop publishing will find this easy to use for on-the-job help. For Version 5.

## WordPerfect Tips and Tricks (Second Edition)
**Alan R. Neibauer**
488pp. Ref. 489-5

This new edition is a real timesaver. For on-the-job guidance and creative new uses for WordPerfect, this title covers all new features of Version 4.2 – including tables of authorities, concordance files, new print enhancements and more.

## WordPerfect Instant Reference SYBEX Prompter Series
**Greg Harvey/Kay Yarborough Nelson**
254pp. Ref. 476-3

When you don't have time to go digging through the manuals, this fingertip guide offers clear, concise answers: command summaries, correct usage, and exact keystroke sequences for on-the-job tasks. Convenient organization reflects the structure of WordPerfect.

## Mastering SAMNA
**Ann McFarland Draper**
503pp. Ref. 376-7

Word-processing professionals learn not just how, but also when and why to use SAMNA's many powerful features. Master the basics, gain power-user skills, return again and again for reference and expert tips.

## The ABC's of MicroSoft WORD
**Alan R. Neibauer**
250pp. Ref. 497-6

Users who want to wordprocess straightforward documents and print elegant reports without wading through reams of documentation will find all they need to know about MicroSoft WORD in this basic guide. Simple editing, formatting, merging, sorting, macros and style sheets are detailed.

## Mastering Microsoft WORD (Second Edition)
**Matthew Holtz**
479pp. Ref. 410-0

This comprehensive, step-by-step guide includes Version 3.1. Hands-on tutorials treat everything from word processing basics to the fundamentals of desktop publishing, stressing business applications throughout.

## Advanced Techinques in Microsoft WORD
**Alan R. Neibauer**
537pp. Ref. 416-X

The book starts with a brief overview, but the main focus is on practical applications using advanced features. Topics include customization, forms, style sheets, columns, tables, financial documents, graphics and data management.

## Mastering DisplayWrite 3
**Michael E. McCarthy**
447pp. Ref. 340-6

Total training, reference and support for users at all levels – in plain, non-technical language. Novices will be up and running in an hour's time; everyone will gain complete word-processing and document-management skills.

## Mastering MultiMate Advantage II
**Charles Ackerman**
407pp. Ref. 482-8

This comprehensive tutorial covers all the capabilities of MultiMate, and highlights the differences between MultiMate Advantage II and previous versions – in pathway support, sorting, math, DOS access, using dBASE III, and more. With many practical examples, and a chapter on the On-File database.

## Mastering MultiMate Advantage
**Charles Ackerman**
349pp. Ref. 380-5

Master much more than simple word processing by making the most of your software. Sample applications include creating expense reports, maintaining customer lists, merge-printing complex documents and more.

## The Complete Guide to MultiMate
**Carol Holcomb Dreger**
208pp. Ref. 229-9

This step-by-step tutorial is also an excellent reference guide to MultiMate features and uses. Topics include search/replace, library and merge functions, repagination, document defaults and more.

# MASTERING
# WORDPERFECT® 5

*SAMPLE FILES AVAILABLE ON DISK*

If you'd like to use the examples in this book without typing them your-self, you can send for a disk containing all the files used in Chapters 2-20, and several extra macro files along with explanations of what they do. To obtain this disk, complete the order form below and return it along with a check or money order for $20.00 per copy (California resi-dents add 6% sales tax), made out to *Susan B. Kelly.*

Susan B. Kelly
P.O. Box 1307
Novato, CA 94948

Name _____

Address _____

City _____

State _____ ZIP _____

Quantity _____

WordPerfect version (4.0, 4.1, 4.2, 5.0) _____

*SYBEX is not affiliated with Susan B. Kelly and assumes no responsibility for any defect in the disk or programs.*

## SYBEX Computer Books
*are different.*

## Here is why . . .

At SYBEX, each book is designed with you in mind. Every manuscript is carefully selected and supervised by our editors, who are themselves computer experts. We publish the best authors, whose technical expertise is matched by an ability to write clearly and to communicate effectively. Programs are thoroughly tested for accuracy by our technical staff. Our computerized production department goes to great lengths to make sure that each book is well-designed.

In the pursuit of timeliness, SYBEX has achieved many publishing firsts. SYBEX was among the first to integrate personal computers used by authors and staff into the publishing process. SYBEX was the first to publish books on the CP/M operating system, microprocessor interfacing techniques, word processing, and many more topics.

Expertise in computers and dedication to the highest quality product have made SYBEX a world leader in computer book publishing. Translated into fourteen languages, SYBEX books have helped millions of people around the world to get the most from their computers. We hope we have helped you, too.

## *For a complete catalog of our publications:*

SYBEX, Inc. 2021 Challenger Drive, #100, Alameda, CA 94501
Tel: (415) 523-8233/(800) 227-2346   Telex: 336311
Fax: (415) 523-2373

## CODES

| CODE | MEANING |
|---|---|
| ‾ | Cursor Position |
| [ ] | Hard Space |
| [-] | Hyphen |
| - | Soft Hyphen |
| / | Cancel Hyphenation |
| ! | Formula Calculation |
| + | Calculate Subtotal |
| = | Calculate Total |
| * | Calculate Grand Total |
| [Adv] | Advance |
| [Align] | Tab Align |
| [Block] | Beginning of Block |
| [BlockPro] | Block Protection |
| [Bold] | Bold |
| [BOX Num] | Caption in Graphics Box |
| [C/A/FlRt] | End of Tab Align or Flush |
| [Center Pg] | Center Page Top to Bottom |
| [Cndl EOP] | Conditional End of Page |
| [Cntr] | Center |
| [Col Def] | Column Definition |
| [Col Off] | End of Text Columns |
| [Col On] | Beginning of Text Columns |
| [Comment] | Document Comment |
| [Color] | Print Color |
| [Date] | Date/Time Function |
| [Dbl Und] | Double Underline |
| [Decml Char] | Decimal/Thousands Separator Character |
| [DefMark:Index] | Index Definition |
| [DefMark:List, *n*] | List Definition |
| [DefMark:ToC] | Table of Contents Definition |
| [EndDef] | End of Index, List, or Table of Contents |
| [Endnote] | Endnote |
| [Endnote Placement] | Endnote Placement |
| [EndOpt] | Endnote Options |
| [Ext Large] | Extra Large Print |
| [Fig Opt] | Figure Box Options |
| [Figure] | Figure Box |
| [Fine] | Fine Print |
| [Flsh Rt] | Flush Right |
| [Font] | Base Font |
| [Footnote] | Footnote |
| [Footer] | Footer |
| [Force] | Force Odd/Even Page |
| [Form] | Form (Printer Selection) |
| [FtnOpt] | Footnote/Endnote Options |
| [Full Form] | Table of Authorities, Full Form |
| [Header] | Header |
| [HLine] | Horizontal Line |
| [HPg] | Hard Page Break |
| [HRt] | Hard Return |
| [Hyph] | Hyphenation |
| [HZone] | Hyphenation Zone |
| [→ Indent] | Indent |
| [→ Indent ←] | Left/Right Indent |
| [Index] | Index Entry |
| [ISRt] | Invisible Soft Return |
| [Italc] | Italics |